Musicians
& Composers
of the 20th Century

Musicians
& Composers
of the 20th Century

Volume 5

Billy Strayhorn—Hans Zimmer
Appendixes
Indexes

Editor

Alfred W. Cramer

Pomona College

SALEM PRESS

Pasadena, California   Hackensack, New Jersey

Editorial Director: Christina J. Moose   *Photograph Editor:* Cynthia Breslin Beres
Developmental Editor: Jeffry Jensen   *Production Editor:* Andrea E. Miller
Acquisitions Editor: Mark Rehn   *Page Design:* James Hutson
Manuscript Editor: Constance Pollock   *Layout:* William Zimmerman
Research Assistant: Keli Trousdale

Cover photo: Tina Turner (Tim Mosenfelder/Getty Images)

Library of Congress Cataloging-in-Publication Data

Musicians and composers of the 20th century / editor Alfred W. Cramer.
    p. cm.
Includes bibliographical references and index.
    ISBN 978-1-58765-512-8 (set : alk. paper) — ISBN 978-1-58765-513-5 (vol. 1 : alk. paper) —
ISBN 978-1-58765-514-2 (vol. 2 : alk. paper) — ISBN 978-1-58765-515-9 (vol. 3 : alk. paper) —
ISBN 978-1-58765-516-6 (vol. 4 : alk. paper) — ISBN 978-1-58765-517-3 (vol. 5 : alk. paper) —
1. Music—20th century—Bio-bibliography—Dictionaries. I. Cramer, Alfred William.
    ML105.M883 2009
    780.92′2—dc22
    [B]
                                                                                    2009002980

First Printing

Contents

Key to Pronunciation

Many of the names of personages covered in *Musicians and Composers of the 20th Century* may be unfamiliar to students and general readers. For these unfamiliar names, guides to pronunciation have been provided upon first mention of the names in the text. These guidelines do not purport to achieve the subtleties of the languages in question but will offer readers a rough equivalent of how English speakers may approximate the proper pronunciation.

Vowel Sounds

Symbol	Spelled (Pronounced)
a	answer (AN-suhr), laugh (laf), sample (SAM-puhl), that (that)
ah	father (FAH-thur), hospital (HAHS-pih-tuhl)
aw	awful (AW-fuhl), caught (kawt)
ay	blaze (blayz), fade (fayd), waiter (WAYT-ur), weigh (way)
eh	bed (behd), head (hehd), said (sehd)
ee	believe (bee-LEEV), cedar (SEE-dur), leader (LEED-ur), liter (LEE-tur)
ew	boot (bewt), lose (lewz)
i	buy (bi), height (hit), lie (li), surprise (sur-PRIZ)
ih	bitter (BIH-tur), pill (pihl)
o	cotton (KO-tuhn), hot (hot)
oh	below (bee-LOH), coat (koht), note (noht), wholesome (HOHL-suhm)
oo	good (good), look (look)
ow	couch (kowch), how (how)
oy	boy (boy), coin (koyn)
uh	about (uh-BOWT), butter (BUH-tuhr), enough (ee-NUHF), other (UH-thur)

Consonant Sounds

Symbol	Spelled (Pronounced)
ch	beach (beech), chimp (chihmp)
g	beg (behg), disguise (dihs-GIZ), get (geht)
j	digit (DIH-juht), edge (ehj), jet (jeht)
k	cat (kat), kitten (KIH-tuhn), hex (hehks)
s	cellar (SEHL-ur), save (sayv), scent (sehnt)
sh	champagne (sham-PAYN), issue (IH-shew), shop (shop)
ur	birth (burth), disturb (dihs-TURB), earth (urth), letter (LEH-tur)
y	useful (YEWS-fuhl), young (yuhng)
z	business (BIHZ-nehs), zest (zehst)
zh	vision (VIH-zhuhn)

Complete List of Contents

Volume 1

Volume 2

Volume 3

Volume 4

Volume 5

Musicians
& Composers
of the 20th Century

Billy Strayhorn

American jazz pianist and composer

An important jazz arranger and composer, Strayhorn is known for his longtime collaboration with Duke Ellington and for his compositions "Lush Life" and "Take the A Train."

Born: November 29, 1915; Dayton, Ohio
Died: May 31, 1967; New York, New York
Also known as: William Thomas Strayhorn (full name)
Member of: The Billy Strayhorn All-Stars

Principal recordings

ALBUMS: *Chelsea Bridge*, 1941; *Caravan*, 1947 (with the Duke Ellington All-Stars and the Billy Strayhorn All-Stars); *Trio*, 1950; *Satin Doll*, 1953; *Historically Speaking: The Duke*, 1956; *A Drum Is a Woman*, 1957; *Such Sweet Thunder*, 1957; *Billy Strayhorn/Johnny Dankworth*, 1958; *The Billy Strayhorn Septet*, 1958; *Cue for Saxophone*, 1959; *Johnny Hodges with Billy Strayhorn and the Orchestra*, 1961; *The Peaceful Side*, 1961; *Lush Life*, 1964; *The Far East Suite*, 1966; *And His Mother Called Him Bill*, 1967.
SINGLES: "Take the A Train," 1941.

The Life

William Thomas Strayhorn (STRAY-hohrn) was born to James and Lillian Strayhorn, and he was raised with four siblings in the Pittsburgh, Pennsylvania, area. By the time Strayhorn finished high school, he was an accomplished pianist performing with youth orchestras. He soon discovered jazz, and he began leading his own trio with success. During this time, he also studied at the Pittsburgh Musical Institute.

Strayhorn met Duke Ellington in 1938, impressing the bandleader with striking interpretations of several Ellington compositions. The following year, Strayhorn moved to New York City to work for Ellington. At that time, he began a serious relationship with a man named Aaron Bridgers. Strayhorn and Bridgers, unafraid to be open about their homosexuality at a time when most were secretive, shared an apartment in Harlem. Their relationship ended in 1947 when Bridgers left for Paris to pursue a career as a cocktail pianist. They remained friends and always reunited when Strayhorn visited Paris.

Later, Strayhorn became active in the Civil Rights movement after his close friends Arthur Logan (a prominent African American doctor) and his wife Marian introduced him to Martin Luther King, Jr. Strayhorn raised funds for King and participated in numerous demonstrations with the Logans and his longtime friend Lena Horne. Logan diagnosed Strayhorn, who was a heavy drinker and a smoker, with cancer of the esophagus in 1964. Bill Grove, Strayhorn's partner, was with him when he died in New York City in 1967.

The Music

Strayhorn was a gifted jazz pianist, composer, and arranger, and he spent the majority of his career working for and with Ellington. Partly because of his homosexuality, Strayhorn never sought the spotlight and worked mainly behind the scenes. Although he was capable of writing raucous swing numbers and simple blues tunes, Strayhorn's most personal works were introspective and revealed the influence of classical composers such as Claude Debussy and Maurice Ravel. During his lifetime, he made just one album as a leader (in 1961) and gave only one significant concert (at the request of the Duke Ellington Society in 1965).

Early Works. Strayhorn's early works are marked by the influence of George Gershwin. His first major work was *Concerto for Piano and Percussion*, which he performed at his high school graduation in 1934. The piece bore such a resemblance to Gershwin's *Rhapsody in Blue* (1924) that many of his classmates remember him playing that piece. After graduation Strayhorn wrote songs and skits for the musical revue *Fascinating Rhythm*, which was a hit in Pittsburgh and on the local African American theater circuit.

"Lush Life." Strayhorn's most important early work was "Lush Life," which he completed in 1936. The song tells the story of a jilted lover who plans to spend life drinking in a low-class bar surrounded by other lonely people. It is a strong example of Strayhorn's songwriting style. In "Lush Life" the chromatic harmony and the melody work alternately with and against the lyrics to create an organic whole. Strayhorn performed the song for

Billy Strayhorn. (Library of Congress)

friends and at parties, but he never intended it to be published or recorded. Nat King Cole decided to record it after hearing it in 1949, leading to broad recognition of the song. "Lush Life" was published that year, and it is one of Strayhorn's most important contributions to the jazz repertoire. Jazz musicians and several popular singers have made the song a standard.

"Take the A Train." Completed by Strayhorn in 1940, "Take the A Train" became the Duke Ellington Orchestra's theme song. Describing subway directions to Harlem, the song is a fast-tempo swing number with an unusually chromatic yet unforgettable melody. The composition was a fitting choice for Ellington's theme because of its energy and memorable melody and because of its musical inspiration from the African American culture of Harlem. Ellington is widely identified with this song, even though he did not write it. Unfortunately, because of this strong association, Strayhorn is often overlooked as the song's composer. "Take the A Train" is an important and regularly heard piece in jazz repertoire.

Such Sweet Thunder. As his career progressed, Ellington focused increasingly on creating large-scale works that challenged the conventions of the jazz idiom, and he relied heavily on Strayhorn's collaboration. Their preferred format was the suite, which allowed them to compile several shorter pieces, often with no direct relation to one another, into a greater and more prestigious whole. Among the most successful of these works was *Such Sweet Thunder*, inspired by the works of William Shakespeare and premiered in 1957 at Town Hall in New York. Included in the suite was Strayhorn's hauntingly beautiful ballad "Star-Crossed Lovers." The composition was actually completed earlier and recorded by Johnny Hodges as "Pretty Girl," but Ellington insisted upon renaming it and adding it to the suite. "Star-Crossed Lovers," referring to *Romeo and Juliet* (1597), is a strong example of Strayhorn's gift for making highly effective use of relatively few melodic and harmonic ideas, and it is considered a high point of the suite.

The Peaceful Side. Strayhorn's only album as a leader features him on piano, accompanied by bass, strings, and voices. His arrangements and performances of "Take the A Train," "Lush Life," "Day Dream," "Passion Flower," and "Chelsea Bridge" are restrained, introspective, and soft. The album provides further insight into Strayhorn's distinct musical personality because the performances of his best-known compositions are so different from the Duke Ellington Orchestra renderings.

Musical Legacy

Strayhorn's complete output as a composer is difficult to assess because he collaborated so extensively with Ellington, frequently without credit for his arrangements or for his entire compositions. Although scholars and musicians may debate the importance of Strayhorn's work, it is clear that his use of chromatic harmony and his comfort with adopting musical devices from bebop style helped to modernize jazz. Many of Strayhorn's compositions are standards of the jazz repertoire that are performed regularly. Interest in Strayhorn's music surged in the 1990's after Joe Henderson released a Grammy Award-winning album of Strayhorn's compositions called *Lush Life* in 1992 and David Hajdu released the excellent book *Lush Life: A Biography of Billy Strayhorn* in 1996.

Sam Miller

Further Reading

Dance, Stanley. *The World of Duke Ellington.* New York: Da Capo Press, 2000. This collection of essays and features by a longtime Duke Ellington Orchestra insider includes an interview with Strayhorn.

Hajdu, David. *Lush Life: A Biography of Billy Strayhorn.* New York: Farrar, Straus and Giroux, 1996. This thoroughly researched biography chronicles the life of the talented, gentle, and shy Strayhorn, who has been described as the alter ego of Ellington.

Leur, Walter van de. *Something to Live For: The Music of Billy Strayhorn.* Oxford, England: Oxford University Press, 2002. This careful examination of Strayhorn's individual contributions to the Ellington repertoire provides ample study of Strayhorn's work outside of the Ellington organization. Based on Strayhorn's actual scores.

Schuller, Gunther. "Duke Ellington." In *The Swing Era.* Oxford, England: Oxford University Press, 1989. This chapter in a lengthy study provides helpful analysis of several Strayhorn compositions as well as commentary on his role in the Duke Ellington Orchestra.

Tucker, Mark, ed. *The Duke Ellington Reader.* Oxford, England: Oxford University Press, 1995. This broad collection of Ellington-related material includes one of the few published interviews of Strayhorn.

See also: Cole, Nat King; Debussy, Claude; Ellington, Duke; Garner, Erroll; Gershwin, George; Gillespie, Dizzy; Horne, Lena; Peterson, Oscar; Ravel, Maurice.

Barbra Streisand

American popular and musical-theater singer-songwriter

In a five-decade career that has encompassed both stage and screen performances as well as studio recordings, Streisand is the most famous singing actress of her generation. Her iconic and ubiquitous presence as an artist, director, and producer has influenced an entire generation on Broadway and in Hollywood.

Born: April 24, 1942; Brooklyn, New York
Also known as: Barbara Joan Streisand (full name)

Principal recordings

ALBUMS: *The Barbra Streisand Album,* 1963; *The Second Barbra Streisand Album,* 1963; *People,* 1964; *The Third Album,* 1964; *My Name Is Barbra,* 1965; *My Name Is Barbra, Two . . . ,* 1965; *Color Me Barbra,* 1966; *Je m'appelle Barbra,* 1966; *A Christmas Album,* 1967; *Simply Streisand,* 1967; *A Happening in Central Park,* 1968; *What About Today?,* 1969; *On a Clear Day You Can See Forever,* 1970 (with Yves Montand); *Barbra Joan Streisand,* 1971; *Stoney End,* 1971; *Barbra Streisand . . . and Other Musical Instruments,* 1973; *Butterfly,* 1974; *The Way We Were,* 1974; *Lazy Afternoon,* 1975; *A Star Is Born,* 1976 (with Kris Kristofferson); *Classical Barbra,* 1976; *Streisand Superman,* 1977; *Songbird,* 1978; *Wet,* 1979; *Guilty,* 1980 (with Barry Gibb); *Yentl,* 1983; *Emotion,* 1984; *The Broadway Album,* 1985; *Till I Loved You,* 1988; *Back to Broadway,* 1993; *Streisand Sings Harold Arlen,* 1993; *Higher Ground,* 1997; *A Love Like Ours,* 1999; *Timeless: Live in Concert,* 2000; *Christmas Memories,* 2001; *The Movie Album,* 2003.

The Life

Barbra Streisand (STRI-zand) was born Barbara Joan Streisand in Brooklyn, New York, to Emanuel and Diana Rosen Streisand. Her father—an observant Jew who held advanced degrees and taught English literature—died when Barbara was only fifteen months old; his premature death would profoundly affect Barbara's personal and professional life. Her mother soon remarried Louis Kind, with whom Barbara had a difficult relationship. Barbara's half sister, Rosalyn Kind, also pursued a career in show business, while her older brother, Sheldon Streisand, stayed away from the public spotlight.

Against her mother's wishes, Streisand, immediately following high school graduation, pursued a career in show business. She gained some immediate success as a nightclub singer and performer in Off-Off-Broadway productions. Her boyfriend at the time, Barry Dennen, helped her to create her own club act, which was first performed in gay bars in Manhattan's Greenwich Village and later taken regionally. It was during this early phase of her career that she shortened her name to "Barbra" to make it more distinctive. She gained some modest fame through this act, appearing on *The Tonight Show* with Jack Paar and on some local and national radio broadcasts, including *60 Minutes* with Mike Wallace and Joyce Davidson.

Her big break, however, came in 1962, when Streisand was cast in the small feature role of Miss Marmelstein in the Broadway production of *I Can Get It for You Wholesale*. Her show-stopping song won her the unanimous affection of critics and audiences alike and led directly to her first recording contract with Columbia Records later that year. The resulting debut album, *The Barbra Streisand Album*, went on to win two Grammy awards. An appearance on *The Ed Sullivan Show* led to a tour with the popular pianist Liberace and secured her even more fame. Two more albums followed rather quickly: *The Second Barbra Streisand Album* and *The Third Album*; at one point, all of her first three albums were in the Top 10 on the *Billboard* chart at the same time—an astonishing feat in the rock-and-roll-dominated charts of the early 1960's.

Streisand returned to Broadway in 1964 in the starring role of Fanny Brice in Jule Styne and Bob Merrill's musical *Funny Girl* (libretto by Isobel Lennart). Her acclaimed performance also introduced two of her signature tunes: "People" and "Don't Rain on My Parade." During this period Streisand also became the youngest woman ever to be featured on the cover of *Time* magazine. Her success in the role of Fanny Brice was reprised twice: once in London's West End and again in the movie

version of *Funny Girl* (1968), for which she won the Academy Award for Best Actress in a Leading Role.

In the late 1960's, Streisand retreated from the live performance area and focused exclusively on recording and film acting. For a brief period, she tried to adapt her singing style to a contemporary rock idiom, but she eventually returned to her forte: melodic tunes of Broadway, the American songbook, and ballads. The anachronistic nature of her later recordings did not seem to alienate her fan base, however, and her albums continued to sell millions of copies. Her iconic grip on public affection was reiterated in 1985 with the surprise number-one hit *The Broadway Album*, which was certified quadruple platinum. To this day, only Elvis Presley and the Beatles have sold more albums than Streisand.

Although Streisand continued to record and make albums, she also began to devote much of her time to producing, directing, and acting in Hollywood films. She also developed a reputation as a political fund-raiser and activist for the Democratic Party. In 1993, Streisand made worldwide headlines when she gave her first public concert appearances in twenty-seven years. With high-end tickets costing in the neighborhood of fifteen hundred dollars each, Streisand became the highest-paid stage performer in history. Repeated limited-run concert events in 2000 and 2006 garnered similar successes. In 2008, *Forbes* magazine ranked Streisand as the second richest woman in the music industry, right behind Madonna.

The Music

Barbra Streisand's musical achievement can be assessed in three different ways: through her roles as a singing actress in Broadway and Hollywood musicals, as a prolific recording artist, and as an occasional composer. Although she also achieved great success as a film director, dramatic actress, writer, and political activist, these endeavors are beyond the scope of her musical legacy.

Although Streisand's early vocal style shows some jazz influence, she never improvised on any of her recordings. Rather, her expression comes through careful attention to text with nuanced embellishments, usually at important words. Her unique phrasing and storytelling capability derive directly from her formidable talent and experience as an actress. Streisand's vocal style and repertoire have remained remarkably consistent throughout her long career. Although she has, on occasion, explored genres as diverse as rock, soul, gospel, and classical music, her voice is heard to best advantage in show tunes, film themes, and contemporary pop ballads.

Broadway, Stage, and Film. Streisand began her singing career and secured her fame in the live area as a stage performer. After a short stint of successful nightclub singing and comedy routines in New York City, Las Vegas, and on television specials, she took Broadway by storm, making star turns as Miss Marmelstein in *I Can Get It for You Wholesale* (1962) and as Fanny Brice in *Funny Girl* (1964). She reprised the role of Fanny Brice in London and Hollywood, starring in the 1968 movie of the same name.

In the late 1960's, Streisand curiously retreated from live performing, focusing instead on recording projects and dramatic acting in the film indus-

Barbra Streisand. (AP/Wide World Photos)

try. She returned to live concert performing—and extraordinary acclaim—in 1993, 2000, and 2006. All of these concert productions have been archived on best-selling DVDs. DVDs of her very first television appearances from the early 1960's have also been made available to the public.

Compositions. While Streisand is primarily remembered as a vocalist and interpreter of songs written by other composers, lyricists, and arrangers, she has actively participated as composer, lyricist, or arranger of about two dozen songs in her extensive output of recordings. As a composer, "Evergreen" (1976) is her most famous song (with lyrics by Paul Williams). It was written for the film *A Star Is Born* (1976) and won a Grammy Award, an Academy Award, and a Golden Globe Award for Best Original Song.

Recordings. As a musician, Streisand's legacy rests largely on the fame and success of her numerous studio recordings. The eclectic nature of Streisand's career has given her a ubiquitous presence in the recording industry. In addition to her own solo recordings, usually marketed as "pop" or "easy listening," she has also contributed to the sound tracks of Broadway cast recordings and Hollywood films.

As the best-selling female recording artist of all time, Streisand is one of the industry's most bankable singers. Most of her steady stream of solo studio recordings (thirty out of thirty-three) have been certified as gold or platinum, and six of them have reached the number-one spot on the *Billboard* chart. The most notable of these recordings are *The Barbra Streisand Album, People, The Christmas Album, The Way We Were, A Star Is Born, Streisand Superman, Guilty, The Broadway Album, Back to Broadway*, and *Higher Ground*. Streisand is better known for her albums than her singles, but many of her singles have also charted well, and she has netted five number-one *Billboard* hits: "The Way We Were" (1974), "Evergreen" (1976), "You Don't Bring Me Flowers" (1978), "No More Tears" (1979), and

"Woman in Love" (1980). She has also recorded successful duets with artists as diverse as Neil Diamond ("You Don't Bring Me Flowers," 1978), Donna Summer ("No More Tears," 1979), Barry Gibb ("Guilty," 1980), Vince Gill ("If Ever You Leave Me," 1998), and Tony Bennett ("Smile," 2006).

As of 2008, Streisand had won a career total of eight competitive Grammy Awards for both albums and singles: *The Barbra Streisand Album* (two Grammy Awards), "People" (from the *Funny Girl* cast recording), *My Name Is Barbra*, "Evergreen" (two, from the sound track to the film *A Star Is Born*), "Guilty" (from *Guilty*), and *The Broadway Album*. In addition, she won the honorary Grammy Legend Award in 1992 and the Grammy Lifetime Achievement Award in 1994—at the age of only fifty-two. The *Funny Girl* original cast recording, *The Barbra Streisand Album*, and "The Way We Were" have all been inducted into the Grammy Hall of Fame.

Musical Legacy

In the fifth decade of her illustrious career, Barbra Streisand was one of the most recognizable names in the entertainment industry and one of America's greatest success stories. As a singer, actress, director, producer, composer, lyricist, and entrepreneur, she is revered as one of the most versatile musical artists of any generation. Moreover, with more than 145 million albums sold, she is the highest-ranking female artist in the history of the American recording industry. She is one of the very few entertainers who has won the "GATE," an acronym for the four principal awards of the entertainment industry: the Grammy, the Academy Award, the Tony, and the Emmy. Although her high profile as an outspoken political activist has at times overshadowed her creative endeavors, she has cemented her place in history as a unique musical and dramatic icon and a major influence on an entire generation of singing stylists.

Matthew Ryan Hoch

Further Reading

Ardia, Bernie. *Barbra Streisand in New York City: A Self-Guided Tour of Landmark Locations in the Career of Barbra Streisand*. Parker, Colo.: Outskirts Press, 2007. This unique publication offers a bio-graphical and geographical retrospective on Streisand's long career in New York City. Special attention is given to Streisand's childhood and formative years.

Dennen, Barry. *My Life with Barbra: A Love Story*. Amherst, N.Y.: Prometheus Books, 1997. Written by Barbra's early costar, mentor, and love interest, this is a revered classic among Streisand fans. Dennen offers a personal glimpse at Streisand's development as an artist during the formative stages of her career.

Edwards, Anne. *Streisand: A Biography*. Boston: Little, Brown, 1997. Of all the Streisand biographies, Edwards's offers the longest and most thorough account of Streisand's career. Painstakingly researched, this biography provides both essential facts and interesting anecdotes.

Pohly, Linda. *The Barbra Streisand Companion: A Guide to Her Vocal Style and Repertoire*. Westport, Conn.: Greenwood Press, 2000. Pohly's book is the best single-volume introduction to Streisand's music. Her entire recorded oeuvre is analyzed within a biographical context, and Streisand's place within the fabric of American popular culture is also assessed.

Santopietro, Tom. *The Importance of Being Barbra: The Brilliant, Tumultuous Career of Barbra Streisand*. New York: Thomas Dunne Books, 2006. In his engaging (and sometimes over-the-top) style, musical-theater stage manager Santopietro critiques Streisand's career. The erudite Santopietro is able to offer intimate details of Streisand's career that are not in print elsewhere.

Waldman, Allison. *The Barbra Streisand Scrapbook: Revised and Updated*. New York: Citadel Press, 2001. This book is often regarded as the definitive retrospective of Streisand's career. In addition to chronicling Streisand's music, films, and production projects, Waldman delves into other literature written about Streisand, separating fact from fiction and debunking myth and rumor.

See also: Bergman, Alan; Coleman, Cy; Diamond, Neil; Elliot, Cass; Gibb, Barry, Maurice, and Robin; Hamlisch, Marvin; Kristofferson, Kris; Latifah, Queen; Legrand, Michel; Merman, Ethel; Sainte-Marie, Buffy; Styne, Jule.

Joe Strummer

English rock singer, songwriter, and guitarist

Strummer was one of the original poets of punk, influencing the punk and rock genres.

Born: August 21, 1952; Ankara, Turkey
Died: December 22, 2002; Broomfield, Somerset, England
Also known as: John Graham Mellor (birth name); Woody Mellor
Member of: The Clash; the Latino Rockabilly War; the Mescaleros

Principal recordings

ALBUMS (solo): *Walker*, 1987; *Earthquake Weather*, 1989.
ALBUMS (with the Clash): *The Clash*, 1977; *Give 'Em Enough Rope*, 1978; *London Calling*, 1979; *Sandinista!*, 1980; *Combat Rock*, 1982; *Cut the Crap*, 1985.
ALBUMS (with the Mescaleros): *Rock Art and the X-Ray Style*, 1999; *Global A Go-Go*, 2001; *Streetcore*, 2003.

The Life

Born in Turkey, Joe Strummer spent most of his childhood in foreign countries because of his father's job. At age ten he was sent back to Britain to attend boarding school with his brother. Idolizing rock and roll, Strummer decided to learn the guitar. During his post-grade school years, he played with part-time bands and made aborted attempts at attending college. In the beginning he called himself Woody Mellor, but eventually he changed his name to Joe Strummer to reflect his rudimentary guitar abilities. After the name change, he joined the Clash in 1976.

The Clash played with success until 1982, when internal troubles derailed the band and permanently ended it in 1986. After the Clash, Strummer moved to limited acting parts and scoring films. In 1989 he had a brief stint with the band the Latino Rockabilly War. This lasted for one album, and then he was back scoring sound tracks and making guest appearances in other bands for tours and recordings.

In 1979 Strummer met Gaby Salter, and they had two children. The couple split in 1993, and in 1995 Strummer married Lucinda Tait. Strummer continued to work with mainstream rockers such as Bono of U2 to promote various charitable causes. In 1999 Strummer started the Mescaleros. On December 22, 2002, Strummer died unexpectedly of an undiagnosed congenital heart defect.

The Music

Strummer was approached by Mick Jones and Paul Simonon to join their next project, and the resulting band was the Clash. Experimenting with punk, rock, ska, reggae, and dub, the Clash forged a unique sound with a purpose. Unlike many punk bands of the day, the Clash chose social activism as a lyrical engine. It was one of the first British punk bands to support a cause other than anarchy. These lyrics can be attributed to Strummer and Jones, who generally shared credit on most Clash songs.

The Clash. The group's debut album, *The Clash*, was released in Great Britain in 1977 on CBS Records. A popular import, the album finally was released in America in 1979. *The Clash* contained multiple songs with political meaning. "White Riot" calls for white youth to become more politically active in their daily life; "Remote Control" rails against conformity. The album achieved great success in Great Britain, establishing the Clash as one of the preeminent British punk bands.

London Calling. *Rolling Stone* and *Time* hailed 1978's *Give 'Em Enough Rope* as album of the year. However, 1979's *London Calling* was the Clash's hallmark. Voted number-one album of the 1980's by *Rolling Stone*, *London Calling* was for the fans. It was twice as long as most releases because the Clash had persuaded Epic Records to produce a double album. *London Calling* experimented with ska, reggae, and classic rock, infusing them into the Clash's signature sound. It featured memorable Clash songs, for example, the title track, which describes a world falling apart. More politically charged tunes include "Spanish Bombs," "Lost in the Supermarket," "Clampdown," and "The Guns of Brixton." *London Calling* was the pinnacle of the Clash's career and the beginning of tensions within the band.

Sandinista! Released in 1980, *Sandinista!*—with its thirty-six tracks—outdid *London Calling*. *Sandi-*

nista! had such political statements as "The Call Up" and "Washington Bullets." It also featured "The Magnificent Seven," one of the first rap songs by a British artist. Heavy ska and reggae influences can be heard in the album. Although the album lists "The Clash" as the author of every song, Strummer wrote the lyrics to most of them, adding his liberal viewpoint.

Combat Rock. The band released *Combat Rock* in 1982. Strummer sang "Know Your Rights" and "Rock the Casbah," both sociopolitical commentaries—the first about personal rights and the second about Iranian censorship. The album also included the Clash classic "Should I Stay or Should I Go?" Like all Clash albums, it is significant for its social commentary, providing a blueprint for other punk bands.

Grosse Pointe Blank. Following the Clash's demise in 1986, Strummer moved on to cinema. He acted as well as put together sound tracks for many films. Among the most famous of these is 1997's *Grosse Pointe Blank*, which starred John Cusack. Besides writing sound tracks, Strummer started the band the Latino Rockabilly War in 1989, producing only one album before breaking up. During the 1990's Strummer kept active with recording and with guest appearances for other bands' shows. In 1999 he started the Mescaleros, returning to the punk roots of the Clash and broadening the sound by working with such artists as Roger Daltrey of the Who and Johnny Cash. The band's album *Streetcore* was released after Strummer died.

Musical Legacy

Strummer was critical to the rock and punk genres, primarily for his lyrical contribution to social activism, which became an essential element of punk bands that followed. His support of humanitarian causes and his benefit concerts made him a role model for all musicians. Strummer notably was dedicated to his fans, and the Clash produced large albums at little cost, grateful to their supporters who were the source of the band's success. Strummer's influence can be heard in the many bands that cover his and the rest of the Clash's songs. The Clash was inducted into the Rock and Roll Hall of Fame in 2003.

Daniel R. Vogel

Further Reading

D'Ambrosio, Antonino. *Let Fury Have the Hour: The Punk Rock Politics of Joe Strummer.* New York: Nation Books, 2004. An analysis of the meaning of Strummer's work. Includes bibliography.

Davie, Anthony. *Vision of a Homeland: The History of Joe Strummer and the Mescaleros.* Northampton, England: Effective, 2004. A history of Strummer's later band, with an account of Strummer's death. Includes complete discography.

Gilbert, Pat. *Passion Is a Fashion: The Real Story of the Clash.* Cambridge, Mass.: Da Capo Press, 2005. A detailed history of the Clash. Includes bibliography, index, and discography.

Needs, Kris. *Joe Strummer and the Legend of the Clash.* London: Plexus, 2005. By a journalist who toured with the band, this is a musical biography of Strummer and the group.

Salewicz, Chris. *Redemption Song: The Ballad of Joe Strummer.* New York: Faber and Faber, 2007. A well-written biography of Strummer. Includes photographs.

See also: Bono; Cash, Johnny; Cliff, Jimmy; Daltrey, Roger.

Jule Styne

American popular music and musical-theater composer and lyricist

Styne's songs from his early days in Hollywood to his successful run on Broadway are firmly established in the popular repertoire. Styne updated the book musical, adapting his style to meet the changing times and audiences.

Born: December 31, 1905; London, England
Died: September 20, 1994; New York, New York
Also known as: Julius Kerwin Stein (birth name)

Principal works

MUSICAL THEATER (music): *High Button Shoes*, 1947 (libretto by Stephen Longstreet; music and lyrics by Jule Styne and Sammy Cahn); *Gentlemen Prefer Blondes*, 1949 (libretto by Joseph Fields and Anita Loos; lyrics by Leo Robin); *Two on the Aisle*, 1951 (libretto and lyrics by Betty Comden and Adolph Green); *Hazel Flagg*, 1953 (libretto by Ben Hecht; lyrics by Bob Hilliard); *Bells Are Ringing*, 1956 (libretto and lyrics by Comden and Green); *Say, Darling*, 1958 (libretto by Richard Bissell, Abe Burrows, and Marian Bissell; lyrics by Comden and Green); *Gypsy*, 1959 (libretto by Arthur Laurents; lyrics by Stephen Sondheim); *Do Re Mi*, 1960 (libretto by Garson Kanin; lyrics by Comden and Green); *Subways Are for Sleeping*, 1961 (libretto and lyrics by Comden and Green); *Fade Out—Fade In*, 1964 (libretto and lyrics by Comden and Green); *Funny Girl*, 1964 (libretto by Isobel Lennart; lyrics by Bob Merrill); *Hallelujah, Baby!*, 1967 (libretto by Laurents; lyrics by Comden and Green); *Darling of the Day*, 1968 (libretto by Nunally Johnson; lyrics by E. Y. Harburg); *Look to the Lilies*, 1970 (libretto by Leonard Spigelgass; lyrics by Cahn); *Sugar*, 1972 (libretto by Peter Stone; lyrics by Merrill); *Lorelei*, 1974 (libretto by Kenny Solms and Gail Parent; lyrics by Comden and Green); *One Night Stand*, 1980 (libretto and lyrics by Herb Gardner); *The Red Shoes*, 1993 (libretto by Marsha Norman; lyrics by Norman and Paul Stryker).

SONGS (music; lyrics by Sammy Cahn): "I'll Walk Alone," 1944; "I Fall in Love Too Easily," 1945; "The Things We Did Last Summer," 1946; "Time After Time," 1947; "There's Nothing Rougher than Love," 1949; "10, 432 Sheep," 1950; "Three Coins in the Fountain," 1954.

Jule Styne. (AP/Wide World Photos)

The Life

Jule Styne (jewl stin) was born Julius Kerwin Stein, the son of Ukrainian Jewish immigrants who moved to Chicago from London when Styne was eight. He was a child prodigy on the piano, and during his teens he played in bands and clubs. Styne moved to Hollywood in the 1930's, where he began his career as a coach and an arranger for actors Alice Faye and Shirley Temple, among others. His first songs at Paramount Pictures were written with Frank Loesser, but when Styne moved to Republic Studios, he began a long, although not exclusive, collaboration with Sammy Cahn that led to fifteen number-one songs, including "Three Coins in the Fountain," "I'll Walk Alone," and "Time After Time."

Styne's first Broadway show, *High Button Shoes*, written with choreographer Jerome Robbins, was a hit, and it ran for more than two years. *Gentlemen Prefer Blondes* made Carol Channing a star. Styne began a long and successful collaboration with Betty Comden and Adolph Green in 1951. Their 1956 hit *Bells Are Ringing* featured Judy Holliday, and it introduced the hit song "Just in Time," the music for which Styne had been playing as a party song until Comden and Green came up with lyrics for it. Styne's biggest hits were *Gypsy* (written with Stephen Sondheim) and *Funny Girl* (for which he teamed with Bob Merrill). His last songs were written for the short-lived Broadway adaptation of *The Red Shoes*. Styne died of heart failure in 1994 at the age of eighty-eight.

The Music

In contrast to other Broadway composers' works, Styne's music often had a big band sound, probably the result of his work in clubs and bands as a teenager and his extensive work in films. His scores in the late 1950's begin to show a sensitivity ("The

Party's Over") that led to the raw depth of emotion in *Gypsy* and *Funny Girl*.

Early Works. Styne's film work is usually remembered for his more nostalgic songs, such as "Three Coins in the Fountain," "I Fall in Love Too Easily," and "The Things We Did Last Summer." However, he also produced brassy showstoppers, such as "There's Nothing Rougher than Love" and the delightful novelty song "10,432 Sheep."

Gypsy. Styne created a tour de force for singer Ethel Merman in *Gypsy*, based on the life of stripper Gypsy Rose Lee and her domineering stage mother. More than the songs in his earlier shows such as *Bells Are Ringing*, the songs in this show reflect Styne's work in film: the dance swing of "All I Need Is the Girl," the brass of "You Gotta Have a Gimmick," the quiet moments of "Little Lamb" and "Small World," and the song that became Merman's trademark, "Everything's Coming Up Roses." Her turbulent showstopper "Rose's Turn" was added late in development of the show. Styne composed the music first, and Sondheim had to fit his lyrics to the composer's symphonic-like monologue. Styne tried this type of onstage confessional again in his next show, *Do Re Mi*, in Phil Silvers's "All of My Life."

Funny Girl. Two of Styne's most famous songs were written for Barbra Streisand, who proved to be an ideal interpreter of his music in the Broadway hit *Funny Girl*. "People" is a soaring, heartfelt ballad that reveals a seldom-seen side of Styne. The fist-shaking brassiness of "Don't Rain on My Parade" echoes Styne's early film work for Doris Day and others. At the same time, Styne could return to themes in *Gentlemen Prefer Blondes* and *Bells Are Ringing* for the sexual tango of "You Are Woman." The composer was not happy with the film version, which jettisoned two top-notch numbers, "Who Are You Now" and "The Music That Makes Me Dance," so Streisand could sing songs made popular by Fanny Brice, the "funny girl" of the title.

Hallelujah, Baby! Styne received his only Tony Award for *Hallelujah, Baby!* This was likely a consolation prize, since his earlier hits had faced stiff competition in the years they were nominated: *Gypsy* went up against *The Sound of Music* (1959), and *Funny Girl* went up against *Hello, Dolly!* (1964). Arthur Laurents's book, which deals with racial relations through the curious conceit of characters

who do not age more than a half century, was too preachy for many audiences, and Comden and Green's lyrics are little more than serviceable. "My Own Morning," the protagonist Georgina's opening number, echoes songs in *Gypsy* and *Funny Girl* as she daydreams about what the future holds. "Being Good," which closes the act, tries to recapture the success of "People" without the earlier song's emotional punch. The title song, in the second act, has a 1960's swing, but it is symptomatic of the uninspired quality of Styne's score.

Musical Legacy

Styne was one of the most prolific songwriters of his generation, with fifteen hundred published songs. Styne did not produce a distinctive sound; rather, he molded his music to the requirements of the words. Styne composed soaring ballads such as "People" as well as volcanic tour de forces such as "Rose's Turn" and comedy numbers such as "What's New at the Zoo." He was known for his affinity for the female voice, and he usually crafted his shows around the female star. The composer won one Academy Award and one Tony Award, although he had multiple nominations in both areas. Nevertheless, his songs are still firmly entrenched in the popular repertoire, as evidenced by reworkings of "Diamonds Are a Girl's Best Friend" by Madonna and by Nicole Kidman in the Baz Luhrmann film *Moulin Rouge* (2001). Styne received the Kennedy Center Honors in 1990.

David E. Anderson

Further Reading

Cahn, Sammy. *I Should Care: The Sammy Cahn Story.* New York: Arbor House, 1974. Styne's longtime and arguably most important collaborator recalls their work together in motion pictures. Cahn's book contains an important firsthand account of Styne's pre-Broadway days.

Mordden, Ethan. *Coming Up Roses: The Broadway Musical in the 1950's.* New York: Oxford University Press, 2000. Mordden is well known for his encyclopedic and catty surveys of Broadway musicals. This volume sheds light on the creation of and original performances of two of Styne's most important shows, *Bells Are Ringing* and *Gypsy*.

_____. *Open a New Window: The Broadway Musical in the 1960's.* New York: Macmillan, 2002.

Mordden's survey of the decade is an important source for readers interested in the Broadway version of *Funny Girl*, but he gives *Hallelujah, Baby!* only a cursory nod.

Taylor, Theodore. *Jule: The Story of Jule Styne.* New York: Random House, 1979. This is a typical popular-style musical biography, but it is not the final word, since the composer lived for fifteen more years.

Wilk, Max. *They're Playing Our Song: Conversations with America's Classic Songwriters.* New York: Da Capo Press, 1997. Styne wrote the preface for this collection of conversations with many illustrious songwriters, and he takes center stage in the chapter "People Who Need People." Wilk's book is important for Styne's extended account of his career as well as for the profiles of other composers.

See also: Cahn, Sammy; Coleman, Cy; Davis, Sammy, Jr.; Fain, Sammy; Green, Adolph, and Betty Comden; Horne, Lena; Loesser, Frank; Madonna; Merman, Ethel; Ronstadt, Linda; Sondheim, Stephen; Streisand, Barbra.

Donna Summer

American rhythm-and-blues singer-songwriter

An international star for over four decades, Summer was the "Queen of Disco" from the mid-1970's into the 1980's. Her unique combination of electronica/techno, disco, rhythm-and-blues, rock, funk, gospel, and soul music led to groundbreaking and bestselling recordings, which earned the top music awards.

Born: December 31, 1948; Boston, Massachusetts
Also known as: LaDonna Adrian Gaines (birth name)

Principal recordings

ALBUMS: *Lady of the Night*, 1974; *Love to Love You Baby*, 1975; *A Love Trilogy*, 1976; *Four Seasons of Love*, 1976; *I Remember Yesterday*, 1977; *Once Upon a Time*, 1977; *Live and More*, 1978; *Bad Girls*, 1979; *The Wanderer*, 1980; *Donna Summer*, 1982; *She Works Hard for the Money*, 1983; *Cats Without Claws*, 1984; *All Systems Go*, 1987; *Another Place and Time*, 1989; *Mistaken Identity*, 1991; *Christmas Spirit*, 1994; *Crayons*, 2008; *Shout It Out*, 2008.

WRITINGS OF INTEREST: *Ordinary Girl: The Journey*, 2003.

The Life

Donna Summer was born LaDonna Adrian Gaines in Boston, Massachusetts. Her father Andrew was a building superintendent and electrician, while her mother Mary worked in a factory. At the age of eight, the musically gifted Summer began singing in church choirs. In her teens, Summer sang with Crow, a Boston rock band. In 1968, she moved to Munich to join the German production of *Hair*. She also performed with the Vienna Folk Opera and won roles in musical theater, including *Godspell* (1970), *Show Boat* (1927), and *Porgy and Bess* (1935).

Summer married actor Helmut Sommor in 1972, and their daughter Mimi was born in 1973. They divorced, but she took "Summer" as her professional name. Working as a backup singer, she met producer-songwriters Giorgio Moroder and Pete Bellotte. They produced a single, "The Hostage," which was a hit in France, Holland, and Belgium. In 1975, they released the single "Love to Love You Baby," which established Summer as an international star. The team produced numerous other award-winning hits.

In 1980 Summer married singer Bruce Sudano. Their daughter Brooklyn was born in 1981, and another daughter, Amanda, was born in 1982. A new album, *Mistaken Identity*, was released in 1991, and Summer's autobiography, *Ordinary Girl*, was published in 2003. In May, 2008, Summer released *Crayons*, her first album of new material in seventeen years.

The Music

Before becoming a disco superstar in the mid-1970's, Summer sang gospel and rock music in the United States and then performed in European musical-theater productions. With her amazing voice, versatility, and remarkable songwriting abilities, Summer was able to have an impact on pop music into the twenty-first century.

"Love to Love You Baby." Released in 1975, this was Summer's first hit, and it helped bring the emerging, subculture disco genre into the mainstream. It also established Summer as the queen of disco. Originally, Summer, Moroder, and Bellotte had recorded the song as a three-and-a-half-minute single. However, at the urging of Casablanca Records president Neil Bogart, the team remixed the track into a seventeen-minute epic, perfect for dance clubs. Thus the 12-inch extended remix was invented. "Love to Love You Baby" featured a pulsating dance beat, a syncopated bass line, steamy groans and sighing, heavy breathing, and high-pitched murmuring. The overt, unabashed sensuality of the song prompted the British Broadcasting Corporation to ban it.

"I Feel Love." Summer's 1977 concept album, *I Remember Yesterday* included the futuristic song "I Feel Love." While previous disco recordings had used acoustic orchestral music for backing tracks, "I Feel Love" had a totally synthesized backing track. "I Feel Love" was Summer's second hit song, reaching number six in the U.S. *Billboard* Hot 100 and number one in the United Kingdom's singles chart. The song featured a driving, hypnotic, and robotic bass line with an off-center counter-rhythm. The pervasive electronic beat was immediately imitated in other disco music and influenced the development of electronica/techno music in the 1980's and 1990's. For her recording of "I Feel Love," Summer was inducted into the Dance Music Hall of Fame in 2004.

"Last Dance." In the 1978 film *Thank God It's Friday*, Summer sang her signature song, "Last Dance." She played the role of aspiring singer Nicole Sims, whose song repeatedly asked the listener to dance the last dance, and take the "last chance for love." With a slow introduction and a slow middle, it was one of the first disco songs to use slow-tempo sections. Summer used this format in subsequent hits, such as "Dim All the Lights," "No More Tears (Enough Is Enough)," and "On the Radio." One of Summer's personal favorites, "Last Dance" won an Academy Award, a Golden Globe, and a Grammy.

"She Works Hard for the Money." Released in 1983, this hit song became a feminist anthem. Summer appeared as a waitress on the cover and sang the praises of the working woman, who labored long hours for low pay. She also produced a music

Donna Summer. (Photoshot/Landov)

video that concluded with an empowering dance in the street by women of various occupations. This was the first music video by a black artist to be extensively promoted on MTV. In 1999, the fast-food restaurant McDonald's used the song for a television campaign but with a variation on the lyrics. The commercials featured Summer singing, "You Get More for the Money."

Crayons. In 2008 Summer released the long-awaited *Crayons*. As track four proclaimed, "The Queen is back!" The album is an eclectic mix of twelve songs of different "colors," sounds, styles, and ethnic traditions. For instance, "Crayons" has a reggae influence, and "Driving Down Brazil" has a Latin/jazz beat. The disco-styled, "I'm a Fire" was the first single from the album and reached number one on the *Billboard* Hot Dance Club play charts. *Crayons* reflects Summer's unique combination of different styles and world cultural experiences.

Musical Legacy

The legendary Summer achieved many firsts. She was the first artist to earn three consecutive number-one platinum double albums and to win the Grammy for Best Rock Vocal Performance (Female), in 1979 for "Hot Stuff." In 1997, she received the first Grammy for Best Dance Recording ("Carry On"). Summer was also the first woman to have four number-one singles in one year. The only artist to have had a number-one dance hit in every decade beginning in the 1970's, Summer has sold more than 130 million records worldwide.

Summer changed music history with "Love to Love You Baby," which brought disco into the mainstream. She has influenced generations of artists. "I Feel Love" inspired Deborah Harry's "Heart of Glass" and Diana Ross's "Love Hangover." Madonna sang "I Feel Love" on a live tour. Beyoncé incorporated "Love to Love You Baby" into one of her songs. Summer's energetic fusion of dance and vocals influenced Whitney Houston and Mariah Carey. Cowritten with her husband, Bruce Sudano, "Starting Over Again" was a hit song for both Dolly Parton and Reba McEntire.

Alice Myers

Further Reading

Gaar, Gillian G. *She's a Rebel: The History of Women in Rock and Roll*. Seattle, Wash.: Seal Press, 2002. This well-researched history of women in rock and roll includes discussions of disco and Summer's career. Illustrated; bibliography and index.

Howard, Josiah. *Donna Summer: Her Life and Music.* Cranberry Township, Pa.: Tiny Ripple Books, 2003. An unauthorized biography based on interviews, televisions shows, and articles. Illustrated; discography and bibliography.

Jones, Alan, and Jussi Kantonen. *Saturday Night Forever: The Story of Disco*. Edinburgh: Mainstream, 2005. Two chapters cover Summer's significance to the disco era. Illustrated. Discography and index.

Shapiro, Peter. *Turn the Beat Around: The Secret History of Disco*. New York: Faber and Faber, 2005. Includes numerous sections about Summer, including her role in Eurodisco and automating the beat. Illustrated; time line, discography, bibliography, and index.

Summer, Donna, and Marc Eliot. *Ordinary Girl: The Journey*. New York: Villard, 2003. A candid autobiography, covering Summer's rise to fame and spiritual transformation. Illustrated; discography and index.

See also: Bowie, David; Gibb, Barry, Maurice, and Robin; Hayes, Isaac; Jay-Z; Lomax, Alan; Stewart, Rod; Streisand, Barbra.

Sun Ra

American jazz pianist and composer

Sun Ra is noted for his unique brand of avant-garde jazz improvisation and his thought-provoking Afrocentric philosophy.

Born: May 22, 1914; Birmingham, Alabama
Died: May 30, 1993; Birmingham, Alabama
Also known as: Herman Poole Blount (birth name); Sonny Blount; Le Sony'r Ra
Member of: The Sun Ra Arkestra; Sun Ra and His Astro Infinity Arkestra; Sun Ra and His Myth Science Arkestra; Sun Ra and His Solar Arkestra

Principal recordings

ALBUMS (with the Sun Ra Arkestra unless otherwise stated): *Angels and Demons at Play*, 1956; *Bad and Beautiful*, 1956 (with Sun Ra and His Myth Science Arkestra); *Interstellar Low Ways*, 1956; *Jazz by Sun Ra*, 1956; *Sun Ra Visits Planet Earth*, 1956 (with Sun Ra and His Solar Arkestra); *Sun Song*, 1956; *Super-Sonic Jazz*, 1956; *We Travel the Spaceways*, 1956 (with Sun Ra and His Myth Science Arkestra); *Sound of Joy*, 1957; *Jazz in Silhouette*, 1958; *The Nubians of Plutonia*, 1959 (with Sun Ra and His Myth Science Arkestra; *Rocket Number Nine*, 1960 (with Sun Ra and His Myth Science Arkestra); *Cosmic Tones for Mental Therapy*, 1961; *Fate in a Pleasant Mood*, 1961 (with Sun Ra and His Myth Science Arkestra; *The Futuristic Sounds of Sun Ra*, 1961 (also released as *We Are in the Future*); *Secrets of the Sun*, 1961 (with Sun Ra and His Solar Arkestra); *When Sun Comes Out*, 1962 (with Sun Ra and His Astro Infinity Arkestra);

Other Planes of There, 1964 (with Sun Ra and His Solar Arkestra); *Art Forms of Dimensions Tomorrow*, 1965 (with Sun Ra and His Myth Science Arkestra); *The Heliocentric Worlds of Sun Ra, Vol. I*, 1965; *The Heliocentric Worlds of Sun Ra, Vol. II*, 1965; *The Magic City*, 1965; *Nothing Is*, 1966; *Strange Strings*, 1966; *Atlantis*, 1967; *Monorails and Satellites*, 1968; *Holiday for Soul Dance*, 1969 (with Sun Ra and His Astro Infinity Arkestra); *My Brother the Wind, Vol. 2*, 1969; *Sound Sun Pleasure!!*, 1970 (with Sun Ra and His Astro Infinity Arkestra); *My Brother the Wind, Vol. 1*, 1971; *Space Is the Place*, 1972; *Saint Louis Blues: Solo Piano*, 1977; *Solo Piano, Vol. 1*, 1977; *Lanquidity*, 1978; *The Other Side of the Sun*, 1978; *Visions*, 1978; *Strange Celestial Road*, 1980; *Sunrise in Different Dimensions*, 1980; *Nuclear War*, 1982; *Hours After*, 1986; *Reflections in Blue*, 1986; *Mayan Temples*, 1990; *Purple Night*, 1990.

The Life

Sun Ra (suhn rah) was born Herman Poole Blount in Birmingham, Alabama. He showed a talent for music at a young age and began composing original songs on the piano by the age of twelve. By the time he was in his mid-teens, he was performing locally with various jazz and rhythm-and-blues groups. During his high school years, Sun Ra began to read books on Freemasonry and other esoteric studies that would later provide core elements to his personal philosophy. Sun Ra graduated from Birmingham Industrial High School at the top of his class. After high school he went to Alabama A&M University on a music-education scholarship but left after one year.

It was during that year that Ra claimed to have had a mystical experience that inspired his particular philosophical path. After leaving college, Sun Ra devoted his time to playing music until October, 1942, when he received his draft notice. Sun Ra attempted to get conscientious-objector status based on his religious convictions but was denied by the draft board. He appealed the decision and was assigned to alternative service at a camp in Pennsylvania. Sun Ra did not report to the camp and was arrested for draft evasion. After pleading his case in court, Sun Ra was sentenced to prison. He spent a few weeks in prison before his conscientious-objector status was reaffirmed and he was taken to

the work camp. Soon, Sun Ra was given a medical status of 4-F because of a hernia and was declared unfit for military service. He left the camp and returned to Birmingham. He moved to Chicago in 1945 and in 1952 legally changed his name to Le Sony'r Ra. In Chicago Ra met Alton Abraham, who would work with Ra for many years.

Ra moved to New York in 1961 and lived communally with his bandmates. They began experimenting with a freer sound, and by 1966 the band had a regular gig at Solug's Saloon. His music began to be appreciated by the growing psychedelic music scene, and in 1968 Sun Ra and his Arkestra toured the West Coast for the first time. The concert in San Jose, California, was reviewed in the new and influential rock music magazine *Rolling Stone*. In the late 1960's the band moved to Philadelphia, which became its base of operations until Sun Ra's death in 1993.

The Music

Sun Ra's musical career began in earnest after his move to Chicago, where he quickly found work backing up blues singer Wynonie Harris, recording two singles in 1946 with her. Working as Sonny Blount, before he had his name legally changed, Sun Ra performed with saxophonist Coleman Hawkins and violinist Stuff Smith in a trio in 1948. By 1952 he was playing with the Space Trio, a group that also included the drummer Tommy "Bugs" Hunter and saxophonist Pat Patrick. Sun Ra and Abraham formed Saturn Records in the mid-1950's, and the label released a few Sun Ra singles and two full-length compilation albums. Sun Ra's album *Sun Song* was released on producer Tom Wilson's Transition Records. While his sidemen changed frequently, John Gilmore on tenor saxophone, alto saxophonist Marshall Allen, and baritone saxophonist Pat Patrick were with him consistently throughout his entire recording career.

The Futuristic Sounds of Sun Ra. This album, released in 1961, is perhaps the first recorded expression of the essential sound of the Sun Ra Arkestra. Also released as *We Are in the Future*, the album is bebop with echoes of traditional jazz. Sun Ra plays piano and is joined by seven other musicians, including Gilmore on tenor saxophone and bass clarinet and Allen on alto saxophone and several other instruments.

Art Forms of Dimensions Tomorrow. This album carried the sound hinted at in Sun Ra's 1961 albums, including *The Futuristic Sounds of Sun Ra*. Electronic reverb and echo combined with percussive rhythms push the more atmospheric sounds of the 1961 albums in a different direction.

The Magic City. This is the best known of Sun Ra's albums from this period. A clash of sounds and vibrations, the 1965 album includes an expanded Arkestra and represents Sun Ra's take on the tumultuous politics and cultural upheavals of the period.

Atlantis. A landmark, the album features a long work led by Sun Ra on organ and followed up by four pieces, also led by Sun Ra, who plays a Clavoline keyboard wired to sound like an electric guitar. This album is the culmination of Sun Ra's late-1960's amalgam of soul, psychedelic, bebop, and (as one critic put it) the "whole of the universe."

Purple Night. Released in 1990, this was one of the last albums to feature Sun Ra on piano. Recorded with a twenty-two-member band, it represents much of Sun Ra's output in the 1980's, with an uplifting, often melodic, and rarely angry sound.

Musical Legacy

Sun Ra experimented with a combination of styles and used instruments to create sounds for which they might not have been originally intended. Sun Ra's music stands alone in its understanding of musicality beyond the standard diatonic scale and its commentary on modern culture. Combining some of the world's most ancient sounds and concepts with new electronic instruments to create unique music, Sun Ra has influenced jazz, rock, and hip-hop artists.

Ron Jacobs

Further Reading

Lock, Graham. *Blutopia: Visions of the Future and Revisions of the Past in the Work of Sun Ra, Duke Ellington, and Anthony Braxton*. Durham, N.C.: Duke University Press, 1999. Lock examines and compares the work of Sun Ra, Ellington, and Braxton in the context of each man's vision of an imagined utopian world. This book looks at each of these artists in relation to his African American heritage and desire to overcome U.S. racism and create a world beyond racism.

Ra, Sun. *Sun Ra: The Immeasurable Equation*. Chandler, Ariz.: Phaelos Books, 2005. This book includes all of Sun Ra's known nonmusical material.

_____. *The Wisdom of Sun Ra: Sun Ra's Polemical Broadsheets and Streetcorner Leaflets*. Edited by Anthony Elms and John Corbett. Chicago: WhiteWalls, 2006. A selection of writings by Sun Ra on race, music, extraterrestrial visitations, and politics. Taken together with his music, this book provides a clearer glimpse of the phenomenon that was Sun Ra.

Swed, John. *Space Is the Place: The Lives and Times of Sun Ra*. New York: Pantheon Books, 1997. Essential biography for anybody interested in Sun Ra's life and music. Swed discusses and analyzes concerts, recordings, and the personal adventures of Sun Ra.

Swenson, John. "Images of Tomorrow Disguised as Jazz." *Rolling Stone*, March 4, 1993. A crisp record review, Swenson's article is a short yet complete overview of Sun Ra's musical history, placing it in historical jazz context while linking it clearly to the artistry of rock and roll.

See also: Coltrane, John; Ellington, Duke; Hawkins, Coleman; Sanders, Pharoah.

Dame Joan Sutherland
Australian operatic soprano

One of the twentieth century's greatest opera singers, Sutherland became known for a voice of immense size and range. She was praised for her phenomenal vocal agility, seamless legato singing, and powerful high notes. She became instrumental in the mid-twentieth century renaissance of bel canto opera.

Born: November 7, 1926; Sydney, Australia
Also known as: Joan Alston Sutherland (full name); La Stupenda

Principal works

OPERATIC ROLES: Dido in Henry Purcell's *Dido and Aeneas*, 1947; Judith in Eugene Goossens's

Judith, 1951; First Lady in Wolfgang Amadeus Mozart's *Die Zauberflöte*, 1952 (*The Magic Flute*); Clotilde in Vincenzo Bellini's *Norma*, 1952; Amelia in Giuseppe Verdi's *Un Ballo in Maschera*, 1952 (*The Masked Ball*); Frasquita in Georges Bizet's *Carmen*, 1953; Gloriana in Benjamin Britten's *Gloriana*, 1953; La Contessa in Mozart's *Le nozze di Figaro*, 1953 (*The Marriage of Figaro*); Aida in Verdi's *Aida*, 1954; Agathe in Carl Maria von Weber's *Der Freischutz*, 1954 (*The Free Shooter*); Eva in Richard Wagner's *Die Meistersinger von Nürnberg*, 1954 (*The Master Singers of Nuremberg*); Woglinde in *Das Rheingold*, 1954; Jennifer in Michael Tippett's *The Midsummer Marriage*, 1955; Pamina in Mozart's *Die Zauberflöte*, 1956 (*The Magic Flute*); Alcina in George Frideric Handel's *Alcina*, 1957; Emilia in Gaetano Donizetti's *Emilia di Liverpool*, 1957; Desdemona in Verdi's *Otello*, 1957; Gilda in Verdi's *Rigoletto*, 1957; Madame Lidoine in Francis Poulenc's *Dialogues des Carmélites*, 1958 (*Dialogues of the Carmelites*); Donna Anna in Mozart's *Don Giovanni*, 1958; Lucia in Donizetti's *Lucia di Lammermoor*, 1959; Elvira in Bellini's *I Puritani*, 1960; Amina in Bellini's *La Sonnambula*, 1960 (*The Sleepwalker*); Violetta in Verdi's *La Traviata*, 1960; Beatrice in Bellini's *Beatrice di Tenda*, 1961; Semiramide in Giacchino Rossini's *Semiramide*, 1962; Cleopatra in Handel's *Giulio Cesare*, 1963 (*Julius Caesar*); Norma in Bellini's *Norma*, 1963; Marguerite in Charles Gounod's *Faust*, 1965; Marie in Donizetti's *La Fille du Régiment*, 1966 (*The Daughter of the Regiment*); Lakmé in Léo Delibes's *Lakmé*, 1967; Maria Stuarda in Donizetti's *Maria Stuarda*, 1971 (*Mary Stuart*); Lucrezia Borgia in Donizetti's *Lucrezia Borgia*, 1972; Rosalinde in Johann Strauss's *Die Fledermaus*, 1973; Esclarmonde in Jules Massenet's *Esclarmonde*, 1974; Lenora in Verdi's *Il Trovatore*, 1975; Amalia in Verdi's *I masnadieri*, 1980 (*The Bandits*); Adriana Lecouvreur in Francesco Cilea's *Adriana Lecouvreur*, 1983; Anna Bolena in Donizetti's *Anna Bolena*, 1984; Ophélie in Ambroise Thomas's *Hamlet*, 1985; Marguerite de Valois in Giacomo Meyerbeer's *Les Huguenots*, 1990.

The Life

Joan Alston Sutherland was the second child of William McDonald Sutherland and Muriel Alston. She received her earliest vocal instruction from her mother, an amateur singer, and began formal voice lessons with John and Aida Dickens at the age of nineteen. During these formative years, Sutherland sang concerts and oratorios in her hometown of Sydney, Australia. She made her operatic debut with the title role in *Judith* by Eugene Goossens at the Sydney Conservatorium in 1951.

In 1951 Sutherland moved to London to continue her studies at the Opera School of the Royal Conservatory of Music. She made her debut at the Royal Opera House at Covent Garden in 1952. In 1954 she married pianist, conductor, and fellow Australian Richard Bonynge. She gave birth to their son, Adam Bonynge, in 1956.

Sutherland made her international debut singing Donna Anna in *Don Giovanni* at the Vancouver Festival in 1958, but it was her success in *Lucia di Lammermoor* in 1959 at Covent Garden that launched her remarkable career. After a performance of George Frideric Handel's *Alcina* in 1960 at La Fenice theater in Venice, Sutherland was given the soubriquet La Stupenda (the stupendous one) by the critics. During her extensive career she traveled to every major opera house in the world, where she sang with some of the twentieth century's greatest artists. Her husband conducted many of her performances and accompanied her in numerous recitals. She made her final performance at Covent Garden on December 31, 1990.

The Music

During the early years at Covent Garden, Sutherland performed a wide variety of soprano roles. These included lyric soprano parts as well as heavier, dramatic soprano roles such as Aida, Eva in *Die Meistersinger von Nürnberg*, and Woglinde in *Das Rheingold*. Because of the large size of her voice, many conductors predicted she would become a great Wagnerian soprano. It was her husband, Richard Bonynge, who encouraged her to specialize in coloratura roles and bel canto opera. With the aid of his coaching, she expanded her range, developed her phenomenal vocal agility, and learned many of her signature operatic roles. Of the fifty-five operas Sutherland performed during her career, *Lucia di Lammermoor*, *I Puritani*, and *Norma* were among her most famous.

Lucia di Lammermoor. Gaetano Donizetti's opera provided the perfect vehicle to display the vocal talents of Joan Sutherland. Her first performance as Lucia was on February 17, 1959, at Covent Garden in London. Franco Zeffirelli directed and Tullio Serafin conducted this production, which was mounted to feature Sutherland. The performances at Covent Garden were so successful that Sutherland was quickly engaged to sing Lucia at many of the world's greatest opera houses. She made her debuts at the Paris Opéra (April 25, 1960), La Scala (May 14, 1961), and the Metropolitan Opera (November 26, 1961) in highly acclaimed productions of *Lucia di Lammermoor*.

In 1961 she recorded the opera for the Decca record label with the chorus and orchestra of the Accademia di Santa Cecilia conducted by John Pritchard. This early recording featured Renato Cioni as Edgardo, Robert Merrill as Enrico, and Cesare Siepi as Raimondo. Sutherland recorded *Lucia di Lammermoor* again for Decca in 1971, this time with Bonynge conducting the Covent Garden Orchestra. This second recording features Luciano Pavarotti, Sherrill Milnes, and Nicolai Ghiaurov. A live recording from the 1959 production at Covent Garden was released in 1998 by the Melodram label. Sutherland sang 211 performances of the opera during her career. Her final appearance as Lucia was in Barcelona in 1988.

I Puritani. Sutherland made her first excursion into the operas of Vincenzo Bellini with the role of Elvira in *I Puritani* at Glyndebourne on May 24, 1960. This demanding role requires a large voice to carry over the orchestra, a strong middle register, a comfortable low range, tremendous flexibility, and secure high notes. Sutherland's voice met these challenges with great success. Between 1960 and 1987 she sang in sixty-eight performances of *I Puritani* in London, New York, Barcelona, Palermo, Genoa, Sydney, Los Angeles, Sacramento, Philadelphia, and Boston. Sutherland and Bonynge recorded *I Puritani* for Decca in 1963 and again in 1973. A live recording from Palermo, conducted by Serafin in 1961, was released by Bella Voce Records in 1997.

Norma. Sutherland furthered her status as one of the foremost interpreters of the bel canto repertoire with her performance of the titular role in Bellini's *Norma* in Vancouver in 1963. This performance also marked her first performance with another noted interpreter of bel canto opera, mezzo-soprano Marilyn Horne, who was to become a frequent collaborator. Sutherland sang 111 performances of *Norma* at the Metropolitan Opera, Covent Garden, San Fransisco Opera, and the Sydney Opera, among many other venues. Her recording of *Norma* for Decca was with the London Symphony under the direction of Bonynge in 1964. Her second studio recording of Norma, with the Welsh National Opera Orchestra, was made in 1984.

Musical Legacy

Sutherland's role in the mid-twentieth century resurgence of interest in the operas of Giacchino Rossini, Bellini, and Donizetti cannot be under-

Dame Joan Sutherland. (CBS/Landov)

stated. In addition, Sutherland was also instrumental in the revival of Handel's music in the 1950's. She was one of the most prolific recording artists of her era, leaving behind a sizable discography. Her career as an operatic and concert singer lasted more than forty years, and she was honored with several awards during her career. In 1975 she was made a Companion of the Order of Australia; in 1978 she was named Dame Commander of the British Empire; and in 1991 Queen Elizabeth II bestowed on her the Order of Merit.

Michael Hix

Further Reading

Adams, Brian. *La Stupenda: A Biography of Joan Sutherland*. Melbourne, Vic.: Hutchinson Group, 1980. Adams wrote this biography shortly after completing his documentary film *Joan Sutherland: A Life on the Move*. The book includes discographies for both Sutherland and Bonynge, a list of Sutherland's first performances of operatic roles, and a bibliography.

Hines, Jerome. "Joan Sutherland." In *Great Singers on Great Singing*. Garden City, N.Y.: Doubleday, 1982. Sutherland discusses concepts related to vocal technique in this interview with Hines.

Major, Norma. *Joan Sutherland: The Authorized Biography*. Boston: Little, Brown, 1994. Major's text is the most extensive biography of Sutherland. It includes a complete catalog of her concert and operatic performances and a comprehensive discography.

Steane, John B. "Let the Florida Music Praise: Rococo Revival." In *The Grand Tradition: Seventy Years of Singing on Record*. New York: Charles Scribner's Sons, 1974. Stean's text discusses the importance of Sutherland's recordings.

Sutherland, Joan. *A Prima Donna's Progress: The Autobiography of Joan Sutherland*. Washington, D.C.: Regnery, 1997. Sutherland's autobiography is an unassuming description of her exceptional career.

See also: Callas, Maria; Pavarotti, Luciano; Sills, Beverly.

Shin'ichi Suzuki
Japanese classical violinist

Driven by his belief that playing music would come as naturally and as early to children as learning to speak, Suzuki developed a method of teaching children as young as three years old to play musical instruments based on listening rather than reading sheet music.

Born: October 17, 1898; Nagoya, Japan
Died: January 26, 1998; Matsumoto, Japan
Also known as: Suzuki Sensei

Principal works

WRITINGS OF INTEREST: *Suzuki Violin School: Suzuki Method*, 1955-1968; *Ai ni ikiru: sainō wa umaretsuki de wa nai*, 1966 (*Nurtured by Love: A New Approach to Education*, 1969); *Sainō kaihatsu no jissai*, 1971; *Suzuki Shin'ichi Zen-Shū*, 1985 (complete works).

The Life

Shin'ichi Suzuki (shin-ee-chee suh-zew-kee) was born to Masakichi and Ryoh Fujie Suzuki, whose factory made musical instruments. In 1915, listening to recordings of violinist Mischa Elman, Suzuki was inspired to teach himself to play the violin.

In 1921 Suzuki traveled to Berlin to study violin with Karl Klinger. He befriended Albert Einstein and fell in love with German soprano singer Waltraud Prange, whom he married on February 8, 1928.

Returning to Japan in 1928, Suzuki and three of his brothers formed the Suzuki Quartet. In 1935 he became a music teacher. After his father's factory was firebombed in World War II, Suzuki left teaching to build wooden aircraft parts. He adopted a war orphan, a boy named Matsui.

In 1946 Suzuki founded a music school for young children that developed into the Talent Education Research Institute. His annual concerts in the 1950's featured performances by his pupils that became famous. Suzuki and his top students were invited to perform at national and international venues.

Throughout the 1960's and continuing to the 1990's, Suzuki's success and fame as a gentle revolutionary music educator grew, and he was awarded many national and international honors and prizes. When Suzuki died in his hundredth year in 1998, a Catholic Mass at his institute commemorated his passing.

The Music

Suzuki's classical education in Germany prepared him for his career as Japan's first professional concert violinist after his return to Japan in 1928. The success of the Suzuki Quartet, playing classical Western music, occurred in the culturally exciting years just before Japanese militarism and war-related austerity measures choked off artistic and aesthetic life.

While still passionately playing the violin and performing in public, Suzuki turned to education. In 1935 he was appointed to teach at the Imperial School of Music and the Kunitachi College of Music, both in Tokyo.

Talent Education Research Institute. The horrors and suffering of World War II deeply affected Suzuki. After he witnessed the loss of his father's music-instrument plant to incendiary bombs, Suzuki relinquished his formal teaching positions. While working in the armaments industry, Suzuki began to teach war orphans, believing that the power of music could restore their hurt souls.

After the war Suzuki moved to Matsumoto and founded his own music school, the Talent Education Research Institute (TERI). His school was based on Suzuki's overriding belief that any talent, including musical talent, was a product of education rather than a gift of genius. Second, Suzuki was convinced that just as children learned to speak their native language early, before they could read or write it, so children could play a musical instrument just by listening to music and then performing it on their own child-sized instruments. Finally, Suzuki thought that teaching

children to play music helped shape their character, so they would become sensitive, disciplined, and able to endure difficulties. His goal was to educate the noble, beautiful hearts of children and young adults who would help rebuild Japan with new, democratic, and peaceful ideas.

At TERI Suzuki encouraged parents to let their children, even as young as three years old, listen to violin music and then play on their custom-made small violins. He demanded that parents actively involve themselves in the musical education of their children, attending their children's classes, listening to their children playing at home, and providing a supportive environment.

Suzuki wrote down the principles of his method in 1948, calling his approach "talent education" and expressing his belief that talent was taught.

Nurtured by Love. The success of his young pupils, whose public performances he organized and supported at both TERI and other venues, earned Suzuki respect and spread acceptance and demand for his method. In 1951 Suzuki received the Chunchi Culture Award. At the 1958 National Music Festival in Japan Suzuki's speech on music education was well received. He earned the Shinmai

Shin'ichi Suzuki. (Hulton Archive/Getty Images)

Culture Award in 1961. After his top pupils' success in 1964 at the Japanese Music Educators' national conference and at the American String Teachers Association, some critics charged Suzuki with trying forcibly to create child prodigies. In response, Suzuki published *Ai ni ikiru: sainō wa umaretsuki de wa nai* (*Nurtured by Love: A New Approach to Education*). The book passionately expressed Suzuki's idea that his method was designed to improve the skill and character of students for their own enjoyment and not geared toward raising professionals.

Nurtured by Love: A New Approach to Education established Suzuki as an internationally recognized, innovative music educator. In 1969 he received the Ysayi Award in Belgium and in 1976 the Mobil Music Award in Japan. In 1982 he was awarded the order of the Palmes Académiques from the French government, and he won the Kohl International Education Award in the United States in 1994. Throughout the decades, Suzuki continued to educate his pupils according to his talent education method and wrote widely to disseminate his ideas. He was involved in music education up to his death.

Musical Legacy

Suzuki was one of Japan's most innovative and influential music educators of the postwar period of the twentieth century. Suzuki's belief in the power of education and the success of his students earned him international respect.

Affectionately called Suzuki Sensei, or teacher Suzuki, Suzuki developed a pedagogic approach well suited to supporting Japan's postwar reconstruction. His method—with its emphasis on pupils' equality, nurturing education, and developing a fine, sensitive character—aided Japan's postwar rejection of the militarism and imperialism of the 1930's and 1940's.

Suzuki's method was adopted internationally. By 2007 approximately 300,000 students in thirty-four countries were learning to play music by the Suzuki method. In Japan more than one hundred music schools are affiliated with regional Suzuki Institutes. There were four international Suzuki Associations, covering Asia, the Americas, Europe, and the Pan-Pacific.

R. C. Lutz

Further Reading

Cannon, Jerlene. *Diamond in the Sky*. Miami, Fla.: Summy-Birchard, 2002. Sympathetic biography of Suzuki, written for young adults. Showcases Suzuki's belief that musical skills can be nurtured in every child.

Collins, David. *Dr. Shinichi Suzuki: Teaching Music from the Heart*. Greensboro, N.C.: Morgan Reynolds, 2002. Appreciative description and analysis of the Suzuki method. Bibliography of Suzuki's writings.

Duke, Robert A. "Teacher and Student Behavior in Suzuki String Lessons." *Journal of Research in Music Education* 47, no. 4 (Winter, 1999): 293-307. Academic report of a study of music teachers employing the Suzuki method and their relationship with their students and the students' parents. Illustrates the benefits of Suzuki's style of early music teaching.

Suzuki, Shin'ichi. *Ability Development from Age Zero*. Van Nuys, Calif.: Alfred, 1999. Expresses Suzuki's belief that talent is a product of the environment; guides parents on how to foster their children's joy in learning to play music from an early age.

_____. *Nurtured by Love*. 2d ed. Van Nuys, Calif.: Alfred, 1986. This edition of Suzuki's 1966 classic is the most widely available in English. Excellent introduction to Suzuki's method and its underpinning philosophy. The principles of the Suzuki method are interspersed with autobiographical stories.

See also: Chung, Kyung-Wha; Kreisler, Fritz.

George Szell

Hungarian classical conductor and pianist

With his legendary musical perfectionism and his extraordinary conducting technique, Szell is credited with establishing the Cleveland Orchestra as one of world's premier symphony orchestras.

Born: June 7, 1897; Budapest, Hungary
Died: July 30, 1970; Cleveland, Ohio
Also known as: György Széll (birth name)

Principal recordings

ALBUMS (as conductor): *Bach: Concerto for Violin No. 2 in E Major*, 1953; *Mozart: Symphony No. 40 in G Minor*, 1955; *Mozart: Le Nozze di Figaro*, 1957; *Dvořák: Symphony No. 8 in G Major, Op. 88*, 1958; *Prokofiev: Symphony No. 5 in B-flat Major, Op. 100*, 1959; *Tchaikovsky: Symphony No. 5/Szell with the Cleveland Orchestra*, 1959; *Mendelssohn: Concerto for Violin in E Minor, Op. 64*, 1961; *Mozart: Symphony No. 33 in B-flat Major*, 1962; *Dvořák: Carnival Overture, Op. 92*, 1963; *Tchaikovsky: Concerto for Violin in D Major, Op. 35*, 1965; *Beethoven: Concerto for Piano No. 1 in C Major, Op. 15*, 1968; *Beethoven: Concerto for Piano No. 3 in C Minor, Op. 37*, 1969; *Beethoven: Symphony No. 5 in C Minor, Op. 67*, 1969.

ALBUMS (as pianist): *Brahms: Quintet for Piano and Strings in F Minor, Op. 34*, 1945; *Mozart: Quartet for Piano and Strings No. 1 in G Minor*, 1946; *Mozart: Sonata for Violin and Piano in C Major*, 1946; *Schubert: Quintet for Piano and Strings in A Major, Op. 114*, 1946.

The Life

George Szell (zehl) was born György Széll in Budapest, Hungary, on June 7, 1897. At age two, Szell already demonstrated remarkable talent; by age three, his father moved the family to Vienna so that the boy could begin proper piano instruction. Szell thrived as a student of renowned pedagogue Richard Robert (who also taught Rudolph Serkin), and at age eleven, the prodigy gave a European concert tour, leading some to dub him "the new Mozart." In addition to piano, Szell studied and mastered harmony, counterpoint, and form, briefly studying composition with Max Reger. At age fourteen, Szell was signed to an exclusive ten-year publishing contract with Vienna's Universal Edition. At age seventeen, Szell appeared with the Berlin Philharmonic as composer, conductor, and pianist.

The turning point to full-time conducting probably came when Szell stepped in for a conductor, who had suddenly injured his arm, at a concert series at the summer resort where Szell and his family were on holiday. In 1946 Szell became director of the Cleveland Orchestra, and he is credited with making it the one of the greatest symphony orchestras of all time. Because they set the standard for orchestral preparation and sound, his legendary rehearsal techniques and recordings continue to be studied.

The Music

Szell is revered as one of the greatest conductors in history, and his name is synonymous with that of the Cleveland Orchestra. Under Szell's direction, it became one of the finest in the world. In addition to insisting on rigorous, extensive rehearsals, Szell increased the number of the orchestra's members and the length of the concert season. He also inaugurated the orchestra's summer series with the opening of the Blossom Music Center. Szell had the orchestra's home, Severance Hall, acoustically redesigned to make it more resonant, and he established the orchestra's well-received international tours. In addition, he made numerous critically and commercially acclaimed recordings of orchestral standards.

Early Career. At age eighteen, Szell won an appointment to Berlin's Royal Opera as an unpaid pianist-coach. He immediately made a great impression on the music director, Richard Strauss. In turn, Szell credited Strauss for his influence on Szell's conducting technique. The two remained lifelong friends.

Szell gradually transitioned from opera to symphony conducting, and he held posts all over Europe, including appointments in Strasbourg (1917), Prague (1919-1921), Darmstadt (1922), and Düsseldorf (1922-1924). From 1924 to 1930, he was principal conductor of the Berlin Opera, which had replaced the Royal Opera. In 1930 Szell made his American debut with the St. Louis Symphony Orchestra. Later in the decade, Szell avoided the roiling political climate on the European continent by conducting in the United Kingdom (where he eventually became conductor of the Scottish Orchestra) and in the Netherlands (where he became principal guest conductor of The Hague's Residence Orchestra). The Australian Broadcasting Commission invited Szell to conduct its celebrity series of concerts during the summers of 1938 and 1939.

United States. Because of the tremendous political tension in Europe, Szell and his wife decided to move to the United States in August, 1939, and he began to teach at New York's New School for Social Research and at Mannes School of Music. Szell soon received conducting invitations to the Detroit Symphony, the Hollywood Bowl, and the Ravinia Festival in Highland Park, Illinois. In 1941 Arturo Toscanini invited Szell to conduct some concerts with the NBC Symphony, and the following year, Szell made his conducting debut with the Metropolitan Opera, where he remained on the conducting staff until 1946. In 1943 Szell made his debut and began his lifelong association with the New York Philharmonic.

Cleveland. In 1946 Szell became a U.S. citizen and the music director of the Cleveland Orchestra. He transformed the local ensemble into a world-renowned musical powerhouse. He dismissed some musicians, and he hired exceptional replacements, subsequently expanding the orchestra to include more than one hundred musicians. His rehearsal technique remains legendary. He demanded perfection from each orchestra member, resulting in an impeccable sound that was likened to the precision of a string quartet. Szell's efforts brought the local orchestra to international attention, placing it on par with the best in the world.

In addition to improving the orchestra's quality, Szell extended its concert season, and he established a summer home, the Blossom Music Center. Severance Hall had acoustical problems from its inception, but they were not amended until Szell had it redesigned to include an acoustical shell, affectionately dubbed the "Szell shell." The result was extremely successful, and Severance Hall became a wonderful venue to showcase the orchestra's unparalleled sound.

Szell is credited with taking the orchestra on annual tours to Carnegie Hall and other East Coast venues, as well as with inaugurating international tours to Europe and Asia. He led the orchestra in numerous critically and commercially acclaimed recording projects, many of which are extant. Szell conducted numerous world premieres, several of which he and the Cleveland Orchestra commissioned. He frequently conducted and made several recordings with Amsterdam's Concertgebouw Orchestra, and he regularly appeared with the London Symphony Orchestra, the New York Philharmonic, the Vienna Philharmonic, and at the Salzburg Festival. He remained with the orchestra until his death in 1970.

Musical Legacy

Szell's musical legacy is truly remarkable, and it is readily evident in his historical recordings and in the high quality of the Cleveland Orchestra. He transformed a regional ensemble to a paramount one with his tireless devotion to perfection and musicality. Szell's legendary rehearsals and precision brought the Cleveland Orchestra to the world's stage, and it set the standard for subsequent music directors to maintain. The numerous recordings he left are authoritative for musicians and music lovers around the globe.

Anastasia Pike

Further Reading

Henahan, Donal. "George Szell, Conductor, Is Dead." *The New York Times*, July 31, 1970. A well-written and extensive tribute to New York City's lifelong friend, Szell, published the day after he died.

Rosenberg, Donald. *The Cleveland Orchestra Story*. Cleveland, Ohio: Gray, 2000. In a book about the Cleveland Orchestra, Rosenberg traces its history, from its inception through its tenure with Christoph von Dohnányi.

Schonberg, Harold. *The Great Conductors*. New York: Simon & Schuster, 1967. The former *New York Times* music critic's book is simply yet elegantly written, and it places Szell in context with other conducting greats.

Slominsky, Nicholas, and Laura Diane Kuhn. *Baker's Biographical Dictionary of Musicians*. New York: G. Schirmer, 2001. A wonderful and extensive resource covering the lives of notable musicians throughout history, with an entry on Szell.

See also: Busch, Adolf; Levine, James; Strauss, Richard; Toscanini, Arturo.

Joseph Szigeti
Hungarian classical violinist

An important concertizing violinist, Szigeti championed the notion that performers must remain faithful to composers' wishes as seen in notations on the printed score, a practice that broke with the current vogue but ultimately gained the respect of violinists, conductors, and critics.

Born: September 5, 1892; Budapest, Hungary
Died: February 19, 1973; Lucerne, Switzerland
Also known as: Jóska Singer (birth name)

Principal recordings
ALBUMS: *Bach: Partita for Violin Solo No. 3 in E Major*, 1908; *Brahms: Violin Concerto in D Major, Op. 77*, 1928; *Hungarian Folk Tunes: Bartók*, 1930; *Beethoven: Violin Concerto in D Major, Op. 61*, 1932; *Mendelssohn: Violin Concerto in E Minor, Op. 64*, 1933; *Mozart: Concerto for Violin, No. 4 in D Major*, 1934; *Prokofiev: Violin Concerto No. 1*, 1935; *Bach: Concerto for Two Violins in D Minor*, 1937; *Handel: Sonata for Violin and Basso Continuo in D Major, Opp. 1 and 3*, 1937; *Mozart: Sonata for Violin and Piano in E Minor*, 1937; *Concerto for Violin: Ernest Bloch*, 1939; *Bartók: Contrasts for Violin, Clarinet, and Piano*, 1940; *Debussy: Sonata for Violin and Piano in G Minor*, 1940; *Rhapsody for Violin and Piano: Béla Bartók*, 1940; *Beethoven: Sonata Nos. 4, 9, and 10*, 1944; *Stravinsky: Duo Concertant for Violin and Piano*, 1945; *Beethoven: Sonata for Violin and Piano, No. 5 in F Major, Op. 24, Spring*, 1948; *Bach: Brandenberg Concerto No. 1 in F Major*, 1950; *Hindemith: Sonata for Violin and Piano in E Major*, 1953; *Ravel: Sonata for Violin and Piano in G Major*, 1953; *Mozart: Sonata for Violin and Piano in B-flat Major*, 1955.
WRITINGS OF INTEREST: *With Strings Attached: Reminiscences and Reflections*, 1947; *A Violinist's Notebook: Two Hundred Music Examples with Notes for Practice and Performance*, 1964; *Beethoven's Violinwerke: Hinweise für Interpreten und Hörer*, 1965; *Szigeti on the Violin*, 1969; *Bach: Six Sonatas and Partitas for Solo Violin*, 2003.

The Life
Joseph Szigeti (SIH-geh-tee) was born Jóska Singer. He acquired the last name he would keep for life when, at the age of three, his mother died, and he moved to live with his grandparents in the town of Máramarous-Sziget in the Carpathian Mountains near modern Slovakia. He took early violin lessons in Hungary, he performed concerts around Europe, and he lived in England for six years (1907-1913). He moved to Switzerland in 1913, teaching at the Geneva Conservatory (from 1917 to 1925) and concertizing throughout Europe and America. In Geneva, he met his wife Wanda Ostrowska, and they were married in 1919. They had a daughter, Irene, shortly thereafter.

Szigeti emigrated to the United States in 1940, and he became a citizen in 1951. By this time, he was internationally acclaimed as a soloist, and he toured the world, performing in recitals and in concerts with orchestra. In the mid-1950's, arthritis began to affect his performances. He returned to Switzerland in 1960, spending the remainder of his life teaching and writing about the violin and its music. He died in 1973, at the age of eighty, in Lucerne.

The Music
Szigeti began to study the violin with his uncle, but his superlative talent was evident early on, and his father soon took him to Budapest to study with Jenö Hubay at the Franz Liszt Academy of Music. Among his fellow students were Stefi Geyer and Ferenc von Vecsey, both of whom established solid solo careers in the early to mid-twentieth century.

At the time that Szigeti began his career, fashion emphasized recitals of salon pieces by composers ranging from Pablo de Sarasate and Henryk Wieniawski to Fritz Kreisler, George Enescu, and František Drdla. The 78-rpm recorded disc was just becoming a household item, and the short side lengths, typically three to four minutes, were also well-suited to character pieces, thus making them an ideal way to supplement a concert career. Szigeti made his solo debut in Berlin in 1905 at age thirteen, but the concert received almost no press, and the result for Szigeti was a few years playing intermission entertainment between acts of operettas and circuses.

Influences: Busoni and Bartók. According to Szigeti, the salon miniatures he emphasized during these early days required little thought, and he began to give consideration to musical masterpieces by composers such as Johann Sebastian Bach, Wolfgang Amadeus Mozart, and Ludwig van Beethoven only after meeting and being mentored by pianist and composer Feruccio Busoni. The artists met in England while they were concertizing, and Busoni's influence was profound, coloring Szigeti's approach to music for the rest of his career as both a performer and a pedagogue.

Szigeti also met Béla Bartók in the first decade of the twentieth century. Several years later, they became fast friends, forming a concertizing duo, with Bartók playing the piano. (There is an important recording made by these two musicians at the Library of Congress in 1940—two days after Bartók arrived as an émigré—including the Sonata for Violin (1917) by Claude Debussy, Ludwig van Beethoven's Sonata No. 9 (1802), also known as the "Kreutzer," and Sonata for Violin No. 2 (1922) and Rhapsody No. 1 for Violin and Orchestra (1928) by Bartók.

Joseph Szigeti. (Library of Congress)

Performances. Szigeti's American debut occurred in 1925 at Carnegie Hall, when he performed Beethoven's Concerto for Violin (1806) with the Philadelphia Orchestra, conducted by Leopold Stokowski. This concert was an unqualified success, and it helped to secure his international performance career, which included concerts during the 1930's in Australia, New Zealand, South Africa, and South America. Until the 1950's, he was known as one of the top concertizing violinists in the world, and—because of his dedication to the composer's written intentions—he was often affectionately known as the "scholarly virtuoso."

Because of his noted commitment to contemporary music, Szigeti received the dedications of several important mid-twentieth century compositions, including violin concerti by Hamilton Harty, Frank Martin, Ernest Bloch, Bartók, and Eugène Ysaÿe. He performed the world premiere of Bloch's Concerto for Violin in Cleveland in 1938.

Writings on Music. Of the books he authored, *Szigeti on the Violin* is probably the most valuable. It presents elements of his biography as a prelude to a detailed analysis of his ideas on interpretation and technique, ranging from a discussion of fingering with respect to string color to larger concepts of phrasing. He also expresses his views on musical life, detailing the change of emphasis throughout the twentieth century from recitals as a proving ground for young musicians to the competition, a change he indicates was not in the best interests of profound music making.

Recordings. Szigeti made numerous recordings throughout his career, including all the major violin concerti and sonatas. Most, if not all, have been remastered to digital format. His last recordings, notably the complete solo sonatas and partitas by Johann Sebastian Bach, met with some criticism for inconsistencies of tone and execution, yet they still reveal Szigeti's legendary deep understanding of the music.

Musical Legacy

As a performer, Szigeti set a standard for faithful adherence to composers' wishes as seen on the printed score, rather than imposing a willful virtuosity upon the music. He was an early champion of twentieth century music, performing and commissioning concerti and chamber music by Igor

Stravinsky, Bartók, Maurice Ravel, Sergei Prokofiev, and Arthur Honegger. He lived in a time of great stylistic individuality in performance, and the concept of careful score study as a path toward understanding a composer's intentions was relatively new.

Szigeti's reception throughout his career was mixed. Some reviews described his tone as small but elegant and interpretations as dry and stiff. At the other end of the spectrum, crowds in Naples, Italy, cheered him for fifteen minutes at a concert in 1956. Nevertheless, Szigeti's adherence to the belief in the overarching value of a composer's intentions ultimately triumphed and became the fundamental rule of interpretation for the next several generations of performers.

Later in his life, when arthritis affected his technique, he retired from concertizing and taught violinists who became prominent musicians, including Arnold Steinhardt (first violinist for the Guarneri String Quartet) and concert soloist Kyung-Wha Chung. His students credit him with increasing their insight into the deep meaning of great music, much as Busoni did for Szigeti fifty years earlier.

Aside from his influence as a teacher, Szigeti's legacy rests upon his scholarly approach to performing, his writing (especially the book *Szigeti on the Violin*, which should be read by any serious student of the violin), and his leadership in commissioning two masterpieces by Bartók: 1940's *Contrasts* for violin, clarinet, and piano (commissioned jointly with clarinetist Benny Goodman) and 1944's *Concerto for Orchestra*. The commission for the latter piece was sprearheaded by Szigeti and conductor Fritz Reiner (ultimately made by conductor Serge Koussevitzky) almost as a charity gesture, because Bartók, near the end of his life, needed the money.

Jonathan A. Sturm

Further Reading

Horowtiz, Joseph. *Artists in Exile: How Refugees from Twentieth-Century War and Revolution Transformed the American Performing Arts*. New York: Harper, 2008. This book examines the lives and careers of performers who migrated to the United States from Russia or Europe, and it contains references to Szigeti.
Szigeti, Joseph. *Szigeti on the Violin*. New York: Dover Books, 1979. This book contains some autobiographical information, but more importantly it explores in detail issues of interpretation, including musical examples from masterpieces in the violin repertoire.
_____. *A Violinist's Notebook: Two Hundred Music Examples with Notes for Practice and Performance*. London: Gerald Duckworth, 1964. A literal master class in book form, with examples drawn from great violin literature, each with its own technical or musical problem that Szigeti explains in English and in German.
_____. *With Strings Attached*. New York: Alfred A. Knopf, 1947. Szigeti's autobiography, written (according to several reviews) rather haphazardly, yet it includes interesting glimpses of Szigeti's teachers, his colleagues, and personal details on his life. Includes a discography.

See also: Bartók, Béla; Busoni, Ferruccio; Goodman, Benny; Hindemith, Paul; Honegger, Arthur; Martin, Frank; Prokofiev, Sergei; Ravel, Maurice; Stokowski, Leopold; Stravinsky, Igor.

Karol Szymanowski

Polish classical composer

Composer Szymanowski developed an original and sophisticated musical style, transforming late Romanticism, Impressionism, and neoclassicism into a highly personal musical language.

Born: October 6, 1882; Tymoszówka, Ukraine, Russian Empire (now Poland)
Died: March 28, 1937; Lausanne, Switzerland
Also known as: Karol Maciej Szymanowski (full name)

Principal works

BALLET (music): *Harnesie*, Op. 55, 1935.
CHAMBER WORKS: *Myths: Three Poems for Violin and Piano*, Op. 30, 1915; *Nocturne and Tarantella*, Op. 28, 1915 (for violin and piano); String Quartet No. 1 in C Major, Op. 37, 1917; *Three Paganini Caprices*, Op. 40, 1918 (for violin and piano); String Quartet No. 2, Op. 56, 1927.

OPERA (music): *Król Roger (King Roger)*, Op. 46, 1926.

ORCHESTRAL WORKS: Violin Concerto No. 1, Op. 35, 1916; Symphony No. 3, 1917 (*Song of the Night*); *Stabat Mater*, 1929; Symphony No. 4, Op. 60, 1932 (for piano and orchestra); Violin Concerto No. 2, Op. 61, 1933.

PIANO WORKS: Piano Sonata No. 1 in C Major, Op. 8, 1910; Twelve Études, Op. 33, 1916.

The Life

Karol Maciej Szymanowski (shih-mah-NAWF-skee) was a child of a landowning family with a prestigious ancestry. He began piano lessons at home at the age of seven, and three years later he went to the neighboring Elisavetgrad to study piano and theory with Gustav Neuhaus. In 1901 Szymanowski moved to Warsaw to attend the Warsaw Conservatory as a part-time student, concentrating on piano, on composition (in the class of Zygmunt Noskowski), and on theory (in the class of Marek Zawirski). With Ludomir Rozycki and Mieczyslaw Karlowicz, fellow composers from the Warsaw Conservatory, Szymanowski formed a group called the Young Poland in Music. In 1905 the group established a small publishing business, the Polish Composers' Press.

During the remaining years before the outbreak of World War I, Szymanowski undertook several international trips, to Germany, Austria, France, England, Italy, Algeria, and Morocco. Fascinated with German culture, he later developed a deep appreciation for Greek, Byzantine, and Islamic (Sufi) traditions.

During his childhood Szymanowski suffered a leg injury that did not heal properly, so he was exempt from military service. He spent the years between the outbreak of World War I and the Bolshevik revolution at home in Tymószowka, with occasional travels to Kiev, Moscow, Odessa, and St. Petersburg. During these formative years Szymanowski appeared as a pianist in concerts of his music, as a soloist and accompanist. He did not like performing, and contradictory reports exist regarding his abilities as a pianist. In 1917 the revolutionaries burned down his family home, and Szymanowski's piano was thrown into a nearby pond. Between 1917 and 1919, the Szymanowski family remained in Kiev and later moved to Elisavetgrad.

In Kiev Szymanowski fell in love with a teenage Borys Kochno (later an assistant and lover of Sergei Diaghilev). The brief romance remains the only documented love affair in Szymanowski's life. At that time Szymanowski worked on a homoerotic novel, "Efebos." Only fragments of the work have been preserved.

In December, 1919, the Szymanowski family relocated to Warsaw. In October, 1920, Szymanowski was sent abroad by the Polish government to arrange concerts of Polish music. The trip included stops in Stockholm, Oslo, Copenhagen, London, and Paris. From London, Szymanowski made his first trip to the United States, where he visited Massachusetts, Pennsylvania, New York, and Florida, and to Cuba. A second trip to the United States was undertaken the following year, with Szymanowski appearing as a pianist in concerts of his music. Among other performances, noteworthy was his concert with violinist Pawel Kochański at Columbia University on December 13, 1921.

During the immediate postwar years, Szymanowski's music became more popular. His compositions were performed in Paris (1922, 1925), London (1921), New York City (1923), Prague (1924), and Vienna (1925). In Poland, a recently reborn country with a growing need for national music, Szymanowski gradually became a symbol of the nation's creative powers.

In 1926 Szymanowski became the director of the Warsaw Conservatory. Because of ongoing conflicts among the faculty, he resigned from this post in 1929. Almost the entire year after his resignation was spent in a sanatorium in Davos, Switzerland, where he took treatment for various respiratory conditions.

Later, in 1930, Szymanowski became the principal of a new music school, the Polish State Academy of Music in Warsaw. The institution was dissolved in 1932. In 1930 and 1931 Szymanowski was awarded an honorary doctorate at Jagellonian University in Kraków, he was elected an honorary member of the International Society of Contemporary Music, and he became an honorary member of the Czech Academy of Arts.

In 1932 Szymanowski's health began a rapid deterioration, and at the same time he found himself in a difficult financial situation. He resided mostly at the villa Atma in his beloved Zakopane, a mountain resort in the Polish Tatra Mountains, which he had visited for ten years.

In the last years of his life, he took several trips abroad: Denmark, Spain, Italy, Yugoslavia, Russia, Bulgaria, and Hungary in 1933; Germany and England in 1934; Sweden, Denmark, Belgium, France, Latvia, and Czechoslovakia in 1935; and southern France in 1936. Many of these trips included Szymanowski performing his newly composed Symphony No. 4. The ailing composer spent Christmas of 1936 in Nice, France, from where he was transferred to the sanatorium Clinique du Signal in Lausanne, Switzerland. He passed away a few months later from cancer of the larynx. His body was buried at the Skalka Cathedral in Kraków, Poland.

The Music

Szymanowski's early output, which included piano variations, songs, preludes, and études, betrayed the clear influence of Frédéric Chopin, a composer who devoted himself almost entirely to the piano. Such was the clear expectation of the Polish public: The "next Chopin" was to be another exceptional composer for the piano. It was not until 1907 that Szymanowski composed his first symphony, at a time when he was under the powerful influence of post-Wagnerian Romanticism and of Aleksandr Scriabin's chromaticism. In 1909 Szymanowski won the second prize in a composers' competition in Berlin, for his prelude and fugue for piano.

Three friendships played an important role in Szymanowski's life: the pianist Artur Rubinstein, the violinist Kochański, and the conductor Grzegorz Fitelberg. They inspired the composer to write a considerable amount of piano and violin music and orchestral works. In addition, Szymanowski's creative powers were enriched by his extensive travels. In France, Szymanowski experienced the music of Igor Stravinsky, which at the time revolutionized the musical world. He knew personally Diaghilev, the director of the famous Ballets Russes in Paris. In Africa and Italy, Szymanowski discovered a source of inspiration that took him away from the Christian world. It seems apparent that Szymanowski dealt with sexual identity problems, and in these countries he discovered a world beyond Christian morality.

Myths: Three Poems for Violin and Piano. Composed in 1915, with the help of Kochański, *Myths: Three Poems for Violin and Piano* consists of pieces inspired by Greek mythology. The first movement, "La Source d'Arethuse" (the source of Arethusa), tells the story of Arethusa, who, while escaping an enamored pursuer, transforms herself into a water spring. However, her follower changes into a river and in this form crosses the ocean to finally join the waters of Arethusa's source. The second composition, "Narcissus," tells the legendary story of a youth who falls in love with his image when he sees it reflected in water and dies instantly. The third movement, "Dryades et Pan" (Dryads and Pan), represents the forest wanderings of nymphs and the god Pan, a half-human, half-goat creature who plays the flute. *Myths, Three Poems for Violin and Piano* is a collection of exquisite studies in tone color, formal discipline, and rhythmic structure.

Symphony No. 3. Composed in 1916 in Tymoszówka, and first performed in February of 1917, Symphony No. 3, *Song of the Night*, is a choral-orchestral composition with a solo tenor part. The text, in Polish translation, was borrowed from the poetry of Mevlana Djalal al-Din Rumi (1207-1273), a Persian Sufi mystic. This poem, typical of Rumi's work, has several levels of meaning. On the mystical level, the poetry expresses an almost sensual yearning for unity with a higher being; on the humanistic level, it portrays yearning for sensual and spiritual fulfillment with an idealized special friend. The musical style suggests North African and Arabic sonorities.

The Influence of Zakopane. In 1922 Szymanowski settled in Zakopane, the mountain resort in the Tatra Mountains, spending many of his winters there. In the local folk song and dance, he discovered a source of inspiration quite different from that of Chopin, who was influenced by the folk music of the Polish central plains. Zakopane was more than a center of folk culture. At the time, the Polish intellectual and artistic elite spent vacations there, a vibrant cultural center where writers, poets, painters, and architects met to discuss their ideas.

Stabat Mater. Based on a Polish translation of the hymn by Jacopone da Todi from the thirteenth century, the work was completed in 1926 and performed first in Warsaw in 1929. International performances during the composer's lifetime included those in Belgium and England. The composition is scored for orchestra, chorus, and three soloists. The composer was reluctant to write a religious work, but he later developed an attachment to this composition. The text, which portrays the sufferings of Mary under the cross on which her Son hangs crucified, expresses the suffering of all humanity. Szymanowski's *Stabat Mater* is considered to be among the finest religious works ever written.

Harnasie. The Polish equivalent of Stravinsky's *The Rite of Spring*, the ballet was completed in 1931. It was first performed in Prague in 1935 and later, in 1936, at the Paris Opera House with the celebrated Serge Lifar dancing the role of the main character. The composer considered the idea of writing a ballet based on a story of Polish mountain people for about ten years. His purpose was to introduce Polish national music to the European scene. Jerzy Rytard, a friend of the composer, wrote the initial story line in 1923. The libretto (which describes a love story resulting in a kidnapping) plays a minor role in this work. The ballet's musical richness relies on folk dances and songs, with rhythmic energy and lyric beauty. The work is one of the most treasured masterpieces of Polish music.

Musical Legacy

Although Szymanowski was the most well-known Polish composer after Chopin, his highly individual musical language did not find immediate followers. Szymanowski's interest in Polish folklore influenced Polish music well into the 1960's. Unlike Chopin, who composed almost entirely for the piano, Szymanowski produced works in a variety of musical genres, all of high artistic quality, an impressive output that inspired new generations of Polish composers.

Slawomir P. Dobrzanski

Further Reading

Downes, Stephen. *Szymanowski, Eroticism, and the Voices of Mythology*. Aldershot, England: Ashgate, 2003. A musicological, philosophical, and psychological study of Szymanowski's works. The book examines Szymanowski's music and the influences of Greek mythology, Sufism, and Slavic paganism in the context of their relationship to the composer's psyche.

Maciejewski, Boguslaw. *Karol Szymanowski: His Life and Music*. London: Poets' and Painters' Press, 1967. A concise account of Szymanowski's life, representing a thorough introduction to the composer and his work. Includes a list of compositions and a calendar of events in Szymanowski's life.

Samson, Jim. *The Music of Karol Szymanowski*. New York: Taplinger, 1981. Musicological analysis of Szymanowski's compositions arranged in three stylistic periods. The author examines in detail the composer's influences, stylistic novelties, harmonic language, and musical form, and he places the compositions in biographical context. Includes a list of compositions.

Szymanowski, Karol. *Szymanowski on Music. Selected Writings of Karol Szymanowski*. Edited and translated by Alistair Wightman. Lancaster, England: Toccata Press, 1999. This publication consists of articles by Szymanowski published in Polish during his lifetime. The composer discusses such issues as folk music, nationalism in music, music of contemporary composers, and the role of musical criticism in society.

Wightman, Alistair. *Karol Szymanowski: His Life and Work*. Aldershot, England: Ashgate, 1999. A thorough look at Szymanowski, his environment, and his music, with several quotes from Szymanowski's correspondence. It discusses the development of his personality and provides a well-written analysis of his music. Includes a chronological list of compositions and a catalog of literary works.

See also: Bartók, Béla; Paderewski, Ignace Jan; Prokofiev, Sergei; Rubinstein, Artur; Scriabin, Aleksandr; Stravinsky, Igor.

T

Tōru Takemitsu

Japanese classical and film-score composer

Takemitsu, one of Japan's leading classical composers, joined Western and Japanese musical traditions, with instruments from both. His impressive film scores helped popularize the works of premier directors such as Akira Kurosawa.

Born: October 8, 1930; Tokyo, Japan
Died: February 20, 1996; Tokyo, Japan

Principal works

CHAMBER WORKS: *Distance de fée*, 1951; *Shitsunai kyosokyoku*, 1955 (*Chamber Concerto*); *Arc*, 1962 (for strings); *Garden Rain*, 1974; *Shuteika—Ichigu*, 1979 (*In the Autumn Garden—Complete Version*); *A Way a Lone*, 1981 (for string quartet); *A Way a Lone II*, 1981 (for string orchestra); *Ame zo furu*, 1982 (*Rain Coming*); *Tree Line*, 1988.

FILM SCORES: *Kurutta kajitsu* (1956; crazy fruit); *José Torres*, 1960; *Kwaidan*, 1964; *Suna no onna*, 1964 (*Woman in the Dunes*); *José Torres, Part II*, 1965; *Tanin no kao*, 1966 (*The Face of Another*); *Dodesukaden*, 1970; *Chinmoku*, 1971 (*Silence*); *Kaseki no mori*, 1973 (*The Petrified Forest*); *Kaseki*, 1975; *Ai no borei*, 1978; *Ran*, 1985; *Kuroi ame*, 1989 (*Black Rain*); *Rikyu*, 1989; *Rising Sun*, 1993.

ORCHESTRAL WORKS: *Saegirarenai kyusoku*, 1952 (*Uninterrupted Rests*); *Requiem*, 1957 (for string orchestra); *Solitude sonore*, 1958; *Ki no kyoku*, 1961 (*Tree Music*); *Pianisuto no tame no corona*, 1962 (*Corona for Pianist[s]*); *Piano Distance*, 1961; *Kaze no uma*, 1962 (*Horse in the Wind*); *Arc Parts I and II*, 1966 (for piano and orchestra); *Chiheisen no doria*, 1966 (*Dorian Horizon*; for string orchestra); *Asterism*, 1967 (for piano and orchestra); *Green*, 1967 (*November Steps*); *Shiki*, 1970 (*Seasons*); *Cassiopeia*, 1971; *Eucalypts II*, 1971; *Fuyu*, 1971 (*Winter*); *Munari by Munari*, 1972; *Aki*, 1973 (*Autumn*); *Shuteika*, 1973 (*In an Autumn Garden*); *Gitimalya*, 1974; *Quatrain*, 1975; *Marginalia*, 1976; *Quatrain II*, 1977; *Tori wa hoshigata no niwa ni oriru*, 1977 (*A Flock Descends into the Pentagonal Garden*); *Umi e*, 1981 (*Toward the Sea*); *Yume mado*, 1985 (*Dream/Window*); *Gémeaux*, 1986; *Twill by Twilight: In Memory of Morton Feldman*, 1988; *Mystère, les yeux clos*, 1990 (*Visions*); *How Slow the Wind*, 1991; *Gunto S.*, 1993 (*Archipelago S.*; for twenty-one players).

VOCAL WORKS: *Kansho*, 1962 (*Coral Island*; for soprano and orchestra); *Stanza I*, 1969 (for female voice and ensemble); *Stanza II*, 1971 (for voice and flute).

WRITINGS OF INTEREST: *Oto, chinmoku to hakariaeru hodoni*, 1971 (*Confronting Silence: Selected Writings*, 1995); *Ongaku no yohaku hara*, 1980; *Yume no inyo*, 1984 (*Quotation of Dream*, 1998); *Ongaku o yobisamasu mono*, 1985; *Yume to kazu*, 1987; *Opera o tsukuru*, 1990; *Oto-kotoba-ningen*, 1992; *Tooi yobigoe no kanatae*, 1992; *Toki no entai*, 1996 (the gardener of time).

The Life

Tōru Takemitsu (toh-roo tah-keh-mee-tsoo) was born on October 8, 1930, in Tokyo, son of the government official Takeo Takemitsu and his wife Reiko. In November his father was posted to the city of Dairen in Manchuria and took his family with him. Takemitsu moved back to Tokyo in 1937 to attend Fujimae Elementary School. When his father died in 1938, Takemitsu was raised by his mother and an aunt who taught the koto, a traditional Japanese stringed instrument.

Soon after enrolling in Keika Middle School, Takemitsu was drafted in late 1944 to help build fortifications. His squad leader secretly played for the boys the French chanson "Parlez-moi d'amour" (speak to me about love), composed by Jean Lenoir and sung by Lucienne Boyer. The song awakened Takemitsu's love of Western music.

After the end of World War II in 1945, Takemitsu ardently listened to the American Forces Network. While working as a waiter in an American post exchange in Tokyo from 1946 to 1947, Takemitsu enjoyed further exposure to popular American and Western European music.

While struggling as a self-taught composer and cofounding Jikken K b (experimental laboratory) to promote new Western-based, antinationalistic music, Takemitsu met and fell in love with Asaka Wakayama, an actress of the Shiki Theater Group. He was hospitalized with tuberculosis from June, 1953, to March, 1954, and on June 15, 1954, married Wakayama. One wedding gift was a piano from the nationalist composer Toshiro Mayazumi, with whom Takemitsu formed a lifelong friendship despite their opposing political views. Beginning in 1955 Takemitsu's film scores were used for Japanese movies.

Hospitalized again in January, 1957, Takemitsu composed *Requiem*, which brought him international recognition when Igor Stravinsky listened to it and praised it in 1959. On December 16, 1961, Takemitsu's daughter Maki was born.

An October, 1962, meeting with American composer John Cage in Tokyo persuaded Takemitsu to fuse Western with Japanese music. His break-through came with the commission of *November Steps* for the New York Philharmonic Orchestra in 1967. In the 1970's Takemitsu's compositions increasingly integrated Japanese and Western musical elements in works with a garden theme.

At the same time Takemitsu flourished as a composer of film music. Of his ninety-three scores, the sound tracks for Akira Kurosawa's *Ran* and the Hollywood blockbuster *Rising Sun* were especially successful.

At the height of his creative work in 1995, Takemitsu was diagnosed with abdominal cancer. His final collection of essays, *Toki no entai* (1995; the gardener of time), appeared in October, 1995. He died on February 20, 1996.

The Music

Takemitsu began composing at seventeen, striving to create works in the style of the Western music he enjoyed. He never received much formal musical training but followed his own inspiration. He joined an amateur choir, where Hiroyoshi Suzuki introduced him to composing.

Takemitsu destroyed his first composition, "Kakehi" (1947), after learning that it sounded Japanese. After some training with composer Yasuji Kiyose from 1948 to 1950, Takemitsu publicly performed his first composition, the piano piece "Lento in Due Movimenti," on December 7, 1950.

Takemitsu's early works were based on his admiration of popular American composers such as Aaron Copland, French Romantics such as Claude Debussy, the Austrian innovators Arnold Schoenberg and Anton von Webern and, most of all, French composer Olivier Messiaen. However, it was only his third work, *Distance de fée* (1951), for violin and piano, that met with his and the critics' approval.

In late 1955 Takemitsu turned briefly to the French avant-garde style of musique concrète, based on everyday sounds and noises. His four-minute "Vocalism A.I." (1956) played on the Japanese word *ai* (love) and featured sounds by a male and a female singer. Takemitsu next started to compose movie scores, and his music for *Kurutta kajitsu* was the third of his ninety-three film scores.

Requiem. While seriously ill in 1957, Takemitsu composed this work for strings for the Tokyo Symphony Orchestra. He declared that *Requiem* was in-

Tōru Takemitsu. (AP/Wide World Photos)

tended to mourn his friend Fumio Hayasaka who died in 1955, although the work carries strong intimations of Takemitsu's own near-death experience.

Formally, *Requiem* represents Takemitsu's break with the musique concrète of the French avant-garde. Exuding a somber tone throughout, *Requiem* introduces its melody with a sudden pitch out of silence. Its slow tempi are designed to convey a mood of pulsating ripples, like those created by raindrops falling on water. Even though Takemitsu argued that his work has no real end or beginning, inspired by a random Tokyo subway ride, critics discerned a three-part *aba* structure. Characteristic of his work to come, silence plays an important part in the melodic contour of the composition.

Requiem led to Takemitsu's international discovery. Stravinsky heard it while visiting Japan in 1959 and praised its composer, whom he met for lunch. Suddenly, Takemitsu became known outside Japan.

November Steps. Takemitsu was commissioned to compose this work for the 125th anniversary of the New York Philharmonic Orchestra in 1967. It was influenced by the work of his composer friend Cage, whom he first met in Tokyo in 1962 and again when Takemitsu was invited to the San Francisco Electronic Music Festival in 1964. Widely disseminated and listened to, it would become Takemitsu's most popular work in the West. In *November Steps* Takemitsu chose to juxtapose biwa (Japanese lute) and shakuhachi (Japanese flute) solos with music from a full Western orchestra. At the New York City performance directed by Takemitsu's friend Seiji Ozawa, the biwa and shakuhachi soloists were seated in front of an evenly divided section of Western string and percussion instruments, with wind instruments forming a bloc at the rear. Throughout *November Steps*, each instrument maintained its own identity, and there was not so much a fusion but rather a juxtaposition of distinct sounds united by a certain harmony. Overall, the work expressed Takemitsu's emerging trademark of sonority.

The title *November Steps* is derived from Takemitsu's play on the Japanese musical term *danmono* (matters of steps). In music, this means "variations on a theme," with *dan* standing for steps or variations. As his composition offers eleven variations

on a theme, Takemitsu took the eleventh month of the year to indicate this. Critics enthusiastically welcomed the work.

Garden Cycle of the 1970's. For Takemitsu, Japanese gardens were free from the militaristic connotations that fueled his early rejection of Japanese music. When he accepted a commission to compose a new work for the Imperial Household's gagaku ensemble of traditional Japanese instruments, Takemitsu chose the theme of a garden. *In an Autumn Garden* was performed on October 30, 1973. It consists of a single movement with the komabue (small transverse bamboo flute) prominently interjecting birdlike sounds piercing Takemitsu's trademark moments of silence.

Encouraged by his success, Takemitsu composed another work centered on the motif of the garden, but this time for Western brass instruments. *Garden Rain* (1974) introduces the theme of water that would characterize many of Takemitsu's later works. In a genuine fusion of Japanese and Western music, Takemitsu composed the substantial brass chords of *Garden Rain* according to the rules for the shō, the mouth organ of the gagaku ensemble. The resulting long duration of the notes and the sonorous, low-pitched timbre of his piece create a unique sonic quality typical of Takemitsu's mature oeuvre.

Takemitsu's orchestral *A Flock Descends into the Pentagonal Garden* fully fuses Japanese and Western instruments with a canny appreciation of moments of silence. Here, the garden is visited by a black bird, played with notes on the pentatonic scale indicated by the black keys of the piano, and a flock of white birds, played on the piano's white keys. Takemitsu completed his garden cycle of compositions with a revised version, *In the Autumn Garden—Complete Version*, that expanded his original composition by five additional movements. It premiered on September 28, 1979. His original piece appears after the movements of "Strophe," "Echo I," and "Melisma" and is followed by "Echo II" and "Antistrophe." The complete version of *Shuteika* is one of Takemitsu's most complex creations, characterized by symmetry, repetition, and recollection of a central theme. Some critics view it as his most outstanding work.

Ran. Takemitsu's lifelong interest in creating film music reached a creative, internationally recognized climax in his score for Akira Kurosawa's *Ran* (1985). The movie is a masterful adaptation of William Shakespeare's *King Lear* set in medieval Japan. For *Ran*, Takemitsu proved equally adept at scoring the early formal meetings of the lord and his retainers as well as the chaos of the betrayed lord's ramblings on a stormy heath. What critics have called "strings that chirp like insects" accompany the evil daughters' scheming, and Takemitsu's trademark haunting, deep-pitched chords intensify the film's climax.

Musical Legacy

Takemitsu has become recognized as one of the outstanding Japanese composers of the second half of the twentieth century. His *November Steps* was hailed in the West as a fusion of Eastern and Western music, even though the different instruments coexist rather than blend. Once Takemitsu abandoned his initial rejection of Japanese music, his garden cycle compositions of the 1970's were pieces of genius and innovation.

Takemitsu's mature compositions brought traditional Japanese music played on the biwa, shakuhachi, and shō into equal interplay with Western instruments and modes of contemporary composition. His middle and final works created world music with its own style and character.

Throughout his musical career, Takemitsu combined the popular and the artistic. His film scores helped win Japanese cinema a large international audience. He did not look down on occasional music but gave it his creative best. For his compositions Takemitsu was honored with many international and Japanese prizes and memberships in foreign academies. He received the Prix Italia in 1958, Japan's Otaka Prize in 1976 and 1981, the Grawemeyer Award in 1994, and the Glenn Gould Award posthumously in 1996. Takemitsu was made a member of the Akademie der Künste of the former East Germany (1979), the American Institute of Arts and Letters (1985), and, in France, the Ordre des Arts et des Lettres (1985) and the Académie des Beaux-Arts (1986). Takemitsu won the Film Award of the Japanese Academy four times, and, with *Ran*, the Los Angeles Film Critics Award for Best Score in 1987.

R. C. Lutz

Further Reading

Burt, Peter. *The Music of Tōru Takemitsu.* Cambridge, England: Cambridge University Press, 2001. Thorough discussion of Takemitsu's career as a composer; placing him in the context of his times. Somewhat brief on Takemitsu's film scores; detailed analysis of brief examples taken from Takemitsu's work. Comprehensive list of Takemitsu's works; bibliography, index.

Cornwell, Lewis. "Tōru Takemitsu's *November Steps.*" *Journal of New Music Research* 31, no. 3 (September, 2002): 211. Review of Takemitsu's early masterpiece combining two traditional Japanese instruments and a Western-style orchestra.

Ohtake, Noriko. *Creative Sources for the Music of Tōru Takemitsu.* Aldershot, Hampshire, England: Scolar Press, 1993. Presentation of Takemitsu's sources and some analysis of his view on the subject. Finds Takemitsu was influenced by both Western and Japanese music and successfully joined both in a creative achievement. Bibliography, index.

Ross, Alex. "Toward Silence: The Intense Repose of Tōru Takemitsu." *The New Yorker*, February 5, 2007. Review of posthumous performances of Takemitsu's works in the United States in 2006 and 2007. Overall reflection on the effect of Takemitsu's use of silence.

Siddons, James. *Tōru Takemitsu: A Bio-Bibliography.* Westport, Conn.: Greenwood Press, 2001. Comprehensive, detailed biography of Takemitsu. Excellent analysis of his major concert pieces organized according to genre, instrument, musical theme. Complete list of Takemitsu's compositions, including film scores. Discography, bibliography that includes English reviews of Takemitsu's works and secondary sources in English. Accessible starting point for analysis of the composer's life and work.

Takemitsu, Tōru. *Confronting Silence: Selected Writings.* Translated and edited by Yoshiko Kakudo and Glenn Glasow. Berkeley, Calif.: Fallen Leaf Press, 1995. Careful selection of substantial essays by Takemitsu written from 1960 to 1993. Enables English readers to learn Takemitsu's personal understanding of his work, his underlying issues and principles, his method and approach to composition, and about fellow composers

Takemitsu credits with influencing his work. Illustrated, index.

Tōru Takemitsu Memorial Edition. *Contemporary Music Review* 21 (December, 2002). Journal issue dedicated to articles by noted scholars on the work of Takemitsu. Articles highlight Takemitsu's personality and his work and offer detailed analysis of his key compositions.

See also: Cage, John; Copland, Aaron; Debussy, Claude; Messiaen, Olivier; Schaeffer, Pierre; Schoenberg, Arnold; Webern, Anton von.

Tan Dun

Chinese American classical and film-score composer

One of the leading Chinese composers to emerge following the turmoil and suppression of the arts during the Cultural Revolution, Tan created a compositional language that was highly personal and at the same time extremely cosmopolitan. It broke down barriers between modernist Western-style composition and Chinese traditional music, encompassing not only instruments and melodic structures, but also more subtle aspects of performance practice and aesthetics.

Born: August 18, 1957; Simao, China

Principal works

CHAMBER WORKS: *Feng ya song*, 1982 (for string quartet); *Two Verses: Erhu, Yangqin*, 1982; *Gu shi*, 1983 (*Drum Poem*; for Chinese drums); *Jin mu shuei huo tu*, 1983 (*Metal, Wood, Water, Fire, Earth*; suite for Chinese plucked instruments); *Zhuji*, 1983 (*Trace of Bamboo*; for bamboo flute); *Nanxiangzi, xiao, zheng*, 1984; *Shan yao*, 1984 (*Mountain Suite*); *In Distance*, 1987 (for piccolo, harp, bass, and drum); *Eight Colors*, 1988 (for string quartet); *Northwest Suite*, 1990 (for Chinese instruments); *Elegy: Snow in June*, 1991 (for cello and percussion); *Golden Sparrow*, 1991; *Circle*, 1992 (for twelve instruments and audience); *Lament: Autumn Wind*, 1993 (for

voices and any six instruments); *Ghost Opera*, 1994 (for string quartet, pipa, water, stone, paper, and metal); *Concerto for Piano and Ten Instruments*, 1995; *Concerto for Six*, 1997 (for bass clarinet, electric guitar, cello, double bass, prepared piano, and percussion); *Music for Pipa and String Quartet*, 1999.

FILM SCORES: *Fallen*, 1998; *Crouching Tiger, Hidden Dragon*, 2000.

OPERAS (music): *Nine Songs*, 1989 (ritual opera for twenty performers); *Marco Polo*, 1996 (libretto by Paul Griffiths).

ORCHESTRAL WORKS: *Li Sao*, 1980 (*Encountering Sorrow*); *On Taoism*, 1985; *Death and Fire: Dialogue with Paul Klee*, 1993; *Symphony 1997 (Heaven Earth Mankind)*, 1997; *2000 Today: A World Symphony for the Millennium*, 1999; *Water Passion After Saint Matthew*, 2000.

PIANO WORKS: *A Child's Diary*, 1978; *Eight Pieces in Hunan Accent*, 1978; *Five Pieces in Hunan Accent*, 1978; *Traces*, 1989; *CAGE: In Memory of John Cage*, 1993.

VOCAL WORKS: *Silk Road*, 1989 (for soprano and percussion); *Bitter Love*, 1999 (for soprano, six performers, slide projections, and video).

The Life

As a child growing up in a village in Hunan province, Tan Dun was able to hear traditional Chinese music and the nature-inspired sounds of shamanistic rituals, which survived in some rural areas, despite having been actively discouraged by the government. While a teenager, he was assigned to a rice-farming commune, where he also assumed some informal duties as a community musician, collecting folk songs and creating music with human voices, tools, and whatever instruments could be found. He managed to learn how to play the violin, and when an accident killed some members of a regional Peking opera troupe, Tan was recruited to join the group. The Cultural Revolution was ending, and when the Central Conservatory of Music reopened in 1978, he was accepted out of thousands of applicants for one of only thirty places. At the conservatory, his horizons and his abilities grew rapidly. In 1986 he attended Columbia University in New York, where he earned a doctor of musical arts degree in 1993. During the 1990's and 2000's, he expanded his range of activities to include opera and film music, and he continued to write symphonic and chamber music.

The Music

During his years at the commune, Tan, in a creative response to limited resources, began to experiment by using common implements for percussion instruments and by working with unconventional combinations of instruments. He also acquired some background in traditional Chinese music. During his studies at the conservatory, he was able to bypass the Soviet-influenced Romantic compositional language that had been favored before the Cultural Revolution; instead, he was influenced by more modernist composers, including some, such as Tôru Takemitsu, George Crumb, Chou Wen-Chung, and others, who visited and lectured at the conservatory. Along with writing in nontonal idioms, some of these composers were interested in integrating Asian aesthetics into their work.

Tan rose to the forefront of new Chinese composers who wrote in modern styles but who were inspired by Asian traditions. In 1979 he completed his first symphony, *Encountering Sorrow*, inspired by an ancient poetic classic from the Warring States Period, and he was awarded a national prize for this work. In 1983 his string quartet *Feng ya song* won the Weber Prize in Dresden. Although this helped to catapult Tan to international recognition, his dissonant writing had attracted unwanted attention from conservative Chinese government officials, and his work was temporarily banned.

On Taoism. In 1985, shortly after his grandmother's death, Tan wrote a highly personal piece, reflecting upon her Daoist funeral and honoring the Daoist aesthetic of avoiding conscious action. Possibly because of its politically risky evocation of traditional belief systems as well as its avant-garde style, which rejected Western conventions of form even though it used Western instruments, the piece greatly displeased Chinese government officials, who saw it as further proof of the composer's supposed degeneracy. In this piece, the instrumentalists are required to perform pitch bends and other techniques associated with Chinese traditional music and certain modern Western composers, and they are asked to chant and sing. This was the last piece Tan wrote before moving to the United States.

Marco Polo. Tan's first major opera debuted in 1996, and employed multiple musical traditions representing cultures along the ancient Silk Road followed by Marco Polo on his historic trip to China. Tan worked with librettist Paul Griffiths so that the work would reflect not only a physical and musical journey, but also a more universal spiritual journey. Along with full orchestra and chorus, instruments included the Indian sitar and tabla (small drums), Tibetan horns and "singing bowls," and the Chinese pipa, a four-stringed lute.

Symphony 1997 (Heaven Earth Mankind). This symphony was composed for the official ceremonies celebrating the reunification of Hong Kong and China in 1997. Written in three movements, reflected in the title and related to traditional Chinese cosmology, the symphony incorporates a children's choir, cello solo (premiered by Yo-Yo Ma), and a full bianzhong orchestra of bells, based on ancient prototypes recently unearthed in China. The compositional style ranges from atonal to popular. In this piece quotation is used for multitemporal as well as multicultural references, conveying a strong feeling of universality. Quoted melodies include Ludwig van Beethoven's "Ode to Joy," traditional Chinese songs, and one of the composer's film sound tracks.

Water Passion After Saint Matthew. Continuing Tan's exploration of the theme of music as ritual, his integration of sounds from nature, and his multicultural palette of instruments and voices, this piece represented water as a sonic element, along with Tuvan throat singing, Peking opera, rural fiddle playing from the United States, and the sound of thunder. These resources were used to tell the story of Christ's Passion as related in the Gospel. Inspired by Johann Sebastian Bach's work, *Saint Matthew Passion* (1727), the *Water Passion After Saint Matthew* was written for the 250th anniversary of Bach's death in 2000.

Crouching Tiger, Hidden Dragon. Tan broke musical stereotypes in composing the score for Ang Lee's highly successful martial-arts film, just as the filmmaker broke free of motion-picture genre conventions. In the music Tan alternated three orchestras (symphonic, Chinese traditional, and Asian percussion ensemble), using cellist Ma to unite them. Released in 2000, the film broadened his audience to include millions of new listeners.

Musical Legacy

Tan set a high standard for the creativity and for the breadth of knowledge required to compose sensitively and appropriately for a vast range of instruments and of voices from multiple cultures. He won the Glenn Gould International Protégé Prize, an Academy Award, the Grawemeyer Award for music composition, and many others.

John Myers

Further Reading

Everett, Yayoi Uno, and Frederick Lau, eds. *Locating East Asia in Western Art Music*. Middletown, Conn.: Wesleyan University Press, 2004. A collection of essays about major composers utilizing East Asian elements in composition. Includes Yu Siu Wah's essay about Tan's *Symphony 1997 (Heaven Earth Mankind)*. Includes illustrations, bibliography, and index.

Kouwenhoven, Frank. *Tan Dun*. New York: Schirmer Books, 1994. One of the first works in English on Tan, this includes a biography, a list of compositions, illustrations, and a bibliography.

Mays, Desirée. *Opera Unveiled: 2007*. Santa Fe, N.Mex.: Art Forms, 2007. Series explores composers, librettists, and context. This volume has a chapter on Tan's *Tea: A Mirror of Soul*. Includes illustrations and bibliography.

Melvin, Sheila, and Cai Jingdong. *Rhapsody in Red: How Western Classical Music Became Chinese*. New York: Algora, 2004. Includes treatment of cultural identification of Chinese people with Western art music, the Cultural Revolution, and recovery. Includes bibliography and index.

Strimple, Nick. *Choral Music in the Twentieth Century*. Portland, Oreg.: Amadeus Press, 2002. Includes discussion of Tan's *Water Passion After Saint Matthew*, with bibliography and index.

Takemitsu, Tōru. *Confronting Silence: Selected Writings*. Translated and edited by Yoshiko Kakudo and Glenn Glasow. Berkeley, Calif.: Fallen Leaf Press, 1995. Essays by one of Tan's most important influences, covering the connections between East Asian aesthetics and Western avant-garde composition and the use of East Asian instruments.

See also: Crumb, George; Ma, Yo-Yo; Takemitsu, Tōru.

Art Tatum
American jazz pianist and composer

Although almost completely blind, Tatum was a master of arpeggios and shifting harmonies and rhythms that helped to chart the direction of jazz.

Born: October 13, 1909; Toledo, Ohio
Died: November 5, 1956; Los Angeles, California

Principal recordings

ALBUMS: *Battle of Jazz, Vol. 2*, 1941; *Art Tatum Concert*, 1949; *At Shrine Auditorium*, 1949; *In Private*, 1949; *Art Tatum*, 1950; *Tatum Piano*, 1950; *Makin' Whoopee*, 1954 (with Benny Carter and Louis Bellson); *More of the Greatest Piano of Them All*, 1954; *Tatum-Carter-Bellson*, 1954 (with Carter and Bellson); *The Three Giants*, 1954 (with Carter and Bellson); *The Art Tatum-Roy Eldridge-Alvin Stoller Trio*, 1955; *The Incomparable Music of Art Tatum*, 1955; *Quartet*, 1955 (with Ben Webster); *Still More of the Greatest Piano of Them All*, 1955; *Art Tatum-Ben Webster Quartet*, 1956; *The Art Tatum-Buddy DeFranco Quartet*, 1956; *The Art Tatum Trio*, 1956 (with Red Callender and Jo Jones); *Presenting the Art Tatum Trio*, 1956 (with Callender and Jones).

The Life

Art Tatum's parents had some musical attainments, but not exceptional ones. Tatum had cataracts in his eyes from birth, and several operations did not save his sight. Diseases, including measles at the age of three, may also have contributed to his condition. Tatum studied at the Jefferson School in Toledo, where he learned to read Braille and to play the violin and piano. At age fifteen he enrolled in a school for the blind in Columbus, and around 1925 he spent some time at the Toledo School of Music. His first musical experience was at church, but he did study classical music, and he had one capable piano teacher named Overton Rainey.

Tatum formed a band of his own in 1926, and he worked at nightclubs in Toledo for the next several years. In 1932 and 1933 he was an accompanist, but for most of his career he was a brilliant soloist. He was married twice, and he died in 1956 of uremia, caused by liver failure, at the age of forty-seven.

The Music

Much of Tatum's early performing was done in clubs in Toledo, Cleveland, New York City, and Chicago. In 1936 he was selected to accompany the great black singer Adelaide Hall, a position that he held for eighteen months. By 1938 he was able to perform in Europe. Although he did play with orchestras and chamber groups, he enjoyed the freedom of being a jazz soloist, and he excelled at it.

Art Tatum. (Hulton Archive/Getty Images)

Concerts in London. In March of 1938, Tatum traveled to England. He found the experience of playing in clubs fulfilling, since London audiences at Ciro's and at the Paradise Club listened intently to his music, instead of regarding his playing as background, the way American audiences did. He played such songs as George Gershwin's "Liza" and Harold Arlen's "Stormy Weather," and he performed for the British Broadcasting Corporation.

Humoresque. In a series of recording sessions in February of 1940, Tatum produced some of his best performances, including Peter De Rose's "Deep Purple," Clifford Burwell's "Sweet Lorraine," Harold Arlen's "Get Happy," and Sam Coswell's "Cocktails for Two." Tatum also included, from the light classical music which he enjoyed playing, a portion of Antonín Dvořák's *Humoresque* (1894). It should be noted that Tatum recorded many of these numbers at other times, but the 1940 recordings are generally regarded as outstanding.

"Willow Weep for Me" *and* **"Aunt Hagar's Blues."** Tatum made about three hundred recordings, most of the best ones in the 1940's. In 1949 he made two masterful performances. One was Ann Ronell's "Willow Weep for Me," where he subordinated the floridities of his style to a respectful attention to the reiterations of the song. When he came to a double-time section of the song, however, he doubled the double-time. He finished with a chimelike figure. In "Aunt Hagar's Blues," he gave each cho-

rus of the song its own character instead of displaying his great array of musical ideas to flow into each. Tatum's enormous skill and dexterity made restraining his effects an important aspect of his development. In this song, as in "Willow Weep for Me," Tatum interpolated another number, in this case a W. C. Handy song called "Black Coffee." This was one of Tatum's most controversial traits, but here it worked unexpectedly and perfectly.

"Mine" *and* **"Too Marvelous for Words."** These songs were performed at a private recording session at the home of Warner Bros. music director Ray Heindorf in 1950. "Mine" was a Gershwin song that Tatum had never played before and never recorded again. The unanimous opinion of critics is that "Too Marvelous for Words," composed by Richard Whiting, was his best performance on that occasion. James Lester chose this as the title of his biography of Tatum.

"Someone to Watch Over Me." Although by 1955 Tatum was suffering from uremia, a disorder of the blood system associated with a severe kidney disease, he went back to Heindorf's house for another session. He played in succession Gershwin's "Someone to Watch Over Me" and Duke Ellington's "In a Sentimental Mood," which have similar opening phrases. In the first he interpolated Stephen Foster's "My Old Kentucky Home" and in the second Foster's "Old Folks at Home." The Gershwin song, which is usually played as a tender ballad, was presented stormily, but he changed to a sentimental mood appropriate to Ellington's song.

Musical Legacy

Tatum's blindness did not deter him, and he had one prominent physical advantage: large hands that could span a great length of piano keys. Tatum enjoyed his freedom, and he worked outside the standard techniques of stride piano. He limited his interest in ensemble playing, although he did on occasion play successfully with some of the jazz greats. He was often called "God," for his pianistic talent that seemed beyond ordinary human proportions.

Tatum's playing was too difficult to encourage much imitation, Oscar Peterson being the most skilled jazz pianist to imitate him. In addition, Tatum was generous in helping young performers. One of the most notable was Teddy Wilson, whom he invited to stand behind him and watch as he played. He would even slow down his usual pace so that Wilson could better follow his movements.
Robert P. Ellis

Further Reading

Giddins, Gary. *Visions of Jazz*. New York: Oxford University Press, 1998. This book has only a few pages on Tatum, but it includes much information on the Heindorf recordings.

Gioia, Ted. *The Imperfect Art: Reflections on Jazz and Modern Culture*. New York: Oxford University Press, 1989. Gioa has one valuable chapter on Tatum.

Green, Benny. *The Reluctant Art: Five Studies in the Growth of Jazz*. Cambridge, Mass.: Da Capo Press, 1991. This book places Tatum in the development of the jazz idiom.

Lester, James. *Too Marvelous for Words: The Life and Genius of Art Tatum*. New York: Oxford University Press, 1994. Although there are many aspects of Tatum's early life that the author was not able to clarify, this book offers a well-written account of the pianist.

Schuller, Gunther. *The Swing Era: The Development of Jazz, 1930-1945*. New York: Oxford University Press, 1989. Schuller illustrates many Tatum passages and discusses Tatum's relationship to Teddy Wilson.

See also: Arlen, Harold; Carter, Benny; Cole, Nat King; Garner, Erroll; Gershwin, George; Hampton, Lionel; Handy, W. C.; Jones, Hank; Mingus, Charles; Parker, Charlie; Peterson, Oscar; Powell, Bud; Previn, Sir André; Turner, Big Joe; Waller, Fats; Webster, Ben.

Sir John Tavener
English classical composer

In his compositions, Tavener combines elements from religious practices, popular influences, and literary sources to achieve a highly spiritual and universal portrayal of beauty in music.

Born: January 28, 1944; London, England
Also known as: John Kenneth Tavener (full name)

Principal works

CHORAL WORKS: *Cain and Abel*, 1966; *Celtic Requiem*, 1971; *The Lamb*, 1982; *Ikon of the Nativity*, 1991; *Song for Athene*, 1993; *Lamentations and Praises*, 2000.

OPERA (music): *Thérèse*, 1979 (libretto by Gerard McLarnon).

ORCHESTRAL WORKS: *The Whale*, 1968 (for voice and orchestra); *The Protecting Veil*, 1989 (for cello and orchestra); *Schuon Lieder*, 2003; *Laila (Amu)*, 2005; *Fragments of a Prayer*, 2006; *The Beautiful Names*, 2007.

The Life

John Kenneth Tavener (TA-veh-nur) is the son of Kenneth and Muriel Tavener, and he is a descendant of his namesake, the Tudor composer John Taverner. At a young age, Tavener showed talent as a pianist and an organist. With a music scholarship, he attended the Highgate School, where he studied keyboard and composition. In 1962 Tavener entered the Royal Academy of Music, intending to become a concert pianist. He instead studied composition with Sir Lennox Berkeley and David Lumsdaine. While pursuing his studies, Tavener served as a church organist; however, he did not intend to make the church his ultimate place of employment. In 1965 Tavener won the prestigious Prince Rainier of Monaco composition prize for his cantata, *Cain and Abel*, which premiered on a radio broadcast by the London Bach Society.

Tavener achieved fame with the 1968 premiere of *The Whale*, composed for the London Sinfonietta. In 1969 he became professor of composition at Trinity College, and he produced *Celtic Requiem* (the piece was admired by the Beatles, who convinced Apple Records to produce a recording). Events in Tavener's personal life, including a brief marriage in 1974, caused agonizing dry spells in his compositional output, which led him to seek solace in faith. In 1977 he formally entered the Orthodox Church, which became a profound source of inspiration. During the 1980's, Tavener was diagnosed with Marfan's syndrome, which caused a stroke and heart abnormalities. At this point, his works became increasingly introspective. Tavener returned to the spotlight in 1989 when *The Protecting Veil* pre-

Sir John Tavener. (AP/Wide World Photos)

miered at the Proms (summer concerts), successfully introducing his music to a wider audience. His personal life improved as well: In 1991, he married his second wife, Maryanna, and he began a close relationship with Mother Thekla, an Orthodox nun. Mother Thekla consoled him as he dealt with his mother's death, and she urged him to continue composing. With the encouragement of his wife and Mother Thekla, Tavener's career was resurrected. Greece became his second home, and in 1993 he received an Apollo Award from the Greek National Opera for his contributions to Greek culture, the first foreigner to receive this honor. His fiftieth birthday was commemorated in 1994 by the BBC's Ikons Festival.

Tavener achieved international stature in 1997 through the broadcast performance of his composition *Song for Athene* at the close of Princess Diana's funeral. In 2000 he was knighted, leading to an increase in overseas commissions. The most notable was *Lamentations and Praises*, written for the choral group Chanticleer, which earned Tavener a 2002 Grammy Award. *The Beautiful Names*, commissioned by the Prince of Wales, premiered at Westminster Cathedral by the BBC Symphony Orchestra in 2007. He remains an active composer, devoted husband, and doting father of three children.

The Music

Tavener has always maintained a close association with religious music. As a child, he was profoundly affected by performances of Johann Sebastian Bach's *St. Matthew Passion* (1727), George Frideric Handel's *Solomon* oratorio (1789), and Igor Stravinsky's *Canticum Sacrum* (1955), musical experiences that he considered crucial to his formation as a composer. While Tavener's inspirations vary widely, the unifying factor is the goal of expressing beauty and truth through music. His study of composition with Lumsdaine focused upon complicated avant-garde techniques, and Tavener eventually drifted away from contemporary technique in favor of a type of minimalism that reflects a profound sense of spirituality. His later works are sparse, making almost exclusive use of diatonic tonality, in contrast to the complex early works.

Early Works. Tavener's early compositions were entirely improvised at the keyboard. As a student at Highgate, his works reflected an unusual mixture of influences, including Stravinsky, George Gershwin, Maurice Ravel, and Handel. Among the works completed at Highgate were a number of pieces written for the school orchestra. One of Tavener's first significant works was *Credo* (1961), scored for tenor soloist, chorus, narrator, oboes, brass, and organ. As a student at the Royal Academy of Music, Tavener delighted in the frequent performance of his pieces, including an opera titled *The Cappemakers* (1964), based on two medieval mystery plays. Lumsdaine's avant-garde influence is evident in Tavener's use of aleatoric bells during Lazarus's resurrection scene, a sound resource to which he would return in later works.

The Whale. *The Whale*, a piece commissioned for the inaugural concert of the London Sinfonietta, first brought the youthful Tavener into the spotlight. It is scored for soloists, chorus, orchestra, and tape, and it offers a creative retelling of the biblical story of Jonah. Tavener's penchant for sonic experimentation resulted in the use of a striking variety of techniques in *The Whale*, such as lengthy opening narrative, jazz motifs, plainchant, fire-engine sounds, stomping, and shouting. The extraordinary conglomeration of techniques impressed audiences, and Tavener became an overnight success.

Celtic Requiem. The *Celtic Requiem* was another London Sinfonietta commission. It combines three different, yet traditional textual elements: the Latin mass of the dead, children's rhymes and games that deal with the subject of death, and ancient Celtic poetry. This piece reflects Tavener's exploration of religious traditions different from those of his childhood, and it first identified him as an artist with strong creative ties to spirituality. One musical technique featured in the *Celtic Requiem* is a sense of static composition, often sensed as harmonic motionlessness; this became an essential part of Tavener's mature style.

The Lamb. *The Lamb* was Tavener's first significantly popular composition after *The Whale*, and it has remained one of his most frequently performed works. It was written in one afternoon in 1982, as a birthday gift for his nephew. The text is William Blake's poem of the same title, published in his 1789 book, *Songs of Innocence and Experience*. Scored for unaccompanied chorus, *The Lamb* contains numerous manipulations of an economic melodic idea set

to simple harmonies and beautifully treated dissonances, all declaimed in homophonic texture.

The Protecting Veil. After his conversion to Orthodox Christianity, Tavener became interested in creating ikons—sacred objects—in music. When Russian-Jewish cellist Steven Isserlis commissioned a work incorporating the qualities of Russian Orthodox music, the composer was eager for the chance to address a metaphysical subject. Like *The Lamb*, *The Protecting Veil* was written in an extremely short span of time. It is scored for solo cello and string orchestra, and it celebrates the Feast of the Protecting Veil of the Mother of God. This feast was established by the Byzantine church in commemoration of the Virgin's appearance in Constantinople around the year 900 to protect the citizens threatened by invasion. The cello's lengthy melodic line, based on various chants sung for feasts in honor of the Virgin Mary, represents the voice of Mary. Tavener attempted to portray the essence of Mary's compassion and power.

The Beautiful Names. *The Beautiful Names* was commissioned by the Prince of Wales, and it premiered in June, 2007, with the BBC Symphony Orchestra and Chorus, and tenor soloist John Mark Ainsley. The piece is a setting of the ninety-nine names of Allah from the Qur'ān, and it incorporates qualities of Sufism, Hinduism, and Buddhism through the use of traditional drums, Tibetan temple bowls, and gongs. Prior to the piece's premiere, Tavener said that he structured the work based upon the sevenfold constitution of man described in Hindu philosophy, and the main sections of the work are arranged on three conjunct triads. In addition, there is little repetition of musical material or text in the entire piece. *The Beautiful Names* reflects Tavener's increased interest in a universalist philosophy, which embraces all religious traditions as expressions of the spiritual realm.

Musical Legacy

Tavener never identified with a school of composition in his early years, though he could have followed numerous avant-garde composers who were already in or past their prime period of musical output. After much exploration of the possibilities, he discovered that the flamboyant qualities of avant-garde did not comply with his innate sense of religious creativity. As a result, Tavener spent nearly two decades gradually shedding the characteristics of his compositional training in order to create his unique aesthetic expression.

Critics occasionally denounce Tavener as a thoughtfully packaged product of popular culture, because of the attention his compositions have received from royalty, celebrities, and pop stars. Admirers often compare Tavener to other mystic composers, such as Olivier Messiaen and Arvo Pärt, because his works evoke a similar intensity of spiritual feeling. Tavener will be remembered for his genius in combining an incongruous collection of compositional techniques and religious ideas in order to present a unified and moving portrait of universal experience.

Kelly A. Huff

Further Reading

Dudgeon, Piers. *Lifting the Veil: The Biography of Sir John Tavener*. London: Portrait, 2003. This major biographical study focuses on the connections between Tavener's life experiences and his musical output, and it is based on extensive interviews with the composer, his close collaborators, and his religious mentors. Includes select discography, photographs, and bibliography.

Haydon, Geoffrey. *John Tavener: Glimpses of Paradise*. London: Victor Gollancz, 1995. Biographical information is organized as small vignettes, following the completion of Haydon's second major film on Tavener. Includes a chronological list of compositions, photographs, and select discography.

Tavener, John. "*Celtic Requiem*: An Introduction." *The Musical Times* 110, no. 1517 (July, 1969): 736-737. A detailed description of the genesis and symbolism of Tavener's *Celtic Requiem*, prior to its premiere by the London Sinfonietta.

_____. *The Music of Silence: A Composer's Testament*. Edited by Brian Keeble. London: Faber & Faber, 1999. This autobiography offers a description of Tavener's compositional processes and his personal philosophies, with in-depth commentaries on selected works. Includes a chronological list of compositions, photographs, and select discography.

Tavener, John, and Malcolm Crowthers. "All at Sea? On the Eve of the Barbican Festival Devoted to His Music, John Tavener Talks to Malcolm Crowthers About the Sea, Bells, Religion, and Life in Greece." *The Musical Times* 135, no. 1811 (January, 1994): 9-14. In an interview, Tavener discusses several lesser-known works that were performed at the 1994 festival of his music, organized by the BBC.

Tavener, John, and Mother Thekla. *Ikons: Meditations in Words and Music (A Fount Book)*. London: HarperCollins, 1994. A personal devotion or meditation book written by Tavener, with the aid of Mother Thekla. Includes a companion compact disc featuring some of Tavener's music.

See also: Lennon, John; McCartney, Sir Paul; Messiaen, Olivier; Pärt, Arvo; Ravel, Maurice; Rutter, John; Stravinsky, Igor.

Cecil Taylor
American jazz pianist and composer

Taylor was a primary leader of the late 1950's avant-garde who pioneered new approaches to improvisation that expanded the boundaries of jazz.

Born: March 25, 1929; New York, New York
Also known as: Cecil Percival Taylor (full name)

Principal recordings

ALBUMS: *In Transition*, 1955; *Jazz Advance*, 1956; *Coltrane Time*, 1958; *Hard Driving Jazz*, 1958; *Looking Ahead!*, 1958; *Cecil Taylor Plays Cole Porter*, 1959; *Love for Sale*, 1959; *Stereo Drive*, 1959; *Air*, 1960; *The World of Cecil Taylor*, 1960; *Cell Walk for Celeste*, 1961; *Jumpin' Punkins*, 1961; *New York City R and B*, 1961; *Nefertiti the Beautiful One Has Come*, 1962; *Conquistador*, 1966; *Student Studies*, 1966; *Unit Structures*, 1966; *Akisakila*, 1973; *Indent*, 1973; *Solo*, 1973; *Spring of Two Blue-J's*, 1973; *Silent Tongues*, 1974; *Dark unto Themselves*, 1976; *Embraced*, 1977 (with Mary Lou Williams); *Cecil Taylor Unit*, 1978; *One Too Many, Salty Swift, and Not Goodbye*, 1978; *Three Phasis*, 1978; *Fly! Fly! Fly! Fly! Fly!*, 1980; *It Is in the Brewing Luminous*, 1980; *The Eighth*, 1981; *Garden*, 1981; *Winged Serpent (Sliding Quadrants)*, 1984; *For Olim*, 1986; *Olu Iwa*, 1986; *Chinampas*, 1987; *Tzotzil*,

Mummers, Tzotzil, 1987; *Erzulie Maketh Scent*, 1988; *The Hearth*, 1988; *Leaf Palm Hand*, 1988 (with Tony Oxley); *Pleistozaen mit Wasser*, 1988 (with Derek Bailey); *Regalia*, 1988 (with Paul Lovens); *Remembrance*, 1988; *Riobec*, 1988 (with Günter Sommer); *Spots, Circles, and Fantasy*, 1988 (with Han Bennink); *Alms/Tiergarten (Spree)*, 1989; *In Florescence*, 1989; *Looking (Berlin Version) Corona*, 1989; *Looking (Berlin Version) Solo*, 1989; *Celebrated Blazons*, 1990; *Thelonious Sphere Monk: Dreaming of the Masters, Vol. 2*, 1992; *Always a Pleasure*, 1993; *Buildings Within*, 1993; *Akisakila, Vol. 2*, 1995; *Mixed*, 1998; *Cecil Taylor/Bill Dixon/Tony Oxley*, 2002; *Piano Solo*, 2002; *Port of Call*, 2002; *Piano Cecil*, 2003; *Algonquin*, 2004; *All the Notes*, 2004; *The Owner of the River Bank*, 2004 (with the Italian Instabile Orchestra).

The Life

Cecil Percival Taylor grew up in Corona, Queens, a metropolitan New York neighborhood that harbored numerous musicians. As a member of a small but growing African American middle class, he was encouraged by his mother to study classical piano from an early age and was exposed to the great breadth and wealth of the arts found in cosmopolitan New York. In 1949 Taylor began a two-year diploma program at the New England Conservatory of Music in Boston. After graduating in 1951, Taylor moved back to New York and began sporadic gigs as both a sideman and a leader. His recording career began in 1956, when he became the leader of both a trio and a quartet. He recorded about one album per year until 1962, when he made his first European tour.

Taylor slowly began to receive recognition and acclaim throughout the 1960's. In the early 1970's he held several short-term posts at universities (University of Wisconsin, Antioch College, Glassboro State College), and he received a Guggenheim grant in 1973. In the 1980's he was consistently winning *Down Beat* magazine's poll for best pianist and had an extraordinary monthlong stint as an artist-in-residence in Berlin, performing with Europe's top improvisers. In 1991 Taylor received the prestigious MacArthur Foundation Fellowship. His collaborators have included John Coltrane, dancers Mikhail Baryshnikov and Dianne McIntyre, pianist Mary Lou Williams, drummers Max Roach and Elvin Jones, the Art Ensemble of Chicago, and saxophonist Anthony Braxton.

The Music

Jazz Advance. Taylor's first commercial recording, *Jazz Advance*, with his first ensemble (bassist Buell Neidlinger, drummer Dennis Charles, and soprano saxophonist Steve Lacy) already revealed an original approach to the piano and improvisation. In his rendition of Thelonious Monk's "Bemsha Swing," for example, he used texture as an organizing principle within the repeating chorus structure. His principal method was to exploit registral contrasts of the left and right hands with static or moving clusters, parallel versus conjunct lines, and a number of other relationships, rather than the standard practice of assigning chords to the left hand and melody to the right hand.

Looking Ahead! Over the next several years this new approach would be developed and documented in jazz-based trios or quartets. *Looking Ahead!*, recorded in 1958 and featuring vibraphonist. Earl Griffith, contains some of Taylor's most intimate and enduring statements. Throughout this period Taylor had a difficult time finding steady work, in part because of the incompatibility of his music with nightclub socializing and in part because his very dynamic and forceful piano technique intimidated club owners, fearful for their pianos.

The World of Cecil Taylor. Recorded in late 1960, *The World of Cecil Taylor* shows Taylor on the verge of breaking through the confines of the twelve- and thirty-two-bar formal structures that were standard in jazz at the time. *Into the Hot*, recorded a year later, debuted Taylor's new ensemble, with long-term associate alto saxophonist Jimmy Lyons, drummer Sunny Murray, and bassist Henry Grimes. During the improvisation section of "Pots," the drummer and the rest of the ensemble are in two different rhythmic strata, with no overriding beat governing the music, despite the piece's loose choral structure.

Live at Montmartre. In late 1962 Taylor, Murray, and Lyons toured Scandinavia, recording *Live at Montmartre*, which shows the final disintegration of a steady beat and regular choral structure, two hitherto sacrosanct characteristics of jazz. This album provided a first glimpse of the ultimate demise of any steady beat in Taylor's music, a feature that Taylor and Murray would develop over the next few years.

Touring Europe. Taylor did not record from 1963 to 1965 and continued to be plagued by difficulties finding work. He eventually recorded two albums on the mainstream Blue Note label in 1966 (*Unit Structures* and *Conquistador*), which showed a new maturity in writing for a medium-sized ensemble (sextet and septet). Throughout the 1960's Taylor found a growing audience in Europe.

In 1973-1974 Taylor recorded a series of live concerts that featured his solo piano playing (*Indent, Akisakila, Spring of Two Blue-J's,* and *Silent Tongues*) and established him as an unparalleled master of the genre. These concert performances reveal an unprecedented style of solo piano improvisation and a flawless command of the instrument. While some melodic motives appear to float from performance to performance, each piece (often consisting of several movements) has its own shape, defined initially by extended opening statements that eventually transform into nonstop barrages all over the instrument, taxing the construction of the piano. The textural improvisation hinted at in his earliest recordings is here in full bloom as a large-scale organizational device.

After 1974. From the mid-1970's Taylor performed and recorded with various formations of his groups, entering into a number of unusual collaborations. A highly touted duo concert with elder piano stateswoman Mary Lou Williams in New York's Carnegie Hall proved disappointing for both, although a 1979 concert with elder drum statesman Max Roach showed more communication and sympathy. Taylor's 1986 solo piano recording *For Olim* continued to develop his long-form works of a decade earlier, providing further evidence of his massive yet subtle command of the piano and now fully consolidated personal musical language.

In the summer of 1988 Taylor enjoyed a month-long residency in Berlin, which yielded an extraordinary eleven-compact-disc boxed set featuring him in concert in duets and trios with some of Europe's most renowned improvisers as well as leading an all-star European orchestra. Taylor continued to give high-profile solo concerts in the 1990's,

enjoying critical acclaim and achieving iconic status as the master of solo improvisation.

In the 2000's Taylor remained in demand in Europe and the United States. He reunited with bassist Grimes for the first time in forty years and gave a series of acclaimed European performances with saxophonist Braxton in 2007, their first musical meeting. Taylor continues to perform with great command and energy for a relatively small but highly devoted global fan base that recognizes him as the wellspring for what came to be known after 1960 as "free improvisation."

Musical Legacy

Besides leaving more than fifty years' worth of deeply personal, virtuosic, and innovative music documented on scores of recordings, Taylor has opened the doors for generations of musicians to new possibilities for playing their instruments and improvising. Starting from a base within jazz in the 1950's, by the mid-1960's Taylor had successfully broken down the boundaries that had previously defined the genre. This freed jazz musicians to devise new conceptions and strategies for improvisation within a solo or an ensemble context. Taylor's steadfast adherence to his initial style, exploring the potential of a music not based in the steady beat so germane to jazz before 1960, has proven to be an enduring inspiration.

Eric Charry

Further Reading

Felver, Christopher. *Cecil Taylor: All the Notes.* DVD. EMotion Studios, 2004. An intimate video documentary of Taylor, featuring him speaking about his life and clips of recent performances with his ensemble.

Jost, Ekkehard. *Cecil Taylor in Berlin '88.* Free Music Production, 1989. A 187-page booklet accompanying an eleven-compact-disc boxed set culled from a residency in Berlin provides analysis of Taylor's music, photographs, and working methods.

_____. *Free Jazz.* New York: Da Capo Press, 1981. This is a classic text focusing on musical analysis. The ten chapters, each devoted to a single musician (including one on Taylor), provide a capsule history of the new movement in jazz in the 1960's.

Spellman, A. B. *Four Lives in the Bebop Business.* New York: Limelight, 1994. Spellman was one of the few African American jazz writers of the era and one of the most perceptive of his generation. The chapter on Taylor provides a great wealth of biographical material, based on interviews, as well as a sympathetic analysis of Taylor's place in American music, yet to be surpassed.

See also: Coleman, Ornette; Coltrane, John; Mingus, Charles; Monk, Thelonious; Porter, Cole; Roach, Max; Williams, Mary Lou.

James Taylor
American folk-rock singer-songwriter

A popular singer-songwriter, Taylor is noted for his autobiographical, melodic, soft rock- and country-flavored tunes, sung in a warm, pleasant voice.

Born: March 12, 1948; Boston, Massachusetts

Principal recordings
ALBUMS: *James Taylor,* 1968; *Sweet Baby James,* 1970; *Mud Slide Slim and the Blue Horizon,* 1971; *One Man Dog,* 1972; *Walking Man,* 1974; *Gorilla,* 1975; *In the Pocket,* 1976; *J. T.,* 1977; *Flag,* 1979; *Dad Loves His Work,* 1981; *That's Why I'm Here,* 1985; *Never Die Young,* 1988; *New Moon Shine,* 1991; *Hourglass,* 1997; *October Road,* 2002; *A Christmas Album,* 2004; *James Taylor at Christmas,* 2006; *One Man Band,* 2007; *Covers,* 2008.
SINGLES: "Mockingbird," 1974 (with Carly Simon); "Devoted to You," 1978 (with Simon).

The Life
One of five children, James Taylor was born into a wealthy family in Boston, Massachusetts, to Isaac and Gertrude (Woodard) Taylor. He grew up in Chapel Hill, North Carolina, where his father served as dean of the School of Medicine at the University of North Carolina. Interested in music from an early age—like siblings Alex, Kate, Hugh, and Livingston Taylor, who also became professional musicians—Taylor took cello lessons, and he learned to play guitar before entering Milton Academy, a Massachusetts prep school. Taylor eventually dropped out of school to play in a band. Later, he underwent treatment for depression and drug addiction, problems that have periodically recurred.

Taylor began recording in 1968, and he has released more than twenty albums, most to critical and commercial success. In 1972 he married singer-songwriter Carly Simon, and they had two children before divorcing in 1983. Taylor was married to actress Kathryn Walker from 1985 to 1995. He has been married since 2001 to Caroline Smedvig, and they have twin sons. A longtime liberal and environmental activist, Taylor and his family settled in Pittsfield, Massachusetts.

The Music
Voluntarily institutionalized in his late teens for drug abuse and for emotional problems, Taylor began writing songs during rehabilitation, and he restored himself through his music. The first artist not associated with the Beatles to sign with Apple Records—his debut there was not successful—Taylor had a hit with his second album in 1970. A consummate professional and a charismatic performer, he has released a steady stream of recordings featuring thoughtful, personal lyrics and lilting melodies with hymn-like progressions and structure, flavored by the country-and-western songs he listened to as a child. Though Taylor's output of original material has slowed since the late 1970's in favor of live albums and compilations, he has remained a popular performer throughout his career. Of his more than twenty-five albums released since 1968, fourteen have been certified as platinum or multiplatinum, and five have been certified as gold—despite the fact that he has garnered only one number-one hit: his 1971 cover of Carole King's "You've Got a Friend."

Sweet Baby James. A 1970 release for Warner Bros., Taylor's second solo effort was backed with a corps of seasoned session musicians (Carole King, piano and vocals; Danny Kortchmar, guitar; Russ Kunkel, drums; Randy Meisner, bass; and Leland Sklar, bass). Together, they produced a series of Taylor-penned hits that have become soft-rock standards: "Sunny Skies," "Country Road," "Fire and Rain," and the title track. In 2003 the triple plat-

James Taylor. (Peter Morgan/Reuters/Landov)

inum album appeared on both VHI's and *Rolling Stone* magazine's lists of the greatest albums of all time.

Mud Slide Slim and the Blue Horizon. Taylor's third album, released in 1971, is notable primarily for producing his sole number-one single: his interpretation of King's "You've Got a Friend," though another song from the album, "Long Ago and Far Away," also made it into the Top 40 charts. "You've Got a Friend" earned Grammy Awards for both Taylor (Best Pop Male Vocal Performance) and King (Song of the Year).

Gorilla. A 1975 release, this was Taylor's sixth album, and, in addition to his regular stable of session musicians (Kortchmar, Kunkel, Sklar), it featured the backing vocals of David Crosby, Graham Nash, Linda Ronstadt, and Simon, his wife at the time. A gold album, *Gorilla* produced two *Billboard* Hot 100 singles: "Mexico" and the Brian Holland-Lamont Dozier-Edward Holland classic "How Sweet It Is (To Be Loved by You)," which rose to number five on the pop charts.

Dad Loves His Work. Released in 1981, this album is the last recording before Taylor divorced Simon. Simon had demanded that the singer reduce his touring to spend more time with his children, and the album title reflects Taylor's attitude toward his wife's ultimatum. The platinum album produced two songs that charted in the Top 20: "Hard Times" and "Her Town Too."

Hourglass. A 1997 release, *Hourglass* yielded no hits, but it received high critical acclaim, and it was commercially successful, becoming certified platinum. Featuring diverse backup personnel (Yo-Yo Ma, cello; Branford Marsalis, soprano saxophone; Stevie Wonder, harmonica; Shawn Colvin, Valerie Carter, and Sting, vocals), *Hourglass* won the Best Pop Album Grammy Award with such tracks as "Little More Time With You," "Yellow and Rose," and "Jump Up Behind Me," the last a tribute to Taylor's father, who came to his son's aid during Taylor's addiction to heroin.

Musical Legacy

In the forefront of a trend of introspective singer-songwriters, Taylor—along with such contemporaries as Joni Mitchell, Jackson Browne, and Crosby, Stills, and Nash—helped pave the way for a softer, more leisurely brand of music in the early 1970's. One of the most accessible and successful of these melodic, down-tempo artists, Taylor had more than twenty of his efforts chart in the Top 100 between 1970 and 1988. Many of his songs, such as "Fire and Rain," "Handy Man," "Shower the People," and "Carolina in My Mind," are mainstays on radio playlists. In addition to his many platinum and gold albums, Taylor has been honored with five Grammy Awards (1971, 1977, 1998, 2001, 2003), and he was the Grammy MusiCares Person of the Year in 2006. He was inducted into both the Songwriters Hall of Fame and the Rock and Roll Hall of Fame in 2000, he received the George and Ira Gershwin Award for Lifetime Musical Achievement in 2004, and in the same year he was named on the *Rolling Stone* list of the 100 Greatest Artists of All Time.

Jack Ewing

Further Reading

Halperin, Ian. *Fire and Rain: The James Taylor Story.* New York: Citadel, 2000. This standard biography of the singer-songwriter—comprising largely articles and interviews—dwells on his family history, which served as the catalyst for much of what followed in Taylor's life.

Mansfield, Ken. *The White Book: The Beatles, the Bands, the Biz—An Insider's Look at an Era.* Nashville, Tenn.: Thomas Nelson, 2007. This memoir from a former Apple Records producer offers insights into the company, particularly during the 1960's and 1970's, when Taylor became the first non-Beatle to be signed by the label.

Risberg, Joel. *The James Taylor Encyclopedia.* Morrisville, N.C.: Joel Risberg, 2005. A definitive reference about the singer-songwriter's life and work.

Weller, Sheila. *Girls Like Us: Carole King, Joni Mitchell, Carly Simon—and the Journey of a Generation.* New York: Atria, 2008. This is a frank account of the struggles of three female singer-songwriters—all whom sang at various times with Taylor—in the male-dominated world of popular music during the 1960's and 1970's.

White, Timothy. *Long Ago and Far Away: James Taylor, His Life and Music.* London: Omnibus Press, 2001. This is an in-depth biography of the singer-songwriter, detailing his ancestry, his drug addiction, and his relationships. Includes photographs.

See also: Babyface; Blackwell, Otis; Brooks, Garth; Buffett, Jimmy; Crosby, David; Grusin, Dave; King, Carole; Krauss, Alison; Lennon, John; Ma, Yo-Yo; Nascimento, Milton; Rush, Tom; Rutter, John; Simon, Carly; Stills, Stephen; Sting; Wonder, Stevie.

Renata Tebaldi

Italian classical and opera singer

Beloved by fans, Tebaldi performed many roles to great success, especially those in the operas of Verdi and Puccini, with her fluent, sensuous singing, her careful attention to words, and her deeply poignant expressiveness.

Born: February 1, 1922; Pesaro, Italy
Died: December 19, 2004; Republic of San Marino

Also known as: Renata Ersilia Clotilde Tebaldi (full name)

Principal works

OPERATIC ROLES: Elena in Arrigo Boito's *Mefistofele*, 1944; Elsa in Richard Wagner's *Lohengrin*, 1946; Prayer Singer in Giacchino Rossini's *Mosè in Egitto*, 1946 (*Moses in Egypt*); Soprano Singer in Giuseppe Verdi's *Te Deum*, 1946; Donna Elvira in Wolfgang Amadeus Mozart's *Don Giovanni*, 1949; Pamyra in Rossini's *Le Siège de Corinthe*, 1949 (*The Siege of Corinth*); Eva in Wagner's *Die Meistersinger*, 1947; Manon in Giacomo Puccini's *Manon Lescaut*, 1949; Aida in Verdi's *Aida*, 1950; Olimpie in Gaspare Luigi Pacifico Spontini's *Olimpie*, 1950; Desdemona in Verdi's *Otello*, 1950; Elisabeth in Wagner's *Tannhäuser*, 1950; Alice in Verdi's *Falstaff*, 1951; Giovanna d'Arco in Verdi's *Giovanna d'Arco*, 1951; Mimi in Puccini's *La Bohème*, 1951; Suzel in Pietro Mascagni's *L'Amico Fritz*, 1951; Amazily in Spontini's *Fernand Cortez*, 1951; Butterfly in Puccini's *Madama Butterfly*, 1952; Mathilde in Rossini's *Guglielmo Tell*, 1953; Wally in Alfredo Catalani's *La Wally*, 1953; Countess Almaviva in Mozart's *Le nozze di Figaro*, 1953 (*The Marriage of Figaro*); Tatiana in Peter Ilich Tchaikovsky's *Eugene Onegin*, 1954; Violetta in Verdi's *La traviata*, 1954; Tosca in Puccini's *Tosca*, 1955; Liù in Puccini's *Turandot*, 1955; Maria Boccanegra in Verdi's *Simon Boccanegra*, 1956; Santuzza in Mascagni's *Cavalleria rusticana*, 1957; Gioconda in Amilcare Ponchielli's *La Gioconda*, 1957; Lenora in Verdi's *Le forza del destino*, 1958 (*The Force of Destiny*); Adriana in Francesco Cilea's *Adriana Lecouvreur*, 1961; Maddalena in Umberto Giordano's *Andrea Chénier*, 1961; Minnie in Puccini's *La Fanciulla del West*, 1961; Giorgetta in Puccini's *Il Trittico*, 1962; Cleopatra in George Frideric Handel's *Giulio Cesare*, 1964; Margherita in Boito's *Mefistofele*, 1966; Amelia in Verdi's *Un ballo in maschera*, 1970 (*The Masked Ball*).

The Life

Renata Ersilia Clotilde Tebaldi (teh-BAHL-dee) was born to Teobaldo Tebaldi, a professional cellist, and his wife Giuseppina, who gave up a potential singing career for a nursing career. When the marriage broke up, Tebaldi was raised by her mother in the small town of Langhirano. Stricken at age three with poliomyelitis, Tebaldi recovered, although her reduced mobility, which persisted through her life, isolated her as a child. She studied piano and planned a career as a teacher. Soon her talent for singing emerged, and she began voice lessons with Giuseppina Passani. At fifteen, she pursued three years of study at the Parma Conservatory (1937-1940) with Ettore Campogaliani, an outstanding teacher of singers. She attracted the attention of the composer-teacher Riccardo Zandonai and his colleague Carmen Melis, with whom she studied at the Pesaro Conservatory (1940-1943). These two, especially Melis, molded Tebaldi carefully, developing her flawless technique and vocal strength, nurturing her range of two octaves. Melis also steered Tebaldi toward roles in the lirico-spinto category (between light, lyric soprano quality and heavy, dramatic singing).

Renata Tebaldi. (DPA/Landov)

Wartime devastation obliged Tebaldi to continue study on her own. She made her operatic debut in Rovigo in 1944, and she sang the following year in Trieste. Engagements in small houses around Italy gained her experience and recognition. In 1946 conductor Arturo Toscanini chose her to participate in his gala concert to open the rebuilt La Scala Opera House in Milan. She received a contract with that company, which served as her working home from 1947 to 1954. She soon emerged as a leading figure in the new generation of outstanding Italian singers.

Though based at La Scala, she sang with major companies throughout Italy, and she won international attention, especially in her London debut in 1950. In the same year she also appeared in San Francisco and in Paris.

In 1948 she signed a contract with British Decca Records, and her recordings—first of arias and excerpts, then of complete operas—furthered her international repute. The true turning point came with her debut in January, 1955, at the Metropolitan Opera in New York. Later that year she sang at the Chicago Lyric Opera. For the next eighteen years, however, the Metropolitan Opera became central to Tebaldi's career, though she did at first divide her time among New York, Milan, and Naples, with guest appearances around the world. She experienced a serious vocal crisis in 1963, but, after a withdrawal of thirteen months, she recovered fully.

Tebaldi confessed to a number of romantic attachments throughout her life, the most serious to conductor Arturo Basile. Totally committed to her career, however, she avoided marriage and children. Tebaldi's mother was utterly devoted to her daughter, and her death in November, 1957, was a devastating blow to Tebaldi, prompting the deeply religious singer to consider becoming a nun. Nevertheless, her housekeeper, manager, and confidant, Ernestina Vigano, helped Tebaldi with a deeply supportive friendship.

With her last Met performance in January, 1973, Tebaldi retired from the stage and then, after some concertizing and an emotional farewell recital in 1976, from all performing. She did some teaching, but she spent most of the remaining three decades of her life in Milan. She died at the age of eighty-two in the Republic of San Marino.

The Music

Early Works. From her early training, Tebaldi cultivated the prima donna roles in the major nineteenth century literature that would become her core repertoire. Nevertheless, she explored at first a novel range of operas. Her Cleopatra in George Frideric Handel's *Giulio Cesare* (1724) was a rare venture into Baroque material. She limited her portrayals in Wolfgang Amadeus Mozart's operas to the Countess in *The Marriage of Figaro* (1786), Donna Elvira in *Don Giovanni*, and Mathilde in his *Guglielmo Tell* (1829), as well as the title role in Gaspare Luigi Pacifico Spontini's *Olimpie* (1821) and Amazily in his *Fernand Cortez* (1809). At La Scala, she appeared in the operas of Richard Wagner—Eva in *Die Meistersinger* (1867), Elsa in *Lohengrin* (1850), and Elisabeth in *Tannhäuser* (1845)—though in Italian translations, as was common then. She also appeared as Tatiana in Peter Ilich Tchaikovsky's *Eugene Onegin* (1879), and she tried one of Giuseppe Verdi's early and then-unfashionable roles, the title character in *Giovanna d'Arco* (1845).

Italian Operatic Roles. In her maturity, however, and especially at the Metropolitan Opera, Tebaldi concentrated almost exclusively on Italian operas, especially in the mainline Verdi and Giacomo Puccini roles. Her signature part was that of Desdemona, in Verdi's *Otello* (1887), in which she first appeared in Trieste, in which she debuted at the Metropolitan Opera, and in which she gave her final performance there. For a while, her portrayals, so beautifully sung, were sometimes criticized as dramatically bland, although she could respond to stimulating onstage colleagues. In later years, her theatrical capacities improved. She even took on new Verdi roles, such as Maria Boccanegra in *Simon Boccanegra* (1857) and Alice in *Falstaff* (1893), plus Minnie in Puccini's *La Fanciulla del West* (1910).

Rivalry with Callas. Superb as she was, Tebaldi had rivals. In her initial years at the Metropolitan Opera, she faced the company's reigning dramatic soprano, Zinka Milanov. More spectacular, however, was her supposed "feud" with Maria Callas. With a coloratura style that stressed dramatic urgency over vocal luster, Callas had a slightly later start than Tebaldi at La Scala, which gradually marginalized Tebaldi in favor of the exciting newcomer. The rivalry escalated when Callas debuted at the Metropolitan Opera in 1956, the year after Tebaldi. Their repertoires were generally as different as their styles, but the tension between them was magnified by Callas, by rival press agents, by journalists, and by obstreperous fans. Tebaldi personally stood aloof, and the two eventually had a meeting of reconciliation in 1968—three years after Callas's ravaged voice and crumbling career forced her withdrawal from stage performance. Tebaldi's personality was famously dignified and placid, but Metropolitan Opera manager Rudolf Bing spoke of her "dimples of iron."

Musical Legacy

First in Italy, and then at the Metropolitan Opera in New York, Tebaldi acquired a legion of devoted fans, who still cherish the memory of her singing, and her career also coincided with a heyday of great opera recordings. Though noncommercial releases have preserved her in some live performances, her studio work, mostly for Decca Records, documented her favorite roles in her mainstream operas: Arrigo Boito's *Mefistofele* (1868), Alfredo Catalani's *La Wally* (1892), Amilcare Ponchielli's *La Gioconda* (1876), Francesco Cilea's *Adriana Lecouvreur* (1902), Umberto Giordano's *Andrea Chénier* (1896), and Pietro Mascagni's *Cavalleria rusticana* (1890).

In addition, she made recordings singing in the operas of her two chief composers: Puccini's *Manon Lescaut* (1893), *La Bohème* (1896), *Tosca* (1900), *Madama Butterfly* (1904), *La Fanciulla del West*, *Il Trittico* (1918), and *Turandot* (1926); Verdi's *La traviata* (1853), *The Masked Ball* (1859), *Aida* (1871), and, in particular, *Otello*. These recordings remain enduring classics, and for many critics her performances are benchmarks against which subsequent singers can still be measured.

John W. Barker

Further Reading

Casanova, Carlamaria. *Renata Tebaldi: The Voice of an Angel*. Dallas, Tex.: Baskerville, 1995. With a subtitle from Toscanini's epithet for her, this is an affectionate survey of Tebaldi's career, her roles, and her recordings.

Harris, Kenn. *Renata Tebaldi: An Authorized Biogra-*

phy. New York: Drake, 1974. Written by a somewhat adoring friend of Tebaldi, this book surveys the personal and professional life of the opera singer.

Rasponi, Lanfranco. *The Last Prima Donnas*. New York: Alfred A. Knopf, 1982. This resource includes the transcript of an extended interview with Tebaldi, in which she offers biographical reflections.

Seroff, Victor. *Renata Tebaldi: The Woman or the Diva*. New York: Appleton-Century-Crofts, 1961. This "intimate portrait" of Tebaldi's life and career includes an overview of her repertoire and her recordings.

See also: Callas, Maria; Puccini, Giacomo; Toscanini, Arturo.

Sonny Terry

American blues singer-songwriter and harmonicist

Terry was one of the foremost exponents of the blues harmonica, playing single-note runs punctuated by falsetto whoops. In addition, the duo he formed with guitarist Brownie McGhee was perhaps the best known in blues history, exemplifying the Piedmont and East Coast blues style.

Born: October 24, 1911; Greensboro, North Carolina
Died: March 11, 1986; Mineola, New York
Also known as: Saunders Terrell (birth name)

Principal recordings

ALBUMS: *Sonny Terry and His Mouth Harp*, 1953; *Brownie McGhee and Sonny Terry Sing*, 1958 (with Brownie McGhee); *The 1958 London Sessions*, 1958 (with McGhee); *Sonny Terry's New Sound*, 1958; *Just a Closer Walk with Thee*, 1960 (with McGhee); *Sonny's Story*, 1960; *Sonny and Brownie at Sugar Hill*, 1961 (with McGhee); *Brownie McGhee and Sonny Terry at the Second Fret*, 1963 (with McGhee); *Sonny Is King*, 1963; *Sonny Terry and Lightnin' Hopkins*, 1963 (with Lightnin' Hopkins); *Sonny Terry and Woody Guthrie*, 1969 (with Guthrie); *Sonny and*

Brownie, 1973 (with McGhee); *Black Night Road*, 1976; *Harmonica Blues*, 1976; *Walk On*, 1977 (with McGhee); *Midnight Special*, 1978 (with McGhee); *Whoopin'*, 1984 (with Johnny Winter and Willie Dixon); *Backwater Blues*, 1999 (with McGhee; recorded 1961).

The Life

Saunders Terrell was raised on a small farm in North Carolina. His parents were musical; his father played the harmonica and his mother sang. Terry learned to play his father's harmonica when he was eight and practiced long hours, experimenting with the sounds that can be coaxed from that small instrument. Unfortunately losing sight in his left eye in an accident when he was eleven years old and most sight in his right eye when he was sixteen, Terry decided to pursue a career as a musician. He moved with his family to Shelby, North Carolina, and played with various bands at fish fries, at medicine shows, at house parties, and on the street.

After a tractor trailer ran over his father, killing him, Terry moved in with his sister Lou Daisy. Around 1934, he began playing with guitarist Blind Boy Fuller and moved in with him. He also worked selling liquor and in a factory for the blind, making mattresses. Fuller and Terry traveled to New York to make their first recordings under the Vocalion label. Terry gained prominence at a famous Carnegie Hall concert, titled "Spirituals to Swing," in 1938. In 1941, Terry formed a duo with Brownie McGhee and they moved to Washington, D.C., for the duration of World War II.

After the war, Terry and McGhee returned to New York, moving into a large house on downtown's Sixth Avenue. Over the next thirty years, Terry was in great demand, performing with McGhee, recording with various other musicians, playing in folk revivals and blues concerts, and starring in Broadway shows. In the late 1970's Terry's partnership with McGhee dissolved, and health problems ended his musical career.

The Music

Terry was already a talented harmonica player when he first heard blues music, at about age fourteen. Harmonica music in the Piedmont area was known for its soundings of rural life, of trains and animal hunts. Terry developed a distinct style of rapid, single-note runs and driving chordal rhythms. Terry's unique vocal style added to the electricity of his harmonica playing (in the context of blues music, often referred to as "harp" playing). He sang with a high falsetto and added arresting "whoops." Incredibly, he seemed to be "whooping" not only between but often during his rapid harmonica runs.

Guitarist Blind Boy Fuller was sufficiently impressed with Terry's street playing that around 1934 the two formed a partnership and played throughout North Carolina. Their first recordings came to the attention of John Hammond, who invited Fuller to play in his pathbreaking "Spirituals to Swing" concert in Carnegie Hall on December 23, 1938. However, Fuller was incarcerated at the time, so Terry traveled to New York by himself. The concert brought Terry instant acclaim. His recorded performance of "Fox Chase" is an incredible mix of whoops, stomping, and relentless single-note runs on the harmonica, all simulating the sound of a fox hunt (the composition originates in the old English ballads "Lost John" and "Louise, Louise"). After the concert, Terry made his first solo recordings at Havers Studio.

"John Henry." Terry returned to Carnegie Hall the following Christmas Eve (1939) for another "Spirituals to Swing" concert. He recorded performances of two of his most celebrated songs. The first, "John Henry," accompanied by Bull City Red on washboard, was a traditional African American song that Terry gave an entirely original and idiosyncratic sound. He tells the story of John Henry with an assortment of whoops, falsetto howls, and short, chugging harmonica blasts.

Terry recorded a much different version of "John Henry" with McGhee twenty years later, on their well-received record, *Brownie McGhee and Sonny Terry Sing*. A smoother version, thanks to McGhee's steady strumming and their unison singing, it features Terry's driving harp playing, simulating John Henry's hammer.

"Mountain Blues." Terry's other favorite song performed at Carnegie Hall on December 24, 1939, was "Mountain Blues." Terry plays it in a slow, mournful style, keeping a steady beat by banging on his harmonica. He wails his tale of abandonment with alternative blasts of harp playing and haunting falsetto.

Sonny Terry. (Hulton Archive/Getty Images)

After Fuller's sudden death during surgery on February 13, 1941, Terry joined with guitarist and vocalist McGhee. With the combination of Terry's ferocious, whooping style and McGhee's smooth singing and dexterous guitar riffs, the duo became celebrated in the blues and folk revival of the late 1950's and early 1960's.

"Stranger Blues." A good example of the work of Terry and McGhee is their recording of "Perfect Strangers," which was captured on videotape. The duo introduce the song by recounting the baleful life of strangers—a classic blues theme. McGhee provides a steady background with his fluid singing and guitar playing. Terry wails away on his harmonica, punctuated by his patented whoops. His two hands flap around his harmonica like birds, bending and scooping his notes at will.

Terry also made appearances in theater, on television, and in film. In the late 1960's, the McGhee and Terry duet toured Australia, India, and Europe. The "British invasion" brought Terry new fans.

"Sonny's Whoopin' the Doop." In 1984, Terry recorded the album *Whoopin'* with Johnny Winter and Willie Dixon. The instrumental number "Sonny's Whoopin' the Doop" is featured on this album. Terry begins the song with virtuosic harmonica playing, punctuated by his old-fashioned falsetto yelps. In the middle of the song, Terry slows the tempo of his playing to accentuate the wails and moans of his harp. He concludes the song with frenetic runs and a flurry of whoops.

Musical Legacy

Terry had a unique harmonica style based on the rural, acoustic blues of the Piedmont Carolina country. Much indebted to the folk tradition as well, Piedmont blues harmonica imitated the locomotion of trains and the sounds of fox chases, accompanied by the frenetic yelps of chased and chasing animals. Terry was a master of tone color, vibrato, and tremolo, accentuated by his vocal falsetto and whoops. A versatile musician, he recorded blues, folk, and gospel music. His partnerships with Blind Boy Fuller and especially Brownie McGhee were without parallel, and along with them, Terry was a seminal figure in the blues and folk revival of the late 1950's and early 1960's.

Howard Bromberg

Further Reading

Bastin, Bruce. *Red River Blues: The Blues Tradition in the Southeast*. Urbana: University of Illinois Press, 1986. This volume in the series Music in American Life focuses on blues from the Piedmont belt and North Carolina. The chapter on Terry is based on an extensive 1974 interview.

Bogdanov, Vladimir, Chris Woodstrata, and Stephen Thomas Erlewine, eds. *All Music Guide to the Blues: The Definitive Guide to the Blues*. 3d ed. San Francisco: Backbeat Books, 2003. In a biographical entry and various essays, this blues reference work explains Terry's importance in Piedmont blues and the development of harmonica blues.

Cooper, Kent, ed. *The Harp Styles of Sonny Terry*. New York: Oak, 1975. Terry's instructional book on playing the blues harmonica, with autobiographical material.

Dicaire, David. *Blues Singers: Biographies of Fifty Legendary Artists of the Early Twentieth Century*. Jef-

ferson, N.C.: McFarland, 1999. A collection of breezy biographies of blues pioneers, including Terry.

See also: Fuller, Blind Boy; Guthrie, Woody; Leadbelly.

Léon Theremin
Russian classical instrumentalist and conductor

Theremin invented a space-controlled monophonic instrument called the theremin, one of the first electronic instruments. Several composers wrote original concert works and film scores incorporating the theremin.

Born: August 15, 1896; St. Petersburg, Russia
Died: November 3, 1993; Moscow, Russia
Also known as: Lev Sergeyevich Termen (birth name)

Principal works

ELECTRONIC/THEREMIN PERFORMANCES: *Music from the Ether*, 1928; Edvard Hagerup Grieg: *Aase's Death*, 1930; Wagner: *Prelude to Lohengrin*, 1930; *Theremin Orchestra*, 1932; "Let the Sun Shine Forever, Let Me Be Forever," 1993 (as conductor).

The Life

Léon Theremin (LAY-ohn THER-eh-mihn) was born to lawyer Sergei Theremin and his wife, Yevgenia Orzhinskaya. At a young age, Theremin was interested in both music and science, so in 1914 he entered St. Petersburg University to study astronomy and physics and St. Petersburg Conservatory to study cello. In 1917 Theremin graduated from both the university and the conservatory. In 1919 he began working in a laboratory at the Petrograd (originally St. Petersburg) Physics-Technical Institute, where he experimented on radio waves and human capacitance (ability to store energy). His work there led to the invention of an electronic instrument that he called the Etherphon; later it became known as the Thereminvox, or theremin. In

1927 he began a tour with his instrument that culminated in New York City, where he lived and worked until 1938. After that time, all traces of Theremin vanished, and most people believed that he had died. Later it was discovered that he worked for the KGB, the intelligence agency of the Soviet Union, first as a prisoner for nearly a decade and then voluntarily until 1964.

Theremin's most famous invention for the KGB was a concealed listening device, the Buran, which went undetected for years at the U.S. embassy in Moscow. From the mid-1960's until his death in 1993, he returned to his musical roots, working with electronic instruments, first at the Moscow Conservatory and later at Moscow State University.

The Music

Although Theremin spent roughly a third of his life working on nonmusical electronic devices, primarily for use by the Soviet state, his greatest achievements involved his work on electronic instruments. Theremin created several, three of which should be noted for their innovations. The first is the widely known theremin, the space-control instrument that bears his name. The second device, the Rhythmicon, created complex rhythm combinations. The third was a small stage that allowed a dancer to create music by bodily motion, much like the theremin, which he called the Terpsitone.

The Theremin. The instrument that bore the inventor's name, the Thereminvox, later known as the theremin, came about because of a chance observation during a laboratory experiment. In 1920 at the Petrograd Physics-Technical Institute, Theremin created a device that measured changes in the density of gases under various conditions. His device included a pair of vacuum tubes used in radios that, when tuned properly, created a pitch. When he attached headphones, he noticed that, as his hand approached the device, it affected the frequency of the pitch. After simple experimentation, he realized that he could control the pitch and create monophonic (or single-voiced) melodies. In 1921 he refined the instrument, adding volume control, and registered a patent. In 1927, after demonstrating his creation to Vladimir Lenin, the leader of the Soviet Union, Theremin embarked on a tour of Europe and the United States.

In 1929 RCA licensed and manufactured the instrument for the mass market. To use a theremin the musician stands in front of a box that has two antennae attached and waves his or her hands around the antennae, without touching them, creating electrical sound signals. One hand controls the pitch, and the other hand controls the volume. RCA's instrument met with limited commercial success, and, in the wake of the Great Depression, RCA began losing money on the project and cancelled its license of the theremin in 1931.

In the late 1920's and early 1930's, the theremin attracted the attention of various musicians, who wanted to create new works for it. Some of these were thereminists Lucie Rosen and Clara Rockmore; composer Joseph Schillinger, who wrote the first composition to feature the theremin, the *First Airphonic Suite*, for RCA Theremin and Orchestra; and conductor Leopold Stokowski, who commissioned and used several variants of the theremin, including a fingerboard and a keyboard model.

The Rhythmicon. In 1931 Theremin received a commission from the New York Musicological Society to create an instrument that could perform complex rhythms. Working with him on the project were composers Schillinger and Henry Cowell. The instrument was the first of its kind, a predecessor to the drum machines that appeared in the later part of the twentieth century. Cowell proposed that the instrument, called the Rhythmicon, should perform rhythmic ratios inherent in the overtone series. When the performer played intervals on the keyboard attached to the instrument, he would hear eighth-note pulses with an octave, triplet eighth notes with a perfect fifth, three sixteenth notes for a perfect fourth, and so on. Upon completion of the instrument in 1932, Cowell composed the unpublished Concerto for Rhythmicon and Orchestra. The only known remaining Rhythmicon, which is no longer operational, is owned by the Smithsonian Institution of Washington, D.C.

The Terpsitone. Theremin's third innovative instrument was based on the principles of the theremin's space control. Instead of a box with antennae for controlling pitch and volume, the Terpsitone consisted of a small dance platform under which a metal plate interacted with a dancer's body to control pitch. Unlike the theremin, the Terpsitone required a second person to control the volume and vibrato. Although the instrument was created for a dancer to perform, Theremin could not find a dancer who could control the pitches enough to create a melody, and so thereminist Rockmore agreed to debut the instrument at Carnegie Hall in 1932. The Terpsitone was not as widely used as the theremin, but the inventor continued to develop and demonstrate the instrument after his retirement from the KGB.

Musical Legacy

Besides Schillinger and Cowell, composers Edgard Varèse, Percy Grainger, Bohuslav Martinů, and Alfred Schnittke wrote works incorporating Theremin's instruments. In addition, Bernard Herrmann and Miklós Rózsa used the theremin in prominent film scores. The eerie sounds of the theremin were used to great effect in films, including *Spellbound* (1945), *The Lost Weekend* (1945), *The Day the Earth Stood Still* (1951), and *The Ten Commandments* (1956). Perhaps the best-known song featuring the instrument was the Beach Boys' "Good Vibrations." Although Theremin's instrument is still being built and used in performances, his greatest influence was upon the work of the pioneer of synthesized sound, Robert Moog. As a teenager, Moog built and sold theremins from his parents' home. Inspired by the concepts behind the theremin, Moog explored other ways of synthesizing sounds, creating the first synthesizers.

Mark D. Porcaro

Further Reading

Galeyev, Bulat M. "L. S. Termen: Faustus of the Twentieth Century." *Leonardo* 24, no. 5 (1991): 573-579. A brief overview of Theremin's life and works, including his life in Russia after 1938.

Galeyev, Bulat M., Leon S. Theremin, Natalia Nesturkh, et al. "Leon Theremin: Pioneer of Electronic Art." *Leonardo Music Journal* 6 (1996): 45-83. This journal devoted a special section to Theremin's life, work, and legacy to commemorate the centenary of his birth.

Glinsky, Albert. *Theremin: Ether Music and Espionage.* Urbana: University of Illinois Press, 2000. With a foreword by Moog, this thorough biography focuses on Theremin's inventions and his espionage work during the Cold War.

Theremin, Leon. "Recollections." *Contemporary Music Review* 18, no. 3 (1999): 5-8. Theremin recalls his musical life from his early years until the time when he was taken back to the Soviet Union in 1938.

Wierzbicki, James. "Weird Vibrations: How the Theremin Gave Musical Voice to Hollywood's Extraterrestrial 'Others.'" *Journal of Popular Film and Television* 30, no. 3 (2002): 125-135. In addition to a discussion of the role of the theremin in film scores, this article presents a short history of Theremin and his instrument.

See also: Cowell, Henry; Grainger, Percy Aldridge; Herrmann, Bernard; Martinů, Bohuslav; Rózsa, Miklós; Schnittke, Alfred; Stokowski, Leopold.

Michael Tilson Thomas
American classical conductor

An acclaimed pianist, composer, educator, and proponent of American music, Thomas has an interest in a diverse array of music, including American jazz, Russian folk, German Romantic, and contemporary pop.

Born: December 21, 1944; Los Angeles, California
Also known as: Michael Tomashevsky (birth name)

Principal works

ORCHESTRAL WORK: *From the Diary of Anne Frank*, 1990.

Principal recordings

ALBUMS (as conductor): *Stravinsky: Suite No. 1 for Small Orchestra*, 1963; *Tchaikovsky: Symphony No. 1 in G Minor, Op. 13, Winter Dreams*, 1970; *Debussy: Images for Orchestra*, 1971; *Stravinsky: Le Sacre du printemps*, 1972; *George Gershwin: Rhapsody in Blue*, 1976; *Steve Reich: The Desert Music*, 1985; *Tchaikovsky: Symphony No. 6 in B Minor, Op. 74, Pathétique*, 1986; *Charles Ives: Symphony No. 4*, 1989; *Tchaikovsky: Nutcracker Suite, Op. 71a*, 1991; *Prokofiev: Romeo and Juliet, Op. 64*, 1995; *Copland: The Modernist*, 1996;

Copland: The Populist, 2000; *Mahler: Symphony No. 1*, 2004; *Mahler: Symphony No. 7*, 2005.

The Life

Michael Tilson Thomas was born to Theodor and Roberta Thomas on December 21, 1944, at Cedars of Lebanon Hospital in Hollywood, California. Thomas's musical lineage runs deep: His father worked on Broadway, and his grandparents starred at New York's Yiddish Theatre after emigrating from Russia to the United States. Thomas began playing piano by ear at a young age, and he studied at the University of Southern California music preparatory school until 1962. He then enrolled as a full-time piano and composition student, with John Crown and Ingolf Dahl, respectively. Thomas's first formal conducting experience came at the age of nineteen, as the music director of the Young Musicians Foundation's Debut Orchestra in Los Angeles. Soon after, he was appointed musical assistant to Friedelind Wagner at the internationally acclaimed Bayreuth Festival.

Thomas's first major breakthrough came in the summer of 1968 when, as a conducting fellow at the Tanglewood Music Festival, he won the coveted Koussevitzky Prize. By the end of the year, he had been appointed assistant conductor of the Boston Symphony Orchestra, and on October 22, 1969, he conducted an impromptu performance in New York, in place of ailing music director William Steinberg, to rave reviews.

International success came quickly thereafter. He stayed as assistant and then associate conductor in Boston until 1974, and then he served as music director of the Buffalo Philharmonic Orchestra (1971-1979), director of the New York Philharmonic's Young People's Concert series (1971-1977), principal guest conductor of the Los Angeles Philharmonic (1981-1985), principal conductor of the London Symphony Orchestra (1988-1995), and, starting in 1995, music director of the San Francisco Symphony. Thomas has also served as founder and artistic director of the New World Symphony, an American training orchestra for recent conservatory graduates in search of full-time orchestral employment. Beginning in 1987, the group has performed at its home in Miami, Florida, and around the world, blending youthful enthusiasm and professional pedigree to create memorable music.

Thomas is active in other musical arenas as well, composing numerous works and performing the piano music of Igor Stravinsky, George Gershwin, Aaron Copland, and Leonard Bernstein. In June, 2000, Thomas hosted a festival celebrating American Maverick composers. He performed a recording cycle of Gustav Mahler's major orchestral works with the San Francisco Symphony, and he hosted Keeping Score, an interactive, multiyear program with the San Francisco Symphony that brings classical music to people of all ages and backgrounds.

The Music

Thomas has multiple musical identities: most prominently as conductor, as pianist, and as composer. As a conductor, Thomas is a premier interpreter and proponent of American music, particularly that of Ives, Copland, and Bernstein. He is dedicated to performing the more difficult, modernist works of these composers, and he continues to premiere works by contemporary composers such as Steve Reich. As a composer, the expansive harmonies and colorful writing of Gershwin, Dahl, and Copland have influenced his own music.

The Desert Music. This is a large, five-movement work for voices and orchestra by American composer Steve Reich. Thomas conducted the premiere in 1984, at the Brooklyn Academy of Music. *The Desert Music* is one of Reich's longest works, lasting nearly forty-five minutes, and it sets text by American poet William Carlos Williams. Thomas's conception of this piece accentuates the wide range of vocal and instrumental textures, as well as the pulsing, repetitive rhythmic layers that are so prevalent in minimalist music. Thomas has a history of collaborating with Reich, performing in and leading the premiere of Reich's *Four Organs* with the Boston Symphony Orchestra in 1971.

From the Diary of Anne Frank. Written and premiered in 1990, *From the Diary of Anne Frank* is Thomas's most well-known composition. The work was conceived for a series of benefits for the United Nations Children's Fund (UNICEF) at the behest of Audrey Hepburn, a goodwill ambassador for the organization, and it sets spoken excerpts from Frank's diary to music for orchestra. The piece takes shape with a series of loose variations on four themes, and it fuses Hebraic music, American pop,

Michael Tilson Thomas. (Hermann Wostmann/DPA/Landov)

Balinese influences, and original tunes to create a compelling musical portrait. While this polystylistic work deals with the terror of the Holocaust through the eyes of an innocent teenager, Thomas emphasizes the joy and hope that persist in Frank's words. The piece was premiered by the New World Symphony and Hepburn at the Philadelphia Academy of Music.

Appalachian Spring. This ballet by American composer Copland has become one of the most popular and recognizable musical works from the twentieth century. Written in 1943 and 1944 for Martha Graham, Copland's *Appalachian Spring* aurally represents the expansive American frontier through traditional folk melodies and expansive harmonies. Thomas studied with Copland, and he has recorded a series of discs dedicated to both the accessible (*Copland the Populist*) and relatively more difficult (*Copland the Modernist*) music of Copland, complete with commentary. As a premier conductor of Copland's music, Thomas juxtaposes an Impressionistic flair with the open harmonies and singable melodies associated with *Appalachian Spring* (1944), and he emphasizes the conglomeration of high art form and texture with simple, traditional folk tunes.

Musical Legacy

Thomas was named Musician of the Year in 1971 and Conductor of the Year in 1995 by *Musical*

America. He has won numerous Grammy Awards with the San Francisco Symphony, and he was named Gramophone's Artist of the Year in 2005. He continues to advocate contemporary American composers and their music, not only verbally but also musically, through commissions and recording projects.

Thomas's lasting contribution is his work with the New World Symphony. For a world-renowned conductor to continually support and actively perform with a training orchestra is a testament to Thomas's commitment to the future of orchestral music. His work with Keeping Score has unified diverse audiences across the globe. Like Bernstein before him, Thomas is a lively and integral part of the American musical scene.

Michael Mauskapf

Further Reading

Hart, Philip. "Buffalo Philharmonic Orchestra." In *Orpheus in the New World.* New York: W. W. Norton, 1973. Written during Thomas's tenure with the Buffalo Philharmonic Orchestra, Hart's exploration of the American symphony orchestra includes a discussion of the conductor's burgeoning career.

Key, Susan, and Larry Rothe, eds. *American Mavericks: Visionaries, Pioneers, Iconoclasts.* Berkeley: University of California Press, 2001. This collection of essays about the American Mavericks festival (2000) provides commentary on numerous twentieth century American composers and their music. Accompanied by a compact disc, it concludes with an essay by Thomas.

Morrison, Richard. *Orchestra: The LSO—A Century of Triumph and Turbulence.* New York: Faber & Faber, 2004. This history of the London Symphony Orchestra includes several passages pertaining to Thomas's time as principal conductor.

Seckerson, Edward, and Michael Tilson Thomas. *Michael Tilson Thomas: Viva Voce—Conversations with Edward Seckerson.* Boston: Faber & Faber, 1994. Extended conversations with Thomas include discussions about his childhood, his relationships with Copland and Bernstein, and his work as a conductor and composer.

Sharpe, Roderick L., and Jeanne Koekkoek Stierman. *Maestros in America: Conductors in the Twenty-first Century.* Lanham, Md.: Scarecrow Press, 2008. Contains brief but up-to-date biographical essays on approximately one hundred American conductors, including Thomas.

See also: Bernstein, Leonard; Copland, Aaron; Gershwin, George; Ives, Charles; Koussevitzky, Serge; Reich, Steve; Stravinsky, Igor; Vaughan, Sarah.

Virgil Thomson

American classical and film composer

The most French-influenced of the twentieth century composers crafting a new "American" identity in music, Thomson was a fluent writer for voice and instruments, a pioneer in film scores, a remarkable composer of operas, and one of America's greatest music critics.

Born: November 25, 1896; Kansas City, Missouri
Died: September 30, 1989; New York, New York
Also known as: Virgil Garnett Thomson (full name)

Principal works

BALLETS (music): *Filling Station*, written 1937, performed 1958 (libretto by Lew Christensen); *The Harvest According*, 1952 (libretto by Agnes de Mille); *Parson Weems and the Cherry Tree*, 1975 (libretto by Erick Hawkins).

CHAMBER WORKS: *Sonata da chiesa*, 1926 (revised 1973); *Portrait of Señorita Juanita de Medina Accompanied by Her Mother*, 1928; *Five Portraits for Four Clarinets*, 1929; *Madame Marthe-Marthine*, 1929; *Portrait of Alice B. Toklas*, 1930; *Miss Gertrude Stein as a Young Girl*, 1938; *Portrait of Jamie Campbell*, 1940; *Concerto for Flute, Strings, Harp, and Percussion*, 1954.

FILM SCORES: *The Plow That Broke the Plains*, 1936; *The River*, 1938; *Tuesday in November*, 1945;

Louisiana Story, 1948; *The Goddess*, 1958; *Power Among Men*, 1958; *Journey to America*, 1964.

OPERAS (music): *Four Saints in Three Acts*, 1934 (libretto by Stein); *The Mother of Us All*, 1947 (libretto by Stein); *Lord Byron*, abridged version 1972, complete version 1991 (libretto by Jack Larson).

ORCHESTRAL WORKS: *Symphony No. 1*, 1928 (*Symphony on a Hymn Tune*); *Symphony No. 2*, 1931 (revised 1941); *Sonata No. 1*, 1932; *The Seine at Night*, 1947; *Wheat Field at Noon*, 1948; *Sea Piece with Birds*, 1952; *Sonata No. 2*, 1964.

PIANO WORKS: *Traveling in Spain: A Portrait of Alice Woodfin Branlière*, 1929; *The John Mosher Waltzes*, 1937; *Portrait of Briggs Buchanan*, 1943; *Bugles and Birds: A Portrait of Pablo Picasso*, 1944.

VOCAL WORKS: *Susie Asado*, 1926 (lyrics by John Rippon); *Capital Capitals*, 1927 (lyrics by Gertrude Stein); *Preciosilla*, 1927 (lyrics by Stein); *Five Songs from William Blake*, 1951; *Four Songs to Poems of Thomas Campion*, 1951; *Praises and Prayers*, 1963.

WRITINGS OF INTEREST: *The State of Music*, 1939; *The Musical Scene*, 1945; *The Art of Judging Music*, 1948; *Music Right and Left*, 1951; *Virgil Thomson*, 1966; *Music Reviewed, 1940-1954*, 1967; *American Music Since 1910*, 1971; *A Virgil Thomson Reader*, 1981.

The Life

From his birth and rearing in America's heartland, Virgil Garnett Thomson absorbed a love of regional identity and a feeling for Protestant hymnody. His early musical training was on the organ. He enlisted in the army and was spared service in France only by the end of World War I. Studying at Harvard University, he was active in conducting and accompanying, but his teachers fired his interest in the newly fashionable musical and cultural life of France. On a fellowship to Paris, he was briefly a student of Nadia Boulanger and came to know important composers of the moment, such as Erik Satie, whose ideals of simplicity and ironic wit would long be an influence on him.

After further studies at Harvard and Juilliard, Thomson returned to Paris, which he made his primary residence from 1925 until 1940. Thomson said that living in France allowed him to understand his American identity better, also prompting him to convey it musically to the French. There he composed his first symphony, *Symphony on a Hymn Tune*.

As World War II loomed, Thomson moved to New York (1940), where he became the music critic for *The New York Herald-Tribune*, a position he retained until 1954. During the decade and a half of his tenure, he introduced a new voice to music criticism, taking to task the conventional and the pompous in favor of new musical values.

Having roomed at the Chelsea Hotel briefly in 1936-1937, upon arriving in New York in 1940 Thomson began a residence that would last for the rest of his life, in this celebrated haven for writers and artists on Twenty-third Street between Seventh and Eighth Avenues. His apartment was modest, but he loved its eccentric ambience. A discreet, lifelong homosexual in a closeted time, he nevertheless had a rich circle of friends, male and female, and became an enduring musical celebrity. He wrote, lectured, conducted, and collected awards, all on a

Virgil Thomson. (Library of Congress)

wide scale and into his last years. He was working on a composition until a week before his death, two months shy of his ninety-third birthday.

The Music

Thomson produced an extensive output. Though he tackled larger forms, such as two string quartets, three symphonies, and a cello concerto, as well as suites from his opera and film scores, he was essentially a miniaturist in feeling and created a vast number of small pieces. He delighted in setting poetry, either for solo voice and piano or for choral forces; one of his masterpieces is his set of *Five Songs from William Blake*, which eventually (1951) took form as a cycle with orchestra. Perhaps his most idiosyncratic practice was having friends or important people to "sit" for him while he composed "portraits" of them on the spot, usually for piano but often for instrumental combinations—in this, extending Stein's creation of "word pictures."

Four Saints in Three Acts. In Paris, Thomson was drawn into the expatriate circle of Gertrude Stein. He had known her writings and even set some of her poems to music. With her he planned a full-length opera, using her free-wheeling libretto. This was *Four Saints in Three Acts*, an eccentric and plotless confection of religious and mystical imagery built around Spanish saints. The libretto was completed in 1927, but it was several more years before the fully composed and orchestrated score was ready, filled with hymns and dances in a deliberately simple and folksy style. With a scenario imposed on it, with an unconventional all-black cast, and in a production of striking visual novelty, Thomson presented it in New York and Chicago, creating a sensation.

Film Scores. Thomson became the first American classical composer to write important film scores. From 1936 through to 1964, he produced nine of them, the most famous being for *The Plow That Broke the Plains* and *The River*, both with Pare Lorenz, as well as *Louisiana Story* with Robert Flaherty. In these scores, as well as in his ballet score *Filling Station* for Lincoln Kirstein, Thomson furthered his very personally "nationalistic" style, assimilating folk songs, traditional tunes, and Protestant hymns with French finesse.

Music Criticism. Thomson had already balanced his composing with extensive writing on music when, in 1939, he published a collection of wide-ranging essays titled *The State of Music*. With such evidence of his literary flair—on the eve of his final departure from France in the face of the impending World War II—he accepted an appointment on the staff of *The New York Herald-Tribune* as its chief music critic. In this position, from October, 1940, to September of 1954, he established himself as America's most penetrating and provocative music critic. Conditioned to French elegance and clarity, he avoided the pomposity and pedantry that marked the writing of so many peers and wrote in a direct, pungent style that electrified the musical scene. He had strong opinions and no fear of taking positions opposed to other critics; he was perfectly willing to disparage then-idolized musicians of the day (such as Jascha Heifetz and Arturo Toscanini) and to hound sacred cows, such as the Metropolitan Opera and the New York Philharmonic (especially its authoritarian manager, Arthur Judson).

Deploring the narrowness of performing repertoires, Thomson created his list of the "Famous Fifty," works most likely to appear in concert programs. His reviews and articles set a new standard for musical writing, rather as George Bernard Shaw in London had done more than a half century before. The four collections Thomson published of his criticism—*The Musical Scene* (1945), *The Art of Judging Music* (1948), *Music Right and Left* (1951), and *Music Reviewed, 1940-1954* (1967)—are still altogether readable and stimulating today (as are Shaw's).

The Mother of Us All. Thomson continued to compose during and especially after his official career as a critic. Perhaps his most important achievement was his renewed collaboration with Stein, in the full-length opera *The Mother of Us All* (1947), a veritable pageant of Americana focused upon the struggle for women's rights as led by Susan B. Anthony. A third opera, *Lord Byron*, with a libretto by Jack Larson, was composed laboriously during the 1960's but not produced untl 1967.

Musical Legacy

Thomson's music has at times been written off as simplistic and superficial, and he was even accused of winning performances by virtue of his influence as a critic. However, if relatively few of his highly individualistic works have won enduring places in the working repertoire, they remain landmarks of American creativity, notably the two Stein operas. He deserves status beside those mid-century composers who established a distinctly "American" musical sound—such as Roy Harris and especially Aaron Copland. Finally, Thomson's writings made him one of the most effective commentators on American musical life in his time.

John W. Barker

Further Reading

Hoover, Kathleen, and John Cage. *Virgil Thomson: His Life and Music*. New York: Thomas Yoseloff, 1959. The earliest biography of Thomson, heavily edited by the composer but still valuable.

Page, Tim, and Vanessa Weeks Page. *Selected Letters of Virgil Thomson*. New York: Summit Books, 1988. A wide-ranging and stimulating collection.

Thomson, Virgil. *Music with Words: A Composer's View*. New Haven, Conn.: Yale University Press, 1989. Thomson's personal analyses of forms and styles.

_____. *The State of Music*. New York: William Morrow, 1939. Rev. ed. New York: Random House, 1962. Trenchant and provocative essays on American musical life.

_____. *Virgil Thomson*. New York: Alfred A. Knopf, 1967. A collection of essays and reminiscences—the closest Thomson came to producing an autobiography.

_____. *A Virgil Thomson Reader*. Edited by Richard Kostelanetz. New York: Routledge, 2002. A generous anthology of articles, reviews, essays, and interviews.

Tommasini, Anthony. *Virgil Thomson: Composer on the Aisle*. New York: W. W. Norton, 1997. The most thorough and authoritative biography to date.

Watson, Steven. *Prepare for Saints: Gertrude Stein, Virgil Thomson, and the Mainstreaming of American Modernism*. Berkeley: University of California Press, 2000. A joint study of the writer and composer, in the context of their creation of *Four Saints in Three Acts*.

See also: Harrison, Lou; Price, Leontyne; Seeger, Ruth Crawford.

Dimitri Tiomkin

Ukrainian film-score composer

A great composer of film music, Tiomkin used his Russian training to create a lush, epic orchestral sound. His comprehensive knowledge of a variety of American music accounts for his success as a composer for Westerns, for which he wrote memorable songs, and his understanding of French music led to his supreme command of Impressionist harmonies.

Born: May 10, 1894; Kremenchuk, Poltava, Ukraine
Died: November 11, 1979; London, England
Also known as: Dimitri Zinovievich Tiomkin (full name)

Principal works

FILM SCORES: *Alice in Wonderland*, 1933; *Lost Horizon*, 1937; *You Can't Take It with You*, 1938; *Mr. Smith Goes to Washington*, 1939; *Only Angels Have Wings*, 1939; *Meet John Doe*, 1941; *A Gentleman After Dark*, 1942; *When Strangers Marry*, 1944; *Angel on My Shoulder*, 1946; *Duel in the Sun*, 1946; *It's a Wonderful Life*, 1947; *The Long Night*, 1947; *Portrait of Jennie*, 1948; *Red River*, 1948; *Tarzan and the Mermaids*, 1948; *Strangers on a Train*, 1951; *The Thing from Another World*, 1951; *The Big Sky*, 1952; *High Noon*, 1952; *Lady in the Iron Mask*, 1952; *The Steel Trap*, 1952; *I Confess*, 1953; *Jeopardy*, 1953; *Dial M for Murder*, 1954; *The High and the Mighty*, 1954; *Friendly Persuasion*, 1956; *Giant*, 1956; *Land of the Pharaohs*, 1956; *Gunfight at the O. K. Corral*, 1957; *Night Passage*, 1957; *Search for Paradise*, 1957; *The Old Man and the Sea*, 1958; *Rio Bravo*, 1959; *The Alamo*, 1960; *The Unforgiven*, 1960; *The Guns of Navarone*, 1961; *Circus World*, 1964; *The Fall of the Roman Empire*, 1964; *Thirty-Six Hours*, 1965.

The Life

Dimitri Zinovievich Tiomkin (DMEE-tree zyih-NOH-vyeh-vich TYEHM-kihn) was born in the Ukraine in 1894. His father was a prominent doctor, and his mother was a music teacher. In 1907 Tiom-kin enrolled at the St. Petersburg Conservatory, where he studied piano with Felix Blumenfeld and composition with Alexander Glazunov. In addition to the classical education he received at the conservatory, Tiomkin soon displayed an affinity for film music, working as an accompanist for silent films. He also became enamored of American popular music, an interest that dated from his exposure to Irving Berlin's "Alexander's Ragtime Band."

After the Russian Revolution, Tiomkin moved to Berlin, where his father had settled earlier. In Berlin the young composer and pianist continued his musical studies with Egon Petri, Michael Zadora, and Ferruccio Busoni. He composed a number of light musical pieces, and he made his professional debut as a piano soloist, performing Franz Liszt's Piano Concerto No. 2 (1857) with the Berlin Philharmonic.

Along with his roommate Michael Kariton, a fellow pianist, Tiomkin left Berlin for Paris, where the two performed piano duets. In 1925 the duo set sail for America, where Tiomkin met Albertina Rasch, a ballerina and choreographer. Tiomkin and Rasch began a professional relationship—Tiomkin accompanied her and her ballet troupe on a national tour—that soon became personal, and the two were married in 1927. In 1928 the couple returned to Paris, where Tiomkin gave recitals that focused on American and new music. There he gave the European premiere of George Gershwin's Piano Concerto in F (1925) and *Rhapsody in Blue* (1924), with Gershwin, Sergei Prokofiev, and Arthur Honegger in the audience.

In 1929 Tiomkin followed his wife to Hollywood, where he provided the music to her dance sequences in musicals produced by Metro-Goldwyn-Mayer. After composing the music for several other films, Tiomkin had his big break. He met and befriended director Frank Capra, who put him in charge of the music for the epic fantasy *Lost Horizon*. This was the first of a number of significant collaborations with Capra, and Tiomkin provided the scores to many Capra classics, including *Mr. Smith Goes to Washington*, *Meet John Doe*, and *It's a Wonderful Life*. During World War II, he wrote music for Why We Fight, a series of seven propaganda films Capra provided for the U.S. Army.

After the war, Tiomkin worked with other directors. For Alfred Hitchcock he wrote the sound tracks for *Strangers on a Train*, *I Confess*, and *Dial M for Murder*. For Fred Zinnemann he provided the sound track for *High Noon*. After the enormous success of that score, Tiomkin became known for his Western sound tracks, and he went on to score such films as *Rio Bravo*, *The Alamo*, and *The Guns of Navarone*. His final film project was *Tchaikovsky* (1969), a Russian-American collaboration on the life of the composer. For the film, Tiomkin arranged Tchaikovsky's music, and he acted as executive producer. In 1968, following Albertina's death, Tiomkin moved to London, where he married Olivia Cynthia Patch in 1972. After his death in 1979, he was buried in Los Angeles.

The Music

When he began to compose for Hollywood, Tiomkin had done little large-scale composition. He had, however, internalized a great deal of music from three sources. First, his studies with Glazunov gave him a thorough grounding in counterpoint, form, and harmony, as well as in Russian Romanticism. Second, Tiomkin was interested from a young age in American music, especially jazz, and he eventually came to know a wide range of American popular and folk music. Third, from his years in Paris, Tiomkin developed a love of French music, including that of Claude Debussy, Maurice Ravel, and the composers of Les Six. These influences were palpable in his film scores. Tiomkin was equally at home with instrumental and vocal forces, and indeed some of his best music combines these two.

Lost Horizon. Capra's decision to put Tiomkin in charge of the music for his film *Lost Horizon* surprised many in Hollywood. Tiomkin was virtually unknown as a composer at the time, and *Lost Horizon* was an epic production of unprecedented scale, initially requiring music to accompany a running time of six hours (the film was ultimately cut to about two and a half hours). In order to assist Tiomkin, Capra hired a number of major orchestrators, including Hugo Friedhofer, Max Reese, and Robert Russell Bennett. Capra also brought in the venerated Max Steiner to conduct, to offer suggestions, and possibly to step in and write the score if Tiomkin was not up to the task.

Capra's worries were groundless; Tiomkin's score was a masterpiece. As Capra wrote in his autobiography, "Tiomkin's music not only captured the mood, but darned near captured the film." The sound track for *Lost Horizon* instantly made a name for its composer. It established Tiomkin's reputation as a master of the epic film score, and it demonstrated his expert handling of a large symphony—the largest orchestra Columbia Studios had ever used to date—paired with chorus. As befits the film's Tibetan setting, the score is peppered with musical exoticisms, including the extensive use of Asian percussion instruments. The film's main theme, set for wordless chorus, has a timeless, almost medieval quality that avoids clichéd representations of the East.

High Noon. Although billed as a Western, the motion picture *High Noon* defies many of the conventions of that genre. It was independently produced, and it avoided the romanticized view of the Old West popularized by the large Hollywood studios at the time. *High Noon* was so gritty and realistic that early previews were panned.

Dimitri Tiomkin. (Hulton Archive/Getty Images)

Tiomkin's score for the film revolves around a single song, "Do Not Forsake Me," with lyrics by Ned Washington. The song appears in various guises and variations, sometimes scored for orchestra alone, sometimes scored for voice and light accompaniment. The song was released prior to the film on a Capitol Records album that featured interpretations of the song by six different singers (in the film, the song is sung by Tex Ritter). Tiomkin noted in his autobiography that "the record was an immediate success, one of the hits of the year . . . the picture was released four months after the record, and packed the theaters, a box-office gold mine. The success of the record promoted it."

Like the film, Tiomkin's score contains many genre-defying elements. First, unlike most conventional sound tracks of the period, *High Noon* begins and ends softly, with "Do Not Forsake Me" being sung by Ritter, accompanied only by guitar, accordion, and drums. Second, the song clamors for attention frequently throughout the film, rather than merely underscoring the action or dialogue. Third, the score slips back and forth between diegetic and nondiegetic music—that is, between music that only we hear and music that the characters seem to hear. Fourth, Tiomkin's orchestration is dominated by winds, brass, and piano, in contrast to the string-dominated textures of most Hollywood music of the time.

The Fall of the Roman Empire. In 1964 Anthony Mann directed *The Fall of the Roman Empire* for Paramount Pictures. The film featured one of Tiomkin's last major sound tracks and one of his grandest. Reversing the pared-down orchestration he had employed for many Westerns, Tiomkin called for a large chorus and an orchestra of 130 players, and he wrote music for about two and one-half hours of the three-hour film. The orchestration features the prominent use of brass, drums, and piano.

The motion picture's main theme uses organ and orchestra, and some have observed that the theme resembles Russian folk music, with its use of modal harmonies and melodic construction and its melancholy quality. It is interesting to see that late in his life, Tiomkin returned to the music of his youth.

Musical Legacy

By the end of his career, Tiomkin was reportedly the highest paid composer in the history of motion pictures. Unlike most composers in the Hollywood studio system, Tiomkin worked as a freelancer, which allowed him to be employed by a wide range of studios and directors. He was often allowed to sit in on film projects in the early stages of production, a rarity in the film business.

Tiomkin was nominated twenty-three times for an Academy Award. He was a three-time winner in the category of Best Score for *The High and the Mighty*, for *The Old Man and the Sea*, and for *High Noon*. The song "Do Not Forsake Me," from *High Noon*, also won for the category of Best Song. Upon receiving his Oscar for *The High and the Mighty*, Tiomkin highly amused the audience at the awards ceremony by thanking Ludwig van Beethoven, Johannes Brahms, Richard Wagner, and Richard Strauss in his acceptance speech.

Although not a native-born American, Tiomkin had a great impact as a film composer on Westerns and on patriotic films. The success of "Do Not Forsake Me" led to a large number of similar efforts by other studios to insert a hit song in their films that could be marketed separately from the film. His scores for *Rio Bravo* and other Western films virtually defined the genre, and scores such as *Mr. Smith Goes to Washington* were highly influential in their incorporation of American folk songs.

Alexander Kahn

Further Reading

Darby, William, and Jack Du Bois. "Dimitri Tiomkin." In *American Film Music: Major Composers, Techniques, Trends, 1915-1990*. Jefferson, N.C.: McFarland, 1990. This chapter on Tiomkin's film music contains a great deal of musical analysis and a consideration of the composer's overall output.

Palmer, Christopher. "Dimitri Tiomkin." In *The Composer in Hollywood*. London: Marion Boyars, 1990. Palmer's account of the composer focuses less on biography and more on identifying trends in Tiomkin's oeuvre.

_____. *Dimitri Tiomkin: A Portrait*. London: T. E. Books, 1984. Palmer's monograph contains illustrations and a filmography. While the biographical data is largely derivative of Tiomkin's autobiography, the analysis of the composer's music and his place in the Hollywood pantheon is well crafted.

Thomas, Tony. "Dimitri Tiomkin." In *Film Score: The Art and Craft of Movie Music.* Burbank, Calif.: Riverwood Press, 1991. This brief chapter on Tiomkin's film music is supplemented by a reprint of Tiomkin's article "Dimitri Tiomkin on Film Music," which originally appeared in the journal *Films in Review* in 1951.

Tiomkin, Dimitri, and Propser Buranelli. *Please Don't Hate Me.* Garden City, N.Y.: Doubleday, 1959. Tiomkin's autobiography, cowritten with Buranelli, is filled with humour and fascinating details regarding the composer's life. Tiomkin paints frank portraits of the many colorful personalities with whom he came in contact over the course of his career.

See also: Berlin, Irving; Busoni, Ferruccio; Debussy, Claude; Eddy, Duane; Gershwin, George; Honegger, Arthur; Prokofiev, Sergei; Ravel, Maurice; Ritter, Tex; Steiner, Max; Strauss, Richard.

Sir Michael Tippett

English classical composer

The protean nature of Tippett's mind, the importance of his dreams, the literary sources that informed his passionately presented musical ideas, and his embrace of contemporary popular music made an unprecedented contribution to English music in the form of operas and orchestral works.

Born: January 2, 1905; London, England
Died: January 8, 1998; London, England
Also known as: Michael Kemp Tippett (full name)

Principal works

BRASS WORKS: *Fanfare No. 1*, 1943; *Fanfare No. 2*, 1953; *Fanfare No. 3*, 1953; *Wolf Trap Fanfare*, 1980; *Festal Brass with Blues*, 1984; *Fanfare No. 5*, 1987.

CHAMBER WORKS: String Quartet No. 1, 1935, revised 1944; Piano Sonata No. 1, 1938, revised 1942 and 1954; String Quartet No. 2 in F-Sharp, 1943; *Preludio al Vespro di Monteverdi*, 1946; String Quartet No. 3, 1946; Sonata for Four

Horns, 1955; Piano Sonata No. 2, 1962; Piano Sonata No. 3, 1973; String Quartet No. 4, 1979; *The Blue Guitar*, 1983; Piano Sonata No. 4, 1985; String Quartet No. 5, 1992.

CHORAL WORKS: *A Child of Our Time*, 1944; *The Heart's Assurance*, 1951; *Crown of the Year*, 1958; *Magnificat and Nunc Dimittis Collegium Sancti Johannis Cantabrigiense*, 1962; *Songs for Ariel*, 1962; *A Vision of St. Augustine*, 1966; *The Mask of Time*, 1984; *Byzantium*, 1991.

OPERAS (music and libretto): *The Midsummer Marriage*, 1952; *King Priam*, 1962; *The Knot Garden*, 1970; *The Ice Break*, 1977; *New Year*, 1989.

ORCHESTRAL WORKS: Concerto for Double String Orchestra, 1940; *Fantasia on a Theme of Handel*, 1942; Symphony No. 1, 1945; Suite in D, 1948; *Fantasia Concertante on a Theme of Corelli*, 1953; *Divertimento on Sellinger's Round*, 1954; Piano Concerto, 1956; Symphony No. 2, 1958; Concerto for Orchestra, 1963; Symphony No. 3, 1972; Symphony No. 4, 1977; Triple Concerto, 1980; *The Rose Lake*, 1995.

The Life

Michael Kemp Tippett was raised in the English countryside of Suffolk. He was drawn to music, but it was not until he experienced concerts and theater in London while studying at the Royal College of Music, beinning in 1923, that he focused on a musical career. In 1928 he moved to Oxted, Surrey, where a performance of his music at the Barn Theater made him realize his need for further study. He studied counterpoint and fugue with R. O. Morris at the Royal College of Music. This period led to the creation of his first published works.

Tippett was music director of Morley College in London from 1940 to 1951, although for three months in 1943 he was imprisoned for pacifism. While at Morley College, Tippett sparked a revival of the music of Henry Purcell, an English composer who deeply influenced him (and Benjamin Britten). After leaving Morley College, Tippett devoted himself exclusively to composition, moving to Wadham, Surrey, then to Wiltshire in 1960, first to Corsham and the hills of Chippenham, and finally to South London. Tippett found his reputation advanced by the appearance of recordings of his works in the 1960's, and he was knighted in 1966.

The Music

A Child of Our Time. Tippett's war oratorio, *A Child of Our Time*, based on events surrounding the Nazi Kristallnacht pogrom of November 9, 1938, is unquestionably his most popular and well-known work, and its story is indicative of Tippett's lifelong interest in contemporary issues. At the prompting of poet T. S. Eliot, Tippett wrote the text, a practice he would continue in his operatic librettos (and for which he was frequently criticized). His decision to base the structure of the work on George Friderich Handel's *Messiah* (1742), incorporating Negro spirituals as commentary on universal suffering, is powerful. It is the earliest indication of Tippett's interest in African American music.

The Midsummer Marriage. Tippett's first opera was drawn from his own dream world, a source of great significance to him, and from several other influences, including Wolfgang Amadeus Mozart's *The Magic Flute* (1791) and the writings of psychoanalyst Carl Jung and of dramatist George Bernard Shaw. The story reflects the journey to individual discovery of Mark and Jennifer, and then the discovery of each other, told through a remarkable outpouring of musical lyricism unique in the history of British opera, and perhaps in the history of the entire genre. (A secondary couple, Jack and Bella, provide a comedic diversion.) Although the action takes place in a single day, Tippett uses seasonal imagery to chart Mark and Jennifer's spiritual progress, embodied in the ritual dances of act 2 and act 3.

Concerto for Orchestra. The Concerto for Orchestra connects the stylistically transitional Symphony No. 2, which moves from early lyricism to starker neoclassicism, to the monumental Symphony No. 3. Tippett's new grittily objective musical manner in Concerto for Orchestra derives from the spare language developed in his second opera, *King Priam* (based on Homer). Tippett breaks the orchestra into smaller groups, which become characters; for example, strings are not used until the second movement, and the full orchestra is reserved for the third movement. Such dry and spare textures are matched by a new blocklike arrangement of form, where development occurs more through musical juxtaposition and superimposition than through the traditional organic thematic method.

The Knot Garden. Tippett's third opera, *The Knot Garden*—the title refers to a rose garden where lovers meet—draws upon William Shakespeare's *The Tempest* (1623), as his Prospero-like Mangus oversees six dysfunctional relationships: Faber and Thea, a married couple on the brink of divorce; their innocent ward, Flora; a homosexual couple, Mel (black) and Dov (white, perhaps representative of Tippett); and Thea's sister, Denise, a political freedom fighter. The rapid cuts and dissolves of the action mirror those seen on a television show, and the music advances in sudden juxtapositions of musical fragments and segments, like a mosaic. The characters are thrown together in different combinations, until they join hands in the conclusion to sing about unity. Tippett's grand achievement in this work is his use of a complex, postmodern urban musical language to reflect the psychodramatic world depicted in the unfolding drama (including a fully developed blues ensemble at the end of act 1). A similar development occurs later in Tippett's Symphony No. 3, in a Charles Ivesian confrontation with Ludwig van Beethoven's Symphony No. 9 (1824).

Triple Concerto. The Triple Concerto for violin, viola, cello, and orchestra represents a blending of Tippett's early lyricism and his midlife musical complexity. In the third of three works constructed in single-movement form (including String Quartet No. 4 and Symphony No. 4), the string soloists are like operatic characters who sing without words. The Indonesian gamelan-inspired second movement celebrates the intense lyrical beauty that is a hallmark of Tippett's style.

Musical Legacy

Tippett's early works exhibit a mood of sonorous optimism at odds with the bleak tone of much of modern music. The spirit of the dance is rarely absent from his musical vision, and he could write propulsive, fast music, as his symphonic scherzos amply demonstrate. However, Tippett's middle-period style established an intensely Expressionistic urban manner, similar to that of Leonard Bernstein, with a musical grammar closer to that of Ives. The works of composers Harrison Birtwistle, Mark-Anthony Turnage, and Thomas Adés testify to Tippett's enduring influence.

Stephen Arthur Allen

Further Reading

Bowen, Meirion. *Michael Tippett*. London: Robson Books, 1997. An essential biography of the composer, which outlines the details of his life and examines in depth his personality and his works.

Clarke, David. *The Music and Thought of Michael Tippett: Modern Times and Metaphysics*. Cambridge, England: Cambridge University Press, 2006. Clarke locates Tippett's music in the nineteenth century, relating it to cultural developments, literary criticism, and gender-sexuality studies.

Kemp, Ian. *Tippett: The Composer and His Music*. Oxford, England: Oxford University Press, 1987. A traditional biography, with personal details not covered elsewhere, and musical insights.

Tippett, Michael. *Selected Letters of Michael Tippett*. Edited by Thomas Schuttenhelm. London: Faber & Faber, 2005. This complements a collection of letters published in *Those Twentieth Century Blues*, Tippett's autobiography.

_____. *Those Twentieth Century Blues: An Autobiography*. London: Hutchinson, 1991. Indispensable insights into the composer's dream life, his letters, and his personal archives.

_____. *Tippett on Music*. Edited by Meirion Bowen. New York: Oxford University Press, 1995. Expands on material from Tippett's earlier books, *Moving Into Aquarius* and *Music of the Angels: Essays and Sketchbooks of Michael Tippett*.

See also: Bernstein, Leonard; Britten, Benjamin; Ives, Charles; Solti, Sir Georg; Sutherland, Dame Joan; Vaughan Williams, Ralph.

Mel Tormé

American jazz singer, composer, and drummer

Tormé's smooth and remarkably controlled tenor voice made him one of the most talented white jazz singers during the height of his career in the 1950's.

Born: September 13, 1925; Chicago, Illinois
Died: June 5, 1999; Los Angeles, California

Also known as: Melvin Howard Tormé (full name); Velvet Fog

Principal recordings

ALBUMS: *Mel Tormé's California Suite*, 1949; *Live at the Crescendo*, 1954; *Musical Sounds Are the Best Songs*, 1954; *It's a Blue World*, 1955; *Lulu's Back in Town*, 1956; *Mel Tormé and the Marty Paich Dek-Tette*, 1956 (with Marty Paich and the Dek-Tette); *Sings Fred Astaire*, 1956; *Songs for Any Taste*, 1956; *Prelude to a Kiss*, 1957; *Tormé Meets the British: The London Recordings, 1956-1957*, 1957; *Mel Tormé Sings About Love*, 1958; *Tormé*, 1958; *Back in Town*, 1959 (with the Mel-Tones); *Olé Tormé: Mel Tormé Goes South of the Border with Billy May*, 1959 (with Billy May); *Broadway, Right Now!*, 1960 (with Margaret Whiting); *The Duke Ellington and Count Basie Songbooks*, 1960 (with the Johnny Mandel Orchestra); *I Dig the Duke! I Dig the Count!*, 1960; *Mel Tormé Swings Shubert Alley*, 1960; *Swingin' on the Moon*, 1960; *My Kind of Music*, 1961; *Comin' Home Baby!*, 1962; *Mel Tormé at the Red Hill*, 1962; *Mel Tormé Sings Sunday in New York and Other Songs About New York*, 1963; *That's All*, 1964; *Right Now!*, 1966; *A Day in the Life of Bonnie and Clyde*, 1968; *A Time for Us (Love Theme from Romeo and Juliet)*, 1969; *Raindrops Keep Fallin' on My Head*, 1969; *Live at the Maisonette*, 1974; *Together Again*, 1978 (with Buddy Rich); *Top Drawer*, 1983; *Mel Tormé, Rob McConnell, and the Boss Brass*, 1986 (with Rob McConnell and the Boss Brass); *Reunion*, 1988 (with Marty Paich and the Dek-Tette); *Mel and George "Do" World War II*, 1990 (with George Shearing); *Fujitsu-Concord Jazz Festival in Japan '90*, 1991; *Christmas Songs*, 1992; *Nothing Without You*, 1992 (with Cleo Lane); *A Tribute to Bing Crosby*, 1994; *Velvet and Brass*, 1995 (with Rob McConnell's Boss Brass).

WRITINGS OF INTEREST: *The Other Side of the Rainbow: With Judy Garland on the Dawn Patrol*, 1970; *It Wasn't All Velvet: An Autobiography*, 1988; *Traps, the Drum Wonder: The Life of Buddy Rich*, 1991; *My Singing Teachers: Reflections on Singing Popular Music*, 1994.

The Life

Melvin Howard Tormé (tohr-MAY) grew up on Chicago's South Side, born to Russian-Jewish parents who sang, played piano, and loved music. His earliest musical influences included African American music, sacred and secular Jewish music, and contemporary popular songs sung at home or heard on the radio. He exhibited very early imitative talents through his voice and drumming. His winning audition for NBC radio producer Walter Wicker at the Chicago World Fair led to his career as a child radio star, as well as acting lessons and appearances in locally made films.

As a child, then, Tormé had an appreciation of jazz greats, like Benny Goodman and Gene Krupa, and he began writing songs at thirteen. Harry James invited him to play drums with his band. When the opportunity fell through, James played and had broadcast an arrangement of the fifteen-year-old's "Lament to Love." At sixteen Tormé became a singer and composer-arranger for Chico Marx's orchestra in California. In 1943 he made his film debut in *Higher and Higher* (also Frank Sinatra's film debut). He also formed his vocal quintet, Mel Tormé and His Mel Tones, with the later famous exotica composer Les Baxter, Ginny O'Connor (who later became a film composer and conductor Henry Mancini's wife), Betty Beveridge, and Bernie Parke. They fronted Artie Shaw and His Orchestra. About four years later, Tormé became a solo act.

Tormé recorded for big and small record labels in the 1940's and 1950's: Decca, Musicraft, Capitol, Bethlehem, and Verve. His repertory often included sentimental songs, whether they were jazz or pop standards. In 1945 he composed "The Christmas Song (Chestnuts Roasting on an Open Fire)" with Bob Wells. A year later, Nat King Cole made the best-known recording of the song. By 1949, Tormé had recorded his first album, *Mel Tormé's California Suite*, with Capitol Records. He collaborated with arranger Marty Paich between 1955 and 1957 on albums for Bethlehem Records and from 1958 to 1961 for Verve.

In the early 1960's, he became the Special Musical Material Writer and Advisor on *The Judy Garland Show* on CBS, although after working only nine months on the show, the tempestuous Garland had him fired. Tormé continued recording, but he had trouble attaining commercial success into the 1970's. At that time, the multitalented Tormé initiated a writing career, which eventually included completing four nonfiction books and one novel.

From the 1980's to the early 1990's he worked with arranger George Shearing. From the late 1980's to the early 1990's, references to Tormé and his appearances as himself in the television situation comedy *Night Court* introduced new audiences to the jazz singer.

In the 1990's, Tormé continued recording albums while making appearances on television shows such as *Seinfeld*. His singing career ended with his stroke in 1996; he died of a subsequent stroke in 1999.

The Music

Tormé lent his smooth tenor with highly controlled vibrato and flourishes to numerous jazz and popular standards, as well as his own compositions. Not only do his best recordings demonstrate his superior performance and interpretive abilities; they also reveal that Tormé had a sensitive understanding of music and a fine musical ear.

It's a Blue World. This 1955 album includes Tormé's renditions of sentimental, sad ballads such as the title song, Duke Ellington and Paul Francis Webster's "I've Got It Bad (and That Ain't Good)," and Jimmy Van Heusen and Johnny Burke's "Polka Dots and Moonbeams." It exhibits the diverse and demanding repertoire that Tormé performed in the early stages of his career while recording for the small jazz label Bethlehem.

Swingin' on the Moon. Here Tormé sings jazz arrangements of popular standards such as Richard Rodgers and Lorenz Hart's "Blue Moon" and John Blackburn and Karl Suessdorf's "Moonlight in Vermont." This 1960 recording for Verve features accompaniment by the Russ Garcia Orchestra.

That's All. On this album, produced by Columbia in 1964, Tormé worked with arranger Robert Mersey to select the most challenging collection of ballads. The album represents the range and various musical interests of both Tormé and Mersey. The songs featured include Alan Brandt and Bob Haymes's "That's All," Cole Porter's "I've Got You Under My Skin," George and Ira Gershwin's "Isn't It a Pity?," Rodgers and Hart's "My Romance," and João Gilberto and Norman Gimbel's "Ho-Ba-La-La." Mersey's careful but lush and highly intricate orchestration never upstages Tormé's soaring vocals, whose phrasing is at its best on this album. For example, in his version of Vernon Duke and E. Y.

Harburg's "What Is There to Say?," Tormé holds the last note at the end of most phrases so that the orchestra appears unable to utter anything between them. This performance of the song evokes a conversation between Tormé and the large studio orchestra. "Ho-Ba-La-La" demonstrates Tormé's formidable skills as a scat singer.

Top Drawer. This 1983 album for Concord Records features Tormé's take on well-known swing standards and demonstrates his appreciation of Johnny Mercer through "How Do You Say 'Auf Wiedersehen'?" and "Here's to My Lady." It showcases Tormé's bebop vocal skills in his version of Sonny Rollins's "Oleo" and features Shearing's accompaniment on piano. The album also contains Tormé's rendition of Hoagy Carmichael and Mitchell Parish's "Stardust."

Fujitsu-Concord Jazz Festival in Japan '90. Tormé's concert at the Jazz Festival in Japan was released in 1991. Tormé is accompanied by the Howard Wess Orchestra, and the album features Tormé on drums and offers an amazing rendition of "Stardust." Other impressive performances include Eric Maschwitz and Manning Sherwin's "A Nightingale Sang in Berkeley Square," Antonio Carlos Jobim's "Wave," and Count Basie's "Swingin' the Blues." Tormé also sings Billy Joel's "New York State of Mind," which was unusual since he hated rock.

Musical Legacy

Tormé recorded definitive versions of "Moonlight in Vermont," "That's All," "'Round Midnight," and "Blue Moon." His songwriting was immortalized through the ubiquitous holiday classic "The Christmas Song." He earned numerous Grammy nominations and two Grammy Awards: in 1962 for Best Male Vocalist and Best Rhythm and Blues Recording for *Comin' Home Baby!*, and in 1999 for Lifetime Achievement.

Melissa Ursula Dawn Goldsmith

Further Reading

Hulme, George. *Mel Tormé: A Chronicle of His Recordings, Books, and Films.* Jefferson, N.C.: McFarland, 2000. This sourcebook offers a historical time line about Tormé and information about his music, acting, and writing projects.

Tormé, Mel. *It Wasn't All Velvet.* New York: Viking, 1988. Tormé's autobiography describes his love of music, his family's support, his show business experiences, and his problems with divorce.

_____. *My Singing Teachers.* New York: Oxford University Press, 1994. Tormé reminisces about his singing teachers and offers advice to readers interested in singing.

_____. *The Other Side of the Rainbow with Judy Garland on the Dawn Patrol.* New York: William Morrow, 1970. This candid autobiographical account focuses on Tormé's time as Special Musical Material Writer and Advisor on CBS's *The Judy Garland Show.*

_____. *Traps, the Drum Wonder: The Life of Buddy Rich.* New York: Oxford University Press, 1991. This biography combines Tormé's personal account of Rich and interviews with Rich's colleagues and family members.

See also: Burke, Johnny; Mercer, Johnny.

Arturo Toscanini

Italian classical conductor

Toscanini parted drastically from the Romantic style of conducting, insisting that musicians adhere to the musical intentions of the composer. In his work with the NBC Symphony Orchestra, he made classical music accessible to large numbers of people.

Born: March 25, 1867; Parma, Italy
Died: January 16, 1957; New York, New York

Principal recordings

ALBUMS: *Mozart: Die Zauberflöte*, 1928; *Beethoven: Symphony No. 6 in F Major, Op. 68, Pastoral*, 1937; *Mozart's Sixth Symphony*, 1937; *Don Quixote: Richard Strauss*, 1938; *Beethoven: Symphony No. 1 in C Major, Op. 21*, 1939; *Beethoven: Symphony No. 2 in D Major, Op. 36*, 1939; *Beethoven: Symphony No. 3 in E-flat Major, Op. 55—Eroica*, 1939; *Beethoven: Symphony No. 4 in B-flat Major, Op. 60*, 1939; *Beethoven: Symphony No. 5 in C Minor, Op. 67*, 1939; *Beethoven: Symphony No. 7 in A Major, Op. 92,*

1939; *Beethoven: Symphony No. 8 in F Major, Op. 93*, 1939; *Beethoven: Symphony No. 9 in D Minor, Op. 125—Choral*, 1939; *Wagner: Götterdämmerung*, 1941; *Wagner: Lohengrin*, 1941; *Mendelssohn: Midsummer Night's Dream*, 1942; *Samuel Barber: Adagio for Strings, Op. 11*, 1942; *Brahms: German Requiem, Op. 45*, 1943; *Prokofiev: Symphony No. 1 in D Major, Op. 25, Classical*, 1944; *Puccini's La Bohème*, 1946; *Arrigo Boito: Mefistofele, Prologue*, 1948; *Tchaikovsky: Romeo and Juliet*, 1948; *Puccini: Manon Lescaut, Intermezzo*, 1949; *Verdi: Aida*, 1949; *Schubert: Symphony No. 8 in B Minor, Unfinished*, 1950; *Verdi: Falstaff*, 1950; *Donizetti: Overture to Don Pasquale*, 1951; *Brahms: Symphony No. 1 in C Minor, Op. 68*, 1952; *Brahms: Symphony No. 2 in D Major, Op. 73*, 1952; *Brahms: Symphony No. 3 in F Major, Op. 90*, 1952; *Brahms: Symphony No. 4 in E Minor, Op. 98*, 1952; *Wagner: Die Walküre*, 1952; *Mendelssohn: Symphony No. 4, Italian*, 1953; *Schubert: Symphony No. 9 in C Major, Great*, 1953; *Tchaikovsky: Symphony No. 6 in B Minor, Op. 74, Pathétique*, 1954; *Un ballo in maschera: Verdi*, 1954.

The Life

Until he was nine years old, Arturo Toscanini (ahr-TUR-oh tah-skah-NEE-nee), the son of Claudio and Paola Montani Toscanini, expected to become a tailor, like his father. In 1876, however, he had instruction at the music conservatory, and that changed the course of his life. Intrigued by classical music, Toscanini took cello lessons and later piano lessons. In 1878 Toscanini was given a full scholarship to the Parma Conservatory of Music, where his remarkable musical ability was appreciated and nurtured. So devoted was Toscanini to music that he sometimes sold his lunch to classmates at the conservatory and used the proceeds to buy sheet music.

In 1885 Toscanini graduated from the Parma Conservatory of Music, winning first prize in cello. Following his graduation, the Reggia, the major opera house in Parma, employed him to play in its orchestra. He also played with traveling orchestras in Italy during his first year out of the conservatory, but he was eager for adventure. In 1886 he became a cellist in an Italian company scheduled to present several operas in Brazil.

Arturo Toscanini. (Library of Congress)

In Brazil the nineteen-year-old cellist stepped in unexpectedly when the temperamental conductor refused to conduct the scheduled opera, Giuseppe Verdi's *Aida* (1871). Because he was severely nearsighted, Toscanini developed a prodigious ability to memorize entire operas and symphonies, so he never had a musical score before him when he conducted. Aware of this ability, the musicians in the orchestra prevailed upon the reluctant musician to conduct so that the performance could proceed.

Therefore, on June 25, 1886, Toscanini began his life as a conductor. Although he had trepidations, he performed magnificently. News of his virtuosity and his ability to memorize scores reached musical circles in Italy.

Upon his return from Brazil, Toscanini was besieged by invitations to be guest conductor for many local orchestras. When he carried out such performances flawlessly, he was invited to conduct some of Italy's most prestigious orchestras. By 1892, he was called upon to conduct the world premiere of Ruggiero Leoncavallo's new opera, *I*

Pagliacci (1892). Four years later, he conducted the world premiere of Giacomo Puccini's *La Bohème* (1896). By this time, Toscanini was generally acknowledged as the best opera conductor in Italy, if not in the world.

In 1898, Toscanini was named principal conductor of Milan's La Scala, Italy's most celebrated opera house. He held this post until 1903 when he was fired because of his intransigence. Toscanini was driven by strong musical scruples. He departed from the practices of Romantic conductors of the last half of the nineteenth century, striving to respect fully the integrity of the composers whose works he conducted. As a conductor, he demanded the highest possible level of performance from each member of his orchestra and was not hesitant to upbraid publicly anyone who did not meet his musical standards. His hair-trigger temper was legendary.

Toscanini refused to allow the encores that were generally provided for audiences in Italy. He discouraged audiences from applauding in the course of a performance as they had often done in the past, arguing that the encores that such applause evoked were a disservice to the composer of the work being performed. He was convinced that continuity was lost when the action of an opera was halted for an encore.

La Scala's directors warned Toscanini that he must change his ways. In 1903, because he refused, they dismissed him. In 1906, however, they rehired him, and he continued as the principal conductor at La Scala until 1908. In that year, he resigned to become a conductor for the Metropolitan Opera in New York City, where he remained until 1915.

With World War I raging, Toscanini felt compelled to return to his native Italy, which entered the war on the side of Britain and her allies. He conducted concerts for Italy's military, and, at war's end, he was decorated for his heroism in leading army orchestras in dangerous combat zones.

Semiretired after the war, Toscanini made a tour of the United States with La Scala during 1920 and 1921, and at the completion of this tour he rejoined La Scala as its lead conductor for eight more years. It was his opposition to the growing Fascism in Italy under the rule of Benito Mussolini that led him to return to the United States in 1929.

Toscanini had served as guest conductor of the New York Philharmonic Orchestra in 1926 and 1927. In 1928 he became its major conductor, a position in which he served until 1936, and then at age seventy, he became conductor of the NBC Symphony Orchestra. This body of musicians was organized specifically for him, so that he could, through regular radio broadcasts, bring classical music to huge audiences. He toured the world with this orchestra and continued to conduct it until 1954, when he made his final recording with NBC.

At eighty-seven, Toscanini divided the last three years of his life between Italy and New York. He suffered a severe stroke shortly before he turned ninety and died on January 16, 1957. Following his death, as homage to him, the NBC Symphony Orchestra played a concert without a conductor.

The Music

Serving the Composer. Unlike many of the major conductors who had preceded him in the late nineteenth century, Toscanini was not an innovator. He had a clear and unshakable philosophy of what a conductor's first duty was. In his mind, conductors had to study with great care the musical scores of the pieces they were to conduct and to make every attempt to present the music exactly the way the composer had indicated in these scores, observing every nuance presented by the musical notations.

This conservative approach to conducting was one that Toscanini observed with unbending devotion. He felt that the composers were the creators and the conductors were their servants. The hands of each composer whose works Toscanini conducted lay heavily upon his shoulders. He studied the scores scrupulously, memorized them with absolute accuracy, and demanded that each member of his orchestra reproduce flawlessly the notes and notations the composer had intended.

Toscanini was the first major conductor to conduct without having a score before him. His nearsightedness would have made it virtually impossible for him to read such a score during a performance, so he studied scores at his leisure and committed them to memory. He also had perfect pitch and extraordinarily keen hearing so that he could detect any deviations from the score and pinpoint the instrumentalist who was making such changes. Toscanini was brutal in tracking down any deviation, humiliating its perpetrator, and eliminating the problem.

Repertoire and Recordings. Early in his career, Toscanini favored compositions by the classical Italian composers who had first influenced him as a student, especially such opera composers as Giacomo Puccini and Giuseppe Verdi. As he matured, his musical parameters broadened, extending to eighteenth and early nineteenth century composers. Toscanini came to be acknowledged as the world's foremost interpreter of the music of Verdi and Ludwig van Beethoven. He observed the rapid tempi of both composers, and he preserved the crisp accents their scores indicated.

Although he ruled with an iron hand, Toscanini gained the respect of the members of his orchestras. He was uncompromising in demanding excellence from them. The result was performances that approached perfection. During his seventeen years as director of the NBC Symphony Orchestra, Toscanini shepherded the orchestra through the creation of more than thirty albums under the RCA Victor label. A major musical achievement was Toscanini's recording of the nine symphonies of Beethoven and the four symphonies of Johannes Brahms.

Making the Classics Accessible. Through his recordings and through his worldwide concert tours with the NBC Symphony Orchestra, Toscanini brought classical music to millions of people who might otherwise never have experienced it. The radio broadcasts of the NBC Symphony Orchestra became the major musical fare of millions of regular listeners. There was nowhere on the globe to which the influence of this orchestra did not extend.

Musical Legacy

Toscanini's chief contribution to music was his dogged adherence to the scores of the composers whose work he was conducting. He felt a direct obligation to them, a keen responsibility to respect every subtlety they indicated in their scores. Although many of these composers were dead, they had a living advocate in Toscanini.

Over and above his close adherence to the musical scores of the compositions he was conducting, Toscanini felt a need to open the world of music to thousands of people who had not had prior access to it. When NBC, a corporate enterprise, approached him with the idea of creating an orchestra that would regularly perform on the radio, thereby expanding the reach of classical music, Toscanini eagerly undertook the assignment, even though he was approaching age seventy at the time. That he was intimately associated with the NBC Symphony Orchestra for seventeen years is remarkable, considering the age at which this association began.

Toscanini is remembered not only as a giant in his field but also for his resistance to Fascism, which was sweeping through much of Europe during the 1920's and 1930's. He had adopted the principles of democracy from his father, who, in his youth, had served with the Italian patriot Giuseppe Garibaldi. These democratic views stirred his populist mentality, which led him to bring music to people throughout the world.

R. Baird Shuman

Further Reading

Frank, Mortimer H. *Arturo Toscanini: The NBC Years.* Portland, Oreg.: Amadeus Press, 2002. This book documents Toscanini's experience with the NBC Symphony Orchestra, and it describes how the conductor promoted modern composers as well as his favorite classical composers. It also provides insights into the man and his career. Includes extended discography.

Freeman, John W., and Walfredo Toscanini. *Toscanini.* New York: Treves Press, 1987. This volume, a collaboration with Toscanini's grandson, is rich with photographs and other illustrations, and it provides a well-written text.

Horowitz, Joseph. *Understanding Toscanini.* New York: Alfred A. Knopf, 1987. The third section of this book is a fifty-one-page discography of Toscanini concerts, an excellent resource.

Matthews, Denis. "The NBC Symphony." In *Arturo Toscanini.* New York: Hippocrene Books, 1982. This chapter outlines a crucial professional period in Toscanini's life.

Sachs, Harvey. "The Dare to Answer No." In *Toscanini.* Philadelphia, Pa.: J. B. Lippincott, 1978. This chapter delves into the reasons that Toscanini finally left La Scala in 1929 after conducting somewhat reluctantly there for a decade following World War I.

_____. "Toscanini and Mussolini." In *Reflections on Toscanini.* New York: Grove Weidenfeld,

1991. This chapter of some forty pages explains the political miasma in which Toscanini found himself as Fascism swept through Italy.

Toscanini, Arturo. *The Letters of Arturo Toscanini.* Edited by Harvey Sachs. New York: Alfred A. Knopf, 2002. The Toscanini letters provide intimate insights into the man, often when he was off guard. An indispensable resource for Toscanini scholars.

See also: Anderson, Marian; Barber, Samuel; Busch, Adolf; Horowitz, Vladimir; Karajan, Herbert von; Klemperer, Otto; Koussevitzky, Serge; Lehmann, Lotte; Levine, James; Melchior, Lauritz; Merrill, Robert; Prokofiev, Sergei; Puccini, Giacomo; Respighi, Ottorino; Serkin, Rudolf; Solti, Sir Georg; Stokowski, Leopold; Szell, George; Tebaldi, Renata; Thomson, Virgil; Walter, Bruno; Willson, Meredith.

Peter Tosh

Jamaican reggae singer, guitarist, and songwriter

Tosh broke out as a ska musician and then moved Jamaican popular music toward the reggae genre.

Born: October 19, 1944; Westmoreland, Jamaica
Died: September 11, 1987; St. Andrew, Jamaica
Also known as: Winston Hubert McIntosh (birth name)
Member of: Bob Marley and the Wailers

Principal recordings

ALBUMS (solo): *Negril*, 1975; *Legalize It*, 1976; *Equal Rights*, 1977; *Bush Doctor*, 1978; *Mystic Man*, 1979; *Wanted Dread and Alive*, 1981; *Mama Africa*, 1983; *No Nuclear War*, 1987; *I Am That I Am*, 2001.

ALBUMS (with the Wailing Wailers): *Soul Rebel*, 1971; *African Herbsman*, 1973; *Burnin'*, 1973; *Catch a Fire*, 1973.

The Life

Peter Tosh was born in Westmoreland, Jamaica, to Alvera Coke, her illegitimate son with James McIntosh, a preacher. With his existence denied by his father and his mother never present, Tosh was raised by his aunt. His aunt moved him to Kingston in 1956, but she soon died, leaving Tosh with no authoritative figure in his life. Tosh reportedly was quite adept at picking up music by ear and at a young age began emulating musicians he had heard. Around fifteen years of age, Tosh met Bob Marley and Neville Livingston, when they all took music lessons from Joe Higgs, a famous Kingston singer. They would form the Wailing Wailers in 1963. Tosh was the only member who could play an instrument, and he later commented that he had taught Marley how to play the guitar. They signed with Clement "Coxsone" Dodd's Studio One label, and they had their first hit in Jamaica in 1964 with the ska song "Simmer Down."

In 1966, when the Ethiopian Emperor Haile Selassie I came to Jamaica, the Rastafarian movement swept the nation, and Tosh and Livingston were immediately caught up in it. When Marley returned from the United States that year, they introduced him to the religion, which viewed Haile Selassie as the living God. Along with their religious conversion, the Wailing Wailers converted their sound first toward rocksteady and then reggae. Disillusioned with Dodd's label, the Wailing Wailers attempted to start their own label, which failed. They next teamed with Lee "Scratch" Perry to produce a few songs. Tosh and the other Wailing Wailers found themselves writing for American singer Johnny Nash.

Nash's rendition of the Marley-Tosh tune "Stir It Up" helped bring fame to the group, but when they signed with Chris Blackwell of Island Records in 1972 the band received their big break. Their second album on the label, *Burnin'*, would be their last together. However, this album helped propel Tosh's and Marley's solo careers. At this point, Tosh took the name Peter Tosh as his new recording name. One of the reasons Tosh left the Wailing Wailers was that the touring life for the group's first record with Island Records was too stressful for him and Livingston. To complicate matters, Tosh was involved in a near-fatal car accident in 1973 that cost his girlfriend her life.

Tosh diverged from his bandmates and let his militant style show in his solo work. He became famous as an advocate for the legalization of marijuana with his first album, *Legalize It*. He also found himself in trouble with Jamaican authorities for preaching against the injustices of society in the country. After he publicly insulted the prime minister of Jamaica at the One Love Peace Concert in 1976, he was often the target of physical harassment. Tosh later signed with the Rolling Stones' label, but he had a belligerent fallout with Keith Richards after three records. After returning from an African soul-seeking trip in the early 1980's, Tosh began to get his career back on track and even won a Grammy in 1987. Unfortunately, on September 11, 1987, Dennis "Leppo" Lobban and three other men entered Tosh's home in Kingston and, after demanding money, shot Tosh in the head. Tosh was pronounced dead at Kingston Hospital.

The Music

After starting the Wailing Wailers, Tosh, Marley, and Livingston took their ska sound to Clement Dodd's Studio One label. However, they seemed to censure the Jamaican Rude Boy culture (which emulated American cinematic gangsters). Their first Jamaican hit, "Simmer Down," told the Rude Boys to put down their guns and give up their ways. Most of the thirty tracks that the Wailing Wailers laid down from 1964 to 1967 emphasized the ska

culture. There were songs about Rude Boys, dance halls, and women. The Wailing Wailers benefited from having the powerhouse ska band the Skatalites as their backing band during these years, producing some of the finest songs of the ska era. However, by 1966, the Rastafarian movement had taken hold of Tosh and his bandmates, and this religious conversion put them at odds with Dodd. Dodd wanted to keep recording the popular ska songs that had brought success to the group, but they wanted to slow down their songs in a laid-back Rastafarian style.

Catch a Fire. The next phase found Tosh and the other Wailing Wailers writing songs for American singer Nash. Marley and Tosh had success with Nash's rendition of their "Stir It Up"; however, it was not until they released their first album with Island Records' Blackwell in 1973 that they came onto the international scene. Their first album, *Catch a Fire*, was mildly successful with fans but did not sell well. It led to a tour in England followed by a truncated tour in the United States. *Catch a Fire* included their own rendition of "Stir It Up" and such social commentary as the songs "Concrete Jungle" and "Slave Driver." Despite limited success, Tosh did not like touring under Blackwell, and the group's second album was their final album. *Burnin'* was a breakthrough for the musicians and included "I Shot the Sheriff," "Get Up, Stand Up," and "Burnin' and Lootin'." Eric Clapton's version of "I Shot the Sheriff" would hit number one on the pop charts in the United States in 1974. This success helped Marley's and Tosh's careers as solo artists.

Legalize It. Tosh's solo album *Legalize It* was released on CBS Records in 1976, and Tosh used his rough, militant style to promote the legalization of marijuana in Jamaica. Like many Rastafarians, he believed that the herb offered an avenue toward a greater state of mind. The title track became an anthem for legalization movements everywhere.

Peter Tosh. (AP/Wide World Photos)

Equal Rights. Tosh's next album was more critical of society, as Tosh moved toward becoming an antiauthority figure. *Equal Rights*, released in 1977, began with "Get Up, Stand Up" and also included "Downpressor Man," "Stepping Razor," and the Pan-African song "African."

Rolling Stones Records. After the One Love Peace Concert, Tosh was noticed by Mick Jagger and signed with Rolling Stones Records. This move benefited Tosh by giving him extra exposure but limited him musically because now he was under the thumb of other artists. *Bush Doctor*, a series of songs put together by Tosh and members of the Rolling Stones, is regarded by many critics as the low point of Tosh's career. Tosh released *Mystic Man* the next year and began to look again to antiwar and antishitstem (system) songs. One of Tosh's trademarks was twisting words to represent what he really thought. For example, he referred to Kingston as "Killsome" and the prime minister as "crime minister." Furthermore, he was notorious for using profane Jamaican slang in his lyrics. His last venture with Rolling Stones Records was *Wanted Dread and Alive*, released in 1981. Tosh was coming back to his former glory on this album, and it included one of his most famous songs, "Reggaemylitis," about a fictional musical sickness. This album set the tone for future reggae artists.

Mama Africa. Tosh's revitalization in Africa produced *Mama Africa* for Capitol Records in 1983. Tosh was in top form on this album, with his famous vocal sincerity and blatant honesty. "Peace Treaty," another plea for world peace, made its debut on this album. It also included a Tosh-esque cover of "Johnny B. Goode," a Chuck Berry song. Other Tosh originals on *Mama Africa* were "Glass House" and "Where You Gonna Run." Both songs spoke about respecting others and facing one's demons.

No Nuclear War. *No Nuclear War* encapsulated all of Tosh's beliefs. The title track was a powerful song about the ridiculousness of the Cold War. "Fight Apartheid" spoke out against the South African system and the exploitation of Africa in general. "Vampire," like many Tosh songs before it, railed against the ruling class, those on top of society who prey on the poor and keep the younger generation down. "Lessons in My Life" was about Tosh's hope for a better future, although he remained wary for his fellow man. "Come Together"

promoted unity, and "Testify" delved into Tosh's belief that spirituality could overcome any obstacle. The album won a Grammy Award. However, the joy would be short-lived. Tosh was murdered that year.

Musical Legacy

Tosh's works are well remembered. *Catch a Fire* and *Burnin'* were listed as *Rolling Stone*'s 500 Greatest Albums of All Time. Tosh's contribution to the ska genre was both a blessing and a curse. With the Wailing Wailers he recorded some of the most memorable and covered ska songs, but he also contributed to the downfall of the genre with his shift to reggae.

As one of the forefathers of reggae, Tosh set the tone for Rastafarian ganja (marijuana) advocates and political activists. His musical subjects spanned many different topics, but he was foremost an activist like his Wailer brother Marley. It was their commitment to causes such as the Pan-African movement that set an example for other musicians, who started taking up their own campaigns. Tosh set an example for other performers, but foremost he was an excellent musician and a soulful vocalist, defining reggae and taking its popularity to an international level.

Daniel R. Vogel

Further Reading

Cumbo, Fikisha. *Bob Marley and Peter Tosh: Get Up! Stand Up! Diary of a Reggaeophile*. New York: CACE International, 2001. This is one of the few books that covers Tosh in depth, along with Marley. The author had access to Tosh in a series of interviews and through a personal friendship. Many original photographs and interviews.

Foster, Chuck. *Roots, Rock, Reggae*. New York: Billboard Books, 1999. Foster goes over many of the ska, rocksteady, and reggae legends in his book and devotes a chapter to Tosh. A useful overall description of Tosh's career.

Potash, Chris, ed. *Reggae, Rasta, Revolution*. New York: Schirmer Books, 1997. Collection of articles about ska, rocksteady, and reggae music from newspapers and other printed sources. Tosh is the subject of some, and the book is useful for comparing how the media and critics portrayed Tosh and other musicians of his genre and time.

Scott, Ricardo. *Scott's Official History of Reggae: The Original Wailers and the Trench-Town Experience.* New York: Cornerstone, 1993. This history of the Wailing Wailers also explores the evolution and influences of reggae, with Tosh covered in depth as a key figure.

Stolzoff, Norman C. *Wake the Town and Tell the People.* Durham, N.C.: Duke University Press, 2000. About the dance-hall culture during the ska, rocksteady, and reggae days out of which Tosh grew.

See also: Berry, Chuck; Clapton, Eric; Marley, Bob; Richards, Keith.

Pete Townshend

English rock guitarist and songwriter

As the guitarist and the primary songwriter of the Who, Townshend assisted in the development of the concept album, in the creation of the rock opera, and in the utilization of the synthesizer as a structural instrument in popular music.

Born: May 19, 1945; London, England
Also known as: Pete Dennis Blandford Townshend (full name)
Member of: The Who

Principal recordings

ALBUMS (solo): *Who Came First*, 1972; *Rough Mix*, 1977 (with Ronnie Lane); *Empty Glass*, 1980; *All the Best Cowboys Have Chinese Eyes*, 1982; *White City: A Novel*, 1985; *Pete Townshend's Deep End Live!*, 1986 (with Deep End); *The Iron Man: A Musical*, 1989; *Psychoderelict*, 1993.

ALBUMS (with the Who): *The Who Sings My Generation*, 1965; *A Quick One*, 1966 (released in the United States as *Happy Jack*, 1967); *The Who Sell Out*, 1967; *Magic Bus*, 1968; *Tommy*, 1969; *Who's Next*, 1971; *Quadrophenia*, 1973; *The Who by Numbers*, 1975; *Who Are You*, 1978; *Face Dances*, 1981; *It's Hard*, 1982; *Endless Wire*, 2006.

The Life

Pete Dennis Blandford Townshend (TOWN-zehnd) was born into a middle-class musical fam-ily. His father Cliff was a professional saxophonist, and his mother Betty was a singer. Townshend demonstrated an interest in music at an early age, and he received his first guitar at the age of twelve, In 1959 he joined his first band, a Dixieland jazz band called the Confederates. In the fall of 1961, Townshend enrolled at Ealing Art College, and his time there played a formative role in his approach to music. Especially influential was Roy Ascot, Ealing's head tutor, who based his education theories on cybernetics. Ascot had students take classes in a variety of disciplines that were typically segregated from one another, and this mixture of high and functional art is displayed in Townshend's solo work and in the Who's *The Who Sell Out* and later albums.

In 1962 Townshend joined a rhythm-and-blues-oriented group called the Detours that also included future Who members John Entwistle and Roger Daltrey. In the following years the group went through several personnel and name changes before ultimately becoming the Who, with Daltrey singing lead vocals, Townshend on guitar, Entwistle on bass, and Keith Moon on drums. Initially the band struggled to find an audience, but eventually it took hold with London's mod culture. In 1964 Townshend composed his first original songs for the group, and he quickly emerged as the group's primary songwriter.

In 1968 Townshend was profoundly affected by the spiritual writings of Indian guru Meher Baba, whose teachings influenced his songwriting from that point. That same year Townshend married Karen Astley, daughter of composer Ted Astley, and the couple had three children before divorcing in 2000. During the early 1980's Townshend struggled with drug and alcohol addiction, an experience he frequently reflects upon in his lyrics.

Townshend's first official solo album, *Who Came First*, was released in 1972, and he continued to compose songs both for his solo albums and for the Who until he left the band in 1983. Since leaving the band, Townshend has continued to take part in the Who reunion concerts, the first of which was held in 1985. Townshend is active as a solo artist, and he has released a variety of projects, such as *White City: A Novel* (a story-based album), *Horse's Neck* (a book of short stories), and *The Iron Man: A Musical* (a musical adaptation of Ted Hughes's children's story).

In December, 2008, Townshend received the Kennedy Center Honors, for his contributions to the performing art of music.

The Music

As the primary creative mind behind the Who, Townshend wrote the majority of the Who's songs, and he determined the artistic direction of the band. Most of the Who's albums are organized around a unifying conceptual element, which is also true of Townshend's solo work. His personal beliefs and experiences are commonly expressed in his songs and those of the Who, even when the other members did not share them. Townshend never shied away from venturing into new sonic territory, and he helped expand the boundaries of what a rock band was capable of producing.

The Who Sell Out. This album, released in 1967, is one of the earliest examples of a concept album. The songs are linked by fictitious advertisements for commercial products in the model of Radio London. The album contains a pop art critique of overconsumption, and it intermingles advertisements with music to demonstrate the commodification of the music itself. "I Can See for Miles" was the only song on the album that was released as a single, and it is an example of the increased utilization of production techniques in the late 1960's through its use of overdubbing and complex vocal harmonies. In songs such as "Tattoo" and "Sunrise," Townshend exposes some of his previously hidden vulnerabilities, while numerous songs, including "Mary Anne with the Shaky Hand," "Silas Stingy," and "Relax," demonstrate hints of psychedelia. "I Can't Reach You" features Townshend on lead vocals, and it exhibits his increased interest in spirituality that came to fruition the following year when he encountered the teachings of Meher Baba. "Rael," a miniature rock opera with a plot and an instrumental second half, hints at what was to follow.

Tommy. *Tommy*, released by the Who in 1969, was one of the first rock operas, and it was pivotal in introducing the term into the popular music vernacular. Townshend was the principal composer of both the music and the story that involves a dumb, deaf, and blind boy named Tommy. At the insistence of the Who, *Tommy* was recorded without additional musicians, avoiding operatic orchestration. Instead, the members of the Who overdubbed

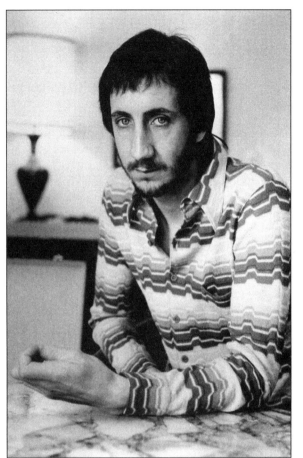

Pete Townshend. (AP/Wide World Photos)

their parts. The most prominent parts were performed on typical rock instruments, which allowed the album to be performed onstage in concert. Although *Tommy* differs greatly from a traditional opera, it retains typical operatic elements, such as an overture, restated themes, and instrumental passages. The evocation of the phrase rock opera elevated the album in the hierarchical structure of popular music, and it demonstrated the musical capabilities of rock music, without alienating the rock audience. Adapted for several different mediums, *Tommy* is the most prominent of all Townshend's works. In 1975 *Tommy* was released as a film starring Daltrey as Tommy and featuring appearances by musicians Elton John, Tina Turner, and Eric Clapton. *Tommy* has also been produced as a Broadway musical that premiered in 1993, for which Townshend won a Tony Award for Best Original Score. The Who also released another rock opera,

Quadrophenia, set in England's Mod culture of the mid-1960's. It was later released as a film in 1979.

Who's Next. Released in 1971, this album was the Who's next major work after *Tommy*. Originally, the songs that appeared on *Who's Next* were intended for Townshend's next great project, *Lifehouse*, which was to be larger in scope than *Tommy*. Townshend's attempt to bring *Lifehouse* to fruition failed, and *Who's Next* is a collection of some of the best songs composed for that project. *Who's Next* was produced during a time when an increased amount of new technology was available for musicians. Townshend utilized these new resources, and he composed most of the songs before presenting his completed demos to the other members of the band. His use of new technology is especially notable in the songs "Baba O'Riley" and "Won't Get Fooled Again," two of the first popular music songs to utilize a synthesizer as a structural element. The synthesizer, and in the case of "Baba O'Riley," a violin, provided greater variety to the Who's typical power trio instrumentation during a time when the synthesizer was a new and novel instrument. Townshend also ran his guitar through synthesizers and filters in songs such as "Bargain" and "Going Mobile," which contributed to the full sound of this album.

Psychoderelict. *Psychoderelict* is one of Townshend's several solo albums. Similar to many of Townshend's albums with the Who, *Psychoderelict* is a conceptual album, and it draws upon several of Townshend's past projects (especially the failed *Lifehouse*). It is a radio play with a mixture of dialogue and music that tells a semiautobiographical story about an aging rock artist named Ray High. Initially unable to compose new material, High is inspired to write again through his correspondence with a reporter who is posing as a fourteen-year-old girl. Dialogue frequently appears in the middle of songs, and, because of its lukewarm reception, a music-only version of the album was also produced. The only single, "English Boy," was released in both dialogue and dialogue-free versions, and it is the lead track on the album. Throughout the song, dialogue from a radio show introduces the story, and the entire song is a youth anthem in the same lyrical vein as Townshend's earlier Who song, "My Generation." In addition, there are several instrumental compositions dedicated to Meher Baba and sections of the original demo version of "Baba O'Riley."

Musical Legacy

Musically and aesthetically, Townshend had a large influence on subsequent generations of rock-and-roll performers. His destruction of guitars and amplifiers on stage sparked a trend among rockers, and his guitar style within the power trio format, especially in the Who's early years, was foundational for later acts, such as Cream and the Jimi Hendrix Experience. As the singular guitarist in the band, Townshend alternated between lead and rhythm roles, and he frequently utilized feedback to fill out the texture. Townshend was influential through his use of the synthesizer, for structural means rather than just short, embellishing figures. Along with other progressive and art rock musicians, Townshend has contributed to the elevation of rock music. His association of rock with visual-arts movements (*The Who Sell Out*) and with Western classical terminology (rock opera) helped rock achieve cultural legitimacy. Other artists, such as Pink Floyd (*The Wall*, 1979) and My Chemical Romance (*The Black Parade*, 2006), have released rock operas, and the rock-opera format has inspired rock musicals, metal operas, and hip-hoperas.

Matthew Mihalka

Further Reading

Barnes, Richard. *The Who: Maximum R & B*. London: Plexus, 1996. Written by Townshend's art school roommate, this book covers the entirety of the Who's career, focusing primarily on the early works. It also contains a large number of photographs, in color and in black and white.

Giuliano, Geoffrey. *Behind Blue Eyes: The Life of Pete Townshend*. New York: Dutton, 1996. Giuliano's biography focuses mainly on the events that shaped Townshend's life and secondarily on the music. It also includes a discography, a diary of events, a 1995 interview with Townshend, and a 1989 interview with Townshend, Daltrey, and Entwistle.

Marsh, Dave. *Before I Get Old*. New York: St. Martin's Press, 1983. This contains an extensive history of the Who, and the social climate that surrounded the band's career.

Schaffner, Nicholas. *The British Invasion: From the*

First Wave to the New Wave. New York: McGraw-Hill, 1983. Includes a chapter on the Who, with several interviews conducted with members of the Who.

Smith, Larry David. *Pete Townshend: The Minstrel's Dilemma.* London: Praeger, 1999. This book explores Townshend's struggle to find the right balance between creativity and commercialism. It discusses his work both with the Who and as a solo artist.

Wolter, Stephen, and Karen Kimber. *The Who in Print: An Annotated Bibliography, 1965 Through 1990.* London: McFarland, 1992. This source consists of annotations of articles about the Who that appeared in music magazines. It also covers books, record and concert reviews, and film, television, and video articles. Contains a section dedicated to Townshend as an author.

See also: Clapton, Eric; Daltrey, Roger; Hendrix, Jimi; John, Sir Elton; Turner, Tina.

Merle Travis

American country singer-songwriter and guitarist

While Travis did not invent the fingerstyle guitar technique called "Travis picking," he made it widely accessible to such disciples as Chet Atkins and Doc Watson through his recordings, radio broadcasts, and television appearances. His deeply folk-flavored country songs have had an enduring impact beyond Travis's original recordings of them.

Born: November 29, 1917; Rosewood, Kentucky
Died: October 20, 1983; Tahlequah, Oklahoma
Also known as: Merle Robert Travis (full name)

Principal recordings

ALBUMS: *Folk Songs of the Hills,* 1947; *Merle Travis Guitar,* 1956; *Back Home,* 1957; *Travis,* 1962; *Songs of the Coal Mines,* 1963; *I'm a Natural Born Gambling Man,* 1964; *Merle Travis and Joe Maphis,* 1964 (with Joe Maphis); *Great Songs of the Delmore Brothers,* 1969; *Strictly Guitar,* 1969;

The Atkins-Travis Traveling Show, 1974; *Country Guitar Giants,* 1979 (with Maphis); *Light Singin' and Pickin',* 1980; *Travis Pickin',* 1981; *Merle and Grandpa's Farm and Home Hour,* 1985 (with Grandpa Jones); *Rough, Rowdy, and Blue,* 1986.

The Life

Merle Robert Travis (TRAH-vihs) was the youngest of four children born to a farmer-turned-miner in Kentucky's coal country. His father played banjo, and at age twelve Merle got a guitar from an older brother whose wife played guitar in the fingerpicking style popular in Kentucky's Muhlenberg County. Guitarists Ike Everly (father of Don and Phil Everly) and Mose Rager were role models for Travis, an eager pupil. Travis made his first radio appearance in Evansville, Indiana, in 1936, and a year later was hired by veteran fiddler and bandleader Clayton McMichen for his Georgia Wildcats. In 1938, Travis began a six-year association with the Drifting Pioneers, a string band that broadcast over Cincinnati's 50,000-watt station WLW.

In 1943, Travis and Louis Marshall "Grandpa" Jones became the first artists to record for the King label. After a brief stint in the Marines, Travis moved to Los Angeles in 1944 and made his first Capitol label recordings as a sideman late that year. His first recordings as leader appeared in 1945, and the next year saw his biggest chart success, "Divorce Me C.O.D." The year 1947 saw the *Folk Songs of the Hills* album, which included Travis's most enduring songs.

The late 1940's found Travis designing a solid-body guitar and continuing to enjoy chart success with his singles. That waned in the 1950's, but his fortunes brightened in 1955, when Tennessee Ernie Ford had a multimillion-selling hit with Travis's "Sixteen Tons." In the 1960's and 1970's, folk audiences rediscovered Travis, and he continued to perform and record into the 1980's. His 1973 album with his star disciple, *The Atkins-Travis Traveling Show,* won a Grammy for Best Country Instrumental Performance.

Travis settled in eastern Oklahoma with fourth wife (and former wife of Hank Thompson) Dorothy, writing his memoirs and recording as late as 1981. In October of 1983 he suffered a heart attack and died in the hospital the next day. A monument dedicated to him in Ebenezer, Kentucky, is the site where his ashes were dispersed.

The Music

Travis was forged in the crucible of "live" radio, where both versatility and virtuosity were highly valued. He absorbed everything from folk songs to 1920's pop tunes, and his work as both guitarist and songwriter freely reflects the range of his influences. The guitar style that came to be called Travis picking was not original with him, though his impressive talent and access to both radio and recording meant he effectively branded it. Characterized by a right-hand thumb-and-finger interaction that somewhat approximated stride-style piano, Travis picking was a sophisticated folk fingerstyle that, with variations, was common to both black and white rural southerners. Travis, equally at home on either acoustic or electric guitar, "took it to town" while keeping the sound grounded enough to be embraced by folk-guitar enthusiasts after it had ceased being novel in country music.

Similarly, his songwriting could be artfully guileless. Commissioned by his record label to write an album's worth of folk songs, he delivered originals that had the stamp of hoary authenticity, even though they were freshly penned. The songs he wrote for the commercial country market tended to be of a novelty bent, though the best of them had a sophistication that would not have been out of place in a late-1940's pop song. Uniquely, Travis the songwriter inhabited a territory somewhere between Woody Guthrie and Johnny Mercer.

"Divorce Me C.O.D." In the 1960's, divorce would become a topic of cliché in country music. In the 1940's, however, it was untried and somewhat taboo. In 1946, Travis changed that with a clever lyric and a bouncy delivery that took this song to number one on *Billboard*'s folk chart for a remarkable fourteen weeks. Unfortunately, this success encouraged Travis to lean toward novelty songs for his future commercial singles.

"Sixteen Tons." Travis never worked in a coal mine, but he saw enough of the miner's life to write detailed songs about it. "Sixteen Tons" was lyrically inspired by family remarks about the miner's life, as well as by an old Josh White song. What Travis made of his raw materials was entirely original, as was, in a very different way, Tennessee Ernie

Ford's later reworking of the song into an international hit.

"Dark as a Dungeon." The bluesy "Sixteen Tons" contrasts with the hymnlike quality of Travis's other great critique of the miner's life, "Dark as a Dungeon." "Sixteen Tons" would become an unlikely pop hit, while "Dark as a Dungeon" would be sung by Pete Seeger and Joan Baez and became a folk revival standard. A lesser songwriter, delivering a topical song in a folk idiom, might have made something mawkish, but Travis's work is genuinely moving.

"Cannonball Rag." Originally recorded in 1949 as "Cannonball Stomp," Travis may have brought this solo guitar showpiece with him from Kentucky. It was not the hottest of his guitar instrumentals, but it was one with a musical smile beaming over its virtuosity and became the most widely performed of all Travis's guitar pieces.

Musical Legacy

Travis will be remembered as a man who gave his name to a style of guitar playing adopted and modified by Chet Atkins and such disciples of his as Jerry Reed. That style continues to be a part of both country and folk music performances in the United States and abroad. Travis also designed a solid-body guitar that may have influenced some of Leo Fender's early creations. Travis was also a catalyst for, and early popularizer of, the Bigsby vibrato bar for electric guitars.

A pleasant if unremarkable singer, Travis enjoyed considerable chart success in his time with now-forgotten novelty songs. Ironically, his enduring compositions are the songs he wrote reluctantly when Capitol wanted a collection of folk songs. These drew on the specifics of his native region and the life of its people and, for all their specificity, struck a universal chord. They remain paragons of the best folk-inspired topical songs, inspiring such later works in the idiom as John Prine's "Paradise." Travis was inducted into the Country Music Hall of Fame in 1977.

Mark Humphrey

Further Reading

Anderson, Bobby. *That Muhlenberg Sound*. Beechmont, Ky.: MuhlBut Press, 1993. While it is tempting to dismiss this book as an amateurishly written regional musical genealogy, it does provide useful background on the region that gave rise to Travis, the people who influenced his guitar style, and later local musicians and singers influenced by Travis.

Green, Archie. *Only a Miner: Studies in Recorded Coal-Mining Songs.* Urbana: University of Illinois Press, 1972. Green's superb scholarly work offers a detailed analysis of Travis's *Folk Songs of the Hills,* particularly "Sixteen Tons" and "Dark as a Dungeon."

Jones, Louis M., with Charles K. Wolfe. *Everybody's Grandpa: Fifty Years Behind the Mike.* Knoxville: University of Tennessee Press, 1984. Jones was a nearly lifelong friend of Travis, whose personal flaws as well as musical brilliance are vividly recalled—along with much else in Jones's colorful life—in this delightful musician's memoir.

Wolfe, Charles K. *Kentucky Country: Folk and Country Music of Kentucky.* Lexington: University Press of Kentucky, 1982. Country music's finest scholar presents Travis in the context of a rich and varied tapestry of musicians from the Bluegrass State.

See also: Atkins, Chet; Watson, Doc.

Ernest Tubb

American country singer-songwriter, bandleader, and guitarist

Tubb was a key transitional figure in country music's evolution from self-accompanied singer-guitarists in the mold of his idol, Jimmie Rodgers, to singer-bandleaders accompanied by amplified instruments. Melodically simple and lyrically direct, many of his songs became country standards. He was influential in making Nashville a recording center and acted as mentor to singers ranging from Hank Williams to Loretta Lynn.

Born: February 9, 1914; near Crisp, Texas
Died: September 6, 1984; Nashville, Tennessee
Also known as: Ernest Dale Tubb (full name); Texas Troubadour
Member of: The Texas Troubadours

Principal recordings

ALBUMS (solo): *Ernest Tubb Favorites,* 1952; *The Importance of Being Ernest,* 1959; *Midnight Jamboree,* 1961 (with others); *Family Bible,* 1963; *Ernest Tubb and Loretta Lynn,* 1965 (with Loretta Lynn); *Mr. and Mrs. Used to Be,* 1965 (with Lynn); *Singin' Again,* 1967 (with Lynn); *Stand by Me,* 1967; *Great Country,* 1969; *If We Put Our Heads Together,* 1969 (with Lynn); *Ernest Tubb,* 1975.

ALBUMS (with the Texas Troubadours): *Jimmie Rodgers Songs,* 1951; *Old Rugged Cross,* 1951; *The Daddy of 'Em All,* 1957; *Ernest Tubb and the Texas Troubadours,* 1960; *Ernest Tubb Record Shop,* 1960; *On Tour,* 1962; *Blue Christmas,* 1964; *Just Call Me Lonesome,* 1964; *The Texas Troubadours,* 1964; *Thanks a Lot,* 1964; *Country Dance Time,* 1965; *Hittin' the Road,* 1965; *My Pick of the Hits,* 1965; *By Request,* 1966; *Ernest Tubb Sings Country Hits, Old and New,* 1966; *Ernest Tubb's Fabulous Texas Troubadours,* 1966; *Another Story,* 1967; *Country Hit Time,* 1968; *Ernest Tubb Sings Hank Williams,* 1968; *The Terrific Texas Troubadours,* 1968; *Let's Turn Back the Years,* 1969; *Saturday Satan, Sunday Saint,* 1969; *Good Year for the Wine,* 1970; *One Sweet Hello,* 1971; *Baby, It's So Hard to Be Good,* 1972; *Say Something Nice to Sarah,* 1972; *I've Got All the Heartache I Can Handle,* 1973.

The Life

Ernest Dale Tubb was the son of a Texas cotton farmer. Though the world of his childhood offered few luxuries, a phonograph player was an exception. The recordings of Jimmie Rodgers were immensely popular, and Tubb first heard them in 1928. Soon, like young men across the South, Tubb was singing Rodgers's songs and attempting to master his so-called blue yodel. What set him apart was geographic good fortune: He was in San Antonio, Texas, where Rodgers's widow lived, when he launched his career. Carrie Rodgers liked Tubb's renditions of her late husband's songs and used her influence to get him on the Bluebird label, where Tubb made his first recordings in 1936.

His initial recordings, reverently imitative of his idol, were unsuccessful, but a change in Tubb's voice—one he blamed on a tonsillectomy—forced him to develop his own distinctive singing style and to write songs to suit it. After a move to the Decca label in 1940, Tubb scored a major hit a year later with "Walking the Floor over You." During and after World War II, he recorded many songs related to wartime separation and longed-for reunions, most successfully "Soldier's Last Letter."

After the war, Tubb would open the Ernest Tubb Record Shop and take the first Grand Ole Opry troupe to Carnegie Hall, both in 1947. He launched a popular "live" radio show following Grand Ole Opry broadcasts called *The Midnight Jamboree*, and he fronted a band, the Texas Troubadours, named for his old tag. In the mid-1960's, Tubb hosted a syndicated television show, even though his hit-making prime was past. He and his Texas Troubadours remained a popular touring act well into the 1970's, but in 1984 Tubb lost his long-running battle with emphysema.

The Music

Tubb's rise followed the repeal of Prohibition in 1933, the reopening of taverns, and the widespread dissemination of jukeboxes to offer their patrons entertainment. It was an ideal environment for songs like "Walking the Floor over You," songs which were unassuming in their production and delivered with an Everyman's relaxed confidence. America's entry into World War II was a disaster from which the so-called big bands never recovered, among them Tubb's rival, Bob Wills and His Texas Playboys. But Tubb's bare-bones production in the 1940's meant loss of drafted personnel was no crisis, so long as he could find a competent electric guitarist to accompany him. After World War II, he would build a bigger band and add drums, but the jazzy "take-off" solos of Western Swing were anathema to Tubb, and his band always hewed close to the melody. The baleful, barely on-pitch sincerity of Tubb's voice epitomized what some ears found intolerable in country music. Yet Tubb's magic was working his limitations in ways that told his fans he was one of them. They rewarded him with a loyalty that extended far beyond his hit-making prime.

"Walking the Floor over You." Widely considered an exemplary first step toward a style of country that would later be labeled honky-tonk, this recording offered an amplified guitar accompanying Tubb in the straightforward, no-frills manner that

characterized most of his future recordings. Electric guitars were not entirely new to country recordings by 1941, but they had tended to appear in the more jazz-tinged context of Western swing bands. Here, Tubb was responding to a jukebox distributor's telling him his records needed to be louder. Tubb's acoustic rhythm guitar still bears the imprint of his idol, Jimmie Rodgers, but his plank-plain vocals lack the honeyed drawl that was Rodgers's calling card. Instead, they offer the audible smile that was Tubb's best defense against his severe limitations as singer. That, coupled with a bounce that owed more to swing than Tubb may have consciously known and lyrics that were a comic—but not corny—portrayal of a domestic breakup, made the song a hit when released and, in time, Tubb's theme song and a much-covered country standard.

"Soldier's Last Letter." As World War II raged, this song topped the so-called folk chart for four weeks in 1944 and even made it to number twenty-nine on the pop side. It may have been the last song of this nature to be so hugely successful. Country music has, more than other genres, retained both maudlin and patriotic themes to this day, but this song is clearly of another era. Even in 1944, it was a throwback to songs like Rodgers's "The Soldier's Sweetheart," though the patriotism of Tubb's dead soldier is underscored more than that of Rodgers. As melodically simple as anything Tubb recorded, its lyrics, penned by an army sergeant, are the contents of a soldier's letter to his mother. The fact that the letter is unsigned reveals that her son died in combat. To call this a tearjerker is an understatement. Yet the success of this song in its time—it was Tubb's greatest chart success—speaks volumes of the era and makes it a cornerstone of Tubb's career. Not surprisingly, he would record other songs related to the experience of soldiers well into the era of the Vietnam conflict.

"Waltz Across Texas." This 1965 recording was never a major chart hit, yet it became, over the remainder of Tubb's life, a second theme song for him. Written by his nephew, Talmadge Tubb, it had the old-fashioned sound of something Tubb might have recorded in the 1940's. He had recorded other songs related to his home state, but this one—simple, sentimental, and sounding vaguely like something Rodgers might have recorded about his adopted home state—became an understated classic.

Musical Legacy

Tubb, by dint of a winning personality and plain hard work, created a persona and legacy far exceeding his limited range as singer. (Johnny Cash would later do the same.) Tubb grew out of a musical world mapped by Jimmie Rodgers, with his "blue yodels" and "heart songs," and Hollywood's singing cowboys, such as Gene Autry. Tubb would forge their prewar sensibilities into a sound that drew nickels to postwar jukeboxes and that would, in time, be labeled honky-tonk. If his music sounded hopelessly dated by the 1960's, Tubb would not waver from it, and he lived to see it celebrated by the likes of Merle Haggard and Hank Williams, Jr. His tireless touring and legendary patience with, and devotion to, his fans gave Tubb's career as performer a longevity beyond his career as hit maker, though that was itself remarkable. In 1979, thirty-eight years after the original, a sixty-five-year-old Tubb, helped by Haggard and Charlie Daniels, climbed to number thirty-one on *Billboard*'s country chart with a remake of "Walking the Floor over You."

Mark Humphrey

Further Reading

Kingsbury, Paul, and Alan Axelrod, eds. *Country: The Music and the Musicians.* New York: Abbeville Press, 1988. Rich with photographs, this book provides topical and chronological information on country music, placing honky-tonk within a larger historical context. Includes selected discography and bibliography.

Russell, Tony. *Country Music Originals: The Legends and the Lost.* New York: Oxford University Press, 2007. Russell is a British researcher of early country music who brings a refreshing and insightful perspective to his work. His two pages on Tubb may tell most readers all they need to know about the man and his music. Other miniessays on vintage country artists, both famous and obscure, provide readers with a context for measuring Tubb's contribution to the country genre.

See also: Frizzell, Lefty; Leadbelly; Lynn, Loretta; Miller, Roger.

Big Joe Turner
American blues singer and songwriter

A blues shouter, Turner was a rhythm-and-blues pioneer who transited smoothly to success in early rock and roll.

Born: May 18, 1911; Kansas City, Missouri
Died: November 24, 1985; Inglewood, California
Also known as: Joseph Vernon Turner, Jr. (full name)

Principal recordings

ALBUMS: *Joe Turner Sings Kansas City Jazz*, 1953; *Big Joe Rides Again*, 1956; *Boss of the Blues*, 1956; *Joe Turner*, 1958; *Rockin' the Blues*, 1958; *Big Joe Is Here*, 1959; *Joe Turner and the Blues*, 1960; *Singing the Blues*, 1967; *Bosses of the Blues*, 1969 (with T-Bone Walker); *Texas Style*, 1971; *Flip, Flop, and Fly*, 1972 (with Count Basie); *Roll 'Em*, 1973; *Life Ain't Easy*, 1974; *The Trumpet Kings Meet Joe Turner*, 1974 (with others); *Every Day I Have the Blues*, 1975; *The Midnight Special*, 1976; *In the Evening*, 1977; *Things That I Used to Do*, 1977; *Nobody in Mind*, 1982; *Blues Train*, 1983 (with Roomful of Blues); *Kansas City Here I Come*, 1984; *Patcha, Patcha All Night Long*, 1985 (with Jimmy Witherspoon).

The Life

Joseph Vernon Turner, Jr., was born in Kansas City, Missouri, home of many swing-era jazz pioneers. With his family, he listened to the recordings of singers Bessie Smith and Ethel Waters, which nurtured his love of singing. By his teens, Turner was leading blind blues singers around Kansas City streets, learning repertoire and vocal projection. Soon he was singing in the Backbiters' Club, where blues and boogie-woogie pianist Pete Johnson had a steady engagement. Turner and Johnson moved on to more prestigious clubs, and they eventually toured with a band that took them as far as Chicago. Talent scout John Hammond heard the duo in Kansas City's Sunset Club, and he invited them to participate in a Carnegie Hall concert, From Spirituals to Swing, celebrating the evolution of African American music. Johnson and Turner were to represent the 1920's piano style called boogie-woogie, and they did it so effectively that boogie-woogie became newly popular.

Turner and Johnson soon had a regular engagement at New York City's Café Society, and they made their first recordings shortly after the 1938 Carnegie Hall concert. Over the next forty-five years, Turner recorded extensively in settings that ranged from blues and rhythm and blues to jazz and rock and roll. Without changing his delivery, he adapted successfully to each in turn, making a poignant return to Kansas City in the documentary film, *The Last of the Blue Devils* (1980). Despite ill health, Turner continued performing and delighting audiences until shortly before his death at age seventy-four.

The Music

Turner had a forceful vocal instrument, and some admirers commented that, under different circumstances, he would have made a great opera singer. His early experience among street-singing bluesmen honed his remarkable ability for rearranging free-floating blues verses as well as for extemporaneously creating fresh ones. Vocal projection, another useful tool for a street singer, was an art he mastered with ease. Hornlike singing power and a knack for spinning blues lyrics made Turner the archetypal urban blues shouter, though calling Turner's singing style shouting is a disservice.

Most blues singers are attached to a specific era or subgenre. For example, Charley Patton embodied the Delta blues prior to the Great Depression; Muddy Waters shaped the electric evolution of the blues music in postwar Chicago. For all their greatness, these artists were defined and limited by their time and place. Turner somehow crossed all such boundaries: For nearly five decades, his musical approach remained remarkably consistent, yet fluid enough to record with pianists ranging from Johnson to Art Tatum and in band settings that encompassed the evolution of popular urban blues-based music from boogie-woogie to rock and roll. Turner effortlessly fit the style of the moment without being confined by it.

"Roll 'Em, Pete." Johnson played more than boogie-woogie piano, but when the patrons of Kansas City's Sunset Club wanted to hear him show off in that style, they shouted, "Roll, 'Em, Pete!" Turner, the expert blues lyricist, readily wrote lyrics to fit Johnson's celebratory piano flourishes, and the result was a sensation at Carnegie Hall's From Spirituals to Swing concert. Their collaboration sparked the spate of boogie-based swing pop that followed, well into the 1940's. Their first recording, with Turner already in supreme command of his trademark style, was solely of piano and vocal, and it took place on December 30, 1938. In 1956 Johnson and Turner re-created the classic for Atlantic Records on *Boss of the Blues*. They performed it together the last time in 1967 at a Carnegie Hall reunion concert.

"Piney Brown Blues." The 1940 original recording, attributed to Joe Turner and His Fly Cats, shows Turner's effectiveness in a slow blues framework. The lyrics recall Turner's Kansas City days,

Big Joe Turner. (Hulton Archive/Getty Images)

when Piney Brown ran the Sunset Club. Johnson's piano is superb, and Turner's voice brings effective emotional nuance to his lyrics. This is another song Turner reworked in various settings throughout his long career.

"Rebecca." This 1944 recording is essentially an expansion of "Roll 'Em, Pete" with new lyrics. Guitar and bass augment the duo this time, and despite its close likeness to the earlier song, the unbridled joy of Turner's hoarse vocals and the pounding velocity of Johnson's piano make this a stunning performance. Alternate-take recordings show Turner's knack for changing the lyrics as he went along. This is another song he performed, in some form, until the end.

"Shake, Rattle, and Roll." Though illiterate, Turner had an ear for lyrics, and he could learn new songs quickly. Atlantic Records songwriter and session pianist Jesse Stone was the composer of what became Turner's biggest hit and his major contribution to the early rock-and-roll repertoire. Stone played the repetitive piano figure that introduces the 1954 recording, one that featured a sound unlike that of Turner's recordings of a decade or more before. Nevertheless, Turner is completely comfortable in the genre, and Atlantic Records' genius for matching an old master with fresh material and arrangements gave Turner's career a new lease on life. Thirty years later, Turner was performing this for the children of rock and roll's first fans at punk-rock clubs in Los Angeles and New York.

Musical Legacy

A powerful presence, Turner left a deep imprint on several genres and generations of American vernacular music. The rollicking boogie duets with Johnson are the foundation of his legacy, but his later Atlantic Records efforts proved him to be more adaptable to emergent rock and roll than some of the rhythm-and-blues singers who more immediately preceded it. Turner provided a blueprint for a host of powerful male blues and rhythm-and-blues singers, who have been tagged blues shouters. Despite his influence on the development of both rhythm-and-blues and early rock vocalists, Turner was also expert at singing blues in a jazz setting. Both his early recordings with Tatum and his later ones with Count Basie and others for Pablo

Records offer proof that Turner was remarkably at home in a range of musical styles without being confined by any of them.

Mark Humphrey

Further Reading

Balliett, Whitney. *American Singers: Twenty-seven Portraits in Song*. New York: Oxford University Press, 1988. The veteran *New Yorker* jazz critic had a long and fond association with Turner, and this wonderful chapter, titled "Majesty," captures Turner completely.

Cohn, Lawrence, ed. *Nothing But the Blues: The Music and the Musicians*. New York: Abbeville Press, 1993. This collection of essays and evocative photographs offers a detailed overview of Turner's career in the context of the evolution of urban blues.

Oakley, Giles. *The Devil's Music: A History of the Blues*. New York: Da Capo Press, 1997. Oakley's well-written history includes a fascinating quote from Turner about the development of his singing style.

See also: Basie, Count; Burke, Solomon; Patton, Charley; Tatum, Art; Walker, T-Bone; Waters, Muddy.

Tina Turner

American soul, rhythm-and-blues, and rock singer

With a significant career in recordings and in concerts, Turner is noted for her powerful stage presence, sultry dance moves, and full-throated vocal delivery.

Born: November 26, 1939; Nutbush, Tennessee
Also known as: Anna Mae Bullock (birth name); Queen of Rock and Roll
Member of: Ike and Tina Turner

Principal recordings

ALBUMS (solo): *Tina Turns the Country On!*, 1974; *Acid Queen*, 1975; *Delilah's Power*, 1977; *Rough*, 1978; *Love Explosion*, 1979; *Private Dancer*, 1984; *Mad Max: Beyond Thunderdome*, 1985; *Break*

Every Rule, 1986; *Foreign Affair*, 1989; *Look Me in the Heart*, 1990; *Simply the Best*, 1991; *What's Love Got to Do with It*, 1993; *Wildest Dreams*, 1996; *Good Hearted Woman*, 1998; *Twenty Four Seven*, 1999.

ALBUMS (with Ike and Tina Turner): *The Soul of Ike and Tina Turner*, 1961; *Dance with Ike and Tina Turner*, 1962; *Don't Play Me Cheap*, 1963; *Dynamite*, 1963; *It's Gonna Work Out Fine*, 1963; *Please, Please, Please*, 1963; *Ooh Poo Pah Doo*, 1965; *Ike and Tina Turner and the Raelettes*, 1966; *River Deep, Mountain High*, 1966; *So Fine*, 1968; *Cussin', Cryin', and Carryin' On*, 1969; *Fantastic*, 1969; *Get It Together*, 1969; *Her Man, His Woman*, 1969; *The Hunter*, 1969; *In Person*, 1969; *Outta Season*, 1969; *Come Together*, 1970; *'Nuff Said*, 1971; *Something's Got a Hold on Me*, 1971; *What You Hear Is What You Get*, 1971; *Workin' Together*, 1971; *Feel Good*, 1972; *Let Me Touch Your Mind*, 1973; *The Gospel According to Ike and Tina*, 1974; *The Great Album*, 1974; *Nutbush City Limits*, 1974; *Strange Fruit*, 1974; *Sweet Rhode Island Red*, 1974; *Airwaves*, 1979.

WRITINGS OF INTEREST: *I, Tina: My Life Story*, 1986 (with Kurt Loder).

The Life

Tina Turner was born Anna Mae Bullock in Nutbush, Tennessee. Her father, Floyd Richard Bullock, was a Baptist deacon, and he worked at a factory and on the farm. Her mother, Zelma Currie, was a factory worker. Turner found support for her singing in the Spring Hill Baptist Church choir, which she joined at nine years old. In addition to church services, throughout her teens, she sang with the blues-based Bootsie Whitelow and His String Band, where she developed her formidable voice.

In 1956 Turner and her sister Alline moved to St. Louis after being abandoned by their father. Later, they were reunited with their mother, and Turner launched her career in St. Louis.

She met Ike Turner when she auditioned for his local group, Kings of Rhythm Band. He gave her the stage name Tina, after the comic-book character Sheena: Queen of the Jungle, and they were married in 1960. Throughout that decade, they teamed up with Sun Records and Wall of Sound producer Phil Spector, which paved the way for success.

Although Turner was busy raising Ike's sons, Ike, Jr. and Michael, her son Craig (with saxophone player Raymond Hill), and her son Ronnie (with Ike), the couple spent a lot of time on the road promoting their hit singles. The travel took a toll on both Turners, leading Ike to escalate his use of drugs and alcohol and to abuse Tina.

The addictions and the abuse grew intolerable, and Turner walked out on her husband before a concert in 1976, and their divorce was finalized two years later. Taking a hiatus from her career, Turner restored her personal life, and she converted to Buddhism. In the 1980's, Turner returned to the concert stage a solo artist, and she has continued to record and to perform.

The Music

Years with Ike. After teaming up with Ike, Turner's first major breakthrough came in 1960 when the pair's single "A Fool in Love" hit the charts. Over the next decade, they released a series of albums backed by the Kings of Rhythm Band. In 1966 "River Deep, Mountain High," produced by Spector, was a radio hit. In 1971 the pair's recording of Creedence Clearwater Revival's "Proud Mary," reached number four on the pop charts, and it was followed by the tribute tune to her hometown "Nutbush City Limits."

Based on Turner's success as a lead vocalist, Ike produced *Tina Turns the Country On!* in 1974, although it did not meet with the pair's previous success. This disappointment, coupled with his addictions and abuse, troubled their already fractured relationship. Turner did have some success with her next album, *Acid Queen*, and she appeared in the feature film *Tommy* (1975), based on the Who's rock opera.

Rough *and* Love Explosion. Things proved tumultuous in 1976 following Turner's personal and professional breakup with Ike, though she kept a high public profile by touring. The 1978 album *Rough* was a departure for Turner, with its rock-and-roll sound, and the following year's *Love Explosion* focused on disco. Both failed to resonate with fans.

Private Dancer. In 1982 Turner recorded, with the British Electric Foundation, the Temptations' "Ball of Confusion," followed by Al Green's "Let's Stay Together." That attracted the attention of

Capitol Records, which signed a recording contract with Turner, and on that label she released *Private Dancer* in 1984. The pop crossover project had the chart-topping "What's Love Got to Do with It" (which won Grammy Awards for Record of the Year, Song of the Year, and Best Female Pop Vocal Performance) and "Better Be Good to Me" (which won the Grammy Award for Best Female Rock Vocal Performance).

Fans and critics responded favorably to her comeback. Bryan Adams asked her to sing a duet on "It's Only Love"; Quincy Jones recruited her for the all-star single "We Are the World"; Mick Jagger invited her to Live Aid for duets on "State of Shock" and the Rolling Stones' "It's Only Rock and Roll." She starred alongside Mel Gibson in *Mad Max Beyond Thunderdome* (1985), and she sang the sound-track hit "We Don't Need Another Hero."

Break Every Rule. In 1986 Turner released *Break Every Rule*, known for the hit "Typical Male" and a tour that landed her in the Guinness Book of World Records (for performing in front of the largest paying audience to ever see a single performer, 184,000 fans in Brazil). Although not as commercially successful, 1989's *Foreign Affair* featured her signature song "The Best" and resulted in a major tour over the next two years.

What's Love Got to Do with It. Turner ended her contract with Capitol Records, and she signed a contract with Virgin Records, which released the sound track to her biographical film *What's Love Got to Do with It* (1993). In 1996 *Wildest Dreams* provided several popular singles, including the duet with Barry White on the title cut, a cover of John Waite's "Missing You," and the James Bond film series sound track hit "Goldeneye."

Later Work. In 1999 Turner released *Twenty Four Seven*, featuring a dance-oriented sound. The standout track, "When the Heartache Is Over," was popular in clubs, and Turner gained a new generation of fans. Her 2000 tour in support of that project took in more than eighty million dollars in the United States alone.

After the *Twenty Four Seven* tour, Turner took a break, although she did perform in benefit concerts. She sang in a duet with Phil Collins on the tune "Great Spirits," on the sound track for Walt Disney Studio's *Brother Bear* (2003), and she released a greatest-hits album in 2005 called *All the Best*.

Tina Turner. (AP/Wide World Photos)

Musical Legacy

Turner began her career singing soul and rhythm and blues, and she blazed trails for women artists in her fiery performances, vocal and dance. Turner's collaboration with her husband Ike in the 1960's and 1970's produced enduring hits that are still played on the radio.

Turner's comeback in the 1980's as a solo performer was notable because she expanded her repertoire to other genres and she proved that age was no barrier to success. She demonstrated her ability to thrive during difficult personal circumstances, providing a powerful example of perseverance, and she expressed powerful emotions in songs that appeal to listeners of all ages. Never afraid to change with the times, Turner nevertheless always maintained her artistic integrity.

Andy Argyrakis

Further Reading

Armani, Eddy. *My Twenty-two Years with Tina Turner*. London: John Blake, 1999. A friend and business associate of Turner relates incidents from the artist's life, beginning with her relationship with Ike and covering the years following their divorce and the rebuilding of her career. The account is generally flattering and considered by some reviewers to be too biased, although it does present inside information.

Bego, Mark. *Tina Turner: Break Every Rule*. New York: Taylor, 2005. Named after her album of the same title, this book addresses Turner's early years with Ike, the couple's tumultuous breakup, her solo career, and career as a superstar. It features several personal stories and carefully researched behind-the-scenes-information on her life in and out of the spotlight.

Brackett, Nathan, and Christian Hoard, eds. *The New Rolling Stone Album Guide*. 4th ed. New York: Simon & Schuster, 2004. This fourth edition guide lists all of Ike and Tina Turner's key studio releases and Turner's solo projects through 2000. Includes detailed reviews of albums.

Campbell, Michael, and James Brody. *Rock and Roll: An Introduction*. New York: Schirmer Books, 1999. This historical account of rock and roll includes references to Turner, particularly during her resurgence of the 1980's.

Shaw, Arnold. *Black Popular Music in America: The Singers, Songwriters, and Musicians Who Pioneered the Sounds of American Music*. New York: Schirmer Books, 1986. A highlight of this resource is a discussion of how Turner transcended racial boundaries to become a successful crossover star.

Turner, Tina, with Kurt Loder. *I, Tina*. New York: William Morrow, 1986. This autobiography was the inspiration for the feature film about her life *What's Love Got To Do With It*. The text candidly traces all facets of her relationship with Ike and how she survived their split.

See also: Collins, Phil; Etheridge, Melissa; Hendrix, Jimi; Jagger, Sir Mick; Jones, Quincy; Pickett, Wilson; Santana, Carlos; Spector, Phil; Townshend, Pete; Wynette, Tammy.

Jeff Tweedy

American rock/country singer, guitarist, and songwriter

Tweedy is one of the leading lights of the 1990's alt-country movement, a genre that combined country music with punk-rock influences.

Born: August 25, 1967; Belleville, Illinois
Also known as: Jeffrey Scott Tweedy (full name); Scott Summit
Member of: Uncle Tupelo; Golden Smog; Wilco; Loose Fur

Principal recordings

ALBUMS (with Golden Smog): *On Golden Smog*, 1992; *Down by the Old Mainstream*, 1995; *Weird Tales*, 1998; *Another Fine Day*, 2006.

ALBUMS (with Loose Fur): *Loose Fur*, 2003; *Born Again in the USA*, 2006.

ALBUMS (with Uncle Tupelo): *No Depression*, 1990; *Still Feel Gone*, 1991; *March 16-20, 1992*, 1992; *Anodyne*, 1993.

ALBUMS (with Wilco): *A.M.*, 1995; *Being There*, 1996; *Mermaid Avenue*, 1998 (with Billy Bragg); *Summerteeth*, 1999; *Mermaid Avenue, Vol. II*, 2000 (with Bragg); *Chelsea Walls*, 2002; *Yankee Hotel Foxtrot*, 2002; *A Ghost Is Born*, 2004; *Sky Blue Sky*, 2007.

The Life

Jeffrey Scott Tweedy is the fourth and youngest child of Bob and Jo Ann Tweedy. Tweedy developed a love of music early, listening to his older siblings' records and buying music by such punk bands as X and the Clash. Soon he began playing guitar, and in 1981, while a high school freshman, Tweedy met another budding musician, Jay Farrar, in English class.

Tweedy and Farrar formed a garage band, the Primitives, and in 1987 the band changed its name to Uncle Tupelo. Tweedy dropped out of college to devote more time to the band, as it toured heavily around the Midwest and developed a devoted cult following. The band began receiving notice from music critics and in 1989 signed with a small New York-based independent label, Rockville Records.

The band went on to release three albums that brought it significant acclaim and expanded its cult audience. In 1993 Uncle Tupelo signed with Sire Records, owned by Warner Bros.

However, while on tour that year, Tweedy and Farrar had a falling out, and the band broke up. Tweedy rallied the other members of Uncle Tupelo and formed a new band, Wilco, in 1994. The band signed with Reprise Records, another subsidiary of Warner Bros. The following year Tweedy married Sue Miller, at the time the owner of a Chicago rock club, the Lounge Ax. That same year their son Spencer was born, and later the Tweedys had a second son, Sam.

In 2001 Tweedy and Wilco garnered controversy when Reprise Records executives told them that their proposed new album, *Yankee Hotel Foxtrot*, was not commercial enough to release. Around the same time the band parted ways with Jay Bennett, who had made contributions over the years as a writer, multi-instrumentalist, and engineer. Wilco would not change the album to appease the label and instead arranged to be released from its contract with Reprise Records, taking the rights to the album with them. This event brought the band a great deal of press. Many music writers who had championed the band over the years wrote articles about the band's dispute with Reprise Records, positioning the band as an innovative victim of an industry more concerned with profits than artistic integrity. The band streamed the album—which had already spread over the Internet through peer-to-peer file-sharing networks such as Napster—on its Web site. In 2002 *I Am Trying to Break Your Heart*, a documentary detailing the making of the album and the controversies that occurred, was released.

In 2004, on the eve of a Wilco tour, Tweedy checked into a drug rehabilitation center, seeking treatment for an addiction to painkillers, which he had used to combat migraine headaches. Since then, the band has continued to tour and record successfully. Tweedy also frequently performs live as a solo artist.

The Music

No Depression. Tweedy's first major released work was the first Uncle Tupelo album, *No Depression*. The band's mix of country and folk music played with punk-rock volume proved to be heavily influential throughout the 1990's. The album took its name from the 1936 Carter Family song "No Depression in Heaven" (which the band also covered on the album). The album and band would soon inspire a wellspring of artists and fans interested in a raw approach to country music.

March 16-20, 1992. The more Uncle Tupelo played and recorded, the more attention it received from the industry. After the success of Nirvana in late 1991, major labels started signing underground and punk-influenced rock bands. While much of the music of this time was characterized by loud guitars and harsh sounds, Uncle Tupelo made a distinctive change for its third album, *March 16-20, 1992*. With R.E.M. guitarist Peter Buck serving as producer, the band made an entirely acoustic album. The album further impressed critics and fans by displaying the band's command of traditional songs.

Being There. By 1996 Tweedy and Farrar had parted ways, and Uncle Tupelo was no more.

Jeff Tweedy. (AP/Wide World Photos)

Tweedy had assembled the band Wilco, but many felt it was not until Wilco's second album, *Being There*, that Tweedy truly moved on from the legacy of his previous band. *Being There* was a double album of Tweedy compositions that drew from a diverse variety of influences and a wider palette of sounds. Wilco's guitarist Bennett assumed keyboard duties as well, and the band began experimenting in the studio more, adding guitar feedback and radio static to songs. This was a marked departure from Uncle Tupelo, who often recorded albums completely live. *Being There* was not a huge commercial success, but it garnered a wide amount of critical praise and helped introduce Wilco to a new audience.

Mermaid Avenue. Tweedy and Wilco gathered more attention with their next project. British folk-rocker Billy Bragg received an invitation from Nora Guthrie, daughter of the late Woody Guthrie, to go through the large archives of lyrics to songs her father had never finished, write new music for them, and record the songs. Bragg invited Wilco to be his backing band, and soon Tweedy and Bennett were also poring over the Guthrie archives, picking lyrics that appealed to them and setting them to music. The results came out on two albums, *Mermaid Avenue* and *Mermaid Avenue Vol. II*. Bragg and Wilco received praise for their work in bringing new light to Guthrie's legacy. *Mermaid Avenue* received a Grammy nomination for Best Contemporary Folk Album.

Yankee Hotel Foxtrot. In 2000 Tweedy and Wilco began working on the album that would change almost everything about the band: *Yankee Hotel Foxtrot*. Tweedy brought in a new drummer, Glenn Kotche, and the band further developed the experimental aspects of their sound. The album boldly mixed sounds, from gentle acoustic guitars to long waves of sonic noise. Tweedy's lyrics explored themes of American identity. The band, having streamed the album on its Web site, went on tour shortly after the terrorist attacks on September 11, 2001. At the time many writers and fans noted the prescient nature of Tweedy's lyrics on *Yankee Hotel Foxtrot*. When the album was finally released, by Nonesuch Records in April, 2002, it debuted on the *Billboard* charts at number twelve. It was Tweedy's most immediately successful album yet.

Yankee Hotel Foxtrot raised Tweedy's profile considerably. Subsequent Wilco albums and tours were successful, and Tweedy also began touring more as a solo artist. One of his tours was chronicled in a 2006 documentary, *Sunken Treasure*. He embarked on other projects as well: He and Kotche formed a side band called Loose Fur with experimental musician Jim O'Rourke. They released two albums, *Loose Fur* and *Born Again in the USA*. In 2004 Tweedy published a book of poetry, *Adult Head*. Over the years, Tweedy has taken part in other side bands, such as Golden Smog and the Minus Five. Wilco's 2007 album, *Sky Blue Sky*, debuted at number one on the *Billboard* charts, another first for Tweedy and the band.

Musical Legacy

With his initial works with Uncle Tupelo and Wilco, Tweedy brought to the forefront a mix of country and rock. While he was not the first to mix these genres, the music he made with those bands inspired many other musicians and writers. Bands such as the Jayhawks, Whiskeytown (led by Ryan Adams), and the Old 97's began playing a similar style of music. In 1994 an America Online message board called "No Depression" discussing Uncle Tupelo and other bands emerged, and later a magazine to cover the music, also called *No Depression*, was launched. Though the music Tweedy made in this period was not commercially successful, it proved to be a viable alternative to both mainstream country and rock music.

As Wilco progressed, Tweedy's reputation evolved. As the band went through different sounds and lineups, Tweedy gained respect from some fans, musicians, and critics for his willingness to change his sound. On the other hand, he also collected criticism from those who preferred his earlier work. In this light he can be seen in company with such artists as Bob Dylan, who assertively challenged perceptions of what defined his style of music.

After *Yankee Hotel Foxtrot*, Tweedy and Wilco moved to a new level of success. The follow-up album, *A Ghost Is Born*, debuted in the *Billboard* Top 10 and eventually won the band their first Grammy Awards, for Best Alternative Album and Best Recording Package.

Michael Pelusi

Further Reading

Alden, Grant, and Peter Blackstock, eds. *The Best of "No Depression": Writing About American Music.* Austin: University of Texas Press, 2005. This anthology collects artist profiles from *No Depression*, the famous alt-country magazine that took its name from the first Uncle Tupelo album. The book contains an article about Wilco, chronicling the making and release of *Yankee Hotel Foxtrot.* There is also a piece about Farrar, Tweedy's former bandmate in Uncle Tupelo.

DeRogatis, Jim, and Carmel Carrillo, eds. *Kill Your Idols: A New Generation of Rock Writers.* Fort Lee, N.J.: Barricade Books, 2004. DeRogatis and Carrillo gathered a group of rock critics to write essays deconstructing and criticizing often-praised rock albums. *Yankee Hotel Foxtrot* is among the albums examined.

Kot, Greg. *Wilco: Learning How to Die.* New York: Broadway Books, 2004. Tells Wilco's story and contains a thorough biography of Tweedy, covering his childhood and adolescence, as well as Uncle Tupelo. Kot, a rock critic for the *Chicago Tribune*, interviewed Tweedy and nearly all of his bandmates from over the years, as well as family, friends, producers, and record executives.

Tweedy, Jeff. *Adult Head.* Lincoln, Nebr.: Zoo Press, 2004. Tweedy's first book is a collection of poetry.

Wilco, Dan Nadel, Peter Buchanan-Smith, Rick Moody, and Fred Tomaselli. *The Wilco Book.* New York: Picturebox, 2004. The members of Wilco collaborated with artists, writers, and musicians to produce this highly unusual book. Along with copious photographs and illustrations, the book contains the band's ruminations on writing, recording, and performing. Moody contributes an essay on the band's music. The book also comes with a compact disc of previously unreleased music.

See also: Carter, Maybelle; Guthrie, Woody.

Conway Twitty

American country and rockabilly singer-songwriter

During a career that spanned several decades, Twitty established himself as one of the most successful and durable stars of country music. With his emotional and sensual approach to singing, he helped to bring adult issues to country music. As a highly charismatic figure, he is remembered not only for his musical diversity and brilliance as a songwriter but also for his sensitivity as an entertainer.

Born: September 1, 1933; Friars Point, Mississippi
Died: June 5, 1993; Springfield, Missouri
Also known as: Harold Lloyd Jenkins (birth name); High Priest of Country Music

Principal recordings

ALBUMS: *Conway Twitty Sings*, 1958; *Saturday Night with Conway Twitty*, 1959; *Lonely Blue Boy*, 1960; *The Conway Twitty Touch*, 1961; *The Rock 'n' Roll Story*, 1961; *Portrait of a Fool and Others*, 1962; *Hit the Road*, 1964; *Look into My Teardrops*, 1966; *Here's Conway Twitty*, 1968; *Next in Line*, 1968; *Darling, You Know I Wouldn't Lie*, 1969; *I Love You More Today*, 1969; *You Can't Take Country out of Conway*, 1969; *Hello Darlin'*, 1970; *To See My Angel Cry*, 1970; *How Much More Can She Stand*, 1971; *I Wonder What She'll Think About Me Leaving*, 1971; *Lead Me On*, 1971 (with Loretta Lynn); *We Only Make Believe*, 1971 (with Lynn); *Conway Twitty*, 1972; *Conway Twitty Sings the Blues*, 1972; *I Can't See Me Without You*, 1972; *Shake It Up*, 1972; *Clinging to a Saving Hand*, 1973; *I Can's Stop Loving You*, 1973; *She Needs Someone to Hold Her*, 1973; *Who Will Pray for Me*, 1973; *You've Never Been This Far Before*, 1973; *Country Partners*, 1974 (with Lynn); *Honky Tonk Angel*, 1974; *I'm Not Through Loving You Yet*, 1974; *Never Ending Song of Love*, 1974; *Feelin's*, 1975 (with Lynn); *High Priest of Country Music*, 1975; *Linda on My Mind*, 1975; *Star Spangled Songs*, 1975; *This Time I've Hurt Her More*, 1975; *Now and Then*, 1976; *Twitty*, 1976; *United Talent*, 1976 (with Lynn); *Dynamic Duo*, 1977 (with Lynn); *I've Already Loved You in*

My Mind, 1977; *Play, Guitar, Play*, 1977; *Conway*, 1978; *Conway Twitty Country*, 1978; *Georgia Keeps Pulling on My Ring*, 1978; *Honky Tonk Heroes*, 1978 (with Lynn); *Country Rock*, 1979; *Cross Winds*, 1979; *Diamond Duet*, 1980 (with Lynn); *Heart and Soul*, 1980; *Rest Your Love on Me*, 1980; *Mr. T.*, 1981; *Two's a Party*, 1981 (with Lynn); *Dream Maker*, 1982; *Southern Comfort*, 1982; *Lost in the Feeling*, 1983; *Merry Twismas*, 1983; *By Heart*, 1984; *Conway Twitty and Loretta Lynn*, 1984 (with Lynn); *Chasin' Rainbows*, 1985; *Don't Call Him a Cowboy*, 1985; *A Night with Conway Twitty*, 1986; *Fallin' for You for Years*, 1986; *Borderline*, 1987; *Still in Your Dreams*, 1988; *House on Old Lonesome Road*, 1989; *Crazy in Love*, 1990; *Even Now*, 1991; *Country Gospel Greats*, 1992 (with Lynn); *Final Touches*, 1993.

The Life

Conway Twitty was born Harold Lloyd Jenkins to Floyd Jenkins and Velma McGinnis Jenkins on September 1, 1933, in Friars Point, Mississippi. He was given the name "Harold Lloyd" in honor of the silent film star of the same name. In addition to being a cotton farmer, his father was the captain of a small ferryboat that carried passengers across the Mississippi River from Friars Point to Helena, Arkansas.

As a young child, Twitty was taught by his father to play the guitar. He loved listening to country music on the jukebox and to gospel music that he heard from a local black church. The family moved to Helena, Arkansas, when he was ten. He became so good on the guitar that by the time of the move to Helena Twitty had begun appearing on local radio stations. At this time, he formed his first band, the Phillips County Ramblers. The family was very poor, and young Twitty had to work in order to help purchase clothes for his sister and brother. By the age of twelve, he was playing on a weekly radio show on KFFA in Helena. In addition to

music, Twitty proved himself to be an excellent baseball player in high school. He was so good at baseball that the Philadelphia Phillies offered to sign him to a contract after he had graduated from high school.

In 1954, Twitty was drafted into the United States Army. While stationed in Japan, he played on an Army baseball team and formed a band, the Cimmarons. He remained in the Army from 1954 to 1956. During his time in the military, Elvis Presley burst onto the music scene and became a monumental phenomenon. Twitty also became caught up in the rockabilly style that had been popularized by Presley and Carl Perkins. Twitty returned to the United States in 1956. While he could have signed with the Phillies to play professional baseball, he decided that he would rather become a professional musician. He would have one of the most extraordinary music careers in the history of popular music.

During his lifetime, Twitty was married three times. He was married to Ellen Matthews from 1953 to 1954. From 1955 to 1985, he was married to Temple Maxine Jaco Medley; they had three children. In 1987, Twitty married Dolores Virginia Henry. Tragically, he died in 1993 as a result of an abdominal aortic aneurysm.

Conway Twitty. (AP/Wide World Photos)

The Music

After being discharged from the Army in 1956, Twitty was signed with Sun Records by the legendary figure Sam Phillips. Although Twitty recorded several songs for Sun Records, none of them was released. Elvis Presley also recorded for Sun Records, and Twitty attempted to work in his rockabilly style.

Creating a Rock Persona. At this point in time, the persona of Conway Twitty had not been created. He recorded as Harold Jenkins, but he did not have the success that he had envisioned. He came to the conclusion that, in order to become a rock star, he needed the right professional name. After looking at a map of the United States, he picked the town of Conway, Arkansas, and the town of Twitty, Texas, to form his new name. With this, Conway Twitty was born.

Twitty's band was given the name the Twitty Birds. In 1957, he signed with Mercury Records and began recording as Conway Twitty, releasing the song "I Need Your Lovin." This was the only single that charted for him with Mercury, so he was released from the label.

In 1958, Twitty signed with Metro-Goldwyn-Mayer (MGM). He finally found the success that he desired with the release of the single "It's Only Make Believe." This single went to number one in many countries around the world and sold more than eight million copies. In the United States, "It's Only Make Believe" went to number one on the pop, country, and blues singles charts. With this single, Twitty became a rockabilly star in his own right.

For the next few years, Twitty continued to release hit singles as a rock musician. Although he had become a successful rock musician, he was not totally satisfied with his achievements. During this period, he had been writing country songs for other recording stars. Not completely comfortable as a rock performer, by the mid-1960's Twitty believed that it was time for him to be true to himself and become a country artist. After letting his contract with MGM expire, he signed with producer Owen Bradley of Decca Records as a country musician.

Going Country. In 1968, Twitty finally had his first number-one country single with "Next in Line." This hit was merely the first of his amazing string of forty-two number-one hits on the *Billboard* country singles charts. As a wonderful songwriter in his own right, Twitty wrote nineteen of his number-one hits himself. Some of the most famous include "Hello Darlin'," "Goodbye Time," "You've Never Been This Far Before," "Linda on My Mind," and "Tight Fittin' Jeans." He also sang many duets with the legendary country artist Loretta Lynn. This partnership became highly successful; together, Twitty and Lynn recorded such country classics as "After the Fire Is Gone," "Lead Me On," and "Louisiana Woman, Mississippi Man."

At his concerts, Twitty was such a consummate entertainer that he earned the nickname the High Priest of Country Music. He was adored by thousands of female fans who considered seeing Twitty in concert to be almost a religious experience. By the 1980's, he had broadened his approach to country music by including elements of rock music. Always an emotional singer, Twitty had a way of connecting with his audience that few performers could equal. With his deep, smooth voice, he was a natural at delivering a passionate ballad. He remained active into the early 1990's with such Top 10 singles as "Crazy in Love" and "I Couldn't See You Leavin'."

Musical Legacy

During his illustrious career, Twitty had a total of fifty-five number-one singles on various music charts. As a songwriter, singer, producer, and entertainer, he was loved by millions of fans. He was honored with more than one hundred awards. His musical partnership with Loretta Lynn garnered several top-selling singles and awards. He was elected to the Country Music Hall of Fame in 1999. At the forty-third annual Academy of Country Music Awards in 2008, the late Conway Twitty was honored with the Cliffie Stone Pioneer Award.

Jeffry Jensen

Further Reading

Cross, Wilbur, and Michael Kosser. *The Conway Twitty Story: An Authorized Biography*. Garden City, N.Y.: Doubleday, 1986. A biography that concentrates on Twitty's work ethic, which took him from an impoverished average guy to music legend.

Escott, Colin. *The Conway Twitty Rock 'n Roll Years*. Bremen, West Germany: Bear Family Records,

1985. A short yet solid account of Twitty's career. Includes photographs and a discography by Richard Weige.

————. "It's Only Make Believe: Conway Twitty." In *All Roots Lead to Rock: Legends of Early Rock 'n' Roll, a Bear Family Reader*, edited by Colin Escott. New York: Schirmer Books, 1999. A critical essay on Twitty's importance.

Wilson, Shirley. *From Aaron Jenkins to Harold Jenkins: Conway Twitty's Roots*. Hendersonville, Tenn.: S. Wilson, 1985. A valuable examination of Twitty's family history.

See also: Lynn, Loretta; Milsap, Ronnie; Presley, Elvis.

McCoy Tyner

American jazz pianist and songwriter

An influential jazz pianist, Tyner is noted for his modal approach to improvisation, his explosive left-hand technique, and his spiritual awareness at the keyboard.

Born: December 11, 1938; Philadelphia, Pennsylvania
Also known as: Alfred McCoy Tyner (full name); Sulaimon Saud
Member of: The John Coltrane Quartet

Principal recordings

ALBUMS (solo): *Inception*, 1962; *Nights of Ballads and Blues*, 1963; *The Real McCoy*, 1967; *Expansions*, 1968; *Asante*, 1970; *Sahara*, 1970; *Four Times Four*, 1976; *Supertrios*, 1977; *Looking Out*, 1982; *It's About Time*, 1985 (with Jackie McLean); *Bon Voyage*, 1987 (with the McCoy Tyner Trio); *Uptown/Downtown*, 1988 (with the McCoy Tyner Big Band); *Things Ain't What They Used to Be*, 1989; *New York Reunion*, 1991 (with the McCoy Tyner Quartet); *The Turning Point*, 1991 (with the McCoy Tyner Big Band); *Manhattan Moods*, 1993 (with Bobby Hutcherson); *Infinity*, 1995; *McCoy Tyner and the Latin All-Stars*, 1999 (with others); *McCoy Tyner with Stanley Clarke and Al Foster*, 2000; *Suddenly*, 2000; *Land of

Giants, 2003; *Illuminations*, 2004; *Monk's Dream*, 2004.

ALBUMS (with the John Coltrane Quartet): *The Avant-Garde*, 1960; *Coltrane's Sound*, 1960; *My Favorite Things*, 1960; *Africa/Brass*, 1961; *Coltrane Jazz*, 1961; *Olé*, 1961; *Ballads*, 1962; *Coltrane Plays the Blues*, 1962; *Standard Coltrane*, 1962; *Impressions*, 1963; *John Coltrane and Johnny Hartman*, 1963; *Crescent*, 1964; *A Love Supreme*, 1964; *Ascension*, 1965; *First Meditations*, 1965; *The John Coltrane Quartet Plays*, 1965; *Kulu Sé Mama*, 1965; *Om*, 1965; *Sun Ship*, 1965; *Transition*, 1965.

The Life

Alfred McCoy Tyner (TI-nur) was born in 1938 in Philadelphia, where his mother first encouraged him in music. At thirteen, Tyner began formal piano study, and he subsequently enrolled in the Granoff School of Music, where he studied harmony and theory. Two early influences were his neighbors, the jazz pianist brothers Bud and Richard Powell. In 1955 Tyner met John Coltrane, and the two formed a strong musical relationship. In the mid-1950's, Tyner converted to Islam, and he adopted the Muslim name Sulaimon Saud.

In 1959 Tyner joined the Benny Golson-Art Farmer Jazztet, recording with the group on its 1960 Argo Records debut *Meet the Jazztet*. Tyner and Coltrane reunited in 1960; with a rotating cast of drummers and bassists (mainly Elvin Jones and Jimmy Garrison), they formed the John Coltrane Quartet, a group that within five years made several landmark recordings in jazz, including *My Favorite Things* and *A Love Supreme*.

Even before leaving Coltrane's quartet in 1965, Tyner had been featured on a number of notable artist debuts for Blue Note records. By the end of the 1960's, Tyner could claim album credits for nearly forty Blue Note releases, along with several releases for Impulse Records as a bandleader.

Beginning in the 1970's, Tyner performed and recorded extensively as a leader, both in trio and in big band settings, many of which explored music of diverse cultures, especially Brazilian, African, and Afro-Caribbean music. Although he has distanced himself from any religious denomination, themes of spirituality remained pervasive in Tyner's music throughout his career.

The Music

Tyner generally avoids analytical and theoretical descriptions of his music, citing instead an approach to jazz that is based on harnessing religious and spiritual energy. While this theological basis for Tyner's musical philosophy is evident in meditative recordings such as *A Love Supreme* and *Sahara*, his live performances have been equally noted for capturing the spiritual aspects of his musical persona. His playing is most often described as powerful and athletic. Melodically, Tyner often employs rapid flourishes of pentatonic and modal scales in his improvisations; harmonically, he emphasizes fourths and fifths, often superimposing these intervals to create ambient polymodal harmonic landscapes. As a pianist, Tyner possesses a technical command of the instrument rarely surpassed in jazz, illustrated in part by his formidable left-hand technique. As a composer, Tyner explores a wide range of textures, many of them inspired by composers such as Igor Stravinsky and Duke Ellington. His big band arrangements are noted for their lush, impressionistic, and well-balanced qualities.

The John Coltrane Quartet. The ability to dismantle a working hierarchy of instrumentalists within a jazz combo proved to be a revolutionary aspect of Coltrane's groups of the early 1960's. Performing on this level of equality provided Tyner the opportunity to explore an essentially new role for the piano in jazz, one that was first executed on the 1960 Atlantic Records album *My Favorite Things*. Here Tyner eschews the traditional role of piano accompanist in favor of adopting an active yet complementary voice to the group. Tyner's solo on the album's title track features the pianist at his most inventive, blending modal harmonies with a series of syncopated vamps that provide Richard Davis (bass) and Jones (drums) ample room for musical interplay. Tyner's adventurous and dynamic playing on *My Favorite Things* is contrasted with an inspired lyricism on the quartet's ballad albums, *Ballads* and *John Coltrane and Johnny Hartman*. The dual nature of Tyner's playing on these early recordings—powerful and rhythmic, yet sensitive and lyrical—meet somewhere halfway on the spiritually oriented albums of the quartet, most notably *A Love Supreme* and *Transition*.

McCoy Tyner. (AP/Wide World Photos)

Blue Note Records. Often overlooked in Tyner's career (because of the overshadowing legacy of the John Coltrane Quartet) is his work as a sideman and soloist for Blue Note Records during the 1960's. The Blue Note debuts of Joe Henderson (*Page One*, 1963) and Wayne Shorter (*Night Dreamer*, 1964) constitute landmark achievements in recorded jazz, and Tyner's unmistakable presence on these albums can be credited as a large part of their appeal and success. Demonstrated on these albums is Tyner's unique ability to adapt to others' playing style while retaining the individual components of his sound (rhythmic and directional modal lines and active parallel chords in the lower registers).

Sahara. Tyner launched his solo career for Blue Note with 1967's *The Real McCoy*, featuring Henderson on saxophone. Despite the maturity and confidence of Tyner's playing in the late 1960's, his musical vision reached unprecedented levels in

1972 with Milestone Records' release of *Sahara*, often viewed as the pianist's most virtuosic and inspired album. Arranged as a series of musical reflections on the African landscape, the Grammy Award-winning *Sahara* features Tyner and his bandmates in dramatic musical form. Fast tempi ("Rebirth") and eruptive musical outbursts ("Ebony Queen") progress alongside lengthy, contemplative piano solos ("A Prayer for My Family"), including Tyner playing the Japanese koto and drummer Alphonse Mouzon incorporating an array of African and Latin American percussion.

McCoy Tyner Big Band. Tyner's career entered a new musical phase in the 1980's with the McCoy Tyner Big Band, a group that quickly garnered a strong New York City following, with the group's appearance at such venues as the Village Vanguard and the Blue Note. The success of the big band, featuring Tyner as a pianist, composer, and arranger, resulted in two Grammy Awards, and it demonstrated Tyner's comprehensive and consummate musicianship.

Musical Legacy

Tyner's albums *Land of Giants* and *Illuminations* showcase Tyner's continued collaboration with old partners (Gary Bartz, Bobby Hutcherson) and interest in newer talent (Christian McBride, Eric Harland). Tyner is a four-time Grammy Award winner, with *Illuminations* being honored as Best Jazz Instrumental Album, Individual or Group. In high demand for jazz festivals and music venues around the world, Tyner was a National Endowment for the Arts Jazz Master award recipient in 2002, and he received an honorary doctorate of music degree from the Berklee College of Music in 2005.

Cory M. Gavito

Further Reading

Kahn, Ashley. *The House That Trane Built: The Story of Impulse Records*. New York: W. W. Norton, 2006. Kahn discusses Tyner's and the John Coltrane Quartet's recordings for Impulse Records within the context of the label's growing status during the 1960's.

Kofsky, Frank. *John Coltrane and the Jazz Revolution in the 1960's*. New York: Pathfinder, 1992. Providing a social and cultural context for the 1960's John Coltrane Quartet, Kofsky illuminates Tyner's role in the rhythm section ("Jazz Rhythm in the Coltrane Quartet"), and he provides an interview featuring Tyner discussing the music of the legendary group.

Lyons, Len. "McCoy Tyner." In *The Great Pianists: Speaking of Their Lives and Music*. New York: William Morrow, 1983. In an in-depth mid-1970's interview, Tyner places his early Philadelphia training in perspective, and he offers personal reflection on religion, spirituality, orchestration, and future musical projects.

Sidran, Ben. "McCoy Tyner." In *Talking Jazz: An Oral History*. New York: Da Capo Press, 1995. Sidran's interview with Tyner provides a rare glimpse into the technical aspects of the pianist's musical language.

Tyner, McCoy, and Stanley Dance. "Tyner Talks." *Down Beat* 24 (October, 1963). Tyner describes the intimate nature of the recordings and the performances of Coltrane's 1960's groups in this early interview.

See also: Bacharach, Burt; Coltrane, John; Corea, Chick; Ellington, Duke; Grappelli, Stéphane; Jarrett, Keith; Jones, Elvin; Palmieri, Eddie; Powell, Bud; Shorter, Wayne; Stravinsky, Igor.

U

Umm Kulthum

Egyptian world music singer

Kulthum rose from poverty in the dusty peasant village in Egypt where she was born to dazzle audiences as far away as Paris with her songs, encompassing Western popular and art music, Arab folk music, and religious music and exhibiting strong Arab and Muslim roots.

Born: December 31, 1898; Tamy al-Zahayrah, Egypt
Died: February 3, 1975; Cairo, Egypt
Also known as: Umm Kulthum Ebrahim Elbeltagi (birth name); Oum Kalthoum

Principal recordings

ALBUMS: *Anta dumri*, 1994; *El soulasia el mokodassa*, 1994; *Keset el ams*, 1994.

SINGLES: "Ana ʿalʾa keefak," 1924; "Il-Khalaaʾah," 1924; "Ma li futint," 1924; "Ya karawan," 1925; "In kuntu assamih," 1928; "Zekrayat," 1930 ("Memories"); "Ouzkourini," 1939; "Raq el habib," 1941 ("The Servitude of Love"); "Hasibak lel-zaman," 1957; "Dalili ehtar," 1958; "Hagartak," 1959 ("I Abandoned You"); "Howwa sahih el-hawa ghallab," 1960; "Kull laylah wi-kull yum (betfakkar fi min?)," 1962; "Arak asey al-damii," 1964; "Siret el-hobb," 1964 ("Tale of Love"); "Amal hayati," 1965 ("Hope of My Life"); "Beeid annak," 1965 ("Away from You"); "Enta el-hobb," 1965 ("You Are My Love"); "Al-Atlal," 1966 ("The Ruins"); "Fakkarooni," 1966 ("They Reminded Me"); "Hadith al-rouh," 1967 ("The Talk of the Soul"); "Toof we shoof," 1967; "Alf leila we leila," 1969 ("One Thousand and One Nights"); "Aqbal al-layl," 1969; "Tareeq wahed," 1969; "Aghadan alqak," 1971; "Ya msaharni," 1972; "Hakam aleina el-hawa," 1973; "Leilet Hobb," 1973 ("Night of Love").

The Life

The father of Umm Kulthum (ewm KUHL-thuhm), al-Shaykh Ibrahim al-Sayyid al-Baltiji, was the devout leader of his village mosque, and her mother was a homemaker. She had a sister, Sayidda, ten years older, and a brother, Khalid, one year older. The family home was in the village of Tamy al-Zahayra near the city of al-Sinbillawayn in the delta province of Daqahliyya. At the age of five, Umm Kulthum was sent to the local Qurʾan school, where she learned to recite Qurʾānic Arabic with proper enunciation and to sing some of the standard religious songs based on the Prophet Muhammad's life. Although these songs were usually sung by men, women sometimes performed them, and so when her brother was ill, Kulthum would sing in his place. Her skill soon identified her as min al-mashayikh (reared among the sheikhs).

After her debut between the ages of five and eight at the home of the village leader, Kulthum started performing at events in neighboring villages, earning the equivalent of fifty cents or more. Traveling around as a public performer meant contact with the disreputable elements of society, and it led to her attentive father's often dressing her as a boy. By 1920 Kulthum's fee had jumped to fifty dollars. With the encouragement of the noted singer Zakariyya Ahmad and with the patronage of one of Cairo's prominent families, Kulthum and her family moved to Cairo sometime in the early 1920's. She began singing in theaters at intermissions, eventually moving up from working-class neighborhoods to the music halls of the main theater district. Between 1924 and 1926 Kulthum released fourteen recordings on Odeon Records, but in 1926 she left Odeon Records to sign a contract with Gramophone Records, which paid her five hundred dollars per disc with a yearly retainer of ten thousand dollars.

Various physical ailments plagued Kulthum after 1937, and in 1946, beset with personal problems, she suffered a serious depression. Treatment at Bethesda Naval Hospital in Maryland in 1949 was followed by marriage to Dr. Hasan al-Hafnawi in 1954 and by a close friendship with Abdel Nasser, the Egyptian prime minister. In the 1960's, she became interested in politics, contributing more than two million dollars to the Egyptian government and earning the resentment of those who saw her as too conservative. Further health problems culminated in the kidney disease that led to her death in 1975. A crowd of mourners carried her body through the streets of Cairo for three hours before taking it to its burial place.

The Music

Umm Kulthum's songs represent a mixture of styles, although her musical idiom has Arab and Muslim roots. It is commonly thought of as asil, or authentic, and it is seen as a contribution to Egyptian cultural life. Her exceptional vocal power and its uniform quality enabled Kulthum to give performances of great length. Her originality inspired the development of both a neoclassical mode of expression and a populist one, and much of this inspiration derived from her close involvement with the composition of the works she sang and her control over the circumstances under which she composed.

Early Works. Kulthum explained that she began singing by imitating her father, who sang religious songs at weddings in their village. When she started singing in Cairo, she performed traditional religious pieces unaccompanied by instruments. Audiences often requested popular songs of the day, and thus she learned many lighthearted love songs in colloquial Arabic. Sophisticated listeners complained of the vapidity of these simple songs, known as taqatiq, but she complemented these with qasaid, which were often long, rhyming poems honoring the Prophet, and also some new qasaid on romantic themes. One of the most popular of these early love songs was "Ma li futint." Other favorites included the taqatiq "Ana ʿalʾa keefak" and "il-Khalaaʾah," a composition judged in bad taste. Kulthum's career continued to prosper; in the 1940's, she reached the peak of her success, singing ughniyyat, love songs combining vocal instrumental sections, and the neoclassical qasaid.

"In kuntu assamih." Kulthum adopted a new genre in the late 1920's, a series of monologues composed for her by al-Qasabji and Ahmad Rami, described as virtuosic, dramatic, romantic, and innovative in genre and style. In classical practice, a composer basically works up from the lower range

of the chosen melodic mode and eventually returns to the original mode. However, in "In kuntu assamih" al-Qasabji introduced triadic passages into the instrumental introduction that listeners knowledgeable about European classical musical found modern and operatic. The recording of "In kuntu assamih" sold in great numbers, and the monologue came to be identified with Kulthum. The texts of these monologues featured themes on love lost and individual struggle.

Widad. *Widad* was the first of six films that Kulthum made, starting in 1935. She invented a story about a singing slave girl in thirteenth century Egypt, and Rami wrote the script. The leading male roles were played by well-known stars, and the production was so successful that it became the first Egyptian entry in an international film festival in London. Kulthum's motion pictures featured exotic locales with exciting characters involved in romantic plots that developed themes of good triumphing over evil. The style of her films was strictly Hollywood. Of her other five films, only a version of the opera *Aida* (1871) made in 1942 failed; her last was *Fatma* (1947), a popular and blatantly didactic production dramatizing the misbehavior of the wealthy, the virtues of closeness with friends and family, and the honor of the woman who resists temptation.

"Al-Atlal." "Al-Atlal" was Kulthum's signature song. It was produced by the famous songwriter Riyad al-Sunbati, a talented composer who enjoyed innovation and who featured a piano in "Arak asey al-damii," the only one of Kulthum's songs to include that instrument. Kulthum showed great respect for al-Sunbati, and she considered him superior to other writers in treating difficult Arabic poems and in expressing their meanings in his melodic adaptations. He understood Kulthum's voice, and he composed with her abilities in mind. She sang "al-Atlal" in Paris in 1967 and in just about every concert she gave before Arab audiences. The words of "al-Atlal" came from two qasaid by the Egyptian poet Ibrahim Naji, mainly from "al-Atlal" (traces) and less so from "al-Wida" (the farewell). "Al-Atlal" was a neoclassical qasaid relying on the old theme of a wanderer in the desert looking for a lost lover or for some other source of loneliness and bereavement, subject matter for which Naji was well known.

Kulthum appropriated "al-Atlal" for her own purposes, streamlining Naji's quatrains by taking the third line out of each. She rearranged the order of Naji's stanzas, replaced a few words, and inserted lines from Naji's "al-Wida" into the middle of the poem. Not all critics appreciated the freedom that Kulthum took with Naji's text. One argued that the original qasaid was not just a lyric, but it was a narrative that recorded events in a specific order. Kulthum's answer to this criticism was that the number and order of lines in the qasaid was less important than the singer's expression of the poet's meaning, a sentiment apparently justified by the work's popularity.

Musical Legacy

Kulthum's reputation lives on in the stories of her life written for children and in the many recordings of her work sold worldwide. Her solid business sense enabled her to demand large fees, and in advancing her own career commercially she achieved an authority that raised the level of respect for singers and that smoothed the way for other women in her profession. Her broad contributions to Egyptian culture made her a historic figure, and her voice resonated with her country's indigenous values. Her songs are now turath, part of Egyptian heritage.

Frank Day

Further Reading

Danielson, Virginia. "Artists and Entrepreneurs: Female Singers in Cairo During the 1920's." In *Women in Middle Eastern History: Shifting Boundaries in Sex and Gender*, edited by Nikki R. Keddie and Beth Baron. New Haven, Conn.: Yale University Press, 1991. An early version of a subject Danielson would explore in her biography of Kulthum.

_____. *The Voice of Egypt: Umm Kulthum, Arabic Song, and Egyptian Society in the Twentieth Century*. Chicago: University of Chicago Press, 1997. A comprehensive, prize-winning study of Kulthum and the society in which she flourished. Includes illustrations, bibliography, and glossary.

Fernea, Elizabeth Warock, and Basima Qattan Bezirgan, eds. *Middle Eastern Muslim Women Speak*. Austin: University of Texas Press, 1977. One of the autobiographical statements in this volume is by Kulthum.

Nassib, Sélim. *I Loved You for Your Voice*. Translated by Alison Anderson. New York: Europa Editions, 2006. A novel based on the life of Kulthum, told in the first person by Rami, the poet-librettist who wrote many of the songs she performed.

See also: Khan, Ali Akbar; Khan, Nusrat Fateh Ali; Kuti, Fela; Makeba, Miriam; Shabalala, Joseph; Shankar, Ravi.

V

Ritchie Valens

American rock singer, songwriter, and guitarist

A rock-and-roll star, Valens, despite a professional career that was tragically cut short, served as an inspiration to musicians of Hispanic origin.

Born: May 13, 1941; Pacoima, California
Died: February 3, 1959; Clear Lake, Iowa
Also known as: Richard Steven Valenzuela (birth name)

Principal recordings

ALBUMS: *Ritchie Valens*, 1959; *In Concert at Pacoima Jr. High*, 1960; *Ritchie*, 1963.
SINGLES: "Come on, Let's Go," 1958; "Donna," 1958; "Framed," 1958; "La Bamba," 1958; "Big Baby Blues," 1959; "Fast Freight," 1959; "In a Turkish Town," 1959; "Little Girl," 1959; "Stay Beside Me," 1959; "That's My Little Suzie," 1959; "We Belong Together," 1959; "Cry, Cry, Cry," 1960; "The Paddiwack Song," 1960.

The Life

Ritchie Valens (VAH-lenz) was born Richard Valenzuela on Mother's Day in 1941 in Pacoima, California. He was the son of World War I veteran and first-generation Mexican American Joseph Steven Valenzuela and Concepción "Connie" (Reyes) Valenzuela. Both parents worked in a munitions plant in Saugus at the time of his birth.

Valens was raised in a poor, English-speaking household in an ethnically diverse working-class community in the San Fernando Valley. He grew up with a half-brother who was four years older, Bob Morales, the product of his mother's previous marriage. Valens became interested in music as a child, thanks to weekend gatherings at the Valenzuela home, where friends and family performed and danced to traditional Mexican folk songs. He obtained his first guitar as a young boy, and by the time he entered Pacoima Junior High he was already proficient on the instrument.

At age sixteen, Valens joined a local band, and he soon became a headliner, imitating the style of singer Little Richard. The following year, a record producer signed him to a contract, and his name was shortened to Valens to broaden his appeal. He recorded several songs that became hits, dropping out of San Fernando High School to perform full time. While on a tour of the American Midwest, Valens, Buddy Holly, and J. P. Richardson (the "Big Bopper") were killed when their chartered plane crashed outside Clear Lake, Iowa, on February 3, 1959.

The Music

Though he died before reaching his eighteenth birthday, Valens left a considerable body of original songs and intriguing versions of cover tunes, many of which were released only posthumously. A self-taught musician with a clear but untrained voice, Valens was steeped in a variety of musical genres, including traditional folk songs, mariachi, flamenco, blues, rhythm and blues, and rockabilly, elements of which he blended to produce a distinctive sound. During performances with the band he joined as a sixteen-year-old, the Silhouettes, he became known for making up lyrics on the spot, for improvising fresh guitar licks, and for his energetic delivery. During his short professional career of less than twelve months, Valens—a star in the making, particularly among Hispanic communities—demonstrated the capacity to reach across ethnic boundaries with simple but poignant lyrics accompanied by inventive guitar techniques.

"Come on, Let's Go." Valens's first recording, released in the summer of 1958 through the Del-Fi label of Keen Records, was inspired by a phrase his mother always used when herding her children together for an outing. A hard-charging song more densely layered than typical tunes of the period, it features a strong backbeat and Valens's crisp, jazzy guitar beneath deceptively simple, repetitive lyrics.

"Come On, Let's Go" eventually reached number forty-two on the pop charts, sold more than 750,000 singles, and propelled Valens to an October, 1958, appearance on *American Bandstand*.

"Donna." Composed for a high school sweetheart, Donna Ludwig (later Fox), "Donna" quickly became the quintessential slow dance number for high school proms in the late 1950's and early 1960's. Cowritten by Valens and record producer Bob Keane (originally Kuhn), the ballad melds doowop, delicate guitar work, and Valens's compelling vocals into an evocative paean to lost love. The song, which Valens sang on a second *American Bandstand* appearance in December, 1958, rose to number two on the pop charts during Valens's lifetime, and it is considered a classic of its type.

"La Bamba." The B side of the single containing "Donna," "La Bamba" was Valens's rock-oriented reworking of an ancient—the original song may be as old as five hundred years—traditional Mexican huapango (a spirited wedding tune intended for dancing on a wooden platform, highlighting intricate counterpoints and nonsense lyrics) from the region of Vera Cruz. One of the first pop hits to be sung entirely in Spanish, the song was also one of the earliest to feature the electric bass to accentuate the complex rhythms. Though "La Bamba" did not fare quite as well on the charts as "Donna" (it reached number twenty-two before Valens's untimely death), it has had incredible durability and worldwide popularity. Since the early 1960's, dozens of artists as diverse as the Ventures, Dusty Springfield, Neil Diamond, and Henry Mancini have all recorded covers of Valens's timeless hit.

Musical Legacy

Though Valens fell into obscurity following his death, his artistry was always appreciated by working musicians. The Beatles, for example, credited his "La Bamba" as the major influence for their early hit, "Twist and Shout."

In 1971 Don McLean commemorated the deaths of Valens, Holly, and Richardson in "American Pie" (as "the day the music died"). In 1987 *La Bamba*, a film portraying Valens's life, exposed a new generation of music fans to his work. Since then, the singer-songwriter has been posthumously flooded with honors: a star on the Hollywood Walk of Fame, induction into the Rockabilly Hall of Fame and the Rock and Roll Hall of Fame, and parks and edifices renamed in his memory. A U.S. postage stamp with his portrait was issued in 1993. Importantly, he has continued to act as an inspiration for Chicano artists—Los Lobos, Freddy Fender, Carlos Santana, Selena, the Ramones, Café Tacuba, and countless others—who have collectively immortalized Valens by recording his songs and expanding on the Latin-American rock breakthrough he pioneered.

Jack Ewing

Further Reading

Huxley, Martin, and Quinton Skinner. *Behind the Music: The Day the Music Died*. New York: MTV, 2000. The book describes the events leading up to the deaths of Valens, Holly, and Richardson, as related by family, friends, band members, and witnesses. Includes photographs.

Keane, Bob. *The Oracle of Del-Fi*. Los Angeles: Del-Fi International Books, 2006. This is the behind-the-scenes story of producer Keane, who signed Valens and many other popular recording artists to recording contracts.

Lehmer, Larry. *The Day the Music Died: The Last Tour of Buddy Holly, the Big Bopper, and Ritchie Valens*. New York: Schirmer Books, 2003. A minute-by-minute examination of the final moments of the ill-fated trio of musicians. Includes photographs.

Mendheim, Beverly. *Ritchie Valens: The First Latino Rocker*. 2d ed. Tempe, Ariz.: Bilingual Review Press, 1996. A detailed biography of the life and death of the young Latino singer-songwriter. Includes illustrations.

See also: Diamond, Neil; Fender, Freddy; Holly, Buddy; Jennings, Waylon; Little Richard; Mancini, Henry; Santana, Carlos.

Vangelis

Greek New Age composer, keyboardist, and synthesizer player

Vangelis shifted from playing rock to composing progressive rock and experimental music, and he achieved tremendous success with such memorable film scores as Chariots of Fire *and* Blade Runner.

Born: March 29, 1943; Volos, Greece
Also known as: Evangelos Odysseas Papathanassiou (birth name)
Member of: The Formynx; Aphrodite's Child; Jon and Vangelis

Principal works

FILM SCORES: *Sex Power*, 1970; *Salut, Jerusalem*, 1972; *Verve*, 1973; *Amore*, 1974; *Ignacio*, 1975; *Ace Up My Sleeve*, 1976; *La Fête sauvage*, 1976; *Chariots of Fire*, 1981; *Blade Runner*, 1982; *Missing*, 1982; *Nankyoku monogatari*, 1983; *The Bounty*, 1984; *Wonders of Life*, 1985; *Francesco*, 1989; *Bitter Moon*, 1992; *1492: Conquest of Paradise*, 1992; *I Hope . . .*, 2001; *Alexander*, 2004; *El Greco*, 2007.

Principal recordings

ALBUMS (solo): *Dragon*, 1971; *Earth*, 1973; *L'Apocalypse des animaux*, 1973; *Heaven and Hell*, 1975; *Albedo 0.39*, 1976; *Spiral*, 1977; *Beaubourg*, 1978; *Hypothesis*, 1978; *China*, 1979; *Odes*, 1979; *Opera Sauvage*, 1979; *See You Later*, 1980; *Soil Festivities*, 1984; *Invisible Connections*, 1985; *Mask*, 1985; *Direct*, 1988; *The City*, 1990; *El Greco*, 1995; *Voices*, 1995; *Oceanic*, 1996; *Rapsodies*, 1996; *Mythodea: Music for the NASA Mission, 2001 Mars Odyssey*, 2001.
ALBUMS (with Aphrodite's Child): *Aphrodite's Child*, 1968; *Rain and Tears*, 1968; *End of the World*, 1969; *It's Five O'Clock*, 1970; *666*, 1971.
ALBUMS (with Jon and Vangelis): *Short Stories*, 1980; *Friends of Mr. Cairo*, 1981; *Private Collection*, 1983; *Page of Life*, 1991.

The Life

Vangelis (van-GEHL-ihs) grew up in Volos, a city on Pagassitikos Bay, about two hundred miles northwest of Athens. He showed early interest and talent in music, composing as early as age four. He was offered formal music lessons, but he decided to teach himself to play piano and then guitar. He studied classical music, painting, and filmmaking at the Academy of Fine Arts in Athens. In the early 1960's, he was a founding member of the Formynx, one of the best known rock groups in Greece. After they disbanded in 1967, Vangelis moved to Paris and formed Aphrodite's Child. Its European hit was the song "Rain and Tears," based on Johann Pachelbel's Canon in D Major (1680). Aphrodite's Child disbanded in 1971. Before moving to London in 1974, Vangelis recorded the successful solo album *Heaven and Hell* and others. He decided against becoming a keyboard replacement for the band Yes, though he became a mentor for the group's vocalist Jon Anderson, working with him on several projects. In his London studio Vangelis's most notable film scores were *Chariots of Fire*, which won the Academy Award for Best Original Score, and *Blade Runner*. Vangelis was composer and musical director for various events and activities, including part of the flag relay of the closing ceremony of the 2000 Summer Olympics in Sydney, Australia.

The Music

Vangelis refused music lessons, so it is interesting that his commercially successful themes, such as "Hymn" from *Opera Sauvage* and "Chariots of Fire," are included in music books to inspire students who are learning to play piano. His early career shifted from playing rock to composing progressive rock and experimental music. The use of the synthesizer marked the beginning of his mature career. The lush sound of his electronic music was created by recording on tape many keyboard parts and then editing and mixing them. A device made for him, called a direct box, enabled him to record multiple tracks, since he composes by playing as many keyboards at a time as possible. He also composes orchestra scores.

Earth. Though this album's first track, "Come On," is weak, other songs, such as "My Face in the Rain" and "Let It Happen," demonstrate a solid combination of music similar to that of Aphrodite's Child and Vangelis's new direction. "A Song" was a complete departure from the band, and it foreshadowed his later music.

Short Stories. This 1980 album is representative of the collaboration between Vangelis and Yes vocalist Anderson. It demonstrates improvisation by both musicians, in the vein of psychedelic rock. "Curious Electric" could be described as an ancestor to New Age or trance music. The album was best known for the song "I Hear You Now," especially Anderson's song text.

Chariots of Fire. Winner of many film-score awards, including the Academy Award for Best Original Score, this 1981 sound track put Vangelis on the international stage. On the album, the best-known pieces were "Theme from *Chariots of Fire*," "Five Circles," and "Eric's Theme." The first reached number one on the *Billboard* Hot 100; the first and second pieces were included on Vangelis's best-selling compilation, *Themes* (1989). With its fanfare opening and striking melody, the exhilarating music of "Chariots of Fire" accompanied runners on the beach in the film effectively. It has also been used frequently both seriously and comically in other films and on television.

Blade Runner. Though it received fewer accolades than *Chariots of Fire*, the music to this 1982 film was notable. The electronic music featured digital sound effects such as sirens, chimes, and heart monitors, exemplified in the "Main Titles Music from *Blade Runner*." The sexy "Love Theme from *Blade Runner*" is also electronic music, but it featured a saxophone-sounding solo. "Memories of Green," which was from Vangelis's solo album *See You Later*, was also used in the film.

1492: Conquest of Paradise. This Academy Award-nominated score was released in 1992, the same year as the film. It is clearly a musical precursor to his score for *Alexander*. This score, however, has more classical music influence (for example, compare the title theme to Antonio Vivaldi's *Variations on La Folia*, 1705) and more New Age music (for example, "West Across the Ocean Sea").

Alexander. Vangelis's sound track to this film combined traditional Greek music with electronic music, studio orchestra, and choir. It was released at the same time as the film. With its large orchestral sound and mixed choir, "Across the Mountains" is reminiscent of the film-composing style of Ernest Gold for the epic *Exodus* (1960). "Eternal Alexander," a similar composition, has a memorable melody.

Musical Legacy

Vangelis's progressive rock and experimental music resembled that of the Moody Blues and Pink Floyd. He preceded New Age composers Enya and Yanni; however, their music does not sound similar to his. In addition to winning the Academy Award for Best Original Score for *Chariots of Fire*, the theme song ranked number one for at least one week on the *Billboard* Hot 100 chart. In 1992 France made him a Knight of the Order of Arts and Letters. In 1993 he earned a nomination for Best Original Score Motion Picture at the Golden Globe Awards for *1492: Conquest of Paradise*. He received a Public Service Medal in 2003 from the National Air and Space Administration, which used his orchestral composition *Mythodea* as the theme for its 2001 Mars Odyssey mission.

Melissa Ursula Dawn Goldsmith

Further Reading

Griffin, Mark J. T. *Vangelis: The Unknown Man: An Unauthorized Biography*. 2d ed. Ellon, England: M. Griffin, 1997. This biography of Vangelis is based on interviews, brief articles, music reviews, and album liner notes.

Hannan, Michael, and Melissa Carey. "Ambient Soundscapes in *Blade Runner*." In *Off the Planet: Music, Sound, and Science Fiction Cinema*. Edited by Philip Hayward. Bloomington: Indiana University Press, 2004. A musical study about Vangelis's film score for *Blade Runner*, this article explores its interaction with sound effects.

Sammon, Paul M. *Future Noir: The Making of "Blade Runner."* London: Orion Media, 1997. This source shows how Vangelis's score interacts with the film, and it discusses the composer's impressions of the film's rough cut and his rapport with director Ridley Scott.

Stiller, Andrew. "The Music in *Blade Runner*." In *Retrofitting "Blade Runner": Issues in Ridley Scott's "Blade Runner" and Philip K. Dick's "Do Androids Dream of Electric Sheep,"* edited by Judith Kerman. Bowling Green, Ohio: Bowling Green State University Popular Press, 2002. This chapter evaluates how the music underscores the film's story, and it gives details about the film score.

Whitesel, Todd. "Jon Anderson: Change He Must." *Goldmine* 32, no. 7 (March 31, 2006): 14-19. Progressive rock vocalist Anderson, front man of the band Yes, discusses what it was like to work with Vangelis.

See also: Bernstein, Elmer; Elfman, Danny; Enya; Newman, Randy; Yanni; Zimmer, Hans.

Eddie Van Halen

American rock guitarist and songwriter

A dominant figure in hard rock music, Van Halen augmented the techniques of the electric guitar, elevating the practice of two-handed tapping, and he promoted the importance of the extended solo in rock music.

Born: January 26, 1955; Amsterdam, the Netherlands
Also known as: Edward Lodewijk Van Halen (full name)
Member of: Van Halen

Principal recordings

ALBUMS (with Van Halen): *Van Halen*, 1978; *Van Halen II*, 1979; *Women and Children First*, 1980; *Fair Warning*, 1981; *Diver Down*, 1982; *1984*, 1984; *5150*, 1986; *OU812*, 1988; *For Unlawful Carnal Knowledge*, 1991; *Balance*, 1995; *Van Halen III*, 1998.

The Life

Edward Lodewijk Van Halen (van HAY-lehn) was the second son of Jan Van Halen and Eugenia Van Beers. A saxophonist and a clarinetist, his father was a professional musician, and he later appeared on the band Van Halen's fifth album, playing the clarinet on "Big Bad Bill Is Sweet William Now." Van Halen and his older brother Alex began the study of classical piano at an early age. In 1962 the family emigrated to Pasadena, California. In addition to the piano, Van Halen learned to play the violin, drum set, and bass. Around 1967, after his brother surpassed his abilities on the drum set, Van Halen took up the guitar. Captivated by the instrument, he practiced the guitar incessantly.

Blues and rock guitarists such as Eric Clapton,

Jimmy Page, Jeff Beck, and Jimi Hendrix served as major musical influences on Van Halen's guitar playing. The use of the pentatonic scale and the call-and-response nature of the blues impacted his musical development. He showed an affinity for using power chords, distorted amplifiers, and feedback associated with rock music. The music of Baroque composer Johann Sebastian Bach served as a model for many of Van Halen's compositions.

The guitarist began performing in public at parties, and, with his growing popularity, he began appearing at local clubs in Southern California. His first group was the teenage power trio the Trojan Rubber Company. He graduated from Pasadena High School in 1971, the same year that he began experimenting with his celebrated finger-tapping technique. He briefly attended Pasadena City College. The following year he formed the band Mammoth, achieving regional success. Van Halen's early rock experiences were primarily in cover bands, infrequently performing original compositions. While the renamed band Van Halen continued to perform and record covers, the opus of the group soon consisted principally of original songs.

In 1976 Gene Simmons of Kiss recognized the talents of Van Halen and band; however, Simmons was unsuccessful in obtaining a record contract for the group. The next year, the band Van Halen signed with Warner Bros., and it began working with producer Ted Templeman. After the release of its self-titled album in 1978, Van Halen went on tour, opening for Journey and later for Black Sabbath. Van Halen headlined its own tour following the release of its second album in 1979. During the 1980's, the keyboard took on a more prominent role for the guitarist. Many successful albums followed, with alternate leading vocalists for the ensemble (David Lee Roth, Sammy Hagar, and Gary Cherone).

Apart from the band Van Halen, the guitarist collaborated in numerous other musical projects. Van Halen provided the guitar solo for Michael Jackson's hit song "Beat It" (1983). The same year, he worked with legendary guitarist Brian May on the short-lived Starfleet Project. As early as 1975, Van Halen had already begun to experiment with guitar construction in the pursuit of an instrument that accentuated elements from both the Gibson Les Paul and Fender Stratocaster, resulting in the

Frankenstrat, with its trademark striped guitar motif.

The Music

The musical opus of guitarist Van Halen stems primarily from his involvement with the successful rock group, which recorded twelve albums. The music of Van Halen crosses several musical styles, reflecting the guitarist's numerous musical influences. The music of the group carefully negotiates characteristics associated with hard rock while still achieving widespread commercial success. As a guitarist, Van Halen surpassed many other musicians in techniques idiomatic to the instrument by constantly pushing the boundaries of the electric guitar. Like other rock guitarists, he used string bending, pick slides, natural and artificial harmonics, slurs, and whammy bar dives; however, it was his two-handed tapping that separated him from other rock musicians. His music often displays the influence of classical music.

"Eruption." Released in 1978 on *Van Halen*, "Eruption" is one of the most influential guitar solos in the history of rock. The monumental guitar instrumental opens simply with a single power chord, establishing a tonal center. Promptly, Van Halen explores the potential of the pentatonic scale, employing a series of passages using hammer-ons and pull-offs as well as artificial harmonics. The guitarist closes the opening section with the use of the whammy bar. The next section also begins with the striking of power chords. Reflecting his eclectic rock influences, he employs string bends reminiscent of legendary rock guitarist Chuck Berry. A tremolo section—that is, a series of rapid repetition of a single note—follows the bending, and Van Halen punctuates with another whammy bar dive. He returns to the use of fast passages involving repeated notes, reintroducing passages with hammer-ons and pull-offs. The climax of the celebrated guitar solo commences with two-handed tapping, outlining chords with arpeggios with the use of the right hand to tap, working in conjunction with the left hand. This section evokes the music of Bach. After a lengthy tapping section, the guitar instru-

mental concludes with harmonics, feedback, and the use of the whammy bar. In less than two minutes, Van Halen exhibits his musical prowess and virtuosity on the electric guitar.

"Cathedral." On the 1982 album *Diver Down* is the brief work "Cathedral," another electric guitar composition that highlights the ingenuity of Van Halen. In a solo performance, the guitarist emulates the sound of a church organ by manipulating the guitar-picking attacks with the use of the volume knob of the instrument in combination with an echo guitar effect. The guitar solo opens with a slow introduction that eventually employs arpeggios reminiscent of the solo works of Bach.

"Little Guitars." In the brief introduction to "Little Guitars" from the album *Diver Down*, Van Halen emulates the playing of flamenco guitarists. Unable to master the traditional Spanish-guitar techniques, he cleverly uses a pick for the tremolo played in combination with left-hand slurs to imitate flamenco music.

Eddie Van Halen. (AP/Wide World Photos)

"Dancing in the Street." This song was first recorded by the Motown group Martha and the Vandellas in 1964, and the band Van Halen covered the song in *Diver Down*, reflecting its formative cover-band years. Van Halen arranged and played the synthesizer as well as the guitar on the recording. In this song, the guitar, uncustomary for the group, played a subordinate role; the only exception was the succinct guitar solo.

"Jump." In 1984 the song "Jump" reached number one on the *Billboard* charts. The radio-friendly song combined hard rock with synthesizer-driven pop music. Uncharacteristically of the band Van Halen, a synthesizer plays an extremely prominent role in the music; in fact, it overshadows the guitar. In addition to the guitar, Van Halen plays the synthesizer on the recording, exhibiting his capabilities on the keyboard that span from his childhood lessons in classical piano. "Jump" includes the requisite guitar solo expected from the legendary guitarist.

Musical Legacy

Van Halen expanded upon and utilized playing techniques idiomatic to the electric guitar. Continuing traditional practices of the rock genre, he employed string bending, pick slides, harmonics, hammer-ons, and pull-offs; however, it was his extreme whammy bar dives and, in particular, his two-handed tapping that most influenced the playing of rock musicians. Although guitarists before Van Halen used tapping to a limited extent, he advanced the technique, and he transformed the approach to guitar soloing of rock musicians of his generation and those that followed. In contrast to many of his contemporaries, Van Halen often borrowed musical devices from classical music.

The guitarist fostered the extended guitar solo in rock music, assuring that the guitar solo became a requisite in both recorded and live performances. While he excelled at his inventive comping behind the singer and the writing of riff-rich songs, Van Halen is best known for his sophisticated and virtuosic guitar solos. His pioneering guitar work elevated the instrument to a high status within rock music.

In addition to his revolutionary guitar playing, he explored the possibilities of guitar construction. Seeking a guitar with the playability of a Fender Stratocaster and the sound of Gibson Les Paul, Van Halen experimented with numerous guitar designs to create an instrument that suited his personal needs. Many of his guitars employed whammy bars, the Floyd Rose tremolo device being the most commonly used. Van Halen worked in conjunction with numerous guitar companies, such as Kramer, Ernie Ball, Peavey, and Charvel, in the creation of signature guitars.

Mark E. Perry

Further Reading

Christe, Ian. *Everybody Wants Some: The Van Halen Saga*. Hoboken, N.J.: Wiley, 2007. A comprehensive book on the lives and the music of the band members, past and present, of Van Halen. Told anecdotally, the book contains numerous appendixes, including a list of unreleased recordings and a list of covers played by the band in Pasadena. Includes illustrations.

Considine, J. D. *Van Halen!* New York: Quill, 1985. A journalistic approach to the early history of the band Van Halen. Includes an appendix with illustrated examples on Van Halen's guitar techniques, discography, and illustrations.

Waksman, Steve. "Contesting Virtuosity: Rock Guitar Since 1976." In *The Cambridge Companion to the Guitar*, edited by Victor Anand Coelho. Cambridge, England: Cambridge University Press, 2003. This chapter examines the concept of virtuosity among rock guitarists such as Van Halen.

_____. "Into the Arena: Edward Van Halen and the Cultural Contradictions of the Guitar Hero." In *Guitar Cultures*, edited by Andy Bennett and Kevin Dawe. Oxford, England: Berg, 2001. The author examines the music of Van Halen and the role the guitarist played in the era of arena rock. The chapter offers a cultural study of the rock figure. Bibliography.

Walser, Robert. "Eruptions: Heavy Metal Appropriations of Classical Virtuosity." *Popular Music* 11 (October, 1992): 263-308. The article analyzes works such as Van Halen's "Eruption," demonstrating parallels with classical music. It contains a transcription of the guitar solo "Eruption." Includes bibliography and discography.

_____. *Running with the Devil: Power, Gender, and Madness in Heavy Metal Music*. Hanover, N.H.: Wesleyan University Press, 1993. The author explores the cultural context surrounding heavy metal music. The music of Van Halen and of other heavy metal musicians is studied, examining such issues as music analysis, gender studies, and postmodernism. Includes illustrations, discography, and bibliography.

See also: Berry, Chuck; Clapton, Eric; Hendrix, Jimi; Jackson, Michael; Johnson, Lonnie; Page, Jimmy.

Jimmy Van Heusen
American musical-theater composer

One of the most gifted popular songwriters between 1940 and the mid-1960's, Van Heusen shaped the musical careers of Bing Crosby and Frank Sinatra with the lilting and award-winning melodies he produced for these two singers.

Born: January 26, 1913; Syracuse, New York
Died: February 7, 1990; Rancho Mirage, California
Also known as: Edward Chester Babcock (birth name)

Principal works

MUSICAL THEATER (music): *Swingin' the Dream*, 1939 (libretto by Gilbert Seldes and Erik Charell; based on William Shakespeare's *A Midsummer Night's Dream*; lyrics by Eddie De Lange); *Nellie Bly*, 1946 (libretto by Joseph Quillan; lyrics by Johnny Burke); *Carnival in Flanders*, 1953 (libretto by Preston Sturges; lyrics by Burke); *Eddie Fisher at the Winter Garden*, 1962 (lyrics by Sammy Cahn); *Come on Strong*, 1962 (libretto by Garson Kanin; lyrics by Cahn); *Skyscraper*, 1965 (libretto by Peter Stone; based on Elmer Rice's play *Dream Girl*; lyrics by Cahn); *Walking Happy*, 1966 (libretto by Roger O. Hirson and Ketti Frings; based on Harold Brighouse's play *Hobson's Choice*; lyrics by Cahn).
SONGS (music): "Deep in Dream," 1938 (lyrics by Eddie De Lange; performed by Artie Shaw Orchestra, with Helen Forrest on vocals); "Oh!

You Crazy Moon," 1939 (lyrics by Johnny Burke; performed by Tommy Dorsey Orchestra, with Jack Leonard on vocals); "Imagination," 1940 (lyrics by Burke; performed by Fred Waring Pennsylvanians); "Polka Dots and Moonbeams," 1940 (lyrics by Burke; performed by Frank Sinatra); "It Could Happen to You," 1944 (lyrics by Burke; performed by Dorothy Lamour); "Like Someone in Love," 1944 (lyrics by Burke; performed by Dinah Shore); "Swinging on a Star," 1944 (lyrics by Burke; performed by Bing Crosby); "But Beautiful," 1947 (lyrics by Burke; performed by Crosby); "Here's That Rainy Day," 1953 (lyrics by Burke; performed by Dolores Gray); "Love and Marriage," 1955 (lyrics by Sammy Cahn; performed by Sinatra); "All the Way," 1957 (lyrics by Cahn; performed by Sinatra); "Come Fly with Me," 1957 (lyrics by Cahn; performed by Sinatra); "Come Dance with Me," 1958 (lyrics by Cahn; performed by Sinatra); "High Hopes," 1959 (lyrics by Cahn; performed by Sinatra and Eddie Hodges); "The Second Time Around," 1960 (lyrics by Cahn; performed by Sinatra); "Call Me Irresponsible," 1963 (lyrics by Cahn; performed by Sinatra).

The Life

Jimmy Van Heusen (van HEW-zehn) was born Edward Chester Babcock in Syracuse, New York, and commenced his songwriting career and musical studies as a high school student. When he went to work for a local radio station, WSYR in Syracuse, the management insisted that he change his name because Babcock seemed potentially and improbably obscene to the station's listeners. Seeing a truck with the title of the Van Heusen shirt company, he opted for that professional name but retained his own name throughout his life. He moved to New York City and began songwriting. By 1938 he had his first hit with the song "Deep in a Dream." Other hits, written with Johnny Mercer, soon followed. Van Heusen was on his way.

In 1940, Van Heusen move to California, where until 1969 he wrote songs with Johnny Burke and Sammy Cahn that attained popularity when Bing Crosby and Frank Sinatra featured the melodies. During World War II (1941-1945), Van Heusen's

Jimmy Van Heusen and Sammy Cahn (behind the piano). (Hulton Archive/Getty Images)

songwriting career was not his only activity. He had learned to fly during the late 1930's and soon became a skilled aviator. When he was not turning out hits, he served as a test pilot for the defense contractor Lockheed in the mornings, returning to the studios to practice his other profession in the afternoons.

Van Heusen won four Academy Awards for his songs. Within the Hollywood community, he enjoyed a reputation as a ladies' man that rivaled the success of his friend Sinatra. He partied with great intensity but could rebound after a hard night on the town to work the next day. He finally married Josephine Brock Perlberg in 1969, the same year in which he retired; the couple had no children. He died in 1990 after a lengthy illness.

The Music

Jimmy Van Heusen is associated with the later phase of what has been called the golden age of

American popular song, from the mid-1920's through the early 1960's. Though he was not an innovator of the stature of George Gershwin, Richard Rodgers, or Jerome Kern, Van Heusen was an adept creator of attractive melodies that resonated with the popular taste of the time. In his work for Bing Crosby and Frank Sinatra, he mastered the genre of the romantic ballad while providing uptempo songs of broad appeal. Among his major hits from that period, "Imagination," "Polka Dots and Moonbeams," and "It Could Happen to You" have all attained the status of standards in the repertoire of jazz signers and musicians.

In his partnerships with Burke and Cahn, Van Heusen several times tried to achieve a Broadway musical hit. Although these shows were flops, some of the songs that Van Heusen wrote for them became standards, including "Here's That Rainy Day" from 1953's *Carnival in Flanders*.

Songs with Burke. In 1940 Van Heusen went to work at Paramount Pictures, where he teamed with Johnny Burke, a popular writer of song lyrics. The team became songwriters both for the up-and-coming singer Frank Sinatra and the established star crooner, Bing Crosby. Van Heusen and Burke wrote the songs for the high-grossing "Road" pictures that starred Crosby and Bob Hope. A song called "Swingin' on a Star" featured in *Going My Way* with Bing Crosby won the Academy Award for best song in 1944, the first of four Oscars that Van Heusen would achieve. The Burke-Van Heusen partnership continued after the war ended but broke up during the mid-1950's because of Burke's chronic alcoholism.

Songs with Cahn. The second important phase of Van Heusen's career came when he teamed with lyric writer Sammy Cahn and the duo began writing songs for Frank Sinatra. Cahn reported that Van Heusen could provide melodies for his lyrics with great ease. If one melody did not work, Van Heusen turned out several others the same day. The professionalism and skill that Van Heusen and Cahn brought to their songs impressed Sinatra, who also liked to work fast. More important, Sinatra's career had been in a downward spiral in the early 1950's, and the songs that Van Heusen and Cahn produced help resurrect the singer's artistic fortunes. Among the hits that they crafted for the crooner were "The Tender Trap," "All the Way" (which won him a second Oscar), and "High Hopes." Van Heusen's ability to keep up with Sinatra's frenetic night routine forged a bond with the singer that spurred them both to an intense artistic collaboration.

Musical Legacy

At his best, Jimmy Van Heusen captured the sense of optimism and confidence that permeated the United States during the height of his career. At the same time, he understood the melancholy that lay just beneath the surface of these emotions. The enduring popularity of "Here's That Rainy Day" among jazz musicians and cabaret singers attests to Van Heusen's ability to evoke deeper emotional feelings with his melodies.

His later work with Sammy Cahn has aged less well, since it was so intimately connected to the Rat Pack ethos of Sinatra and the "swinging" attitudes of the late 1950's and early 1960's. The "booze, broads, and Sinatra" image that Van Heusen cultivated has become a stale cliché of an era that now seems dated and distant. Yet "The Second Time Around" and "Call Me Irresponsible" are still popular among fans of the music of this period. In the "Road" pictures with Hope and Crosby and in the other songs that he wrote with Johnny Burke, however, Van Heusen proved himself a songwriter of great versatility and a winning style. His work is still underrated; his best songs merit greater attention for what he contributed to a unique American art form.

Lewis L. Gould

Further Reading

Cahn, Sammy. *I Should Care: The Sammy Cahn Story.* New York: Arbor House, 1974. These memoirs by one of Van Heusen's collaborators illuminate their work for Frank Sinatra.

Ewen, David. *American Songwriters.* New York: H. W. Wilson, 1987. Contains a chapter on Van Heusen and his career.

Hemming, Roy. *The Melody Lingers On: The Great Songwriters and Their Movie Musicals.* New York: Newmarket Press, 1986. Includes an essay on Van Heusen and a listing of the films in which his songs appeared.

Sheed, Wilfred. *The House That George Built with a Little Help from Irving, Cole, and a Crew of About Fifty.* New York: Random House, 2007. Provides an incisive and thoughtful chapter on Van Heusen as a songwriter.

Wilder, Alec. *American Popular Song: The Great Innovators, 1900-1950.* New York: Oxford University Press, 1972. Includes an examination of Van Heusen's work from the perspective of one of his fellow songwriters.

See also: Burke, Johnny; Cahn, Sammy; Crosby, Bing; Horne, Lena; Tormé, Mel.

Dave Van Ronk

American folk and blues singer, guitarist, and songwriter

With his gravelly voice and ribald performances, Van Ronk came to prominence in the early Greenwich Village folk music scene, with his unique blend of ragtime, blues, and other musical styles.

Born: June 30, 1936; Brooklyn, New York
Died: February 10, 2002; New York, New York

Principal recordings

ALBUMS: *Black Mountain Blues*, 1959; *Dave Van Ronk Sings Ballads, Blues, and a Spiritual*, 1959; *Dave Van Ronk and the Ragtime Jug Stompers*, 1960 (with the Ragtime Jug Stompers); *Dave Van Ronk Sings Earthy Ballads and Blues*, 1961; *Dave Van Ronk Sings the Blues*, 1961; *Van Ronk Sings*, 1961; *In the Tradition*, 1963; *With the Red Onion Jazz Band*, 1963 (with the Red Onion Jazz Band); *The Genius of Dave Van Ronk*, 1964; *Just Dave Van Ronk*, 1964; *Gambler's Blues*, 1965; *No Dirty Names*, 1966; *Dave Van Ronk and the Hudson Dusters*, 1967 (with the Hudson Dusters); *Dave Van Ronk, Folksinger*, 1967; *Van Ronk*, 1969; *Songs for Ageing Children*, 1973; *Sunday Street*, 1976; *Hummin' to Myself*, 1990; *Peter and the Wolf*, 1990; *A Chrestomathy*, 1992; *Going Back to Brooklyn*, 1994; *Chrestomathy*,

Vol. 2, 1995; *From . . . Another Time and Place*, 1995; *Statesboro Blues*, 1996; *Somebody Else Not Me*, 1999; *Sweet and Lowdown*, 2001.

The Life

Dave Van Ronk was born to working-class parents during the Great Depression. His father left soon after the birth, and Van Ronk was raised by his mother and her family and friends. Van Ronk wrote that he never missed his father since he never knew him. He spent his early life on the streets of his Brooklyn neighborhood, getting in trouble at school for his impudent nature and absorbing the jazz music of the period. In 1945 he and his mother moved to Richmond Hill in Queens, a suburban neighborhood. He took piano lessons for a few years, and then he taught himself the ukulele. He dropped out of high school, and he began taking guitar lessons from jazz guitarist Jack Norton. When he was around seventeen, he began playing jazz professionally but not regularly. In addition to playing guitar, Van Ronk sang.

He made very little money playing music, so, tired of being broke, he joined the merchant marines. After a year or two as a sailor, he lost his seaman's papers in a mishap. In 1957 he moved back to New York City to try making a living playing music once more. Around this time, he moved to Greenwich Village, where he began taking part in the weekly impromptu gatherings of amateur musicians in Washington Square. It was there that Van Ronk was introduced to folk music. During this period, Van Ronk perfected a fingerpicking style he learned mostly from Tom Paley of the folk group the New Lost City Ramblers. This style was modified and elaborated upon after Van Ronk met and studied the style of Reverend Gary Davis.

At the time, the influence of leftist politics was prominent in the folk music scene, and Van Ronk helped organize and perform in several benefits to support its causes. He also wrote a regular column for the folk music scene broadsheet titled *CaraVan*.

Playing in coffeehouses and bars, Van Ronk enjoyed a moderate success, and he released his first solo album in 1958, followed by another in 1959. By 1961 the folk music scene was a national phenomenon, and Van Ronk was well known. He continued to record, releasing eight more albums before the end of the 1960's. He was also a regular feature on the festival circuit.

Van Ronk was married to Terri Thal in the 1960's. When that marriage ended, he lived for many years with Joanne Grace, and then he married Andrea Vuocolo, with whom he spent the rest of his life. He was working on his memoirs when he died of a heart attack during treatment for colon cancer.

The Music

Van Ronk's sound is a unique synthesis of jazz and blues that blends the harmony and melody in one line. Critics noted its similarity to piano playing and to traditional jazz. His technique developed as he matured, and his voice maintains its gravelly quality from his first album until his final work recorded in 2002. Van Ronk occasionally departed from the singer-songwriter persona, recording with jug bands and even a traditional ragtime band.

Dave Van Ronk. (AP/Wide World Photos)

Early Works. On *Dave Van Ronk Sings Ballads, Blues, and Spirituals*, Van Ronk is a bit raw. His fingerpicking style is still being worked on, and his voice is not as raspy as it would become. However, this album represents what he does the best: interpret standards and other people's songs.

Dave Van Ronk and the Hudson Dusters. In this album, Van Ronk appears with an electric backing group. Although folk purists were dismayed, interpreting this as another folksinger going commercial, Van Ronk and the band are a convincing blues-rock combo with echoes of Paul Butterfield's Blues Band and the electric Bob Dylan.

Going Back to Brooklyn. Made up completely of Van Ronk compositions, this album highlights his songwriting abilities. Sometimes dry and other times more overt, his humor is apparent in the lyrics, and his guitar playing excels.

Musical Legacy

Van Ronk was an innovative force in the U.S. folk music scene of the late 1950's and early 1960's. His introduction of blues and jazz guitar stylings influenced such artists as Dylan, Phil Ochs, and Joni Mitchell. His support for these and other young folksingers helped them launch their careers. His social influence on the folk music scene was pronounced. After his death, a section of Sheridan Square, where Barrow Street meets Washington Place, in Greenwich Village was renamed in his honor.

Ron Jacobs

Further Reading

Brookhiser, Richard. "A Village Voice." *National Review* (September 9, 2001). A brief article details the writer's discovery of Van Ronk, and it provides a concise and accurate description of Van Ronk's musical approach and performance style.

Dylan, Bob. *Chronicles, Vol. 1.* New York: Simon & Schuster, 2004. Van Ronk rates several mentions in Dylan's first volume of his memoirs. Dylan's impressions of Van Ronk are revealing, demonstrating the reverence younger musicians in the Greenwich Village scene of the early 1960's held for Van Ronk.

Perlman, Ken. "Back-picking." *Sing Out!* (Spring, 2005). Perlman discusses Van Ronk's guitar playing, and he describes in words and in nota-tion how to learn the guitarist's technique. He uses examples from Van Ronk's version of "Cocaine Blues."

Van Ronk, Dave, with Elijah Wald. *The Mayor of MacDougal Street.* New York: Da Capo Press, 2005. This posthumously published autobiography is a colorful detailing of Van Ronk's life and career. Most of the book covers the first twenty years of Van Ronk's career, with many anecdotes about this period. It includes his reminiscences of the various musical and political scenes in which he was involved.

See also: Dylan, Bob; Hurt, Mississippi John; Mitchell, Joni.

Townes Van Zandt

American folk/country singer, guitarist, and songwriter

Van Zandt's combination of country-blues fingerpicking, comically dark songwriting, and nontraditional vocal stylings inspired other country and rock musicians.

Born: March 7, 1944; Fort Worth, Texas
Died: January 1, 1997; Nashville, Tennessee

Principal recordings

ALBUMS: *In the Beginning*, recorded 1966, released 2003; *First Album: For the Sake of the Song*, 1968; *Our Mother the Mountain*, 1969; *Townes Van Zandt*, 1969; *Delta Momma Blues*, 1971; *High, Low, and in Between*, 1972; *The Late Great Townes Van Zandt*, 1972; *Live at the Old Quarter, Houston, Texas*, 1977; *Flyin' Shoes*, 1978; *At My Window*, 1987; *The Nashville Sessions*, 1994; *Roadsongs*, 1994; *No Deeper Blue*, 1995; *Abnormal*, 1996; *The Highway Kind*, 1997; *A Far Cry from Dead*, 1999.

The Life

Townes Van Zandt was born into a Texas family of oil barons and cattle ranchers. He lived a fairly conventional life until he reached puberty, when he was diagnosed as bipolar (then known as manic de-

Townes Van Zandt. (AP/Wide World Photos)

pression) with schizophrenic tendencies and began a series of electroshock treatments. He spent most of his early youth moving around the country with his family as his dad went from job to job. Some time during this period, enamored with rock and roll and the music of bluesman Lightnin' Hopkins, he began playing guitar. After graduating from high school, he began attending the University of Colorado in Boulder in 1962. During his first two years at the university he was abusing alcohol and was eventually brought back to Texas by his parents. He was admitted to the University of Texas Medical Branch Hospital in Galveston, where he received three months of insulin shock therapy. Van Zandt later told music writer Robert Greenfield that he had staged the nervous breakdown to avoid being drafted into the U.S. military. In 1965 he entered the University of Texas in Houston as a pre-law student. He also began to perform at coffeehouses and taverns, playing humorous songs he wrote to "keep the patrons happy." As he became more accomplished at songwriting, his material began to tell stories about people he had met—drifters, workingmen, and other street characters. He claimed Bob Dylan and Ramblin' Jack Elliott as influences.

Van Zandt was living an itinerant life at the time, sleeping at friends' apartments and houses, drink-

ing, and living day to day. At the same time he began opening for such blues and bluegrass acts as Hopkins and Doc Watson. In 1968 he met songwriter Mickey Newbury, who convinced Van Zandt to try his luck in Nashville. He took the advice, and Newbury introduced him to Cowboy Jack Clement, who became one of Van Zandt's producers. Van Zandt recorded the album titled *First Album: For the Sake of the Song* on the Poppy label in 1967. He recorded four more albums over the course of the next five years. In 1976 he hired John Lomax III as his new manager, moved back to Nashville, and signed a recording contract with Tomato Records. He recorded a live album in 1976 and another studio disc in 1978. After that he did not record another album for almost ten years, although he did continue to tour. In 1987 he signed with Sugar Hill Records and recorded his eighth studio album, *At My Window.* He released three more live albums in the next few years, and in 1990 he toured with the Canadian rock group the Cowboy Junkies. In 1994 Sugar Hill Records released a live album and a studio album Van Zandt recorded in Ireland. He died unexpectedly in 1997 following hip surgery. Several more albums and a movie about his life were released posthumously.

The Music

Our Mother the Mountain. Produced by Kevin Eggers and released in 1969, this is considered by many to be Van Zandt's masterpiece. His plaintive voice and subtle guitar stylings create a unique and often heartbreaking sound.

High, Low, and in Between. Produced by Clement, the album features some of Van Zandt's finest songs, including "No Deal" and "To Live Is to Fly." His sardonic humor is apparent throughout the album, and many of the songs are backed by a country rock band. Van Zandt plays both guitar and piano.

The Late Great Townes Van Zandt. This is the last album attributed to producer Eggers. The followup to *High, Low, and in Between*, this includes two of Van Zandt's most recorded songs, "Pancho and Lefty" and "If I Needed You." It also features covers of songs by Guy Clark and Hank Williams. Van Zandt plays no guitar, only piano.

Live at the Old Quarter, Houston, Texas. Recorded in 1973, this album perfectly captures Van Zandt in performance. The Old Quarter was one of the first places Van Zandt ever performed and a favorite haunt of his. All of the songs feature Van Zandt solo with his acoustic guitar.

The Highway Kind. Released in 1997 only three months after Van Zandt's death, this was recorded on tour in the United States and Europe. Featuring new and old material and some covers, the disc is at once depressing and light, as only Van Zandt can be. Some critics commented that the performances here were the songs of a man weary beyond his years. The backing band is, as usual, almost perfect in its approach to the nuances of Van Zandt's performance.

Musical Legacy

Van Zandt was one of those rare artists whose legacy began almost as soon as he recorded an album. His song's stories of ironic tragedy became the favorite of critics and musicians almost as soon as they were heard. Like Dylan on a smaller scale, his singing style remains unique despite the efforts of others to imitate it. Country musicians such as Merle Haggard, Willie Nelson, and Emmylou Harris have recorded his songs, as well as those identified more with Americana music, such as Steve Earle.

Ron Jacobs

Further Reading

Kruth, John. *To Live's to Fly: The Ballad of the Late Great Townes Van Zandt*. Cambridge, Mass.: Da Capo Press, 2007. Kruth's posthumous biography utilizes interviews with friends and family and articles and interviews written by others to provide a detailed and realistic account of Van Zandt's life and music. He also includes perceptive readings of Van Zandt's songs and performances.

_____. "Townes Van Zandt: The Self-Destructive Hobo Saint." *Sing Out* (Summer, 2004): 54-62. This article in a folksingers' magazine discusses

Van Zandt's bouts with depression and his friendships with other musicians. Makes the claim that one day Van Zandt will be recognized as one of America's best twentieth century poets.

Tom, Luke. "Songs like Voices from Beyond the Grave." *The Wall Street Journal*, June 25, 2003, p. D8. Keenly observant discussion of Van Zandt, with highlights of his career and his influence on his peers.

Zollo, Paul. "Townes Van Zandt." In *Songwriters on Songwriting*. Cambridge, Mass.: Da Capo Press, 2003. Among interviews with dozens of modern songwriters is one with Van Zandt that provides an intimate look at his creative process.

See also: Dylan, Bob; Earle, Steve; Haggard, Merle; Harris, Emmylou; Hopkins, Lightnin'; Lovett, Lyle; Nelson, Willie.

Edgard Varèse

French classical composer

A visionary composer, Varèse created musical works that demonstrated a remarkably organic integration of electronic and acoustic materials.

Born: December 22, 1883; Paris, France
Died: November 6, 1965; New York, New York
Also known as: Edgard Victor Achille Charles Varèse (full name)

Principal works

ORCHESTRAL WORKS: *Un grand sommeil noir*, 1906; *Offrandes*, 1922; *Hyperprism*, 1923; *Octandre*, 1924; *Intégrales*, 1925; *Amériques*, 1926; *Arcana*, 1927; *Ionisation*, 1933; *Ecuatorial*, 1934; *Density 21.5*, 1936; *Étude pour Espace*, 1947; *Déserts*, 1954; *La Procession de Vergés*, 1955; *Poème électronique*, 1958; *Nocturnal*, 1961.

The Life

Edgard Victor Achille Charles Varèse (EHD-gahr VEE-tohr ah-KEEL shahrl vah-REH-zeh) was born in Paris on December 22, 1883, and he was raised in Burgundy and northern Italy before returning to Paris as a young adult. His childhood was difficult, in particular, his relationship with his father, which resulted in the relocations during his youth. Varèse began his musical training at the Schola Cantorum in 1904, and he continued his studies at the Paris Conservatory the following year. In 1907 he moved to Berlin, where he met and married actress Suzanne Bing. Their short-lived marriage produced a daughter, Claude, in 1910. In 1915, after a stint in the French army during World War I, Varèse emigrated to the United States, attaining American citizenship in 1927.

Almost immediately upon his arrival in the United States, Varèse found fertile ground for his musical pursuits. The title of the first work he composed in the United States, *Amériques*, not only paid homage to his newly adopted home but also was a reference to the metaphorical new world of sound that he was beginning to explore during this period.

Along with harpist-composer Carlos Salzedo, Varèse founded the International Composers Guild in 1921, the manifesto of which included a well-known phrase associated with Varèse: "The present-day composer refuses to die." In 1928 Varèse returned to Paris to work for several years, during which time his interest in electronic music began to grow as he investigated ways of developing and incorporating electronic instruments in his music. Varèse was the first major composer to use the newly invented theremin, an electronic instrument, in his work *Ecuatorial*, which was premiered by Nicolas Slonimsky in April, 1934. Upon his subsequent return to the United States, Varèse lived in Santa Fe, New Mexico; San Francisco; and Los Angeles before returning to New York City in 1938.

Throughout his life, Varèse enjoyed associations with major literary and artistic figures, including Le Corbusier, Henry Miller, Alexander Calder, Joán Miró, Joseph Stella, Fernand Léger, Romain Rolland, Man Ray, and Marcel Duchamp. In 1918 Varèse married Louise McCutcheon Norton, an established literary figure who was later recognized for her English translations of French literature, most notably that of Arthur Rimbaud. Throughout their life together, Louise was an important collaborator and supporter of her husband, and the two remained extremely close until the composer's death nearly fifty years later.

Frustrated by unrealized projects that depended upon electronic resources that were either unavail-

able or not yet developed, Varèse entered a long period of compositional dormancy from the late 1930's through the early 1950's. Among the ambitious projects he attempted during this period was *Espace*, a multilingual choral work requiring radiophonic synchronization of simultaneous performances in New York City, Paris, Moscow, and Beijing. While such a work would be entirely possible in an age of satellite feeds and Internet communication, just conceiving of such a work at that time is a testament to Varèse's remarkable vision.

The advent of new technology following World War II reinvigorated Varèse, and such developments allowed him to continue his musical pursuits as he had envisioned them decades earlier. It was during this final stage of Varèse's life that he began to achieve the recognition he deserved, including an invitation to join the Royal Swedish Academy (1962) and the receipt of a Koussevitzky International Recording Award (1963). Varèse died in New York City on November 6, 1965, just short of his eighty-second birthday.

The Music

Early Influences. Varèse's initial musical training was fairly traditional, his teachers including such mainstream French composers as Albert Roussel and Charles Widor. Additional studies with Feruccio Busoni during his formative years established an early interest in sound for its own sake and in the use of unusual sounds as the basis of his compositions. Varèse's early musical style is difficult to assess, as the only extant work from his youth is a setting of Paul Verlaine's poem *Un grand sommeil noir*, composed in 1906. The remaining works from this period were either lost, destroyed in a Berlin warehouse fire, or (in the case of the symphonic poem *Bourgogne*) destroyed by the composer's own hand.

Because of his unique approach to musical sound and the emphasis on noise elements, Varèse is often associated with the Futurist movement, which originated in Italy prior to World War I and was musically defined by Luigi Russolo's manifesto *The Art of Noises* (1913). Among the most significant influences on Varèse's concept of music were the writings of nineteenth century Polish philosopher and mathematician Józef Maria Hoene-Wronski, whose definition of music as "the corporealization of the intelligence that is in sound" would become the touchstone of Varèse's compositional philosophy. In order to avoid the historical and aesthetic baggage associated with the word music, Varèse referred to his work as "organized sound" and to himself as a "worker in rhythms, frequencies, and intensities" rather than as a composer.

Amériques *to* Arcana. Perhaps Varèse's most productive compositional period was during the time he cofounded the International Composers Guild in the early 1920's, when he composed *Amériques*, *Offrandes*, *Hyperprism*, *Octandre*, and *Intégrales*. In addition to the orchestral work *Arcana*, completed later in the decade, these works established Varèse's mature style, which remained unusually consistent throughout the remainder of his life.

An important characteristic of his compositional style is the careful attention to all musical parameters. Varèse became increasingly interested in musical elements that had been previously subjugated

Edgard Varèse. (Library of Congress)

by pitch concerns—timbre, density, register, texture, dynamics—and his works reflected this shift by emphasizing percussion and wind instruments, particularly those that allowed him to explore registral and dynamic extremes (such as piccolo, E-flat clarinet, contrabass trombone, tuba). While string instruments were reduced to a supportive role (mostly for coloristic and percussive effects) in *Amériques*, he eventually eliminated them altogether from many of his ensemble works because of their strong association with what he perceived as an outmoded Romanticism inherent to their style of playing. The one exception to this was the contrabass, which Varèse found useful in extending the low end of the ensemble in his chamber work *Octandre*.

Ionisation *and* Density 21.5. Varèse was fascinated by scientific phenomena and mathematical formulas, but he approached these ideas philosophically or conceptually rather than literally in his works. This interest is clearly exemplified in titles such as *Ionisation* for percussion ensemble, *Density 21.5* for solo flute (named for the density of platinum, as the work was originally composed for a platinum flute), and *Hyperprism* for winds and percussion. Even his explanation of musical processes seems more appropriate to a science journal than a theory text, incorporating phrases such as "shifting planes," "colliding sound-masses," "penetration and repulsion," and "transmutation." When listening to Varèse's work, such descriptions seem entirely apt, as his approach to sound is so effectively derived from these conceptual models. Completed in 1931 and premiered by an ensemble conducted by Slonimsky at Carnegie Hall in 1933, *Ionisation* is significant for being the first work written exclusively for percussion ensemble. Because the piece is composed primarily for indefinitely pitched instruments (with the exception of chimes and piano, which are used only in the coda), Varèse was able to focus almost entirely on other musical elements in the unfolding of sonic blocks. *Density 21.5* presents a contrasting listening experience: Composed for flutist Georges Barrère in 1936, this is the only monophonic work in Varèse's catalogue, demonstrating the composer's approach to linear pitch and rhythmic development with a relatively limited use of timbral and dynamic materials because of the nature of the instrument. In spite of the inherent restrictions of a single-line instrument, Varèse uses contrasting pitch materials and extreme registral placement to create a polyphonic effect.

Déserts *and* Poème électronique. During the final decade of his life, Varèse produced his seminal electronic works, following years of unsuccessful attempts to realize his musical vision. Completed in 1954, *Déserts* is structured as a set of episodes that alternate music for a large ensemble of wind and percussion instruments with purely electronic sounds. Although the separation of acoustic and electronic forces in this composition would seem to argue against integration, the musical material and the similarity of developmental processes within each section result in a cohesive and organic work. *Poème électronique* was created at the insistence of architect Le Corbusier, who designed the Philips Pavilion for the 1958 World's Fair in Brussels, Belgium. Varèse composed this purely electronic work as part of an installation within the pavilion, using more than four hundred loudspeakers that enabled the sound to be physically projected through space, a radical concept at the time. Varèse's final composition was *Nocturnal*, a setting of texts by Anaïs Nin for solo soprano, male chorus, and orchestra.

Musical Legacy

Largely underappreciated during his lifetime, Varèse has since his death had a profound influence on new generations of composers. He has come to be considered by many as an important and original voice, and his relatively small catalog—less than twenty extant compositions—is notable for the uncompromising quality and significance of each work. Works such as *Ionisation*, *Density 21.5*, and *Poème électronique* are established in the contemporary classical repertoire, and they receive regular performances in professional and academic settings. Other works are performed less frequently, primarily because of the unusual personnel requirements or practical difficulties involved.

Varèse's consistent and inherently musical approach to electronic music sets him apart from other early practitioners working in that medium, many of whom seemed more concerned with technical issues than musical ones. As a result, the electronic materials in *Déserts* and *Poème électronique*, while admittedly dated, sound less so than works

by Varèse's contemporaries. These works also demonstrate an organic integration of electronic and acoustic materials to a degree that is unique for the time, and which has served as an important model for subsequent generations of electronic music composers. Although his importance is particularly notable among composers within the experimental classical tradition, such as Pierre Boulez, John Cage, Iannis Xenakis, Chou Wen-chung, and Roger Reynolds, Varèse also influenced jazz legend Charlie Parker, guitarist and postmodern composer Frank Zappa, and the rock band Pink Floyd. Varèse was commemorated in a 2006 exhibit at the Tinguely Museum in Basel, Switzerland, titled "Edgard Varèse: Composer, Sound Sculptor, Visionary."

Joseph Klein

Further Reading

Bernard, Jonathan. *The Music of Edgard Varèse*. New Haven, Conn.: Yale University Press, 1987. Bernard's exploration of Varèse's work is innovative and insightful, taking into account the composer's unique approach to texture, timbre, and register in his application of analytical tools.

Meyer, Felix, and Heidy Zimmermann. *Edgard Varèse: Composer, Sound Sculptor, Visionary*. Rochester, N.Y.: Boydell and Brewer, 2006. An important collection of facsimile scores, letters, art reproductions, and essays by dozens of leading American and European scholars, including Jonathan Bernard, David Schiff, Kyle Gann, and Chou Wen-chung. Based on a major 2006 exhibition of Varèse's life and work associated with the Paul Sacher Foundation in Basel, Switzerland.

Nattiez, Jean-Jacques. "Varese's *Density 21.5*: A Study in Semiological Analysis." *Music Analysis* 1, no. 3 (October, 1982): 243-340. Translated by Anna Barry. This extensive and controversial analysis of the composer's most frequently performed work sheds light on his distinctive compositional process, particularly with regard to motivic transformation.

Ouellette, Fernand. *Edgard Varèse*. Translated by Derek Coltman. London: Calder and Boyars, 1973. The first major biography about the composer was originally published in French in 1968, just a few years after his death. The book includes a great deal of information, and it is divided into chapters devoted to significant milestones in Varèse's life.

Varèse, Edgard. "The Liberation of Sound." In *Contemporary Composers on Contemporary Music*, edited by Elliot Schwartz and Barney Childs. New York: Da Capo Press, 1998. This collection of lectures presented by Varèse between 1936 and 1959 was compiled and edited by his closest pupil, Wen-chung, and it is perhaps the most direct and cogent presentation of the composer's conceptual, aesthetic, and technical approach to organized sound.

Varèse, Louise. *Varèse: A Looking Glass Diary*. Vol. 1. London: Davis-Poynter, 1972. The first of a proposed two-volume journal by the composer's widow (the second volume was incomplete at the time of her death in 1989). The book presents an extensive narrative account of events from Varèse's early life as well as rare photographs, correspondence, and personal insights unavailable elsewhere.

See also: Adams, John; Babbitt, Milton; Boulez, Pierre; Busoni, Ferruccio; Cage, John; Carter, Elliott; Chávez, Carlos; Dodge, Charles; Dolphy, Eric; Feldman, Morton; Parker, Charlie; Seeger, Ruth Crawford; Still, William Grant; Theremin, Léon; Xenakis, Iannis; Zappa, Frank.

Sarah Vaughan

American jazz singer

With her exceptional range and pitch control, her instinct for harmony and improvisation, and her phrasing, Vaughan elevated the role of the jazz vocalist to a level equal to other performers in the jazz bands of the 1940's.

Born: March 27, 1924; Newark, New Jersey
Died: April 3, 1990; Hidden Hills, California
Also known as: Sarah Lois Vaughan (full name); Sassy; Divine One

Principal recordings

ALBUMS: *I'll Wait and Pray*, 1944 (with Billy Eckstine); *It Might as Well Be Spring*, 1946 (with John Kirby); *It's Magic*, 1947; *Mean to Me*, 1950; *Divine Sarah Sings*, 1954; *Lullaby of Birdland*, 1954; *Rodgers and Hart Songbook*, 1954; *Sarah Vaughan with Clifford Brown*, 1954; *The George Gershwin Songbook, Vol. 1*, 1955; *The George Gershwin Songbook, Vol. 2*, 1955; *In the Land of Hi-Fi*, 1955; *Sassy*, 1956; *At Mister Kelly's*, 1957; *The Irving Berlin Songbook*, 1957; *Sarah Vaughan Sings George Gershwin*, 1957; *Sarah Vaughan Sings Great Songs from Hit Shows*, 1957; *Swingin' Easy*, 1957; *Broken-Hearted Melody*, 1958; *No Count Sarah*, 1958; *Vaughan and Violins*, 1959; *Dreamy*, 1960; *After Hours*, 1961; *The Divine One*, 1961; *Sarah + 2*, 1961; *Sarah Vaughan*, 1961; *You're Mine You*, 1962; *Sarah Sings Soulfully*, 1963; *Sarah Slightly Classical*, 1963; *Sassy Swings the Tivoli*, 1963; *Snowbound*, 1963; *The Lonely Hours*, 1964; *Sweet 'n' Sassy*, 1964; *Sarah Vaughan Sings the Mancini Songbook*, 1965; *¡Viva! Vaughan*, 1965; *The New Scene*, 1966; *Sassy Swings Again*, 1967; *A Time in My Life*, 1971; *With Michel Legrand*, 1972; *Send in the Clowns*, 1974; *I Love Brazil*, 1977; *How Long Has This Been Going On?*, 1978; *Copacabana*, 1979; *The Duke Ellington Songbook, Vol. 1*, 1979; *The Duke Ellington Songbook, Vol. 2*, 1979; *Songs of the Beatles*, 1981; *Crazy and Mixed Up*, 1982; *The Mystery of Man*, 1984; *Brazilian Romance*, 1987; *Deep Purple*, 1990.

The Life

Sarah Lois Vaughan (vahn), daughter of Asbury and Ada Vaughan, was born in 1924 in Newark, New Jersey. As a young girl, she played piano and sang in the choir of the Mount Zion Baptist Church. Along with taking piano lessons, she majored in music at Newark's Arts High School. More important, she spent her teenage years listening to recordings of jazz and blues artists, skipping school to seek out performances in Newark's many clubs and theaters. By the age of fifteen, she was playing and singing in local clubs.

In 1943 Vaughan competed in an amateur contest at Harlem's Apollo Theater. She attracted the attention of popular singer Billy Eckstine and bandleader Earl Hines. At the age of eighteen, her professional career was launched when Hines hired her to play piano and sing in his band. Touring with the Hines band was her training

Sarah Vaughan. (AP/Wide World Photos)

ground. Singing with Eckstine, listening to and learning from the talented and innovative players Dizzy Gillespie on trumpet, Charlie Parker on saxophone, and J. J. Johnson on trombone, Vaughan refined her vocal style, learning to improvise and use her voice as an instrument.

In late 1943 Eckstine left the Hines band, which played a danceable style of music, to start his own band, specializing in the new, aggressive jazz style known as bebop. Gillespie, Parker, and Vaughan were major elements of the new band. The only woman in the band, Vaughan was a trouper on the road, energetic and tireless. She earned the nickname Sassy for her tough, fresh attitude, and the name stayed with her throughout her life.

In late 1944 Vaughan left Eckstine's band to become a soloist, singing and accompanying herself on piano with a variety of back-up instrumentalists, including Parker and Gillespie. In 1946 she married jazz trumpeter George Treadwell, who became her manager. She continued to record for small labels and to tour and to sing in clubs, receiv-

ing good reviews and winning awards for her jazz singing. By the 1950's, her recordings on the Columbia and Mercury labels, with their blend of jazz and pop, were frequently listed on the *Down Beat* and pop charts. In addition to her club appearances, she was singing regularly on radio and television shows and touring the country with theater and concert bookings.

In 1958 Vaughan divorced Treadwell and married Clyde B. Atkins; in 1961 Vaughan and Atkins adopted a daughter, Debra Lois, who later took the professional name Paris Vaughan. The marriage was not a success, and Vaughan left Atkins in 1962. Vaughan spent much of her time on the road, but she maintained a house in Newark where her mother cared for Vaughan's daughter while she was on the road.

By the late 1960's and early 1970's, jazz was being overtaken by the increasingly popular sound of rock and roll, and fewer small club engagements were available. However, Vaughan and her trio were still busy with concerts, jazz festivals, and recording contracts. In 1974 Vaughan began singing with symphony orchestras, and such George Gershwin tunes as "Summertime" and "The Man I Love" became part of her performing repertoire.

Vaughan married a third time, to Waymon Reed, a trumpeter with the Count Basie Band, in 1978. The couple separated in 1981.

In spite of a lifetime of hard work, touring, smoking, drinking, and staying up all night, Vaughan retained a voice of exceptional flexibility and quality. She continued to record, tour, and appear on television and with orchestras until her death from lung cancer in 1990.

The Music

Vaughan's recordings generally fall into two categories: the commercial pop material with large studio groups and the intimate, spontaneous jazz work with a trio of piano, bass, and drums. Rather than broaden her repertoire, Vaughan performed many of the same signature songs over and over again in clubs and concerts, changing her interpretation and improvisation to make each performance unique. Later in her career Vaughan performed and recorded with symphony orchestras, during which her voice would take on an operatic quality.

"Lover Man." One of Vaughan's earliest and most loved recorded vocals, this Roger "Ram" Ramirez ballad, made in 1945 for the independent Guild label, featured a quintet led by Gillespie on trumpet, Parker on alto sax, Al Haig on piano, Curly Russell on bass, and Big Sid Catlett on drums. The young instrumentalists, with their complicated ranges, melodies, rhythms, and harmonies, signaled the transition from the swing era to the new bebop sound. The recording opens with Vaughan's straight rendition of the tune in her elegant midrange. Parker's adventurous accompaniment weaves around and through her melody, followed by Gillespie's solo improvisation in his high register. Then Vaughan's voice returns in its instrumental mode, forming an exquisite trio with the trumpet and alto sax. Vaughan recorded this tune many times, including in a 1954 session with her jazz trio of John Malachi on piano, Joe Benjamin on bass, and Roy Haynes on drums.

"The Lord's Prayer." Recorded in New York City in 1947 with the Ted Dale Orchestra, this song is one of the few that references her early experience in the choir of the Mount Zion Baptist Church. Her rendition showcases the richness of her contralto, the sweetness of her soprano, the great joy in her singing, and the spiritual power of her sound.

"Tenderly." A new tune in 1947 when she first recorded it, "Tenderly" reached the top of the pop charts, and it was Vaughan's signature song for many years. Her performances were instrumental in turning the ballad into a jazz standard. Recordings and performances of "Tenderly" feature her famous bent notes and exquisite control of vibrato in her contralto range.

"Lullaby of Birdland." Recorded in 1954 in New York City with Clifford Brown on trumpet, Herbie Mann on flute, Paul Quinichette on tenor sax, Jimmy Jones on piano, Benjamin on bass, and Haynes on drums, "Lullaby of Birdland" was a staple of Vaughan's jazz performances. The recording is a notable example of her extraordinary scat-singing ability as well as her agility in moving from her high to low range, her voice becoming one of the instruments in the ensemble.

"Misty." The song that became Vaughan's jazz tour de force was recorded several times, beginning in 1958 with Quincy Jones's orchestra and strings in Paris. Vaughan's renditions of this tune highlight the instrumental quality of her voice, as she seems to become part of the saxophone section. In live performance, she became known for her embellishments of this song, ranging from her highest soprano to her lowest, nearly baritone, range.

"Send in the Clowns." Recorded in 1974 on the Mainstream label, this Stephen Sondheim ballad blends Vaughan's jazz, pop, and operatic instincts. It is sometimes referred to as her aria for its almost classical cadenzas. Once again Vaughan's exquisite control over her wide range is evident. This song replaced "Tenderly" as her signature song in her later career.

"Summertime." Vaughan recorded "Summertime" many times over the course of her career, beginning as early as 1949. The aria is a perfect vehicle for the operatic quality and wide range of her voice, as her high soprano soars and her contralto thrills. The music of Gershwin would become a significant part of her later career, when she performed with symphony orchestras. She recorded "Summertime" live with her trio in Tokyo in 1973.

Musical Legacy

From the beginning of her career in the mid-1940's, Vaughan, along with Gillespie, Parker, and others, was in the vanguard of the new bebop movement in jazz. The complicated chord structure, harmonies, and rhythms of bebop distinguish her work from such other contemporary jazz singers as Ella Fitzgerald and Billie Holiday. A tension between her work with bebop and her more commercial pop recordings existed throughout much of her career. Best known for her expressive ballads, Vaughan had a vocal quality and range that, with training, could have taken her beyond jazz and pop work into an operatic career. She is noted for her range and control, her instincts in improvisation, her grasp of chord structure, and her clear sense of pitch. She used her voice like an imaginative instrumentalist, bending notes, moving flexibly through her range, improvising freely, yet always with a certainty of where she had come from and where she was going. Noted characteristics of her voice include a rich, controlled tone and vibrato, a broad range from a sweet soprano to a deep contralto, and exceptional sureness of pitch. She used her improvisational ability, her knowledge of chord structure, her sophisticated style, her hornlike phrasing, and her ease with complicated melodies, rhythms, and harmonies to win a new respect and importance for the vocalist in jazz ensembles.

Dubbed the Divine One by television host Dave Garroway, Vaughan won many *Down Beat* and *Metronome* awards and polls as a jazz and pop vocalist from 1947 through the mid-1950's. She won the Grammy Award for Best Jazz Vocal Performance in 1982 for *Gershwin Alive!* with Michael Tilson Thomas and the Los Angeles Philharmonic and the Grammy Award for Lifetime Achievement in 1989.

Susan Butterworth

Further Reading

Crowther, Bruce, and Mike Pinfold. *Singing Jazz: The Singers and Their Styles.* San Francisco: Miller Freeman Books, 1997. An enlightening discussion of jazz singing styles and personalities. Discusses Vaughan's career in detail, her influence on other singers, and the potential conflict between jazz and commercial singing.

Feather, Leonard. *The Jazz Years: Earwitness to an Era.* New York: Da Capo Press, 1987. Jazz promoter, critic, historian, and educator Feather's memoir includes an account of his helping Vaughan obtain her first recording dates.

Gates, Henry Louis, Jr., and Cornel West. *The African-American Century: How Black Americans Have Shaped Our Country.* New York: Free Press, 2000. The authors present a decade-by-decade look at the twentieth century through the lives of prominent African Americans. Vaughan is included as an influence on the decade 1950-1959.

Gillespie, Dizzy, with Al Fraser. *To Be or Not . . . to Bop.* New York: Doubleday, 1979. In this autobiography, Gillespie discusses his relationship with many of the musical personalities of his era. Includes comments by and about Vaughan.

Gourse, Leslie. *Sassy: The Life of Sarah Vaughan.* New York: Charles Scribner's Sons, 1993. Authoritative biography of Vaughan covers information from interviews with many people who knew and worked with her. Includes extensive discography.

Smith, Jessie Carney, ed. *Epic Lives: One Hundred Black Women Who Made a Difference.* Detroit, Mich.: Visible Ink Press, 1993. Includes a chapter on Vaughan, showcasing her career as a role model of a successful and influential black woman.

Williams, Martin. *The Jazz Tradition.* 2d rev. ed. New York: Oxford University Press, 1993. A series of essays presents the evolution of jazz through the contributions of two dozen major figures, including Vaughan.

See also: Basie, Count; Blakey, Art; Burke, Johnny; Davis, Sammy, Jr.; Gershwin, George; Gillespie, Dizzy; Gordon, Dexter; Jones, Quincy; Legrand, Michel; Nascimento, Milton; Parker, Charlie; Robinson, Smokey; Smith, Bessie; Sondheim, Stephen; Washington, Dinah; Webb, Jimmy.

Stevie Ray Vaughan

American rock guitarist and songwriter

An influential guitarist, Vaughan bridged the gap between blues and rock, infusing the two with his fiery, yet soulful, guitar playing.

Born: October 3, 1954; Dallas, Texas
Died: August 27, 1990; East Troy, Wisconsin
Also known as: Stephen Ray Vaughan (full name)
Member of: Stevie Ray Vaughan and Double Trouble

Principal recordings

ALBUMS (solo): *The Fire Meets the Fury*, 1989 (with Jeff Beck); *Family Style*, 1990 (with Jimmie Vaughan).

ALBUMS (with Stevie Ray Vaughan and Double Trouble): *Texas Flood*, 1983; *Couldn't Stand the Weather*, 1984; *Soul to Soul*, 1985; *Live Alive*, 1986; *In Step*, 1989.

The Life

Stephen Ray Vaughan (vahn) was born in Dallas to Jim and Martha Vaughan. Vaughan's parents introduced him to music, and in 1963 he began playing the guitar, taught by his older brother, Jimmie, who later founded the Fabulous Thunderbirds. Jimmie's influence weighed heavily on Vaughan, and the brothers immersed themselves in the sounds of Albert King, Freddie King, Albert Collins, and other blues guitarists, and they also listened to jazz-blues players, such as Kenny Burrell. As a teenager, Vaughan became interested in Jimi Hendrix and the aggressive style of rock and roll.

Vaughan dropped out of school in 1972, and he moved to Austin. While in Austin, Vaughan married Lenora (Lenny) Bailey, and they divorced in 1988. After playing in several bands and making a name for himself, Vaughan put together his own power trio, Double Trouble, in 1979. The band—which consisted of Vaughan on guitar and vocals, Tommy Shannon on bass, and Chris Layton on drums—quickly earned a favorable reputation in the Austin music scene, and it caught the attention of rhythm-and-blues producer Jerry Wexler, who got the band booked at the 1982 Montreux Jazz Festival in Switzerland.

Although Double Trouble had a cool reception from the festival audience, David Bowie and Jackson Browne enjoyed the band's performance. Bowie approached Vaughan with the idea of recording on his album *Let's Dance* (1983), and Browne offered his recording studio to the band, free of charge, to record a demo. Both of these opportunities resulted in more exposure for the band. The demo found its way into the hands of noted producer John Hammond, who decided to produce the band's debut album, *Texas Flood*, which went gold in 1983. The follow-up album, *Couldn't Stand the Weather*, ended up selling more than a million copies, and in 1985 the band released *Soul to Soul*, with Reese Wynans taking on keyboard duties.

In 1986 Vaughan's addiction to alcohol and cocaine caused him to collapse on stage in London. After that, Vaughan checked himself into rehab, emerging with a newfound sobriety that infused his next recording: the critically acclaimed and Grammy Award-winning *In Step*. In 1990 Vaughan and his brother recorded *Family Style*, and they made plans to tour together in support of the album. However, following an appearance with Eric Clapton, Buddy Guy, and others at Alpine Valley on August 26, 1990, the helicopter carrying Vaughan and three members of Clapton's entourage crashed, killing everyone onboard. Following his death, a number of Vaughan's studio and live recordings were released, achieving large sales numbers and winning more Grammy Awards.

The Music

Steeped in the classic blues sounds of King, Collins, Otis Rush, Johnny "Guitar" Watson, and Muddy Waters, Vaughan's signature style grew from his love of the blues mixed with his admiration for rock and roll and also jazz, most notably in the playing of Hendrix, Lonnie Mack, and Burrell. With his older brother's influence and guidance, Vaughan developed a robust, yet emotive style of guitar playing, which often incorporated simultaneous lead and rhythm lines, in a manner similar to Hendrix, and he demonstrated a gritty, yet passionate vocal style, reminiscent of that of Larry Davis. Vaughan's guitar tone was also highly regarded—produced through the combination of vintage Fender amplifiers and guitars, heavy-gauge guitar strings, and effects pedals—though most of Vaughan's distorted tone came from his overdriven tube amplifiers. Though he often covered classic blues songs and Jimi Hendrix tunes live and on his albums, Vaughan was also a competent songwriter, which became more apparent toward the end of his life.

Texas Flood. Vaughan's debut album, *Texas Flood*, was released in 1983, bringing him unexpected success and launching a blues revival. While the album contained some covers, including the title track, which showcased Vaughan's influences, it also provided a platform for Vaughan's own compositions. Tracks such as "Pride and Joy" and the instrumental "Rude Mood" highlight his instrumental prowess, while the jazz-infused "Lenny" provides a contrast to the high energy blues-rock tunes with a virtuosic but sentimental performance. The album was nominated for a Grammy Award for Best Blues Recording.

Couldn't Stand the Weather. The follow-up to *Texas Flood, Couldn't Stand the Weather* solidified Vaughan's reputation as a formidable guitarist, earning another Grammy Award nomination and selling better than its predecessor. The album's title track adds a tinge of funk to Vaughan's repertoire, and his cover of Hendrix's classic "Voodoo Chile (Slight Return)" pays homage to the original. The instrumental tracks, "Scuttle Buttin'" and "Stang's Swang," highlight Vaughan's boogie chops and jazz leanings, respectively.

In Step. Vaughan's final studio effort with Double Trouble before his death, *In Step* earned

Vaughan a Grammy Award. It is with this album that a sober Vaughan presented his strong songwriting skills. His sobriety, echoed not only in the album's title but also in the lyrics of several of the album's songs, enabled him to exhibit an emotional and personal quality not found in previous efforts. The guitar playing is expressive, including blistering solos and lyrical melodies.

Musical Legacy

Following Vaughan's death, several albums of previously recorded material were released, including *The Sky Is Crying* and *Family Style*, which earned Vaughan several more Grammy Awards. In 1992 the Fender music company introduced a signature series guitar based on Vaughan's "Number One" guitar. His influence is apparent not only in the instruments and equipment that guitarists use, but also in the style with which they play. Musicians such as Kenny Wayne Shepard, John Mayer, and others have all cited Vaughan as a primary influence. Additionally, his music is featured in commercials, films, and video games.

Gabriel Weiner

Further Reading

Dickerson, James L. *The Fabulous Vaughan Brothers: Jimmie and Stevie Ray.* Lanham, Md.: Taylor, 2004. A portrait of the Vaughan brothers' rise to popularity in the Austin music scene and in recording sessions in Memphis, Tennessee. Includes photographs and discography.

Gregory, Hugh. *Roadhouse Blues: Stevie Ray Vaughan and Texas Rhythm and Blues.* San Francisco: Backbeat Books, 2003. While this book does include a biography of Vaughan, it also traces the history of Vaughan's predecessors, contemporaries, and followers within the Southwest music scene.

Kitts, Jeff, Harold Steinblatt, and Brad Tolinski, eds. *Guitar World Presents: Stevie Ray Vaughan.* Milwaukee, Wis.: Hal Leonard, 1997. A collection of articles taken from *Guitar World* magazine, including interviews with Vaughan, a discography, and guitar instructional materials.

Leigh, Keri. *Stevie Ray: Soul to Soul.* Dallas: Taylor, 1993. Written by a friend of Vaughan, this book details the guitarist's love for music and his battles with addiction. The book includes personal letters, handwritten music, rare photographs and other memorabilia, in addition to interviews with Vaughan, his bandmates, and his friends.

Patoski, Joe Nick, and Bill Crawford. *Stevie Ray Vaughan: Caught in the Crossfire.* Boston: Little, Brown, 1993. This comprehensive biography of Vaughan is supported by extensive research and penetrating interviews, providing a compelling depiction of Vaughan's life.

See also: Beck, Jeff; Bowie, David; Browne, Jackson; Clapton, Eric; Guy, Buddy; Hendrix, Jimi; King, Albert; Rush, Otis; Waters, Muddy.

Ralph Vaughan Williams
English classical composer

One of the most important English composers of the twentieth century, Vaughan Williams did much to establish a distinct national style of concert music. His intense study and promotion of rich English musical traditions, ranging from folk songs to a variety of church music, provided the impetus for a highly individual idiom and inspired a whole generation of contemporaries.

Born: October 12, 1872; Down Ampney, England
Died: August 26, 1958; London, England

Principal works

BALLETS (music): *Old King Cole*, 1923 (libretto by Vaughan Williams); *Job*, 1931 (libretto by Geoffrey Keynes and Gwen Raverat; based on *Illustrations of the Book of Job* by William Blake).

CHAMBER WORKS: String Quintet in C Minor, 1903; String Quartet No. 1 in G Minor, 1909 (revised 1921); *Phantasy Quintet*, 1912 (for two violins, two violas, and one cello); *Six Preludes in English Folksongs*, 1926 (for cello and piano); String Quartet No. 2 in A Minor, 1944; *Three Preludes on Welsh Hymn Tunes*, 1956 (for organ).

CHORAL WORKS: Mass in G Minor, 1921; *Three Shakespeare Songs*, 1951 (includes *Full Fathom Five*, *The Cloud-capp'd Towers*, and *Over Hill, Over Dale*).

OPERAS (music): *Riders to the Sea*, 1937 (libretto by John Millington Synge); *The Pilgrim's Progress*,

1951 (libretto by John Bunyan); *Hugh the Drover*, 1956 (also known as *Love in the Stocks*; libretto by Harold Child).

ORCHESTRAL WORKS: *In the Fen Country*, 1904 (revised 1935); *Norfolk Rhapsody No. 1 in E Minor*, 1906 (revised 1914); *Norfolk Rhapsody No. 2 in D Minor*, 1906; *Norfolk Rhapsody No. 3 in G Major*, 1906; *Fantasia on a Theme by Thomas Tallis*, 1910 (revised 1919; for two string orchestras); *The Wasps, Aristophanic Suite*, 1912; Symphony No. 2 in G Major, 1914 (*A London Symphony*); Symphony No. 3, 1922 (*Pastoral Symphony*); *The Lark Ascending*, 1920 (for violin and orchestra); *English Folk Suite*, 1924 (for a military band); *Toccata marziale in B-flat Major*, 1924 (for a military band); *Flos Campi*, 1925; Piano Concerto in C Major, 1931; *Fantasia on Greensleeves*, 1934 (for harp, flute, and strings); Suite for Viola and Orchestra, 1934; Symphony No. 4 in F Minor, 1935; *Five Variants of Dives and Lazarus*, 1939 (for harp and string orchestra); Symphony No. 5 in D Major, 1943 (revised 1951); Oboe Concerto in A Minor, 1944; Symphony No. 6 in E Minor, 1948; *Partita*, 1949 (for double string orchestra); Symphony No. 7, 1953 (Sinfonia Antartica); Symphony No. 8 in D Minor, 1956 (revised 1956); *Variations*, 1957 (for a brass band); Symphony No. 9 in E Minor, 1958.

VOCAL WORKS: *Linden Lea*, 1902 (based on the poetry of William Barnes); *The House of Life*, 1903 (based on the poetry of Dante Gabriel Rossetti); *Songs of Travel*, 1904 (based on the poetry of Robert Louis Stevenson); *Toward the Unknown Region*, 1906 (based on the poetry of Walt Whitman); Symphony No. 1, 1910 (*A Sea Symphony*; based on the poetry of Whitman); *Five Mystical Songs*, 1911 (based on the poetry of George Herbert); *On Wenlock Edge*, 1924 (based on the poetry of Alfred Edward Housman); *Sancta Civitas*, 1925 (*The Sacred City*; based on the Bible); *Dona nobis pacem*, 1936 (*Grant Us Peace*; based on the poetry of Whitman); *Serenade to Music*, 1938 (based on *The Merchant of Venice* by William Shakespeare); *A Song of Thanksgiving*, 1944 (based on Thanksgiving songs); *Hodie*, 1954 (*This Day*; based on Christmas cantatas).

The Life

Ralph Vaughan Williams (rayf vahn WIHL-yumz) was born the third and youngest child of the Reverend Arthur Vaughan Williams, a vicar hailing from a family of prominent lawyers, and Margaret Wedgwood, a niece of Charles Darwin among whose relations were successful makers of fine china. After the death of his father in 1875, the young Ralph spent much of the remainder of his early youth in Surrey, where he demonstrated ample musical promise. By 1890 Vaughan Williams had completed several successful years at Charterhouse School and was prepared to embark upon advanced musical study.

During the early and middle 1890's, Vaughan Williams studied at the Royal College of Music in London with Hubert Parry and Charles Stanford, and at Cambridge University with Charles Wood. While he learned much from each of these men, it was his instruction with Parry that Vaughan Williams recalled with particular warmth later in his career. Parry encouraged his pupil's love for the rich English choral tradition and insisted that he study the works of the German masters. Another important relationship began at this time: Vaughan Williams's friendship with Gustav Holst. Their correspondence and support for each other proved to be mutually beneficial for many years.

The years following 1900 saw Vaughan Williams embark upon the important tasks of collecting and arranging folk songs and of editing *The English Hymnal*. Both activities kindled his creative imagination and provided him a means by which to establish an original voice. Further study abroad in Berlin with Max Bruch (1897) and in Paris with Maurice Ravel (1908) rounded out Vaughan Williams's student education. All of these experiences took place around the time he produced his first masterworks. Among them was the *Fantasia on a Theme by Thomas Tallis* of 1910, which brought its composer much of his later international fame.

The beginning of World War I in 1914 saw Vaughan Williams volunteer for the medical corps of the British army. His experiences on the French front as an ambulance driver significantly colored his next works, notably the *Pastoral Symphony* and *Flos Campi*. In the decades after the war, Vaughan Williams divided his time between teaching, conducting, writing on music, and composing. Each new major work that appeared added to his success and reputation.

In the last twenty years of his life, Vaughan Williams continued to compose and involve himself in the English musical scene. His concert music showed no signs of drying up. The dark and mysterious Symphony No. 6 was completed in 1947 and received scores of performances within its first years of existence. The year 1951 proved more difficult. First, the premiere in April of a last completed opera and long labor of love, *The Pilgrim's Progress*, elicited puzzlement and even some disapproval from its first audience. Then, sadly but not unexpectedly, his first wife Adeline died in May after long years of sickness. (In 1953 Vaughan Williams married his assistant, Ursula Wood.) All of this, however, did little to stymie Vaughan Williams's autumnal productivity, and by the time he died peacefully in August of 1958, he was the venerated figure of English music.

The Music

The long compositional career of Vaughan Williams spanned an eventful period in history, both musically and historically. His various works exhibit the successful integration of indigenous English musics into traditional European concert forms and a desire to create distinctive sounds.

Fantasia on a Theme by Thomas Tallis. His long study of Tudor polyphony inspired Vaughan Williams to create a work that would invoke the spirit of Elizabethan England while still belonging in the concert halls of his own time. The result was this fantasia scored for double string orchestra and lasting around fifteen minutes in performance. For the theme, Vaughan Williams borrowed the "Third Mode Melody" from a collection of church tunes that Tallis wrote in the 1560's. The work is a fantasia in the sense that it recalls characteristics of several forms—most noticeably theme-and-variations and sonata—without strictly conforming to any of them. To create the music's

Ralph Vaughan Williams. (Hulton Archive/Getty Images)

unique sound, Vaughan Williams uses triadic, but not strictly diatonic, harmonies under the solemn modal theme, and he uses accompanying strings to dovetail and double key voices, giving the whole an open, shimmering sound.

Pastoral Symphony. When this symphony first appeared, it created a great deal of confusion as to its character and its aims. Audiences long considered this largely subdued music to be a portrait of the English countryside. However, Vaughan Williams later revealed that the four-movement work was closely associated in spirit with his military service in France. At turns mournful and contemplative, the music can be seen as an inward coming to terms with the psychological impact of war. From a technical standpoint, it presents a watershed in how Vaughan Williams approached harmony. Combinations of several diatonic pitch collections provide many parts of the work with a new-sounding harmonic language that inhibits traditional triadic analysis. Unconventional treatment of cadences and layered instrumentation help to provide a sense of seamless continuity.

Symphony No. 6 in E Minor. If traditional harmonic analysis proves difficult with the *Pastoral Symphony*, it borders on the obsolete in the case of Symphony No. 6. Though the piece is nominally in E minor, the sequence of movements follows an unexpected harmonic course, evoking tonal centers as remote as B-flat minor at the beginning of the second movement. Throughout the work, initial motives play a crucial part in the overall form, and they can be used analytically where tonal design becomes ambiguous. The form is highly developmental throughout, and textures vary from static homophony in the second movement to the intense contrapuntal passages of the third. Each section is played without interruption.

Of all Vaughan Williams's compositions, Symphony No. 6 has provoked perhaps the most speculation as to possible meanings. The overall sinister tenor of the music has led many to agree that the work takes its inspiration from the recently ended World War II. Some early commentators even suggested that the eerie pianissimo epilogue depicts a world devastated by nuclear war. Vaughan Williams vehemently denied this notion, and in reference to the finale he quoted lines from William Shakespeare's *The Tempest* (1610-1611), notably:

"our little life is rounded with a sleep." Whatever the programmatic implications, the symphony has since earned widespread admiration as one of the composer's finest creative efforts.

The Pilgrim's Progress. Vaughan Williams's last completed opera, *The Pilgrim's Progress*, was perhaps nearer to his heart than any other of his compositions. The trope of the traveling pilgrim, facing persecution and hardship en route to his goal, resonated with him on many levels with regard to his life and work. Vaughan Williams had involved himself professionally with the tale as early as 1906, when he was commissioned to write incidental music for a staged play on the subject. Over the next four decades he worked on the music on and off. Some of the resulting product shares material with some other compositions, most notably parts of Symphony No. 5. Vaughan Williams coined the work a "morality" rather than an opera, suggesting that he intended its nature to be spiritual and contemplative rather than strictly dramatic. This notion did little to pacify early critics who relegated *The Pilgrim's Progress* to the cathedral rather than to the stage. Certainly the music identifies with such an image. Much of the material borrows heavily from church music styles and the subdued modality of his earlier pastoral works, such as *The Lark Ascending*. Moments of conflict exist, however, and glimpses of the dark nature of works such as Symphony No. 4 and Symphony No. 6 can be discerned from time to time, making studies involving such comparisons highly compelling. Overall, the work favors thoughtfulness and a beautiful solemnity.

Musical Legacy

In many of his writings, Vaughan Williams addressed what he considered to be the ideal goals of a composer. Prominent among them was his insistence that one's music have pertinence to and meaning for the community in which it was created. Only by being a product of its own surroundings could a given music then begin to have real meaning abroad, he argued. Vaughan Williams placed a lot of emphasis, then, on traditions and local customs. He did so at a time when traditions of every sort were being rejected and called into question in the name of progress, and he often paid for it via others' charges that he was narrow in his own work. Vaughan Williams himself, however, rejected the notion of artistic merit, or lack thereof, being tied to mere technical currency. He advocated the forging of one's own distinctive style, regardless of how old or new the music sounded, by means of studying tradition and of being sensitive toward the issues of one's present time and place.

Such values not only permeate the music of Vaughan Williams but also proved highly influential to subsequent composers in Britain. A number of younger musicians who went on to become notable British composers in their own right—Gerald Finzi and Herbert Howells among them—benefited from Vaughan Williams's guidance and knack for fostering creativity. Their mentor could be seen exerting considerable efforts on behalf of relatively unknown composers (often many years his juniors) in the name of promoting those he felt showed promise and originality. Even British artists more sympathetic to prevailing contemporary views of the middle twentieth century, such as Benjamin Britten and Michael Tippett, acknowledged some debt to the example of Vaughan Williams. With the onset of serialism and the avant-garde in the 1950's and beyond, Vaughan Williams's music and ideas waned a bit internationally. Now, however, his music is as popular as it ever was, and musicians of numerous leanings continue to benefit from its diversity and instruction.

Ryan Ross

Further Reading

Adams, Byron, and Robin Wells, eds. *Vaughan Williams Essays*. Aldershot, England: Ashgate, 2003. Each chapter in this book presents an in-depth study on a topic germane to the life and work of Vaughan Williams.

Frogley, Alain, ed. *Vaughan Williams Studies*. Cambridge, England: Cambridge University Press, 1996. Frogley's volume offers an extremely valuable and diverse array of essays by foremost experts on Vaughan Williams and on English music.

Kennedy, Michael. *The Works of Ralph Vaughan Williams*. 2d ed. New York: Oxford University Press USA, 1994. A thorough life-and-works study on Vaughan Williams.

Pike, Lionel. *Vaughan Williams and the Symphony*. London: Toccata Press, 2003. A significant study on Vaughan Williams's music, this volume offers incisive analysis for each of the symphonies.
Vaughan Williams, Ralph. *National Music and Other Essays*. 2d ed. Oxford, England: Oxford University Press, 1987. This volume comprises one of the largest collection of writings on music by Vaughan Williams, covering a wide range of topics, including the evolution of folk songs, the history of nationalism in music, Johann Sebastian Bach, and Holst.

Vaughan Williams, Ursula. *R. V. W.: A Biography of Ralph Vaughan Williams*. London: Oxford University Press, 1964. An authoritative account of her husband's life and work by Ursula Vaughan Williams.

See also: Britten, Benjamin; Holst, Gustav; Previn, Sir André; Ravel, Maurice; Tippett, Sir Michael.

Suzanne Vega
American folksinger, songwriter, and guitarist

A singer and songwriter, Vega expanded the vocabulary of folk music, bridging the gap to mainstream popular music. Her songs are personal and socially responsible, delivered in a unique vocal style.

Born: July 11, 1959; Santa Monica, California
Also known as: Suzanne Nadine Vega (full name); Mother of the MP3

Principal recordings
ALBUMS: *Suzanne Vega*, 1985; *Solitude Standing*, 1987; *Days of Open Hand*, 1990; *99.9 F°*, 1992; *Nine Objects of Desire*, 1996; *Songs in Red and Gray*, 2001; *Beauty and Crime*, 2007.

The Life
Suzanne Nadine Vega (sew-ZAN nay-DEEN VAY-gah) was born in Santa Monica, California, and by her first birthday, her parents had divorced. Her mother quickly married Ed Vega, a Puerto Rican writer, and the family moved to East Harlem in New York City. Vega was an outsider, and she was not well suited to life on the streets, finding comfort

in books and in her fantasies. She began writing poetry at age six, and at age eleven she began to teach herself the guitar. Composing music based on her poetry, she wrote her first song at the age fourteen.

Vega attended New York's High School for the Performing Arts, where she studied modern dance. Although she won numerous awards and graduated in the top five of her class, she was unsure of her potential as a dancer, and she turned to music. While an English major at Barnard College, Vega performed in New York coffeehouses, giving her first public performance in a church basement on January 2, 1976. Vega signed her first recording contract in 1984. In 1994 she gave birth to her daughter Ruby. Vega and Ruby's father, producer Mitchell Froom, were married from 1995 to 1998.

The Music

Although Vega is frequently labeled a folk-singer, her songs incorporate a wide variety of acoustic and electronic instrumental forces and rhythmic styles (among them samba, industrial, and techno). A gradual progression in her musical experimentation can be charted in her discography, from her self-titled 1985 debut album, which was praised by critics for its courageous straying from the typical confines of folk music. *Solitude Standing* also met with great critical acclaim, containing her hits "Luka" and "Tom's Diner." Her musical unpredictability continues through each of her albums: *Days of Open Hand, 99.9 F°, Nine Objects of Desire, Songs in Red and Gray,* and *Beauty and Crime.* In addition to these albums, Vega has contributed songs to film sound tracks: *The Haunted Mansion* (2003), *The Truth About Cats and Dogs* (1996), *Dead Man Walking* (1995), and *Pretty in Pink* (1986). She collaborated with minimalist composer Philip Glass on two pieces, "Lightning" and "Freezing," from his *Songs for Liquid Days* (1986). Consistent in all of Vega's work is her unique singing style, straightforward and plaintive with no vibrato, a reflection of her vocal influences (Astrud Gilberto, Leonard Cohen, Lou Reed, and Lotte Lenya among them). Her chilling vocal delivery fits well with her poignant poetry, consisting of illustrative images in short, simple phrases, a style influenced by writers such as John Steinbeck and Sylvia Plath. Vega describes her poetic writing as almost uncivilized, a nod to the reality of the subjects on which she

Suzanne Vega. (AP/Wide World Photos)

writes, which include child abuse ("Luka"), HIV/ AIDS ("Blood Makes Noise"), post-traumatic stress disorder ("Men in a War"), and childbirth ("Birthday [Love Made Real]"). Vega's songs are introspective and personal, inspired by her interaction with society. However, Vega is not directly political in her music, nor does she use her work as a confessional: Rather than admonish society for problematic issues, Vega prefers to frame these issues in musical vignettes, drawing the listener into her dramatic world as either an observer or an active participant.

"Luka." Vega's signature song, "Luka," which reached number three on the *Billboard* charts in 1987, is a prime example of Vega's simple vocal and compositional styles. The song tells the story of Luka, a nine-year-old boy physically abused by his parents, from his perspective, bringing the listener face-to-face with him. The matter-of-fact singing reflects the childlike innocence of the narrator, rendering him neither victimized nor empowered, a position for which children's rights advocates criticized Vega. No matter how the message was received, "Luka" brought Vega from the sheltered world of folk music into the spotlight of mainstream pop.

"Tom's Diner." The unaccompanied "Tom's Diner" recounts a forlorn lover reminiscing about a failed relationship while watching life continue as usual. Illustrative of Vega's characteristic simplicity, "Tom's Diner" is one of her most influential songs, and at least twenty-five artists have incorporated it into their own works. Among the most successful was the originally unauthorized remix by the British group DNA. Vega later approved of the remix, and she released it on *Tom's Album* with other artists' renditions of the song. "Tom's Diner" also earned Vega the nickname Mother of the MP3, because it was chosen by Karlheinz Brandenburg to refine the compression algorithm on the now-ubiquitous digital music format.

Nine Objects of Desire. Vega's 1996 album shows a sensual turn in her music, influenced primarily by the birth of her daughter Ruby and her marriage to Froom. A song cycle, the album is unified and inspired by nine objects of desire: Ruby; Froom; Lolita (of Vladimir Nabokov's novel); death; three men (unnamed); one woman (unnamed); and a plum. The increased use of electronic instruments and rhythmic beats continues the trend begun on *99.9 F°*, but this album is marked by a more sultry and intimate tone. The bossa nova-inspired "Caramel" was used on the film sound track for *The Truth About Cats and Dogs*.

Musical Legacy

Vega's dedication to truth in her music inspired many folksingers and songwriters, especially women. She is cited by such artists as Tracy Chapman, Sinéad O'Connor, and Shawn Colvin (who sang backup on *Solitude Standing*) as an pioneering force for women in music. Amy Ray of the Indigo Girls once hoped her group would become important enough to open a Vega concert. Vega's influence was also rewarded at the first Lilith Fair in 1997; she was the first artist to take the stage at the groundbreaking all-women's event. Her significance as a renegade performer led to her 2003 hosting of the Minnesota Public Radio show *American*

Mavericks, a thirteen-episode series dedicated to American composers who extended the boundaries of classical music.

Phillip J. Klepacki

Further Reading

DeMain, Bill. *Behind the Muse: Pop and Rock's Greatest Songwriters Talk About Their Work and Inspiration*. Cranberry Township, Pa.: Tiny Ripple Books, 2001. Songwriter and journalist DeMain interviews forty songwriters, including Vega, about their approaches to the craft, their sources of inspiration, and their style.

Farinella, David. "Suzanne Vega: Colors of Her Life." *Mix* 26, no. 4 (March, 2002): 165, 172-173. This interview addresses the writing and production process of Vega's sixth album, *Songs in Red and Gray*. It also discusses previous projects, relating changes and constants in her musical style.

Vega, Suzanne. *The Passionate Eye: The Collected Writing of Suzanne Vega*. New York: Avon Books, 1999. A volume of Vega's poetry and lyrics, as well as journal entries, short stories, and selected journalistic interviews.

Woodworth, Marc, ed. *Solo: Women Singer-Songwriters in Their Own Words*. New York: Delta Books, 1998. A collection that provides personal accounts from nineteen artists, including Vega, discussing their lives, their creative processes, and the intersection of the two. Includes photographs.

See also: Cohen, Leonard; Glass, Philip; Reed, Lou.

Heitor Villa-Lobos

Brazilian classical composer

Villa-Lobos was a significant composer of Brazilian art music and an influential music educator. He popularized the sound of worldwide MPB, Música Popular Brasileira.

Born: March 5, 1887; Rio de Janeiro, Brazil
Died: November 17, 1959; Rio de Janeiro, Brazil

Principal works

BALLETS: *Amazonas*, composed 1917, first performed 1929; *Uirapuru*, composed 1917, first performed 1935; *Possessão*, 1929; *Caixinha de boas festas*, 1932 (children's ballet); *Pedra Bonita*, 1933; *Gênesis*, composed 1954, first performed 1969; *Rudá*, 1954; *Emperor Jones*, 1956 (based on Eugene O'Neill's play).

CHAMBER WORKS: Piano Trio No. 1, 1911; Trio, 1913 (for flute, cello, and piano); Piano Trio No. 2, 1915; Sonata No. 1, 1915 (for cello and piano); Sonata No. 1, 1915 (for violin and piano); Sonata No. 2, 1915 (for violin and piano); String Quartet No. 1, 1915; String Quartet No. 2, 1915; Sonata No. 2, 1916 (for cello and piano); String Quartet No. 3, 1916; *Sexteto místico*, 1917 (for flute, oboe, saxophone, harp, cello, and guitar); String Quartet No. 4, 1917; Piano Trio No. 3, 1918; Sonata No. 3, 1920 (for violin and piano); Trio, 1921 (for oboe, clarinet, and bassoon); Sonata No. 4, 1923 (for violin and piano); Quartet, 1928 (for flute, oboe, clarinet, and bassoon); *Quinteto em forma de chôros*, 1928 (for flute, oboe, clarinet, English horn/horn, and bassoon); *Bachianas brasileiras, No. 1*, 1930; String Quartet No. 5, 1931; *Corrupio*, 1933 (for bassoon and string quartet); *Bachianas brasileiras, No. 6*, 1938; String Quartet No. 6, 1938; String Quartet No. 7, 1941; String Quartet No. 8, 1944; Piano Trio No. 4, 1945; String Quartet No. 9, 1945; String Quartet No. 10, 1946; String Quartet No. 11, 1947; String Quartet No. 12, 1950; String Quartet No. 13, 1951; String Quartet No. 14, 1953; String Quartet No. 15, 1954; String Quartet No. 16, 1955; Quintet, 1957 (for flute, violin, viola, cello, and harp); String Quartet No. 17, 1957.

CHORAL WORKS: *Nonetto (Impressão rápida de todo o Brasil)*, 1923 (for chorus and ensemble); *Bachianas brasileiras, No. 9*, 1945; *Bendita sabedoria*, 1958; *Floresta do Amazonas*, 1959 (*Forest of the Amazon*; symphonic poem for voice, male chorus, and orchestra).

FILM SCORE: *O Descobrimento do Brasil*, 1937 (*Discovery of Brazil*).

GUITAR WORKS: *Suite popular brasileira*, 1912 (*Suite populaire brésilienne*); *Chôros No. 1*, 1920; *Twelve Études*, 1929; *Five Preludes*, 1940; Guitar Concerto, 1951.

OPERAS (music): *Izath*, Op. 4, composed 1914, first performed 1940 (libretto by A. Júnior and Villa-Lobos); *Yerma*, Op. 4, composed 1956, first performed 1971 (based on Federico García Lorca's play).

ORCHESTRAL WORKS: Cello Concerto No. 1, 1913; *Chôros No. 10 (Rasga o coração)*, 1926; *Momoprecoce Fantasy*, 1929 (for piano and orchestra); *Bachianas brasileiras, No. 2 (O trenzinho do Caipira)*, 1930; *Bachianas brasileiras, No. 4*, 1936; *Descobrimento do Brasil*, 1937 (four suites); *Bachianas brasileiras, No. 3*, 1938; *Bachianas brasileiras, No. 7*, 1942; *Bachianas brasileiras, No. 8*, 1944; Cello Concerto No. 2, 1953; Harp Concerto, 1953; *Odisséia de uma raça*, 1953 (symphonic poem); Harmonica Concerto, 1956.

PIANO WORKS: *A prole do bebê, No. 1*, 1918; *Carnaval das crianças brasileiras*, 1920 (*Children's Carnival*); *A prole do bebê, No. 2*, 1921 (*Baby's World*); *Cirandinhas*, 1925 (twelve pieces); *Chôros No. 5 (Alma brasileira)*, 1925; *Cirandas*, 1926 (sixteen pieces); *Rudepoema*, 1926 (*Savage Verse*); Piano Concerto No. 1, 1945; Piano Concerto No. 2, 1948; Piano Concerto No. 4, 1952; Piano Concerto No. 5, 1954; Piano Concerto No. 3, 1957.

VOCAL WORKS: *Três canções indígenas*, 1930; *Canções típicas brasileiras*, 1935 (*Cansons typiques brésiliennes*; thirteen folk songs); *Serestas*, 1943 (fourteen songs); *Bachianas brasileiras, No. 5*, 1945.

The Life

Heitor Villa-Lobos (AY-tawr vee-lah-LOH-bohsh) was born in Rio de Janeiro on March 5, 1887, to Noêmia Monteiro and Raúl Villa-Lobos, who worked in the rare-books section of the National Library. Although the boy's formal schooling was uneven, his musical training was rigorous, managed by his father, an amateur musician. Emphasizing classical music, the father cultivated his son's interest in the cello, which became a signature instrument in his compositions. Independently, the young musician cultivated his love of popular music, learning to play another identifying instrument of his work, the guitar. Earning income by playing in music halls, on stage, in film theaters, and for private functions, he joined the circle of leading popular musicians, including Nazaré (Ernesto Nazareth).

Villa-Lobos journeyed throughout Brazil as a young man, gathering voluminous examples of Brazilian folk music. In 1915 he married Lucília Guimarães, a pianist, and he settled in Rio de Janeiro, beginning a career marked by prolific composition. By the end of the decade, he had come to the attention of composer Darius Milhaud and pianist Artur Rubinstein while they were in Brazil. His participation during 1922 in the avant-garde Week of Modern Art consolidated his emerging reputation as a vanguard innovator in Brazilian music.

Promoted by Rubinstein, Villa-Lobos settled in Paris, and he visited other parts of Europe from 1923 to 1930. He gave major concerts of his music, and his work was well received, making him familiar to Maurice Ravel, Manuel de Falla, and Igor Stravinsky. He returned to Brazil in 1930, and he initiated a project that continued for more than a quarter century and singularly advanced musical education. Backed by a nationalist regime in power from 1930 to 1945, Villa-Lobos incorporated basic musical training in schools throughout the country,

emphasizing the study of Brazilian music. He sponsored massive concerts of choral music with tens of thousands of voices. Separating from his wife in 1936 (divorce was not then allowed in Brazil), he took as a companion a former student, Arminda Neves d'Almeida, with whom he remained until the end of his life.

Toward the end of World War II, the American government sponsored performances by Villa-Lobos in the United States. His international reputation grew further when he was invited on numerous occasions to perform his work throughout Europe and Japan. His music's vibrant sinuosity, of Amazonic resonance, became singularly recognizable and identified as Brazilian. In 1945 Villa-Lobos established the Brazilian Academy of Music. He served as its head until his death from cancer in 1959.

The Music

Chôros. The music of Villa-Lobos is noted for its nationalistic content and its personal and innovative style. These were the fundamental characteristics of Brazilian modernism, of which he was the musical leader. Representing these characteristics from the beginning of his career was the chôro, a musical genre emerging in Rio de Janeiro as he came of age. Such music consisted of samba-based improvisation on polkas and waltzes that were popular in late nineteenth century Rio de Janeiro. It was performed as street music or in music halls, and the instrumentation essentially consisted of a flute, a guitar, and a cavaquinho (a small, four-string Brazilian guitar). However, it could include several other instruments or consist of solo piano or guitar performance. Chôro was a lively music, but it had a plaintive aspect resulting from a string technique that gave a "weeping" or chôro effect (from the Portuguese chorar, to cry or weep). Of his chôros, using a wide range of instrumentation, especially notable are *Chôros No. 5* (*Alma brasileira*; Brazilian soul), a lyrical serenade, and *Chôros No. 10* (*Rasga o coraçåo*; tear my heart), a work of richly textured polyphony.

Heitor Villa-Lobos. (AP/Wide World Photos)

Nationalist Emphasis. Nationalist themes dominate many of his dramatic works, such as the ballets *Amazonas* and *Uirapuru*, and the film score of *Discovery of Brazil*. Nonetheless, his work exhibits a cosmopolitan character. He wrote the opera *Yerma*, which was based on the work of the Spanish poet Federico García Lorca. The early compositions of Villa-Lobos reflect French Romantic and Impressionist influences. Moreover, *Uirapuru* echoes Igor Stravinsky's *The Firebird* (1910).

Solo instrumental works of Villa-Lobos concentrated on the piano, guitar, and cello. Among his piano works are *Children's Carnival*, *Baby's World* (based on themes of an infant's toys and figurines), *Savage Verse* (written for and first performed by Rubinstein), and the children's music *Cirandinhas*. Villa-Lobos composed guitar music throughout his career, and the *Suite populaire bresilienne* is especially known. Much of his chamber music includes piano instrumentation. Among such works is a nonetto, *Impressão rápida de todo o Brasil*.

Bachianas brasileiras. The *Bachianas brasileiras* reflect the musical techniques of the works of Johann Sebastian Bach, whom Villa-Lobos considered the supreme master of composition and the epitome of measured, formal Baroque music. The nine *Bachianas brasileiras* suites, appearing from 1932 to 1944, combine the oldest and most influential musical tradition in Brazil, the Baroque, with a modernist revival of Brazilian folk and popular music, blending formalized and improvisational music. The rich tones and weight of the *Bachianas brasileiras* emanate from the resonant dimensions of the cello. Among the most noted of the *Bachianas brasileiras* is number five. Its famous soprano aria, *Cantilena*, soars with limpid purity suffused with the echoing tonalities of deep, vibrant cellos and the masterful balance of feminine and masculine coloring. The famous Brazilian opera star of the Metropolitan Opera of New York, Bidu Sayão, promoted an international dimension for the creations of Villa-Lobos.

Prolific in his production, Villa-Lobos also composed five concerti for piano and one each for guitar, harp, cello, and harmonica. There are twelve symphonies, appearing throughout his career from 1920 to 1957. His oeuvre further includes string quartets, operas, and ballets. (Early in his career, Villa-Lobos discarded the use of opus numbers.)

Much of his work is replete with sounds of nature, particularly birdsong and forest reverberations, together with indigenous rhythms. Onomatopoeia is a striking feature in his compositions. *Trenzinho do caipira* (*Rustic Train*, the last movement of *Bachianas brasileira No. 2*) vividly echoes the sounds of a small train chugging through the valleys and struggling up a hill of the interior.

Books by Villa-Lobos are mainly instructional, including an eleven-volume practical guide to singing, a collection of vocal exercises, and patriotic songs for schoolchildren. In this regard, he worked on establishing a definitive version of the Brazilian national anthem.

Musical Legacy

The music of Villa-Lobos is part of the cultural renaissance that flourished in Brazil during the first half of the twentieth century. The arching, mounting fullness of his characteristic sound is integral to and reflective of the sinuosity of the architecture of Oscar Niemeyer in Brasília; the organically flowing gardens of the landscape architecture of Roberto Burle-Marx; the lyrical, linear sculpture of Bruno Giorgi; and the captivating primitiveness of the paintings of Tarsila do Amaral, Alberto Guignard, and Cândido Portinari.

Villa-Lobos ceaselessly promoted the concept and the content of Brazilian national music. Such music had already begun to appear at the end of the nineteenth century, especially in the works of Alexander Levy and later Alberto Nepomuceno, and Villa-Lobos continued and magnified this trend. Although not the founder of a school, he was the keystone of a nationalist musical movement that included Mozart Camargo Guarnieri, Francisco Mignone, and Oscar Lorenzo Fernandez. Hans-Joachim Koelreutter established an internationalist atonal school of music in Brazil, yet it was Villa-Lobos's students—such as Cláudio Santoro and César Guerra-Peixe—who synthesized this innovation with the nationalist tradition.

Performing rights for the works of Villa-Lobos (who was a member of the Brazilian Composers Union) have been complicated over the years because of the terms of various contracts with publishers in Brazil, France, Italy, and the United States. These documents have now been reviewed and standardized, largely through the work of the

Villa-Lobos Music Society in New York City and the Villa-Lobos Museum in Rio de Janeiro, founded by Neves d'Almeida.

Beyond his international projection of the character of Brazilian music, Villa-Lobos exercised a decisive influence on how and what musical education occurred in schools. Musical ability was considered a quality of the Brazilian character, and knowing how to produce and participate in music was valued and encouraged. Throughout the country, Villa-Lobos conducted tens of thousands of schoolchildren in concerts of choral music performed before massive audiences, encouraging generations of students and parents. The music of Villa-Lobos was appreciated by national audiences for popular music and by international connoisseurs of art music.

Edward A. Riedinger

Further Reading

Appleby, David P. *Villa-Lobos: A Life (1887-1959)*. Lanham, Md.: Scarecrow Press, 2002. Based on extensive use of primary sources, this is a well-researched biography of Villa-Lobos, written by a specialist in Brazilian music.

Béhague, Gerard. *Heitor Villa-Lobos: The Search for Brazil's Musical Soul*. Austin: University of Texas, 1994. A biography of Villa-Lobos and a musicological analysis of fifty-two of his works by a noted scholar of Latin American music.

Oliveira, J. "Black Key vs. White Key: A Villa-Lobos Device." *Latin American Music Review* 5 (1984): 33-47. This article describes the way in which Villa-Lobos devised alternating sequences of black and white keys on the piano to achieve part of his characteristic style.

Peppercorn, Lisa M. *Villa-Lobos, the Music: An Analysis of His Style*. London: Kahn & Averill, 1991. Relevant to lay and scholarly interests, this work provides a critical review of biographical sources and a close analysis of bibliography on Villa-Lobos.

Vassberg, David E. "Villa-Lobos, Music as a Tool for Nationalism." *Luso-Brazilian Review* 6, no. 2 (1967): 55-65. This article analyzes how Villa-Lobos systematically used music as a means of defining Brazilian national character, particularly through choral music programs in schools.

See also: Chávez, Carlos; Gil, Gilberto; Jobim, Antônio Carlos; Milhaud, Darius; Nascimento, Milton; Ravel, Maurice; Rubinstein, Artur; Segovia, Andrés; Steiner, Max.

Gene Vincent

American rock singer, songwriter, and guitarist

An early rockabilly-rock performer, Vincent combined a soulful, penetrating vocal style with a dynamic onstage presence.

Born: February 11, 1935; Norfolk, Virginia
Died: October 12, 1971; Newhall, California
Also known as: Vincent Eugene Craddock (birth name)
Member of: Gene Vincent and His Blue Caps

Principal recordings

ALBUMS (solo): *A Gene Vincent Record Date*, 1958; *Hot Rod Gang*, 1958 (with others); *Shakin' Up a Storm*, 1964; *Gene Vincent*, 1967; *I'm Back and I'm Proud*, 1969; *If You Could Only See Me Today*, 1970; *The Day the World Turned Blue*, 1971.

ALBUMS (with Gene Vincent and His Blue Caps): *Bluejean Bop!*, 1956; *Gene Vincent and His Blue Caps*, 1957; *Gene Vincent Rocks! And the Blue Caps Roll*, 1958; *Sounds Like Gene Vincent*, 1959; *Crazy Times*, 1960; *Crazy Beat*, 1963.

SINGLES (with Gene Vincent and His Blue Caps): "Be-Bop-A-Lula," 1956; "Race with the Devil," 1956; "Woman Love," 1956; "Lotta Lovin'," 1957; "Dance to the Bop," 1958.

The Life

Gene Vincent was born Vincent Eugene Craddock in Norfolk, Virginia. He was one of four children of Ezekiah Jackson Craddock and Mary Louise Craddock, proprietors of a general store. Vincent grew up interested in country, rhythm-and-blues, and gospel music, and he acquired his first guitar at the age of twelve.

In 1952 Vincent dropped out of high school to join the U.S. Navy, and he was stationed in Korea. In 1955 he was severely injured in a motorcycle accident that left him with a permanently damaged leg. The injury—a source of constant pain—eventually led to dependence on painkillers and alcohol abuse. During his long recovery, Vincent wrote a rockabilly tune, "Be-Bop-A-Lula," that landed him music publishing and recording contracts. In 1956, the year he married for the first of four times, the song propelled Vincent toward fame. With his band, the Blue Caps, Vincent released a string of hits in the late 1950's and early 1960's, before rockabilly was supplanted by rock and roll, which caused his fade in popularity in the United States. A devastating 1960 auto crash, in which fellow rockabilly artist Eddie Cochran was killed, further damaged Vincent's bad leg.

Moving to England in the early 1960's, Vincent experienced a fresh surge in popularity among loyal rockabilly fans abroad, thanks in part to his revamped image as a black-leather-wearing rebel. A dynamic performer at live shows throughout his brief career, Vincent died of bleeding ulcers at the age of thirty-six.

The Music

Vincent's musical career divides into two phases. The first, which lasted about five years, was marked by up-tempo songs—authored by Vincent or by members of his backup band—reaching the Top 40 on American pop charts. Notable among these were "Be-Bop-A-Lula," "Race with the Devil," "Bluejean Bop," "Lotta Lovin'," and "Dance to the Bop." "Be-Bop-A-Lula" and "Bluejean Bop" earned Vincent gold records. The hits were marked by Vincent's strong, confident vocals, usually aided by heavy echo effects to add depth. The Blue Caps ably supported Vincent (the original band consisted of "Galloping" Cliff Gallup, lead guitar; "Wee" Willie Williams, rhythm guitar; "Jumpin'" Jack Neal, upright string bass; Dickie "Be-Bop" Harrell, drums). Gallup's virtuoso lead guitar work was often a highlight on recordings. When Vincent entered the musical scene, he parlayed his sudden fame into appearances on television programs (*Town Hall Party*, *The Ed Sullivan Show*) and in rock-oriented films (*The Girl Can't Help It* in 1956, *Hot Rod Gang* in 1958, and *Live It Up!* in 1960) that added to his allure.

The second phase, encompassing the last decade of his life, witnessed Vincent's descent into obscurity in the United States and his concurrent rise to cult figure in Great Britain and France. While based in England, he scored several minor hits, including "She She Little Sheila" and "I'm Going Home," but he never regained his earlier career momentum.

"Be-Bop-A-Lula." The song that launched Vincent's career in 1956 was, as indicated by its title, a product of bebop, a style of jazz that evolved from swing during the early 1940's. The extemporaneous quality of bebop and its special language became an integral part of the nonconformist Beat period. Possibly inspired by Helen Humes's 1945 hit "Be-Baba-Leba," Vincent's song, like its predecessor, had an improvisational feel and meaningless syllables to provide a rhythmic hook. Vincent added a steady, driving tempo, supplementing his voice with reverb, and he produced a classic example of rockabilly, an important musical bridge between country, rhythm and blues, and rock and roll. Vincent's biggest hit, the song rose to number seven and spent twenty weeks on U.S. pop charts.

Bluejean Bop! A first album hastily compiled to capitalize on the popularity of "Be-Bop-A-Lula," it was recorded two months after the hit single's release. The title tune provided a second hit single, a million-seller. The album presented an eclectic combination of numbers that effectively showcased Vincent's singing range and the Blue Caps' versatility. Some cuts were composed on the spot (such as "Jumps, Giggles, and Shouts" and "Who Slapped John?"). There was new material from a variety of sources (such as Jerry Reed's "Crazy Legs," Bobby Carroll's "Well I Knocked Bim Bam," and Danny Wolfe's "Gonna Back Up Baby"). The remainder of the album featured down-tempo covers ("Up a Lazy River," "Jezebel," and "Peg o' My Heart") augmented by fine instrumental work and by Vincent's smooth renditions, so unlike his urgent, harder rocking tunes.

Crazy Times. A 1960 release and Vincent's best-selling album, this reinforces the singer's reputation for covering a wide range of material and musical styles. The album featured old standards ("Blue Eyes Crying in the Rain" and "Green Back Dollar") and original new material ("She She Little Sheila"; a ballad Vincent wrote for his wife, "Darlene"; and two songs that reflected wistfully on the touring life: "Everybody's Got a Date But Me" and "Mitchiko from Tokyo").

Musical Legacy

The influence of rockabilly—an evolving blend of country, gospel, rhythm and blues, and fledgling rock and roll—on contemporary music is incalculable. Vincent, Elvis Presley, Carl Perkins, Buddy Holly, Roy Orbison, Little Richard, and Eddie Cochran were true pioneers. Vincent, however, was the prototype: first to adapt a swaggering, rebellious stage persona; first to dress the part of a society outcast; first to win wide acceptance while singing suggestive lyrics to frankly sexual driving rock beats. Vincent earned a star on Hollywood's Walk of Fame, he became a charter inductee into the Rockabilly Hall of Fame in 1997, and he was enshrined in the Rock and Roll Hall of Fame in 1998. The Everly Brothers, the Beatles, Jim Morrison, Bob Dylan, Jeff Beck, Van Morrison, the Stray Cats, Dave Edmunds and other artists emulated or paid homage to Vincent.

Jack Ewing

Further Reading

Cochran, Bobby, and Susan Van Hecke. *Three Steps to Heaven: The Eddie Cochran Story*. Milwaukee, Wis.: Hal Leonard, 2003. A biography of the seminal rocker linked with Vincent on their 1960 tour to England, when Vincent was involved the crash that killed Cochran.

Collis, John. *Gene Vincent and Eddie Cochran: Rock 'n' Roll Revolutionaries*. London: Virgin, 2004. The story of two tragic rock figures, told against the backdrop of their groundbreaking joint 1960 tour to England. Includes photographs.

Morrison, Craig. *Go Cat Go! Rockabilly Music and Its Makers*. Urbana: University of Illinois Press, 1998. An overview of the musical style that was a precursor to rock and roll, this contains biographies of the genre's biggest stars, including Vincent's, and discographies.

Naylor, Jerry, and Steve Halliday. *The Rockabilly Legends: They Called It Rockabilly Long Before It Was Called Rock 'n' Roll*. Milwaukee, Wis.: Hal Leonard, 2007. Complete coverage of the dynamic rockabilly genre. Includes photographs, brief biographies of rockabilly artists, and a DVD sampler of period music.

Van Hecke, Susan. *Race with the Devil: Gene Vincent's Life in the Fast Lane*. New York: St. Martin's Minotaur, 2000. This is an in-depth biography of the performer, containing many behind-the-scenes details and photographs.

See also: Beck, Jeff; Blackwell, Otis; Everly, Don and Phil; Lewis, Jerry Lee; Little Richard; Morrison, Jim; Morrison, Van; Perkins, Carl; Presley, Elvis.

W

Tom Waits

American rock singer, songwriter, pianist, guitarist and film-score composer

A prolific singer-songwriter and multi-instrumentalist, Waits is best known for his gritty, blues-inflected vocal style with evocative lyrics depicting bygone eras and snapshots of life on the road.

Born: December 7, 1949; Pomona, California
Also known as: Thomas Alan Waits (full name)

Principal works

FILM SCORES: *One from the Heart*, 1982 (with Crystal Gale); *Night on Earth*, 1991; *Don't Say a Word*, 2005.

Principal recordings

ALBUMS: *Closing Time*, 1973; *The Heart of Saturday Night*, 1974; *Nighthawks at the Diner*, 1975; *Small Change*, 1976; *Foreign Affairs*, 1977; *Blue Valentine*, 1978; *Heartattack and Vine*, 1980; *Swordfishtrombones*, 1983; *Tom Waits*, 1984; *Rain Dogs*, 1985; *Frank's Wild Years*, 1987 (with Benoit Christîe); *Bone Machine*, 1992; *The Black Rider*, 1993 (with William S. Burroughs and Robert Wilson); *Mule Variations*, 1999; *Alice*, 2002; *Blood Money*, 2002; *Real Gone*, 2004.

The Life

Tom Waits was born Thomas Alan Waits in Pomona, California, to Jesse Frank Waits and Alma Johnson McMurray. He grew up in Southern California, learning to play piano and performing in a soul band during his high school years. In 1971 Waits recorded his first demos for Herb Cohen and Frank Zappa's Los Angeles-based Bizarre/Straight Records. In the following year, he signed a contract with Asylum Records on which he would release *Closing Time*, his first album.

Over the course of the 1970's, life on the road be-gan to take its toll on Waits, leading to alcoholism, a subject that appeared in many of his songs from that era. In 1980 Waits began working with director Francis Ford Coppola, writing music for the feature film *One from the Heart* (1982). He met playwright Kathleen Brennan through his work on the film, and they married, which had a positive impact on Waits's health and on his career. His interest in film and theater would grow over the following years resulting in a number of film scores, musical-theater pieces, and even acting roles. While Waits's music had always conveyed a strong sense of drama, his relationship with Brennan heightened his creative and artistic process, influencing his staged and his unstaged musical works.

Although Waits's recordings have never achieved wide commercial success, his music has attracted a devoted following of fans, including prominent recording artists. The most commercially successful cover of a Waits's song was Rod Stewart's 1989 version of "Downtown Train," which reached number three on the *Billboard* charts. Testifying to his critical success and his musical eclecticism, Waits won a Grammy Award for his album *Bone Machine* in the Best Alternative Album category and a Grammy Award for *Mule Variations* in the Best Contemporary Folk Album category.

The Music

Although Waits began his career as a crooning balladeer and a lounge pianist, he matured musically with the development of his gravel-voiced hobo persona. In his portraits of life on city streets, at truck stops, in smoky saloons, and at carnival sideshows, Waits conjures images of broken people in decrepit surroundings—the seedy yet honest underside of Americana. His songwriting draws on the musical storytelling tradition of Woody Guthrie and Bob Dylan as well as the poetic prose of Jack Kerouac and Charles Bukowski. To match this troubadour lyricism, Waits's musical palette features gravelly vocals (reminiscent of Louis Armstrong) with an eclectic blend of instrumental ensembles and stylistic traditions. Indeed, his compositions run the stylistic gamut from blues, folk, country, rock, swing, and soul to avant-garde jazz and classical music.

Early Ballads. After the release of *Closing Time*, Waits released a series of albums: *The Heart of Saturday Night*, the double live album *Nighthawks at the Diner*, *Small Change*, *Foreign Affairs*, and *Blue Valentine*. In these early albums, Waits established his drifter aesthetic and refined his Beat poet lyricism. In one noteworthy example from *Small Change*, his semiautobiographical "Tom Traubert's Blues (Four Sheets to the Wind in Copenhagen)" spins a melancholic yarn about a drunk stranded and rambling about in a foreign country. The recording is typical of Waits's early ballad style, featuring the composer on piano with an intimate string accompaniment. In "Step Right Up," another track from the album, Waits plays the role of a traveling salesman, pitching dozens of imagined products with comically hyperbolic claims. The jazz trio accompaniment with a repeated acoustic bass ostinato here typifies Waits's early up-tempo compositions.

Tom Waits. (AP/Wide World Photos)

Experimentation. *Swordfishtrombones* completed Waits's shift from blues-tinged balladeer to avant-garde maverick. With this recording, Waits began experimenting with new atmospheric and industrial effects that would also appear on *Rain Dogs* and the Grammy Award-winning *Bone Machine*. Mixing the percussive sounds of hubcaps and pans with marimba, bagpipes, organs, and the angular, near-atonal lines of guitarist Marc Ribot, Waits developed a new sound to complement his poetry. He describes this diverse sonic palette of modern electric and acoustic instruments coupled with found objects and instrumental oddities including the Stroh violin and Chamberlain as a "junkyard orchestra." On the song "Cemetery Polka" (from *Rain Dogs*), Waits uses such an ensemble to great effect, performing on Farfisa and pump organ with an accompaniment of metal and wood percussion effects evoking the rattling of bones.

Music for Theater. During this period, Waits became more involved in music for theater. Following an Academy Award nomination for his music to Coppola's *One from the Heart*, Waits collaborated with Brennan on the musical-theater piece *Frank's Wild Years*, which was produced at Chicago's Steppenwolf Theater in 1986 and which starred Waits in the title role. Following a number of other film and theater projects, Waits collaborated with director Robert Wilson and Beat author William S. Burroughs on the production of *The Black Rider: The Casting of the Magic Bullets* (1990), based on the German folktale *Der Freischütz* and performed in Hamburg in 1990. Waits drew inspiration for the musical from the collaborations of composer Kurt Weill and author Burtolt Brecht.

Late Works. In 1998 Waits released a compilation album entitled *Beautiful Maladies*, and in 1999 he released the Grammy Award-winning *Mule Variations*. Nominated in the Contemporary Folk category, the album highlighted the blues and country-roots-music side of Waits's influences while retaining the odd musical timbres of his previous work. On the album's final track, "Come on up to the House," Waits offers a lyrical viewpoint that reflects a newfound maturity.

In 2002 Waits simultaneously released albums of music from two recent theatrical projects: a musical based on Georg Büchner's *Woyzeck* (1913) entitled *Blood Money* and an adaptation of Lewis Carroll's

Alice in Wonderland (1865) entitled *Alice*. Eschewing the rustic tone of *Mule Variations*, his 2004 album *Real Gone* is notable for its frenetic, guitar-driven songs, with Waits's signature piano accompaniments replaced by the singer's beat boxing.

Musical Legacy

Waits's body of work in the fields of popular music, film, and theater will be remembered as a major contribution to the American maverick singer-songwriter tradition. Waits has made his mark in popular music with his unmistakable voice and his lyrical drifter persona. His critical successes as well as the numerous recordings of his compositions by other musicians also testify to the impact of Waits's music.

J. Griffith Rollefson

Further Reading

Humphries, Patrick. *The Many Lives of Tom Waits*. New York: Omnibus, 2007. An overview of the thirty years of Waits's career, with his output of twenty albums and his songs covered by prominent artists. Includes discography and filmography.

Jacobs, Jay S. *Wild Years: The Music and Myth of Tom Waits*. Toronto, Ont.: ECW Press, 2000. This biographical work chronicles Waits's career, and it demonstrates that after the singer-songwriter conquered his personal problems, his music became more experimental. Includes discography and a list of guest appearances.

See also: Armstrong, Louis; Burke, Solomon; Dylan, Bob; Guthrie, Woody; Howlin' Wolf; Leadbelly; Lovett, Lyle; Sibelius, Jean; Stewart, Rod; Weill, Kurt.

T-Bone Walker

American blues singer, songwriter, and guitarist

Walker pioneered the use of the electric guitar as a lead instrument in a blues band, and he enjoyed a string of hits in the new rhythm-and-blues field.

Born: May 26, 1910; Linden, Texas
Died: March 16, 1975; Los Angeles, California
Also known as: Aaron Thibeaux Walker (full name); Oak Cliff T-Bone

Principal recordings

ALBUMS: *I Get So Weary*, 1961; *Great Blues Vocals and Guitar*, 1963; *The Legendary T-Bone Walker*, 1967; *Stormy Monday Blues*, 1967; *Blue Rocks*, 1968; *I Want a Little Girl*, 1968; *The Truth*, 1968; *Bosses of the Blues, Vol. 1*, 1969; *Feelin' the Blues*, 1969; *Funky Town*, 1969; *Good Feelin'*, 1969; *Every Day I Have the Blues*, 1970; *Dirty Mistreater*, 1973; *Fly Walker Airlines*, 1973; *Well Done*, 1973.

SINGLES: "I Got a Break Baby," 1942; "Mean Old World," 1942; "Bobby Sox Baby," 1946; "Call It Stormy Monday (But Tuesday Is Just as Bad)," 1947; "T-Bone Shuffle," 1947.

The Life

Aaron Thibeaux "T-Bone" Walker was the only child of Rance Walker and Movelia Walker Randall. His parents separated when Walker was two, and both his mother and stepfather, Marco Washington, were musicians. Raised in the Oak Cliff section of Dallas, Walker was exposed to a wide variety of African American popular music, particularly blues, from his singing, guitar-playing mother and her circle of friends, which included Blind Lemon Jefferson. In 1929 Walker made a record under the name Oak Cliff T-Bone, and he worked medicine shows, as a dancer and a multi-instrumentalist. Playing a banjo, he developed an act in which he billed himself as the Cab Calloway of the South. During this time, he crossed paths with Charlie Christian, who brought the electric guitar to jazz. Around 1936, Walker moved to Los Angeles, where he performed as a dancer with bandleader Big Jim Wynn's show. His often-overlooked talent as singer took him on the road with bandleader Les Hite in 1939. The following year saw him honing his new skills on the electric guitar as well as on his flamboyant stage show at the Little Harlem Club in Los Angeles. In 1942 his signature guitar style first appeared on "I Got a Break Baby." The hits started coming after World War II on the Los Angeles-based Black & White Records, recordings that paired Walker with small combos featuring the best West Coast rhythm-and-blues session men. Although he later made fine recordings for the Imperial and Atlantic labels, Walker's career never regained its post-World War II momentum. Still, he remained a beloved legend in the Los Angeles rhythm-and-blues community, and he was widely mourned following his death from pneumonia in 1975.

The Music

Just as his friend Christian did for the electric guitar in jazz, Walker invented the vocabulary for that instrument in blues. His single-string phrases, double-string slurs, and punchy chordal vamps were ingenious pairings of idiom with instrument. The tone of early electric guitars enabled Walker to emulate the staccato punch of a horn. The sustain associated with later electric guitars was absent in the 1940's, which encouraged Walker to create clipped, conversationally syncopated single-string phrases. While the originality of his guitar style cannot be overemphasized, his talent as both singer and songwriter provided a successful framework for that style's display. Walker epitomized an urbane extension of guitar-based blues into the more horn-driven sound of emergent rhythm and blues.

"Mean Old World." Recorded for the fledgling Capitol label in July, 1942, this was a song Walker would revisit throughout his career. The relaxed tempo of the tune and the cool assurance of Walker's minute-plus guitar solo as the record opens contrast with the high-pitched urgency of his vocals. The lyrics are striking for representing an existential philosophy of the blues. Walker's strong vocals and stinging guitar lines are ably abetted by pianist Freddie Slack and by an effectively understated bass-and-drums rhythm section.

"Bobby Sox Baby." This 1946 song, written by Dootsie Williams, was an influential hit that com-

bined an after-hours blues groove with novelty lyrics about a teenage girl seeking autographs of popular singers such as Frank Sinatra. If the combination seems odd in retrospect, it was effective in its day. The widespread popularity of the recording brought Walker's distinctive guitar approach to the attention of Lowell Fulson and others, who have cited this performance as the incentive to emulating Walker's style.

"Call It Stormy Monday (But Tuesday Is Just as Bad)." This 1947 recording became one of the enduring standards of the blues genre. Walker wrote the song, which catalogs the character of the days of the week. Expert playing by an ensemble that includes trumpeter Teddy Buckner and pianist Lloyd Glenn neatly augments the original nature of the song's lyrics. Walker brings a witty resignation to his vocal performance, and his guitar weaves tastefully punctuate the vocals. B. B. King points to this recording as a major influence on his later development as a blues singer and guitarist.

"T-Bone Shuffle." Walker's tendency toward slow blues is broken by this boogie-based showpiece in the dance rhythm tagged a shuffle. Soloing in the company of another expert small ensemble, Walker makes economic but effective statements on guitar in the midst of unusually celebratory lyrics. This became a signature song he reworked later in his career.

Musical Legacy

Although he was not the first bluesman to record with electric guitar, Walker may be been the first to realize its potential beyond mere amplification. The single-string soloing of such pioneering bluesmen as Lonnie Johnson gained new dimension and vocabulary in Walker's hands, thanks to his intuitive understanding of the electric guitar's expressiveness as a blues voice. He was also a fine singer and a flamboyant showman, and other artists emulated his performance style.

Mark Humphrey

Further Reading

Cohn, Lawrence, ed. *Nothing But the Blues: The Music and the Musicians*. New York: Abbeville Press, 1993. This collection of essays and evocative photographs offers an overview of Walker's career in the context of the evolution of urban blues.

Dance, Helen Oakley. *Stormy Monday: The T-Bone Walker Story.* Baton Rouge: Louisiana State University Press, 1987. An affectionate jazz and blues insider's portrait of Walker's life and career.

Shaw, Arnold. *Honkers and Shouters: The Golden Years of Rhythm and Blues.* New York: Collier Books, 1978. Shaw's expansive overview of rhythm and blues includes a fascinating 1973 interview with Walker.

Welding, Pete, and Toby Byron, eds. *Bluesland: Portraits of Twelve Major American Blues Masters.* New York: Dutton, 1991. Includes a chapter on Walker's music, his life, and his significance by Helen and Stanley Dance, his early champions and longtime friends.

See also: Christian, Charlie; Jefferson, Blind Lemon; Johnson, Lonnie; King, B. B.; Turner, Big Joe.

Fats Waller

American jazz pianist and composer

An enormously popular stride pianist, comic entertainer, and composer of enduring jazz and popular standards, Waller, with his impeccable piano technique and humorous patter, was a dominant influence on musical entertainment.

Born: May 21, 1904; New York, New York
Died: December 15, 1943; Kansas City, Missouri
Also known as: Thomas Wright Waller (full name)

Principal works

MUSICAL THEATER (music): *Keep Shufflin'*, 1928 (with Clarence Todd; lyrics by Andy Razaf and Henry Creamer; libretto by Flournoy Miller and Aubrey L. Lyles); *Hot Chocolates*, 1929 (with Harry Brooks; lyrics and libretto by Razaf); *Early to Bed*, 1943 (lyrics and libretto by George Marion, Jr.).

Principal recordings

SINGLES: "Squeeze Me," 1923; "Wild Cat Blues," 1923 (with Clarence Williams); "Anybody Here Want to Try My Cabbage," 1924; "In Harlem's

Araby," 1924; "Georgia Bo-Bo," 1926; "Come on and Stomp, Stop, Stomp," 1927; "I'm Goin' Huntin'," 1927 (with James C. Johnson); "Ain't Misbehavin'," 1929; "Blue, Turning Grey over You," 1929; "Handful of Keys," 1929; "Honeysuckle Rose," 1929; "My Fate Is in Your Hands," 1929; "My Feelin's Are Hurt," 1929; "Smashin' Thirds," 1929; "Sweet Savannah Sue," 1929; "What Did I Do to Be So Black and Blue," 1929 (with Harry Brooks); "Zonky," 1929; "I'm Crazy 'bout My Baby and My Baby's Crazy 'bout Me," 1931; "How Can You Face Me," 1932; "Keepin' out of Mischief Now," 1932; "Strange as It Seems," 1932; "I'm Gonna Sit Right Down and Write Myself a Letter," 1934; "Ain't Cha Glad," 1933; "You're Breakin' My Heart," 1933; "Stealin' Apples," 1936; "Joint Is Jumpin'," 1938; "Spider and the Fly," 1938; "The Sheik of Araby," 1939; "You Can't Have Your Cake and Eat It," 1939; "Your Feets Too Big," 1939; "Old Grand Dad," 1940; "All That Meat and No Potatoes," 1941; "Slightly Less than Wonderful," 1943.

The Life

Thomas Wright "Fats" Waller was born in 1904 in Harlem, New York, one of five surviving children of Edward and Adeline Lockett Waller. At the earliest age Waller was exposed to the richness of African American music at church services and in his home, where his musically talented mother led the family in hymn singing. He also learned to play the harmonium, the organ, and the piano. Waller acquired the nickname Fats because of his love of eating.

His prodigious musical talent already in evidence, Waller left school in 1918 and began playing organ and piano in motion-picture houses, vaudeville theaters, and dance clubs throughout Harlem. Waller also began learning stride piano from its master, James P. Johnson.

In 1921 Waller married Edith Hatchett, and they had a son, Thomas, Jr., although they soon divorced. In the 1920's Waller began composing hit after hit. The money he earned from composing and performing he quickly spent on his divorce settlement, lavish lifestyle, and carousing. In 1927 he married Anita Rutherford; their sons were Ronald and Maurice. In the 1930's Waller became a radio and recording star and appeared in numerous short films. Having just achieved a Broadway triumph with his musical score of *Early to Bed* in 1943, Waller caught pneumonia on his way back to New York from an engagement in California with his manager, W. T. (Ed) Kirkeby. Weakened by a lifetime of indulgence, Waller collapsed on a train platform in Kansas City and died.

The Music

In 1922 Waller's musical career launched in earnest. He began playing piano at Harlem rent parties, where tenants pass the hat for donations to help pay their rent, which he commemorated in his hit song "The Joint Is Jumpin'." As the "professor of piano," Waller had ample opportunity to practice his unique combination of keyboard artistry, spoken asides, and comic mannerisms. He also began making records for the Okeh label, and he was popular as an accompanist for such stars as Louis Armstrong, Alberta Hunter, and Bessie Smith. His composition "Squeeze Me" was his first hit.

Stride Pianist. Over the next two decades, Waller perfected his talents as a pianist, entertainer, and composer. He became the foremost exemplar of stride piano, a complex style in which the left hand alternates between low single bass notes on the first and third beats and chords one octave higher on the second and fourth beats of each measure. This stride provides a rollicking percussive bounce as the right hand roams the high keys, playing syncopated melodies and embellishments. The swiftly shifting hands provide rhythmic accents and a polyphonic, orchestral feel. Waller's virtuosic recordings of his piano compositions "Handful of Keys" and "Smashin' Thirds" are rich with cross-rhythms, counterpoint, and fast tempi.

Jazz Standards. In 1934 Waller attained international stardom: He had a weekly radio show on CBS, he began recording for RCA Victor, and he toured in the United States and in Europe. Waller also began performing with his septet known as Fats Waller and His Rhythm, including such highly professional musicians as Herman Autrey, Gene "Honeybear" Sedric, and Al Casey. Waller and His Rhythm eventually made more than four hundred recordings. Waller made appearances in films, performing "Spreadin' Rhythm Around" in *King of Burlesque* (1935), accompanying Bill "Bojangles"

Robinson in *Hooray for Love* (1935), and performing the title song in the short films (known as "soundies") *Honeysuckle Rose* (1941), *Your Feets Too Big* (1941), and *The Joint Is Jumping* (1942).

As a composer of jazz standards, Waller is second only to Duke Ellington. Waller teamed up with talented lyricist Andrew Razaf to produce enduring songs. Waller's compositions show an innate melodic gift, surprising but engaging harmonies, and a sense of rhythm that always swings. Waller's hits include such classics as "Honeysuckle Rose," "I'm Crazy 'bout My Baby, and My Baby's Crazy 'bout Me," "Keepin' out of Mischief Now," "All That Meat and No Potatoes," and "Blue, Turning Grey over You." Waller demonstrated his love for the organ with his composition "Jitterbug Waltz," with its lilting, descending melody. Waller's recordings of the novelty songs "I'm Gonna Sit Right Down and Write Myself a Letter," "The Sheik of Araby," and the fantastic "Your Feets Too Big" are comedic classics. Both Armstrong and Ellington recorded Waller's "What Did I Do to Be So Black and Blue" in 1929 as eloquent pleas against racism.

"Ain't Misbehavin'." Few songs have spanned jazz history as much as Waller's greatest composition, "Ain't Misbehavin'," with lyrics by Razaf. The song is delightful with its catchy melody, midsong doubling of tempo, and delightful internal rhymes. Armstrong scored a nightly hit with his rendition of the song in the 1929 revue *Chocolate Babies*, at Harlem's Connie's Inn, as well as in his bravura recording on July 19, 1929. In 1941 Waller played "Ain't Misbehavin'" in a soundie.

In the celebrated 1943 race film *Stormy Weather*, with such African American stars as Robinson, Lena Horne, Dooley Wilson, and the Nicholas brothers, Waller and His Rhythm accompany Ada Brown in "That Ain't Right" and perform "Ain't Misbehavin'." Several critics claim Waller stole the film with his trademark rolling eyes, fluttering eyebrows, comical falsetto singing, and masterful stride piano. While Brown sings, Waller comically bobs his head, jauntily covered by his too-small brown derby, and engages in a call and response of his classic comic patter: "Mercy," "One never knows, do one," "Tell these fools anything, but tell me the truth," "Aw, beef to me, Mama, beef to me, I don't like pork no how," and "Suffer, suffer, excess baggage, suffer."

Although Waller died shortly after the film was made, "Ain't Misbehavin'" remains one of the most performed of jazz standards. In 1978 a delightful Broadway hit musical, *Ain't Misbehavin'*, introduced the title song and other Waller compositions to a new generation.

Musical Legacy

With his extravagant showmanship, Waller was the "clown prince" of jazz. His comic banter and persona, entertaining to this day, should not obscure two points. First, Waller was one of the most talented pianists and composers in jazz history. Many of his songs are enduring standards. His piano playing represented the high point of stride and influenced a generation of pianists. Count Basie, Ellington, Art Tatum, Teddy Wilson, and even the cerebral bop pianists Thelonious Monk and Dave Brubeck have acknowledged a debt to Waller. Jamming at Harlem's after-hour clubs in the early 1940's, Waller is rumored to have contributed ideas to, and even the name of, the new jazz style, bop. Second, Waller's surreal treatment of the most banal material reflects a satirical view of social conventions, race relations, and the human condition. Thus Waller, like fellow entertainers W. C. Fields and the Marx brothers, made his own zany contribution to the absurdist aesthetic of the interwar period.

Howard Bromberg

Further Reading

Giddins, Gary. *Visions of Jazz: The First Century*. Oxford, England: Oxford University Press, 1999. This collection of thoughtful essays on the most important jazz musicians emphasizes Waller's extensive influence on subsequent pianists.

Kirkeby, Ed, Duncan Schiedt, and Sinclair Trail. *Ain't Misbehavin': The Story of Fats Waller*. New York: Da Capo Press, 1976. Sympathetic memoir of Waller's life and music by his personal manager, Kirkeby.

Shipton, Alyn. *Fats Waller: The Cheerful Little Earful*. London: Continuum, 2005. A new chapter for this revised edition surveys Waller's reissued compact discs.

Vance, Joel. *Fats Waller: His Life and Times*. Chicago: Contemporary Books, 1977. Informal biography emphasizing the religious roots of Waller's music and outlook.

Waller, Maurice, and Anthony Calabrese. *Fats Waller*. New York: Shirmer Books, 1997. Larger-than-life story of Fats Waller as told by his son, Maurice Waller.

See also: Armstrong, Louis; Basie, Count; Blake, Eubie; Brubeck, Dave; Carter, Benny; Ellington, Duke; Garner, Erroll; Gillespie, Dizzy; Grappelli, Stéphane; Hunter, Alberta; Jones, Hank; Jordan, Louis; Kirk, Rahsaan Roland; McPartland, Marian; Monk, Thelonious; Powell, Bud; Smith, Bessie; Tatum, Art; Washington, Dinah.

Bruno Walter
German classical conductor and composer

As a conductor, Walter was a celebrated interpreter of Austro-German music, and he was a strong advocate of the works of Gustav Mahler.

Born: September 15, 1876; Berlin, Germany
Died: February 17, 1962; Beverly Hills, California
Also known as: Bruno Schlesinger (birth name)

Principal works

CHAMBER WORKS: String Quartet, 1903; Sonata in A Major, 1910 (for violin and piano).

ORCHESTRAL WORKS: *Symphonische Phantasie*, 1904; Symphony No. 1 in D Minor, 1907; Symphony No. 2 in E Major, 1910.

Principal recordings

ALBUMS (as conductor): *Beethoven: Concerto for Violin in D Major, Op. 61*, 1932; *Wagner: Die Walküre, Act I*, 1935; *Brahms: Concerto for Piano No. 1 in D Minor, Op. 15*, 1936; *Mahler: Symphony No. 9*, 1938; *Beethoven: Symphony No. 1 in C Major, Op. 21*, 1939; *Beethoven: Fidelio*, 1941; *Tchaikovsky: Concerto for Piano No. 1 in B-flat Minor, Op. 23*, 1948; *Mahler: Kindertotenlieder*, 1949; *Brahms: Concerto for Piano No. 2 in B-flat Major, Op. 83*, 1951; *Mahler: Das Lied von der Erde*, 1952; *Beethoven: Sonata for Violin and Piano No. 5 in F Major, Op. 24—*

Spring, 1953; *Mozart: Concerto for Piano No. 14 in E-flat Major*, 1954; *Beethoven: Symphony No. 6*, 1958 (*Pastoral*); *Brahms: Symphony No. 4 in E Minor, Op. 98*, 1959; *Brahms: Symphony No. 2 and No. 3*, 1960.

WRITINGS OF INTEREST: *Von den moralischen Kräften der Musik*, 1935; *Gustav Mahler*, 1936 (English translation, 1937); *Theme and Variations: An Autobiography*, 1946; *Von der Musik und vom Musizieren*, 1957 (*Of Music and Music Making*, 1961).

The Life

In 1876 Bruno Walter (BREW-noh VAHL-tur) was born Bruno Schlesinger to Joseph and Johanna Schlesinger, a middle-class Jewish family in Berlin. Walter learned piano from his mother in his early childhood, and at the age of eight, he entered the Stern Conservatory in Berlin. Although Walter made great progress in piano under the tutelage of Heinrich Ehrlich, he decided to become a conductor after seeing Hans von Bülow conducting an orchestra. Walter made his conducting debut at the Cologne Opera in 1894, and he moved to Hamburg the following year. There, he met Gustav Mahler, who had great influence on Walter's development as a musician. Walter frequently visited Mahler's house, where the two men played piano duets and talked about music, literature, and science. Their close relationship continued while Walter worked at opera houses in Breslau (where he changed his surname from Schlesinger to Walter), Pressburg, Riga, and Berlin between 1896 and 1900. In 1901 Walter moved to Vienna to work at the Court Opera, where Mahler was music director, and he remained there for eleven years.

In 1913 Walter became the Royal Bavarian General Music Director in Munich, and he conducted in three opera houses in the city for the next ten years. He directed various German operas, such as Richard Wagner's *Parsifal* (1882) and *Tristan und Isolde* (1859), and the premiere of Hans Erich Pfitzner's *Palestrina* (1915). In 1925 he was appointed as music director of the Berlin State Opera, and in 1929 he became the music director of the Leipzig Gewandhaus. Walter made many guest appearances in the 1920's and early 1930's, with performances throughout the Europe and the United States.

After Adolf Hitler came to power in 1933, Walter left Germany, and in 1936 he became the artistic director of the Vienna State Opera. During the Anschluss, in March, 1938, when Germany annexed Austria, he fled, eventually settling in the United States, where he became a citizen in 1946. After his arrival in New York in 1939, Walter conducted many American orchestras, such as the NBC Symphony Orchestra, the New York Philharmonic, and the Los Angeles Philharmonic. He made his debut at the Metropolitan Opera in 1941, conducting Ludwig van Beethoven's *Fidelio* (1805). In 1949 he moved to Los Angeles, and he appeared as guest conductor with many prominent orchestras in North America and in Europe. In his final years, Walter made various recordings with the Columbia Symphony Orchestra. On February 17, 1962, he died of a heart attack at age eighty-five in Beverly Hills, California.

The Music

During the 1910's and 1920's, Walter directed various German operas, such as Wagner's Ring cycle, and he championed the music of Mahler, making it an integral part of his repertoire throughout his career. Walter became involved in recording in the mid-1920's, and his involvement continued until the 1960's, by which time stereo recording technique had been well established. His music is Romantic and lyrical, and Walter frequently instructed the orchestra members to sing the melodies of the music, as seen in videos and recordings of his rehearsals.

Mahler's Symphony No. 9. Walter gave the world-premiere performance of Mahler's Symphony No. 9 with the Vienna Philharmonic Orchestra in 1912. He made a live recording of this work on January 16, 1938, with the same orchestra, and this is the first complete recording of the symphony. Overall, Walter conducted at fast tempi. He performed this symphony in about seventy minutes; it took ten minutes longer when he recorded the same symphony about twenty years later with the Columbia Symphony Orchestra. The fast tempi of the earlier performance might reflect the tension at this concert, which took place two months before the Nazis invaded Austria, prompting Walter to leave the country.

The same symphony was recorded again in 1961 in Hollywood with the Columbia Symphony Or-

Bruno Walter. (Library of Congress)

chestra. The new stereo recording features modern sound quality and well-prepared orchestra playing. Missing, however, is the urgency of the old Vienna recording.

Beethoven's Symphony No. 6. After his retirement from concert activities, Walter was approached by Columbia Records to undertake a series of stereo recordings of classical and Romantic repertoires with the Columbia Symphony Orchestra, a pick-up orchestra formed by the members of the Los Angeles Philharmonic and freelance musicians on the West Coast. The 1958 recording of Beethoven's Symphony No. 6 in F Major (1808) represents one of the best among such recordings. Walter's lyrical interpretation depicts the program music—titled *Pastoral Symphony* or *Recollection of the Life in the Countryside* in the first edition—in every respect, as he believed that one must understand nature in order to understand Beethoven's music.

Brahms's Symphony No. 4. Recorded in Hollywood, in February, 1959, with the Columbia Symphony Orchestra, this performance of Johannes Brahms's Symphony No. 4 in E Minor (1885) embodies the musical style of Walter's later years. In general, he took slow tempi, and he let the orchestra sing melodies elegantly with frequent use of ritardando (slowing down of the tempo) at the end of phrases, which are not indicated in the score. This style differs from his 1951 recording of the same work with the New York Philharmonic, where the music moves in a faster tempo with less noticeable use of tempo changes.

Musical Legacy

Walter left a large amount of recordings, including stereo recording, because of his long career that lasted until 1961. His repertoire included not only Austro-German music, such as that of Wolfgang Amadeus Mozart, Beethoven, and Brahms, but also the music of Hector Berlioz, Antonín Dvořák, Peter Ilich Tchaikovsky, and others.

Walter described himself as "educational conductor," and he trained orchestras by explaining to them in detail the characteristics of the music during rehearsals. This approach, which differed from that of other conductors, who adopted a more authoritative style, became a standard in orchestra rehearsals.

Walter was a writer as well as a performer. His books are great resources for the study of Austro-German music because he witnessed the performances of great musicians in the early twentieth century, an era before recording techniques had been developed.

Fusako Hamao

Further Reading

Holden, Raymond. *The Virtuoso Conductors: The Central European Tradition from Wagner to Karajan.* New Haven, Conn.: Yale University Press, 2005. As a professional conductor, the author covers the rehearsal techniques, the performance practices, and other topics of nine European conductors after Wagner, including Walter.

Ryding, Erik, and Rebecca Pechefsky. *Bruno Walter: A World Elsewhere.* New Haven, Conn.: Yale University Press, 2001. A major biographical study based on Walter's numerous unpublished letters, which are archived at the New York Public Library, and on interviews with more than sixty acquaintances.

Walter, Bruno. *Gustav Mahler*. Translation from the German supervised by Lotte Walter Lindt. New York: Alfred A. Knopf, 1958. This brief biography of Mahler presents Walter's recollections and reflections on the master.

_____. *Of Music and Music Making*. Translated by Paul Hamburger. New York: Norton, 1961. Outlines Walter's ideas on the education of orchestra members, solidifying his role as an educational conductor.

_____. *Theme and Variations: An Autobiography*. Translated by James A. Galston. New York: Alfred A. Knopf, 1946. Walter's autobiography provides detailed information about his life as conductor, and it includes fascinating insights on music and on the musicians of his time.

See also: Bernstein, Leonard; Busch, Adolf; Karajan, Herbert von; Klemperer, Otto; Lehmann, Lotte; Mahler, Gustav; Melchior, Lauritz; Menuhin, Sir Yehudi; Strauss, Richard; Toscanini, Arturo.

Sir William Walton

English classical and film-score composer

A leading British composer, Walton incorporated a variety of European influences into his works, introducing a new cosmopolitanism into his country's music.

Born: March 29, 1902; Oldham, Lancashire, England
Died: March 8, 1983; Ischia, Italy
Also known as: William Turner Walton (full name)

Principal works

BALLETS: *The Wise Virgins*, 1940 (based on Johann Sebastian Bach's music); *The Quest*, 1943; *Varii capricci*, 1983.
CELLO WORK: *Passacaglia*, 1980 (for cello).

CHAMBER WORKS: Piano Quartet, 1921; String Quartet No. 1, 1922; String Quartet No. 2 in A Minor, 1946; Sonata for Violin and Piano, 1949.
CHORAL WORKS: *A Litany*, 1916; *Belshazzar's Feast*, 1931; *In Honour of the City of London*, 1937; *Set Me as a Seal upon Thine Heart*, 1938; *Where Does the Uttered Music Go?*, 1946; *Coronation Te Deum*, 1952; *Gloria*, 1961 (for solo voices, chorus, and orchestra); *What Cheer?*, 1961; *The Twelve*, 1965 (for chorus and organ; based on a text by W. H. Auden); *Missa Brevis*, 1966 (for chorus and organ); *Jubilate Deo*, 1972 (for chorus and organ); *Cantico del sole*, 1974; *Antiphon*, 1977 (for chorus and organ).
FILM SCORES: *As You Like It*, 1936; *Dreaming Lips*, 1937; *A Stolen Life*, 1938; *Major Barbara*, 1941; *The First of the Few*, 1942; *The Foreman Went to France*, 1942; *Next of Kin*, 1942; *Went the Day Well?*, 1942; *Henry V*, 1944; *Hamlet*, 1948; *Richard III*, 1955; *Three Sisters*, 1970.
GUITAR WORK: *Five Bagatelles*, 1971 (for guitar).
OPERAS (music): *Troilus and Cressida*, 1954 (libretto by Christopher Hassall); *The Bear*, 1967 (libretto by Paul Dehn and Walton; based on Anton Chekhov's play).
ORCHESTRAL WORKS: *Portsmouth Point*, 1925 (concert overture); *Sinfonia Concertante*, 1927 (for piano and orchestra); Viola Concerto, 1929; Symphony No. 1, 1935; *Crown Imperial*, 1937 (ceremonial march); Concerto in B Minor for Violin and Orchestra, 1936; *Façade, Suite No. 2*, 1938; *Scapino Overture*, 1940; *Orb and Sceptre*, 1953 (composed for the coronation of Queen Elizabeth II); Cello Concerto, 1956; *Johannesburg Festival Overture*, 1956; Partita, 1957; Symphony No. 2, 1960 (*Liverpool*); *Variations on a Theme by Hindemith*, 1963; *Capriccio burlesco*, 1968; *Improvisations on an Impromptu of Benjamin Britten*, 1969; *Façade II: A Further Entertainment*, 1977.
PIANO WORK: *Duets for Children*, 1940.
VOCAL WORKS: *Façade, Suite No. 1*, 1929 (for voice and chamber ensemble; based on Edith Sitwell's poetry); *Anon. in Love*, 1960 (song cycle for tenor and guitar or orchestra); *A Song for the Lord Mayor's Table*, 1962 (six songs for soprano and piano or orchestra).

The Life

William Turner Walton's father was a music teacher as well as a church organist and choirmaster, and the boy grew up singing in his father's choir. Walton also studied piano, organ, and violin, and won a scholarship to study singing at Christ Church, Oxford, in 1912.

Despite his obvious talent, Walton left Christ Church in 1920 without a degree and survived the following decade thanks to his close friendship with the culturally active Sitwell family—the brothers Sacheverell and Osbert and their sister Edith. His trip to Italy with the family in 1920 broadened his cultural horizons, and Edith and Sacheverell respectively were instrumental in the composition of his two most important early works, *Façade* and *Belshazzar's Feast*.

In the 1930's the financial and critical success of his Symphony No. 1 and his scores to such films as *Escape Me Never* allowed Walton to live free of the Sitwells, a step that reinvigorated his music. A 1948 visit to Buenos Aires, Argentina, led to his marriage to Susana Gil Passo. Shortly afterward the couple built a villa on the Italian island of Ischia, where Walton completed work on what would prove to be an unsuccessful opera, *Troilus and Cressida*. He died on the island in 1983.

The Music

Walton's earliest works demonstrate his firsthand knowledge of choral performance, which he drew upon throughout his life. For a time he exhibited an interest in the atonal techniques then gaining critical ground in European music, but he soon abandoned outright experimentation for a more accessible style.

Façade. A series of seemingly nonsensical poems by Edith Sitwell set to music, *Façade* is regarded as a signature British composition of the 1920's. Walton wrote the accompaniments in a variety of popular musical styles, but also borrowed elements from such continental composers as Erik Satie and Arnold Schoenberg. In performance, a speaker sits behind a curtain reciting Sitwell's poems through a kind of megaphone while a small chamber ensemble plays Walton's witty accompaniments. The jazzy, bittersweet work was first performed privately in 1922 and received its public premiere the following year. Subsequently Walton revised *Façade* several times and extracted two suites from it.

Belshazzar's Feast. When Walton received a commission from the British Broadcasting Corporation (BBC) in 1929 to write a cantata, his friend Osbert Sitwell prepared a libretto drawn from the Old Testament story of the fall of Babylon, adding passages from Psalms and Revelation. Walton composed the music during 1930 and 1931, and the work—grown too large for radio broadcast—received its premiere at the Leeds Triennial Festival in 1931. Intensely dramatic, frequently abrasive, and subtly critical of Edwardian society, *Belshazzar's Feast* is scored for a large orchestra augmented with additional ranks of trumpets and trombones. The composition was an immediate success and is considered by many the most important English work of its kind since *The Dream of Gerontius* (1900), by Edward Elgar.

Symphony No. 1. Walton began work on his first symphony in 1932 but found its completion delayed by personal difficulties and was forced to agree to a performance of its first three movements in late 1934. Although the truncated symphony was received enthusiastically, another year passed before it was performed in its entirety. Its dynamic first movement develops fragmentary motifs announced in its opening bars into a stirring but oddly troubled conclusion. A sinister second movement leads to a bleak third. It is only in the final bars of the climactic fourth movement that the accumulated tension of the first three movements is relieved. A large and emotionally charged work, the symphony is generally regarded as Walton's masterpiece and one of the three or four most important symphonies of the twentieth century.

Concerto in B Minor for Violin and Orchestra. In 1936 violinist Jascha Heifetz approached Walton to write a concerto for him, a work that Walton began two years later when he was staying on the Amalfi coast of Italy. He completed the concerto, after conferring with the virtuoso in New York City, in 1939, and Heifetz gave its premiere later that year. Although Walton had accepted the commission with some reluctance, the work's sensuous colors and languorous, beguiling melodies have made it one of his most popular compositions. It is also perhaps the work that best displays the Italianate lyricism that distinguishes his mature style.

Symphony No. 2. By the time Walton finished his second symphony in 1960, his reputation had waned. Although conversant with the latest trends in the musical world, he had for the most part remained true to a tonal tradition regarded after World War II as outdated. Yet he had learned to write more concisely and orchestrate more economically. While not as emotionally expansive as his first symphony, Walton's second is more tightly organized, and its slow second movement contains a flowing, haunting melody. The work's third and final movement is a set of striking variations on an angular, dissonant theme and brings the work to an ecstatic conclusion.

Musical Legacy

In finding his musical voice, Walton worked through a series of styles, including atonalism and jazz. He never forgot the lessons he had learned, employing a nearly atonal theme in the final movement of his Symphony No. 2 and producing a late sequel to *Façade* in *Façade II: A Further Entertainment* in 1977. Analysts have identified a number of contemporary European influences in Walton's first symphony, including Jean Sibelius, but they are integrated so successfully that the symphony was proclaimed immediately as a triumph for English music. The Italian world exercised the greatest overt influence on Walton, as reflected in the sensuous lyricism of his Viola Concerto and especially his Concerto in B Minor for Violin and Orchestra.

A slow, meticulous craftsman who revised repeatedly, Walton suffered from a lack of academic training—which may explain the relative paucity of his works. His reputation suffered after World War II, but since his death critics have approached his later works more positively.

Grove Koger

Further Reading

Burton, Humphrey, and Maureen Murray. *William Walton: The Romantic Loner—A Centenary Portrait Album*. Oxford, England: Oxford University Press, 2002. A biography in words and pictures, including selections from interviews and letters. Numerous illustrations and musical examples.

Craggs, Stewart R., ed. *William Walton: Music and Literature*. Brookfield, Vt.: Ashgate, 1999. Collection of essays assessing Walton's choral, orchestral, operatic, and film music. Bibliography.

Kennedy, Michael. *Portrait of Walton*. New York: Oxford University Press, 1989. Sympathetic biography by a noted music critic. Illustrations, musical examples, classified list of works, discography of Walton conducting his own works, select bibliography.

Lloyd, Stephen. *William Walton: Muse of Fire*. Rochester, N.Y.: Boydell Press, 2001. Biography concentrating on Walton's earlier years and profiting from newly released works on his contemporaries. Illustrations, list of works, bibliography.

Walton, Susana. *William Walton: Behind the Facade*. New York: Oxford University Press, 1988. Anecdotal memoir by Walton's widow. Illustrations.

See also: Britten, Benjamin; Elgar, Sir Edward; Heifetz, Jascha; Previn, Sir André; Satie, Erik; Schoenberg, Arnold.

Clara Ward

American gospel singer

Ward was a popular gospel singer and composer known for her stirring vocals and dramatic phrasing. Her well-polished, all-female group brought show-business theatricality to their gospel performances.

Born: August 21, 1924; Philadelphia, Pennsylvania
Died: January 16, 1973; Los Angeles, California
Also known as: Clara Mae Ward (full name); Little Clara
Member of: The Ward Singers; the Famous Ward Singers; the Clara Ward Singers

Principal recordings

ALBUMS (with various versions of the Ward Singers): *Surely God Is Able*, 1955; *Lord Touch Me*, 1956; *Down by the Riverside*, 1958; *That Old Landmark*, 1958; *Hallelujah*, 1960; *Hang Your Tears Out to Dry*, 1966.

The Life

Clara Mae Ward grew up in Philadelphia, the daughter of George and Gertrude Ward. Clara and older sister Willarene (Willa) sang in their church choir and received piano instruction. In straitened circumstances, the Ward family was compelled to move twenty-four times in nineteen years. Clara dropped out of high school to pursue her musical career. At the age of seventeen, Ward married Richard Bowman. The Ward Singers, aggressively managed by mother Gertrude, became nationally popular with gospel music fans after a spectacular performance at the National Baptist Conference in 1943.

Shortly after suffering a miscarriage, Ward divorced Bowman and began to date women surreptitiously. In 1952, the Ward Singers became the first Gospel group to headline a show at the famous Apollo Theater. Gertrude dressed the group in flamboyant sequined gowns, a novelty for gospel singers. Ward was composing, recording, and performing nationally on a relentless schedule. In 1953, she opened Ward's House of Music, a publishing company for gospel sheet music.

Ward had a long-term romantic relationship with the Reverend C. L. Franklin, a gospel singer and the father of Aretha Franklin, whose interest in singing Ward encouraged. Her success allowed her and Gertrude to move to an exclusive neighborhood in Los Angeles and purchase such luxuries as a purple, twelve-passenger 1957 Chrysler limousine. In the late 1950's she began performing in nightclubs, such as New York's Village Vanguard. In 1957, the Famous Ward Singers performed at the Newport Jazz Festival. In October, 1958, the National Clara Ward Fan Club was founded.

The 1958 departure of the talented Marion Williams, who shared lead singing with Ward, was a blow to the group. In 1962 Ward began performing at the New Frontier Hotel in Las Vegas, an engagement that lasted five years. In 1963, she starred as Birdie Lee in the Broadway show, *Tambourines to Glory*. During this period, Ward had a fling with baseball great Roberto Clemente.

However, Clara was suffering under the strain of her relentless performance schedule, aggravated by her mother, who demanded more work, more money, and more shows. In the late 1960's, she began performing for U.S. troops in Vietnam but also

Clara Ward. (Hulton Archive/Getty Images)

began to experience severe headaches, brought on to some extent by alcoholism. During a performance in 1967 in Miami, Ward collapsed from a stroke. Rushed to the hospital, she recovered in three weeks. Gertrude proclaimed her a "miracle girl" and arranged for her to resume her relentless performing schedule. On December 8, 1972, Ward suffered a second stroke. She died about a month later, not yet forty-nine years old. In 1998, the United States commemorated Ward on a postage stamp.

The Music

Clara Ward's talents as a singer were noted early and brought the Ward sisters to prominence in the world of gospel music. Clara had a high-pitched alto voice, a sweet tone, and a nasal quality capable of producing a stirring legato at the end of her phrases. She was much influenced by gospel pioneer Mary Johnson Davis in the blues-inflected rhythms she brought to her delivery. In addition to Ward, her sister Willa, and mother Gertrude, other members of the Ward singers at various times included such talented singers as Williams, Henrietta Waddy, Kitty Parham, and Frances Stedman. The

Ward Singers were variously known as Gertrude Ward and Daughters, the Consecrated Gospel Singers, the Clara Ward Singers, and, most popularly, the Famous Ward Sisters. With Ward's success, the Famous Ward Sisters early on secured a multiyear contract with the Savoy Recording Company.

"Just One Moment." Ward made her first recording, "Just One Moment," in 1948. Her high-register singing, unique nasal tone, quivering moans, varied rhythms, and intense vocal delivery established her as an instant gospel music recording star.

"Surely God Is Able." Ward was much taken with William Herbert Brewster's composition "Our God Is Able," and in 1949 she decided to record a new arrangement of the song, titled "Surely God Is Able." Ward changed the tempo to three-quarter time, a waltz meter rare in gospel music, and added background refrains of "surely, surely," in an infectious call-and-response. The Ward Singers' release of "Surely God Is Able" in 1950 under the Gotham label became the first million-seller record by a gospel music group. The song begins with a five-note piano introduction from which the initial call-and-response springs. In a clarion voice, Ward calls out "surely" four times, with the chorus of background singers responding each time. As the piano lead is reinforced by an organ, Ward and the chorus repeat the phrase "God is able." Midway through the song, Williams picks up the lead, repeating Ward's phrases in her rougher, more earthy timbre. The lyric recounts the help God provides his chosen vessels, including Daniel, Ezekiel, Moses, Joshua, and Solomon. The Ward Singers often performed "Surely God Is Able," notably in a historic concert in Carnegie Hall in October, 1950.

"How I Got Over." Ward's most popular song was her reworking of the spiritual "How I Got Over," first recorded in 1951. Ward sings the lead throughout, her pulsing, high-register voice rising above the called responses of her background singers. Ward brings great drama to her singing, overcoming every obstacle she sings about with passionate, electrifying phrasing.

Musical Legacy

Clara Ward's legacy is manifold. In popularity as a female gospel singer in the 1940's and 1950's,

Ward was outshone only by Mahalia Jackson. Ward was also a talented arranger of gospel music. She and her singers were the first all-female gospel group organized on a permanent basis. Under Gertrude's aggressive and demanding management, Ward and her singers pioneered numerous techniques. They excelled in a lead-switching style. They sang in perfect harmony and synchronization. Their songs featured a call and response that was one of the most exciting elements of their gospel style. Ward's singing incorporated jazz and blues elements with gospel, and Gertrude had the singers abandon their church robes for elegant dresses, sequined gowns, beehive hairstyles, and coiffured wigs. Shocking to many religious fans, Ward and Gertrude brought their gospel singing to nightclubs, jazz spots, and even Las Vegas. Their theatricality was praised by some fans and considered tawdry by others.

Ward's singing style remain her most important legacy. Her voice was high-pitched and nasal but pure-toned and capable of great agility in the higher registers. Equally important, Ward was able to instill a dramatic quality in all of her songs, characterized by blues-like inflections, stirring rhythms, rapid ascents and descents on the scale, and a moving sincerity. Although criticized in later years for commercialism, Ward and her group had a significant influence on gospel and popular singers, including notably Aretha Franklin, and helped transform gospel into a dominant mainstream genre.

Howard Bromberg

Further Reading

Boyer, Horace Clarence. *How Sweet the Sound: The Golden Age of Gospel.* Washington, D.C.: Elliott and Clark, 1995. History of gospel music by a scholar and former gospel performer.

Cohn, Lawrence, ed. *Nothing but the Blues: The Music and the Musicians.* New York: Abbeville Press, 1993. A survey of blues history, brisk in tone. Includes discussion of Ward, emphasizing her theatricality.

Moore, Alan, ed. *Cambridge Companion to Blues and Gospel Music.* New York: Cambridge University Press, 2003. Analyzes Ward's 1952 recording of "Precious Lord" as one of twelve key blues and gospel music recordings.

Ward-Royster, Willa, and Toni Rose. *How I Got Over: Clara Ward and the World-Famous Ward Singers*. Philadelphia: Temple University Press, 1997. A revealing family biography by Clara's sister. Includes a perceptive introduction by gospel music historian Horace Boyer and appendixes that list recordings, shows, and awards.

See also: Cleveland, James; Crouch, Andraé; Dorsey, Thomas A.; Franklin, Aretha; Grant, Amy; Jackson, Mahalia; Smith, Michael W.; Staples, Pops.

Dionne Warwick

American rhythm-and-blues singer-songwriter

Warwick, the number-two female vocalist of the rock era (after Aretha Franklin), recorded fifty-six Top 100 songs between 1962 and 1987 and continued recording in various genres into the next century. Her classically trained voice and her gospel roots made her an international favorite, often imitated.

Born: December 12, 1940; East Orange, New Jersey
Also known as: Marie Dionne Warwick (full name); Dionne Warwicke
Member of: The Gospelaires

Principal recordings

ALBUMS (solo): *Presenting Dionne Warwick*, 1963; *Anyone Who Had a Heart*, 1964; *Make Way for Dionne Warwick*, 1964; *Here I Am*, 1965; *The Sensitive Sound of Dionne Warwick*, 1965; *Dionne Warwick in Paris*, 1966; *Here Where There Is Love*, 1967; *On Stage and in the Movies*, 1967; *The Windows of the World*, 1967; *The Magic of Believing*, 1968; *Promises, Promises*, 1968; *The Valley of the Dolls*, 1968; *Freewheelin'*, 1969; *Soulful*, 1969; *I'll Never Fall in Love Again*, 1970; *Very Dionne*, 1970; *Dionne*, 1972; *Just Being Myself*, 1973; *Then Came You*, 1975; *Track of the Cat*, 1975; *In Concert: Recorded with the Edmonton Symphony Orchestra*, 1977; *Love at First Sight*, 1977; *Dionne*, 1979; *No Night So Long*, 1980;

Friends in Love, 1982; *Heartbreaker*, 1982 (with Barry Gibb); *How Many Times Can We Say Goodbye*, 1983; *Finder of Lost Loves*, 1985; *Friends*, 1985 (with others); *Reservations for Two*, 1987; *Dionne Warwick Sings Cole Porter*, 1990; *Friends Can Be Lovers*, 1993; *Celebration in Vienna*, 1994 (with Plácido Domingo); *Aquarela do Brazil*, 1995; *My Favorite Time of the Year*, 2004; *Soulful Plus*, 2004; *My Friends and Me*, 2006; *Dionne Warwick Sings Bacharach and David*, 2008; *Why We Sing*, 2008.
ALBUMS (with the Gospelaires): *Camp Meeting*, 1961; *Just Faith*, 1961; *Bones in the Valley*, 1963.
WRITINGS OF INTEREST: *My Point of View*, 2004.

The Life

Dionne Warwick (DEE-awn WAHR-wihk) was born Marie Dionne Warrick in East Orange, New Jersey. The slight spelling change in her professional name was the result of a misspelling on a record label that the singer decided to keep. Her father, Mancel Warrick, worked various jobs before finding moderate success as a record promoter for Chess Records, a gospel label. He later became a certified public accountant. Her mother, Lee Drinkard Warrick, was the business manager for her family's gospel group, the Drinkard Singers. Dionne sang with the group at the age of six.

Both parents encouraged her musical talent, which was good enough to gain for her a scholarship to the competitive Hartt College of Music at the University of Hartford, where she matriculated in 1959. She formed a gospel group known as the Gospelaires, which was tapped for background singers in recording sessions for various vocalists. While singing background for the Drifters, Warwick was heard by Burt Bacharach and Hal David, who asked her to record demo songs for their music. This chance meeting began a collaboration that would launch Warwick's career as a solo singer.

The Music

Dionne Warrick was already a local celebrity in East Orange, New Jersey, as a teenager in the mid-1950's, appearing on local television with the Drinkard Singers, but her breakthrough was her solo work for Burt Bacharach's Scepter Records. In fact, a convenient method of charting Warwick's career is by her recording labels.

Bacharach and Scepter, 1963-1972. Warwick began singing demos for Bacharach, and one of those demos, "Make It Easy on Yourself," was supposed to be her first single as a solo artist. However, when Bacharach gave the song to singer Jerry Butler instead, Warwick angrily told Bacharach, "Don't make me over, man!" Delighted with the phrase, Hal David turned it into a song with Bacharach and gave it to Warwick as a peace offering. Warwick turned it into her first hit, which peaked at number twenty-one on *Billboard*'s Hot 100 chart and number five on the rhythm-and-blues chart. It would be followed by twenty-one more Bacharach/David hits on the Hot 100, fourteen of them in the Top 10.

One of these was the song that had been promised her, "Make It Easy on Yourself," which Warwick finally recorded in 1970. It climbed to number two on the adult contemporary charts. Warwick twice had hits with songs Bacharach and David had written for male vocalists and that David had advised her not to change, thinking they were too tied to the male point of view. She turned "Message to

Dionne Warwick. (AP/Wide World Photos)

Martha" into her 1966 hit "Message to Michael," which reached number five in the rhythm-and-blues charts, and "This Guy's in Love with You," a 1968 number-one hit for Herb Alpert, into her 1969 cover "This Girl's in Love with You," which reached the number-two spot (adult contemporary).

The Warner Years, 1972-1978. When Warwick left Bacharach's label in 1972 (though she would work with Bacharach and David off and on for decades after), many critics thought that it would damage her career, and for a few years after her departure from Scepter, she did not crack *Billboard*'s Hot 100. Then, in 1974, she had her first number-one hit (and her first non-Bacharach hit) with "Then Came You," recorded with the Spinners. While this was Warwick's only hit single for the Warner label, she made five albums with respectable sales: *Dionne, Just Being Myself, Then Came You, Track of the Cat,* and *Love at First Sight.* The *Dionne* album was produced by Bacharach, but the breakup of the Bacharach/David partnership at that time left Warwick without the resources on which she had counted in signing with Warner. Warwick was forced to file a breach-of-contract suit against her former partners. These troubles were no doubt a factor in her dearth of hits for Warner.

Arista Records, 1979-1995. When her Warner contract ended, Warwick signed with Arista Records and went into the studio with Barry Manilow as producer, resulting in the 1979 album *Dionne* (not to be confused with the 1972 Warner album of the same name) and "I'll Never Love This Way Again," which went to number five. Another song from the same album, "Déjà Vu," hit number fifteen on the Hot 100 and number one in adult contemporary. She hit the Top 40 eight more times for Arista. Warwick's 1983 album *How Many Times Can We Say Goodbye* teamed her with producer Luther Vandross, who sang a duet with her on the title song, which climbed to number four. Warwick's greatest hit for the label was a Bacharach composition, this time with lyricist Carole Bayer Sager, "That's What Friends Are For," which was *Billboard*'s number one for four weeks, and was the best-selling song of 1986.

Concord Records. After a decade as an independent recording artist, Warwick signed with Concord in 2005, resulting in the 2006 compact disc *My Friends and Me*, produced by Warwick's son and including duets with other famous vocalists. She returned to her gospel roots with the 2008 release *Why We Sing*.

Musical Legacy

In the second half of the twentieth century, according to *Billboard* magazine, Warwick is second only to Aretha Franklin in the number of charted hits. She hit the *Billboard* Hot 100 a total of 56 times. *Billboard*'s turn-of-the-century retrospective of the rock era, *Top Pop Singles, 1955-1999* rated the Top 200 recording artists, and placed Warwick at number twenty. Her partnership with songwriters Burt Bacharach and Hal David must be considered a creative element of the songs they wrote for her, because her skill and classical training allowed her to sing the melodically and rhythmically complex work Bacharach wanted to write, allowing him to write increasingly challenging melodies.

John R. Holmes

Further Reading

Johnstone-Guerra, Mary. *Celebrities as Fans.* New York: Nadine Press, 2005. In her contribution to this book, Warwick switches roles and comments as a fan on other celebrities.

Nathan, David. *Soulful Divas: Personal Portraits of Over a Dozen Divine Divas.* New York: Watson-Guptill, 1999. This collection of interviews and sketches of women vocalists includes a readable and informative piece on Warwick.

Warwick, Dionne. Introduction to *What the World Needs Now, and Other Love Lyrics*, by Hal David. New York: Trident Press, 1968. Warwick's introductory portrait of David is a moving tribute to their artistic collaboration.

_____. *My Point of View.* New York: Lighthouse Press, 2004. Warwick's autobiography is valuable for its insights not only into her career but also into many of the major names in the entertainment industry with whom she has worked.

See also: Bacharach, Burt; Carpenter, Karen; David, Hal; Hayes, Isaac; Horne, Lena; Wonder, Stevie.

Dinah Washington
American jazz singer

With her dynamic voice and precise enunciation, Washington sang in a wide variety of styles, moving from jazz and rhythm and blues into the pop mainstream.

Born: August 29, 1924; Tuscaloosa, Alabama
Died: December 14, 1963; Detroit, Michigan
Also known as: Ruth Lee Jones (birth name); Queen of the Blues; Queen of the Jukebox; Miss D

Principal recordings

ALBUMS: *Evil Gal Blues*, 1943; *Mellow Mama*, 1945; *Dinah Washington Songs*, 1950; *Blazing Ballads*, 1952; *Dynamic Dinah*, 1952; *After Hours with Miss D*, 1953; *Dinah Jams*, 1954; *Jazz Sides*, 1954; *For Those in Love*, 1955; *Dinah!*, 1956; *In the Land of Hi-Fi*, 1956; *The Swingin' Miss D*, 1956; *Dinah Washington Sings Bessie Smith*, 1957; *Dinah Washington Sings Fats Waller*, 1957; *The Fats Waller Songbook*, 1957; *Music for a First Love*, 1957; *Music for Late Hours*, 1957; *The Queen*, 1959; *Unforgettable*, 1959; *What a Diff'rence a Day Makes!*, 1959; *I Concentrate on You*, 1960; *Two of Us*, 1960 (with Brook Benton); *For Lonely Lovers*, 1961; *September in the Rain*, 1961; *Dinah '62*, 1962; *Drinking Again*, 1962; *In Love*, 1962; *Tears and Laughter*, 1962; *Back to the Blues*, 1963; *Dinah '63*, 1963; *The Good Old Days*, 1963; *In Tribute*, 1963; *The Late, Late Show*, 1963; *This Is My Story*, 1963; *A Stranger on Earth*, 1964; *Queen and Quincy*, 1965 (with Quincy Jones); *Dinah Discovered*, 1967.

The Life

Dinah Washington was born Ruth Lee Jones in 1924, in Tuscaloosa, Alabama, into a family with deep Baptist and gospel roots. Four years later, they moved to Chicago to escape the oppressive segregation of the South. Washington began singing at home, and her mother Asalea encouraged her to sing in the gospel genre. Nevertheless, Washington was hired by bandleader Lionel Hampton to sing with his orchestra. She changed her name for the stage, some say choosing Dinah for the Ethel Waters single of the same name and choosing Washington for the first president of the United States.

At eighteen, when Washington began to work with Hampton, she married and divorced John Young. In the summer of 1945, Washington, who was pregnant, married drummer George Jenkins. She left him after three weeks, and she later gave birth to a son, George Kenneth. Despite her troubled personal life, she continued to record and to perform. At twenty-two, Washington married Robert "Bobby" Grayson, and they had a son, Bobby, Jr. The marriage lasted less than three years. In 1950 Walter Buchanan, a bass player from Arnett Cobb's orchestra, became Washington's fourth husband. After three months, they divorced.

Seven years later, Washington married saxophonist Eddie Chamblee, a union that lasted only a few months. While on a trip overseas, she married taxicab driver Horatio "Rusty" Maillard, and when that relationship ended, she married Rafael Campos. Her last husband was Richard "Night Train" Lane. In 1963 Washington overdosed on prescription medication, and she died in her bed at the age of thirty-nine.

Dinah Washington. (AP/Wide World Photos)

The Music

Early Recordings. In 1943 Keynote Records had Washington record several songs, including "Evil Gal Blues," "Homeward Bound," "Salty Papa Blues," and "I Know How to Do It." The recordings landed on the *Billboard* Harlem Hit Parade Top 10. After a year touring with Hampton, Washington left the orchestra, and she did more recordings for Decca Records. The label, which specialized in big band music, did not heavily support the jazz singer.

Washington went to Santa Monica, California, where she signed a contract with Apollo Records to do twelve songs with a band called the Lucky Thompson All-Stars. The group included Lucky Thompson on saxophone, Gene Porter on baritone saxophone, Jewel Grant on alto saxophone, Karl George on trumpet, Milt Jackson on vibraharp, Wilbert Baranco on piano, Lee Young (Lester's younger brother) on drums, and Charles Mingus on bass. She recorded the blues songs "No Voot,

No Boot," "Chewin' Mama's Blues," "My Lovin' Papa," "Mellow Mama Blues," "My Voot Is Really Vout," and "Blues for a Day."

Soon Washington was back in Chicago, ready to sign a contract with Mercury Records. In January of 1946, Washington worked with Gus Chappell, a trombonist in Chicago, and together they made the memorable "Embraceable You" and "I Can't Get Started with You."

Blues, Jazz, Pop, and Country. Soon, Washington began to work with producers who understood her abilities. She sang blues, then jazz, then pop. Her popularity grew, and record labels (Apollo, Mercury, EmArcy) began to vie for her attention. In 1951 Washington recorded for Mercury the pop songs "I Wanna Be Loved," "My Heart Cries for You," and "I Won't Cry Anymore," and they all landed in the Top 5. Washington also recorded in the country genre: a rendition of Hank Williams's "Cold, Cold Heart."

Approaching thirty years old, Washington and a new producer from Mercury, Hal Mooney, collaborated to release more songs to boost her popularity. "I Don't Hurt Anymore," "Dream," "Soft Winds," "Teach Me Tonight," and "If It's the Last Thing I Do" became hits almost instantly. Washington used these songs to define her own style, moving away from the stylings of other jazz singers (such as Ella Fitzgerald and Sarah Vaughan) and pronouncing every syllable clearly and concisely. Quincy Jones helped her on another album, which produced hit songs such as "Blue Gardenia." Washington demonstrated her ability to work in several genres, releasing blues albums, touring with jazz orchestras, and topping the pop charts.

"What a Diff'rence a Day Makes." With the release of "What a Diff'rence a Day Makes"—an amalgam of blues, pop, and Washington's signature sound—she became a mainstream success. The song won a Grammy Award for Best Rhythm and Blues Performance. In 1960 she released another hit, "Baby (You've Got What It Takes)," under the same producer who made "What a Diff'rence a Day Makes," Clyde Otis.

The Allegros. The Allegros became Washington's new backing trio, and in 1962 they helped to define her style with a new record label, Roulette. They contributed to *Dinah '62* (with the popular tracks "Where Are You" and "You're Nobody 'Til Somebody Loves You") and four other albums, *Drinking Again, In Love, Back to the Blues,* and *Dinah '63.*

Musical Legacy

Although Washington lived at a time when segregation hampered African Americans, she surmounted racial boundaries to become a success on stage and in recordings. An inspiration to black female artists, she used her dynamic voice, compelling stage presence, and versatility to create a prosperous career in spite of her highly publicized and turbulent personal life. In 1993 the U.S. Postal Service issued a commemorative first-class stamp bearing the likeness of Washington. She was inducted into the Rock and Roll Hall of Fame in 1993, and in 1984 she was inducted into the Big Band and Jazz Hall of Fame.

Samantha Giarratani

Further Reading

Awkward, Michael. *Soul Covers: Rhythm and Blues Remakes and the Struggle for Artistic Identity.* Durham, N.C.: Duke University Press, 2007. The author looks at the lives of modern artists and their influences. Aretha Franklin honors Washington as a profound influence on her career.

Cohodas, Nadine. *Queen: The Life and Music of Dinah Washington.* New York: Pantheon Books, 2004. This thorough biography of Washington covers the singer's life, music, and passions.

Haskins, Jim. *Queen of the Blues: A Biography of Dinah Washington.* New York: William Morrow, 1984. This biography offers a look at the life and career of the talented and complex singer.

Starr, Larry, and Christopher Waterman. *American Popular Music: From Minstrelsy to MTV.* New York: Oxford University Press, 2003. This music history highlights the importance of jazz, blues, and pop in a time of racism during the 1960's, with references to Washington.

See also: Fitzgerald, Ella; Franklin, Aretha; Hampton, Lionel; James, Etta; Jones, Quincy; Mingus, Charles; Smith, Bessie; Webster, Ben; Williams, Hank; Williams, Lucinda.

Muddy Waters
American blues guitarist, singer, and songwriter

Waters defined postwar electric Chicago blues, adding the innovation of amplification, and the songs he wrote became blues classics.

Born: April 4, 1915; Issaquena County, Mississippi
Died: April 30, 1983; Westmont, Illinois
Also known as: McKinley Morganfield (birth name)

Principal recordings

ALBUMS: *Muddy Waters at Newport,* 1960; *Sings Big Bill Broonzy,* 1960; *Folk Singer,* 1964; *Muddy Waters,* 1964; *Down on Stovall's Plantation,* 1966; *Blues from Big Bill's Copacabana,* 1967; *Brass and* the *Blues*, 1967; *Electric Mud*, 1968; *Super Blues*, 1968; *After the Rain*, 1969; *Fathers and Sons*, 1969; *Sail On*, 1969; *Back in the Good Old Days*, 1970; *Good News*, 1970; *Vintage Mud*, 1970; *The London Muddy Waters Sessions*, 1971; *Can't Get No Grindin'*, 1973; *London Revisited*, 1974; *Muddy and the Wolf*, 1974; *Woodstock Album*, 1975; *Chess*, 1977; *Hard Again*, 1977; *Unk in Funk*, 1977; *I'm Ready*, 1978.

SINGLES: "Country Blues," 1941; "I Be's Troubled," 1941; "Ramblin' Kid Blues," 1942; "You Got to Get Sick and Die Some of These Days," 1942; "Little Anna Mae," 1947; "Hard Days," 1948; "I Can't Be Satisfied," 1948; "I Feel Like Going Home," 1948; "Last Time I Fooled Around with You," 1949; "Rollin' and Tumblin'," 1950; "Rolling Stone," 1950; "Howlin' Wolf," 1951; "Honey Bee," 1951; "I Just Want to Make Love to You," 1954; "(I'm Your) Hoochie Coochie Man," 1954; "Trouble No More," 1955; "Sugar Sweet," 1955; "Got My Mojo Working," 1957; "Good Lookin' Woman," 1957; "Goin' Down Louisiana," 1959; "I Want You to Love Me," 1959; "Deep Down in My Heart," 1960; "Going Home," 1962; "My Home Is on the Delta," 1964; "Canary Bird," 1966; "Mud in Your Ear," 1968; "Blues and Trouble," 1969; "Strange Woman," 1971; "Evans Shuffle," 1972; "My Pencil Won't Write No More," 1972; "Muddy Waters Shuffle," 1973; "Drive My Blues Away," 1974; "Born With Nothing," 1975; "Crosseyed Cat," 1977; "She's Nineteen Years Old," 1979; "Forever Lonely," 1981.

The Life

Born McKinley Morganfield in 1913 in Issaquena County, Mississippi—the nearest town is Rolling Fork, which he referred to as his home—Muddy Waters spent his childhood and youth on Stovall's Plantation outside Clarksdale. Because he lost his mother when he was three years old, he was raised by his grandmother, who gave him his nickname for playing in the muddy puddles near the Mississippi River. Muddy Waters learned slide-guitar techniques from legendary Delta blues performer Son House. In 1941 and 1942, African American musicologist John Work III and folklorist Alan Lomax, a team from the Cohoma County Study for

Fisk University and the Library of Congress, visited Muddy Waters and recorded his performances. After he heard the playback of his songs for the first time, his ambition to become a professional musician was unshakable.

In 1943 he moved to Chicago, where he continued musical activities. He made some unsuccessful recordings, but in 1947 he got another chance from Aristocrat Records (later Chess Records). His record from the April, 1948, session, "I Can't Be Satisfied" coupled with "I Feel Like Going Home" was an unprecedented commercial success for both Muddy Waters and Aristocrat Records.

Until the early 1950's, Muddy Waters recorded with a small ensemble, which consisted of his own electric guitar supported by a stand-up bass. Gradually, he extended the personnel for his recording sessions, his early band including guitarist Jimmie Rodgers, harmonica player Little Walter, and drummer Leroy Foster (later replaced with Elgin Evans). In 1953, with the addition of pianist Otis Spann, Muddy Waters established his definitive sound, which became Chicago blues. In 1954 Muddy Waters recorded his commercially successful song, "(I'm Your) Hoochie Coochie Man," written by the house songwriter for the label, Willie Dixon, who also played bass on the recording.

During the 1950's, Muddy Waters's name was generally unknown outside African American communities, but his enthusiastic performance at the Newport Jazz Festival (in Newport, Rhode Island) in July, 1960, helped him acquire a new, white audience. Muddy Waters stayed with Chess Records until its closure in 1975. In 1976 he signed with Columbia Records' subsidiary, Blue Sky Records. With his new musical partner Johnny Winter, Muddy Waters recorded four albums for Blue Sky Records, including three that won Grammy Awards. In his later years, as a legendary figure of Chicago blues, he performed in Europe and in Japan, as well as in the United States.

The Music

It is no exaggeration to say that the development of Muddy Waters's music is the history of postwar Chicago blues. His music was deeply rooted in the acoustic Delta blues tradition, and through the process of urbanization, his music added the element of amplification, an innovative concept for the time, and it acquired the louder sound of an extended combo. With his increasing popularity outside the African American community, his musical style changed to reflect musical trends as required by his audience.

Plantation Recordings. Muddy's earliest existing recordings were field recordings made by the Cohoma County Study team. Work and Lomax recorded eighteen songs by Muddy Waters and his band, the Son Simms Four, in Stovall in the summer of 1941 and 1942. These recordings show his musical roots, especially the strong influence of his mentor Son House. "Country Blues" was a reworking of House's "My Black Mama." "You Got to Get Sick and Die Some of These Days," which is based on House's "Mississippi County Farm Blues," shows how seriously Muddy Waters studied House's guitar techniques.

"I Can't Be Satisfied" *and* **"I Feel Like Going Home."** Muddy Waters's first successful record was mainly supported by the African American working class who migrated from the South to Chicago. With lyrics about frustrated feelings in a new urban environment and nostalgia for the South sung with an amplified slide guitar and an acoustic bass, these songs formed the basis of a successful commercial formula for his early records.

"Rolling Stone." Another recurring theme in Muddy Waters's early records is womanizing. "Rolling Stone," based on Delta blues performer Robert Petway's "Catfish Blues," contains Muddy Waters's favorite melodic pattern.

"Rollin' and Tumblin'." Until the early 1950's, Muddy Waters used different ensembles for recordings and live performances, because label owner Leonard Chess was reluctant to change a successful formula. Instruments in his early records were only his amplified guitar with an acoustic bass. However, even before his first successful record from the Aristocrat-Chess label, Muddy Waters was performing with Rogers (guitar), Little Walter (amplified harmonica), and Foster (drums). Two versions of "Rollin' and Tumblin'"—released in 1950 under Little Walter and Baby Face Leroy from Parkway Records because of Muddy Waters's exclusive contract with Chess Records—capture the sound of Muddy Waters's live band of the time. This band departed from the tradition of Delta blues and created from the Delta anthem a frenzied

city blues sound. After hearing this record, Chess Records allowed Muddy Waters to bring more musicians into the studio.

"Evans Shuffle." With the larger band, Muddy Waters expanded his musical potential and dynamism. One highly noticeable musical exploration was his introduction of different beat patterns from his earlier recordings, which usually had slow- or medium-tempo walking-bass beat patterns. His innovative technique appears in "Evans Shuffle," which has a busy shuffle beat pattern.

"I Want You to Love Me." A different beat pattern is seen in "I Want You to Love Me." This song has recurring stop-time riffs played throughout by all the band members (now including pianist Spann). The combination of this beat pattern and the sexually charged lyrics became Muddy Waters's trademark. This song was a test piece for the arrangement of "(I'm Your) Hoochie Coochie Man," written by Dixon.

Muddy Waters. (Hulton Archive/Getty Images)

"(I'm Your) Hoochie Coochie Man." Dixon, the savvy house songwriter of Chess Records, thought that Muddy Waters's energetic performance should be boosted by a composition that would help him develop a menacing performing persona. "(I'm Your) Hoochie Coochie Man," a womanizing character aided by a hoodoo (African American folk magic) power, is based on Southern lore. He is an offshoot of characters of the post-Civil War black badman tales (such as Stackolee-Stagolee and Railroad Bill), an important basis for creating a blues performer's persona. In this folk-ballad-type song, Dixon amalgamates the old Delta tradition with the urban sounds of stop-time riffs, emphasized by an extended blues combo, including two electric guitars, amplified harmonica, piano, and bass. This was Muddy Waters's signature song. After the success of "(I'm Your) Hoochie Coochie Man," Dixon's compositions for Muddy Waters became important in his repertoire.

Muddy Waters at Newport. Muddy Waters's live performance at the Newport Jazz Festival of 1960 was a catalyst for extending his popularity outside African American communities. This live album (visual footage is also available) captures exciting moments of blues history. When Muddy Waters and harmonica player James Cotton dance to "Got My Mojo Workin'," the audience's enthusiasm reaches its peak.

Electric Mud. When Muddy Waters's name became known to the white community, Chess Records made some marketing decisions to sell his records to his new audience. His *Folk Singer* reflected the folk-music boom among college students, and *Super Blues*, with label mates Little Walter and Bo Diddley, was influenced by the musical trend of the time, "super sessions." *Electric Mud*, made in response to the popularity of psychedelic music, was extremely alien to Muddy Waters's traditional musical style. The music in this record is decorated by excessive psychedelic effects, such as noisy guitar sounds with a fuzz box and a wah-wah pedal, overdubbed cat's caterwaul, and a stereo effect rapidly moving from right to left. Some of the tracks, such as "I Just Want to Make Love to You," with strong emphasis on funky syncopation, sound as if the musicians are exploring a new musical realm while working on traditional material.

While this was Muddy Waters's first album to be ranked on the *Billboard* and *Cash Box* album charts, it received severe criticism. Nevertheless, this record became a cult favorite.

Hard Again. When Muddy Waters teamed up with Winter, their musical concept was the revival of the Chess Records sounds of the early 1950's. They hired skillful musicians, including Cotton (harmonica) and "Pine Top" Perkins (piano), who were familiar with Muddy Waters's good old style, and they recorded all the tracks live, that is, without overdubbing. The resulting *Hard Again*, with Muddy Waters's classic numbers "Mannish Boy" and "I Can't Be Satisfied," is a well-produced record by the legendary boss of Chicago blues and his student. Although this work can be interpreted as a pretentious reproduction of a highly established style without new experiments, Muddy Waters powerfully demonstrates his pride in having created a musical tradition.

Musical Legacy

Playing in Muddy Waters's band was an important milestone for many musicians. As well as the personnel of Muddy Waters's classic band—Little Walter, Rogers, and Spann—many of the Muddy Waters alumni became successful bandleaders: harmonica players Cotton, Junior Wells, Paul Oscher, George "Harmonica" Smith, Willie "Big Eyes" Smith, and Jerry Portnoy and guitarists Bob Margolin and Luther Johnson.

When Chuck Berry visited Muddy Waters in Chicago in 1955 and asked where he should take a demo tape, Muddy Waters directed Berry to Leonard Chess. In addition, Muddy Waters was one of those, including Dixon, who urged Chess to release Berry's debut record "Maybellene," although Chess was initially reluctant.

In his last years, Muddy Waters opened Eric Clapton's shows, and he appeared in the Band's final concert, the Last Waltz. He also enjoyed a jam session with the Rolling Stones. Needless to say, this group was named after Muddy Waters's early record "Rolling Stone," which also inspired the name of a counterculture magazine and the title of a famous folk-rock song.

Muddy Waters's achievements were honored with his induction into the Rock and Roll Hall of Fame (early influence category) in 1987 and the Record Academy's Lifetime Achievement Award in 1992. On the South Side of Chicago, the former Forty-third Street has been renamed Muddy Waters Drive.

Mitsutoshi Inaba

Further Reading
Gordon, Robert. *Can't Be Satisfied: The Life and Times of Muddy Waters*. New York: Little, Brown, 2002. Gordon conducted interviews with Muddy Waters's family members, friends, and close associates, gleaning detailed information. His research on the archives of the Cohoma County Study in the appendix is especially valuable.

O'Neal, Jim, and Amy van Singel. *The Voices of the Blues: Classic Interviews from Living Blues Magazine*. New York: Routledge, 2002. One chapter includes several long interviews with Muddy Waters conducted in 1974, 1980, and 1981.

Palmer, Robert. *Deep Blues*. New York: Penguin, 1982. This book is about the historical development of the blues, from the Delta blues tradition to postwar electric Chicago blues, and one of the focal figures is Muddy Waters.

Tooze, Sandra B. *Muddy Waters: The Mojo Man*. Toronto, Ont.: ECW Press, 1997. This informative biography of Muddy Waters discusses his personality and his relationships with his bandmates and with Chess Records. Includes updated discography.

See also: Berry, Chuck; Burke, Solomon; Butterfield, Paul; Clapton, Eric; Cotton, James; Diddley, Bo; Dixon, Willie; Guy, Buddy; Hopkins, Lightnin'; House, Son; Howlin' Wolf; Jagger, Sir Mick; James, Elmore; Jefferson, Blind Lemon; Lomax, Alan; Morrison, Van; Plant, Robert; Raitt, Bonnie; Reed, Jimmy; Robertson, Robbie; Rush, Otis; Seger, Bob; Turner, Big Joe; Vaughan, Stevie Ray; Williamson, Sonny Boy, II.

Roger Waters
English rock singer, bassist, guitarist, and songwriter

Waters was a cofounder of Pink Floyd and, with his intensely personal lyrics, instrumental in shifting the band's emphasis from psychedelia to social criticism and introspection.

Born: September 6, 1943; Great Bookham, Surrey, England
Also known as: George Roger Waters (full name)
Member of: Pink Floyd

Principal recordings
ALBUMS (solo): *Music from "The Body,"* 1970; *The Pros and Cons of Hitch Hiking*, 1984; *Radio K.A.O.S.*, 1987; *Amused to Death*, 1992; *Ça Ira*, 2005; *Hello (I Love You)*, 2007.
ALBUMS (with Pink Floyd): *The Piper at the Gates of Dawn*, 1967; *A Saucerful of Secrets*, 1968; *More*, 1969; *Atom Heart Mother*, 1970; *Meddle*, 1971; *Relics*, 1971; *Obscured by Clouds*, 1972; *The Dark Side of the Moon*, 1973; *Wish You Were Here*, 1975; *Animals*, 1977; *The Wall*, 1979; *The Final Cut*, 1983.

The Life
George Roger Waters is the younger of two sons born to Eric and Mary Waters. Only an infant when his father died in World War II, Waters's critical worldview was shaped by this loss. His schoolteacher mother influenced Waters with her forceful personality and radical politics. As a youth, Waters participated in Britain's Campaign for Nuclear Disarmament. Formal education was less appealing: Waters lost interest in architecture school upon discovering blues and rock and roll in the early 1960's. Two fellow students, Nick Mason and Rick Wright, became Waters's bandmates in Pink Floyd when the group formed in 1966 with Syd Barrett as leader. Barrett's instability led to his replacement by David Gilmour and a larger role for Waters, who became increasingly authoritarian during Pink Floyd's decade of spectacular success (1973-1983). Waters departed in the 1980's for a solo career that would be far less financially rewarding than the activities of

his estranged colleagues, who continued as Pink Floyd into the 1990's. Waters kept a fairly high profile, with international tours and commitment to environmental, peace, and antipoverty causes. A surprising reunion of Waters with the three surviving Pink Floyd members took place in 2005. Married and divorced several times, Waters had several children from these relationships.

The Music

In addition to Waters, the original Pink Floyd lineup was Barrett (guitarist, singer, and songwriter), Mason (drummer), and Wright (keyboards). In 1968 Gilmour (guitarist and singer) replaced Barrett. Waters formally left the band in 1985 and unsuccessfully sued to prevent Gilmour, Mason, and Wright from recording and touring under the Pink Floyd name.

The Dark Side of the Moon. Recorded at the fabled Abbey Road studios, where the Beatles had cut their later albums, *The Dark Side of the Moon* turned Pink Floyd into a supergroup. A technical tour de force that still sounds lush and innovative, the album showcased the skills of all Pink Floyd members. Its lyrics, however, belonged only to Waters, making his role in the album's and group's success a source of friction. As a whole, *The Dark Side of the Moon* provides a stunning listening experience, but each song has individual strengths. "Time" and "Us and Them" address human futility and mortality from an alternately angry and melancholy perspective. Gilmour's guitar and Waters's cynical yet celebratory lyrics make "Money" a hard-rock peak. "Brain Damage" alludes to the breakdown of Barrett, whose memory shadowed Waters.

Wish You Were Here *and* Animals. Difficulties that emerged during 1975's *Wish You Were Here* sessions would worsen in the remainder of Waters's tenure. Calling on long-absent Barrett as his muse, Waters composed the elegiac "Shine on You Crazy Diamond," one of Pink Floyd's signature songs. "Have a Cigar," a trenchant music-industry satire, captured the fame-induced anxiety that is one of Waters's enduring themes. Band infighting aside, *Wish You Were Here* was a best seller even if it did not match *The Dark Side of the Moon*. In 1977 *Animals* also found a huge and devoted audience, despite caustic lyrics and a harsh aural environment that contrasted sharply with its predecessors. With Gilmour on the margins, Waters dominated *Animals* as vocalist and lyricist.

The Wall *and* The Final Cut. The double album *The Wall* was Pink Floyd's only release after *The Dark Side of the Moon* to rival its commercial success and cultural impact. Using a crude yet effective metaphor of an all-encompassing wall to illustrate alienation, Waters put himself at the center of the band's angriest, most ambitious project. *The Wall* chronicled the travails of Waters's alter ego, "Pink," a sensitive but spoiled rock star who rejects all human relationships, develops a fascist persona, and sees his self-imposed exile crumble after his tormentors confront him in an agonizing trial. A sense of finality pervades the album, demanding an end to a situation in which Waters and Pink Floyd are indistinguishable. Relationships with his bandmates seemed important to Waters only to realize his vision, as proven by *The Wall*'s bitter recording sessions. Although Gilmour and Waters detested each other, the guitarist retained a vital role, especially on the album's major hit "Comfortably Numb." Wright, who played as a session musician after Waters fired him, was less fortunate, while Mason's contributions were severely scaled back. The aptly titled *The Final Cut* was Waters's last work with Gilmour and Mason, whose diminished stature was clarified by a subtitle: *A Requiem for the Postwar Dream by Roger Waters, Performed by Pink Floyd*. Considered an unofficial start to Waters's solo career, *Final Cut* eulogizes lost idealism represented by his father Eric Waters and denounces former British prime minister Margaret Thatcher, whose military action against Argentina in 1982 disgusted Waters.

Solo Works. On his own in 1984, Waters's first efforts were poorly received. *The Pros and Cons of Hitchhiking*, which included rejected Pink Floyd material, had scant critical and audience appeal despite stellar support from guitarist Eric Clapton. *Radio K.A.O.S.* was stronger and boasted a story line centered on possibilities of human communication but fell short of standards that reviewers and record buyers expected. Although *Amused to Death* earned Waters his best solo reviews for exploring the impact of global media and militarism, the general public remained largely indifferent. Aside from concert recordings, Waters has not released a rock album since. *Ça Ira* is an opera based on the

French Revolution that took almost ten years to finish.

Musical Legacy

Waters proved that some of the most lucrative lyrics in popular music could be also be painfully personal and often contemptuous of one's audience. Citing Bob Dylan, John Lennon, and Randy Newman as influences, Waters conveyed individual and social concerns in musical contexts that were far more extravagant than those artists' works. One of many paradoxical elements in Waters's career is that his work is relentlessly autobiographical, but his arrangements are lavish and his stage shows spectacular. On one hand, Waters is altruistic, even utopian; on the other, his songs almost always contain cynicism, even misanthropy. Ambitious and impressive as his uneven solo works are, Waters's musical legacy will likely remain primarily and uncomfortably entwined with Pink Floyd.

Ray Pence

Further Reading

Felix, Justin. "'That Space Cadet Glow': Science Fiction Narratives in Roger Waters's *Radio K.A.O.S.* and *Amused to Death.*" *Extrapolation* 41, no. 4 (2005): 375-385. Two underappreciated Waters solo albums are the subject of scholarly analysis highlighting their unique storytelling.

Harris, John. *"The Dark Side of the Moon": The Making of the Pink Floyd Masterpiece.* Cambridge, Mass.: Da Capo Press, 2005. In-depth, not-always-flattering account of the creative process behind the blockbuster album, with attention on Waters and his difficult personality.

Mason, Nick. *Inside Out: A Personal History of Pink Floyd.* San Francisco: Chronicle Books, 2005. Mason, whose relations with Waters have been more cordial than those of his bandmates, offers a lively, lavishly illustrated memoir.

Reising, Russell, ed. *"Speak to Me": The Legacy of Pink Floyd's "The Dark Side of the Moon."* Burlington, Vt.: Ashgate, 2005. Collection of scholarly essays covering a range of topics related to the album's significance in various historical and cultural contexts.

Schaffner, Nicholas. *Saucerful of Secrets: The Pink Floyd Odyssey.* New York: Harmony Books, 1991.

Popular book covering the band from its Barrett period to its post-Waters phase. Schaffner's focus on conflict within the band is sensationalistic, but the book's comprehensive scope is valuable.

See also: Clapton, Eric; Dylan, Bob; Lennon, John; Newman, Randy.

Doc Watson

American country singer, guitarist, and banjoist

Watson's flat-picking approach to the guitar became integral to bluegrass. His sagacious avuncular presence coats all old and new music—from ballads, to blues, to rockabilly—with a patina of deep-rooted tradition.

Born: March 2, 1923; Stoney Fork Township, North Carolina
Also known as: Arthel Lane Watson (full name)
Member of: The Doc Watson Family

Principal recordings

ALBUMS: *The Doc Watson Family*, 1963; *Doc Watson*, 1964; *Treasures Untold*, 1964; *Doc Watson and Son*, 1965; *Home Again*, 1966; *Southbound*, 1966; *Ballads from Deep Gap*, 1967; *Strictly Instrumental*, 1967; *Doc and Merle Watson's Guitar Album*, 1972; *The Elementary Doctor Watson!*, 1972; *Will the Circle Be Unbroken, Vol. I*, 1972 (with the Nitty Gritty Dirt Band and others); *Then and Now*, 1973; *Memories*, 1975; *Doc and the Boys*, 1976; *The Doc Watson Family: Tradition*, 1977; *Lonesome Road*, 1977; *Look Away*, 1978; *Red Rocking Chair*, 1981; *Down South*, 1984; *Riding the Midnight Train*, 1986; *Portrait*, 1987; *Will the Circle Be Unbroken, Vol. II*, 1989 (with the Nitty Gritty Dirt Band and others); *On Praying Ground*, 1990; *Songs for Little Pickers*, 1990; *Remembering Merle*, 1992; *Songs from the Southern Mountains*, 1994; *Docabilly*, 1995; *Doc and Dawg*, 1997; *Mel, Doc, and Del*, 1997; *Third Generation Blues*, 1999; *Legacy*, 2002; *Round the Table Again*, 2002; *Will the Circle Be Unbroken,*

Vol. III, 2002 (with the Nitty Gritty Dirt Band and others); *The Three Pickers*, 2003.

The Life

Arthel Lane Watson was sixth of nine children of General Dixon and Nancy Anne Watson. By the second year of his life, Watson had lost his vision to an eye infection. General Watson was a farmer and a song leader in church, while Nancy Anne was a housewife who sang around the house. His parents as well as a number of Watson's neighbors were musical repositories of traditional material. From his mother Watson heard such old hymns as "There Is a Fountain" and "The Lone Pilgrim." Watson's first instrument was the diatonic harmonica; his father bought him one each year as a Christmas present after he turned six. When he was about ten, Watson received his first banjo, a fretless homemade version that his father built and on which he taught the young Arthel his first banjo tune, "Reuben's Train," which continued as a fixture in Watson's performances.

In the mid-1930's the Watson family acquired their first radio and record player. Radio exposed Watson to the music of such country artists as the Blue Sky Boys, the Monroe Brothers, J. D. Mainer, the Delmore Brothers, and Merle Travis. The family had an eclectic collection of records that included Tin Pan Alley balladeer Gene Austin backed by a guitarist, alternating-thumb-style blues guitarist Mississippi John Hurt, and the works of country guitar pioneers Riley Puckett, Maybelle Carter, and Jimmie Rodgers. These musicians as well as the Delmore Brothers and Travis inspired Watson's development on guitar, the instrument with which he is most strongly associated.

At age ten Watson started attending the Raleigh School for the Blind. Not interested in either classical music or the piano, Watson had not taken up the musical training available at that school. Still, with some basic instruction on guitar from his friend Paul Montgomery, Watson showed some talent, and his father bought Watson his first guitar. In the 1940's Watson occasionally played music on the street in Boone and Wilkesboro. His first paid musical job was performing at the American Legion House in Boone with Charlie Osborne's square dance band. At eighteen Watson picked up his famous nickname "Doc" when he appeared with

Paul Greer on a radio show in Lenoir, North Carolina, and broadcast on WHKY, Hickory. In 1947 Watson married Rosa Lee Carlton, daughter of legendary local fiddler Gaither Carlton. Around 1953 Watson joined Jack Williams and the Country Gentlemen, a country-and-western swing band, and soon acquired a Gibson Les Paul electric guitar. Missing a fiddler, the band relied on Watson to play the lead on interpretations of fiddle tunes. Taking his cue from country session musicians Hank Garland and Grady Martin, Watson developed a style that, when transposed to acoustic guitar, became known as country flat-pick guitar.

In 1960 Smithsonian curator and folk revival musician Ralph Rinzler traveled to Mountain City, Tennessee, to record Clarence "Tom" Ashley, a banjo player who had previously recorded in 1929. Watson was among the cream of area musicians Ashley invited for the sessions. Impressed by Watson's musicianship and deep traditional roots, Rinzler persuaded the younger musician to accompany Ashley to major folk revival venues in the North. Following well-received solo performances in 1963 at the Newport and Berkeley Folk Festivals and a concert with Bill Monroe in 1964 at the Town Hall in New York City, Watson became a darling of the folk revival and was signed to a contract with Vanguard Records. Joined that summer by his fifteen-year-old son Merle, Watson traveled and recorded prolifically on the folk revival circuit.

By 1968 folk rock had displaced acoustic folk revival music, and Watson followed the lead of Bob Dylan, Joan Baez, and Lester Flatt and Earl Scruggs to Nashville studios, recording an album enhanced by electric instruments and drums (to which Watson was not alien, having honed his guitar skills in an electrified country dance band). With acoustic folk music's popularity on the wane, Watson's career was at a low ebb when he appeared alongside country music legends Maybelle Carter, Roy Acuff, Merle Travis, and Jimmy Martin on the Nitty Gritty Dirt Band's *Will the Circle Be Unbroken*, a seminal three-disc collaboration between early commercial country and contemporary folk-rock musicians. The album was exceptionally successful with a rock audience that was just beginning to appreciate country music through country-rock amalgams and proved a shot in the arm for Watson's career. A similar audience of literate roots-conscious audiences has since supported his career. The Watsons, with T. Michael Coleman on bass and other musicians, traveled continuously and recorded a number of commercially and critically successful albums, in the process earning four Grammy Awards.

After Merle's death in a tractor accident in October, 1985, Doc Watson resumed his career with Merle's protégé, Jack Lawrence, on second guitar. He has occasionally been joined by Merle's son, Richard, an accomplished blues-influenced flat-pick guitarist like his father. Watson is also the patron saint at MerleFest, one of the largest roots music festivals in North America held in memory of his son each year since 1988 on the campus of Wilkes Community College in Wilkesboro, North Carolina.

The Music

Folkways Records' *The Doc Watson Family* emphasized Watson's deep traditional roots and betrayed the disparate soils feeding those roots—Old World ballads, regional native ballads, blues ballads, widespread as well as local fiddle tunes, banjo tunes, Baptist hymns, and the blues.

From 1964 to 1967, when Watson continuously traveled across the country to play at folk revival venues, almost each year Vanguard released two of his albums, which largely stuck to a spare acoustic sound. The quality of Watson's performances and recordings would stay sturdily consistent for the next four decades. In *Doc Watson and Son*, he found an exceptionally able accompanist and partner in his son Merle, who continued to be his father's road and musical companion until his accidental death in 1985.

Held in high esteem by acoustic musicians, Watson has collaborated with many and appeared on recordings alongside such stalwarts as Monroe, Flatt and Scruggs, Mac Wiseman, Chet Atkins, Jean Ritchie, Ricky Skaggs, and Bryan Sutton. He has also appeared on cross-genre collaborative albums

Doc Watson. (AP/Wide World Photos)

with Dan Fogelberg, Michelle Shocked, the Chieftains, and James Cotton.

Doc Watson. On Watson's first solo album for Vanguard Records, he appears without accompanist. The album features the first recording of Watson's signature flat-pick guitar adaptation of the fiddle tune "Black Mountain Rag," which forever changed the role of the guitar in traditional American music. Emulating the constant sawing motion typical of Appalachian fiddle playing on up-tempo tunes, Watson devised an unrelenting, strictly alternating plectrum or flat-pick motion that allowed transposition of fiddle and banjo tunes to the guitar and elevated the guitar to the role of a lead instrument. On this album, this style is also featured on "Nashville Blues" and a version of the murder ballad "Tom Dooley," which had been recorded by the Kingston Trio years earlier. Watson's different version of the story and the music, however, were passed down from his own grandmother. The album also reveals Watson's command of Travis-style fingerpicking on his adaptation of the Delmore Brothers' "Deep River Blues" and on another instrumental showcase, "Doc's Guitar." On "Little Omie Wise" and "St. James's Hospital," both later standards in his repertoire, Watson accompanies himself with continuously cascading fingerpicked rolls that are rarely heard in his later work with accompanists. On "Georgie Buck" and Doc Boggs's "Country Blues," he accompanies himself on frailing banjo. An all-round entertainer, Watson includes two comical songs, "Intoxicated Rat" and "Born About Six Thousand Years Ago," the latter also featuring a rack-worn harmonica.

Southbound. Although the quality of his previous work was unimpeachable, *Southbound* was exceptional in a number of respects. While on the preceding two albums, the young Merle had served as reliable accompanist, here he stepped up to assume the role of a second contrapuntal voice and also composer. Merle's "Southbound" has since remained a centerpiece of Watson's repertoire. With *Southbound* Watson's talent for arranging and reinterpreting older and contemporary artists' material and stamping it with his own personality became undeniable with his arrangements of John D. Loudermilk's "Windy and Warm," Mel Tillis's "Walk on Boy," Jimmie Driftwood's "Tennessee Stud," Leadbelly's "Alberta," the Delmore Brothers' "Blue Railroad Train," and Tom Paxton's "Last Thing on My Mind." The instrumentals "Sweet Georgia Brown" and "Nothing to It" also helped bring swing-based instrumentals into the acoustic flat-pick guitar repertoire.

Then and Now. With this album, Watson established himself with the audience that favored roots music played acoustically, a niche market that developed after folk influences had been sidelined by mainstream rock. With an enhanced sound featuring drums, bass, pedal steel guitar, and also subtle washes of strings on some tracks, the album proved once again that the Watsons were not strict folk purists, and they could subtly dress up innovation with an overall traditional aura. The core of the album featured full-band interpretations of a number of songs from the African American repertoire, including "Matchbox Blues," "Milkcow Blues," "Frankie and Johnny," "Corrina Corrina," and many other songs interpreted in styles that emphasized the blues influence on hillbilly music.

Musical Legacy

Watson's legacy is manifold. With an immediately recognizable magisterial baritone, he could have had an exceptional career as a popular vocal-

ist. His additional strong instrumental talents with straight harp, cross harp, clawhammer banjo, and alternating-thumb fingerpicking guitar made him an exceptional solo entertainer on folk-revival stages and then in country-folk music and Americana circuits. His innovative flat-pick guitar stylings, however, have mesmerized three generations of audiences and musicians around the world. That guitar style became integral to progressive, and even traditional, bluegrass music and begat a worldwide fraternity of flat-pick guitarists and enthusiasts. Some of his followers might have equaled and arguably surpassed him with regard to facility on the guitar, but unchallenged is Watson's stature as the embodiment of constantly innovative but sturdily traditional music making. The Presidential Medal for the Arts (1997), a National Heritage Fellowship (1988), and a National Academy of Recording Arts and Sciences (NARAS) Lifetime Achievement Award presented at the 2004 Grammy Awards are just some of the official recognitions Watson has received for his contributions to American music.

Ajay Kalra

Further Reading

Havighurst, Craig. "Living Legacy: Doc Watson's Immeasurable Influence on the Guitar and Folk Community." *Acoustic Guitar* (June, 2003): 54-64. Evaluation of Watson's life and legacy.

Holt, David, and Doc Watson. *Legacy.* Fairview, N.C.: High Windy Audio, 2002. Multi-instrumentalist and longtime folk music enthusiast Holt's seventy-two-page booklet, which accompanies a three-disc audio documentary, includes interviews with Watson's family, friends, and musical compatriots Baez and Ry Cooder. This Grammy-winning project is perhaps the best introduction to Watson's life and music.

Ledgin, Stephanie. "Father and Son: The Rich Musical Legacy of Doc and Merle Watson." *Acoustic Guitar* (March/April, 1993): 49-57. Comprehensive article-length biography with interview, accompanied by an analysis of the Watsons' distinctive guitar styles in relation to their influences.

Metting, Fred. *The Life, Work, and Music of the American Folk Artist Doc Watson.* Lampeter, England: Edwin Mellen, 2006. The only book-length, detailed account of Watson's life, his musical and social worlds, and his influences.

Sievert, Jon. "Doc Watson." *Frets* (March, 1987): 30-67. Fairly detailed interview with Watson regarding his life and music, accompanied by guitar transcriptions in tablature.

See also: Acuff, Roy; Baez, Joan; Carter, Maybelle; Cotton, James; Dylan, Bob; Flatt, Lester; Hurt, Mississippi John; Ritchie, Jean; Rodgers, Jimmie; Scruggs, Earl; Travis, Merle; Van Zandt, Townes.

André Watts

American classical pianist

A virtuoso, Watts is the first African American pianist to have won international acclaim as a first-rank classical instrumentalist.

Born: June 20, 1946; Nuremberg, Germany

Principal recordings

ALBUMS: *André Watts Plays Liszt, Album 1*, 1986; *André Watts Plays Liszt, Album 2*, 1986; *Beethoven: Sonatas No. 13 in E-Flat, No. 14—Moonlight, and No. 23—Appassionata*, 1987; *Chopin: Piano Concertos Nos. 1 and 2*, 1990; *The Chopin Recital*, 1992; *Tchaikovsky—Piano Concerto No. 1/Saint Saëns—Piano Concerto No. 2*, 1995; *MacDowell—Piano Concerto No. 2/ Liszt—Piano Concertos Nos. 1 and 2*, 1996; *Rachmaninoff: Piano Concertos Nos. 2 and 3*, 2003.

The Life

André Watts (AHN-dray wahts) was born in 1946 in Nuremberg, Germany, where his father, an African American Army sergeant named Herman Watts, married the Hungarian Maria Alexandra Gusmits. Watts learned to play the violin at age four, and about three years later, his mother taught him to play the piano. When he was ten, the Watts family moved to the United States, settling in Philadelphia, where Watts studied the piano with Genia Robinor, student of the Polish pianist Theodor Leschetizky, at the Philadelphia Academy of Music

(now part of the University of the Arts). When his parents divorced in 1962, Watts stayed with his mother.

In January, 1963, conductor Leonard Bernstein selected the sixteen-year-old Watts to perform Franz Liszt's Piano Concerto No. 1 in E-flat Major (1855) for the nationally televised *Young People's Concert* with the New York Philharmonic. About three weeks later, Bernstein invited him to substitute for Glenn Gould at the regular New York Philharmonic subscription concert. Watts performed the same concerto, reportedly receiving an eight-minute standing ovation. He quickly became one of the popular piano virtuosos on the international classical music scene. Despite his success, he continued to study with Leon Fleischer at the Peabody Institute, in Baltimore, Maryland, through 1974. He frequently plays at benefit concerts, and he is one of the leaders of the nonprofit organization Classical Action: Performing Arts Against AIDS.

The Music

Watts started his career in the early 1960's by performing Romantic repertory by Ludwig van Beethoven, Franz Schubert, Camille Saint-Saëns, Frédéric Chopin, Liszt, Johannes Brahms, and Sergei Rachmaninoff. Over the decades he has expanded his repertory to include works by Alessandro Scarlatti, Johann Sebastian Bach, Wolfgang Amadeus Mozart, Claude Debussy, George Gershwin, Edward MacDowell, Modest Mussorgsky, Maurice Ravel, Béla Bartók, György Ligeti, and even Luciano Berio. His technique is impeccable, his touch crisp and clear; his playing offers a sense of caprice and subtlety. When performing a concerto, he considers himself an accompanist as much as a soloist, and he pays close attention not only to the conductor but also to the individual orchestral players. Listening to the breathing of a clarinetist, for example, helps him bring coherence to the performance. Watts applies similar thinking to his playing in general, and he is known to bring out musical nuances and their structural significance in a piece. In his interpretations, even trills adopt different personalities at different points in a composition. In this way, his interpretations bring an ongoing sense of freshness and vitality.

Concerto Soloist. Watts is famous primarily as a concerto player. His legendary 1963 performance of Liszt's Piano Concerto No. 1 in E-flat Major launched his performance career. For more than four decades, he has performed the major Romantic concerti of Tchaikovsky, Saint-Saëns, and Beethoven. At the Mostly Mozart Festival in New York, Watts performed Mozart's Piano Concerto No. 24 in C Minor (1786). As a specialist of Romantic masterpieces, Watts interpreted this concerto, one of the most emotional pieces that Mozart wrote, with expressive intensity and dramatic weight, characterized by free pedaling and a chromatic, emotionally intense cadenza. In addition to Romantic and select classical repertories, Watts played twentieth century piano concerti, including those by Dmitri Shostakovich, Gershwin, and MacDowell.

André Watts. (Hulton Archive/Getty Images)

Recitalist. In his recitals Watts played classical and Romantic repertory, including songs and sonatas by Schubert, Mozart, and Beethoven. Although he was sometimes criticized for having a narrow repertory, he has expanded it considerably. In 2001 he performed Modest Mussorgsky's *Pictures at an Exhibition* (1874) at Cornell University. In the celebration of the fiftieth anniversary of the Metropolitan Museum of Art in the 2004-2005 season, he added a Francis Poulenc piece to the Mozart and Brahms program. He has been known for his electrifying transcription of Bernstein's *Candide* (1956). In June, 2004, he opened Black Music Month in Chicago by playing his own transcription of Bach's chorale prelude *Ich ruf zu dir* (1713) and Ferruccio Busoni's transcription of Bach's *In dir ist Freude* (1713). Watts continued to bring surprises to his audiences by playing Ravel's *Miroirs* (1906), four pieces from Ligeti's *Musica ricercata* (1951-1953), and Sergei Prokofiev's Sonata for Violin and Piano No. 1 in F Minor with the violinist Cho-Liang Lin.

Recording Artist. Watts won a Grammy Award for Best New Classical Artist in 1963. A compilation of his recordings from 1963 through 1980 was released by Philips in 1999 as part of its great pianists of the twentieth century series.

Musical Legacy

At age twenty-six, Watts was the youngest recipient of an honorary doctorate from Yale in 1972, and he received honorary doctorates from the Juilliard School in 1994 and from the Peabody Institute in 1997. In addition, he received honorary degrees from Miami University of Ohio and Albright College in Pennsylvania. He was honored by the president of the Congo with the Order of the Zaire, the highest honor for a civilian, and he was recipient of the University of the Arts Medal from the University of the Arts in Philadelphia. In 1998 he hosted the thirtieth anniversary gala of the Chamber Music Society of Lincoln Center, New York. In 2000 he was appointed artist-in-residence of the University of Maryland, and in 2004 he was named to the Jack I. and Dora B. Hamlin Endowed Chair of the Jacobs School of Music of Indiana University in Bloomington. In 2006 he was inducted into the Hollywood Bowl Hall of Fame.

Hedy Law

Further Reading

Dubal, David. *Reflections from the Keyboard: The World of the Concert Pianist.* New York: Schirmer Books, 1997. A must-read for music lovers, this books provides interviews with forty-three pianists, including Watts.

Isacoff, Stuart, ed. *Great Lessons from Great Pianists.* Bedford Hills, N.Y.: Ekay Music, 1997. The source offers an interview with Watts and his transcription of Bach's *Ich ruf zu dir.*

Mach, Elyse. *Great Contemporary Pianists Speak for Themselves.* New York: Dover, 1991. A valuable compilation of autobiographies for and anecdotes about twentieth century pianists. Includes a detailed interview of Watts.

Southern, Eileen. *Biographical Dictionary of Afro-American and African Musicians.* Westport, Conn.: Greenwood, 1982. Written by the first tenured African American woman professor in musicology at Harvard University, this dictionary is one of the most significant references on American music, and it includes an entry on Watts.

_____. *The Music of Black Americans: A History.* New York: Norton, 1997. This seminal music history of black Americans is a standard text in studies of American music, and it explains Watts's contribution to classical music.

See also: Bartók, Béla; Berio, Luciano; Bernstein, Leonard; Busoni, Ferruccio; Gould, Glenn; Ligeti, György; Poulenc, Francis; Rachmaninoff, Sergei; Ravel, Maurice.

Franz Waxman

German film-score composer

A creative and prolific composer of Hollywood film scores, Waxman used his extensive knowledge of art music and popular idioms to create music that effectively mirrored a film's dramatic structure and supplied added information about the story line.

Born: December 24, 1906; Königshütte, Upper Silesia, Germany (now Chorzów, Poland)
Died: February 24, 1967; Los Angeles, California
Also known as: Franz Wachsmann (birth name)

Principal works

FILM SCORES: *Einbrecher*, 1930 (*Murder for Sale*); *Bride of Frankenstein*, 1935; *Fury*, 1936; *Sutter's Gold*, 1936; *The Bride Wore Red*, 1937; *Captains Courageous*, 1937; *A Christmas Carol*, 1938; *The

Young in Heart, 1938; *The Philadelphia Story*, 1940; *Rebecca*, 1940; *Dr. Jekyll and Mr. Hyde*, 1941; *Suspicion*, 1941; *God Is My Co-Pilot*, 1945; *Objective, Burma!*, 1945; *Humoresque*, 1946; *Possessed*, 1947; *Dark City*, 1950; *The Furies*, 1950; *Sunset Boulevard*, 1950; *Ann of the Indies*, 1951; *He Ran All the Way*, 1951; *A Place in the Sun*, 1951; *Come Back, Little Sheba*, 1952; *Phone Call from a Stranger*, 1952; *I, the Jury*, 1953; *Rear Window*, 1954; *The Silver Chalice*, 1954; *Mister Roberts*, 1955; *Peyton Place*, 1957; *Run Silent, Run Deep*, 1958; *The Nun's Story*, 1959; *Return to Peyton Place*, 1961; *Taras Bulba*, 1962.
VOCAL WORK: *The Song of Terezin*, 1965.

The Life

Franz Waxman was the last of seven children born to Otto and Rosalie Wachsmann. Waxman's father worked in the steel business, providing the family with a comfortable upper-middle-class lifestyle. Waxman studied piano as a child, exhibiting a talent for playing both classical and popular music. Discouraging him from seriously pursuing music, his father acquired the sixteen-year-old Waxman a job as a bank teller. Waxman's work in the bank was short-lived, and he began his musical studies in Dresden in 1923. Soon, he transferred to the Berlin Music Conservatory. While in Berlin, Waxman worked as a pianist in cafés to support himself, eventually obtaining a job as the pianist for the Weintraub Syncopaters, a popular jazz orchestra in Europe. The connections he established in that group led to a job in the music department at Universum Film AG, Germany's internationally acclaimed film company. In 1934, after being brutalized by Nazis in Berlin, Waxman emigrated to Los Angeles (via Paris), where he prospered as a film composer, earning twelve Academy Award nominations. Waxman was also a successful composer and conductor of concert music, and he founded the Los Angeles Music Festival in 1947, a venture in which he displayed a commitment to programming the music of avant-garde twentieth century composers. In 1967 Waxman died of cancer at age sixty in Los Angeles.

The Music

Waxman's film scores established a precedent for film music composers to integrate sophisticated and up-to-date musical procedures into their scores. Many of his film scores, such as *Humoresque* and *Possessed*, creatively transform the themes of famous composers, such as Georges Bizet and Robert Schumann. When using this technique Waxman put the quoted theme in a diegetic context, but it continually resurfaces and mutates in ways that ultimately capture the film's overriding thematic ideas.

Bride of Frankenstein. Waxman made his mark in Hollywood with his first American film score, for James Whale's *Bride of Frankenstein*. The score became a huge asset to Universal Pictures' music library, and portions of it were reused for years in numerous second-rate productions, leading it to be recognized as archetypal horror film music. The score displays Waxman's creative use of distinctive leitmotifs to characterize the Bride, the Monster, and Dr. Praetorius, which appear immediately in the opening cue and are increasingly developed and combined contrapuntally as the film progresses. When ritualistic activities are depicted, Waxman often mimics the conventional musical codes of European art music. For example, a funeral march plays for the premature funeral procession of Baron Frankenstein, and an idyllic pastoral passage, denoted by harp arpeggios and a languid flute melody, accompanies the Monster's journey into the countryside. In technological and frightening, Waxman adopts common devices—harmonic ambiguity, agitated ostinati, and eerie trills and tremolos—reminiscent of the dissonant Expressionistic music of the Second Viennese School.

Sunset Boulevard. Waxman's score for *Sunset Boulevard*, the story of the downfall of an aging Hollywood starlet, is one of his great masterpieces, and it is his first to be honored with an Academy Award. The three prominent themes of *Sunset Boulevard*'s score subtly enact the emergence of a love triangle among Norma, Joe Gillis (her scriptwriter lover), and Betty (a younger woman who captivates Gillis). The score reaches explosive heights when the delusional Norma greets the media after murdering Gillis. Believing they are there to document her comeback, she descends a winding staircase, playing the role of Salome (the seductive biblical dancer and the subject of Richard Strauss's controversial 1905 opera). Waxman accentuates the exotic trill that pervades Strauss's opera, and he in-

fuses the final incantation of Norma's theme with dark instrumentation, low registers, and aggressive syncopation to convey the protagonist's misfortune.

The Song of Terezín. *The Song of Terezín*, a dramatic orchestral song cycle scored for mezzo-soprano, mixed chorus, and children's chorus, is a poignant statement on the repercussions of fascism and genocide. The music is set to poetry written by children who spent the final days of their lives in the Theresienstadt concentration camp (often called Terezín). Waxman selected eight songs from the collection entitled *I Never Saw Another Butterfly*, alternating between settings for solo voice and for choir in the seven movements preceding the finale, "Fear," where all of the voices recognize that death is near, and they join together in a reflective lament. Waxman thought of the mezzo-soprano as a mother separated from her child. The score assembles stylistic and technical devices endemic to the Austro-Germanic tradition: the use of a passacaglia structure and a twelve-tone row in the first song, a fleeting and playful melodic flurry invoking a symphonic scherzo in the third song, and jarring Expressionistic textures and ostinati in the fifth song. Waxman hauntingly quotes Ludwig van Beethoven's "Moonlight" Sonata (1801) in the sixth song, as the text describes a deserted piano and the excision of music from daily life. With *The Song of Terezín* Waxman attests that music can serve as a vehicle to combat injustice in the world and to act as a living tribute to victims who succumbed to political and moral corruption.

Musical Legacy

Waxman was one of the first composers in Hollywood to regard film scoring as a serious art form, affirming that film music could be aesthetically equivalent to concert music. Although his income came primarily from composing music for motion pictures, Waxman's interests in film composition were always second to his interests in European art music, as he immersed himself in the intensive study of both canonic and contemporary concert music. He admirably composed and conducted concert scores, encouraging other film composers, such as Elmer Bernstein, Leonard Rosenman, and John Williams, to uphold this duality.

Jessica Payette

Further Reading

Cook, Page. "Franz Waxman Was One of the Composers Who Thought Film Music Could Be an Art." *Films in Review* 19, no. 7 (August/September, 1968): 415-430. Cook commemorated Waxman's death with a biographical and artistic sketch in a popular periodical.

Darby, William, and Jack Du Bois. *American Film Music: Major Composers, Techniques, Trends, 1915-1990*. Jefferson, N.C.: McFarland, 1990. This presents an overview of Waxman's film scores, and it is particularly noteworthy for commentary on Waxman's inspired scores in critically bashed films such as *Taras Bulba*.

Palmer, Christopher. *The Composer in Hollywood*. London: Marion Boyars, 1990. A film composer offers firsthand knowledge of legendary Hollywood film composers and their musical output. Palmer's discussion includes stylistic and technical analyses of several of Waxman's scores.

Thomas, Tony. *Music for the Movies*. Los Angeles: Silman-James Press, 1997. Features a chapter on Waxman's life and works by one of the most highly regarded experts on the history of film music.

Waxman, Franz. "Interview on *Music from the Films*: A CBC Broadcast." *Hollywood Quarterly* 5, no. 2 (Winter, 1950): 132-137. Typescript of Lawrence Morton's interview with Waxman recorded for the Canadian Broadcasting Company's series *Music from the Films*.

See also: Bernstein, Elmer; Elfman, Danny; Rózsa, Miklós; Steiner, Max; Strauss, Richard; Williams, John.

Jimmy Webb

American country/pop singer, pianist, songwriter, and film-score composer

Webb's signature songwriting style—an adventuresome combination of Tin Pan Alley, rock-and-roll, country, and folk sensibilities—is an entertaining bridge between pop and rock and roll.

Born: August 15, 1946; Elk City, Oklahoma
Also known as: James Layne Webb (full name)

Principal works

FILM SCORE: *The Last Unicorn*, 1982.
SONGS: "By the Time I Get to Phoenix," 1967; "MacArthur Park," 1968; "Wichita Lineman," 1968; "Highwayman," 1977.

Principal recordings

ALBUMS: *Jim Webb Sings Jim Webb*, 1968; *Words and Music*, 1970; *And So: On*, 1971; *Letters*, 1972; *Land's End*, 1974; *El Mirage*, 1977; *Angel Heart*, 1982; *Suspending Disbelief*, 1993; *Ten Easy Pieces*, 1996; *Last Unicorn*, 1998; *Twilight of the Renegades*, 2005; *Live and at Large*, 2007.
WRITINGS OF INTEREST: *Tunesmith: Inside the Art of Songwriting*, 1998.

The Life

James Layne Webb was born to Robert Lee and Sylvia Ann Webb in the Oklahoma panhandle. Webb's father was a Baptist minister, and James and siblings Beth, Gary, and Susan were raised under strict religious guidelines. In 1963, after years of struggle, the senior Webb moved his family to California for better job prospects. Webb entered Colton High School to finish his senior year, but it was marred by the premature death of his mother at the age of thirty-six. Her death traumatized the family, and Webb's father moved the family back to Oklahoma. Webb decided to stay in California to attend San Bernardino College and pursue his dream of being a songwriter.

Webb began working as a copyist for several small Hollywood publishers, including Jobete Music. His contract was later purchased by rock-pop star Johnny Rivers, and it was under Rivers's tutelage that Webb began writing songs for the Versatiles, a group Rivers had signed to his Soul City Records label. The group later changed its name to the Fifth Dimension. When up-and-coming singer Glen Campbell found one of Webb's songs, "By the Time I Get to Phoenix," on Rivers's *Rewind* album (1967) and recorded it the same year (1967) as the Fifth Dimension's recording of another Webb song, "Up, Up, and Away," the young songwriter had two hit singles before his twenty-first birthday. Dubbed the wunderkind of pop sensibility, Webb would go on to have more hit singles with the Fifth Dimension, Campbell, Richard Har-

Jimmy Webb. (AP/Wide World Photos)

ris, Art Garfunkel, Linda Ronstadt, and others throughout the next two decades.

In the 1970's Webb returned to performing, releasing five solo albums in that decade alone. None was commercially successful, and his five albums released between 1982 and 2007 fared no better. His 1974 marriage to former teen model Brigitta Patricia Sullivan, daughter of actor Barry Sullivan, ended in divorce in the mid-1990's. By then the Webbs had lived in upstate New York for almost fifteen years as Webb, frustrated by a shrinking set of opportunities in Hollywood, had turned his attention to writing musicals for Broadway.

The Music

Bridging the Generations. For a brief period, between rock and roll's first assault against the airwaves in the late 1950's and its conquest of the same by the early 1970's, it was possible to hear such pop and jazz crooners as Tony Bennett, Jack Jones, Ella Fitzgerald, and Sarah Vaughan on the same sta-

tions that played the Beatles, the Supremes, and Chubby Checker. During the transitional period, Broadway show music, jazz instrumentals, and Tin Pan Alley crooners gradually lost radio airtime to pop, rhythm and blues, and rock and roll. In musical terms, this meant a declining emphasis on melody and harmony and a reemphasis on rhythm (guitars and drums for rock and roll; bass and drums for rhythm and blues). In this respect, the importance of Motown Records cannot be overstated, for Berry Gordy's genius was to combine blues and rhythm and blues with the string and horn orchestrations typical of show tunes. This desire for popular rawness and classical elegance would usher in a new type of song, as different from the compositions of Harold Arlen and Sammy Cahn as it was from those of early John Lennon-Paul McCartney and Mick Jagger-Keith Richards tunes.

In such a cross-fertilizing context, it is no surprise that among Webb's first jobs as a professional songwriter was a stint with Motown Records. Nor is it surprising that his songs—a hybrid of show music and rock and roll—would dominate the pop charts between 1967 and 1969. His songs made instant pop stars of the Fifth Dimension ("Up, Up, and Away," "Paper Cup," "Carpet Man," "The Girls' Song"), Campbell ("By the Time I Get to Phoenix," "Wichita Lineman," "Where's the Playground, Susie?," "Galveston"), and Harris ("MacArthur Park," "Didn't We?"). Webb's songs combined literate but folksy lyrics with largely minor-key melodies grounded in gospel and classical traditions. In short, Webb forged a music that paid homage to the present and past, to both pop spontaneity and emotion and classical form and intelligence.

Solo Albums. Webb's commercial success at the end of the 1960's provoked a backlash from countercultural rock-and-roll artists and critics, affecting Webb's self-perception. His decision to strike out on his own in 1970 with *Words and Music*, featuring Webb in Rivers-style black leather, can be read as an attempt to show his critics that he was as steeped in the present as they were. The problem was that the album alienated his straight pop audience and failed to mollify his critics. Moreover, both the straight pop audience and the underground rockers were put off by Webb's unpolished, unpredictable singing, which echoes blues and gospel singing traditions more than it does the pop traditions his songs honor.

Webb released only one album in the 1980's, 1982's *Angel Heart*. However, two albums of the 1990's, *Suspending Disbelief* and *Ten Easy Pieces*, received a great amount of critical acclaim, notwithstanding their commercial failure. In 2005 Webb remarried and released his tenth solo album, *Twilight of the Renegades*. This was followed in 2007 by the release of his first live recording, *Live and at Large*. Though Webb never scored hits as a performer, he established himself as a successful, well-received cabaret artist, playing to sold-out venues in England and the United States.

Musical Legacy

Webb influenced a new generation of straight pop songwriters such as Diane Warren, singer-songwriters such as Freedy Johnston, and country songwriters such as Vince Gill. Mainstream and underground rock acts (such as R.E.M. and Boo Radleys) have gravitated toward his classic and newer songs, turning Webb into something of a cult figure. As a performer in the line of other legendary singer-songwriters whose vocal stylistics test the limits of pop and rock—such as Bob Dylan, Randy Newman, and Neil Young—Webb compels one to experience his music and words in a voice which, precisely because it is raw and unpolished, sings with conviction of romance chastened, ambition shattered, and desire undeterred, the staples of all American popular music.

Tyrone Williams

Further Reading

Blaine, Hal, with David Goggin. "Jimmy Webb and the Fifth Dimension." In *Hal Blaine and the Wrecking Crew*. Emeryville, Calif.: Mix Books, 1990. Writing with the same gusto and drive that made his drumming legendary among some of the best-known 1960's pop stars, Blaine takes the reader behind the scenes of some of his more significant recording sessions, including those he did for the Fifth Dimension's pioneering second album, *Magic Garden*, written and orchestrated entirely by Webb.

DeMain, Bill. "Jimmy Webb." *Performing Songwriter*, March/April, 2007, 120-122. Although DeMain begins by going over old ground, most of the interview concentrates on newer projects, including two Broadway shows Webb was writing.

Webb, Jimmy. *Memorabilia*. Port Chester, N.Y.: Cherry Lane, 1990. Part memoir (photographs of family, friends, telegrams, and ticket stubs) and part songbook (guitar and piano parts for some of Webb's best-known songs up through the late 1980's), this book is multifunctional. The casual fan can browse through these memories of Webb's life, while the musician can play some of the most sophisticated popular songs of the mid- and late twentieth century.

_____. *Tunesmith: Inside the Art of Songwriting*. New York: Hyperion Books, 1998. One of the best books on songwriting ever written. Webb moves back and forth between interesting, wry, and dark-humored tales of the songwriter's precarious existence and thorough, even technical, descriptions of lyric writing and music composition. As useful for the professional as it is entertaining for the fan.

See also: Bacharach, Burt; Campbell, Glen; Garfunkel, Art; Hayes, Isaac; Newman, Randy; Young, Neil.

Anton von Webern

Austrian classical composer

Webern, with Arnold Schoenberg and Alban Berg, is one of the three main composers of the Second Viennese School. Following World War II, avant-garde composers adopted Webern's approach to twelve-tone composition as their primary compositional model. More recently, his compositions have been appreciated for their profound lyricism.

Born: December 3, 1883; Vienna, Austria
Died: September 15, 1945; Mittersill, Austria
Also known as: Anton Friedrich Wilhelm von Webern (full name)

Principal works

CHAMBER WORKS: *Langsamer Satz*, 1905 (for string quartet); *Five Movements*, Op. 5, 1909 (for string quartet); *Four Pieces*, Op. 7, 1910 (for violin and piano); *Five Pieces*, Op. 10, 1913 (for small orchestra); *Six Bagatelles*, Op. 9, 1913 (for string quartet); *Three Little Pieces*, Op. 11, 1914 (for cello and piano); String Trio, Op. 20, 1927; Quartet, Op. 22, 1930 (for violin, clarinet, tenor saxophone, and piano); Concerto, Op. 24, composed 1934, first performed 1948 (for nine instruments); *Variations*, Op. 30, 1941 (for string quartet).

CHORAL WORKS: *Entflieht auf leichten Kähnen*, Op. 2, composed 1908, first performed 1921 (for a cappella choir; text by Stefan George); *Das Augenlicht*, Op. 26, 1935 (*The Light of the Eyes*; for mixed chorus and orchestra; text by Hildegard Jone); Cantata No. 1, Op. 29, 1939 (for soprano, chorus, and orchestra; text by Jone); Cantata No. 2, Op. 31, 1943 (for soprano, bass, chorus, and orchestra; text by Jone).

ORCHESTRAL WORKS: *Im sommerwind*, 1904; *Passacaglia*, Op. 1, 1908; *Six Pieces*, Op. 6, 1909 (for large orchestra); Symphony, Op. 21, 1929.

PIANO WORK: *Variations*, Op. 27, 1936 (for piano).

VOCAL WORKS: *Eight Early Songs*, 1901-1904; *Zwei Lieder*, Op. 8, 1910 (*Two Songs*; for voice and chamber orchestra; text by Rainer Maria Rilke); *Three Orchestral Songs*, 1913-1914; *Vier Lieder*, Op. 13, 1918 (*Four Songs*; for soprano and orchestra or piano); *Fünf Lieder aus "Der siebente Ring,"* Op. 4, 1919 (*Five Songs from "The Seventh Ring"*; for voice and piano; based on Stefan George's poetry volume); *Five Latin Canons*, Op. 16, 1924 (for soprano, clarinet, and bass clarinet).

The Life

Born Anton Friedrich Wilhelm von Webern and raised in the Carinthian region of Austria, Anton von Webern (AN-tahn fuhn VAY-burn) developed a lifelong love for the Austrian mountains and a youthful allegiance to the operas of Richard Wagner. He attended the University of Vienna, where under the direction of the pioneering musicologist Guido Adler he received his doctorate with a dissertation on Renaissance music in 1906. Along with Alban Berg, he began studying with Arnold Schoenberg in 1904. Schoenberg's teaching challenged traditional pedagogy, emphasizing the pursuit of high artistic aims through adherence to basic principles. These lessons and Schoenberg's uncom-

promising personal intensity reinforced Webern's fanatical idealism, a trait that lies behind the intense lyrical mysticism of his compositions and also may have contributed to his impracticality, which hampered his ability to earn a secure living.

After Webern unofficially graduated from his studies with Schoenberg in 1908, he took a series of assistant conductor posts at provincial opera houses, from which he had a tendency to resign whenever he sensed artistic compromise or whenever he felt a need to live closer to Schoenberg. Eventually a small amount of interest in his compositions developed, but Universal Edition's plans to publish several of his works in 1914 were interrupted by World War I. In 1917, after his army service ended, Webern became assistant conductor at the opera house in Prague, but he left in less than a year to rent an apartment near Schoenberg in the Viennese suburb of Mödling. During this period, Schoenberg found work for Webern arranging music and coaching rehearsals of Schoenberg's Society for Private Musical Performances, until economic pressures ended the society's work in 1922.

Webern dropped "von," which signified nobility, from his name, and it was his work with ordinary people, rather than in professional settings, that set the stage for his only public success during his lifetime—as a conductor. During the 1920's, he conducted workers' choruses in Mödling and Vienna. Their riveting performances won him opportunities to conduct performances of the Vienna Symphony, and later he occasionally conducted orchestras in cities such as Munich, Barcelona, and London. His fanatically zealous attention to detail often elicited stunning, inspired performances, but it could backfire, for there were occasions when an apparent lack of commitment on the orchestra's part caused him such pain that he would walk out on the rehearsals, forcing a search for a substitute conductor at the last minute.

Webern's fortunes waned as the Nazi Party gained influence in and, in 1938, finally took over Austria. His compositions were banned, his choral posts were terminated, and international opportunities ceased with the outbreak of war. Moreover, he was left in artistic isolation by the death of Berg in 1935 and the emigration of many of his close friends and associates, including Schoenberg in 1933. There was some compensation in the new artistic friendship that developed between Webern and the poet Hildegard Jone.

Webern passed the war in the company of his family and remaining friends, many of whom were ardent supporters of the Nazi regime. Webern himself was sympathetic to the Nazi cause because the utopian aspect of the Third Reich resonated with his own idealism and his belief in the universality of Germanic culture. On the other hand, he did nothing to aid the Nazi cause. No anti-Semite, he maintained at personal risk regular social contact with a Jewish friend well into 1942. Webern and his family lived the last desperate years of the war in poverty and sadness. After the war ended, an American soldier, seeking to arrest Webern's son-in-law who was wanted for illegal trade in currency, accidentally shot and killed Webern.

The Music

Early Works. When Webern began studying composition with Schoenberg, he was already an accomplished cellist and experienced composer, and he was halfway through the work for his doctorate in historical musicology. He had already completed *Im Sommerwind*, a large symphonic poem in late nineteenth century style. During his studies with Schoenberg, he composed numerous works, which were stylistically a few years behind his teacher's innovations. The *Passacaglia*, Op. 1 presents late seventeenth century form and counterpoint Romantically in a manner earlier explored by composers such as Johannes Brahms and Max Reger. It served as a "graduation piece" to mark the end of Webern's formal studies with Schoenberg in 1908.

Atonal Expressionism. While Webern never ceased to regard Schoenberg as his teacher and guide, from 1909 Webern no longer held himself back in terms of modern innovation. Schoenberg's move that year to an intuitive style of composition, free from the tonal harmony that had organized Western music since the late seventeenth century, seems to have been prompted by his realization that Webern was already there in his *Five Movements*, Op. 5, for string quartet.

Like Schoenberg's, Webern's work between 1909 and World War I can be called expressionist or intuitive. Most of Webern's compositions during this period are called Sätze (movements) or Stücke

(pieces). Noise is present in this music: deep percussive noises, whistling high notes, and even sounds without pitch. Overlapping instrumental notes and lines blend to produce a single evolving sonority.

Six Pieces. Webern's *Six Pieces*, Op. 6, for large orchestra, was composed in response to the death of his mother. He later explained that the work depicted the fragrances of mountain plants as well as premonitions of catastrophe, remembrance, and resignation. The first of the six pieces captures an anxious swirl of consciousness. The fourth, which alludes to the funeral marches found in some of Gustav Mahler's symphonies, seems to represent the sounds of a march filtered through the disjunct consciousness of a mourner. Throughout the *Six Pieces*, thin, evanescent wisps of sound suggest the world of fragrances and other fleeting perceptions indicated in Webern's program notes—this despite the fact that the *Six Pieces* is scored for an enormous orchestra typical of symphonic music in the years before World War I.

Anton von Webern. (Hulton Archive/Getty Images)

Middle Period. By the start of World War I, Webern began to compose almost exclusively vocal music accompanied by small instrumental chamber ensembles. The vocal lines (like the instrumental lines) came to be characterized by wide jumps between low and high pitches and by great rhythmic variety. Reflecting his training as a scholar of Renaissance music, Webern often used rigorous polyphonic procedures, such as canon, in his atonal compositions during and following the war. Perhaps for this reason, around 1923, when Schoenberg revealed his twelve-tone system (in which a single composition was based rigorously on a specific ordering of the twelve tones of the chromatic scale), Webern adapted to the new method quickly. He wrote exclusively in the twelve-tone system until his death.

Late Works. Webern's ornate middle style culminated in his String Trio, Op. 20, his first full-scale work for instruments without voices in more than a decade. Following this work, he began moving toward a more economical style. Rhythms became straighter; in the place of the earlier overlapping sounds, relationships between instrumental (and vocal) lines became more clearly delineated. The play of contrasts became more central. All this was partly because the twelve-tone method provided Webern with new ways to delineate musical structure using symmetry.

Cantata No. 2. Webern's music continued to consist of brief movements full of intensely shaped gestures. In contrast to Schoenberg, for whom the twelve-tone system provided a way to return to large forms, and Berg, who always composed long works quite comfortably, Webern produced works that expanded only modestly in scope. His Symphony consists of only two short movements, instead of the customary four longer ones. His six-movement Cantata No. 2, his final completed composition and his longest mature work, is only fifteen minutes long. This work alludes to Bach's cantatas in its alternation of solo with chorus and its closing chorale with words about Christ. The text is by the little-known poet Jone, and its images connect the colors, sounds, and silences of nature with an exalted spiritual state. Like Webern, Jone consistently sought to express a mystical correspondence between inner mental life, rarefied perceptions of nature, and elevations of the soul, and her poems

supply the words for all of Webern's later texted works.

Musical Legacy

When Webern's reputation was at its peak, from the 1950's to the 1970's, he was regarded by such composers as Pierre Boulez, Karlheinz Stockhausen, and even Igor Stravinsky as perhaps the greatest visionary of twentieth century music. They were attracted to the symmetrical construction of Webern's twelve-tone rows and to his compositions based on these tone rows, which they interpreted as crystalline structures built out of relationships between pitches. They saw in Webern a more complete break with the past than they observed in Schoenberg or Berg, who seemingly integrated the twelve-tone method with a traditional melodic approach. Moreover, Webern's seemingly pure mathematical structures appeared to show the way toward a new music free of the ideological baggage that they associated with the cataclysms that had led to World War II. These artists were perceiving Webern in a vacuum: By 1951 the three main composers of the Second Viennese School were dead, surviving members of the Schoenberg Circle were dispersed all over the world, and virtually no histories of the music were yet available. Webern's image began to change as the fervor of the 1950's avant-garde died down and as scholars learned more.

In fact, Webern conceived of his works as deeply expressive of extramusical meanings. All of Webern's work seems to aim for a state of exaltation akin to that which he experienced while engaged in his favorite activity of mountain climbing, or which he found in the mystical writings of Emanuel Swedenborg and August Strindberg or the poems of Rainer Maria Rilke and Jone. This exaltation has to do with a rarefied state of elevated perception in which minute differences in sensation are thrown into relief. His works' subtlety, brevity, calculation, and difficulty come from the tremendous care lavished by Webern as he sought to condense his ideas to their inner essentials.

Alfred W. Cramer

Further Reading

Bailey, Kathryn. *The Life of Webern*. Cambridge, England: Cambridge University Press, 1998. Written by a leading scholar of Webern's music, this readable biography is concise and willing to expose the composer's flaws. Typical of Bailey's comprehensive approach is her treatment of Webern's view of Hitler. Includes vivid descriptions of Webern's music.

_____. *The Twelve-Note Music of Anton Webern: Old Forms in a New Language*. Cambridge, England: Cambridge University Press, 1991. This resource is a technical but accessible introduction to Webern's twelve-tone music.

_____, ed. *Webern Studies*. Cambridge, England: Cambridge University Press, 1996. Various scholars provide close studies of Webern's works and how he composed them.

Hayes, Malcolm. *Anton von Webern*. London: Phaidon, 1995. This is a general-interest biography, richly illustrated and written with attention to the culture in which Webern lived.

Johnson, Julian. *Webern and the Transformation of Nature*. Cambridge, England: Cambridge University Press, 1999. By showing how Webern held an idealistic view of nature, this book attempts to correct the view of the composer as a mathematical composer of abstract music.

Moldenhauer, Hans, and Rosaleen Moldenhauer. *Anton von Webern: A Chronicle of His Life and Work*. New York: Knopf, 1979. This monumental biography gives a detailed history of the events of Webern's life as well as a chronicle of his musical and intellectual development. This work is drawn from a relatively complete study of letters, diaries, other documentary sources, and reminiscences about Webern.

Shreffler, Anne C. *Webern and the Lyric Impulse: Songs and Fragments on Poems of Georg Trakl*. New York: Oxford University Press, 1994. This is an important study of the works of Webern's middle period.

See also: Berg, Alban; Boulez, Pierre; Crumb, George; Hindemith, Paul; Holst, Gustav; Karajan, Herbert von; Kodály, Zoltán; Mahler, Gustav; Nancarrow, Conlon; Nono, Luigi; Poulenc, Francis; Rota, Nino; Schnittke, Alfred; Schoenberg, Arnold; Stockhausen, Karlheinz; Stravinsky, Igor; Takemitsu, Tōru; Zappa, Frank.

Ben Webster

American jazz saxophone player and composer

Webster was a signature stylist on the tenor saxophone, showing off his expressive tone in ballads and blues.

Born: March 27, 1909; Kansas City, Missouri
Died: September 20, 1973; Amsterdam, the Netherlands
Also known as: Benjamin Francis Webster (full name)

Principal recordings

ALBUMS: *Ben Webster Plays Music with Feeling*, 1945; *King of the Tenors*, 1953; *Ballads*, 1954; *Consummate Artistry of Ben Webster*, 1954; *Sophisticated Lady*, 1954; *The Big Tenor*, 1955; *The Soul of Ben Webster*, 1957; *Soulville*, 1957; *Tenor Giants*, 1957; *Trav'lin' Light*, 1957; *Ben Webster and Associates*, 1959; *Ben Webster Meets Oscar Peterson*, 1959; *Gerry Mulligan Meets Ben Webster*, 1959; *The Warm Moods*, 1960; *Ben and Sweets*, 1962 (with Harry Edison); *Soulmates*, 1963 (with Joe Zawinul); *See You at the Fair*, 1964; *Blue Light*, 1965; *Duke's in Bed*, 1965; *Gone with the Wind*, 1965; *The Jeep Is Jumping*, 1965; *Stormy Weather*, 1965; *There Is No Greater Love*, 1965; *Big Ben Time*, 1967; *Ben Webster Meets Bill Coleman*, 1967; *Ben Webster Plays Ballads*, 1967; *Ben Meets Don Byas*, 1968; *Ben Webster at Work in Europe*, 1969; *Blow Ben Blow*, 1969; *For the Guv'nor (Tribute to Duke Ellington)*, 1969; *No Fool, No Fun*, 1970; *Did You Call*, 1972; *Makin' Whoopee*, 1972.

The Life

Benjamin Francis Webster was the only child of Mayme Barker and Walter Webster, who divorced shortly after his birth. Raised by his mother and his great-aunt, Ben lived in comfortable surroundings, spoiled by doting relatives. At an early age, he demonstrated musical prowess, including perfect pitch, and he was given violin lessons. He expressed his initial interest in piano.

Fascinated with the new stride piano style, Webster made a point to hear the talented pianists who passed through Kansas City during his school days, picking up elements of their technique and using them to get into bands. After returning to his hometown following a year at Wilberforce University, Webster met pianist Bill (later Count) Basie, who was stranded in Kansas City. Webster beat Basie out of a job playing for silent films despite being well behind him in experience. Nevertheless, Basie gave Webster some informal piano instruction, and the two began a lifelong friendship.

In 1928 Webster began touring the Southwest in a succession of territory bands, including one led by Willis Young, which included his son, tenor saxophonist Lester Young. Webster had already been given some instruction on saxophone, but it was the Young family who taught him to read music and develop his instrumental technique. After beginning on alto, Webster switched to tenor by the time he played with Gene Coy, Jap Allen, and Blanche Calloway (with whom he made his first recordings) in 1930 and 1931.

Webster's first big-name band was that of Bennie Moten, with whom he toured beginning in the fall of 1931. Following the breakup of that band in 1932, he played with Andy Kirk for about a year and a half before being summoned to join Fletcher Henderson in New York in July, 1934. This launched Webster into the front ranks of jazz. Henderson's band broke up four months later, and most of his musicians joined Benny Carter's band for a brief period.

Following this, Webster played for Willie Bryant (six months), Cab Calloway (two years), Henderson again (ten months), and Teddy Wilson (nine months) before joining Duke Ellington and His Orchestra in January, 1940. This proved to be the most important musical association of his life, lasting until the summer of 1943 and being immortalized in dozens of recordings, films, and airchecks (demonstration recordings). Webster credited the experience with reshaping his musical approach.

Webster spent the next five years based in New York, playing frequently on Fifty-second Street, both as leader and as sideman, before rejoining Ellington for nine months in October, 1948. It was around this time that his heavy drinking affected his performance, forcing him to stop playing briefly and enter a sanatorium. He returned to Kansas City

in 1949 to care for his aging mother and great-aunt, playing in local groups and recording occasionally before relocating to Los Angeles in 1950. There he performed infrequently (occasionally with Carter), but he recorded often, usually backing vocalists such as Dinah Washington and Little Esther. Tours with the Jazz at the Philharmonic show kept him working, but for the remainder of the decade he bounced among New York, Chicago, and Los Angeles in search of gigs.

A professional association with blues singer Jimmy Witherspoon occupied Webster from late 1959 until January, 1963, at which point his mother and great-aunt both died, plunging him into a depression that he tried to alleviate with more drinking. Two years of personal struggle ensued before he was engaged to play at Ronnie Scott's jazz club in London in December, 1964. This booking led to a tour of Scandinavia, and Webster was never to return to America. At first settling in Copenhagen until 1966, followed by shorter periods in the Netherlands and England, Webster played and recorded constantly, enjoying audience appreciation he never found in the United States. He spent the last four years of his life in Copenhagen before dying while on tour in Amsterdam.

The Music

"Toby." Containing one of Webster's first long recorded solos, this recording of Moten and his orchestra demonstrates his early style, based on the punchy phrasing of 1920's-vintage Coleman Hawkins style and a rough technical command of his instrument. Nevertheless, Webster shows a nascent grasp of phrasing and structure, proving himself to be on equal footing with most of his tenor-saxophone contemporaries.

"Cotton Tail." This tune is one of the few Webster compositions not classified as a blues variation. It was, instead, based on George Gershwin's "I Got Rhythm" (1930). Ellington arranged it (with Webster's input) as a tenor sax feature, and it remained in his band's repertoire well into the 1960's. One of his few really successful up-tempo features, Webster played it until the end of his life.

"Stardust." Recorded on location at a dance with Ellington's orchestra, this version of the Hoagy Carmichael standard (arranged by Webster and bassist Jimmy Blanton) is a three-chorus feature demonstrating Webster's voluptuous tone and his refined melodic sense. Although he introduces numerous variations in this continuously building performance, Webster never loses sight of the melody.

"Danny Boy." Done in the unusual key (for saxophones) of concert D, this Irish melody was loved by Webster, and he performs it in his classic ballad style. Almost completely unadorned, the tune is played twice by Webster, sounding cello-like on the second, higher-pitched one. The somewhat menacing finale serves to illustrate the remarkably dual nature of his music and his personality.

"Poutin'." A blues composed by Webster showing off his feeling for the genre, this performance is by turns forceful and reflective, and it illustrates the range of expressive tone colors he could produce from his instrument.

Musical Legacy

Webster's legacy rests primarily on his ballad artistry, although his abilities as a blues player should not be overlooked. His tone, phrasing, and breath control have served as benchmarks for tenor saxophone players since the 1940's, although "Cotton Tail" (his best-known recording) shows the more forceful (even violent) side of his playing. Those two seemingly contradictory elements were amply evident in his personal nature as well.

John L. Clark, Jr.

Further Reading

Büchmann-Møller, Frank. *Someone to Watch Over Me: The Life and Music of Ben Webster*. Ann Arbor: University of Michigan Press, 2006. A thorough examination of Webster's life, using interviews, reviews, and recording data to present a detailed picture.

Dance, Stanley. "Ben Webster." In *The World of Duke Ellington*. New York: Charles Scribner's Sons, 1970. This interview with Webster from 1964, which appeared originally in *Down Beat*, concentrates on his years with Ellington and before.

See also: Basie, Count; Carter, Benny; Ellington, Duke; Hawkins, Coleman; Henderson, Fletcher; Holiday, Billie; Peterson, Oscar; Tatum, Art; Washington, Dinah; Young, Lester.

Kurt Weill

German American classical composer

One of the great composers to emerge from the Weimar Republic, Weill created operas and musicals noted for their complex characters, sophisticated harmonic vocabularies, and imaginative orchestrations.

Born: March 2, 1900; Dessau, Germany
Died: April 3, 1950; New York, New York
Also known as: Kurt Julian Weill (full name)

Principal works

CHAMBER WORKS: Sonata for Cello and Piano, 1920; String Quartet, Op. 8, 1923.

CHORAL WORK: *Der Neue Orpheus*, Op. 16, 1927 (cantata for soprano, solo violin, and orchestra).

MUSICAL THEATER (music): *Die Zaubernacht*, 1922 (*The Magic Night*; lyrics by Vladimir Boritch); *Knickerbocker Holiday*, 1938 (libretto by Maxwell Anderson); *Railroads on Parade*, 1939 (pageant; libretto by Edward Hungerford); *Lady in the Dark*, 1940 (lyrics by Moss Hart and Ira Gershwin); *One Touch of Venus*, 1943 (lyrics by Ogden Nash; libretto by S. J. Perelman and Nash); *The Firebrand of Florence*, 1945 (lyrics by Gershwin); *Love Life*, 1948 (lyrics and libretto by Alan Jay Lerner).

OPERAS (music): *Der Protagonist*, Op. 15, 1926 (libretto by Georg Kaiser); *Royal Palace*, Op. 17, 1927 (ballet-opera in one act; libretto by Iwan Goll); *Die Dreigroschenoper*, 1928 (*The Threepenny Opera*; libretto by Bertolt Brecht and Elisabeth Hauptmann; based on John Gay's *The Beggar's Opera*); *Der Zar lässt sich photographieren*, Op. 21, 1928 (*The Czar Has His Photograph Taken*; one-act opera; libretto by Kaiser); *Happy End*, 1929 (libretto by Hauptmann and Brecht); *Der Jasager*, 1930 (libretto by Brecht); *Aufstieg und Fall der Stadt Mahagonny*, 1930 (*Rise and Fall of the City of Mahagonny*; libretto by Brecht); *Die Bürgschaft*, 1932 (*The Pledge*; libretto by Caspar Neher; based on Johann Gottfried Herder's story *Der afrikanische Rechtsspruch*); *Der Silbersee*, 1933 (*Silver Lake*; libretto by Kaiser); *Johnny Johnson*, 1936 (lyrics and libretto by Paul

Green); *Der Weg der Verheissung*, 1937 (*The
Eternal Road*; libretto by Franz Werfel); *Street
Scene*, 1947 (libretto by Elmer Rice and
Langston Hughes; base on Rice's play); *Down
in the Valley*, 1948 (folk opera; libretto by
Arnold Sundgaard); *Lost in the Stars*, 1949
(libretto by Maxwell Anderson; based on Alan
Paton's novel *Cry, the Beloved Country*).
ORCHESTRAL WORKS: Symphony No. 1, 1921;
Quodlibet, 1923 (suite for orchestra); Concerto for
Violin and Wind Orchestra, Op. 12, 1924; *Berlin
im Licht*, 1928 (march for military band); *Kleine
Dreigroschenmusik*, 1929 (*A Little Threepenny
Music*; suite for wind orchestra; based on *The
Threepenny Opera*); Symphony No. 2, 1934.
VOCAL WORKS: *Frauentanz*, Op. 10, 1923 (seven
medieval songs for soprano, flute, viola,
clarinet, horn, and bassoon); *Mahagonny-
Songspiel*, 1927 (cantata; *The Little Mahagonny*;
lyrics by Weill and Bertolt Brecht); *Die sieben
Todsünden*, 1933 (*The Seven Deadly Sins*; for
voices and orchestra; lyrics by Brecht); *Marie
Galante*, 1934 (for voices and small orchestra;
libretto and lyrics by Jacques Deval).

The Life

Kurt Julian Weill (vil) was born in Dessau, a
small city north of Leipzig and south of Berlin,
where his father, Albert Weill, served as chief cantor of the local synagogue. Early exposure to music
and a teenage interest in composition led to private
lessons with a local teacher.

In 1918 Weill entered the Berlin Hochschule,
where he studied composition (with Engelbert
Humperdinck) as well as counterpoint and conducting. Weill considered his opportunities in
Berlin at the time to be limited, however, and he
contacted Arnold Schoenberg in the hope of studying in Vienna. When financial obstacles prevented
Weill from studying in Vienna, he returned to
Dessau, accepting the post of municipal theater
conductor in Lüdenscheid, northeast of Cologne. In
1921 he was accepted into Ferruccio Busoni's class
in Berlin, and he also studied counterpoint with
Philipp Jarnach. Weill's period of study with Busoni
and Jarnach was a critical stage in his musical development. His first notable composition, *Zaubernacht*, appeared in 1922.

In 1924 he began to collaborate with the playwright Georg Kaiser, with whom he would work
until he left Germany. In 1926 he married Lotte
Lenya, and in the following year he began another
collaborative relationship, this one with Bertolt
Brecht. The period of the late 1920's and the early
1930's was productive for Weill. Unfortunately, the
ascension of fascism led to a rapid deterioration of
the artistic scene, and Weill was an easy target for
the Nazis. His new works were shunned by many
theaters, and some productions were disrupted by
protests and riots. On March 14, 1933, Weill moved
to Paris. Although he began working relatively
soon after his arrival, the results were disappointing. When an opportunity arose to participate in a
New York endeavor, Weill traveled to the United
States. When the production was delayed, Weill decided to stay in America.

When Weill started working in the New York
musical-theater scene, he was essentially starting
over. He initially had some mixed results, with his
first notable American success being *Knickerbocker
Holiday*, from which a number of Weill's songs
achieved considerable popularity. The 1940's can
be considered his second maturity, in that he had
two major successes, *Lady in the Dark* and *One Touch
of Venus*. Weill considered *Street Scene* to be his best
work, and it was followed by *Love Life* and *Down in
the Valley*. A string of collaborative works was envisioned, primarily to have been composed with lyricist Alan Lerner, but Weill died rather suddenly of a
heart ailment before these plans could come to fruition.

The Music

Weill can be seen as two different composers: the
first working in Germany and the second emerging
after his immigration to the United States. Stylistically Weill's early works reveal his considerable
skills and varied inspiration. Some sections of his
Concerto for Violin and Wind Orchestra, for example, feature a chromatic, dissonant, and angular
melodic style, while other parts seem more restrained, introspective, and lyrical. The second
movement hints at his interest in American popular
music styles, in particular the foxtrot. In 1924 Weill
dedicated himself to composing for the theater, for
which the Weimar Republic possessed an active environment. Between 1926 and 1929, Weill composed seven major works for the stage.

Kurt Weill. (AP/Wide World Photos)

The Czar Has His Photograph Taken. Weill rejected a formulaic approach to compositional design, so each of his works features a unique approach. His early output includes works considered expressionist (*Der Protagonist*) and surreal (*Royal Palace*). The 1920's was a period of considerable stylistic variety: The Second Viennese School explored atonality, and Igor Stravinsky and others embraced neoclassicism, Berlin became the center of a style particularly suited to its postwar environment. During the Weimar Republic, Berlin was a center for serious artistic endeavor (opera) as well as a bawdier cabaret. Composers such as Ernst Krenek, Paul Hindemith, and Weill composed *Zeitoper*, or opera of the time. This genre made dramatic use of contemporary technology and took a pluralistic approach to composition, which sometimes included popular music styles.

Composed in collaboration with Georg Kaiser in 1927, *The Czar Has His Photograph Taken* is Weill's only extant comic opera from the last half of the 1920's. A one-act intended by Weill to be programmed with *Der Protagonist*, *The Czar Has His Photograph Taken* focuses on the role and perceptions of individuals in society. The czar has decided to have his picture taken by a leading photographer, Angèle. Knowing this, assassins kidnap Angèle and modify her camera by adding a pistol rigged to fire when activated by the bulb. Facing a false Angèle, the czar participates in the process as planned by the conspirators until just before the photo is taken. At that point, he impulsively decides that he should take Angèle's photo first, then attempts to seduce his assassin. Ultimately, both fail—the conspirators are arrested and the czar is unable to complete the seduction.

While the bulk of the opera is composed in a free tonal style, Weill chose to focus on the perception of the czar by the two main characters. The czar wants to be seen as an ordinary person, and Weill chose the popular foxtrot dance to portray this desire. The assassin sees the czar as representing hated authority, a view supported musically with a march. Utilizing a phonograph record (for playing the tango used to accompany the seduction) is an example of the *Zeitoper* interest in technology. Weill parodies the Greek chorus by placing a male choir in the orchestra pit, from which they comment upon the action and assure the audience that the story is a farce.

Rise and Fall of the City of Mahagonny. The works resulting from his partnership with Bertolt Brecht are among the best known of Weill's output. Their first success was the *Mahagonny-Songspiel*, a work featuring six songs composed by Weill, interspersed with spoken dialogue. Mahagonny is a fictional city placed by Brecht near the gold coast of Florida. Subsequently, Weill and Brecht expanded the *Songspiel* into a much longer work, *Rise and Fall of the City of Mahagonny*, a three-act opera and one of Weill's largest works.

The six original songs are also in the opera, but the spoken dialogue was replaced by arioso and recitative. Brecht's message is political. Capitalism is portrayed as a system in which good people are taken advantage of and their financial wealth and morality siphoned off. Mahagonny can be seen as Brecht's image of Berlin, from the beginning of the twentieth century through World War I and into the Weimar Republic. Foxtrot and other popular styles are featured, and the work maintains some of the *Zeitoper* tradition through its use of projected images and onstage music resources, such as a player piano and a jazz band. While the American-style songs, such as "Alabama Song," were received enthusiastically, the free-tonal style of the remainder of the opera seems compromised by the work's long length.

The Threepenny Opera. With *The Threepenny Opera*, which was composed simultaneously with *The Rise and Fall of the City of Mahagonny*, Weill's style and philosophies coalesced into a strongly unified work. It was based upon John Gay's eighteenth century ballad opera *The Beggar's Opera* (1728), and in it Brecht once again targets capitalism. While Gay, using arrangements of popular English songs, was satirizing eighteenth century English society and Handelian opera, *The Threepenny Opera* is a parody of a parody that attacks the culture of the postwar European bourgeois and the state-supported opera system. *The Threepenny Opera* was a huge success in Germany and also enjoyed international popularity.

Weill based much of this work on popular music, finding inspiration in Tin Pan Alley songs, cabaret, tango, and recordings that collectively (although inaccurately) were labeled jazz. As in Gay's work, spoken dialogue is substituted for recitative, and bar songs sung in a non-virtuosic vocal style replace the Wagnerian arioso style. Similarly, Weill scored the work for a dance-cabaret band in lieu of an opera orchestra. Some of the songs Weill composed for *The Threepenny Opera* became popular, the most famous being "Die Moritat von Mackie Messer," better known as "Mack the Knife."

Lady in the Dark. Weill's most successful American musical represented a shift in the artistic lives of all three of its collaborators. It was the first major project for lyricist Ira Gershwin since the death of his brother George. For playwright Moss Hart, *Lady in the Dark* represented his departure from musical comedy. For Weill *Lady in the Dark* was his most significant and fulfilling venture since leaving Germany. The musical comprises three dream sequences that present the lead character's subconscious as she undergoes psychoanalysis. Weill adapted European operatic elements (recitative, arioso, colorful orchestration) to the American popular and Broadway idiom (spoken dialogue, thirty-two-measure song form), lending substance and unity to the three dream sequences. The dream sequences call upon dance idioms to evoke the emotional tenor of each scene, and the music chronicles the psychological journey of the heroine as she chooses among the three men in her life. The dances (rumba, bolero, and circus march) and their inclusion in dream sequences harkens back to some of

Weill's German works, particularly *Royal Palace*. Weill was meticulous in composing for *Lady in the Dark* and regarded it as some of his best work; its rich orchestration demonstrates it was accomplished with considerable skill.

Musical Legacy

The Second Viennese School was often characterized as academic, and Igor Stravinsky's neoclassical works were seen as unemotional. It was understandable that the catchy and sentimental tunes that peppered Weill's works found a wide audience, and Weill became known as a composer who could compose jazz. Unfortunately, political events in Germany led to such radical changes in the artistic climate that following Weill's path was impossible. In America Weill had to compete in an arena dominated by standardized approaches, and although he found some success, there is little in the way of formula in his approach to composition. In the later 1940's and 1950's, however, a new generation of composers emerged. Weill's impact on these—perhaps best represented by Leonard Bernstein and Stephen Sondheim—can be seen in their rich orchestration, expressive character settings, and stylistic pluralism.

Although Weill enjoyed considerable popularity with the public, his true abilities as a composer have not been adequately recognized, and uninformed interpretations of works such as *The Threepenny Opera* tend to reinforce a view of Weill as a composer of lighter music. He should be admired for the care with which he set characters and his sophisticated harmonic vocabulary, imaginative orchestrations, and interest in integrated pluralism.

Dane O. Heuchemer

Further Reading

Farneth, David, with Elmer Juchem and Dave Stein. *Kurt Weill: A Life in Pictures and Documents.* Woodstock, N.Y.: Overlook Press, 2000. This source, helpful to scholars yet accessible to general readers, documents Weill's life through photographs and facsimiles of documentary sources.

Hinton, Stephen, ed. *Kurt Weill: "The Threepenny Opera."* Cambridge, England: Cambridge University Press, 1990. This collection of essays on Weill's most popular work is a combination of primary sources and secondary-source studies. Brief articles by such Weill contemporaries as Theodor Adorno and Ernst Bloch are followed by later studies by Eric Blom, David Drew, Stephen Hinton, and others.

Kowalke, Kim, ed. *A New Orpheus: Essays on Kurt Weill*. New Haven, Conn.: Yale University Press, 1986. This anthology includes seventeen articles by many leading Weill scholars and the music of his time, including Kowalke, Susan Cook, Drew, and Hinton.

McClung, Bruce D. *"Lady in the Dark": Biography of a Musical*. Oxford, England: Oxford University Press, 2006. A detailed study of the musical that also establishes a solid cultural context for the work, this book won the 2006 Theatre Library Association's George Freedley Memorial Award.

Sanders, Ronald. *The Days Grow Short: The Life and Music of Kurt Weill*. Los Angeles: Silman-James Press, 1980. This unauthorized but substantial biography includes information on Weill's life and professional career.

See also: Bernstein, Leonard; Busoni, Ferruccio; Collins, Judy; Gershwin, Ira; Hindemith, Paul; Klemperer, Otto; Lerner, Alan Jay; Morrison, Jim; Schoenberg, Arnold; Simone, Nina; Sondheim, Stephen; Waits, Tom.

August Wenzinger

Swiss classical cellist

Wenzinger was a pioneer in reviving the viol and its repertoire, and he was instrumental in developing modern viol technique. He was one of the founders of the Schola Cantorum Basiliensis, an institution for continuing education in the field of early music.

Born: November 14, 1905; Basel, Switzerland
Died: December 25, 1996; Basel, Switzerland

Principal recordings

ALBUMS: *Brahms: Sextet for Strings No. 1 in B-flat Major, Op. 18*, 1949; *The Brandenburg Concertos No. 5 in D Major and No. 6 in B Major*, 1951; *The Brandenburg Concertos No. 2 in F Major and No. 3 in G Major*, 1953; *Monteverdi: L'Orfeo*, 1955 (as conductor); *Fifteen Fantasias, Vocal Works*, 1956; *Water Music/Music for the Royal Fireworks*, 1962; *Four Concertos*, 1963; *Anthems, Madrigals, and Fantasies*, 1964; *Great Masters of the Baroque and Classical Era*, 1966; *The Glory of Handel*, 1973; *Marais: The 250th Commemoration*, 1979; *Byrd and His Age*, 1996.

WRITINGS OF INTEREST: *Gambenübung*, 1935, 1938 (*Viol Practice*, 1977); *Gambenfibel*, 1943 (with Marianna Majer).

The Life

Born into a musical family, August Wenzinger (AW-goost VEHN-zihn-gur) began his cello studies at the age of nine. After studying philosophy and ancient languages for two years at Basel University, he transferred to the Basel Conservatory, studying cello with Willi Treichler and Hermann Beyer-Hané. He also attended the lectures of musicologist Karl Nef, who introduced him to the viola da gamba. In 1927, after graduating from the conservatory, he went to the Hochschule für Musik in Cologne, studying composition with Philippe Jarnach and cello with Paul Grümmer, who encouraged him to do research on viol manuscripts in archives and on the performance practice of the viol. In 1929 he was invited by the publishing house Bärenreiter-Verlag to teach a special course on viol playing.

Wenzinger was first cellist with the Bremen orchestra (1929-1933) and with the Basel Allgemeine Musikgesellschaft (1936-1970), and he was a member of the Basel String Quartet (1933-1947). In 1933, together with Paul Sacher and Ina Lohr, he founded the Schola Cantorum Basiliensis, where he taught viola da gamba and directed ensembles until 1970. Beginning in 1953, he was a frequent guest professor at several institutions in the United States. He was the founder and conductor of the Cappella Coloniensis in Cologne from 1954 to 1958, and he directed performances of Baroque concerts and operas at Herrenhausen in Hanover from 1958 to 1966. On December 25, 1996, at the age of ninety-one, Wenzinger died in Basel.

The Music

A pioneer in the study of music of the Renaissance and Baroque periods, Wenzinger was responsible not only for the revival of the viol and its repertoire but also for the revival of early instruments in the twentieth century. In the late 1930's, he founded a trio with flutist Gustav Scheck and keyboardist Fritz Neumeyer, and they performed on period instruments. Starting in 1945, the chamber group, with the addition of other members, toured throughout Europe and the Near East. Wenzinger recorded extensively for Deutsche Grammophone Archiv, including the viol music of Samuel Scheidt, Marin Marais, François Couperin, and Johann Sebastian Bach. In addition, he recorded orchestral concerti and suites by Bach, George Frideric Handel, Georg Philipp Telemann, and others. Together with the Consort of Viols of the Schola Cantorum Basiliensis, he toured internationally with countertenor Alfred Deller, and he recorded works by William Byrd and Orlando Gibbons.

In 1955 Wenzinger conducted the first recorded performance of Claudio Monteverdi's *L'Orfeo* (1607) using period instruments. Subsequently he had conducting engagements in Cologne, Hanover, Stockholm, London, and elsewhere. Besides early music, he also devoted considerable attention to twentieth century compositions. He premiered Frank Martin's Ballade for Cello and Orchestra (1949) and Othmar Schoeck's Cello Concerto (1948), and he performed new works with the Viola da Gamba Trio of the Schola Cantorum Basiliensis, including pieces by Rudolf Kelterborn, Conrad Beck, and David Loeb.

Viol Practice. Published by Bärenreiter-Verlag, Wenzinger's two-volume *Gambenübung* is the first modern method for the viola da gamba. With the use of illustrations and photographs, in the first volume, he discusses the fundamentals of viol playing, including hand, arm, and finger positions, as well as bowing technique. In the second volume, he discusses more advanced issues, such as "the elaboration of the bow stroke" and "the development of the left hand." Numerous exercises are included; his musical examples are drawn from the works of viol composers such as Christopher Simpson, Michael Praetorius, Matthew Locke, and Marais. In 1943 Wenzinger published a second treatise titled *Gambenfibel*, coauthored with Marianna Majer, focusing on children's viol-playing skills.

Monteverdi: L'Orfeo. One of the earliest operas, Monteverdi's *L'Orfeo* is based on the ancient Greek legend of Orpheus, who attempts to rescue his bride, Eurydice, from the underworld. First performed in Mantua in 1607, it has a prologue and five acts. One of the first conductors to revive *L'Orfeo* in the twentieth century, Wenzinger directed the first recorded performance of *L'Orfeo* using period instruments in 1955. Under his direction were Helmut Krebs singing the title role, Hanni Mack-Cosack singing Eurydice, the Choir of the Staatliche Hochschule für Musik of Hamburg, and the Hitzacker Summer Festival 1955 Orchestra. The recording was released in the same year on Deutsche Grammophone Archiv in a two-album collection. An edition of Wenzinger's realization was published by Bärenreiter-Verlag.

Marais: The 250th Commemoration. Performed by the Oberlin Baroque Ensemble under Wenzinger's direction in 1978, the program of this recording commemorated the 250th anniversary of Marin Marais's death. The Ensemble, which was composed of historical performance faculty members of the Oberlin Conservatory of Music, recorded several works by the great viol composer, including *Sonnerie de Ste. Geneviève du Mont de Paris* (1723), Suite for Three Viols in G (1717), *Allemande la Singulière* (1717), *L'Arabesque* (1717), and Pièces en Trio in E Minor (1692). In 1972 Wenzinger began a longtime affiliation with the summer Oberlin Baroque Performance Institute, where he served as musical director for eighteen years.

Musical Legacy

Wenzinger died at the age of 91, leaving a legacy of more than 100 recordings ranging from Guillaume de Machaut to Wolfgang Amadeus Mozart. He published numerous articles in German and two method books for the viola da gamba. Besides *L'Orfeo*, his early music editions include the *Six Suites for Violoncello Solo* and the *Six Brandenburg Concertos* by Bach, *Il pastor fido* by Handel, trio sonatas by Dietrich Buxtehude, and works by Johann Christoph Friedrich Bach and Joseph Haydn.

Not only did Wenzinger make notable contribution to the teaching of early music in Germanic countries, but also he influenced the development of viol playing in the United States. He was Visiting Professor at Harvard University and Brandeis University, as well as the musical director of the Baroque Performance Institute at Oberlin College.

Several of his important students were Jordi Savall, Catharina Meints, and James Caldwell. Wenzinger received honorary doctorates from Brandeis University, Schola Cantorum Basiliensis, and Oberlin College.

Sonia Lee

Further Reading

Bram, Marjorie. "An Interview with August Wenzinger." *Journal of the Viola da Gamba Society of America* 12 (1975): 77-83. This article focuses on Wenzinger's musical background and training, as well as his early performing and teaching activities on the viol.

Loeb, David. "The Lyffe and Times of a Viol Composer (Late 20th c.)" *Journal of the Viola da Gamba Society of America*, 22 (1985): 29-34. This article discusses Wenzinger's interests in modern compositions for the viol. It focuses on Loeb's works written for Wenzinger and his colleagues.

Wenzinger, August. "The Revival of the Viola da Gamba: A History." In *A Viola da Gamba Miscellany: Proceedings of the International Viola da Gamba Symposium; Utretcht 1991*, edited by Johannes Boer and Guido van Oorschot. Utrecht: STIMU, 1994. Wenzinger traces the history of the revival of the viola da gamba from the nineteenth century, and he included a discussion on his contribution to the field.

See also: Casadesus, Henri; Dolmetsch, Arnold; Harnoncourt, Nikolaus; Landowska, Wanda; Martin, Frank; Schweitzer, Albert.

Paul Whiteman

American jazz violinist and composer

A major big band leader during the 1920's and 1930's, Whiteman led the transition in musical styles from ragtime to jazz, providing music for Broadway shows and recordings.

Born: March 28, 1890; Denver, Colorado
Died: December 29, 1967; Doylestown, Pennsylvania
Also known as: King of Jazz
Member of: Paul Whiteman and His Orchestra

Principal recordings

SINGLES (solo): "It Happened in Monterey," 1930; "You Brought a New Kind of Love," 1930; "A Faded Summer Love," 1931; "Lover," 1932; "Rise 'n' Shine," 1932; "Three on a Match," 1932; "Willow, Weep for Me," 1932; "You're an Old Smoothie," 1932; "It's Only a Paper Moon," 1933; "Smoke Gets in Your Eyes," 1933; "All Through the Night," 1934; "Anything Goes," 1934; "I Get a Kick Out of You," 1934; "Love in Bloom," 1934; "Wagon Wheels," 1934; "If the Moon Turns Green," 1935; "Wah-Hoo!," 1936.

SINGLES (with Paul Whiteman and His Orchestra): "Avalon," 1920; "Japanese Sandman," 1920; "Wang-Wang Blues," 1920; "Whispering," 1920; "Cherie," 1921; "Cho-Cho-San," 1921; "My Mammy," 1921; "Say It with Music," 1921; "Song of India," 1921; "Do It Again!," 1922; "Hot Lips," 1922; "I Found a Four Leaf Clover," 1922; "I'll Build a Stairway to Paradise," 1922; "Pack Up Your Sins and Go to the Devil," 1922; "Stumbling," 1922; "Three o'Clock in the Morning," 1922; "Bambalina," 1923; "Linger a While," 1923; "Parade of the Wooden Soldiers," 1923; "Shake Your Feet," 1923; "Swanee River Blues," 1923; "All Alone," 1924; "California Here I Come," 1924; "Somebody Loves Me," 1924; "What'll I Do?," 1924; "Birth of the Blues," 1926; "In a Little Spanish Town," 1926; "Valencia," 1926; "Among My Souvenirs," 1927; "Changes," 1927; "Five Step," 1927; "It Won't Be Long Now," 1927; "Mississippi Mud," 1927; "Muddy Water," 1927; "My Blue Heaven," 1927; "Sugar," 1927; "Washboard Blues," 1927; "C. O. N. S. T. A. N. T. I. N. O. P. L. E.," 1928; "Mississippi Mud," 1928; "My Angel," 1928; "Ol' Man River," 1928; "Ramona," 1928; "Together," 1928; "Blue Hawaii," 1929; "Button Up Your Overcoat," 1929; "Great Day," 1929.

The Life

Paul Whiteman was born in Denver, Colorado, to Wilberforce and Elfrida Dallison Whiteman. His father was superintendent of music for the Denver school system, and he greatly influenced Whiteman's training on the violin and the viola and instilled in his son the self-discipline to become a world-class orchestra leader. Paul played viola in the Denver Symphony Orchestra from 1907 to 1914. He studied music in New York under Henry Schradieck, a violinist and a teacher at the American Institute of Applied Music, and under Max Bendix, conductor of the Metropolitan Opera from 1911 to 1914.

Whiteman left Denver for San Francisco 1914, and he played the viola for the Panama-Pacific Exposition Orchestra in 1915. A number of visiting conductors proved good mentors—Camille Saint-Saëns, John Philip Sousa, Richard Hageman (of the Metropolitan Opera), George Georgescu, Walter Damrosch, and Victor Herbert. He played the viola with the San Francisco Symphony from 1915 to 1918, and he also played in upscale hotels and attended the city's jazz clubs. Whiteman joined the Navy in 1918, and he led a twelve-piece Mare Island Naval Training Camp Symphony Orchestra, an experience that served him well when he later formed the Whiteman Orchestra. He had four wives: Nellie Stack (1908-1914), Jimmy Smith

Paul Whiteman. (AP/Wide World Photos)

(1917-1920), Mildred Vanderhoff (1922-1931), and Margaret Livingston (1931-1967). Whiteman died at the age of seventy-seven in Doylestown, Pennsylvania.

The Music

While playing with the Denver Symphony, Whiteman began "ragging" classical compositions to give them popular appeal, a skill that later interested him in the new sounds of jazz. In San Francisco's clubs, he learned the nuances of jazz, although he believed that improvisations and spontaneity should be preserved with scoring, by writing down jazz music for repeat performances. Later, he encouraged improvisations that were "off the score." Whiteman had considerable orchestral experience, and he promoted what he termed "symphonic jazz" from a solid musical background.

"Whispering" *and* "Avalon." Through jazz, Whiteman found a creative outlet for his considerable musical talent and fulfilled his dream of forming a band. He played in upscale hotels, opening at San Francisco's Fairmont Hotel after World War I with his Rainbow Lane Orchestra. It was composed of jazz musicians, including Gus Mueller (sax), Henry Busse (trumpet), and Buster Johnston (trombone), and Whiteman employed Ferde Grofé, a gifted arranger and pianist.

Whiteman's Orchestra expanded by 1920, playing at the Alexandria Hotel in Los Angeles and the Ambassador in Atlantic City. Added to Grofé, Mueller, Busse, and Johnston were Hale "Pee Wee" Byers (reeds), Mike Pingitore (banjo), Sammy Heiss (string bass and tuba), and Harold McDonald (drums and percussion). The Whiteman Orchestra played in a style referred to as Jazz Classique.

Early Whiteman sound stemmed from Grofé's arrangements, using a harmony chorus of four parts with two brass and two saxophones. Rhythm was indicated by the piano, the banjo, a soft pizzicato bass, or a whispered drum tap, and the melody was given to the first trumpet supported by two saxophones and a trombone. This new style was represented by "Whispering" and "Avalon," and it produced warm, smooth, lush danceable sounds.

The Whiteman Orchestra recorded "Whispering," "Japanese Sandman," "Avalon," and "Wang-Wang Blues" at its first Victor session in Camden,

New Jersey, in 1920. (Later, Whiteman recorded with Columbia Records, Decca Records, and Capitol Records.) "Whispering" became a national hit, selling more than two and a half million copies. Vincent Rose wrote "Avalon" based on an aria from Giacomo Puccini's opera *Tosca* (1900), and Grofé created the Whiteman arrangement, allowing for ad-libs and solos. When the records were released, the Whiteman Orchestra was playing at the café of the Palais Royal in New York.

"Cho-Cho-San" *and* **"Song of India."** In 1921 in New York, Whiteman played at the Metropolitan Opera House and on Broadway. He recorded "Cho-Cho-San" based on Puccini's *Madama Butterfly* (1904) and "Song of India" from the opera *Sadko* (1896) by Nikolay Rimsky-Korsakov. He formed Paul Whiteman, Inc. to develop satellite dance bands (totaling fifty-eight), performing under his name, he and became a successful entrepreneur. His orchestra toured Europe, and by 1923 he was called the King of Jazz.

"I'll Build a Stairway to Paradise." In 1922 Whiteman recorded "Hot Lips" and "Three o'Clock in the Morning," which opened with chimes like those of London's Big Ben. Whiteman popularized George Gershwin's songs from George White's *Scandals* (1922) "I Found a Four Leaf Clover" and "I'll Build a Stairway to Paradise," which featured a sax chorus with musicians Ross Gorman, Donald Clark, and Byers and a bluesy trumpet solo by Tommy Gott. Whiteman recorded and popularized Irving Berlin's song "Pack Up Your Sins and Go to the Devil" from the *Music Box Revue* (1922) and tunes from the 1923 *Ziegfeld Follies* "Shake Your Feet" and "Swanee River Blues," with Frank Siegrist's trumpet solo. Whiteman worked with Al Jolson recording "California Here I Come" in 1924.

Rhapsody in Blue. Whiteman's Experiment in Modern Music concert held February 12, 1924, at Aeolian Hall in New York featured *Rhapsody in Blue* (1924) written by Gershwin. Commissioned and premiered by Whiteman, *Rhapsody in Blue* was played by Gershwin, and it is considered one of the most beautiful songs ever written. In 1925 the Gramophone Company recorded the Whiteman Orchestra at Royal Albert Hall in London. Over the years, additional Whiteman Experiment in Modern Music concerts were played at venues such as Carnegie Hall.

"It Won't Be Long Now." Bing Crosby and Al Rinker were selected by Whiteman as vocalists in 1926. Crosby appeared as soloist on "Muddy Water" in 1927. Crosby, Rinker, and Harry Barris were featured as the Rhythm Boys in "Mississippi Mud," "Five-Step," and "It Won't Be Long Now," with the Dorsey Brothers.

"Washboard Blues." Bix Beiderbecke plays the trumpet in "Washboard Blues" from 1927, the first arrangement by Bill Challis, with Hoagy Carmichael as vocalist. Challis's "Changes" used three baritone saxes, and it allowed Bix to improvise in solo. Challis's arrangements featured hot jazz, showcasing Beiderbecke and Trumbauer. Beiderbecke began to lead a trio with Jimmy Dorsey on clarinet and Tommy Dorsey on trombone, as in "Smile." Challis arranged "Ol' Man River" for Bing Crosby, as well as "Sugar" for Beiderbecke's most famous jazz improvisation. Whiteman was able to take risks in his music, leading it in new directions.

The King of Jazz. Whiteman recorded tunes from *Show Boat* (1927), but after 1927 he allowed his hot brass trio to shine—in symphonic jazz at its best. He recorded songs for the films *The King of Jazz* (1930) and *Coquette* (1929), and vocals were usually sung by Crosby. Whiteman selected the best musicians for his band and paid the highest salaries.

Musical Legacy

A pioneer of symphonic jazz, Whiteman was an impresario in the big band and orchestra era that promoted dance music. He employed all the early jazz musicians of prominence, and he introduced eminent composers. He made more than six hundred recordings, which offered opportunities for new vocalists. Duke Ellington praised Whiteman for making jazz respectable.

Barbara Bennett Peterson

Further Reading

Berrett, Joshua. *Louis Armstrong and Paul Whiteman: Two Kings of Jazz.* New Haven, Conn.: Yale University Press, 2004. This book parallels the musical and personal lives of the "two kings of jazz."

DeLong, Thomas A. *Pops: Paul Whiteman, King of Jazz.* Piscataway, N.J.: New Century, 1983. This laudatory biography explains how Whiteman hired his musicians and vocalists.

Rayno, Don. *Paul Whiteman: Pioneer of American*

Music. Lanham, Md.: Scarecrow Press, 2003. This well-researched biographical study contains a discography, a complete chronology of Whiteman's life, and profiles of other musicians.

Whiteman, Paul, and Mary Margaret McBride. *Jazz.* New York: J. H. Sears, 1926. This resource explains the numerous classical sources for Whiteman's songs.

See also: Beiderbecke, Bix; Crosby, Bing; Ellington, Duke; Gershwin, George; Goodman, Benny; Grappelli, Stéphane; Henderson, Fletcher; Herbert, Victor; Rachmaninoff, Sergei; Sousa, John Philip; Still, William Grant.

Hank Williams

American county singer, guitarist, and songwriter

A mesmerizing performer and skilled musician, Willams had awe-inspiring songwriting abilities, and with them he defined modern country music.

Born: September 17, 1923; Georgiana, Alabama
Died: January 1, 1953; Oak Hill, West Virginia
Also known as: Hiram King Williams (full name)
Member of: The Drifting Cowboys

Principal recordings

ALBUMS (with the Drifting Cowboys): *Hank Williams Sings*, 1952; *Hank Williams as Luke the Drifter*, 1955.

SINGLES (with the Drifting Cowboys): "Move It on Over," 1947; "I'm a Long Gone Daddy," 1948; "Lovesick Blues," 1949; "Mind Your Own Business," 1949; "My Bucket's Got a Hole in It," 1949; "You're Gonna Change, or I'm Gonna Leave," 1949; "Long Gone Lonesome Blues," 1950; "Moanin' the Blues," 1950; "Why Don't You Love Me?," 1950; "Cold Cold Heart," 1951; "Hey Good Lookin'," 1951; "Half as Much," 1952; "I'll Never Get out of This World Alive," 1952; "Jambalaya (On the Bayou)," 1952; "I Won't be Home No More," 1953; "Kaw-Liga," 1953; "Take These Chains from My Heart," 1953.

The Life

Hiram King Williams was the second surviving child of the union of Lonnie and Lilly Williams, a marriage that later ended in divorce. The Williams family lived in a shack in rural Alabama, and the prospect of their son achieving any degree of fame or financial success was remote at best. His father left the family when Williams was young, and the two had little contact. His mother struggled mightily to support Williams, a beloved but sickly child, and Irene, his sister.

A skilled singer and guitarist, Williams eventually secured a radio program to promote his career, and he then signed contracts to record for Sterling Records and MGM Records. He met Audrey Shepherd Erskine at a concert in 1942, and they married in 1944. Ultimately ending in divorce, the marriage did produce Randall Hank Williams, who became known as Hank Williams, Jr. After being fired from the Grand Ole Opry (a weekly radio show and live performance of country music in Nashville, Tennessee) because of his drinking, Williams married Billie Jean Jones shortly before his death on New Year's Day, 1953.

The Music

His aunt taught Williams to play the guitar, but his primary musical influence was a local street musician named Rufus Payne, known as Tec Tot. Williams put together a backing group called the Drifting Cowboys, and by 1946 he had begun a recording career that lasted a short seven years.

Early Works. Williams's first big hit was "Move It on Over," a novelty song he wrote about an errant husband being forced to sleep in the doghouse. This song had a faster tempo than most of his later recordings, and some music observers claim it was a harbinger of rock and roll. The song that established him as a recording giant and budding country-music superstar was "Lovesick Blues," one of the few he did not write and which first had been recorded in the early 1920's. Williams remodeled the song almost beyond recognition, adding a fiddle and a steel guitar and inserting yodeling interludes. It was country in sound and feel, and it was a tremendous number-one hit for Williams. His next three number-one smashes all dated from 1950 ("Long Gone Lonesome Blues," "Why Don't You Love Me?," and "Moanin" the Blues"), and all

Hank Williams. (AP/Wide World Photos)

of them told the story of a man suffering from an ongoing tempestuous relationship with a woman.

"Cold Cold Heart." His next huge hit revolutionized the music industry. Producer and arranger Mitch Miller had heard Williams's music and believed it would appeal to markets that generally would not hear country music, so he persuaded singer Tony Bennett to record a version of the song, and it became a huge hit on the pop charts, too. From that time, Williams's compositions have been widely covered with great success by a variety of musical stylists.

"Hey Good Lookin'." His next number-one hit was "Hey Good Lookin'." This upbeat and bouncy song told the story of a man asking a woman for a date, with the usual emotions associated with that situation.

"Jambalaya (On the Bayou)." "Jambalaya" did not conform to Williams's previous musical formula. It had more than one instrumental break, and it featured Williams singing some Cajun French words and some words he apparently made up for the song. The name Yvonne is mentioned in the lyr-

ics several times, apparently in reference to an infant. When this song was recorded, Williams's girlfriend Bobbie Jett was pregnant with a little girl they intended to call Yvonne. The baby was born after her father's death.

"I'll Never Get out of This World Alive." This song proved tragically prophetic when Williams died only two months later. Some observers point to this song and other circumstantial evidence as proof that he foresaw his death.

"Kaw-Liga." "Kaw-Liga" was a novelty song about a wooden cigar-store Indian falling in love with an Indian maid also carved from wood. The premise was original, and this is the only known Williams record to feature a drum (an underappreciated instrument in country music at that time) and to end in a fade-out (rare then, although common now).

"Your Cheatin' Heart." The song most closely associated with Williams in the years since his death is "Your Cheatin' Heart," one he almost certainly did not have the opportunity to perform live before an audience. In all likelihood the song was written about his former wife, Audrey. His final number-one song was "Take These Chains from My Heart," an upbeat tune thought to be about his relationship with Audrey.

Musical Legacy

Williams suffered from a variety of physical ailments, all made worse by his chronic drug abuse and alcoholism, and his death at twenty-nine helped create the mystique of the tortured artistic genius. His compositions were recorded by a variety of artists representing many different genres, thus universalizing the appeal of country music and solidifying his place as a giant in the field of popular music.

Thomas W. Buchanan

Further Reading

Escott, Colin, with George Merritt and William MacEwen. *Hank Williams, the Biography*. Boston: Little, Brown, 1994. Well researched and thorough, this is an excellent resource on the singer's life. Covering Williams from cradle to grave, the work also includes interesting supplementary material, such as a complete history of all his recording sessions.

Flippo, Chet. *Your Cheatin' Heart: A Biography of Hank Williams*. New York: Simon & Schuster, 1981. This work provides interesting information about Williams's personal life, especially his tortured relationships with his mother and first wife.

Jones, Tim, with Harold McAlindon and Richard Courtney. *The Essential Hank Williams*. Nashville, Tenn.: Eggman, 1996. This work is largely a pictorial history of Williams combined with facts and related memories.

Rivers, Jerry. *Hank Williams: From Life to Legend*. Denver, Colo.: Heather Enterprises, 1967. Rivers, a fiddler in the Drifting Cowboys, knew Williams intimately. A good resource, this book consists of Rivers's direct experiences with and observations of the troubled entertainer.

Williams, Jett, with Pamela Thomas. *Ain't Nothing as Sweet as My Baby*. San Diego, Calif.: Harcourt Brace Jovanovich, 1990. Williams's illegitimate daughter describes her decades-long struggle to be recognized as one of his heirs. This work contains information about Williams provided to the author by her father's relatives and associates.

See also: Acuff, Roy; Atkins, Chet; Bennett, Tony; Cash, Johnny; Frizzell, Lefty; Haggard, Merle; Harris, Emmylou; Holly, Buddy; Jones, George; Joplin, Janis; Lewis, Jerry Lee; Monroe, Bill; Morrison, Van; Orbison, Roy; Tubb, Ernest; Van Zandt, Townes; Washington, Dinah.

John Williams

American film-score composer

A celebrated and prolific film scorer, Williams exhibits in his works the influence of classical music and jazz. His scores not only reflect the action on the screen but also tie together plot elements.

Born: February 8, 1932; Flora Park, New York
Also known as: John Towner Williams (full name)

Principal works

CHAMBER WORK: Cello Concerto, 1994.
FILM SCORES: *Daddy-O*, 1958; *I Passed for White*, 1960; *The Secret Ways*, 1961; *Bachelor Flat*, 1962; *Gidget Goes to Rome*, 1963; *The Killers*, 1964; *John Goldfarb, Please Come Home*, 1965; *How to Steal a Million*, 1966; *Not with My Wife, You Don't!*, 1966; *The Rare Breed*, 1966; *A Guide for the Married Man*, 1967; *Heidi*, 1968 (television); *Goodbye, Mr. Chips*, 1969; *Jane Eyre*, 1970 (television); *Fiddler on the Roof*, 1971; *The Poseidon Adventure*, 1972; *The Long Goodbye*, 1973; *Earthquake*, 1974; *The Sugarland Express*, 1974; *The Towering Inferno*, 1974; *Jaws*, 1975; *Family Plot*, 1976; *Close Encounters of the Third Kind*, 1977; *Star Wars*, 1977; *Jaws 2*, 1978; *Superman*, 1978; *Dracula*, 1979; *The Empire Strikes Back*, 1980; *Raiders of the Lost Ark*, 1981; *E.T.: The Extraterrestrial*, 1982; *Return of the Jedi*, 1983; *The Witches of Eastwick*, 1987; *The Accidental Tourist*, 1988; *Born on the Fourth of July*, 1989; *Indiana Jones and the Last Crusade*, 1989; *Home Alone*, 1990; *Hook*, 1991; *JFK*, 1991; *Home Alone 2: Lost in New York*, 1992; *Jurassic Park*, 1993; *Schindler's List*, 1993; *Nixon*, 1995; *The Lost World: Jurassic Park*, 1997; *Seven Years in Tibet*, 1997; *Saving Private Ryan*, 1998; *Angela's Ashes*, 1999; *Star Wars Episode I: The Phantom Menace*, 1999; *Artificial Intelligence: AI*, 2001; *Harry Potter and the Sorcerer's Stone*, 2001; *Harry Potter and the Chamber of Secrets*, 2002; *Minority Report*, 2002; *Star Wars Episode II: Attack of the Clones*, 2002; *Harry Potter and the Prisoner of Azkaban*, 2004; *Memoirs of a Geisha*, 2005; *Munich*, 2005; *Star Wars Episode III: Revenge of the Sith*, 2005; *Indiana Jones and the Kingdom of the Crystal Skull*, 2008.
ORCHESTRAL WORKS: *Essay for Strings*, 1965; *Sinfonietta for Wind Ensemble*, 1968.
VOCAL WORK: *Seven for Luck*, 1998.

The Life

John Towner Williams is the son of John Williams, a jazz drummer and percussionist, and Esther, a homemaker. He studied piano from the age of six, and he learned to play the bassoon, cello, trombone, trumpet, and clarinet. In 1948 the family moved to Los Angeles, where Williams's father worked in film studio orchestras. At North Hollywood High School, Williams organized a small band, and he discovered that since the clarinet and piano are in different keys, they could not be played from the same music. Consequently, he studied orchestration books, and he learned to transpose music. After graduating from high school, he took courses in piano and composition at the University of California at Los Angeles and at Los Angeles City College. He also studied privately with pianist-arranger Robert Van Epps and Italian composer Mario Castelnuovo-Tedesco. Williams composed a piano sonata at age nineteen. During the Korean War, Williams joined the U.S. Air Force, orchestrating for and conducting military bands. In 1954 he returned to New York, enrolled at the Juilliard School, and studied piano with Rosina Lhévinne. To make money, he played jazz piano in nightclubs and for recording studios. In 1956 he returned to Los Angeles, and he began working as a studio pianist at Columbia and Twentieth Century-Fox, where he met Morris Stoloff and Alfred and Lionel Newman. Working with these composers and others, he became interested in writing for film. Established film scorers, such as Franz Waxman and Bernard Herrmann, observed Williams's skills in orchestration, and they invited him to orchestrate cues for their music. The composers he worked with also encouraged him to focus on his own composing.

While scoring low-budget films, Williams also worked in television. In addition to playing the piano in Henry Mancini's theme to the *Peter Gunn* series, he acted in *Johnny Staccato*, a detective series, playing a jazz musician. However, his major interest continued to be composing. Under contract to Revue Studios, a division of Universal Studios, he was writing as many as thirty-nine scores a year. Working at the intense pace required to produce fifteen to thirty minutes of original music a week, for shows such as *Playhouse 90* and the *Kraft Playhouse*, introduced him to the same time-intensive process as writing for films. He married Barbara Ruick in 1956, and they had three children. Ruick died in 1974, and he married Samantha Winslow in 1980.

In 1958 Williams scored his first film, *Daddy-O*. During the 1960's he scored other films, generally light comedies, such as *Bachelor Flat* and *Gidget Goes to Rome*. For television, he wrote the themes to the *Gilligan's Island* and *Lost in Space* series. Although

he wrote the music for several television films, winning an Emmy Award for both *Heidi* and *Jane Eyre*, the main focus of his work turned to film. By 1968 he was being nominated for Academy Awards, and he won his first as a conductor-arranger for *Fiddler on the Roof*. *The Poseidon Adventure* proclaimed his mastery of disaster film scoring; however, it was his work with Steven Spielberg in *The Sugarland Express* that led to one of the longest director-composer collaborations in Hollywood history, and it had a profound effect on Williams's success.

During this time Williams continued to compose classical music, and he developed a reputation as a conductor, resulting in his appointment as conductor of the Boston Pops Orchestra from 1980 to 1993. He has conducted for a number of orchestras, and in 1993 he was appointed artist in residence at Tanglewood, in Lenox, Massachusetts, teaching young film scorers how to develop their craft.

The Music

Early Works. Most of Williams's early work was for television. With the increasing number of television shows in the 1950's, he had plenty of opportunities. Williams's early work in film was as an orchestrator for established film composers, providing cues for films such as *The Apartment* (1960) and *The Guns of Navarone* (1961). Composing his own music, he ranged from comedies (such as *John Goldfarb, Please Come Home*), to disaster films (such as *The Towering Inferno*), to cowboy dramas (such as *The Missouri Breaks*), to Alfred Hitchcock's final film, *Family Plot*.

However, it was his work on Spielberg's film *Jaws* that brought him fame. His score is influenced by Claude Debussy's *La Mer* (1905) as well as by Igor Stravinsky's *The Rite of Spring* (1913). It is from the latter that the theme representing the great white shark grew. Years later, just a few notes of this theme are instantly recognized as the *Jaws* theme. Critic Timothy Scheurer comments that Williams's score found the emotional core of the film, a mix of romance, mystery, and terror. For *Jaws*, Williams won his second Academy Award, and it was his first for original composition. Collaborating again with Spielberg—on the mystic, otherworldly *Close Encounters of the Third Kind*—Williams developed another memorable theme: a distinctive series of five notes, played on a synthesizer.

John Williams. (AP/Wide World Photos)

Star Wars. In addition to working with Spielberg, Williams began working with director George Lucas for the *Star Wars* series of films. The music for *Star Wars* has been described as a throwback to the grand style of film music, characterized by the work of Max Steiner and Erich Wolfgang Korngold in the 1930's. Like Korngold's work, the score includes both romance and adventure. The score also uses leitmotifs to represent different characters as well as actions. For example, the Princess Leia motif signifies the love between her and Han Solo. *Star Wars* was one of the first films to utilize a full orchestra. Williams knew his score would not work with a ten-piece orchestra, so he hired the London Symphony Orchestra. Williams's score gained mainstream popularity, and it helped legitimize symphonic film music on record. The two-disc album was a commercial success, selling more than four million copies, and the film earned Williams another Academy Award.

Williams composed six scores for the *Star Wars* films. What was unusual was composing music for three prequel films after *Star Wars*. Williams had to use previous themes and create new ones, refashioning the associations and memories of the earlier films into fresh themes. In *Star Wars Episode I: The Phantom Menace*, for example, "Anakin's Theme" has hints of the earlier "Imperial March." Of particular note was the theme "Across the Stars," introduced in *Star Wars Episode II: The Attack of the Clones* and representing the love of Anakin Skywalker and Padme Amidala. *Star Wars Episode III: Revenge of the Sith* has the most powerfully emotional music of the series, particularly the "Immolation Scene," Williams's elegy for a fallen hero. The *Star Wars* series includes more than twelve hours of music, as much music as Richard Wagner's Ring cycle of operas.

Other Major Films. Over the years, other scores have brought additional awards for Williams as well as countless hours of pleasure for his listeners. Williams's score for *Raiders of the Lost Ark* is reminiscent of music for the early Hollywood Saturday-afternoon film serials, with their close calls for the hero and their musical assertions to underscore the hero vanquishing a villain or a physical obstacle. When Indiana Jones runs from the massive boulder at the beginning of the film and later successfully flees the Nazis, a brassy march theme, signifying Jones's triumph, is used. Other recurrent themes are a religious-sounding motif, referencing the Ark of the Covenant, and the love theme underscoring the relationship between Jones and Marion. In another vein, Williams's rich orchestral score for *E.T.: The Extraterrestrial*, which resulted in his fourth Academy Award, includes themes reflecting innocence, friendship, and the exhilaration of flight. The final chase and farewell sequence is unusual in film history in that the on-screen action was reedited to conform to Williams's music.

Other scores feature specific instruments, such as the elegiac violin solo, played by world-class violinist Itzhak Perlman, for *Schindler's List*. For this film, which earned Williams his fifth Academy Award, he wrote a theme reminiscent of a Hebrew lullaby. The theme is introduced halfway into the film, then presented again at certain intervals. Toward the end of the film, the solo piano, played by Williams, reiterates the theme.

In a number of films Williams effectively employs choral music. For *Saving Private Ryan*, Williams uses humming, rather than words, to express emotion.

Classical Works. In addition to writing for film, Williams has written classical music. His *Essay for Strings* has been widely played. Many works, such as his *Sinfonietta for Wind Ensemble*, have been recorded. He has written a number of works featuring a specific instrument. In 1994 his Cello Concerto, composed for cellist Yo-Yo Ma, celebrated the opening of Ozawa Hall at Tanglewood. His song cycle *Seven for Luck*, for soprano and orchestra, based on the poetry of Rita Dove, premiered at Tanglewood in 1998, with Williams conducting the Boston Symphony Orchestra.

Conductor. In addition to guest-conducting for a number of symphony orchestras, Williams was appointed conductor for the Boston Pops in 1980, following legendary conductor Arthur Fiedler. Williams said one of the reasons for his accepting the position was to "win some respect" for film composers. When Williams left the Boston Pops, he retained his ties to the organization as Laureate Conductor. He conducts Boston Pops concerts each year, and he has used Symphony Hall in Boston to record music.

Musical Legacy

Williams brought symphonic music to film scores. More than previous film composers Steiner and Korngold, Williams contributed to increased respectability for those who compose for film. Not only did he use music to underscore the images on the screen, the dialogue, and the sound effects, but also he brought music forward as a principal ingredient in the film. He used full orchestras, and he highlighted individual instruments. His film music is distinctive for its ability to stand on its own, apart from the film. Consequently, recordings of his scores have been commercially successful.

Although he has composed for a variety of venues, including themes for several Olympics Games and for the dedication of the refurbished Statue of Liberty, it is through his music for film that Williams has made his most significant contribution.

His music has reawakened the filmgoing public and studio executives to the value of traditional symphonic music as an important element in a film's success, contributing to the storytelling and to the emotional content being developed by the director.

Marcia B. Dinneen

Further Reading

Bazelon, Irwin. *Knowing the Score: Notes on Film Music*. New York: Van Nostrand, 1975. An in-depth interview with Williams focuses on his career in writing for film and on his innovative use of instruments.

Bond, Jeff. "God Almighty! FSM Finally Talks to John Williams." *Film Score Monthly* 8, no. 1 (January, 2003): 10-13. An interview with Williams in which he discusses his later films.

Darby, William, and Jack Du Bois. "John Williams." In *American Film Music: Major Composers, Techniques, Trends, 1915-1990*. Jefferson, N.C.: McFarland, 1990. This chapter discusses Williams's style in composing and various themes he develops in specific films. Includes a filmography.

Dyer, Richard. "Latest *Star Wars* Score Is an Emotional Adventure." *Boston Globe*, June 6, 2005, p. B7. A review of *Star Wars Episode III: Revenge of the Sith* includes references to previous *Star Wars* films.

Larson, Randall D. *Musique Fantastique: A Survey of Film Music in the Fantastc Cinema*. Metuchen, N.J.: Scarecrow Press, 1985. An overview of Williams's career, stressing his importance to the genre of film music.

Scheurer, Timothy E. "John Williams and Film Music Since 1971." *Popular Music and Society* 21, no. 1 (Spring, 1997): 59-72. The article compares Williams to Korngold, and it includes themes to specific films.

Sullivan, Jack. "John Williams: Close Encounters with a Modest Icon." *American Record Guide* (July/August, 2006): 69. Williams reflects on the global appeal of film music.

See also: Anderson, Leroy; Bergman, Alan; Fiedler, Arthur; Goldsmith, Jerry; Korngold, Erich Wolfgang; Ma, Yo-Yo; Newman, Alfred; Perlman, Itzhak; Segovia, Andrés; Steiner, Max; Waxman, Franz; Williams, Mary Lou.

Lucinda Williams

American country guitarist, singer, and songwriter

Dubbed America's Best Songwriter by Time *magazine in 2001, country-blues-folk songwriter Williams and her work are noted for an introspective, intense lyrical content and a roots-rock combination of electric and acoustic instrumentation.*

Born: January 26, 1953; Lake Charles, Louisiana

Principal recordings

ALBUMS: *Ramblin'*, 1979; *Happy Woman Blues*, 1980; *Lucinda Williams*, 1988; *Sweet Old World*, 1992; *Car Wheels on a Gravel Road*, 1998; *Essence*, 2001; *World Without Tears*, 2003; *West*, 2007.

The Life

Lucinda Williams was born in Lake Charles, Louisiana, on January 26, 1953, to mother Lucille and father Miller Williams, a literature professor and published poet. Williams absorbed her father's expertise in the English language and her mother's affinity for 1960's folk rock, creating her pedigree as a singer-songwriter. After she was expelled from high school for refusing to say the Pledge of Allegiance, Williams continued her education by studying books in her father's collection, and she spent time in Texas and New York throughout the 1970's and in California in the early 1980's. After that she lived in Tennessee, New York, and California.

In the 1970's Williams's demo recordings created a buzz on the folk-country music scene, and she began producing solo records in 1979. Since then, she has released critically acclaimed records on many different labels (among them Smithsonian Folkways, Rough Trade, RCA, Chameleon, American, Mercury, and Lost Highway). Many labels have found her perfectionism in the studio and her refusal to release a record until she deemed it ready for public consumption a challenge.

The Music

Ramblin'. After shopping around demo recordings in Texas, Williams recorded her first solo rec-

ord for the Smithsonian Folkways label in 1979. *Ramblin'* was recorded in Jackson, Mississippi, and was an introduction to Williams's style in an assortment of blues, folk, country, and gospel cover songs. The high-quality performances on this album are somewhat overlooked because of the lack of original material.

Happy Woman Blues. Williams released her second album for Smithsonian Folkways in 1980, and it was her first with original material performed with a full band. The album began a trend in Williams's songwriting career of composing country-folk songs heavily infused with rock and blues elements. Highlights include "Lafayette," "Happy Woman Blues," and "I Lost It," the last a staple of Williams's live shows.

Lucinda Williams. A staggering eight years after *Happy Woman Blues*, Williams released her self-titled third album (and the second of original material) on the British record label Rough Trade. It received glowing reviews, many proclaiming the arrival of a skilled songwriter who had found the perfect balance of country, folk, blues, and rock. It is this same praise, however, that began a long run of strained relationships with record companies that were not sure how to market her omni-genre work. "I Just Wanted to See You So Bad," "Passionate Kisses," "Changed the Locks," and "Crescent City," while tributes to Williams's talents as a singer and songwriter, defied the mass market. Nonetheless, along with her fans, critics and musicians admired Williams and her work. Her fellow musicians began rerecording her songs: Patty Loveless recorded "The Night's Too Long"; Mary Chapin Carpenter recorded "Passionate Kisses"; Emmylou Harris recorded "Crescent City"; and Tom Petty recorded "Changed the Locks." With her third release in the course of nearly ten years, Williams had become a singer's songwriter.

Sweet Old World. Four years later, Williams released *Sweet Old World* on Chameleon Records. Hailed by critics, fans, and fellow musicians, it earned her the opportunity to tour with one of her musical heroes, Rosanne Cash. The irony of the album's title becomes clear in the haunting tales of suicide on "Pineola" and "Sweet Old World." This dark, moody record introduced Williams's audiences to her revealing and unflinching songwriting.

Car Wheels on a Gravel Road. Williams's legendary reputation for perfectionism in the studio, which resulted in several years between albums, came to a head, with Grammy Award-winning results, on *Car Wheels on a Gravel Road*. Williams recorded tracks for *Car Wheels on a Gravel Road* as early as 1995, when she signed with Rick Rubin's American Recordings. When she moved to Nashville, Tennessee, a year later, she met with fellow musician Steve Earle, and she decided to abandon her previous work and rerecord the entire album. Williams took the new tracks to ex-E Street Band member Roy Bittan to overdub the rerecorded sessions, eliminating the overproduced sound of the Earle sessions. Finally released by Mercury Records, *Car Wheels on a Gravel Road* received widespread critical praise, this time accompanied by increased sales, going all the way to gold, and a Grammy Award for Best Contemporary Folk Album.

Later Works. *Essence*, *World Without Tears*, 2005's *Live at the Fillmore*, and *West*—three studio records and one double-live release, all on Lost Highway records—continued the streak of critical praise. *Essence*, a quiet, peaceful record coproduced by Williams and Charlie Sexton, features legendary studio musicians Tony Garnier (bass) and Jim Keltner (drums). *World Without Tears* and *Live at the Fillmore* feature the longest-standing complete band of Williams's career: Doug Pettibone (guitar), Taras Prodaniuk (bass), and Jim Christie (drums). *West*, a tribute to Williams's late mother, features optimistic lyrical content.

Musical Legacy

Williams was a pioneering influence in the alternative-country movement, which is characterized by country artists who incorporate American roots elements (gospel, folk, blues, and especially rock) into their music. Williams's blueprint for artistic success paved the way for other female songwriters, who have written dark autobiographical material (among them Fiona Apple and Tori Amos).

Eric Novod

Lucinda Williams. (AP/Wide World Photos)

Further Reading

Hornby, Nick, ed. *Da Capo Best Music Writing 2001: The Year's Finest Writing on Rock, Pop, Jazz, Country, and More*. New York: Da Capo Press, 2001. This collection includes Bill Buford's feature on Williams from *The New Yorker*, "Delta Nights: A Singer's Love Affair with Loss," a revealing look at her life and work that Williams criticized for revealing too much family information.

Lindall, Anders Smith. *Lucinda Williams: 33 1/3*. London: Continuum, 2008. Focuses on the making of *Lucinda Williams* and includes interviews with Williams.

Rouda, Bill. *Nashville's Lower Broad: The Street That Music Made*. Washington, D.C.: Smithsonian, 2004. In this book's foreword, Williams discusses the music scene in Nashville.

Zimmerman, Keith. *Sing My Way Home: Voices of the New American Roots Rock*. San Francisco: Backbeat Books, 2004. Takes a look at roots-rock musicians in general, and one chapter, "Lucinda Williams: The Modern Day Hank," discusses her songwriting style and persona.

See also: Domino, Fats; Earle, Steve; Harris, Emmylou; Parsons, Gram; Petty, Tom.

Mary Lou Williams

American jazz singer, pianist, and songwriter

Williams adapted her style of playing and composition to such trends as ragtime, the blues, boogie-woogie, swing, and bebop, each of which she mastered and renovated. She came to view jazz as deeply spiritual music, and after her conversion to Catholicism, she composed religious works.

Born: May 8, 1910; Atlanta, Georgia
Died: May 28, 1981; Durham, North Carolina
Also known as: Mary Elfrieda Scruggs (birth name); Mary Lou Burley; Mary Winn; Queen of Jazz
Member of: Andy Kirk and His Twelve Clouds of Joy; the Mary Lou Williams Trio

Principal recordings

ALBUMS (solo): *Little Joe from Chicago*, 1944 (with Henry Wells); *Rehearsal, Vol. 1*, 1944; *Jazz Variations*, 1950; *Piano Moderns*, 1950; *Mary Lou Williams with Barbara Carroll*, 1951; *Piano Contempo*, 1952; *The First Lady of the Piano*, 1953; *Mary Lou Williams in London*, 1953; *Piano*, 1953; *Mary Lou*, 1954; *A Keyboard History*, 1955; *Messin' 'Round in Montmartre*, 1959; *Mary Lou Williams Presents Black Christ of the Andes*, 1963; *The History of Jazz*, 1970; *Music for Peace*, 1970; *From the Heart*, 1971; *Nite Life*, 1971; *Zoning*, 1974; *Free Spirits*, 1975; *Mary Lou's Mass*, 1975; *Embraced*, 1977 (with Cecil Taylor); *My Mama Pinned a Rose on Me*, 1977.

ALBUMS (with Andy Kirk and His Twelve Clouds of Joy): *Corky Stomp*, 1929; *Lotta Sax Appeal*, 1929; *Messa Stomp*, 1929; *Froggy Bottom*, 1936; *Walkin' and Swingin'*, 1936 (with Wells); *In the Groove*, 1937; *Mary's Idea*, 1938; *Instrumentally Speaking, 1936-1942*, 1942.

ALBUM (with the Mary Lou Williams Quartet): *Mary Lou Williams Quartet*, 1953 (with Don Byas).

ALBUMS (with the Mary Lou Williams Trio): *Roll 'Em*, 1944; *Zodiac Suite*, 1945; *Mary Lou Williams Trio*, 1951.

The Life

Born in Atlanta, Georgia, as Mary Elfrieda Scruggs, the daughter of Joseph Scruggs (who abandoned the family) and Virginia Riser, Mary Lou Williams grew up in Pittsburgh, Pennsylvania, where, at a very early age, she manifested a talent for playing the piano. As the "little piano girl," she played at parties, dances, and churches and for silent films. She completed elementary school, but she left high school at fifteen to tour with a vaudeville act. She met and married John Williams, a saxophonist, in 1927, and they eventually became associated with Andy Kirk's orchestra. As "The Lady Who Swings the Band," she developed into an influential soloist as well as a gifted arranger and composer. During the 1930's she supplied scores to such distinguished swing-era bands as those of Benny Goodman, Earl Hines, Jimmy Lunceford, and Tommy Dorsey.

Tired of touring and feeling creatively constrained, Williams left Kirk in 1942, when she divorced her husband. She then settled in New York City, where, with her second husband, trumpeter Harold "Shorty" Baker, she played in small groups and provided arrangements and compositions for Duke Ellington and Dizzy Gillespie. After a stay in Europe in the early 1950's and her conversion to Catholicism in 1957, she devoted herself to composing sacred works and ministering to down-and-out musicians. Under the guidance, then management, of a Jesuit priest, Father Peter O'Brien, she played at New York clubs and the Newport Jazz Festival, in addition to giving church and college concerts. Williams taught at several institutions, including Duke University in North Carolina, where she died of cancer of the spine in 1981.

The Music

Although Williams was initially identified with ragtime and stride styles, with their rhythmic chords played by the left hand, she later adopted, with her own innovations, the boogie-woogie and swing styles of the 1930's. Unlike many traditional jazz musicians, she adeptly navigated the transition to bebop or modern jazz. In her final transformation, she blended jazz and gospel music with such classic forms as the hymn and the mass. During her tenure with Kirk, from the late 1920's to the early 1940's, she achieved fame as a pianist, arranger, and composer.

From Stride to Modern Jazz. Williams's first solo piano recordings reveal the influence of Willie "the Lion" Smith and Earl "Fatha" Hines as well as her mastery of the stride style. In 1936 her compositions "Walkin' and Swingin'" and especially "Froggy Bottom" became best sellers on jukeboxes. In 1937 she created the theme "Camel Hop" for Benny Goodman's radio show, which was sponsored by Camel cigarettes. Her popular boogie-woogie composition "Little Joe from Chicago" was dedicated to her agent, Joe Glaser.

Kirk's Twelve Clouds of Joy orchestra recorded her "What's Your Story, Morning Glory?," based on an old blues tune, in 1938; Jimmy Lunceford's band later made it into a hit. In "Close to Five" and "Big Jam Blues" (from 1939), "Why Go on Pretending" (1940), and "Big Time Crip" (1941) she articulated melodies that captured a jazz sensibility that appealed to many musicians. She also arranged or composed nearly fifty pieces for Duke Ellington's orchestra, including "Trumpets No End," her imaginative take on Irving Berlin's "Blue Skies." Other small groups and big bands used her arrangements and compositions, including those of Louis Armstrong, Cab Calloway, and Glen Gray.

Through her friendship and collaboration with such innovators as Dizzy Gillespie, Bud Powell, Tadd Dameron, and Thelonious Monk, she exerted a powerful influence on the origin and development of modern jazz. For example, her composition "In the Land of Oo-bla-dee" was popular with bebop musicians.

The Zodiac Suite. During this time, Williams became intrigued by an astrology book, and she conceived the idea of creating portraits in sound of musicians she knew based on their astrological signs. Blending modern jazz techniques and her knowledge of such twentieth century composers as Béla Bartók, she composed her magnum opus, *Zodiac Suite*, parts of which she played as early as 1945. In 1946 she played excerpts of *Zodiac Suite* at Carnegie Hall with members of the New York Philharmonic Orchestra, the first time that a symphonic group played music by a jazz composer. Notable later performances include the Newport Jazz Festival in 1957 and over Vatican Radio in 1969.

Sacred Themes. From the 1950's until her death in 1981, Williams continued to play and compose in her version of the modern jazz idiom, but most of her creative energies found an outlet in her work on sacred themes. Her hymn in honor of St. Martin de Porres, a mulatto Peruvian who became the patron saint of interracial justice, was her pioneering effort to integrate jazz, Latin American rhythms, and traditional religious forms. In 1962 she premiered the piece at St. Francis Xavier Church in New York. In 1966 she premiered her first mass at Saint Paul's Cathedral in Pittsburgh, Pennsylvania. The Vatican commissioned the third and most famous of her masses. Initially entitled *Mass for Peace*, it later became known as *Mary Lou's Mass*. During the 1970's, it was performed at St. Patrick's Cathedral in New York as well as in many other churches. She also adapted it for the Alvin Ailey Dance Theater, through which her celebration of God, humanity, and peace added to the work's fame.

Musical Legacy

An influential woman in jazz, Williams was praised by such distinguished musicians as Ellington, who saw her as "perpetually contemporary" and her music as "timeless." Her achievements

Mary Lou Williams. (AP/Wide World Photos)

merited a Guggenheim Fellowship and honorary degrees, bestowed for her humanitarian and musical contributions, from such institutions as Fordham University, Manhattan College, and Loyola University of New Orleans. Her musical legacy has been extended not only by the jazz musicians she influenced but also through a publishing company (Cecilia Music), a record company (Mary Records), and a foundation (The Mary Lou Williams Foundation). Father O'Brien, who played an important role in the foundation after Williams's death, also saw it as a way of preserving and enhancing her musical legacy. Through documentaries, recordings, and many books and articles, Williams remains one of the most revered women of jazz.

Robert J. Paradowski

Further Reading

Dahl, Linda. *Morning Glory: A Biography of Mary Lou Williams.* Berkeley: University of California Press, 2001. This standard biography is based on Williams's extensive archives and the author's interviews with family, colleagues, and friends. Includes sources and notes, a selective bibliography and discography, a compositions and arrangements section, and an index.

_____. *Stormy Weather: The Music and Lives of a Century of Jazz Women.* New York: Pantheon Books, 1984. In this "most complete history of women in jazz," the author devotes considerable space to Williams in her chapter on "The Ladies at the Keyboard." Includes discography, bibliography, and index.

Gottlieb, Robert, ed. *Reading Jazz: A Gathering of Autobiographies, Reportage, and Criticism from 1919 to Now.* New York: Pantheon Books, 1996. Williams's most extensive autobiographical reminiscences appeared in the British magazine *Melody Maker*, and they are now more accessible in this anthology. No index.

Kirchner, Bill, ed. *The Oxford Companion to Jazz.* New York: Oxford University Press, 2000. Williams's achievements are discussed in the chapters on "Pianists of the 1920's and 1930's" and on "Pianists of the 1940's and 1950's." Includes a selected bibliography, an index of names and subjects, and an index of songs and recordings.

Schuller, Gunther. *The Swing Era: The Development of Jazz, 1930-1945.* New York: Oxford University Press, 1989. In the section on Kirk, Schuller analyzes, with musical examples, Williams's contributions to a "great black band." Includes glossary and index.

See also: Armstrong, Louis; Bartók, Béla; Blakey, Art; Ellington, Duke; Gillespie, Dizzy; Goodman, Benny; McPartland, Marian; Monk, Thelonious; Presley, Elvis; Taylor, Cecil.

Sonny Boy Williamson I
American blues harmonica player, singer, and songwriter

With his catchy harmonica stylings, Williamson was noted for his roots in the rural traditions of the blues, yet his popular recordings pointed the way toward the amplified band sounds of post-World War II Chicago. His lyrics, though autobiographical, resonated with working-class African Americans of the 1930's and 1940's.

Born: March 30, 1914; Jackson, Tennessee
Died: June 1, 1948; Chicago, Illinois
Also known as: John Lee Williamson (full name)

Principal recordings

SINGLES: "Blue Bird Blues," 1937; "Early in the Morning," 1937; "Good Morning, School Girl," 1937; "Blue Bird Blues Pt. 2," 1938; "Decoration Blues," 1938; "Honey Bee Blues," 1938; "Whiskey Headed Woman Blues," 1938; "Deep Down in the Ground," 1939; "Low Down Ways," 1939; "My Little Machine," 1939; "T. B. Blues," 1939; "Tell Me Baby," 1939; "Dealing with the Devil," 1940; "Jivin' the Blues," 1940; "Ground Hog Blues," 1941; "My Black Name," 1941; "Sloppy Drunk Blues," 1941; "Western Union Man," 1941; "My Black Name Ringing," 1943; "Check Up on My Baby," 1944; "Miss Stella Brown Blues," 1944; "Mean Old Highway," 1945; "Stop Breaking Down," 1945; "Hoo-Doo Man," 1946; "Biscuit Baking Woman," 1947; "Shake That Boogie," 1947; "Better Cut That Out," 1948; "Susie Q.," 1948.

The Life

John Lee Williamson was born and raised in Jackson, Tennessee, where his grandmother gave him the "Sonny Boy" nickname. By his late teens, Williamson had become proficient enough on harmonica and confident enough as a singer to perform with mandolinist Yank Rachell and guitarist Homesick James Williamson at clubs in the Jackson area. Williamson had an uncle living in St. Louis, home of many established blues performers, and Williamson reportedly became a fixture of the St. Louis blues scene. He is believed to have visited Chicago for the first time in 1934, the year entrepreneur Lester Melrose convinced two of the era's major record labels, RCA Victor and Columbia, to record blues artists for the jukeboxes then springing up in taverns, newly opened in the wake of Prohibition's repeal. In May, 1937, Melrose summoned Williamson and guitarists Robert Lee McCoy (Robert Nighthawk) and Big Joe Williams to record at a hotel in Aurora, Illinois.

The first recording, "Good Morning, School Girl," became a hit, and between 1937 and 1947, Williamson recorded more than a hundred songs. Attacked and robbed on his way home from Chicago's Plantation Club in the early hours of June 1, 1948, Williamson succumbed to his wounds the same day.

The Music

The harmonica was the most widely disseminated free reed instrument for good reasons: It was cheap, relatively easy to play, and as portable as a pocket knife. This German instrument was adapted by rural Americans to play traditional melodies, and it was also "choked" in order to imitate train whistles and baying hounds. In the early days of recording, novelty recordings of harmonica solos were common. From the 1920's through the 1930's, the recorded stars of the blues idiom who wrote and sang original material accompanied themselves either on piano (such as Leroy Carr) or on guitar (Lonnie Johnson). The notion of a harmonica player creating songs of equal caliber was unprecedented. On May 5, 1937, during his debut recording session, twenty-three-year-old Sonny Boy Williamson changed that forever. His power as a blues lyricist and singer, along with his prowess as a harmonica player, made the harmonica

player as blues group leader viable for future generations. His lyrics, populated by such ordinary folks as beauticians and insurance collectors, are well-crafted slices of his era's African American life. That made him something of a folk hero during his thirty-four years, and the popularity of his recordings inspired many young African Americans to emulate his unique strengths, both instrumental and lyrical.

"Good Morning, School Girl." This song's loping rhythm and catchy, atypical blues structure were borrowed from an earlier work ("Airplane Blues," by Sleepy John Estes, 1935). Williamson's striking lyrics, punctuated by assertive harmonica lines, were sung with a hesitant yet dynamic vocal delivery, which was destined to become his trademark. The overall effect was a sort of relaxed urgency. Williamson's first recording was an instant hit that would, over time, become a much-covered blues classic.

"Blue Bird Blues." Williamson's second recording likewise achieved commercial success, and it saw future revisions by such later blues legends as

Sonny Boy Williamson I. (Hulton Archive/Getty Images)

Howlin' Wolf. The original offers one of the most lyrically creative uses of metaphor in all recorded blues. The blue bird of its title is asked to deliver a message to Williamson's wife, Lacey Belle, often mentioned in his lyrics. The bird as messenger— especially of love—is an ancient and universal icon. However, Williamson modernized it and gave it dual meanings it by making it a blue bird: The record label for which Williamson recorded was named Bluebird, and an image of its namesake appeared on each side of its 78-rpm records. Williamson's blues became a sung letter, delivered by the medium of a commercial recording. Williamson's knack for drawing listeners into his personal world was his guileless genius, and he was aptly supported in his endeavor by the guitars of Williams and McCoy. The success of his second recording would inspire him to record "Blue Bird Blues Pt. 2" in 1938.

"Decoration Blues." The harmonica's ability to mimic the human voice and to make sounds akin to choking and crying is put to stunning use in this performance. It opens with Williamson's sobbing harmonica, answered by trilled figures on the mandolin of Rachell. Williams's guitar joins them as Sonny Boy sings a blues elegy for a dead woman he has promised to bring flowers "every Decoration Day." While death was no stranger to blues lyrics, Williamson sharpens the topic by use of details associated with observance of the holiday now called Memorial Day. The trio's playing builds to crescendos of mournful passion even as Williamson's focused lyrics drive home the theme, every verse ending with a reference to Decoration Day as its tag. This darkly emotional, lyrically crafted performance made a deep impression on listeners. It would be covered by such later blues artists as John Lee Hooker and Sonny Boy Williamson II.

Musical Legacy

Williamson inspired younger musicians to take up the harmonica, and many informally claimed the "Sonny Boy" name, as if it were a brand for blues harmonica players and singers. His untimely death cleared the way for one artist, Rice Miller, to use the name on records. Miller extended Williamson's legacy into the amplified blues sound that emerged after World War II, but, as early as 1940, Williamson had recorded with a drummer in per-

formances that hinted at the future direction of blues. Additionally, Williamson's observational skills and natural songwriting abilities would influence not only harmonica players who fronted bands but also the entire next generation of blues songwriters, most significantly Willie Dixon.

Mark Humphrey

Further Reading

Field, Kim. *Harmonicas, Harps, and Heavy Breathers: The Evolution of the People's Instrument.* New York: Fireside, 1993. Field offers an entry on Williamson's career and influence in a work that chronicles the history of the harmonica and its best-known players in a variety of musical genres.

Palmer, Robert. *Deep Blues.* New York: Viking Press, 1981. Palmer's excellent book offers deft observations, framing Williamson in the larger context of the evolution of the blues.

Rowe, Mike. *Chicago Blues: The City and the Music.* New York: Da Capo Press, 1975. Rowe's thorough and well-written account of the development of the blues in Chicago offers an appraisal of Williamson's unique contribution to the blues.

Santelli, Robert. *The Big Book of Blues.* New York: Penguin, 1993. The entry on Williamson offers a succinct overview of his style and influence.

See also: Cotton, James; Dixon, Willie; Hooker, John Lee; Howlin' Wolf; James, Elmore; Williamson, Sonny Boy, II.

Sonny Boy Williamson II
American blues singer, songwriter, and harmonica player

Williamson was the first blues harmonica player known to use amplification and was among the first Delta blues artists to perform live on radio.

Born: December 5, 1899; Glendora, Mississippi
Died: May 25, 1965; Helena, Arkansas
Also known as: Aleck Ford Miller (birth name); Rice Miller

Principal recordings

ALBUMS: *Down and Out Blues*, 1959; *Sonny Boy Williamson and Memphis Slim in Paris*, 1963 (with Memphis Slim); *Help Me*, 1964; *In Memorium*, 1965.

SINGLES: "Eyesight to the Blind," 1951; "Nine Below Zero," 1951; "Don't Start Me to Talkin'," 1955; "Keep It to Yourself," 1956.

The Life

Born near Glendora in the Mississippi Delta, the son of Millie Ford and Jim Miller was given the name Aleck, though he was known by many as Rice. He probably began playing harmonica in his early teens. It ceased to be a pastime when a reported fight with his stepfather prompted him to leave home and to begin the itinerant life of a bluesman. By the early 1930's, he was becoming well known across a wide area encompassing parts of Mississippi, Arkansas, Tennessee, and Missouri. In his travels, he frequently teamed with other itinerant bluesmen, notable among them the singer-guitarists Robert Johnson, Elmore James, and Howlin' Wolf (Chester Burnett), to whom he passed some of his expertise on harmonica.

In 1935 Williamson settled briefly in Helena, Arkansas, a town to which he would return throughout his life. In the late 1930's, Robert Junior Lockwood became his partner, and they jointly explored the then-novel electrical amplification of instruments. Blues songwriter Willie Dixon vividly recalled hearing the Williamson-Lockwood team playing on the streets of Greenville in the late 1930's. By 1941 the duo was bringing a bold new blues sound to live radio broadcasts on Helena's station KFFA, sponsored by King Biscuit Flour. The daily King Biscuit Time broadcasts were heard throughout the Delta.

Williamson recorded for the first time in 1951 for the Jackson-based label Trumpet. When it folded four years later, Williamson's recording contract was sold to the Chicago-based Chess label. His first recordings for Chess featured the band of Muddy Waters, and he would later record with his old friend Lockwood and such new talents as Buddy Guy.

European tours between 1963 and 1965 introduced him to new audiences, and he recorded in

Sonny Boy Williamson II. (Hulton Archive/Getty Images)

England with popular rock bands the Yardbirds and the Animals. He returned to Helena in 1965, he resumed his old King Biscuit Time broadcasts, and he died there on May 25.

The Music

Williamson was a key figure in the development of blues after World War II, in which amplified ensembles were the dominant force. He had pioneered the amplification of the harmonica prior to World War II, and his live radio broadcasts in the 1940's were as influential among developing Delta-based blues players as his later recordings would be nationally. The fact that he appropriated the name of an established recording artist may simply have been a promotional convenience at a time when the media were localized, and few would have noticed that he was not the Williamson who recorded for Bluebird. This Williamson was an individual who, borrowed name aside, created a musical persona entirely distinct from the first Sonny Boy Williamson. Indeed, he was one of the great "characters" in all American vernacular music, one never forgotten by anyone who worked with him or who saw him perform.

"Eyesight to the Blind." Williamson's first recording at his debut session in 1951 was of an original song that was one of his best and that would be closely associated with him throughout his career. Williamson's witty lyrical bragging dares his listeners to believe the magical powers he attributes to his beloved. He credits his woman with rousing a dying man to leave his deathbed to praise her beauty. This is the sort of clever fantasy in which Williamson reveled. His performance at his initial session bristles with the enthusiasm of an artist who knows he has a great song at hand and who delights in delivering it. The performance suffers only from the quality of the recording: Trumpet was a small regional label with far from first-rate equipment. Six years later, Williamson rerecorded the song at Chess with professional engineering and backing from pianist Otis Spann from Muddy Waters's band and his old friend Robert Lockwood on guitar. The song, inexplicably retitled "Born Blind," was performed in a more subdued manner and at a more relaxed pace, but the clever lyrics and assertive harmonica solo benefit from the vastly improved sound quality.

"Nine Below Zero." This song was recorded early in Williamson's career, and he returned to it later. Again, his lyrics employ exaggeration for dramatic effect: in this instance, to underline the cruelty of a woman who waits till sub-zero temperatures set in before putting him out "for another man." The 1951 Trumpet recording finds Williamson delivering vocals that are plaintive as he pleads his case against such injustice. His harmonica solo is front and center, though the badly balanced recording renders Elmore James's guitar nearly inaudible. By contrast, the 1961 Chess recording of the same song is a minor masterpiece benefiting from a radically different arrangement and vastly superior audio engineering. This time Williamson's voice sounds worn out, yet his backing musicians use their combined skills to support him musically.

Spann's piano is a steady bulwark, Luther Tucker's stinging lead guitar punctuates Williamson's litany of injuries, and Lockwood's distorted rhythm guitar frames the bass lines of Willie Dixon and the crack drumming of Fred Below. The overall impact has as strong an impact as any Chicago blues recording of its time.

"Don't Start Me to Talkin'." This was the second song Williamson recorded at his first session for Chess. It became his first single release on the Chess subsidiary label, Checker, and it became his biggest chart hit: It peaked at number seven on the rhythm-and-blues charts in 1955. Williamson's energy and the crack backing of Muddy Waters and his band in their prime demonstrate why this was Williamson's biggest hit: It represents the cream of the era's blues crop in action.

"Keep It to Yourself." This recording opens with a blaring flourish on harmonica, Williamson riveting the listener's attention to his tale of infidelity and the advice he offers in the song's title. The guitars of Lockwood and Tucker blend as a single strong instrument, Spann's piano sits this one out, and the resulting sound is a more developed version of what Delta listeners heard on the King Biscuit Time radio shows of the 1940's. Williamson's second greatest chart success, this peaked at number fourteen on the rhythm-and-blues charts in 1956.

"Help Me." Although this song appeared late in Williamson's career, it did show up on the rhythm-and-blues charts. It is essentially a groove tune built around a framework lifted from Booker T. and the MGs' 1962 hit, "Green Onions." Compared with the lyrical wit displayed in his earlier songs, this one sounds like what it is: an instrumental with words added. However, the change in instrumentation—as with Booker T., an electric organ appears instead of piano—and the evident effort to update Williamson's sound for a younger audience make this a noteworthy performance. The instrumental emphasis allows Williamson to play more harmonica than usual, and there is an urgent intimacy to his plea for help.

Musical Legacy

Williamson left three distinct legacies. First, there is the legion of harmonica players who were directly influenced by his radio performances, his live shows, and his recordings. They include Howlin' Wolf, Junior Wells, James Cotton, and Little Walter Jacobs. Stylistically, Williams was a master of economy; he was less interested in virtuosic displays than in musically punctuating a song's stories. Second, his songs are marked by wit, imagination, sly humor, and a slightly bent worldview. The best of his seventy recordings for the Chess label rank with the finest Chicago blues recordings of the 1950's and early 1960's. Unlike such major contemporaries as Muddy Waters and Howlin' Wolf, Williamson rarely utilized the Chess house songwriter, Willie Dixon. Thus, Williamson's songs stand out in their originality. Unlike those whose music is heard evolving through their recordings, Williamson came to record fully formed as an artist. Any obvious changes reflect the musicians who accompanied him or the state of his health at the time of the recordings.

Third, performances Williamson made for European television while touring Europe between 1963 and 1965 have been unearthed. These showcase his unique talents and on-stage antics. They are a wonderful complement to his recorded legacy, and they help us understand how he made such a terrific impression on young European blues fans, especially those in England, where he recorded with such British beat groups as the Animals and the Yardbirds.

Mark Humphrey

Further Reading

Oakley, Giles. *The Devil's Music: A History of the Blues.* New York: Da Capo Press, 1997. Oakley's well-written overview of the genre includes a finely crafted description of a Williamson performance.

Palmer, Robert. *Deep Blues.* New York: Viking Press, 1981. Palmer effectively conveys the world of the King Biscuit entertainers and their audience.

Rowe, Mike. *Chicago Blues: The City and the Music.* New York: Da Capo Press, 1975. Rowe writes about Williamson's role in the richly creative blues milieu of 1950's Chicago.

Santelli, Robert. *The Big Book of Blues.* New York: Penguin, 1993. Santelli's blues encyclopedia entry on Williamson neatly encapsulates the man, his music, and the impact of both.

See also: Cotton, James; Howlin' Wolf; James, Elmore; Johnson, Robert; Waters, Muddy; Williamson, Sonny Boy, I.

Meredith Willson

American popular music, musical-theater, film-score, and classical composer

Willson is best known for his first two Broadway musicals, The Music Man *and* The Unsinkable Molly Brown, *as well as the fight songs for both the University of Iowa and the Iowa State University.*

Born: May 18, 1902; Mason City, Iowa
Died: June 15, 1984; Santa Monica, California
Also known as: Robert Meredith Reiniger (birth name)

Principal works

FILM SCORES: *The Lost Zeppelin,* 1929; *The Great Dictator,* 1940; *The Little Foxes,* 1941.

MUSICAL THEATER (music, lyrics, and libretto): *The Music Man,* 1957; *The Unsinkable Molly Brown,* 1960 (libretto by Richard Morris); *Here's Love,* 1963; *1491,* 1969 (libretto by Morris).

ORCHESTRAL WORKS: *Parade Fantastique,* 1924; Symphony No. 1 in F Minor, 1936 (*A Symphony of San Francisco*); Symphony No. 2 in E Minor, 1940 (*The Missions of California*); *The Jervis Bay,* 1942; *O. O. McIntyre Suite,* 1956.

SONGS (music and lyrics): "You and I," 1941; "May the Good Lord Bless and Keep You," 1950; "It's Beginning to Look a Lot Like Christmas," 1951; "Banners and Bonnets," 1952; "I See the Moon," 1954; "Chicken Fat," 1961.

The Life

Meredith Willson was born into a musical family, and by age ten he had joined the Mason City Municipal Band, playing the flute. Willson moved to New York in 1919, studying at the Damrosch Institute (later known as the Juilliard School), and he moonlighted in orchestras for film houses and theaters. Willson toured throughout the Americas (1921 to 1924) as flutist and piccolo soloist in the Sousa Band, which his brother Cedric joined in 1923. Between tours, Willson assisted scientist Lee deForest in experiments developing sound for motion pictures.

In 1924 Willson joined the New York Philharmonic, spending five years under the baton of such notables as Arturo Toscanini. In 1929 Willson moved to the West Coast to work for NBC Radio, becoming musical director of the Western division. In 1936 Willson conducted the San Francisco Symphony Orchestra in the premiere of his Symphony No. 1 in F Minor. His Symphony No. 2 in E Minor premiered in Los Angeles in 1940, the same year that Frank Sinatra and Glenn Miller recorded songs by Willson and that Willson composed the score for Charlie Chaplin's first "talkie," *The Great Dictator.*

During World War II, Willson headed the music division of the Armed Forces Radio Service. His most influential radio work came after the war with hits such as "May the Good Lord Bless and Keep You" and "It's Beginning to Look a Lot Like Christmas."

In 1957 Willson's career reached a new high when *The Music Man,* for which he had composed the book, lyrics, and music, premiered on Broadway. Drawing on the experience of his boyhood in Iowa, *The Music Man* was an instant hit. In 1960 Willson wrote the lyrics and composed the music for *The Unsinkable Molly Brown,* which ran for more

than a year on Broadway. In 1962 *The Music Man* was made into an award-winning film. Willson's 1963 show, *Here's Love,* ran for 334 performances on Broadway. Willson's success continued in 1964, when *The Unsinkable Molly Brown* was made into an Academy Award-nominated film.

Willson spent most of the remainder of his life traveling and performing the songs he had composed. His popularity continued after his death, with a Broadway revival of *The Music Man* (2000-2001), a Disney television remake of the film in 2003, and dozens of amateur productions every year. Willson died in Santa Monica, California, at the age of eighty-two, and he is buried in Mason City, Iowa.

The Music

Although he is remembered primarily for his music for Broadway shows, Willson began his musical career composing classical music, film scores, and music for radio.

Early Works. Willson's early compositions include the Symphony No. 1 in F Minor, which he conducted at the premiere in 1936, and the Symphony No. 2 in E Minor, which the Los Angeles Symphony Orchestra premiered in 1940. Both works were for the first time by the Moscow State Symphony Orchestra in 1999. Willson's score for Chaplin's first sound film, *The Great Dictator* (1940), received an Academy Award nomination, as did his score for the 1941 film *The Little Foxes.*

Willson also had numerous successes, including number-one hits, as a composer for radio. "May the Good Lord Bless and Keep You" sold more than one million copies, and it was recorded by such diverse singers as Bing Crosby, Gene Autry, Frankie Laine, and Tammy Wynette. "It's Beginning to Look a Lot Like Christmas" became a Christmas standard, recorded by Perry Como, Dean Martin, Bing Crosby, Johnny Mathis, and numerous other artists.

Meredith Willson leading the band. (Hulton Archive/Getty Images)

The Music Man. Willson's major success, however, came with his compositions for Broadway. Willson never lived in Mason City again after leaving at age seventeen, but he considered "River City" his home, and he used it as the basis for *The Music Man*, his show about an itinerant band-instrument salesman in turn-of-the-century Iowa. Today Mason City proudly boasts Music Man Square and the Meredith Willson Museum, and the city is respected for its excellent school and municipal band programs.

After five years of development and revisions, *The Music Man* opened on Broadway in December, 1957. Willson combined his classical and popular music knowledge to create a score that pleases audiences without being trite. After a traditional overture, the audiences were surprised with a spoken chorus imitating the sound of the train on which the passengers were traveling, a clever technique based on Willson's earlier radio advertising innovation, the "Talking People"—a chorus that used rhythmic speech to tout the sponsor's products. Willson's ingenuity is also clear when he interweaves Harold Hill's brash march "Seventy-six Trombones" with Marian Paroo's gentle ballad "Goodnight My Someone," and when he composes a counter-melody to the famous barbershop song, "Goodnight, Ladies," creating "Pick a Little, Talk a Little."

The Music Man won eight Tony Awards in 1958, including Best Musical, Author, Composer and Lyricist, defeating Leonard Bernstein's *West Side Story* (1957). The cast recording of *The Music Man* won the 1958 Grammy Award for Best Original Cast Album. In 1962 *The Music Man* was made into a film, which won the Academy Award for best film score, and it was nominated in several other categories. In 1963 the Beatles had a hit with Paul McCartney singing a ballad ("Till There Was You") from the film, and they included the song in their famous 1964 U.S. debut on *The Ed Sullivan Show*.

The Unsinkable Molly Brown. Willson's 1960 musical about *Titanic* survivor Margaret Brown was also a success on Broadway, running for more than a year, and it was made into a film in 1964. Still, he never surpassed the success of *The Music Man*, and his next two attempts were less successful: *Here's Love* (based on the 1947 film *Miracle on Thirty-fourth Street*) closed in less than a year, and *1491* never made it to Broadway.

Musical Legacy

The Music Man forms the foundation of Willson's legacy. One of the most often performed Broadway musicals, it also serves as a source of individual songs performed by choruses, soloists, bands, and orchestras, guaranteeing Willson's continuing popularity as a composer.

In addition to his Academy Awards, Grammy Awards, and Tony Awards, Willson received honors from Presidents John F. Kennedy, Lyndon Johnson, and Ronald Reagan. Willson was a great supporter of higher education, and he was granted honorary degrees from two Iowa colleges: Parsons College (1956) and Coe College (1960). Willson later honored Coe with a donation, used to fund an electronic music studio. His library is housed at the University of Iowa. In 1990, after his widow made a substantial donation, the Juilliard School named its only residence hall after its famous alumnus.

William S. Carson

Further Reading

Skipper, John C. *Meredith Willson, The Unsinkable Music Man*. Mason City, Iowa: Savas Woodbury, 2000. Journalist Skipper, a fellow resident of Mason City, weaves a folksy tale of Willson. Includes illustrations.

Willson, Meredith. *And I Stood There with My Piccolo*. New York: Doubleday, 1948. An amusing autobiographical sketch that precedes Willson's Broadway fame.

_____. *But He Doesn't Know the Territory*. New York: G. P. Putnam's Sons, 1959. Willson tells the story of the birth of *The Music Man* in his own words.

_____. *Eggs I Have Laid*. New York: Henry Holt, 1955. A tongue-in-cheek account of some of the less successful moments of Willson's career, with particular emphasis on his work in radio.

_____. *Who Did What to Fedalia?* New York: Doubleday, 1952. Willson's only novel, about a young Iowa girl who heads to New York to become a singer.

See also: Bernstein, Leonard; Crosby, Bing; Elliot, Cass; Loesser, Frank; McCartney, Sir Paul; Mathis, Johnny; Miller, Glenn; Sinatra, Frank; Sousa, John Philip; Toscanini, Arturo; Wynette, Tammy.

Brian Wilson

American rock bassist, pianist, singer, and songwriter

Wilson combined intricate vocal harmonies, the energy of early rock and roll, and wall-of-sound production techniques with lyrics that evoked the simple and sunny joys of youth.

Born: June 20, 1942; Hawthorne, California
Also known as: Brian Douglas Wilson (full name)
Member of: The Beach Boys

Principal recordings

ALBUMS (solo): *Brian Wilson*, 1988; *I Just Wasn't Made for These Times*, 1995; *Orange Crate Art*, 1995; *Imagination*, 1998; *Gettin' in over My Head*, 2004; *Smile*, 2004; *What I Really Want for Christmas*, 2005; *That Lucky Old Sun*, 2008.

ALBUMS (with the Beach Boys): *Surfin' Safari*, 1962; *Surfin' USA*, 1963; *Surfer Girl*, 1963; *Little Deuce Coupe*, 1963; *Shut Down, Vol. 2*, 1964; *All Summer Long*, 1964; *The Beach Boys' Christmas Album*, 1964; *The Beach Boys Christmas Special*, 1964; *Today!*, 1965; *Summer Days (And Summer Nights!!)*, 1965; *Pet Sounds*, 1966; *Smiley Smile*, 1967; *Wild Honey*, 1967; *Friends*, 1968; *Stack-O-Tracks*, 1968; *20/20*, 1969; *Sunflower*, 1970; *Surf's Up*, 1971; *Carl and the Passions—So Tough*, 1972; *Holland*, 1973; *Fifteen Big Ones*, 1976; *Love You*, 1977; *M.I.U. Album*, 1978; *L.A. (Light Album)*, 1979; *Keepin' the Summer Alive*, 1980; *The Beach Boys*, 1985; *Still Cruisin'*, 1989; *Summer in Paradise*, 1992.

SINGLES (with the Beach Boys): "Surfin' USA," 1963; "Barbara Ann," 1965; "Help Me Rhonda," 1965; "Kokomo," 1988.

WRITINGS OF INTEREST: *Wouldn't It Be Nice*, 1991.

The Life

Brian Douglas Wilson was the oldest of three musically talented sons born to Murry and Audree Wilson in Hawthorne, California. A typical middle-class child, Wilson distinguished himself at an early age with his ability to re-create the sophisticated jazzy harmonies of his favorite vocal groups. At his insistence, his younger brothers, Carl and

Dennis, and his cousin, Mike Love (three-fifths of the future Beach Boys), learned to sing the rudiments of what would become Wilson's trademark Beach Boys vocal arrangements.

Wilson's outwardly gregarious nature—he was a popular high school athlete and a natural leader—masked inner turmoil, particularly a tumultuous relationship with his father. Wilson later described his formation and prolific activity on behalf of the Beach Boys as a struggle to assert his independence and to earn the approval of his father.

From 1963 to 1965, the Beach Boys placed nine songs and eight albums in the Top 10. Finding himself at twenty-two a millionaire responsible for maintaining and continuously improving the nation's top hit machine, Wilson began to manifest the symptoms of mental illness. By the time he oversaw the elaborate recording of the group's seminal *Pet Sounds* album and "Good Vibrations" single, he had quit touring and began to seek solace in drugs.

After his inability to complete the ambitious *Smile* album, Wilson withdrew from public life and became as famous for his drug- and paranoia-fueled eccentricities as he had been for his prodigious and inventive music. Although nominally a Beach Boy, his contributions to the group's music dwindled.

From 1975 to 1985, Wilson became an overweight, often incoherent caricature. Even Wilson's partial recovery, with the aid of a controversial therapist, ended when a medical board forced the therapist to surrender his license.

Wilson began a personal and professional renaissance in the mid-1990's, marrying his second wife (Melinda Ledbetter) and finding in the Los Angeles rock band the Wondermints and in musical director-guitarist Jeffrey Foskett partners with whom he could resume not only touring but also recording. With this ensemble and the help of lyricist Van Dyke Parks, Wilson released a complete version of *Smile* in 2004, to strong sales and rapturous critical acclaim.

The Music

Although his younger brother Dennis gave him the idea to write about the Southern California surfing fad, and the other Beach Boys (plus a rotating stable of lyricists) helped bring his compositions to life, it was Wilson's inventive combination of 1950's vocal-group harmony, rock and roll, painstaking production, and, in the Beach Boys' first five years, frequent lead singing that made the Beach Boys' songs an indelible fixture in American pop culture. The California of Wilson's imagination was not a tourist attraction but a state of mind representing the transient innocence of youth and the misfortune awaiting those who cling to it. Ironically, Wilson found himself adrift for most of his adult life, depressed by his inability to match the quality or quantity of his early output and emotionally and psychologically depleted by his self-destructive attempts at coping with this failure. That he continued composing during his bleakest decades testifies to the durability of his talent. That he recovered and returned to public performing in the late 1990's, completing his long-unfinished masterpiece *Smile* in 2004, testifies to the durability of his will and to the inspirational power of his music.

Surfer Girl. The third Beach Boys album (and the second to appear in 1963) gave Wilson production credit for the first time. Although the high-energy hits "Little Deuce Coupe" and "Catch a Wave" were typical beach-crazed anthems, the title song and "In My Room" unveiled the vulnerability, introspection, and harmonic sophistication for which Wilson would ultimately become best known.

Summer Days (and Summer Nights!!). The highlight of this 1965 album was "California Girls," a song that found Wilson achieving creative heights that he would not surpass until he constructed "Good Vibrations" over a six-month period one year later.

Pet Sounds. This album, the instrumental portions of which Wilson recorded with a studio ensemble in 1966 while the rest of the Beach Boys were on tour, garnered a lot of attention. It was not truly rock and roll; in fact, some of the music nearly qualified as easy listening. The Beatles, nevertheless, found it so impressive that they recorded *Sgt. Pepper's Lonely Hearts Club Band* in an effort to compete. Although *Pet Sounds'* moody tone may have confused Beach Boys fans, it made the Top 10 on the strength of the singles "Wouldn't It Be Nice," "Sloop John B.," "Caroline No," and "God Only Knows," one of the most sophisticated and gorgeous songs in Wilson's body of work.

Smiley Smile. Released in the wake of Wilson's abandonment of *Smile*, this 1967 oddity documented the Beach Boys' collapse into disarray in general and Wilson's descent into drugs in particular. Were it not for "Good Vibrations" and "Heroes and Villains," neither of which would be available elsewhere for years, it undoubtedly would have sold even fewer copies than it did.

Fifteen Big Ones. Accompanied on its appearance in 1976 by a massive "Brian's Back" promotional campaign, this best-selling album consisted largely of covers of 1950's and 1960's hits and was actually a group Beach Boys effort, although one that included more participation from Wilson than any other Beach Boys album in a decade.

Love You. Released in 1977, this album (also known as *The Beach Boys Love You*) became a cult favorite on the strength of its playfully catchy melodies. However, Wilson's lyrics revealed that he was, as many suspected, a dysfunctional eccentric.

Brian Wilson. Lavishly produced, this album appeared in 1988 to high praise from most critics. The public, however, found the partially rehabilitated Wilson's heavily assisted attempt at recapturing his youthful glories cumbersome.

I Just Wasn't Made for These Times. This 1995 sound track to the documentary produced by Don Was represented an important step in reintroducing Wilson to serious performing and audiences to the fully rehabilitated Wilson.

Smile. By the time Wilson and his touring Foskett-led Wondermints band recorded what had been for almost forty years the most famous "lost" album in rock-and-roll history, they had already become proficient at presenting it onstage. What had in 1966 and 1967 been so difficult to construct, Wilson completed with relative ease in 2004. There was pre-release apprehension about whether *Smile* would live up to the promise of the parts of the original that had been released piecemeal over the years. Nevertheless, the work's high quality dispelled doubts among fans and critics alike. Perhaps the biggest surprise was Wilson's use of Tony Asher's original lyrics to "Good Vibrations" instead of the Mike Love lyrics with which fans had long been familiar.

Musical Legacy

Besides writing, arranging, singing, and playing on more than two dozen of the rock-and-roll era's most popular singles and launching the surf-music craze, Wilson pioneered a technologically sophisticated style of production that would influence not only the Beatles but also a generation of post-1960's acts. Long after Wilson had retreated from public life, echoes of and homages to his style and approach could be heard in the recordings of acts as diverse as the Electric Light Orchestra, the Carpenters, Chicago, Todd Rundgren, Three Dog Night, and the Raspberries. "Bohemian Rhapsody," the six-minute signature song of the British hard-rock band Queen, an international Top 10 single in 1976 and 1991, was in many ways a direct descendant of Wilson's "Good Vibrations," consisting of several separately recorded and stylistically diverse sections edited into a dazzling whole.

Inducted as a Beach Boy into the Rock and Roll Hall of Fame in 1988, Wilson would, upon his return to mental stability and public performing in the 1990's, become the recipient of other honors as well, including inductions into the Vocal Group Hall of Fame (with the Beach Boys) in 1998 and the UK Music Hall of Fame in 2006. On December 1, 2007, he was recognized, along with Steve Martin, Leon Fleisher, Martin Scorsese, and Diana Ross, at the prestigious annual Kennedy Center Honors ceremony, for the excellence of his contribution to the culture of the United States.

Arsenio Orteza

Further Reading

Carlin, Peter Ames. *Catch a Wave: The Rise, Fall, and Redemption of the Beach Boys' Brian Wilson*. New York: Rodale, 2006. Ending on a note of optimism, this well-written and comprehensively researched biography was completed after Wilson's successful return to the stage as a touring performer and the 2004 release of *Smile*.

Gaines, Steven. *Heroes and Villains: The True Story of the Beach Boys*. New York: Da Capo, 1986. The book demythologizes the Beach Boys by detailing the band members' real-life turmoil, and its tabloid-like focus gives short shrift to the music.

Granata, Charles L. *Wouldn't It Be Nice: Brian Wilson and the Making of the Beach Boys' Pet Sounds*. Chicago: Chicago Review Press, 2003. A painstaking investigation into the making of *Pet Sounds*, what many consider to be Wilson's finest mo-

ment as a singer, a songwriter, a producer, and a pop cultural force.

Leaf, David. *The Beach Boys and the California Myth*. New York: Grosset & Dunlap, 1978. The first extensive treatment of Wilson's music as a significant cultural phenomenon.

White, Timothy. *The Nearest Faraway Place: The Beach Boys and the Southern California Experience*. New York: Henry Holt, 1996. Entertaining Wilson-Beach Boys narrative, although there may be too much emphasis on the role played by Wilson's ancestors in his artistic and temperamental development.

Williams, Paul. *Brian Wilson and the Beach Boys: How Deep Is the Ocean?* London: Omnibus Press, 2003. Several decades' worth of essays on Wilson and the Beach Boys by the rock critic and the founder of *Crawdaddy* magazine.

See also: Bacharach, Burt; Burke, Solomon; Campbell, Glen; Carpenter, Karen; Newman, Randy; Spector, Phil.

Jackie Wilson
American rhythm-and-blues singer and songwriter

An important transitional figure, Wilson led rhythm and blues toward soul, and in the process he helped music largely associated with African Americans cross over to achieve success on the pop charts. He was noted for blending an evocative voice with crowd-pleasing dance moves.

Born: June 9, 1934; Detroit, Michigan
Died: January 21, 1984; Mount Holly, New Jersey
Also known as: Jack Leroy Wilson (full name); Mr. Excitement
Member of: Billy Ward and the Dominoes

Principal recordings

ALBUMS (solo): *He's So Fine*, 1958; *Dogging Around*, 1959; *Lonely Teardrops*, 1959; *So Much*, 1959; *A Woman, a Lover, a Friend*, 1960; *Jackie Sings the Blues*, 1960; *Night*, 1960; *By Special Request*, 1961; *Try a Little Tenderness*, 1961; *You Ain't Heard Nothin' Yet*, 1961; *Body and Soul*, 1962;

Baby Workout, 1963; *Merry Christmas from Jackie Wilson*, 1963; *Shake a Hand*, 1963; *The World's Greatest Melodies*, 1963; *Somethin' Else!*, 1964; *Soul Time*, 1965; *Spotlight on Jackie Wilson*, 1965; *Whispers*, 1966; *Higher and Higher*, 1967; *Do Your Thing*, 1968; *I Get the Sweetest Feeling*, 1968; *Manufacturers of Soul*, 1968; *Two Much*, 1968 (with Count Basie); *This Love Is Real*, 1970; *It's All a Part of Love*, 1971; *You Got Me Walking*, 1971; *Beautiful Day*, 1973; *Nowstalgia*, 1974; *Nobody but You*, 1976.

ALBUMS (with Billy Ward and the Dominoes): *Billy Ward and His Dominoes*, 1954; *Billy Ward* (with Jackie Wilson and His Dominoes), 1957.

The Life

Jack Leroy Wilson was born in Detroit, Michigan, the only child of Jack and Eliza Mae Wilson. Though he began singing as a child and led a performing group—the Ever Ready Gospel Singers—as a teen, Jackie was also a member of the Shakers street gang, and he was frequently in trouble. Confined to a juvenile detention facility in Lansing, he learned to box, and later he competed in the Golden Gloves tournament as a welterweight.

In 1950 Jackie dropped out of ninth grade at Highland Park High School. The following year, he married Freda Hood, who was pregnant, and their daughter was born in March, 1951. At the time, Wilson sang with a group known as the Thrillers. In 1953 he successfully auditioned to replace Clyde McPhatter—who left to form the Drifters—as lead singer of the Dominoes. The group had several rhythm-and-blues hits before Wilson left to pursue a solo career in 1957.

As a soloist, Wilson produced a steady stream of hits until the early 1970's. Along the way he survived gunshot wounds inflicted by a jealous girlfriend in 1961 and the 1970 shooting death of his oldest son, Jackie. In 1975, while performing at a Dick Clark-produced show, Wilson suffered a heart attack, resulting in severe brain damage. He remained semi-comatose for more than eight years until his death in 1984.

The Music

Blessed with a pure tenor voice and perfect pitch, Wilson added athletic dance moves to his repertoire during live performances. His exhilarating,

Jackie Wilson. (CBS/Landov)

frankly sexual entertainment style earned him a distinctive nickname from avid fans (particularly females): Mr. Excitement. Though he had several hits with the Dominoes in the early 1950's, most of Wilson's best work was done as a solo artist, where he demonstrated a wide vocal range, from rumbling growls to soaring falsetto, and an uncanny ability to convincingly sing an incredible variety of material. Songs ranged from his forte, rhythm and blues, to doo-wop, rock and roll, love ballads, and easy-listening standards. Much of Wilson's early success came from tunes he sang by the songwriting partnership of Berry Gordy, Jr. (a former boxer, who used royalties from Wilson's hits to found Motown Records), and Roquel "Billy" Davis (who later wrote songs for Chess Records). During his prematurely curtailed career, Wilson made rhythm-and-blues and Top 40 charts more than forty-five times, released more than twenty albums, and scored six number-one hits.

"Reet Petite (The Sweetest Girl in Town)." Wilson's first single as a solo performer, this Gordy-Davis composition hit the Top 100 on *Billboard* charts in 1957, and it rose to the Top 10 in England. Nearly thirty years later, in 1986, Wilson's version was used in England for a television commercial, and it was the number-one single in England for four weeks.

"Lonely Teardrops." Another Gordy-Davis composition, this 1958 release hit number one on rhythm-and-blues charts, and it made the Top Ten on pop charts. The tune most closely identified with Wilson, and a showcase for his vocal range, it was the last song he ever sang. As he stood on stage September 29, 1975, at the Latin Casino in Cherry Hill, New Jersey, and launched into the opening lyrics, "My heart is cryin', cryin'," he was stricken with a massive heart attack and fell unconscious to the floor. Initially, the audience thought it was a gesture to dramatize the song, and spontaneously began to cheer and applaud until it became obvious something was wrong with Wilson.

"(Stop) Doggin' Around." Another 1960 number-one rhythm-and-blues hit, this was harder edged than most of Wilson's material. It was one of four double-sided singles released during 1960-1961, in which seven of eight songs—"Night"/ "Doggin' Around," "All My Love"/"A Woman, a Lover, a Friend," "Alone at Last"/"Am I the Man," and "My Empty Arms"/"The Tear of the Year"— made the pop or rhythm-and-blues Top 10 charts.

"Baby Workout." Wilson cowrote this hit with Alonzo Tucker of the Midnighters. The song was an obvious attempt to capitalize on the early 1960's fad of introducing hot new dances—such as the Twist, the Mashed Potato, the Frug, and the Watusi—in the lyrics. "Baby Workout" urged listeners to "Put your hands on your hip/And let your backbone slip/And work out."

"(Your Love Keeps Lifting Me) Higher and Higher." This Motown-flavored song, written by Gary Jackson, Raynard Miner, and Carl Smith— with background vocals from the Andantes and instrument work from the Motown house band, the Funk Brothers—was recorded in Chicago and became a big hit for Wilson in 1967. It was on Top 40 charts for twelve weeks, peaking at number six. It also reached number eleven on the British charts in 1969.

"I Get the Sweetest Feeling." Following a mid-1960's slump in popularity that lasted for several years, Wilson hit the charts again in 1968 with a Van

McCoy-Alicia Evelyn tune recorded with Chicago soul music producer Carl Davis that climbed to number nine in England.

Musical Legacy

A posthumous inductee into the Rock and Roll Hall of Fame in 1987, Wilson was instrumental in helping rhythm and blues grow into soul and funk. At the same time, he was a driving force in broadening the appeal of what was perceived as solely an ethnic genre of music, and he was one of the first black artists to achieve success on the mainstream pop charts. Though his abundant recordings were often overproduced and featured songs more appropriate for middle-of-the-road crooners, Wilson's distinctive voice always improved the material. A dynamic performer who enlivened shows with spins, twirls, splits, leaps, and fancy footwork, Wilson greatly influenced the performance styles of such artists as Elvis Presley, James Brown, Prince, and Michael Jackson. Jackson acknowledged Wilson's influence, dedicating 1984's Grammy Award-winning Album of the Year, *Thriller*, to Wilson.

Jack Ewing

Further Reading

Carter, Doug. *The Black Elvis: Jackie Wilson*. Berkeley, Calif.: Heyday, 1998. A complete and thoroughly researched biography of Wilson, Includes photographs and discography.

Douglas, Tony. *Jackie Wilson: Lonely Teardrops*. New York: Routledge, 2005. An in-depth biography of Wilson focusing on his self-destructive behavior. Includes numerous photographs.

_____. *Jackie Wilson: The Man, the Music, the Mob*. Edinburgh, Scotland: Mainstream, 2001. An illustrated story of the singer told by his colleagues and his paramours, this deals with some shady, behind-the-scenes characters in Wilson's life.

Miller, James. *Flowers in the Dustbin: The Rise of Rock and Roll, 1947-1977*. New York: Fireside/Simon & Schuster, 2000. This is a chronicle of the musical world during the three decades between Wynonie Harris's 1947 "Good Rockin' Tonight" and Presley's 1977 death, a period that encompassed Wilson's entire career.

Pruter, Robert. *Jackie Wilson—Mr. Excitement!* Milwaukee, Wis.: Hal Leonard, 1995. This songbook contains a brief biography of Wilson, plus photographs and a complete discography.

See also: Basie, Count; Brown, James; Green, Al; Jamerson, James; Jarrett, Keith; Presley, Elvis; Prince.

Julia Wolfe

American classical composer

In the late 1980's, Wolfe emerged as a leading composer in the postminimalist generation. She helped establish the Bang on a Can Festival in New York City, an important venue for new music.

Born: December 18, 1958; Philadelphia, Pennsylvania

Principal works

KEYBOARD WORKS: *my lips from speaking*, 1993; *East Broadway*, 1996; *Compassion*, 2001; *Earring*, 2001.

OPERA (music): *Carbon Copy Building*, 1999 (with Michael Gordon and David Lang; words by Ben Katchor).

ORCHESTRAL WORKS: *on seven-star-shoes*, 1985; *Song at Daybreak*, 1986; *Amber Waves of Grain*, 1988; *Girlfriend*, 1988; *The Vermeer Room*, 1989; *Four Marys*, 1991; *Window of Vulnerability*, 1991; *Arsenal of Democracy*, 1993; *Early That Summer*, 1993; *Lick*, 1994; *Tell Me Everything*, 1994; *Steam*, 1995; *Believing*, 1997; *Mink Stole*, 1997; *Close Together*, 2000; *Dark Full Ride*, 2002; *My Beautiful Scream*, 2003; *Cruel Sister*, 2004; Accordion Concerto, 2005.

The Life

Julia Wolfe studied composition at the University of Michigan in Ann Arbor, focusing on serial techniques. While there, she helped found the Wild Swan Theater with three other female students, and their productions featured folk-inspired stories for which Wolfe composed the music, often singing while accompanying herself on the dulcimer, an Appalachian folk instrument. During her stay in Ann Arbor, Wolfe met and later married fellow composer Michael Gordon in 1984. The pair subse-

quently enrolled at Yale University for graduate study with composer Martin Bresnick. As Wolfe confessed in an interview with arts writer David Krasnow, she found her instruction in serialism suffocating and felt a renewed freedom under Bresnick. After graduating from Yale, Wolfe and Gordon collaborated with fellow alumnus David Lang in 1987 to form the Bang on a Can festival. They intended the festival to be a haven for genre-defying music, pieces that blurred the boundaries among art, popular, and world music, much in the way their own compositions did. The festival met with great success and developed into an organization complete with its own recording label, Cantaloupe. In addition, the festival generated a critically acclaimed performing ensemble, a sextet called Bang on a Can All-Stars, and a commissioning fund to support new composers.

In 1992, a pivotal point in Wolfe's career, she received a Fulbright Fellowship to work with the Amsterdam-based Orkest de Volharding. The orchestra was founded by Louis Andriessen, a highly regarded Dutch composer who was an important influence on Wolfe's aesthetic outlook. Wolfe has continued to compose, garnering for her work praise and commissions, and she has maintained her involvement with Bang on a Can and its projects.

The Music

Wolfe's style is often labeled postminimalist or totalist, although these categories do not fully explain the variety of her music. Above all, Wolfe's style is a conglomeration of her personal musical experiences: singing show tunes at the piano with her mother; discovering composers George Crumb, György Ligeti, Steve Reich, and Ludwig van Beethoven at college; and a late exposure to Led Zeppelin and James Brown. The majority of Wolfe's compositions are cast in one movement and rarely feature soloists. Her music often displays a dense texture, rhythmic complexity, and an expert use of color. Certain works, such as *Window of Vulnerability*, *Early That Summer*, and *Arsenal of Democracy*, carry political connotations. The calm yet fiercely loud *Window of Vulnerability* combines the literal meaning of the military term with a reflection on humanity's fragility, while *Arsenal of Democracy*, commissioned by Andriessen's Orkest de Volharding, is a thunderously dissonant antiwar assault. Wolfe's political orientation may well stem from her teachers, notably Bresnick and Andriessen, whose music sometimes engages in political commentary.

Carbon Copy Building. In 1999 Wolfe, Gordon, and Lang collaborated with comic-book artist Ben Katchor on the opera *Carbon Copy Building*. Dubbed a comic-book opera, the work premiered at Settembre Musica Festival in Torino, Italy. Though it received a Village Voice Obie award, given to honor excellence in Off-Broadway productions, its New York premiere was met with mixed reviews.

The Vermeer Room. Written in 1989, this one-movement piece for orchestra takes its inspiration from seventeenth century Dutch painter Jan Vermeer's *A Girl Asleep*. The work has a programmatic tinge as Wolfe depicts the girl's dreams with tumultuous sounds. Wolfe limits her pitch material, but she does not rely on strictly minimalist repetition. Rather, the piece derives its structure from the gradual layering of timbres. It begins with a drawn-out crescendo, punctuated by clanging interjections. It becomes more insistent as it restates the opening material, leading to a slow decrescendo. The work ends abruptly, like a sleeper being startled awake. Interestingly, for this work, Wolfe chose for her inspiration a painter known for his sensitivity to light and color, qualities prominent in her own works.

Four Marys. Wolfe wrote *Four Marys* for the Cassatt Quartet, which premiered it at the Bang on a Can festival of 1991. The shifting microtonal fabric of the one-movement work alludes to the dulcimer, recalling Wolfe's days at the Wild Swan Theater. Wolfe translates the dulcimer's idiomatic drone and melodic pitch-bending into the medium of the string quartet. The piece has a nearly inaudible beginning, and then it juxtaposes sections of static wailing with driving, rhythmically active ones. Three-quarters of the way through the composition, a melody emerges from a background of sirenlike glissandi. This tune is reminiscent of the Scottish folk song of the title without being a direct quotation. *Four Marys* concludes with a gradual diminuendo.

Lick. Wolfe composed *Lick* for the Bang on the Can All-Stars in 1994. The work showcases the sextet's abilities, becoming the ensemble's signature piece. Scored for soprano saxophone, cello, double bass, electric guitar, piano, and percussion, the work betrays an instrumentation with decidedly popular leanings. About *Lick*, Wolfe mentioned that her approach to its rhythm was influenced by funk artist Brown and his predilection for tugging at the beat. *Lick* also took a melodic cue from Led Zeppelin, especially the guitar riffs that evoke Jimmy Page.

Musical Legacy

Wolfe has one foot in the classical world and the other foot in the popular world, which is reflected in her compositions. As a young composer in the late 1980's, Wolfe worked outside academia, creating an outlet for her music through the Bang on a Can festival, which developed into an ongoing event. In 2003 Wolfe began to teach composition at the Manhattan School of Music, taking the new role of pedagogue. Wolfe's compositions have fared well, receiving multiple performances in an era when many new works get only one hearing. Bang on a Can and its offshoots are among her most memorable achievements.

Alyson Payne

Further Reading

Gann, Kyle. *American Music in the Twentieth Century*. New York: Schirmer Books, 1997. Composer and critic Gann situates Wolfe in the larger twentieth century panorama.

Krasnow, David. "Julia Wolfe." *BOMB Magazine* 77 (2001): 14-21. An interview with Wolfe encompassing her style, influences, and everyday life with composer-husband Gordon.

Swed, Mark. "American Composer: Julia Wolfe." *Chamber Music* 13 (1996): 12. A short overview of Wolfe and her compositions, focusing on her earlier works.

See also: Brown, James; Crumb, George; Ligeti, György; Page, Jimmy.

Stevie Wonder

American rhythm-and-blues singer, songwriter, and pianist

A popular recording artist for Motown Records, Wonder is a critically acclaimed singer-songwriter working in the rhythm-and-blues tradition. His songs combine complex modulations and rhythms with socially aware lyrics.

Born: May 13, 1950; Saginaw, Michigan
Also known as: Stevland Hardaway Judkins (birth name); Little Stevie Wonder

Principal recordings

ALBUMS: *The Jazz Soul of Little Stevie*, 1962; *Tribute to Uncle Ray*, 1962; *With a Song in My Heart*, 1963; *Workout Stevie, Workout*, 1963; *Stevie at the Beach*, 1964; *Stevie Wonder*, 1965; *Down to Earth*, 1966; *Uptight*, 1966; *I Was Made to Love Her*, 1967; *Someday at Christmas*, 1967; *For Once in My Life*, 1968; *My Cherie Amour*, 1969; *Signed, Sealed, and Delivered*, 1970; *Where I'm Coming From*, 1971; *Music of My Mind*, 1972; *Talking Book*, 1972; *Innervisions*, 1973; *Fulfillingness' First Finale*, 1974; *Songs in the Key of Life*, 1976; *Journey Through the Secret Life of Plants*, 1979; *Hotter than July*, 1980; *The Woman in Red*, 1984 (with Dionne Warwick and Ben Bridges); *In Square Circle*, 1985; *Characters*, 1987; *Jungle Fever*, 1991; *Conversation Peace*, 1995; *A Time to Love*, 2005.

The Life

Stevie Wonder was born Stevland Hardaway Judkins in Saginaw, Michigan, to Lula Hardaway and Calvin Judkins. Born prematurely, he became blind as an infant and never regained his sight. Growing up a musical prodigy in Detroit, the nine-year-old singer and harmonica player was signed by Motown Records' Tamla label and promoted under the name Little Stevie Wonder. At the age of thirteen, his harmonica feature "Fingertips, Pt. 2" rose to number one on the *Billboard* pop and rhythm-and-blues charts. Following this early success, Wonder went to study music at the Michigan School for the Blind in Lansing. In 1964 he returned to his recording career, minus the designation "Little," scoring the next in a string of chart-toppers for Motown with 1965's "Uptight." The song would be his first of many hit singles as a songwriter.

In 1970, Wonder married the singer Syreeta Wright, with whom he had collaborated on his song "Signed, Sealed, Delivered, I'm Yours." After demonstrating an interest in the production of his own recordings with the album *Signed, Sealed, and Delivered*, Wonder fought for and obtained artistic control over his music from Motown in 1971. The result was *Where I'm Coming From*, an album that had little commercial success but foreshadowed the direction that Wonder's later albums would take.

In 1972 Wonder's marriage to Wright ended. As Wonder's artistic voice matured, so did his progressive political identity. Over the course of his career Wonder would record a number of "issue" songs promoting social activism with regard to inner-city struggles (epitomized by 1973's "Livin' for the City"), excessive materialism (1976's "Pastime Paradise"), racial equality (1982's "Ebony and Ivory" with Paul McCartney), AIDS awareness (1985's ensemble piece "That's What Friends Are For"), world hunger (1985's ensemble piece "We Are the World"), and working for a Martin Luther King, Jr., holiday (1980's "Birthday"). Wonder's moral aspirations are summed up in his 1973 hit "Higher Ground," in which the songwriter implores his listeners to keep on doing their part to make the world a better place.

In later years, Wonder is a widely admired and recognized icon of popular culture, for both his songwriting and his political activism. He is also among the most critically acclaimed popular artists of all time, winning twenty-five Grammy Awards—including a remarkable string of Best Album awards for *Innervisions*, *Fulfillingness' First Finale*, and his masterwork, *Songs in the Key of Life*. Along with the albums *Music of My Mind* and *Talking Book*, these albums define Wonder's "classic period."

Following this period, Wonder turned his attention to writing music for the 1979 film *Journey Through the Secret Life of Plants*. He has since written film music for *The Woman in Red* and *Jungle Fever*, among others. He has remained active as a singer, songwriter, producer, and arranger.

The Music

Wonder's mature musical palette matched the progressive nature of his politics during the 1970's. After gaining artistic control over his recordings in 1971, Wonder pulled the Motown sound out of the 1960's, favoring arrangements featuring the modern electronic timbres of the Clavinet and Moog synthesizer. On many of the tracks from his classic period, Wonder would perform the parts for every instrument himself, perfectly rendering his compositional ideas in his studio recordings. Indeed, the intricately syncopated rhythmic patterns and subtle tonal inflections of Wonder's work demand a singular attention to detail. While his work on harmonica and piano continued throughout the 1970's, 1980's, and 1990's, he continually updated the style and instrumentation of his arrangements to match prevailing trends.

Motown Roots. Wonder's early recordings are characterized by their roots in the Motown tradition. Although extremely successful commercially and artistically, the record label was considered a top-down organization, allowing little freedom for its artists. Wonder nonetheless grew artistically within the Motown system, producing the 1965 hit "Uptight," with its characteristic backing vocals, reverb-laden guitar, and drum backbeat. Wonder's production work on 1970's "Signed, Sealed, Delivered I'm Yours" resulted in a single for Motown that embraced more active guitar and horn arrangements over a funk drum beat. His growing career also saw Wonder refining his craft of songwriting for other acts, resulting in a 1967 hit for Smokey Robinson and the Miracles with "Tears of a Clown," among others.

Talking Book. Wonder established the mature sound of his classic period with *Talking Book*. The album features the hit single "Superstition," on which Wonder performs a rollicking and funky ostinato on clavinet—an amplified clavichord that produces a dry, piercing tone well suited to Wonder's percussively rhythmic arrangement. The track also highlights Wonder's ability to write for a horn section, featuring both aggressively syncopated lines as well as fluid ones to evoke the message conveyed in the lyrical content. Finally, Wonder's vocals on "Superstition" feature early examples of his signature growl—an emphatic stylistic device in the rhythm-and-blues tradition that he

Stevie Wonder. (AP/Wide World Photos)

employs throughout his oeuvre. While "Superstition" tends toward the rhythm-and-blues and funk side of Wonder's musical language, the album also features a good example of his writing in the pop ballad style on the track "You Are the Sunshine of My Life." Where Wonder uses the percussive clavinet on the up-tempo "Superstition," in "You Are the Sunshine of My Life" he uses the subdued tones of the Rhodes keyboard—another amplified acoustic instrument that uses small metal bars rather than strings to produce tone.

Innervisions. A broadly ambitious and emotionally stirring album, *Innervisions* features a good mix of love songs and Wonder's trademark social activism. A classic ballad, the melancholy single "All in Love Is Fair" recalls Wonder's then-recent divorce told through a spare piano and drum arrangement. "Don't You Worry 'Bout a Thing" exemplifies Wonder's ever-expanding musical palette, featuring Latin percussion such as guiro (a percussion instrument) and cowbell and the syncopated tumbao salsa rhythm in the piano. On the epic seven-minute "Living for the City," Wonder uses his complement of keyboards, including Moog and ARP synthesizers as well as the Rhodes, to lay improvisational contrapuntal lines that form the foundation of a musical narrative about the trials of city life. The story traces a family's move from "hard-time Mississippi" to New York, where the parents work hard to provide "just enough." The song is notable for its increasing tension developed dynamically and through Wonder's growling vocals as he describes confrontations with racial inequality and lack of opportunity. In the song's famous dramatic interlude are heard the atmospheric sounds of New York City, wherein a seemingly innocent recent arrival is arrested, sentenced to ten years in jail, and thrown into a cell by a racist policeman. Like the title of the album, the scene is evocative of Wonder's blindness, helping the listener imagine the inner turmoil caused by racial prejudice through the sonic drama. Notably, the militant tone of this track is balanced by tracks with messages of unity, such as that found in another hit from the album, "Higher Ground." The Grammy Award-winning album is thus a morally coherent social statement about the larger challenges of life.

Fulfillingness' First Finale. Wonder's second classic-period album—the alliterative *Fulfillingness' First Finale*—is a less-ambitious but well-balanced album, featuring a number of ballads and medium-tempo pop tracks. The standout ballad is "They Won't Go When I Go," a track that begins with a subdued and classically inspired piano introduction. As the introduction progresses, the trilling formality of the arpeggiated piano figures begins to give way to blues inflections. Wonder uses the stepwise harmonic progression of the piece to build slowly throughout, eventually adding contrapuntal lines with the space-age sounds of an Odyssey synthesizer and singing passionately with gospel-inspired lyrics and phrasing. The fusion of musical styles and instrumental devices is especially noteworthy, seamlessly juxtaposing classical and gospel idioms and acoustic and electric instruments. "Boogie on Reggae Woman" is a similar experiment in genre, adding his signature synthesizer funk to the syncopated rhythms of reggae. The most prominent political statement on the album comes in "You Haven't Done Nothin'," a direct and penetrating criticism of then-President Richard Nixon.

Songs in the Key of Life. Widely considered Wonder's masterpiece, *Songs in the Key of Life* is an epic recording in concept and in format, breaking from the standard of LP in favor of a double album with an added seven-inch EP, comprising a total of twenty-one tracks. Outlining his ambitious goals, Wonder begins the album with the track "Love's in Need of Love." The tracks that follow cover several issues of societal concern, from the impoverished black ghetto ("Village Ghetto Land") and the dangers of materialism and apathy ("Pastime Paradise") to utopian statements of racial and economic equality ("Saturn"). Wonder's special attention to African American concerns is especially pronounced on "Black Man" and "Sir Duke," in which the singer pays tribute to advancements made by black Americans in the fields of science, politics, and music. Notably, while ostensibly statements of black pride, both tracks make a concerted effort to be racially inclusive. Just as "Black Man" notes the contributions of Hispanic, Asian, Indian, and white Americans, the tribute to Duke Ellington and other jazz pioneers in "Sir Duke" also includes a reference to the influential white jazz musician Glenn Miller.

Wonder's musical repertoire is typically wide-ranging on this album, ranging from the jazz and reggae influences of "Sir Duke" and the vaudeville style of "Ebony Eyes" to the lyrical harp accompaniment of "If It's Magic" and distorted rock guitar of "All-Day Sucker." The strongest tracks on the album are inevitably those on which Wonder performs in his singular synthesizer-infused funk style. Of these, "I Wish" stands out for its propulsively percussive and many-layered clavinet ostinato—a definitive construction that can only be described as Wonderesque. Like his arrangement for "Superstition," Wonder again pairs the clavinet with expertly composed horn parts, at times punching through the texture and at others providing a flowing accompaniment for the lyrical foreground.

Musical Legacy

Although Wonder's career is usually connected with his work from the 1970's, his extensive musical talents and his political interests enriched the decades following that time period. With his *In*

Square Circle, Wonder reinvented himself to work in a mainstream pop style, and he redoubled his commitment to social justice, including on that album a track entitled "It's Wrong (Apartheid)." While Wonder's popularity waned over the course of the 1980's, giving way to the next generation of popular singers—such as Michael Jackson, Madonna, and Prince—his influence on popular and rhythm-and-blues music has been substantial. In his role as one of Motown's premier recording artists, he played a critical part in bridging the gap between the 1960's rhythm-and-blues style and the rhythm-and-blues-influenced popular music that came to dominate the early twenty-first century.

J. Griffith Rollefson

Further Reading

Fong-Torres, Ben. "Not-So-'Little' Stevie Wonder." In *The Pop, Rock, and Soul Reader: Histories and Debates*, edited by David Brackett. Oxford, England: Oxford University Press, 2005. This anthology of a hundred entries on popular music from magazines, journals, and newspapers is arranged chronologically, and it includes a piece on Wonder by a journalist who covers rock music.

Peisch, Jeffrey. *Stevie Wonder*. New York: Ballantine, 1985. An overview of the personal and professional life of Wonder. Includes photographs.

Swenson, John. *Stevie Wonder*. New York: Plexus, 1986. Swenson, the coeditor and cocreator of *The Rolling Stone Record Guide*, chronicles the life of Wonder.

Werner, Craig. *Higher Ground: Stevie Wonder, Aretha Franklin, Curtis Mayfield, and the Rise and Fall of American Soul*. New York: Random House, 2005. This cultural history looks at the lives of three entertainers, including Wonder, and tells how their music was informed by the gospel genre and how they used their music as a powerful expression in the struggle for racial equality.

See also: Babyface; Beck, Jeff; Blackwell, Otis; Ellington, Duke; Galway, Sir James; Holiday, Billie; Iglesias, Julio; Jackson, Michael; Jamerson, James; Jones, Quincy; Lewis, Jerry Lee; McCartney, Sir Paul; Makeba, Miriam; Masekela, Hugh; Miller, Glenn; Prince; Robinson, Smokey; Sting; Taylor, James.

Tammy Wynette
American country singer, songwriter, and guitarist

Wynette developed a trademark vocal style: a catch in her voice that infused her songs with great emotion. Her tunes dealt with subjects her listeners identified with—love and loss, pain and pleasure, heartbreak and triumph, and breakup and reconciliation.

Born: May 5, 1942; Itawamba County, Mississippi
Died: April 6, 1998; Nashville, Tennessee
Also known as: Virginia Wynette Pugh (birth name); First Lady of Country Music

Principal recordings

ALBUMS: *My Elusive Dreams*, 1967 (with David Houston); *Your Good Girl's Gonna Go Bad*, 1967; *D-I-V-O-R-C-E*, 1968; *Stand by Your Man*, 1968; *Inspiration*, 1969; *The Ways to Love a Man*, 1969; *Christmas with Tammy*, 1970; *The First Lady*, 1970; *Tammy Wynette*, 1970; *Tammy's Touch*, 1970; *The World of Tammy Wynette*, 1970; *It's Just a Matter of Time*, 1971; *We Go Together*, 1971 (with George Jones); *We Sure Can Love Each Other*, 1971; *Bedtime Story*, 1972; *Me and the First Lady*, 1972 (with Jones); *My Man*, 1972; *'Til I Get It Right*, 1972; *We Love to Sing About Jesus*, 1972 (with Jones); *The First Songs of the First Lady*, 1973; *Kids Say the Darndest Things*, 1973; *Let's Build a World Together*, 1973 (with Jones); *Another Lonely Song*, 1974; *We're Gonna Hold On*, 1974 (with Jones); *Woman to Woman*, 1974; *George and Tammy and Tina*, 1975 (with Jones and Tina Denise Byrd); *I Still Believe in Fairy Tales*, 1975; *Golden Ring*, 1976 (with Jones); *'Til I Can Make It on My Own*, 1976; *You and Me*, 1976; *Let's Get Together*, 1977; *One of a Kind*, 1977; *From the Bottom of My Heart*, 1978; *Womanhood*, 1978; *Just Tammy*, 1979; *Only Lonely Sometimes*, 1980; *Together Again*, 1980 (with Jones); *Encore: George Jones and Tammy Wynette*, 1981 (with Jones); *You Brought Me Back*, 1981; *Soft Touch*, 1982; *Even the Strong Get Lonely*, 1983; *Good Love and Heartbreak*, 1983; *Sometimes When We Touch*, 1985; *Higher Ground*, 1987; *Next to You*, 1989; *Heart over Mind*, 1990;

Honky Tonk Angels, 1993 (with Loretta Lynn and Dolly Parton); *Without Walls*, 1994; *One*, 1995 (with Jones).

The Life

Tammy Wynette (wi-NEHT) was born Virginia Wynette Pugh on the Mississippi-Alabama border, the only child of William Hollice Pugh and Mildred Faye Russell Pugh. Her father, a farmer and part-time musician, died when Wynette was an infant. Wynette grew up picking cotton while learning to play a variety of instruments, and she listened constantly to country music.

A basketball star at Tremont High School, Wynette married Euple Byrd and dropped out her senior year. Byrd was often unemployed, so Wynette worked menial jobs to help support a growing family of three daughters. In the early 1960's, Wynette left the shiftless Byrd. To make ends meet, she occasionally sang on television, and in 1966 she moved to Nashville, Tennessee, where she eventually signed a contract with Epic Records. There she became Tammy, because of a resemblance to Debbie Reynolds in the film *Tammy and the Bachelor* (1957). She had a succession of chart-topping country hits between 1966 and the early 1980's, and she became a major headliner.

Her personal life, however, was not as successful. She married and divorced a second husband before marrying country singing star George Jones, to whom she was wed for six tumultuous years. Following a brief fourth marriage, she wed for a fifth and final time to George Richey, remaining with him for the final two decades of her life. In 1978 she was kidnapped in a case that remains controversial. Plagued by medical problems for decades, Wynette underwent dozens of operations, and for many years she was addicted to painkillers. In failing health, she died of a blood clot at age fifty-five.

The Music

Autobiographical musical material was prominent during and after her six-year marriage to Jones, a period of great creativity and, because of Jones's alcoholism, of tremendous personal volatility. The two stars, nicknamed the President and the First Lady of Country Music, had a number of hits together. Blessed with a powerful, tremulous voice despite her petite frame, Wynette throughout her career—particularly during the 1960's and 1970's—represented the epitome of the woman who perseveres in the face of adversity.

"Your Good Girl's Gonna Go Bad." A 1967 release that rose to number three on country charts, this was Wynette's second single and first big hit. Apparently aimed at her philandering second husband, Don Chapel, to whom Wynette was married from 1967 to 1968, the song scathingly denigrates her erstwhile partner's sleazy taste in women.

"I Don't Wanna Play House." Cowritten by Billy Sherrill and Glenn Sutton, this song—which focuses on a mother eavesdropping on two kids playing house and overhearing her young daughter reflect upon the sorrow caused by her parents engaging in the adult version of the game—earned Wynette a Grammy Award in 1967 for Best Female Country Vocal Performance.

"D-I-V-O-R-C-E." Bobby Braddock and Curly Putman wrote this 1968 hit, which continued

Tammy Wynette. (AP/Wide World Photos)

Wynette's theme of examining the effects of grown-ups' problems on innocent children. In this case, the singer spells out certain words in an attempt to delay as long as possible the hurt that the dissolution of the family will cause her young son.

"Stand by Your Man." Cowritten by Wynette and Sherrill, this 1968 single remained at the top of the country charts for three weeks, made the Top 20 on the pop charts the same year, and hit number one in England in 1975. The song most identified with Wynette, it is deemed a classic, and it won the singer a Grammy Award for Best Female Vocal Performance. It has been covered by dozens of artists, including the Dixie Chicks, Tina Turner, Elton John, Lyle Lovett, Lynn Anderson, and Wendy O. Williams, and it has been featured prominently in several films, notably *The Crying Game* (1992). When it was released, feminists harshly criticized the song for its suggestion that women should overlook men's faults for the sake of keeping a marital union intact. Today, it is rated among country music's one hundred greatest hits.

Musical Legacy

A consistent, popular performer, Wynette embodied the image of the strong woman who maintains dignity and femininity in the midst of tribulation. Before medical issues and the music industry (which withheld recording contracts from female vocalists over forty) slowed her momentum in the late 1980's, Wynette scored twenty number-one singles. More than thirty million of her records sold around the world. Her lead vocals—singing esoteric lyrics about "Mu-Mu Land"—on the upbeat, dance-oriented pop tune "Justified and Ancient (Stand by the JAMS)" produced an unexpected international hit for the short-lived British band KLF, and the song rose to number one in eighteen countries.

For her work, Wynette received many honors, including two Grammy Awards (1967, 1969). She was the Country Music Association's Female Vocalist of the Year three times (1967, 1969, 1970), and in 1976 she won a similar British award. Late in life, she accepted many accolades: The Nashville Network's Living Legend (1991), the American Music Award of Merit (1996), and induction into the Country Music Hall of Fame (1998) and into the Grammy Hall of Fame (1998). Posthumous recognition includes the Academy of Country Music's Pioneer Award.

Jack Ewing

Further Reading

Daly, Jackie. *Tammy Wynette: A Daughter Recalls Her Mother's Tragic Life and Death*. New York: Putnam, 2000. Wynette's daughter provides an intimate portrait, with many photographs, of her famous mother.

Hagar, Andrew G. *Women of Country: Dolly Parton, Patsy Cline, Tammy Wynette and More*. New York: Friedman/Fairfax, 1994. This is an overview of the careers of some of country's top female vocalists. Includes photographs.

Jones, George, and Tom Carter. *I Lived to Tell It All*. New York: Dell, 1997. A companion piece to Wynette's memoir, this is Jones's autobiography.

Wynette, Tammy, and John Dew. *Stand by Your Man: An Autobiography*. New York: Simon & Shuster, 1979. Wynette's candid recollection of her rise from poverty to stardom served as a basis for a 1981 made-for-television film of her life.

See also: John, Sir Elton; Jones, George; Lovett, Lyle; Lynn, Loretta; Parton, Dolly; Turner, Tina; Willson, Meredith.

X

Iannis Xenakis

Greek classical composer

Never aligning himself with a trend or school in composition, Xenakis pursued his own vision, utilizing mathematics and probability theory as techniques with which he could control and manipulate sonic textures and organize dense masses of sound.

Born: May 29, 1922; Brăila, Romania
Died: February 4, 2001; Paris, France

Principal works

BRASS WORKS: *Keren*, 1986; *Xas*, 1987.
CHAMBER WORKS: *Nomos alpha*, 1966; *Kottos*, 1977.
CHORAL WORKS: *Nuits*, 1967; *Cendrées*, 1973; *Kassandra*, 1987.
ORCHESTRAL WORKS: *Metastasis*, 1955; *Pithoprakta*, 1957; *Achorripsis*, 1958; *Analogique B*, 1959; *Stratégie*, 1963; *Polytope de Montréal*, 1967; *Terretektorh*, 1967; *Nomos gamma*, 1968; *Anaktoria*, 1969; *Persephassa*, 1969; *Duel*, 1971; *Jonohaies*, 1977; *Shaar*, 1983; *Jalons*, 1986; *Keqrops*, 1986; *La Déesse Athéna*, 1992; *O-Mega*, 1997.
PERCUSSION WORKS: *Psappha*, 1976; *Dmaathen*, 1976; *Pléïades*, 1978; *Rebonds*, 1988.
PIANO WORKS: *Eonta*, 1963; *Herma*, 1963; *Evryali*, 1973; *Pour Maurice*, 1982.

The Life

Son of Greek importer-exporter Clearchos Xenakis and Photini Pavlou, Iannis Xenakis (YAH-nihs zeh-NAH-kihs) was born in Romania, the eldest of three boys. The family encouraged him to take music lessons. At a young age, he lost his mother, who died while giving birth to a fourth child. Xenakis was cared for by nannies until 1927, when he was sent to a boarding school in Greece, on the small island of Spetses. There he studied music, literature, and math. In 1938 Xenakis left for Athens to enroll in a prep school for the Greek university system. At the same time, he studied music theory privately with Aristotle Koundourov.

Shortly after he was accepted at the Athens Polytechnic Institute to study civil engineering in 1940, Italy declared war on Greece, and all educational institutes closed indefinitely. Xenakis joined the resistance and later the ELAS (National Popular Army), and during these years, he was imprisoned, tortured, and wounded by the Italian and the German armies. His most serious injury occurred in 1945, after the German occupation had ended, and British troops had established martial law in Athens. Xenakis was hit by shrapnel, losing his left eye and most of the left side of his face. Rescued by his father, Xenakis was nursed back to health, though he was permanently disfigured. He completed his degree at the Polytechnic Institute in 1947, despite his continuing active involvement in the civil war that followed World War II, between right-wing and communist forces. Captured and imprisoned repeatedly, he managed to flee the country after escaping from a prison camp and hiding out for six months. He decided to go to the United States, where he had relatives. When Xenakis was unable to get there, he decided to stay in Paris. At the time, he was sentenced to death in Greece. He got a job as an engineer for the architect Le Corbusier, and he was soon entrusted to create and to implement his own designs. In fact, he became an accomplished and respected architect, experimenting with new materials and construction shapes, and he worked on several important projects in France and elsewhere, most notably the Philips Pavilion for the 1958 Brussels World's Fair, the space for which Edgard Varèse's *Poème électronique* (1958) was composed, designed with surfaces derived entirely from the hyperbolic paraboloid.

Still interested in music, Xenakis had approached and had been rejected by all the important composition teachers in Paris, including Arthur Honegger, Darius Milhaud, and Nadia Boulanger. Eventually he met Olivier Messiaen, who, impressed by Xenakis's personality and originality, allowed him to audit his classes, advising him to compose music based on what he already knew well and to use his scientific training rather than pursue musical training. Xenakis responded by applying his architectural models on music, seeing a direct link between sound and space. His first published composition, *Metastasis*, was an instant success, and it catapulted Xenakis to the top tiers of the avant-garde.

Soon after *Metastasis*, he explored assigning the complex calculations essential to his approach to computers rather than doing them manually. During the 1960's, Xenakis contributed a great deal to research and development of computer systems for electronic music. He founded, directed, and secured financing for several computer music organizations, including the Centre d'Études de Mathématiques et Automatique Musicales in Paris and the Center for Mathematical Automated Music at Indiana University. He also conceived and developed an autonomous graphic-oriented computer system for composition and sound generation (UPIC), which reflected his ideas of sound-space relationships and his concept of freely transferring structures to different domains. In this spirit, he also produced throughout his career a series of multimedia works, essentially installations of integrated music, laser, and light shows and architectural designs, presented in several international locations, such as the *Persepolis* project, set among the ruins and the mountains at Persepolis, Iran (1971); the series titled *Polytopes*, presented in Montreal (1967), at the Roman baths at the Musée de Cluny in Paris (1972), and at the ruins of Mycenae, Greece (1978); and the *Légende d'éer* (Diatope) in Paris (1978).

Eventually recognized internationally, Xenakis received many honors and was invited to teach at several institutions, such as the Sorbonne (1972-1989), Indiana University (1967-1972), and City University London (1975). He married French writer Françoise Gargouil in 1953, and they had a daughter, Mâkhi, born in 1955. Xenakis remained active and innovative as a composer well into the 1990's, until Alzheimer's disease gradually deprived him of his ability to compose. His last composition, *O-Mega* (after the last letter of the Greek alphabet), premiered at the Huddersfield Contemporary Music Festival, held in Yorkshire, England, in 1997.

Iannis Xenakis. (AP/Wide World Photos)

The Music

Xenakis referred to his method of composing through the use of probabilities as stochastic music (from the Greek word stochos, meaning goal). In general, he developed a model that described a physical system and its laws, and then he applied that model to control the elements of a construction in a specific domain: music, architecture, visuals, or a combination of them. Throughout his career, Xenakis developed and implemented several different models, based on diverse scientific research, which he applied to compositional projects, pursuing each one to its fullest potential before moving on to the next. It is important to mention, however, that Xenakis never rigidly adhered to his models. Instead, his music reveals a keen ear that constantly adjusts and modifies the elements. He claimed to have been inspired by the sounds of crowds demonstrating outside his hospital in Athens, where he was being treated for his wounds, as well as by the behavior of cicadas and flocks of birds. Despite the rigorous formal control in its conception, his music retains an elemental energy. It's clear that Xenakis's thinking was deeply musical, and he was in complete control of his medium and fully aware of the limits of musical perception.

Equally important to his scientific approach is Xenakis's fascination with ritualism and with dramatic form, most often associated with themes from ancient Greece (as revealed in his compositions' titles). Philosophically, Xenakis found meaning by exploring continuums and their extremes: from ancient mythology to modern science, from the visceral to the cerebral, and from intimate insight to public spectacle.

Though extremely creative with the exploration and extension of conventional instrumental techniques, Xenakis also experimented widely with electronic sounds, and he used magnetic tape (and eventually computers) to realize his compositions. He was interested in sounds that did not carry the associations or limitations of conventional instruments. He used computers for calculations and handling large amounts of data rather than for algorithmic composition purposes.

Early Works. Xenakis wrote twenty-four pieces for piano or voice and piano between 1949 and 1952, which were mostly based on Greek folk material and influenced by Béla Bartók. His first completed large-scale work, an orchestral triptych titled *Anastenaria*, followed a similar approach for its two first movements: *Procession vers les eaux claires* (completed early in 1953) and *Le Sacrifice* (summer of 1953), but Xenakis broke all conventions in the third movement, *Metastasis*. (The entire work has never been performed.)

Metastasis. This work exhibits a direct transfer of the continuous displacement of a straight line—the most prominent feature in the architecture of the Philips Pavillion—to musical parameters. It is transformed to a web of glissandi, each with a different duration and trajectory, and it is scored for sixty-one individual strings.

Pithoprakta. *Pithoprakta* is scored for forty-nine musicians, and it utilizes Daniel Bernoulli's law of large numbers in conjunction with Ludwig Boltzmann's kinetic gas theory to create a model of handling a large number of elements, based on gas molecules and their velocities. Molecular speeds are translated into asynchronous pizzicato glissandi events, with the slope of each glissando proportional to the corresponding particle's speed. Xenakis used the chance operations of stochastics to represent a phenomenon that defies accurate measurement.

Achorripsis. Xenakis's third major work is an application of probability. A matrix of activity determines interaction among timbral elements and event types over time. The number of events from each timbral group per time unit is distributed according to the Poisson distribution (a probability theory).

Analogique B. Realized for electronically generated sinusoidal sounds in 1959, this piece deals with granular sounds scattered onto time grids, organized in a order-disorder continuum with Markovian chain principles.

Stratégie *and* Duel. These two pieces are based on conditional processes, where game theory (by John von Neumann and Oskar Morgenstern) is applied. The different outcomes for the piece are all precalculated and organized into rules. Two conductors play the game, choosing from the precomposed outcome possibilities.

Herma. This is Xenakis's version of set theory using Boolean algebra, where all notes of the keyboard form a referential set out of which several subsets are generated, resulting in a vast number of possibilities, organized in a coherent large form structure.

Nomos alpha. Scored for solo cello, *Nomos alpha* was composed in 1966, and its structure is determined by group theory. This was later applied to *Nomos gamma*, for orchestra.

Persephassa. Composed in 1969 for six percussionists dispersed around the audience, this piece treats space as a musical parameter, an interest of Xenakis's throughout the 1960's. The percussionists use a wide range of instruments, and they play a series of imitative passages that are passed around the space.

Légende d'éer (Diatope). A multimedia work conceived entirely by Xenakis for the opening of the Centre Pompidou in Paris in 1977-1978, it included a visual component with computer-controlled laser lights and a seven-channel electroacoustic composition with material stemming from instrumental sounds, noises, and electronically generated sounds, intended for diffusion in "Le Diatope," a curvaceous architectural construction designed by the composer. The work is surrounded by a compilation of five texts, reflecting or reacting to each other across time, space, and cultural distances.

Musical Legacy

While Xenakis is remembered for his use of mathematical formulas to compose music, that does not describe fully his methods of composition or the breadth of his innovation. Highly critical of serial procedures from early on, regarding them to be arbitrary and mostly inaudible, Xenakis steered musical thought toward formal constructions that are integrated, global, and cohesive, with a complexity in need of mathematical formulas for accurate expression. He conceived a new form of meta-art, which transcends individual art forms and refers to out-of-time structures that exist as entities before their implementation in a specific in-time musical construction. With his constantly curious and evolving mind, Xenakis redefined his own style several times in his career. His scientific approach offered fresh perspective on many related topics, and his ideas, many of them well ahead of their time, are actively pursued in research centers.

Yiorgos Vassilandonakis

Further Reading

Harley, James. *Xenakis: His Life in Music*. New York: Routledge, 2004. A general description and reflection upon Xenakis's life and thought processes, intended for the musician, rather than the scientific reader, explaining most concepts in easy-to-understand language. Includes diagrams and musical examples.

Matossian, Nouritza. *Xenakis*. London: Kahn & Averill, 1990. A good source for biographical and light analytical information geared toward the general reader.

Vargas, Balint. A. *Conversations with Iannis Xenakis*. London: Faber & Faber, 1996. Vargas focuses on biographical, political, conceptual, and musical topics and engages the composer in insightful conversation. This book explores Xenakis's life, from the bleak formative years living in exile in Paris to his success as an architect and modern thinker.

Xenakis, Iannis. *Formalized Music: Thought and Mathematics in Composition*. Hillsdale, N.Y.: Pendragon Press, 2001. The quintessential source for Xenakis's ideas by the composer, this collection of essays describes in depth his various approaches and theories, aesthetics, and philosophical issues, including several analyses of specific works as well as technical formulas and diagrams.

See also: Bartók, Béla; Boulanger, Nadia; Honegger, Arthur; Messiaen, Olivier; Milhaud, Darius; Nono, Luigi; Varèse, Edgard.

Y

Yanni

Greek New Age composer and keyboardist

Yanni is largely responsible for popularizing the contemporary musical style known as New Age and remains identified with that genre, even as he dissociates himself with that label, preferring the more diverse and expansive "contemporary instrumental." Furthermore, the integration of his physical appearance into his musical persona has helped make him one of the most visually recognizable and commercially successful New Age/ contemporary musicians in history.

Born: November 14, 1954; Kalamata, Greece
Also known as: Yiannis Hrysomallis (birth name); Yanni Chrysomallis

Principal works

FILM SCORES: *Heart of Midnight*, 1988; *A Taste of Freedom*, 1991; *Faith*, 1998.

Principal recordings

ALBUMS: *Optimystique*, 1984; *Keys to Imagination*, 1986; *Out of Silence*, 1987; *Chameleon Days*, 1988; *Niki Nana*, 1989; *In Celebration of Life*, 1991; *Dare to Dream*, 1992; *In My Time*, 1993; *Live at the Acropolis*, 1993; *I Love You Perfect*, 1995; *Tribute*, 1997; *Steal the Sky*, 1999; *If I Could Tell You*, 2000; *Ethnicity*, 2003; *Live: The Concert Event*, 2006.

WRITINGS OF INTEREST: *Yanni in Words*, 2002.

The Life

Born Yiannis Hrysomallis in a small, picturesque coastal town in Greece, Yianni (YAH-nee) was surrounded by music from a young age. In addition to having a father who played the guitar and a mother who sang, he was influenced by the folk music of his homeland, taking an interest in both piano and accordion as a child. It was also during his youth that he proved himself an adept athlete by setting a new national record in freestyle swimming. Nevertheless, he left Greece after high school, not to return for several years, to pursue a degree in psychology from the University of Minnesota. While in college, he began experimenting with synthesizers and electronic keyboards, eventually performing for a short time with the local rock band Chameleon.

Though largely self-taught as a musician, Yanni successfully recorded his first instrumental album, *Optimystique*, in 1980, releasing it in 1984. After a brief attempt as a sound track composer, the artist organized a small band of keyboards and percussion in 1987 to promote and record his music. Numerous studio albums and associated tours followed.

Yanni performed and recorded monumental concerts during the mid-1990's at iconic outdoor venues: the Acropolis in Athens, Greece; the Taj Mahal in Agra, India; and the Forbidden City in Beijing, China. Extremely successful, these three events marked the pinnacle of the artist's career. After 2000, his output declined but he continued to work on his music and release new albums.

The Music

Complicating any discussion of Yanni's music is the challenge of determining the best descriptor of his style. Though his name has become synonymous with New Age music—due in part to the romantic, sentimental nature of some of his piano-based pieces—he personally prefers the label "contemporary instrumental." The need for such a distinction is strongly supported by Yanni's many upbeat compositions, featuring prominent orchestration and keyboard-driven rhythms, which contradict the peaceful, meditative mood usually associated with New Age music. His use on his "live" albums of full symphony orchestra—including multiple soloists, both instrumental and vocal, and heavy use of percussion—reinforces that distinction.

On the other hand, the fact that many of the artist's popular pieces are constructed using traditional song structures, employ a drum kit, and serve well as "background music" due to their lack of complex musical material would suggest the smooth jazz style. To complicate matters further, Yanni's interest in various indigenous instruments and other ethnic musical material, coupled with his stated "One World, One People" philosophy, suggests a more world-based style. For these reasons, it is difficult to assign Yanni to a particular genre; he is perhaps best described as a keyboardist and composer of short, primarily instrumental, pop-influenced and emotionally charged pieces.

Early Works. During the first twelve years of his career, Yanni recorded and released several albums, including two that basically were compilations. The albums of new material range in style from 1984's progressive-rock-influenced *Optimystique*—featuring keyboards, electric guitars, percussion, and other instruments—to the more colorful pop-oriented *Niki Nana* (1989). Several of these early albums find Yanni consciously attempting to simulate a full orchestra through the use of three keyboard players, including himself, and a drummer. Though in general not as commercially successful as his later albums, Yanni's early albums of new material nevertheless include several of the artist's most popular numbers.

Dare to Dream *and* In My Time. Two albums from the middle of Yanni's career represent the more energetic, upbeat and the overtly sentimental sides of his style, respectively. These albums garnered the artist's first Grammy nominations. *Dare to Dream* includes such popular numbers as "You Only Live Once" and "Aria," the latter being a loose arrangement of the famous "Flower Duet" from the nineteenth century opera *Lakmé* by Léo Delibes. *In My Time*, on the other hand, is perhaps the most stylistically consistent album of Yanni's career, featuring eleven romantic pieces for solo piano and small ensemble, notably "In the Morning Light," "To Take . . . to Hold," and "Until the Last Moment."

Live at the Acropolis *and* Tribute. Yanni's most commercially successful projects are his two live albums (also released as DVDs), the first being recorded live at the Acropolis and the second being recorded live at the Taj Mahal and the Forbidden City. While both albums are essentially compilations of previously released material, all of the pieces are greatly expanded to include numerous soloists (both instrumental and vocal), an enlarged band, and a full symphony orchestra. Performed live before huge audiences, the pieces on these albums are also marked by a greater sense of energy and immediacy than those captured on Yanni's studio albums, while also being focused more on the ensemble as a whole than on the individual artist.

If I Could Tell You *and* Ethnicity. Following his two monumental live projects, Yanni's career slowed considerably. *If I Could Tell You* is a fairly introspective album compared to most of his earlier projects, while *Ethnicity* is specifically focused on the artist's "One World, One People" philosophy, merging various indigenous instruments with a Western ensemble. *Ethnicity* also features Yanni's most extensive use of the human voice to date, including his rare use of full-fledged lyrics. Particularly notable is his arrangement of the Greek folk song "Jivaeri."

Yanni. (AP/Wide World Photos)

Musical Legacy

Yanni's musical legacy is to bring a unique hybrid of world, New Age, and contemporary instrumental music to a fan base committed not only to his musical style but also to his performance and style and his inclusive "One World, One People" philosophy. His popularity owes as much to his management of the way his music is presented as it does to his ability to commandeer and combine many styles and talents in a unified program that touches his audiences at many levels.

Yanni's many albums, as well as his numerous compilations and sound tracks, testify to his prodigious energy and creative ability. The fact that the majority of these albums—even those several that basically rehash previously released material—achieved impressive rankings on various *Billboard* charts speaks to Yanni's superior ability to communicate effectively with his fans. Exposure to his music through television commercials and programs—as well as through such high-publicity sports events as the Olympics, the Super Bowl, the U.S. Open, the Tour de France, and the World Figure Skating Championships—has only increased his name recognition and popularity. Also noteworthy, in addition to his Grammy Award nominations, is his Emmy Award nomination for *Live at the Acropolis* and the honorary doctorate he received from the University of Minnesota.

Frederick Key Smith

Further Reading

Rosen, Craig. "Yanni's *Time* in the Sun Has Come." *Billboard*, April 24, 1993, 10-11. Discusses the release of *In My Time* and its associated concert tour.
Russel, Deborah. "Yanni's PBS Gig Sparks Sales." *Billboard*, April 16, 1994, 1-2. Discusses the immense success of the *Live at the Acropolis* project.
Schnakenberg, Robert E. "Yanni, 1954-   ." In *St. James Encyclopedia of Popular Culture*, edited by Sara Pendergast and Tom Pendergast. Vol. 5. Detroit: St. James Press, 2000. An encyclopedia article about the artist's life and his signature "Yanni sound."
Yanni and David Rensin. *Yanni in Words*. New York: Hyperion, 2002. An autobiography that focuses on the artist's life and personal relationships, as well as his career and creative philosophy.

See also: Cliff, Jimmy; Enya; Harrison, Lou; Khan, Nusrat Fateh Ali; Kitarō; Kuti, Fela; McFerrin, Bobby; Masekela, Hugh; Oldfield, Mike; Sanders, Pharoah; Shankar, Ravi; Takemitsu, Tōru; Umm Kulthum; Vangelis.

Lester Young
American jazz saxophone player and songwriter

Young revolutionized modern jazz tenor-saxophone playing, and his light, lyrical sound was featured in orchestras such as Count Basie's, in his partnering of such singers as Billie Holiday, and in his combo work with both traditional and modern jazz musicians.

Born: August 27, 1909; Woodville, Mississippi
Died: March 15, 1959; New York, New York
Also known as: Lester Willis Young (full name); the Pres

Principal recordings
ALBUMS: *Kansas City Style*, 1944; *Lester Warms Up*, 1944; *Coleman Hawkins and Lester Young*, 1946 (with Coleman Hawkins); *Lester Young: Buddy Rich Trio*, 1946 (with Buddy Rich); *Lester Young: Nat King Cole Trio*, 1946 (with Nat King Cole); *Lester Young Quartet and Count Basie Seven*, 1950 (with Count Basie); *Lester Young Swings Again*, 1950; *The Pres*, 1950; *Pres Is Blue*, 1950; *Lester Young Collates*, 1951; *Lester Young Trio*, 1951 (with Lester Young Trio); *Pres*, 1951; *It Don't Mean a Thing*, 1952; *Pres and His Cabinet*, 1952 (with others); *Pres and Teddy and Oscar*, 1952 (with Oscar Peterson and Teddy Wilson); *Lester Young with the Oscar Peterson Trio*, 1952 (with Peterson); *Battle of the Saxes*, 1953 (with others); *Just You, Just Me*, 1953; *Lester Young Collates No. 2*, 1953; *Lester Young: His Tenor Sax*, 1954; *Lester Young with the Oscar Peterson Trio, Vol. 1*, 1954 (with Peterson); *Lester Young with the Oscar Peterson Trio, Vol. 2*, 1954 (with Peterson); *Mean to Me*, 1954; *The President*, 1954; *Pres and Sweets*, 1955 (with Harry Sweets Edison); *Pres Meets Vice Pres*, 1955 (with Paul Quinichette); *The Jazz Giants '56*, 1956 (with Roy Eldridge); *Lester*

Swings Again, 1956; *Lester's Here*, 1956; *Nat King Cole: Buddy Rich Trio*, 1956 (with Cole and Buddy Rich); *Pres and Teddy*, 1956 (with Wilson); *Tops on Tenor*, 1956; *Going for Myself*, 1957; *If It Ain't Got That Swing*, 1957; *Laughin' to Keep from Cryin'*, 1958; *The Lester Young/Teddy Wilson Quartet*, 1959 (with Wilson).

The Life

The oldest of three children, Lester Willis Young grew up near New Orleans, where his father, a minstrel-show musician, instructed him on playing the trumpet, saxophone, and drums. Young toured several midwestern states with the family band, and, at age thirteen, he decided to concentrate on mastering the saxophone. Later, he often said that his distinctive sound was the result of his attempt to imitate on his tenor saxophone the C-melody saxophone timbre of his idol Frankie Trumbauer. During the late 1920's and early 1930's, Young played for various bands in Kansas, Missouri, Oklahoma, and Minnesota, including the orchestras of King Oliver, Andy Kirk, and Walter Page. His most extensive and important association was with Count Basie's big band and small groups, which led to his first recordings.

After leaving Basie in 1940, Young played in several combos led by himself and by other musicians. In 1944, when he won first place in the *Down Beat* poll for the best tenor saxophonist, he was drafted into the Army, which proved disastrous for his personal and professional life. He was court-martialed for using marijuana, and he spent several months in a Georgia military prison. When he was released at the end of 1945, he resumed playing, recording, and touring. However, the racism that he had experienced before and during the war created deep emotional distress, which was exacerbated by the breakup of his first two marriages to white women. During the 1950's, his alcoholism and his inadequate diet contributed to a precipitous decline in his health. In 1959, after returning from an engagement in Paris, he died at the Hotel Alvin, located on "the musician's crossroad" at Fifty-second Street and Broadway in New York City.

The Music

Young had a deep and lasting influence on the development of modern jazz by creating a unique improvisatory style and a new type of jazz, sometimes called cool, because of its avoidance of emotional excess. By his nonconformity in music, dress, and behavior, and through the jazz argot he helped to popularize, Young influenced not only jazz musicians but also such Beat writers as Jack Kerouac and Allen Ginsberg. In fact, his jazz solos have often been characterized in terms of poetry, since his improvisations flowed like a good conversation. He reveled in surprising combinations of sounds, the way a poet delights in a revelatory ordering of words.

Sax Style. During his early career, Young's songlike style was sometimes compared unfavorably to the robust approach of Coleman Hawkins on the tenor saxophone. Young had a light tone, whereas Hawkins had a rich, rounded tone. Young had a slow vibrato, while Hawkins's was fast. Young's phrasing was smooth, melodic, and economical, where unplayed notes often had as important a role as played ones. Hawkins, on the other hand, constructed his expressive solos with a Baroque profusion of notes. One critic called Hawkins the "Rubens of jazz," while Young was its Cézanne. Young took Hawkins's place in Fletcher Henderson's orchestra, but he was quickly let go because he refused to duplicate Hawkins's sound and style.

Young's graceful, melodic approach to tenor-saxophone playing achieved success largely through his recordings with the Count Basie Orchestra and with small groups of Basie sidemen. His solos on such big band favorites as "One o'Clock Jump" and "Jive at Five" were so admired that Young imitators memorized them note for note. Even more influential were Young's solos in Basie sextets and septets. For example, some jazz musicians view his improvisations on the 1936 version of "Lady Be Good" as the best solo he ever recorded. In 1939 his recording of "Lester Leaps In," with the Kansas City Seven, was so successful that it became his signature tune (it was supposedly named because Lester arrived late for a take on his composition).

Working with Billie Holiday. Young's recordings with the vocalist Holiday are legendary. She gave him the nickname "Pres" because he was the "President" of all saxophone players, and he affectionately nicknamed her "Lady Day." Holiday was attracted to Young's shy, sensitive personality, and she found his melodic and conversational improvisations compatible with the way she interpreted songs. Young believed that a song's lyrics were important in his improvisations, both when he soloed and when he accompanied singers. In his improvisations he edited, reworked, and transformed the song's melody, while managing to create a unified solo or accompaniment that deepened and expanded the song's message and mood. So intimate was the rapport he achieved with Holiday on songs such as "The Man I Love" and "All of Me" that they seem to be thinking each other's thoughts. Something similar happened when Young collaborated with such talented instrumentalists as the guitarist Charlie Christian and the clarinetist Benny Goodman.

After Prison. A controversy exists among aficionados and jazz critics over the quality of Young's music after his release from prison in 1945. Some believe that emotional and physical suffering sapped his will to create, and his work in small groups and large orchestras rarely equaled, and never surpassed, the high quality of his work in the late 1930's and the early 1940's. Other critics and such jazz musicians as Sonny Rollins dispute this evaluation. They observe Young conquering the depths of his despair to achieve his greatest musical creativity. For example, these commentators view his recording of "These Foolish Things," in his first session as a free man, as a masterpiece. Furthermore, his solos on "Lester Leaps In" during the Jazz at the Philharmonic tours exhibit consistently inspiring musicianship. Even as late as 1957, when he appeared for the last time with Holiday on the CBS television show *Sound of Jazz*, the sensitivity and creativity of their collaboration on Holiday's tune "Fine and Mellow" left musicians and viewers deeply moved.

Musical Legacy

Some scholars consider Young to be the greatest tenor player of all time, whereas others pair him with Hawkins as the two most vital creators of how the tenor is used in modern jazz. Young introduced a new sensibility into improvisations by creating a rhythmic flexibility and melodic richness that was malleable enough to transform both ballads and up-tempo tunes into a new jazz style that some called cool, a term that Young may have coined. He

had a major influence on many young tenor players, including Stan Getz, Zoot Sims, Al Cohn, Illinois Jacquet, and Dexter Gordon. Paul Quinichette based his style so closely on Young's that he was given the nickname "Vice Pres."

Young also had an influence on other instrumentalists, including trumpeters, trombonists, and pianists. Some have claimed that Charlie Parker's alto sound was reminiscent of Young's tenor sound, but Parker responded that, though he deeply admired Young, his (Young's) style was in an entirely different musical world. Some have described Miles Davis's *Birth of the Cool* album as an orchestration of Young's tenor sound.

Young's influence extended even into motion pictures. In the film *'Round Midnight* (1986), which some have called the best jazz film ever made, the principal character is largely based on Young. Bertrand Tavernier, the director, dedicated the film to Young and Bud Powell, and Dexter Gordon, who played the central figure, received an Academy Award nomination for his performance. In this way, through recordings and films, Lester Young's legacy lives on.

Robert J. Paradowski

Further Reading

Büchmann-Møller, Frank. *You Just Fight for Your Life: The Story of Lester Young*. New York: Praeger, 1990. Based on interviews with those who knew and worked with Young, this survey of his life and career also contains a sensitive analysis of his music. Includes helpful appendixes on Young's performances and the personnel of his recordings and live engagements.

Daniels, Douglas Henry. *Lester Leaps In: The Life and Times of Lester "Pres" Young*. Boston: Beacon Press, 2002. Douglas presents a sympathetic, revisionist account of Young seen against the background of the history of jazz and of twentieth century African American social and cultural life. Includes extensive notes, selected discography, and index.

Porter, Lewis. *Lester Young*. Ann Arbor: University of Michigan Press, 2005. This revised edition of a biography originally published in 1985 contains a new preface and updated discography. In its first publication, Porter's book was praised as "a major contribution to jazz scholarship" that illuminates Young's life and music. Transcribed solos of Young add to this book's value.

_____, ed. *A Lester Young Reader*. Washington, D.C.: Smithsonian Institution Press, 1991. Porter creates "a symposium of Young, the man and his music" by collecting important primary and secondary sources that he structures in three parts: biographical essays, interviews of Young, and musical analyses.

Schoenberg, Loren. "Lester Young." In *The Oxford Companion to Jazz*, edited by Bill Kirchner. New York: Oxford University Press, 2000. A good brief survey of Young's life and his contributions to jazz. This massive work has a selected bibliography as well as an index of songs and recordings and an index of names and subjects.

See also: Basie, Count; Christian, Charlie; Cole, Nat King; Coltrane, John; Goodman, Benny; Gordon, Dexter; Hawkins, Coleman; Henderson, Fletcher; Holiday, Billie; Jones, Hank; Jordan, Louis; Kirk, Rahsaan Roland; Lewis, John; Mingus, Charles; Parker, Charlie; Peterson, Oscar; Webster, Ben.

Neil Young

Canadian rock guitarist and singer-songwriter

A major voice of rock music for more than forty years, Young established himself as a restless musical spirit willing to use whatever musical genre that he found appropriate to present his message. Whether employing a blistering electric guitar or a more subdued acoustic guitar, Young has composed some of the most gripping songs in rock music.

Born: November 12, 1945; Toronto, Ontario, Canada

Also known as: Neil Percival Young (full name)

Member of: Buffalo Springfield; Crazy Horse; Crosby, Stills, and Nash; Crosby, Stills, Nash, and Young

Principal works

FILM SCORES: *Where the Buffalo Roam*, 1980; *Dead Man*, 1995; *Greendale*, 2003.

Principal recordings

ALBUMS (solo): *Neil Young*, 1969; *After the Gold Rush*, 1970; *Harvest*, 1972; *Time Fades Away*, 1973; *On the Beach*, 1974; *Tonight's the Night*, 1975; *Long May You Run*, 1976 (with the Stills-Young Band); *American Stars 'n' Bars*, 1977 (with Nicolette Larson); *Comes a Time*, 1978 (with Larson); *Hawks and Doves*, 1980; *Everybody's Rockin'*, 1983 (with the Shocking Pinks); *Trans*, 1983; *Old Ways*, 1985; *Landing on Water*, 1986; *This Note's for You*, 1988; *Freedom*, 1989; *Harvest Moon*, 1992; *Unplugged*, 1993; *Mirror Ball*, 1995 (with Pearl Jam); *Dead Man*, 1996; *Silver and Gold*, 2000; *Are You Passionate?*, 2002; *Prairie Wind*, 2005; *Living with War*, 2006; *Chrome Dreams II*, 2007; *Live at Massey Hall 1971*, 2007; *Sugar Mountain: Live at Canterbury House 1968*, 2008; *Fork in the Road*, 2009.

ALBUMS (with Buffalo Springfield): *Buffalo Springfield*, 1966; *Buffalo Springfield Again*, 1967; *Last Time Around*, 1968.

ALBUMS (with Crazy Horse): *Everybody Knows This Is Nowhere*, 1969; *Zuma*, 1975; *Live Rust*, 1979; *Rust Never Sleeps*, 1979; *Re-ac-tor*, 1981; *Life*, 1987; *Ragged Glory*, 1990; *Arc*, 1991; *Weld*, 1991; *Sleeps with Angels*, 1994; *Broken Arrow*, 1996; *Year of the Horse*, 1997; *Live at the Fillmore East*, 2006.

ALBUMS (with Crosby, Stills, and Nash): *Déjà Vu*, 1970; *So Far*, 1974; *American Dream*, 1988; *Looking Forward*, 1999.

The Life

Neil Percival Young was born on November 12, 1945, in Toronto, Ontario, Canada, to Scott Young and Edna Ragland "Rassy" Young. His father, a sports reporter and author, became something of a celebrity on local television. As a child, Young lived in the small Ontario town of Omemee. He and his brother, Bob, loved to hunt, fish, and play with Lionel model trains.

Young was not a healthy child. He suffered from polio, diabetes, and epilepsy. His parents eventually divorced, and Rassy and her sons moved to Winnipeg. Young attended Kelvin High in Winnipeg. While there, he played the guitar, banjo, and ukulele in various instrumental bands. He finally formed the Squires and with this band released the single "The Sultan," which became a hit in the immediate area. With his mother's approval, Young dropped out of high school in order to concentrate on being a musician. After leaving the Squires, Young worked as a solo performer.

In 1966, Young and Bruce Palmer drove to Los Angeles. Young married Susan Acevedo in 1968; the marriage ended in 1970. In that year, he began a relationship with the actress Carrie Snodgrass. Tragically, their son was born in 1972 with cerebral palsy. In a cruel twist of fate, another son was born with the same terrible disease in 1978 to Young and his second wife, Pegi. They founded the Bridge School, located in Hillsborough, California, in 1986. The school specializes in working with children who are challenged verbally and physically.

In March of 2005, Young had to be admitted to a New York hospital to treat a brain aneurysm. During this period, he continued to write songs. These songs were used for his 2005 album *Prairie Wind*. Young was successfully treated for his medical condition and was able to return to performing in July of that year.

The Music

Young proved himself to be one of the most inventive and prolific rock songwriters of his generation. Always restless, he became a master at several music genres, including rock, country, and folk. Few performers are able to sustain the creative spark with as much fervor as Young and for such a long period of time. While frustrating fans and critics alike on occasion with some of his creative choices, Young would always remain true to his own spirit.

Early Inspiration. After settling in Southern California, Young and Palmer joined forces with Stephen Stills, Richie Furay, and Dewey Martin to form the band Buffalo Springfield. Young previously had met both Stills and Furay in Canada. The mixing of rock with folk and country helped to bring the band critical acclaim. The band's first album, *Buffalo Springfield*, was released in 1966 (re-released in 1967) and sold respectably well. Although a second album was released toward the end of 1967, the group was showing signs of falling

Neil Young. (AP/Wide World Photos)

apart. The three songs that Young contributed to the new album—"Broken Arrow," "Mr. Soul," and "Expecting to Fly"—serve as stunning examples of the breadth of Young's songwriting skills. By May, 1968, Buffalo Springfield was no longer viable as a group. Young decided to become a solo artist. His first solo album, *Neil Young*, was released in early 1969. Although the album did not sell extremely well, it did include the moody and crackling song "The Loner." In 1969, Young joined forces with Crosby, Stills, and Nash. As Crosby, Stills, Nash, and Young, the band performed at the legendary Woodstock festival in August of 1969. In 1970, their album *Déjà Vu* was released to almost universal acclaim. One of the most gripping songs of the album was Young's song "Helpless." He also wrote the politically charged song "Ohio." The group released this song in 1970 as a single in response to the killing of four students by the Ohio National Guard on the campus of Kent State University. The single became an anthem for student activists across the country.

The Solo Road. For his next solo album, Young gathered together a strong backing band that became known as Crazy Horse. With the release of *Everybody Knows This Is Nowhere* in the summer of 1969, Young established himself as a rising rock star. The album was a solid success both critically and commercially. It included such blistering songs as "Cinnamon Girl" and "Down by the River."

During the 1970's, Young established himself as one of the leading singer-songwriters in rock music. With the release of such albums as *After the Gold Rush* and *Harvest*, he became recognized as a major voice of his generation. Both of these albums were commercial and critical successes. *After the Gold Rush* included such poignant songs as "Only Love Can Break Your Heart," "Don't Let It Bring You Down," and "Southern Man."

On the country-flavored album *Harvest*, Young included the song "Heart of Gold," which became a number-one single for him and something of a signature tune. He released many more standout albums during the 1970's, including *On the Beach, Tonight's the Night, Zuma,* and *Rust Never Sleeps*. He had proven himself to be equally adept at producing quality acoustic material and hard-edged electric songs.

Revival and Grunge. For much of the 1980's, Young seemed to lose his musical direction. It was not until the late 1980's that he seemed to find his musical way once again. With the release of *Freedom* and *Ragged Glory*, he blazed the trail for what would be called grunge music during the 1990's. His song "Rockin' in the Free World" from the *Freedom* album must be considered one of the most politically potent songs of the period.

Young became known as the "godfather of grunge," a towering influence for several leading grunge bands. During the 1990's, he continued to wear several creative hats. While he did work again with Crosby, Stills, and Nash, it was his solo work that seemed to excite him most. In 2003, he released the conceptual album *Greendale*. A film version of

the album also was made. Young entered the political fray in 2006 with the release of *Living with War*.

Musical Legacy

Never one to shy away from creative challenges, he remained relevant on the musical landscape for more than four decades and across many musical genres. In 1995, Young was inducted into the Rock and Roll Hall of Fame. He was recognized as one of rock and roll's most important performers and songwriters. Over the vast landscape of his career, he inspired numerous younger musicians, including Eddie Vedder of the band Pearl Jam. In 2005, Young was honored with the American Society of Composers, Authors, and Publishers (ASCAP) Founders Award.

Jeffry Jensen

Further Reading

Echard, William. *Neil Young and the Poetics of Energy*. Bloomington: Indiana University Press, 2005. A theoretical foray into what makes Young the artistic force that he is.

Einarson, John. *Neil Young: Don't Be Denied*. Kingston, Ont.: Quarry Press, 1992. A penetrating look at Young from his early years in Canada to his life-changing move to Los Angeles.

McDonough, Jimmy. *Shakey: Neil Young's Biography*. New York: Random House, 2002. At more than seven hundred pages, this biography can be wildly uneven, yet it offers a compelling chronicle of the life of this major rock musician and iconic figure.

Williams, Paul. *Neil Young, Love to Burn: Thirty Years of Speaking Out, 1966-1996*. New York: Omnibus Press, 1997. A striking portrait of a musician who has kept driving himself to produce music that matters.

See also: Cash, Johnny; Cohen, Leonard; Crosby, David; Domino, Fats; Dylan, Bob; Harris, Emmylou; Jansch, Bert; McGuinn, Roger; Reed, Jimmy; Robertson, Robbie; Stills, Stephen; Webb, Jimmy.

Z

Frank Zappa

American rock singer, guitarist, songwriter, and classical composer

Zappa considered all aspects of his creative life—albums, concerts, books, interviews, and television appearances—as interrelated projects within the context of his overall output. His goal was to create virtuosic music that incorporated complex rhythmic structures, angular melodic lines, and tightly coordinated ensemble work.

Born: December 21, 1940; Baltimore, Maryland
Died: December 4, 1993; Los Angeles, California
Also known as: Frank Vincent Zappa (full name); FZ
Member of: The Mothers of Invention

Principal recordings

ALBUMS (solo): *Lumpy Gravy*, 1967; *The Ark*, 1969; *Hot Rats*, 1969; *Freaks and Motherfu*#@%!*, 1970; *Two Hundred Motels*, 1971; *The Grand Wazoo*, 1972; *Just Another Band from L.A.*, 1972; *Waka/Jawaka*, 1972; *Apostrophe (')*, 1974; *Poot Face Boogie*, 1975; *Safe Muffinz*, 1975; *Zoot Allures*, 1976; *Studio Tan*, 1978; *Joe's Garage, Act I*, 1979; *Joe's Garage, Acts II and III*, 1979; *Orchestral Favorites*, 1979; *Sheik Yerbouti*, 1979; *Sleep Dirt*, 1979; *Shut Up 'n' Play Yer Guitar*, 1981; *Tinseltown Rebellion*, 1981; *You Are What You Is*, 1981; *Ship Arriving Too Late to Save a Drowning Witch*, 1982; *Baby Snakes*, 1983; *London Symphony Orchestra, Vol. 1*, 1983; *The Man from Utopia*, 1983; *Rare Meat*, 1983; *Boulez Conducts Zappa: The Perfect Stranger*, 1984; *Francesco Zappa*, 1984; *Them or Us*, 1984; *Thing-Fish*, 1984; *Frank Zappa Meets the Mothers of Prevention*, 1985; *Does Humor Belong in Music?*, 1986; *Jazz from Hell*, 1986; *London Symphony Orchestra, Vol. 2*, 1987; *Broadway the Hard Way*, 1988; *Guitar*, 1988; *As an Am*, 1991; *The Best Band You Never Heard in Your Life*, 1991; *Make a Jazz Noise Here*, 1991; *The Yellow Shark*, 1993; *Civilization, Phaze III*, 1994; *Strictly Commercial*, 1995; *Lather*, 1996; *The Lost Episodes*, 1996; *Have I Offended Someone?*, 1997; *Everything Is Healing Nicely*, 1999.

ALBUMS (with the Mothers of Invention): *Freak Out!*, 1966; *Absolutely Free*, 1967; *Cruising with Ruben and the Jets*, 1968; *We're Only in It for the Money*, 1968; *Uncle Meat*, 1969; *Burnt Weeny Sandwich*, 1970; *Chunga's Revenge*, 1970; *Weasels Ripped My Flesh*, 1970; *Over-Nite Sensation*, 1973; *Roxy and Elsewhere*, 1974; *Bongo Fury*, 1975 (with Captain Beefheart); *One Size Fits All*, 1975; *Playground Psychotics*, 1992; *Ahead of Their Time*, 1993.

WRITINGS OF INTEREST: *The Real Frank Zappa Book*, 1989 (autobiography; with Peter Occhiogrosso).

The Life

Frank Vincent Zappa (ZAP-puh) was born in Baltimore, Maryland, on December 21, 1940. As the son of immigrants (of Italian-Sicilian and Greek-Arab descent), Zappa developed a sense of being an outsider at an early age. Due to Zappa's chronic health problems, the family moved to a warmer locale, eventually ending up in California. The family continued to relocate throughout the state, moving from Monterey to the San Gabriel Valley, El Cajon, San Diego, and Lancaster in the Mojave Desert northeast of Los Angeles. These constant relocations reinforced Zappa's outsider status, and he found himself associating primarily with other marginalized members of society—namely, the African American and Hispanic families who represented the fringe elements of the Lancaster community at that time.

Following graduation from high school, Zappa attended Chaffey Junior College but dropped out after one semester. This experience no doubt contributed to his lifelong disdain for formal education. After a stint producing and composing for a number of low-budget films (which ended abruptly when he was arrested on a trumped-up pornography charge—exacerbating his cynical view of the government), Zappa joined the band the Soul Giants, which under his leadership became the Mothers of Invention. Following a brief period in New York City during the late 1960's, Zappa spent the remainder of his life in Los Angeles, where he lived with his wife Gail and their four children, Moon Unit, Dweezil, Ahmet, and Diva.

In addition to his varied musical pursuits, Zappa was an outspoken critic of political and religious figures, and he spent much of the 1980's taking his activism beyond the realm of his music. Perhaps most notable was his appearance before the U.S. Senate Committee on Commerce, Science, and Transportation in September, 1985, when he testified against censorship and efforts by the Parents Music Resource Center to label music albums that they perceived as having offensive content. Following the collapse of the Berlin Wall in 1989, Zappa became politically active on the international stage, befriending the newly elected president of the Czech Republic, Václav Havel. Zappa's potential run for the U.S. presidency was cut short by a diagnosis of prostate cancer in 1990. He eventually succumbed to the disease at his home on December 4, 1993.

The Music

Early Years. Inspired by his growing interest in rhythm and blues, Zappa began his first serious musical pursuits at age fifteen, playing drums and later guitar in a number of ethnically and racially diverse bands. Around this same time, Zappa discovered the music of avant-garde composer Edgard Varèse—whom he later referred to as "the idol of my youth"—which eventually led him to discover works by Igor Stravinsky, Anton von Webern, Béla Bartók, and other important classical composers. Other influences were such rhythm-and-blues artists as Johnny "Guitar" Watson, Guitar Slim, and Howlin' Wolf and the relatively sanitized doo-wop style of the 1950's—most prominently parodied in the album *Cruising with Ruben and the Jets*. Extramusical influences included such pop-culture detritus as science-fiction B-movies and television commercials.

The Project/Object and Conceptual Continuity. Zappa's artistic vision was unique in that he considered all aspects of his creative life—albums, concerts, books, interviews, and television appearances—as interrelated projects within the context of his overall output, the object. This approach re-

flects the influence of American composer John Cage, whose own philosophy blurred the boundaries between life and art. What Zappa referred to as the "Project/Object" was unified by a web of "conceptual continuities"—an encyclopedic array of musical and cultural references spanning the gamut from the profound (religious fanaticism, political corruption, racism) to the absurd (poodles, tweezers, chrome, vacuum cleaners). The extensive use of musical quotation, from classical repertoire (Stravinsky in particular) to popular music (as in the seemingly ubiquitous "Louie, Louie"), is characteristic of a quintessentially postmodern approach to composition.

The Mothers of Invention. Knowing that there was little chance of supporting himself as a composer of avant-garde music, Zappa formed the Mothers of Invention primarily as a means to support his concert music projects. In spite of this apparent concession, Zappa managed to bring his avant-garde sensibilities to his work as a bandleader. From the beginning, the Mothers of Invention's work was unlike that of any other musical group of the time, their distinctive sound a combination of technical complexity and Cageian indeterminacy. Entire albums and even individual songs were characterized by sharp juxtapositions of unrelated musical styles, perhaps most evident in "Brown Shoes Don't Make It" (*Absolutely Free*). Their live performances were more like Dadaist happenings that incorporated audience participation and an abundant use of props. Zappa's inclusive approach to music may be summed up in his own words: "You can't always write a chord ugly enough to say what you want to say, so sometimes you have to rely on a giraffe filled with whipped cream." While not as technically proficient as later manifestations of the band, the early Mothers of Invention brought a raucous edge to Zappa's music, culminating around 1971 in the absurdist and sexually explicit vaudeville version of the band that featured front men Mark Volman and Howard Kaylan (also known as Flo and Eddie), formerly of the pop band the Turtles.

Zappa University. Throughout the 1970's, the Mothers of Invention's lineup changed constantly, because Zappa had taken sole artistic control of the band and became increasingly interested in creating virtuosic music that incorporated complex

Frank Zappa. (AP/Wide World Photos)

rhythmic structures, angular melodic lines, and tightly coordinated ensemble work. Because of the incredible demands placed on his musicians, a stint in one of Zappa's bands was often referred to as Zappa University, and many of his band members went on to lead impressive careers in their own right. Among the most notable were violinist Jean-Luc Ponty, keyboardist George Duke, guitarists Steve Vai and Adrian Belew, and drummers Terry Bozzio and Vinnie Colaiuta.

The Studio as Instrument. Zappa used the recording studio as yet another instrument in his arsenal, adopting the musique concrète techniques developed by such postwar composers as Pierre Schaeffer and later used by Varèse. These techniques included tape manipulation (reversing tape direction, overdubbing, altering tape speed) as well as a technique Zappa called xenochrony (experimental resynchronization), whereby recorded material from completely unrelated sessions was combined to form an entirely new work. Notable examples of this technique include "Friendly Little Finger" (*Zoot Allures*) and "Rubber Shirt" (*Sheik Yerbouti*).

Zappa as Guitarist. While Zappa's guitar technique does not compare to the pyrotechnic shredding of such guitarists as Yngwie Malmsteen or Vai, he considered his guitar solos as purely func-

tional, a means to an end—namely, the unfolding of a musical composition. His sound is easily identifiable, incorporating the sharp twang of Watson's style with a propensity for long, elegantly spun lines that mimic natural speech patterns rather than following regular metrical structures.

Independence. By the end of the 1970's, Zappa exerted an increasing degree of independence as an artist and entrepreneur, eventually abandoning the name the Mothers of Invention and breaking with Warner Bros. Records to form his own company, Barking Pumpkin. In the early 1980's Zappa acquired a Synclavier, an early digital keyboard that allowed him to create complex musical structures beyond human possibility. The Grammy Award-winning album *Jazz from Hell* was almost entirely realized on this instrument. His use of the Synclavier forced Zappa to confront a paradox within his own work: While a machine was able to reproduce to perfection any degree of complexity that the composer desired, it lacked the ability to react to situations that arise in performance, the latter often resulting in transcendent musical experiences.

Later Years. During the last decade of his life, Zappa continued his prolific output with projects that included symphonic works (*London Symphony Orchestra, Vol. 1* and *London Symphony Orchestra, Vol. 2*), a musical (*Thing-Fish*), transcriptions of classical works (*Francesco Zappa*), collections of solo guitar improvisations (*Shut Up 'n' Play Yer Guitar*), a world tour with a twelve-piece big band in 1988 (ultimately canceled mid-tour because of personnel problems), and an ambitious project to digitally remaster all of his earlier albums for compact-disc release. Perhaps the culmination of his entire musical career was the collaboration, beginning in 1991, with the German-based Ensemble Modern, resulting in *The Yellow Shark*, an evening-long performance of Zappa originals and transcriptions that was eventually released as an album of the same name.

Musical Legacy

Because of his extensive musical, cultural, and political impact during his lifetime, Zappa's influence on future generations is already being felt. His contributions to popular music were recognized by a posthumous induction into the Rock and Roll Hall of Fame and a Grammy Lifetime Achievement Award. Zappa's iconoclastic persona, provocative music, and antiestablishment views continue to inspire people worldwide. He has been memorialized by a bronze bust in Bad Doberan, Germany; a monument in the town of Vilnius, Lithuania; and the dedication of Frank-Zappa-Strasse in Berlin.

Zappa's legacy would be controlled primarily by his widow Gail and the Zappa Family Trust, which would release posthumous albums from Zappa's extensive archive of recorded documents, adding to the more than sixty albums released during his lifetime. Ensembles devoted to his music include the Zappa Family Trust-sponsored Zappa Plays Zappa touring band, formed in 2006 and led by Zappa's son, Dweezil; Project/Object and Banned from Utopia, both formed exclusively to cover Zappa's works; and Ensemble Modern (Germany), the Ed Palermo Big Band (New York), and the Baroque Ensemble Ambrosius (Finland), which have released entire albums of Zappa's works. Given the continued interest in Zappa's concert music, it is conceivable that some of these works may find their way into the classical canon. With the increasing amount of scholarly research relating to Zappa's work, there is little doubt as to the significance of his contributions as a cultural icon and postmodernist composer.

Joseph Klein

Further Reading

Kostelanetz, Richard. *The Frank Zappa Companion.* New York: Schirmer Books, 1997. A collection of writings from authors as varied as Ben Watson, Nicholas Slonimsky, and Havel, this book provides an excellent introduction to Zappa's work and clearly demonstrates the breadth of his influence as a musical and cultural figure.

Lowe, Kelly Fisher. *The Words and Music of Frank Zappa.* Westport, Conn.: Praeger, 2006. A detailed study of the lyrical and musical content of Zappa's work through a chronological survey of his albums. Considers Zappa's role as a satirist and his importance as a social and cultural critic.

Miles, Barry. *Zappa: A Biography.* New York: Grove Press, 2004. While the majority of this book covers familiar ground, the author often provides a degree of detail not found in comparable books.

Sheff, David. "Playboy Interview: Frank Zappa." *Playboy* (April, 1993). One of the last interviews Zappa gave before his death later that year, including discussion of the collapse of the Soviet Union and Zappa's life following his cancer diagnosis.

Vai, Steve. *The Frank Zappa Guitar Book.* Milwaukee, Wis.: Hal Leonard, 1982. Amazingly precise transcriptions of Zappa's most significant guitar solos provide unique insight into the complexities of the composer-performer's distinctive musical language.

Watson, Ben. *Frank Zappa: The Negative Dialectics of Poodle Play.* New York: St. Martin's Press, 1993. Written by a foremost Zappa authority, this book is impressive in the depth of its coverage. Although the author's strongly held political and philosophical convictions are prominent, it is nonetheless an important and recommended source of information.

Zappa, Frank, with Peter Occhiogrosso. *The Real Frank Zappa Book.* New York: Poseidon Press, 1989. Entertaining and informative autobiography provides the composer with a platform to air his views on a wide variety of topics, including music (rock, jazz, classical, electronic), capitalism, marriage, fatherhood, politics, and religion. Also includes the obligatory chapter on crude road stories detailing the exploits of various band members and groupies.

See also: Bartók, Béla; Cage, John; Howlin' Wolf; James, Elmore; Sting; Stravinsky, Igor; Varèse, Edgard; Waits, Tom; Webern, Anton von.

Hans Zimmer

German film-score composer and keyboard player

Zimmer integrated acoustical instrumentation with electronic and rock sources in his film scores, giving his musical style a balance of traditional and contemporary elements.

Born: September 12, 1957; Frankfurt, Germany
Also known as: Hans Florian Zimmer (full name)
Member of: The Buggles; Krisma

Principal works

FILM SCORES: *The Zero Boys*, 1986; *Rain Man*, 1988; *A World Apart*, 1988; *Driving Miss Daisy*, 1989; *Twister*, 1989; *Bird on a Wire*, 1990; *Days of Thunder*, 1990; *Backdraft*, 1991; *Regarding Henry*, 1991; *Thelma and Louise*, 1991; *A League of Their Own*, 1992; *Cool Runnings*, 1993; *The Lion King*, 1994; *Crimson Tide*, 1995; *The Preacher's Wife*, 1996; *The Rock*, 1996; *As Good as It Gets*, 1997; *The Last Days*, 1998; *The Prince of Egypt*, 1998; *The Thin Red Line*, 1998; *Gladiator*, 2000; *Mission: Impossible II*, 2000; *Black Hawk Down*, 2001; *Hannibal*, 2001; *Pearl Harbor*, 2001; *The Ring*, 2002; *Spirit: Stallion of the Cimarron*, 2002; *The Last Samurai*, 2003; *Spanglish*, 2004; *The Weather Man*, 2005; *The Da Vinci Code*, 2006; *The Holiday*, 2006; *Pirates of the Caribbean: At World's End*, 2007; *The Simpsons Movie*, 2007.

Principal recordings

ALBUM (with the Buggles): *The Age of Plastic*, 1980.
ALBUM (with Krisma): *Cathode Mama*, 1981.

The Life

Though born in Germany, Hans Florian Zimmer (ZIHM-mur) received his early musical influences in England, where he was raised and educated. In London, Zimmer began composing jingles for the music company Air-Edel Associates, and he became a member of various pop bands, including Ultravox, Krisma, and the Buggles. Unable to read music and having almost no formal training, Zimmer primarily worked with a synthesizer and computers live on stage. He had his first commercial success when the Buggles' single, "Video Killed the Radio Star" (1979), became an international hit and the first music video aired on MTV in 1981.

Shortly after the Buggles' success, Zimmer met film and television composer Stanley Meyers, who mentored Zimmer in the art of film composing. They collaborated on numerous projects, combining Zimmer's extensive ability with electronic media and Meyers's knowledge of acoustic instrumentation. Realizing the benefit of blending their approaches, the composers formed Lillie Yard Studio in London, a post-production facility specifically dedicated to cutting-edge electronic music work.

Through his collaboration with Meyers, Zimmer was introduced to various Hollywood producers and directors, and in 1988 he was asked to compose the music for *A World Apart*, a small-budget, revolutionary film about South Africa. The film was a turning point in Zimmer's career. He began getting more contracts in Hollywood, and in 1989 he set up a studio in California. One of the most prolific composers in Hollywood, he has composed more than one hundred film scores.

The Music

Zimmer is a self-taught composer, having acquired most of his skills through his work. His early years playing and composing jingles, rock music, and electronic music prepared him well for his career in film, and his prolific output attests to his varied background. He has become well known for his melodic sensibilities and his ability to transform thematic material to follow the overt or the hidden implications of the dialogue. Zimmer achieves his fusion of popular, electronic, and classical elements mainly through his innovative instrumentation; for example, his scores frequently feature a percussive use of the orchestra combined with drumbeats. Zimmer also employs the orchestra atmospherically in a manner similar to soundscaping in electronic music, such as in the sound track for *The Thin Red Line*.

Early Works. Zimmer's output up to the 1980's was almost exclusively jingles and pop themes, usually written with synthesizers. Working with Meyers in the 1980's undoubtedly influenced Zimmer's compositional process, especially in combining acoustical and electronic sources. Their musical score for *My Beautiful Laundrette* (1985) demonstrates the dramatic sensitivity and classically oriented harmonic awareness Zimmer would learn from Meyers. Unfortunately, it is difficult to ascertain among Zimmer's early work with Meyers how much each contributed to the score. Nevertheless, the musical aesthetic in terms of distinct instrumentation, harmonic language, and melodic clarity is clearly apparent in later Zimmer scores.

Rain Man. Zimmer's musical score for *A World Apart* attracted the attention of Barry Levinson, who hired Zimmer for his new film about two brothers and a road trip. Almost exclusively using synthesized sounds and percussion, the musical score for *Rain Man* demonstrates Zimmer's compositional aptitude and his technical competence in capturing complex emotions in the music, as one of the brothers in the film struggles to cope with the other's autism. Zimmer's placement of his understated music in the film reveals the film's lyrical moments, highlighting the connection between the brothers rather than their differences. This, along with an Academy Award nomination for Best Musical Score, helped establish Zimmer as a bankable, dramatic film music composer.

The Lion King. After working for Meyers, Zimmer gradually incorporated more symphonic elements into his primarily synthesizer-based scores.

The Lion King demonstrates Zimmer's maturity as a symphonic composer and an arranger. The musical score blends electronic elements, a live orchestra and chorus, and African percussion instruments to portray the varying on-screen action. Beyond merely repeating associative themes, Zimmer develops the thematic content through orchestration and harmony, matching the film's progress. Zimmer sets the film's songs in various arrangements as part of the musical background too, showcasing not only his skill as an arranger but also his concern for homogeneity within a film score.

Gladiator. Director Ridley Scott approached Zimmer to score *Gladiator* in 1997, before production even began. Hence Zimmer was present during some of the film's shooting, and he was able to spend time working out musical ideas before the film was even in print. Collaborating on some of the melodic material with Lisa Gerrard, Zimmer created one of his most enduring scores, showcasing his full ability as a musical dramatist. Zimmer integrates a pastiche of different styles into a thematically driven, almost Wagnerian leitmotif-based work. Two prevalent themes recur in various guises throughout the work: one for Maximus, the main character, and an earth theme, referring to the ground and Maximus's work as a farmer. Throughout the film's musical score, characteristic traits of Zimmer's orchestral style are found used in innovative ways. A dissonant, tritone-based waltz sets the stage for two important battle sequences, using the orchestra in a primarily percussive manner. The dialogue between Maximus and his rival Commodus is set in a typical dramatic nineteenth century operatic recitative style, again with punctuating instrumentation. At the other extreme, the sustained strings provide an ethereal soundscape for Gerrard's voice during lyrical moments of the film. The dichotomy between these two moments is inherent in the film itself as a distinction between Rome and the afterlife. Zimmer's score is a clas-

Hans Zimmer. (AP/Wide World Photos)

sic example of how an anachronistic score can be emotionally effective.

Musical Legacy

Zimmer's innovative combination of electronic and acoustic sources has become an influential trends in Hollywood. His musical scores are frequently used as temp tracks (guide tracks) for other films and for numerous film trailers. In 2003, in recognition of his contribution to film music, Zimmer was awarded the Henry Mancini Award for Lifetime Achievement from the American Society of Composers, Authors, and Publishers (ASCAP).

Zimmer has concentrated on mentoring and promoting young composers in Hollywood, replicating his experience with Meyers. In 1989 Zimmer and his long-standing business partner Jay Rifkin founded Media Ventures, a postproduction facility specifically catering to film music. (It has since been renamed Remote Control Productions.) Having greatly expanded over the years, the facility and its services are offered by Zimmer to emerging film music composers, many of whom have gained successful careers continuing the use of Zimmer's mix of traditional and contemporary elements.

Jamshed Turel

Further Reading

Chion, Michel. *Thin Red Line*. London: British Film Institute, 2004. Chion includes a detailed and insightful analysis of the construction and the influence of music and sound on the film's narrative.

Marans, Michael. "Hans Zimmer." *Keyboard* 15, no. 6 (June, 1989): 74-80, 146. The article is an interview with Zimmer at the start of his Hollywood career. Zimmer discusses aesthetic choices in film music, the technical aspects of film scoring, and his general approach to scoring.

See also: Elfman, Danny; Horner, James; Williams, John.

Appendixes

General Bibliography

Reference Works and General Studies

Baines, Anthony. *The Oxford Companion to Musical Instruments*. New York: Oxford University Press, 1992.

Cary, Tristram. *Dictionary of Musical Technology*. New York: Greenwood Press, 1992.

Contemporary Musicians. 65 vols. Detroit: Gale Research, 1989-2008.

Cook, Nicholas, and Anthony Pople, eds. *The Cambridge History of Twentieth-Century Music*. New York: Cambridge University Press, 2004.

Crawford, Richard. *America's Musical Life: A History*. New York: W. W. Norton, 2001.

Day, Timothy. *A Century of Recorded Music: Listening to Musical History*. New Haven, Conn.: Yale University Press, 2000.

DuPree, Mary, ed. *Musical Americans: A Biographical Dictionary, 1918-1926*. Berkeley, Calif.: Fallen Leaf Press, 1997.

Ewen, David. *The Complete Book of Twentieth Century Music*. Englewood Cliffs, N.J.: Prentice Hall, 1959.

_____. *Men and Women Who Make Music*. New York: The Reader's Press, 1945.

Fink, Robert, and Robert Ricci. *The Language of Twentieth Century Music: A Dictionary of Terms*. New York: Schirmer Books, 1975.

Gann, Kyle. *American Music in the Twentieth Century*. New York: Schirmer Books, 1997.

Griffiths, Paul. *The Thames and Hudson Encyclopaedia of Twentieth-Century Music*. London: Thames and Hudson, 1986.

Harrap's Illustrated Dictionary of Music and Musicians. New ed. London: Harrap's Reference, 1990.

Hitchcock, H. Wiley, and Stanley Sadie, eds. *The New Grove Dictionary of American Music*. New York: Grove's Dictionaries of Music, 1986.

Huang, Hao, et al., eds. *Music in the Twentieth Century*. 3 vols. Armonk, N.Y.: Sharpe Reference, 1999.

Jones, Barrie, ed. *The Hutchinson Concise Dictionary of Music*. Chicago: Fitzroy Dearborn, 1999.

Kuhn, Laura. *Music Since 1900*. 6th ed. New York: Schirmer Reference, 2001.

Latham, Alison, ed. *The Oxford Dictionary of Musical Terms*. New York: Oxford University Press, 2004.

Lebrecht, Norman. *The Complete Companion to Twentieth Century Music*. 2d ed. London: Simon & Schuster, 2000.

Morton, Brian. *The Blackwell Guide to Recorded Contemporary* Music. Cambridge, Mass.: Blackwell, 1996.

Pickering, David. *Cassell Companion to Twentieth-Century Music*. London: Cassell, 1997.

Randel, Don Michael, ed. *The Harvard Biographical Dictionary of Musicians*. Cambridge, Mass.: Belknap Press of Harvard University, 1996.

_____. *The Harvard Dictionary of Music*. 4th ed. Cambridge, Mass.: MacMillan Press of Harvard University Press, 2003.

Sadie, S., and J. Tyrell, eds. *The New Grove Dictionary of Music and Musicians*. 2d ed. 29 vols. London: Macmillan, 2001.

Sadie, Stanley, ed. *The New Grove Dictionary of Musical Instruments*. 3 vols. New York: Grove's Dictionaries of Music, 1984.

Seeger, Charles. *Studies in Musicology, 1935-1975*. Berkeley: University of California Press, 1977.

_____. *Studies in Musicology II, 1929-1979*. Edited by Ann M. Pescatello. Berkeley: University of California Press, 1994.

Slonimsky, Nicolas. *Lectionary of Music*. New York: McGraw-Hill, 1989.

_____. *Webster's New World Dictionary of Music*. Edited by Richard Kassel. New York: Macmillan, 1998.

_____, ed. emeritus. *Baker's Biographical Dictionary of Musicians*. Centennial ed. New York: Schirmer Books, 2001.

Thompson, Clifford, ed. *World Musicians*. New York: H. W. Wilson Co., 1999.

Vinton, John, ed. *Dictionary of Contemporary Music*. New York: E. P. Dutton, 1974.

African Americans and Music

Baker, David N., Lida M. Belt, and Herman C. Hudson, eds. *The Black Composer Speaks*. Metuchen, N.J.: Scarecrow Press, 1978.

Banfield, William C. *Musical Landscapes in Color: Conversations with Black American Composers.* Lanham, Md.: Scarecrow Press, 2003.

Baraka, Imamu Amiri. *Blues People: Negro Music in White America.* Reprint. New York: William Morrow, 1999.

Baraka, Imamu Amiri, and Amina Baraka. *The Music: Reflections on Jazz and Blues.* New York: Morrow, 1987.

Barnett, LaShonda K. *I Got Thunder: Black Women Songwriters on Their Craft.* New York: Thunder's Mouth Press, 2007.

Brooks, Tilford. *America's Black Musical Heritage.* Englewood Cliffs, N.J.: Prentice-Hall, 1984.

Brooks, Tim, and Dick Spottswood. *Lost Sounds: Blacks and the Birth of the Recording Industry, 1890-1919.* Urbana: University of Illinois Press, 2004.

Burnim, Mellonee V., and Portia K. Maultsby, eds. *African American Music: An Introduction.* New York: Routledge, 2006.

Costen, Melva Wilson. *In Spirit and in Truth: The Music of African American Worship.* Louisville, Ky.: Westminster John Knox Press, 2004.

Crazy Horse, Kandia, ed. *Rip It Up: The Black Experience in Rock 'n' Roll.* New York: Palgrave Macmillan, 2004.

Davis, Nathan. *African American Music: A Philosophical Look at African American Music in Society.* Needham Heights, Mass.: Simon & Schuster Custom Publishing, 1996.

De Lerma, Dominique-René, and Marsch J. Reisser. *Black Music and Musicians in the "New Grove Dictionary of American Music" and the New "Harvard Dictionary of Music."* Chicago: Center for Black Music Research, Columbia College, 1989.

Fernett, Gene. *Swing Out: Great Negro Dance Bands.* New introduction by Dan Morgenstern. New York: Da Capo Press, 1993.

Floyd, Samuel A. *International Dictionary of Black Composers.* 2 vols. Columbia College Center for Black Music Research. Chicago: Fitzroy Dearborn, 1999.

Hennessey, Thomas J. *From Jazz to Swing: African-American Jazz Musicians and Their Music, 1890-1935.* Detroit: Wayne State University Press, 1994.

Horne, Aaron, comp. *Woodwind Music of Black Composers.* New York: Greenwood Press, 1990.

Jones, Ferdinand, and Arthur C. Jones, eds. *The Triumph of the Soul: Cultural and Psychological Aspects of African American Music.* Westport, Conn.: Praeger, 2001.

Kelley, Norman, ed. *R&B, Rhythm and Business: The Political Economy of Black Music.* New York: Akashic, 2002.

Mahon, Maureen. *Right to Rock: The Black Rock Coalition and the Cultural Politics of Race.* Durham, N.C.: Duke University Press, 2004.

Merlis, Bob, and Davin Seay. *Heart and Soul: A Celebration of Black Music Style in America, 1930-1975.* New York: Billboard Books, 2002.

Neal, Mark Anthony. *What the Music Said: Black Popular Music and Black Public Culture.* New York: Routledge, 1999.

Peterson, Bernard L., Jr. *A Century of Musicals in Black and White: An Encyclopedia of Musical Stage Works by, About, or Involving African Americans.* Westport, Conn.: Greenwood Press, 1993.

Phinney, Kevin. *Souled American: How Black Music Transformed White Culture.* New York: Billboard Books, 2005.

Radano, Ronald. *Lying up a Nation: Race and Black Music.* Chicago: University of Chicago Press, 2003.

Ramsey, Guthrie P., Jr. *Race Music: Black Cultures from Bebop to Hip-Hop.* Berkeley: University of California Press, 2003.

Reed, Teresa L. *The Holy Profane: Religion in Black Popular Music.* Lexington: University Press of Kentucky, 2003.

Riis, Thomas L. *More than Just Minstrel Shows: The Rise of Black Musical Theatre at the Turn of the Century.* Brooklyn: Institute for Studies in American Music, Conservatory of Music, Brooklyn College of the City University of New York, 1992.

Shaw, Arnold. *Black Popular Music in America: The Singers, Songwriters, and Musicians Who Pioneered the Sounds of American Music.* New York: Schirmer Books, 1986.

Smith, Eric Ledell. *Blacks in Opera: An Encyclopedia of People and Companies, 1873-1993.* Jefferson, N.C.: McFarland, 1995.

Southern, Eileen. *Biographical Dictionary of Afro-American and African Musicians.* Westport, Conn.: Greenwood, 1982.

_____. *The Music of Black Americans: A History.* New York: Norton, 1997.

Stewart, Earl L. *African American Music: An Introduction.* New York: Schirmer Books. 1998.

Story, Rosalyn M. *And So I Sing: African-American Divas of Opera and Concert.* New York: Warner Books, 1990.

Tate, Eleanora E. *African American Musicians.* New York: Wiley, 2000.

Thomas, Lorenzo. *Don't Deny My Name: Words and Music and the Black Intellectual Tradition.* Edited and with an introduction by Aldon Lynn Nielsen. Ann Arbor: University of Michigan Press, 2008.

Avant-Garde, Electronic, and Experimental Music

Berghaus, Günter. *Avant-Garde Performance: Live Events and Electronic Technologies.* New York: Palgrave Macmillan, 2005.

Born, Georgina. *Rationalizing Culture: IRCAM, Boulez, and the Institutionalization of the Musical Avant-Garde.* Berkeley: University of California Press, 1995.

Darter, Tom, comp. *The Art of Electronic Music: The Instruments, Designers, and Musicians Behind the Artistic and Popular Explosion of Electronic Music.* New York: William Morrow, 1984.

Dobson, Richard. *A Dictionary of Electronic and Computer Music Technology: Instruments, Terms, Techniques.* New York: Oxford University Press, 1992.

Dodge, Charles. *Composers and the Computer.* Los Altos, Calif.: William Kaufmann, 1985.

_____. *Current Directions in Computer Music Research.* Cambridge, Mass.: The MIT Press, 1989.

Dodge, Charles, and Thomas Jerse. *Computer Music: Synthesis, Composition, and Performance.* 2d ed. New York: Schirmer Books, 1997.

Duckworth, William. *Talking Music: Conversations with John Cage, Philip Glass, Laurie Anderson, and Five Generations of American Experimental Composers.* New York: Schirmer, 1995.

Hegarty, Paul. *Noise/Music: A History.* London: Continuum, 2007.

Huxley, Michael, and Noel Witts, eds. *The Twentieth-Century Performance Reader.* New York: Routledge, 2002.

Mertens, Wim. *American Minimal Music: La Monte Young, Terry Riley, Steve Reich, Philip Glass.* London: Kahn & Averill, 1983.

Nicholls, David, ed. *American Experimental Music, 1890-1940.* New York: Cambridge University Press, 1990.

Nyman, Michael. *Experimental Music: Cage and Beyond.* New York: Da Capo Press, 1999.

Potter, Keith. *Four Musical Minimalists: La Monte Young, Terry Riley, Steve Reich, Philip Glass.* Cambridge, England: Cambridge University Press, 2000.

Prendergast, Mark J. *The Ambient Century: From Mahler to Moby—the Evolution of Sound in the Electronic Age.* London: Bloomsbury, 2003.

Reynolds, Roger. *Mind Models: New Forms of Musical Experience.* 2d ed. New York: Routledge, 2005.

Schwarz, K. Robert. *Minimalists.* London: Phaidon Press, 1996.

Sitsky, Larry, ed. *Music of the Twentieth-Century Avant-Garde: A Biocritical Sourcebook.* Westport, Conn.: Greenwood Press, 2002.

Taylor, Timothy D. *Strange Sounds: Music, Technology, and Culture.* New York: Routledge, 2001.

Toop, David. *Exotica: Fabricated Soundscapes in a Real World.* London: Serpent's Tail, 1999.

_____. *Ocean of Sound: Aether Talk, Ambient Sound, and Imaginary Worlds.* London: Serpent's Tail, 1995.

Young, Rob. *Undercurrents: The Hidden Wiring of Modern Music.* London: Continuum, 2002.

Bluegrass

Artis, Bob. *Bluegrass: From the Lonesome Wail of a Mountain Love Song to the Hammering Drive of the Scruggs-Style Banjo, the Story of an American Musical Tradition.* New York: Hawthorn Books, 1975.

Cantwell, Robert. *Bluegrass Breakdown: The Making of the Old Southern Sound.* New York: Da Capo Press, 1992.

Goldsmith, Thomas, ed. *The Bluegrass Reader.* Urbana: University of Illinois Press, 2004.

Erbsen, Wayne. *Rural Roots of Bluegrass: Songs, Stories and History.* Includes a compact disc. Pacific, Mo.: Mel Bay, 2003.

Fleischhauer, Carl, and Neil V. Rosenberg. *Bluegrass Odyssey: A Documentary in Pictures and Words, 1966-86.* Urbana: University of Illinois Press, 2001.

Kochmann, Marilyn, ed. *The Big Book of Bluegrass.* New York: W. Morrow, 1984.

Musicians and Composers of the 20th Century

Ledgin, Stephanie P. *From Every Stage: Images of America's Roots Music*. Jackson: University Press of Mississippi, 2005.

———. *Homegrown Music: Discovering Bluegrass*. Westport, Conn.: Praeger, 2004.

McGee, Marty. *Traditional Musicians of the Central Blue Ridge: Old Time, Early Country, Folk, and Bluegrass Label Recording Artists, with Discographies*. Jefferson, N.C.: McFarland, 2000.

Price, Steven D. *Old as the Hills: The Story of Bluegrass Music*. New York: Viking Press, 1975.

Rosenberg, Neil V. *Bluegrass: A History*. 20th anniversary rev. ed. Urbana: University of Illinois Press, 2005.

Smith, Richard D. *Bluegrass: An Informal Guide*. Chicago: Chicago Review Press, 1995.

Willis, Barry R., Dick Weissman, Art Menius, and Bob Cherry, eds. *America's Music: Bluegrass—a History of Bluegrass Music in the Words of Its Pioneers*. Franktown, Colo.: Pine Valley Music, 1997.

Wilson, Joe. *A Guide to the Crooked Road: Virginia's Heritage Music Trail*. Winston-Salem, N.C.: John F. Blair, 2006.

Blues

Barlow, William. *Looking up at Down: The Emergence of Blues Culture*. Philadelphia: Temple University Press, 1989.

Bastin, Bruce. *Red River Blues: The Blues Tradition in the Southeast*. Chicago: University of Illinois Press, 1995.

Bogdanov, Vladimir, Chris Woodstrata, and Stephen Thomas Erlewine, eds. *All Music Guide to the Blues: The Definitive Guide to the Blues*. 3d ed. San Francisco: Backbeat Books, 2003.

Bourgeois, Anna Stong. *Blueswomen: Profiles and Lyrics, 1920-1945*. Jefferson, N.C.: McFarland, 1996.

Charters, Samuel. *The Bluesmen: The Story and the Music of the Men Who Made the Blues*. New York: Oak, 1967.

———. *The Country Blues*. 1959. Reprint. New York: Da Capo Press, 1975.

———. *Walking a Blues Road: A Selection of Blues Writing, 1956-2004*. New York: Marion Boyars, 2005.

Cohn, Lawrence, ed. *Nothing but the Blues: The Music and the Musicians*. New York: Abbeville Press, 1993.

Davis, Angela. *Blues Legacies and Black Feminism: Gertrude "Ma" Rainey, Bessie Smith, and Billie Holiday*. New York: Pantheon Books, 1998.

Davis, Francis. *The History of the Blues: The Roots, the Music, the People, from Charley Patton to Robert Cray*. New York: Hyperion, 1995.

Dicaire, David. *Blues Singers: Biographies of Fifty Legendary Artists of the Early Twentieth Century*. Jefferson, N.C.: McFarland, 1999.

Evans, David. *Big Road Blues: Tradition and Creativity in the Folk Blues*. New York: Da Capo Press, 1988.

Guralnick, Peter. *Feel Like Going Home: Portraits in Blues and Rock 'n' Roll*. New York: Harper & Row, 1989.

Harris, Sheldon. *Blues Who's Who: A Biographical Dictionary of Blues Singers*. New Rochelle, N.Y.: Arlington House, 1979.

Harrison, Daphne Duval. *Black Pearls: Blues Queens of the 1920's*. New Brunswick, N.J.: Rutgers University Press, 1990.

Jackson, Buzzy. *A Bad Woman Feeling Good: Blues and the Women Who Sing Them*. New York: W. W. Norton, 2005.

Keil, Charles. *Urban Blues*. With a new afterword. Chicago: University of Chicago Press, 1991.

Locke, Alain. 1936. Reprint. *The Negro and His Music: Negro Art, Past and Present*. Salem, N.H.: Ayer, 1991.

Lomax, Alan. *The Land Where the Blues Began*. New York: New Press, 2002.

Moore, Alan, ed. *Cambridge Companion to Blues and Gospel Music*. New York: Cambridge University Press, 2003.

Oakley, Giles. *The Devil's Music: A History of the Blues*. New York: Da Capo Press, 1997.

Obrecht, Jas, ed. *Blues Guitar: The Men Who Made the Music, from the Pages of "Guitar Player Magazine."* San Francisco: GPI, 1990.

———. *Rollin' and Tumblin': The Postwar Blues Guitarists*. San Francsico: Miller Freeman Books, 2000.

O'Neal, Jim, and Amy van Singel. *The Voices of the Blues: Classic Interviews from "Living Blues Magazine."* New York: Routledge, 2002.

Oliver, Paul. *Blues off the Record: Thirty Years of Blues Commentary*. New York: Da Capo Press, 1984.

———. *Broadcasting the Blues: Black Blues in the Segregation Era*. New York: Routledge, 2006.

_____. *The Story of the Blues.* Boston: Northeastern University Press, 1997.

_____, et al. *Yonder Come the Blues: The Evolution of a Genre.* New York: Cambridge University Press, 2001.

Palmer, Robert. *Deep Blues.* New York: Viking Press, 1981.

Rijn, Guido van. *Kennedy's Blues: African-American Blues and Gospel Songs on JFK.* Jackson: University Press of Mississippi, 2007.

Rowe, Mike. *Chicago Blues: The City and the Music.* 1975. Reprint. New York: Da Capo Press, 1981.

_____. *Chicago Breakdown.* London: Eddison Press, 1973. Reprint. New York: Da Capo Press, 1979

Russell, Tony. *The Blues: From Robert Johnson to Robert Cray.* New York: Schirmer Books, 1997.

Santelli, Robert. *Big Book of Blues.* New York: Penguin, 2001.

Stewart-Baxter, Derrick. *Ma Rainey and the Classic Blues Singers.* New York: Stein and Day, 1970.

Titon, Jeff Todd. *Early Downhome Blues: A Musical and Cultural Analysis.* 2d ed. Chapel Hill: University of North Carolina Press, 1994.

Wald, Elijah. *Escaping the Delta: Robert Johnson and the Invention of the Blues.* New York: HarperCollins, 2004.

Waterman, Dick. *Between Midnight and Day: The Last Unpublished Blues Archive.* New York: Thunder's Mouth Press, 2003.

Weissman, Dick. *Blues.* American Popular Music series. New York: Facts On File, 2006.

Welding, Peter, and Toby Byron, eds. *Bluesland: Portraits of Twelve Major American Blues Masters.* New York: Dutton, 1991.

Williamson, Nigel. *The Rough Guide to the Blues.* London: Rough Guides, 2007.

Brazilian Music

Buenosaires, Oscar de. *Bossa Nova and Samba: History, People, Scores, Books, Lyrics, Recordings.* Albuquerque, N.Mex.: FOG, 1999.

Castro, Ruy. *Bossa Nova: The Story of the Brazilian Music That Seduced the World.* Chicago: A Cappella Books, 2000.

Leu, Lorraine. *Brazilian Popular Music: Caetano Veloso and the Regeneration of Tradition.* Burlington, Vt.: Ashgate, 2006.

McCann, Bryan. *Hello, Hello Brazil: Popular Music in the Making of Modern Brazil.* Durham, N.C.: Duke University Press, 2004.

McGowan, Chris, and Ricardo Pessanha. *The Brazilian Sound: Samba, Bossa Nova, and the Popular Music of Brazil.* 2d ed. Philadelphia: Temple University Press, 1998.

Murphy, John P. *Music in Brazil: Experiencing Music, Expressing Culture.* New York: Oxford University Press, 2006.

Perrone, Charles A. *Masters of Contemporary Brazilian Song: MPB 1965-1985.* Austin: University of Texas Press, 1989.

Perrone, Charles A., and Christopher Dunne, eds. *Brazilian Popular Music and Globalization.* Gainesville: University Press of Florida, 2001.

Schreiner, Claus. *Música Brasileira: A History of Popular Music and the People of Brazil.* Translated from the German by Mark Weinstein. 1993. Reprint. New York: Marion Boyars, 2002.

Veloso, Caetano. *Tropical Truth: A Story of Music and Revolution in Brazil.* Translated by Isabel de Sena, edited by Barbara Einzig. New York: Alfred A. Knopf, 2002.

Vianna, Hermano. *The Mystery of Samba: Popular Music and National Identity in Brazil.* Edited andtranslated by John Charles Chasteen. Chapel Hill: University of North Carolina Press, 1999.

Classical

Adamenko, Victoria. *Neo-Mythologism in Music: From Scriabin and Schoenberg to Schnittke and Crumb.* Hillsdale, N.Y.: Pendragon Press, 2007.

Ainsley, Robert, ed. *The Ultimate Encyclopedia of Classical Music.* London: Carlton, 1995.

Albright, Daniel, ed. *Modernism and Music: An Anthology of Sources.* Chicago: University of Chicago Press, 2004.

Applebaum, Samuel, and Sada Applebaum. *The Way They Play.* 14 vols. Neptune City, N.J.: Paganiniana, 1972-1986.

Ashby, Arved, ed. *The Pleasure of Modernist Music: Listening, Meaning, Intention, Ideology.* Rochester, N.Y.: University of Rochester Press, 2004.

Bagar, Robert, and Louis Biancolli. *The Concert Companion.* New York: McGraw-Hill, 1947.

Bailey, Walter B., ed. *Schoenberg, Berg, and Webern: A Companion to the Second Viennese School.* Westport, Conn.: Greenwood Press, 1999.

Beyer, Anders. *The Voice of Music: Conversations with Composers of Our Time.* Edited and translated by Jean Christensen and Beyer. Burlington, Vt.: Ashgate, 2000.

Bredeson, Carmen, and Ralph Thibodeau. *Ten Great American Composers.* Berkeley Heights, N.J.: Enslow, 2002.

Campbell, Margaret. *The Great Violinists.* New York: Doubleday, 1980.

Chotzinoff, Samuel. *A Little Night Music: Intimate Conversations with Jascha Heifetz, Vladimir Horowitz, Gian Carlo Menotti, Leontyne Price, Richard Rodgers, Artur Rubinstein, Andrés Segovia.* London: Hamish Hamilton, 1964.

Cope, David. *Techniques of the Contemporary Composer.* New York: Schirmer Books, 1997.

Craven, Robert R., ed. *Symphony Orchestras of the World: Selected Profiles.* New York: Greenwood Press, 1987.

Cummings, David, ed. *Random House Encyclopedic Dictionary of Classical Music.* New York: Random House, 1997.

Davison, Peter, ed. *Reviving the Muse: Essays on Music After Modernism.* Brinkworth, England: Claridge, 2001

DeLio, Thomas. *Circumscribing the Open Universe: Essays on Cage, Feldman, Wolff, Ashley, and Lucier.* Lanham, Md.: University Press of America, 1984.

Dubal, David. *The Essential Canon of Classical Music.* New York: North Point Press, 2001.

_____. *Reflections from the Keyboard: The World of the Concert Pianist.* New York: Schirmer Books, 1997.

Epstein, Helen. *Music Talks: Conversations with Musicians.* New York: McGraw-Hill, 1987.

Etter, Brian K. *From Classicism to Modernism: Western Musical Culture and the Metaphysics of Order.* Burlington, Vt.: Ashgate, 2001.

Gagne, Cole, and Tracy Caras. *Soundpieces: Interviews with American Composers.* Metuchen, N.J.: Scarecrow Press, 1982.

Gammond, Peter. *The Harmony Illustrated Encyclopedia of Classical Music: An Essential Guide to the World's Finest Music.* New York: Harmony Books, 1988.

Griffiths, Paul. *Modern Music and After: Directions Since 1945.* New York: Oxford University Press, 1995.

Hill, Brad. *Classical.* American Popular Music series. New York: Facts On File, 2006.

Hoffman, Miles. *The NPR Classical Music Companion: Terms and Concepts from A to Z.* Boston: Houghton Mifflin, 1997.

Holden, Raymond. *The Virtuoso Conductors: The Central European Tradition from Wagner to Karajan.* New Haven, Conn.: Yale University Press, 2005.

Horowitz, Joseph. *Classical Music in America: A History of Its Rise and Fall.* New York: W. W. Norton, 2005.

Jacobs, Arthur. *The Penguin Dictionary of Musical Performers: A Biographical Guide to Significant Interpreters of Classical Music, Singers, Solo Instrumentalists, Conductors, Orchestras, and String Quartets Ranging from the Seventeenth Century to the Present Day.* New York: Penguin Books, 1991.

Johnson, Julian. *Who Needs Classical Music? Cultural Choice and Musical Value.* New York: Oxford University Press, 2002.

Kater, Michael H. *Composers of the Nazi Era: Eight Portraits.* New York: Oxford University Press, 2000.

Kilpatrick, John, et al., eds. *The New Grove Twentieth-Century American Masters: Ives, Thomson, Sessions, Cowell, Gershwin, Copland, Carter, Barber, Cage, Bernstein.* New York: Norton, 1988.

Kramer, Lawrence. *Why Classical Music Still Matters.* Berkeley: University of California Press, 2007.

Lampert, Vera, et al., eds. *The New Grove Modern Masters: Bartók, Stravinsky, Hindemith.* London: Macmillan, 1984.

Lebrecht, Norman. *The Life and Death of Classical Music: Featuring the One Hundred Best and Twenty Worst Recordings Ever Made.* New York: Anchor Books, 2007.

Lee, Douglas A. *Masterworks of Twentieth Century Music: The Modern Repertory of the Symphony Orchestra.* New York: Routledge, 2002.

Leeuw, Ton de. *Music of the Twentieth Century: A Study of Its Elements and Structure.* Translated from the Dutch by Stephen Taylor. Amsterdam: Amsterdam University Press, 2005.

Libbey, Ted. *The NPR Guide to Building a Classical CD Collection.* 2d ed., rev. and updated. New York: Workman, 1999.

_____. *The NPR Listener's Encyclopedia of Classical Music*. New York: Workman, 2006.

Mach, Elyse. *Great Contemporary Pianists Speak for Themselves*. New York: Dover, 1980.

McVeagh, Diana, et al., eds. *The New Grove Twentieth-Century English Masters: Elgar, Delius, Vaughan Williams, Holst, Walton, Tippett, Britten*. London: Macmillan, 1986.

Morrish, John, ed. *The Classical Guitar Book: A Complete History*. San Francisco: Backbeat Books, 2002.

Nectoux, Jean-Michel, et al., eds. *The New Grove Twentieth-Century French Masters: Fauré, Debussy, Satie, Ravel, Poulenc, Messiaen, Boulez*. London: Macmillan, 1986.

Neighbour, Oliver, Paul Griffiths, and George Perle, eds. *The New Grove Second Viennese School: Schoenberg, Webern, Berg*. New York: W. W. Norton, 1983.

Noyle, Linda. *Pianists on Playing: Interviews with Twelve Concert Pianists*. Metuchen, N.J.: Scarecrow Press, 1987.

Pincus, Andrew L. *Musicians with a Mission: Keeping the Classical Tradition Alive*. Boston: Northeastern University Press, 2002.

Radice, Mark A. *Concert Music of the Twentieth Century: Its Personalities, Institutions, and Techniques*. Upper Saddle River, N.J.: Prentice Hall, 2003.

Rehding, Alexander, ed. *Music Theory and Contemporary Music*. Abingdon, England: Routledge, 2006.

Rochberg, George. *The Aesthetics of Survival: A Composer's View of Twentieth-Century Music*. Rev. and expanded ed. Ann Arbor: University of Michigan Press, 2004.

Rockwell, John. *All American Music: Composition in the Late Twentieth Century*. New York: Knopf, 1983.

Roig-Francolí, Miguel A. *Understanding Post-Tonal Music*. Boston: McGraw-Hill, 2008.

Ross, Alex. *The Rest Is Noise: Listening to the Twentieth Century*. New York: Farrar, Straus and Giroux, 2007.

Sadie, Stanley, and Vladimir Ashkenazy. *The "Billboard" Illustrated Encyclopedia of Classical Music*. New York: Billboard Books, 2000.

Salzman, Eric. *Twentieth-Century Music: An Introduction*. Upper Saddle River, N.J.: Prentice Hall, 2002.

Schonberg, Harold C. *The Glorious Ones: Classical Music's Legendary Performers*. New York: Times Books, 1985.

_____. *The Great Conductors*. New York: Simon & Schuster, 1967.

_____. *The Lives of the Great Composers*. 3d ed. New York: W. W. Norton, 1997.

Schwartz, Elliot, and Barney Childs, eds. *Contemporary Composers on Contemporary Music*. New York: Da Capo Press, 1998.

Schwartz, Elliott, and Daniel Godfrey. *Music Since 1945: Issues, Materials, and Literature*. New York: Schirmer Books, 1993.

Sharpe, Roderick, and Jeanne Stierman. *Maestros in America: Conductors in the Twenty-first Century*. Lanham, Md.: Scarecrow Press, 2008.

Simmons, Walter. *Voices in the Wilderness: Six American Neo-Romantic Composers*. Lanham, Md.: Scarecrow Press, 2006.

Staines, Joe, and Duncan Clark, eds. *The Rough Guide to Classical Music*. 4th ed., rev. and expanded. London: Rough Guides, 2005.

Stevens, Lewis. *Composers of Classical Music of Jewish Descent*. London: Vallentine Mitchell, 2003.

Struble, John Warthen. *The History of American Classical Music: MacDowell Through Minimalism*. New York: Facts On File, 1995.

Summerfield, Maurice. *The Classical Guitar: Its Evolution, Players, and Personalities Since 1800*. Blaydon on Tyne, England: Ashley Mark, 2003.

Swafford, Jan. *The Vintage Guide to Classical Music*. New York: Vintage Books, 1992.

Webb, Barrie, ed. *Contemporary Performance*. Abingdon, England: Routledge, 2007.

Whittall, Arnold. *Exploring Twentieth-Century Music: Tradition and Innovation*. New York: Cambridge University Press, 2003.

Woodstra, Chris, Gerald Brennan, and Allen Schrott, eds. *All Music Guide to Classical Music: The Definitive Guide to Classical Music*. San Francisco: Backbeat Books, 2005.

Country

Alden, Grant, and Peter Blackstock, eds. *The Best of "No Depression": Writing About American Music*. Austin: University of Texas Press, 2005.

Bane, Michael. *The Outlaws: Revolution in Country Music*. New York: Doubleday, 1978.

Bogdanov, Vladimir, Chris Woodstra, and Stephen Thomas Erlewine, eds. *All Music Guide to Coun-*

try: The Definitive Guide to Country Music. 2d ed. San Francisco: Backbeat Books, 2003.

Brown, Garrett, ed. *Legends of Classic Country*. Richmond, Va.: Time-Life Books, 2000.

Bufwack, Mary. *The Encyclopedia of Country Music: The Ultimate Guide to the Music*. New York: Oxford University Press, 1998.

Bufwack, Mary A., and Robert K. Oermann. *Finding Her Voice: Women in Country Music, 1800-2000*. Nashville, Tenn.: The Country Music Foundation Press and Vanderbilt University Press, 2003.

Bush, Johnny, and Rick Mitchell. *Whiskey River (Take My Mind): The True Story of Texas Honky Tonk*. Austin: University of Texas Press, 2007.

Byworth, Tony, ed. *The "Billboard" Illustrated Encyclopedia of Country Music*. New York: Billboard Books, 2007.

Carlin, Richard. *Country*. American Popular Music series. New York: Facts On File, 2006.

Carr, Patrick, ed. *The Illustrated History of Country Music*. New York: Random House, 1995.

Ching, B. *Wrong's What I Do Best: Hard Country Music and American Culture*. Oxford, England: Oxford University Press, 2001.

Cocoran, Michael. *All over the Map: True Heroes of Texas Music*. Austin: University of Texas Press, 2005.

Dawidoff, Nicholas. *In the Country of Country: People and Places in American Music*. New York: Pantheon Books, 1997.

Dew, Joan. *Singers and Sweethearts: The Women of Country Music*. Garden City, N.Y.: Doubleday, 1977.

Dicaire, David. *The First Generation of Country Music Stars: Biographies of Fifty Artists Born Before 1940*. Jefferson, N.C.: McFarland, 2007.

Ellison, Curtis. *Country Music Culture: From Hard Times to Heaven*. Jackson: University of Mississippi Press, 1995.

Escott, Colin. *The Grand Ole Opry: The Making of an American Icon*. New York: Center Street, 2006.

_____. *Lost Highway: The True Story of Country Music*. Washington, D.C.: Smithsonian Books, 2003.

Feiler, Bruce. *Dreaming out Loud: Garth Brooks, Wynonna Judd, Wade Hayes, and the Changing Face of Nashville*. New York: Avon Books, 1998.

Hagan, Chet. *Country Music Legends in the Hall of Fame*. Nashville, Tenn.: Thomas Nelson, 1982.

Hagar, Andrew G. *Women of Country: Dolly Parton, Patsy Cline, Tammy Wynette and More*. New York: Friedman/Fairfax, 1994.

Havighurst, Craig. *Air Castle of the South: WSM and the Making of Music City*. Urbana: University of Illinois Press, 2007.

Jensen, J. *The Nashville Sound: Authenticity, Commercialism, and Country Music*. Nashville, Tenn.: Vanderbilt University Press, 1998.

Kingsbury, Paul. *The Grand Ole Opry History of Country Music: Seventy Years of the Songs, the Stars, and the Stories*. New York: Villard Press, 1995.

_____, ed. *The Encyclopedia of Country Music: The Ultimate Guide to the Music*. New York: Oxford University Press, 1998.

Kingsbury, Paul, Alan Axelrod, and Susan Costello, eds. *Country: The Music and the Musicians—from the Beginnings to the '90's*. 2d ed. New York: Abbeville Press, 1994.

Kingsbury, Paul, and Alanna Nash, eds. *Will the Circle Be Unbroken: Country Music in America*. New York: DK, 2006.

Kosser, Michael. *How Nashville Became Music City, U.S.A.: Fifty Years of Music Row*. Milwaukee, Wis.: Hal Leonard, 2006.

LaChapelle, Peter. *Proud to Be an Okie: Cultural Politics, Country Music, and Migration to Southern California*. Los Angeles: University of California Press, 2007.

McCloud, Barry. ed. *Definitive Country: The Ultimate Encyclopedia of Country Music and Its Performers*. New York: Perigee, 1995.

Malone, Bill. *Country Music, U.S.A.* 2d rev. ed. Austin: University of Texas Press, 2002.

Malone, Bill, and Judith McCulloh, eds. *Stars of Country Music*. New York: Da Capo Press, 1975.

Millard, Bob. *Country Music: Seventy Years of America's Favorite Music*. New York: HarperPerennial, 1993.

Nash, Alanna. *Behind Closed Doors: Talking With the Legends of Country Music*. New York: Cooper Square Press, 2002.

Peterson, Richard. *Creating Country Music*. Chicago: University of Chicago Press, 1997.

Russell, Tony. *Country Music Originals: The Legends and the Lost*. New York: Oxford University Press, 2007.

St. John, Lauren. *Walkin' After Midnight: A Journey to the Heart of Nashville*. London: Picador, 2000.

Stambler, Irwin, and Grelun Landon. *Country Music: The Encyclopedia.* New York: St. Martin's Press, 1997.

_____. *The Encyclopedia of Folk, Country, and Western Music.* 2d ed. New York: St. Martin's Press, 1984.

Streissguth, Michael. *Voices of the Country: Interviews with Classic Country Performers.* New York: Routledge, 2004.

Tosches, Nick. *Country: Living Legends and Dying Metaphors in America's Biggest Music.* New York: Charles Scribner's Sons, 1985.

Tribe, Ivan. *Country: A Regional Exploration.* Westport, Conn.: Greenwood Press, 2006.

Whitburn, Joel, ed. *The "Billboard" Book of Top 40 Country Hits.* 2d ed. New York: Billboard Books, 2006.

Willman, Chris. *Rednecks and Bluenecks: The Politics of Country Music.* New York: The New Press, 2005.

Wolfe, Charles K. *Classic Country: Legends of Country Music.* New York: Routledge, 2001.

_____. *Kentucky Country: Folk and Country Music of Kentucky.* Lexington: University Press of Kentucky, 1982.

Wolfe, Charles K., and James E. Akenson, eds. *The Women of Country Music: A Reader.* Lexington: University Press of Kentucky, 2003.

Wolfe, Charles K., and Ted Olson, eds. *The Bristol Sessions: Writings About the Big Bang of Country Music.* Jefferson, N.C.: McFarland, 2005.

Zanderbergen, George. *Nashville Music: Loretta Lynn, Mac Davis, Charlie Pride.* New York: Crestwood House, 1976.

Film Music

Bazelon, Irwin. *Knowing the Score: Notes on Film Music.* New York: Van Nostrand, 1975.

Brown, Royal S. *Overtones and Undertones: Reading Film Music.* Berkeley: University of California Press, 1994.

Burlingame, Jon. *Sound and Vision: Sixty Years of Motion Picture Sound Tracks.* New York: Watson-Guptill, 2000.

Burt, George. *The Art of Film Music.* Boston: Northeastern University Press, 1995.

Cordes, Cynthia Ann, et al. *On the Track: A Guide to Contemporary Film Scoring.* New York: Routledge, 2004.

Darby, William, and Jack Du Bois. *American Film Music: Major Composers, Techniques, Trends, 1915-1990.* Jefferson, N.C.: McFarland, 1990.

Davis, Richard. *Complete Guide to Film Scoring.* Boston: Berklee Press, 2000.

Evans, Mark. *Soundtrack: The Music of the Movies.* New York: Hopkinson and Blake, 1975.

Faulner, Robert R. *Music on Demand: Composers and Careers in the Hollywood Film Industry.* Piscataway, N.J.: Transaction, 2003.

Hayward, Philip, ed. *Off the Planet: Music, Sound, and Science Fiction Cinema.* Bloomington: University of Indiana Press, 2004.

Hemming, Roy. *The Melody Lingers On: The Great Songwriters and Their Movie Musicals.* New York: Newmarket Press, 1986.

Hickman, Roger. *Reel Music: Exploring One Hundred Years of Film Music.* New York: W. W. Norton, 2005.

Hischak, Thomas S. *The American Musical Film Song Encyclopedia.* Westport, Conn.: Greenwood Press, 1999.

Karlin, Fred. *Listening to Movies: The Film Lover's Guide to Film Music.* New York: Books, 1994.

Kubernik, Harvey. *Hollywood Shack Job: Rock Music in Film and on Your Screen.* Albuquerque: University of New Mexico Press, 2006.

Larson, Randall D. *Musique Fantastique: A Survey of Film Music in the Fantastc Cinema.* Metuchen, N.J.: Scarecrow Press, 1985.

Marmorstein, G. *Hollywood Rhapsody: Movie Music and Its Makers, 1900 to 1975.* New York: Schirmer Books, 1997.

Morgan, David. *Knowing the Score: Film Composers Talk About the Art, Craft, Blood, Sweat, and Tears of Writing for Cinema.* New York: Harper Paperbacks, 2000.

Palmer, Christopher. *The Composer in Hollywood.* London: Marion Boyars, 1990.

Prendergast, Roy M. *Film Music, a Neglected Art: A Critical Study of Music in Films.* 2d ed. New York: Norton, 1992.

Rona, Jeff. *The Reel World: Scoring for Pictures.* San Francisco: Miller Freeman Books, 2000.

Russell, Mark, and James Young. *Film Music.* Boston: Focal Press, 2000.

Smith, Jeff. *The Sounds of Commerce: Marketing Popular Film Music.* New York: Columbia University Press, 1998.

Thomas, Tony. *Film Score: The Art and Craft of Movie Music.* Burbank, Calif.: Riverwood Press, 1991.

———. *Music for the Movies.* 2d ed. Los Angeles: Silman-James Press, 1997.

Folk and Folk Rock

Alarik, Scott, and Robert Corwin. *Deep Community: Adventures in the Modern Folk Underground.* Cambridge, Mass.: Black Wolf Press, 2003.

Brocken, Michael. *The British Folk Revival, 1944-2002.* Aldershot, England: Ashgate, 2003.

Cantwell, Robert S. *When We Were Good: The Folk Revival.* Cambridge, Mass.: Harvard University Press, 1997.

Carlin, Richard. *Folk.* American Popular Music series. New York: Facts On File, 2006.

Cohen, Norm. *Folk Music: A Regional Exploration.* Westport, Conn.: Greenwood Press, 2005.

———. *Long Steel Rail: The Railroad in American Folksong.* 2d ed. Music edited by David Cohen. Urbana: University of Illinois Press, 2000.

———, ed. *Ethnic and Border Music: A Regional Exploration.* Westport, Conn.: Greenwood Press, 2007.

Cohen, Ronald D. *Folk Music: The Basics.* New York: Routledge, 2006.

———. *Rainbow Quest: The Folk Music Revival and American Society, 1940-1970.* Amherst: University of Massachusetts Press, 2002.

Courlander, Harold. *Negro Folk Music U.S.A.* New York: Columbia University Press, 1963. Reprint. New York: Dover, 1992.

Filene, Benjamin. *Romancing the Folk: Public Memory and American Roots Music.* Chapel Hill: University of North Carolina Press, 2000.

Green, Archie. *Only a Miner: Studies in Recorded Coal-Mining Songs.* Urbana: University of Illinois Press, 1972.

Gruning, Tom. *Millennium Folk: American Folk Music Since the Sixties.* Athens: University of Georgia Press, 2006.

Hajdu, David. *Positively 4th Street: The Lives and Times of Joan Baez, Bob Dylan, Mimi Baez Farina, and Richard Farina.* New York: Farrar, Straus, and Giroux, 2001.

Hampton, Wade. *Guerrilla Minstrels.* Knoxville: University of Tennessee Press, 1986.

Hood, Phil. *Artists of American Folk Music: The Legends of Traditional Folk, the Stars of the Sixties, the Virtuosi of New Acoustic Music.* New York: Quill, 1986.

Lankford, Ronald D. *Folk Music U.S.A.: The Changing Voice of Protest.* New York: Schirmer Books, 2005.

Lornell, Kip. *The NPR Curious Listener's Guide to American Folk Music.* New York: Berkley, 2004.

Nettl, Bruno, and Helen Myers. *Folk Music in the United States: An Introduction.* 3d ed. rev. and expanded by Helen Myers. Detroit: Wayne State University Press, 1976.

Ritchie, Jean. *Folk Songs of the Southern Appalachians.* 2d ed. Lexington: University Press of Kentucky, 1997.

Rosenberg, Neil V., ed. *Transforming Tradition: Folk Music Revivals Examined.* Urbana: University of Illinois Press, 1993.

Santoro, Gene. *Highway 61 Revisited: The Tangled Roots of American Jazz, Blues, Folk, Rock, and Country Music.* New York: Oxford University Press, 2004.

Seeger, Ruth Crawford. *"The Music of American Folk Song" and Selected Other Writings on American Folk Music.* Edited by Larry Polansky with Judith Tick. Forewords by Pete, Mike, and Peggy Seeger. Rochester, N.Y.: University of Rochester Press, 2001.

Stambler, Irwin, and Lyndon Stambler. *Folk and Blues: The Encyclopedia.* New York: St. Martin's Press, 2001.

Unterberger, Richie. *Eight Miles High: Folk-Rock's Flight from Haight-Ashbury to Woodstock.* San Francisco: Backbeat Books, 2003.

———. *Turn! Turn! Turn! The Sixties Folk-Rock Revolution.* San Francisco: Backbeat Books, 2002.

Vassal, Jacques. *Electric Children: Roots and Branches of Modern Folkrock.* New York: Taplinger, 1976.

Weissman, Dick. *Which Side Are You On? An Inside History of the Folk Music Revival in America.* London: Continuum, 2005.

Woliver, Robbie. *Bringing It All Back Home: Twenty-five Years of American Music at Folk City.* New York: Pantheon Books, 1986.

Gays and Lesbians and Music

Brett, Philip, Elizabeth Wood, and Gary C. Thomas, eds. *Queering the Pitch: The New Gay and Lesbian Musicology.* 2d ed. New York: Routledge, 2006.

Fleming, Lee, ed. *Hot Licks: Lesbian Musicians of Note*. Charlottetown, P.E.I.: Gynergy, 1996.

Fuller, Sophie, and Lloyd Whitesell, eds. *Queer Episodes in Music and Modern Identity*. Urbana: University of Illinois Press, 2002.

Gill, John. *Queer Noises: Male and Female Homosexuality in Twentieth Century Music*. Minneapolis: University of Minnesota Press, 1995.

Hadleigh, Boze. *Sing Out! Gays and Lesbians in the Music World*. New York: Barricade Books, 1997.

_____. *The Vinyl Closet: Gays in the Music World*. San Diego, Calif.: Los Hombres Press, 1991.

Smith, Richard. *Seduced and Abandoned: Essays on Gay Men and Popular Music*. London: Cassell, 1995.

Studer, Wayne. *Rock on the Wild Side: Gay Male Images in Popular Music of the Rock Era*. San Francisco: Leyland, 1994.

Summers, Claude J., ed. *The Queer Encyclopedia of Music, Dance, and Musical Theater*. San Francisco: Cleis Press, 2004.

Whiteley, Sheila, and Jennifer Rycenga, eds. *Queering the Popular Pitch*. New York: Routledge, 2006.

Gospel

Boyer, Horace Clarence. *The Golden Age of Gospel*. Photography by Lloyd Yearwood. Urbana: University of Illinois Press, 2000.

_____. *How Sweet the Sound: The Golden Age of Gospel*. Washington, D.C.: Elliott and Clark, 1995.

Broughton, Viv. *Too Close to Heaven: The Illustrated History of Gospel Music*. London: Midnight Books, 1996.

Carpenter, Bil. *Uncloudy Days: The Gospel Music Encyclopedia*. San Francisco: Backbeat Books, 2005.

Cusic, Don. *The Sound of Light: The History of Gospel and Christian Music*. Milwaukee, Wis.: Hal Leonard, 2002.

Darden, Bob. *People Get Ready! A New History of Black Gospel Music*. New York: Continuum, 2004.

Goff, James R., Jr. *Close Harmony: A History of Southern Gospel*. Chapel Hill: University of North Carolina Press, 2002.

Graves, Michael P., and David Fillingim, eds. *More than Precious Memories: The Rhetoric of Southern Gospel Music*. Macon, Ga.: Mercer University Press, 2004.

Heilbut, Anthony. *The Gospel Sound: Good News and Bad Times*. New York: Limelight, 2002.

Hillsman, Joan R. *Gospel Music: An African American Art Form*. New York: McGraw-Hill, 1998.

Jackson, Jerma A. *Singing in My Soul: Black Gospel Music in a Secular Age*. Chapel Hill: University of North Carolina Press, 2004.

McNeil, W. K. *Encyclopedia of American Gospel Music*. New York: Routledge, 2005.

Oliver, Paul, Max Harrison, and William Bolcom. *The New Grove Gospel, Blues, and Jazz, with Spirituals and Ragtime*. New York: Norton, 1986.

Pollard, Deborah Smith. *When the Church Becomes Your Party: Contemporary Gospel Music*. Detroit: Wayne State University Press, 2008.

Reagon, Bernice Johnson. *If You Don't Go, Don't Hinder Me: The African American Sacred Song Tradition*. Lincoln: University of Nebraska Press, 2001.

_____. *We'll Understand It Better By and By: Pioneering African American Gospel Composers*. Washington, D.C.: Smithsonian Institution Press, 1992.

Terry, Lindsay. *Stories Behind Fifty Southern Gospel Favorites*. Grand Rapids, Mich.: Kregel, 2005.

Young, Alan. *Woke Me up This Morning: Black Gospel Singers and the Gospel Life*. Jackson: University Press of Mississippi, 1997.

Hip-Hop and Rap

Berger, Arion. *Hardcore Rap: A Fusion of Metal, Rock, and Hip-Hop*. New York: Universe, 2001.

Brown, Ethan. *Queens Reigns Supreme: Fat Cat, 50 Cent, and the Rise of the Hip-Hop Hustler*. New York: Anchor Books, 2005.

Brown, Jake. *Dr. Dre in the Studio: From Compton, Death Row, Snoop Dogg, Eminem, 50 Cent, the Game, and Mad Money, the Life, Times, and Aftermath of the Notorious Record Producer, Dr. Dre*. New York: Colossus Books, 2006.

Campbell, Kermit E. *Gettin' Our Groove On: Rhetoric, Language, and Literacy for the Hip Hop Generation*. Detroit: Wayne State University Press, 2005.

Cepeda, Raquel, ed. *And It Don't Stop: The Best American Hip-Hop Journalism of the Last Twenty-five Years*. New York: Faber and Faber, 2004.

Chang, Jeff. *Can't Stop, Won't Stop: A History of the Hip-Hop Generation*. New York: St. Martin's Press, 2005.

Chuck D and Yusuf Jah. *Lyrics of a Rap Revolutionary*. New York: Offda Books, 2007.

Chuck D, Yusuf Jah, and Spike Lee. *Fight the Power: Rap, Race, and Reality*. New York: Delta, 1997.

Dyson, Michael Eric. *Know What I Mean? Reflections on Hip-Hop*. New York: Basic Civitas, 2007.

Fernando, S. H., Jr. *The New Beats: Exploring the Music, Culture, and Attitudes of Hip-Hop*. New York: Anchor Books, 1994.

Forman, Murray, and Mark Anthony Neal, eds. *That's the Joint! The Hip-Hop Studies Reader*. Oxford, England: Routledge, 2004.

Fricke, Jim, and Charlie Ahearn. *Yes Yes Y'All: The Experience Music Project Oral History of Hip-Hop's First Decade*. New York: Da Capo Press, 2002.

George, Nelson. *Hip-Hop America*. New York: Penguin, 2005.

Green, Jared, ed. *Rap and Hip-Hop: Examining Pop Culture*. San Diego, Calif.: Greenhaven Press, 2003.

Hess, Mickey. *Is Hip Hop Dead? The Past, Present, and Future of America's Most Wanted Music*. Westport, Conn.: Praeger, 2007.

_____, ed. *Icons of Hip Hop: An Encyclopedia of the Movement, Music, and Culture*. Westport, Conn.: Greenwood Press, 2007.

Hisama, Ellie M., and Evan Rapport, eds. *Critical Minded: New Approaches to Hip-Hop Studies*. Brooklyn, N.Y.: Institute for Studies in American Music, 2005.

Keyes, Cheryl L. *Rap Music and Street Consciousness*. Urbana: University of Illinois Press, 2002.

Kitwana, Bakari. *Why White Kids Love Hip-Hop: Wankstas, Wiggers, Wannabes, and the New Reality of Race in America*. New York: Basic Civitas Books, 2005.

Light, Alan, ed. *The "Vibe" History of Hip-Hop*. New York: Three Rivers Press, 1999.

McFarland, Pancho. *Chicano Rap: Gender and Violence in the Postindustrial Barrio*. Austin: University of Texas Press, 2008.

McQuillar, Tayannah Lee. *When Rap Music Had a Conscience: The Artists, Organizations, and Historic Events That Inspired and Influenced the "Golden Age" of Hip-Hop from 1987 to 1996*. New York: Thunder's Mouth Press, 2007.

Ogbar, Jeffrey O. G. *Hip-Hop Revolution: The Culture and Politics of Rap*. Lawrence: University Press of Kansas, 2007.

Ogg, Alex, and David Upshal. *The Hip Hop Years: A History of Rap*. New York: Fromm International, 2001.

Oliver, Richard, and Tim Leffel. *Hip-Hop, Inc.: Success Strategies of the Rap Moguls*. New York: Thunder's Mouth Press, 2006.

Perry, Imani. *Prophets of the Hood: Politics and Poetics in Hip Hop*. Durham, N.C.: Duke University Press, 2004.

Pough, Gwendolyn D. *Check It While I Wreck It: Black Womanhood, Hip Hop Culture, and the Public Sphere*. Boston: Northeastern University Press, 2004.

Quinn, Eithne. *Nuthin' but a "G" Thang: The Culture and Commerce of Gangsta Rap*. New York: Columbia University Press, 2005.

Reeves, Marcus. *Somebody Scream! Rap Music's Rise to Prominence in the Aftershock of Black Power*. New York: Faber & Faber, 2008.

Reynolds, Simon. *Bring the Noise: Twenty Years of Writing About Hip Rock and Hip Hop*. London: Faber, 2007.

Rose, Tricia. *Black Noise: Rap Music and Black Culture in Contemporary America*. Hanover, N.H.: Wesleyan University Press/New England, 1994.

Shapiro, Peter. *The Rough Guide to Hip-Hop*. London: Rough Guides, 2005.

Strode, Tim, and Tim Wood, eds. *The Hip Hop Reader*. New York: Pearson Longman, 2008.

Toop, David. *The Rap Attack: African Jive to New York Hip-Hop*. New York: Serpent's Tail, 1991.

_____. *Rap Attack 2: African Rap to Global Hip Hop*. London: Serpent's Tail, 1994.

_____. *Rap Attack 3: African Rap to Global Hip Hop*. London: Serpent's Tail, 2000.

Vibe Magazine. *Hip-Hop Divas*. New York: Three Rivers Press, 2001.

Wang, Oliver, ed. *Classic Material: The Hip-Hop Album Guide*. Toronto: ECW Press, 2003.

Watkins, S. Craig. *Hip-Hop Matters: Politics, Pop Culture, and the Struggle for the Soul of a Movement*. Boston: Beacon Press, 2005.

Woodstra, Chris, John Bush, and Stephen Thomas Erlewine, eds. *Old School Rap and Hip-Hop*. New York: Backbeat Books, 2008.

Jazz

Alexander, Charles. *Masters of Jazz Guitar: The Story of the Players and Their Music*. San Francisco: Backbeat Books, 2002.

Balliett, Whitney. *American Musicians II: Seventy-

two Portraits in Jazz. New York: Oxford University Press, 1986.

_____. *American Singers: Twenty-seven Portraits in Song.* New York: Oxford University Press, 1988.

Barnhart, Scotty. *The World of Jazz Trumpet: A Comprehensive History and Practical Philosophy.* Milwaukee, Wis.: Hal Leonard, 2005.

Budds, Michael J. *Jazz in the Sixties: The Expansion of Musical Resources and Techniques.* Iowa City: University of Iowa Press, 1978.

Case, Brian, and Stan Britt. *The Harmony Illustrated Encyclopedia of Jazz.* 3d ed. New York: Harmony Books, 1986.

Collier, James Lincoln. *The Making of Jazz: A Comprehensive History.* New York: Dell, 1978.

Cook, R. M., and Brian Norton. *The Penguin Guide to Jazz Recordings.* 8th ed. London: Penguin, 2006.

Crouch, Stanley. *Considering Genius.* New York: Basic Civitas Books, 2006.

Crowther, Bruce, and Mike Pinfold. *The Jazz Singers: From Ragtime to the New Wave.* New York: Blandford Press, 1986.

_____. *Singing Jazz.* San Francisco: Miller Freeman Books, 1997.

Dahl, Linda. *Stormy Weather: The Music and Lives of a Century of Jazz Women.* New York: Pantheon Books, 1984.

Dance, Stanley. *The World of Swing.* New York: Da Capo Press, 1979.

Doerschuk, Robert. *88: The Giants of Jazz Piano.* San Francisco: Backbeat Books, 2001.

Enstice, Wayne, and Janis Stockhouse. *Jazzwomen: Conversations with Twenty-one Musicians.* Bloomington: Indiana University Press, 2004.

Feather, Leonard. *The Encyclopedia of Jazz.* New York: Da Capo Press, 1960.

_____. *Encyclopedia of Jazz in the Sixties.* New York: Horizon Press, 1967.

_____. *From Satchmo to Miles.* New York: Da Capo Press, 1972.

_____. *The Jazz Years: Earwitness to an Era.* New York: Da Capo Press, 1987.

_____. *The New Encyclopedia of Jazz.* Oxford, England: Oxford University Press, 1999.

_____. *The Passion for Jazz.* New York: Horizon, 1980.

_____. *The Pleasures of Jazz: Leading Performers on*

Their Lives, Their Music, Their Contemporaries. New York: Horizon Press, 1976.

Feather, Leonard, and Ira Gitler. *The Biographical Encyclopedia of Jazz.* Oxford, England: Oxford University Press, 2007.

Friedwald, Will. *Jazz Singing.* Cambridge, Mass.: Da Capo Press, 1996.

Giddins, Gary. *Riding on a Blue Note: Jazz and American Pop.* New York: Oxford University Press, 1981. Reprint. New York: Da Capo Press, 2000.

_____. *Visions of Jazz: The First Century.* New York: Oxford University Press, 1998.

Gioia, Ted. *The History of Jazz.* New York: Oxford University Press, 1997.

_____. *The Imperfect Art: Reflections on Jazz and Modern Culture.* New York: Oxford University Press, 1989.

_____. *West Coast Jazz: Modern Jazz in California, 1945-1960.* Berkeley: University of California Press, 1998.

Glaser, Matt and Stéphane Grappelli. *Jazz Violin.* New York: Oak, 1981.

Goldberg, Joe. *Jazz Masters of the Fifties.* New York: Da Capo Press, 1965.

Gottlieb, Robert, ed. *Reading Jazz: A Gathering of Autobiographies, Reportage, and Criticism from 1919 to Now.* New York: Pantheon Books, 1996.

Gourse, Leslie. *Louis' Children: American Jazz Singers.* New York: Cooper Square Press, 2001.

_____. *Madame Jazz: Contemporary Women Instrumentalists.* New York: Oxford University Press, 1995.

Green, Benny. *The Reluctant Art: Five Studies in the Growth of Jazz.* Cambridge, Mass.: Da Capo Press, 1991.

Gridley, Mark. *Jazz Styles: History and Analysis.* Englewood Cliffs, N.J.: Prentice Hall, 1994.

Hadlock, Richard. *Jazz Masters of the 1920's.* New York: Da Capo Press, 1972.

Hentoff, Nat. *Jazz Is.* New York: Random House, 1976.

Holmes, Thom. *Jazz.* American Popular Music series. New York: Facts On File, 2006.

Jenkins, Todd S. *Free Jazz and Free Improvisation: An Encyclopedia.* Westport, Conn.: Greenwood Press, 2004.

Jost, Ekkehard. *Free Jazz.* New York: Da Capo Press, 1981.

Kernfeld, Barry, ed. *The New Grove Dictionary of*

Jazz. 2d ed. New York: Grove's Dictionaries, 2002.

Kirchner, Bill, ed. *The Oxford Companion to Jazz*. New York: Oxford University Press, 2000.

Korall, Burt. *Drummin' Men: The Heartbeat of Jazz—the Bebop Years*. Oxford, England: Oxford University Press, 2002.

Larson, Thomas. *Fragmentation: The Piano Trio in History and Tradition of Jazz*. Dubuque, Iowa: Kendall/Hunt, 2005.

Lees, Gene. *Waiting for Dizzy: Fourteen Jazz Portraits*. New York: Oxford University Press, 1991. Reprint. New York: Cooper Square Press, 2000.

_____. *You Can't Steal a Gift: Dizzy, Clark, Milt, and Nat*. New Haven, Conn.: Yale University Press, 2001.

Lyons, Len. *The Great Jazz Pianists: Speaking of Their Lives and Music*. New York: Da Capo Press, 1983.

Lyons, Len, and Don Perlo. *Jazz Portraits. The Lives and Music of the Jazz Masters*. New York: William Morrow, 1989.

Lyttleton, Humphrey. *The Best of Jazz: Basin Street to Harlem*. New York: Penguin Books, 1980.

Martin, Henry. *Enjoying Jazz*. New York: Schirmer Books, 1986.

Martin, Henry, and Keith Waters. *Jazz: The First Hundred Years*. Belmont, Calif.: Wadsworth/Thomson Learning, 2002.

Mathieson, Kenny. *Giant Steps: Bebop and the Creators of Modern Jazz, 1945-1965*. Edinburgh: Payback, 1999.

Megill, David W., and Paul O. W. Tanner. *Jazz Issues: A Critical History*. Dubuque, Iowa: William C. Brown and Benchmark, 1995.

Morgenstern, Dan, and Sheldon Meyer. *Living with Jazz*. New York: Pantheon Books, 2004.

Nicholson, Stuart. *Jazz-Rock: A History*. New York: Schirmer Books, 1998.

Oliphant, Dave. *The Early Swing Era, 1930 to 1941*. Westport, Conn.: Greenwood Press, 2002.

Ostransky, Leroy. *Understanding Jazz*. Englewood Cliffs, N.J.: Prentice-Hall, 1977.

Peterson, Lloyd. *Music and the Creative Spirit: Innovators in Jazz, Improvisation, and the Avant Garde*. Lanham, Md.: Scarecrow Press, 2006.

Porter, Lewis, and Michael Ullman. *Jazz, from Its Origins to the Present*. Englewood Cliffs, N.J.: Prentice Hall, 1993.

Ratliff, Ben. *Jazz: A Critic's Guide to the Hundred Most Important Recordings*. New York: Henry Holt, 2002.

Rosenthal, David H. *Hard Bop: Jazz and Black Music, 1955-1965*. New York: Oxford University Press, 1992.

Rowland, Mark, and Tony Scherman, eds. *The Jazz Musician*. New York: St. Martin's Press, 1994.

Schuller, Gunther. *Early Jazz: Its Roots and Musical Development*. New York: Oxford University Press, 1968.

_____. *The Swing Era: The Development of Jazz, 1930-1945*. Oxford, England: Oxford University Press, 1989.

Shadwick, Keith. *The Encyclopedia of Jazz and Blues*. London: Quantum, 2007.

Shapiro, Nat, and Nat Hentoff, eds. *Hear Me Talkin' to Ya: The Story of Jazz as Told by the Men Who Made It*. New York: Dover, 1966.

Shipton, Alyn. *Handful of Keys: Conversations with Thirty Jazz Pianists*. New York: Routledge, 2004.

_____. *A New History of Jazz: Revised and Updated Edition*. New York: Continuum, 2007.

Sidran, Ben. *Talking Jazz: An Oral History*. New York: Da Capo Press, 1995.

Spagnardi, Ronald. *The Great Jazz Drummers*. Cedar Grove, N.J.: Modern Drummer Publications, 1992.

Spellman, A. B. *Four Lives in the Bebop Business*. Ann Arbor: University of Michigan Press, 2004.

Stearns, Marshall W. *The Story of Jazz*. New York: Oxford University Press, 1970.

Stewart, Rex. *Jazz Masters of the Thirties*. New York: Macmillan, 1972.

Taylor, Billy. *Jazz Piano: A Jazz History*. Dubuque, Iowa: William C. Brown, 1982.

Tirro, Frank. *Jazz: A History*. 2d ed. New York: W. W. Norton, 1993.

_____. *Living with Jazz*. Orlando, Fla.: Harcourt Brace, 1996.

Walser, Robert. *Keeping Time: Readings in Jazz History*. New York: Oxford University Press, 1999.

Ward, Geoffrey, and Ken Burns. *Jazz: A History of America's Music*. New York: Alfred Knopf, 2000.

Weinstein, Norman C. *A Night in Tunisia: Imaginings of Africa in Jazz*. Metuchen, N.J.: Scarecrow Press, 1992.

Williams, Martin. *Jazz Changes*. New York: Oxford University Press, 1992.

_____. *Jazz Heritage*. New York: Oxford University Press, 1985.

_____. *Jazz Masters in Transition, 1957-1969*. London: Macmillan, 1970. Reprint. New York: Da Capo Press, 1982.

_____. *Jazz Masters of New Orleans*. New York: Da Capo Press, 1979.

_____. *The Jazz Tradition*. 2d rev. ed. New York: Oxford University Press, 1993.

Yanow, Scott. *Afro-Cuban Jazz: Third Ear—The Essential Listening Companion*. San Francisco: Miller Freeman, 2000.

Yarrow, Scott. *Trumpet Kings: The Players Who Shaped the Sound of Jazz Trumpet*. San Francisco: Back Beat Books, 2001.

Yudkin, Jeremy. *Miles Davis, Miles Smiles, and the Invention of Post-Bop*. Bloomington: Indiana University Press, 2008.

Latin American Music

Alava, Silvio H. *Spanish Harlem's Musical Legacy, 1930-1980*. New York: Arcadia, 2007.

Aparicio, Frances R. *Listening to Salsa: Gender, Latin Popular Music, and Puerto Rican Cultures*. Hanover, N.H.: University Press of New England, 1998.

Baim, Jo. *Tango: Creation of a Cultural Icon*. Bloomington: Indiana University Press, 2007.

Béhague, Gerard. *Music in Latin America: An Introduction*. Englewood Cliffs, N.J.: Prentice Hall, 1979.

Boggs, Vernon. *Salsiology: Afro-Cuban Music and the Evolution of Salsa in New York City*. Westport, Conn.: Greenwood Press, 1992.

Burr, Ramiro. *The Billboard Guide to Tejano and Regional Mexican* Music. New York: Billboard Books, 1999.

Calvo Ospina, Hernando. *Salsa! Havana Heat, Bronx Beat*. Translated by Nick Caistor. London: Latin America Research Bureau, 1995.

Croppa, Carlos G. *The Tango in the United States*. Jefferson, N.C.: McFarland, 2004.

Fernandez, Raul A. *From Afro Cuban Rhythms to Latin Jazz*. Berkeley: University of California Press, 2006.

Figueroa, Rafael, comp. *Salsa and Related Genres: A Bibliographical Guide*. Westport, Conn.: Greenwood Press, 1992.

Flores, Juan. *From Bomba to Hip-Hop*. New York: Columbia University Press, 2000.

Gerard, Charley. *Music from Cuba: Mongo Santamaría, Chocolate Armenteros, and Cuban Musicians in the United States*. Westport, Conn.: Praeger, 2001.

Gerard, Charley, with Marty Sheller. *Salsa! The Rhythm of Latin Music*. New ed. Tempe, Ariz.: White Cliffs Media, 1998.

Leymarie, Isabelle. *Cuban Fire: The Story of Salsa and Latin Jazz*. London: Continuum, 2002.

Lowinger, Rosa, and Ofelia Fox. *Tropicana Nights: The Life and Times of the Legendary Cuban Nightclub*. Orlando, Fla.: Harvest Books, 2005.

Moore, Robin D. *Music and Revolution: Cultural Change in Socialist Cuba*. Berkeley: University of California Press, 2006.

Morales, Ed. *The Latin Beat: The Rhythms and Roots of Latin Music, from Bossa Nova to Salsa and Beyond*. New York: Da Capo Press, 2003.

Olsen, Dale A., and Daniel E. Sheehy, eds. *The Garland Handbook of Latin American Music*. 2d ed. Includes two compact discs. New York: Garland, 2008.

Orovio, Helio. *Cuban Music from A to Z*. Durham, N.C.: Duke University Press, 2004.

Padura Fuentes, Leonardo. *Faces of Salsa: A Spoken History of the Music*. Translated by Stephen J. Clark. Washington. D.C.: Smithsonian Books, 2003.

Peña, Manuel. *Música Tejana: The Cultural Economy of Artistic Transformation*. College Station: Texas A&M University Press, 1999.

Primero, Max Salazar. *Mambo Kingdom: Latin Music in New York*. New York: Schirmer, 2002.

Roberts, John Storm. *Latin Jazz: The First of the Fusions, 1880's to Today*. New York: Schirmer Books, 1999.

_____. *The Latin Tinge: The Impact of Latin American Music on the United States*. 2d ed. New York: Oxford University Press, 1999.

Rondón, César Miguel. *The Book of Salsa: A Chronicle of Urban Music from the Caribbean to New York City*. Translated by Frances R. Aparicio with Jackie White. Chapel Hill: University of North Carolina Press, 2008.

Salazar, Max. *Mambo Kingdom: Latin Music in New York*. New York: Schirmer Books, 2002.

San Miguel, Guadalupe, Jr. *Tejano Proud: Tex-Mex*

1685

Music in the Twentieth Century. College Station: Texas A&M University Press, 2002.

Steward, Sue. *Musica! Salsa, Rumba, Merengue, and More*. San Francisco: Chronicle Books, 1999.

Sublette, Ned. *Cuba and Its Music: From the First Drums to the Mambo*. Chicago: Chicago Review Press, 2004.

Waxer, Lise. *The City of Musical Memory: Salsa, Record Grooves, and Popular Culture in Cali, Colombia*. Middletown, Conn.: Wesleyan University Press, 2002.

_____. *Situating Salsa: Global Markets and Local Meanings in Latin Popular Music*. New York: Routledge, 2002.

Musical Theater

Block, Geoffrey. *Enchanted Evenings: The Broadway Musical from "Show Boat" to Sondheim*. New York: Oxford University Press, 1997.

Bloom, Ken. *American Song: The Complete Musical Theatre Companion, 1877-1995*. 2 vols. New York: Gale Group, 1996.

Bloom, Ken, and Frank Vlastnik. *Broadway Musicals: The 101 Greatest Shows of All Time*. New York: Blackdog & Leventhal, 2004.

Brantley, Ben, ed. *The New York Times Book of Broadway: On the Aisle for the Unforgettable Plays of the Last Century*. New York: St. Martin's Press, 2001.

Bryer, Jackson R., and Richard A. Davison. *The Art of the American Musical: Conversations with the Creators*. New Brunswick, N.J.: Rutgers University Press, 2005.

Citron, Stephen. *Stephen Sondheim and Andrew Lloyd Webber: The New Musical*. New York: Oxford University Press, 2001.

_____. *The Wordsmiths: Oscar Hammerstein II and Alan Jay Lerner*. New York: Oxford University Press, 1995.

Davis, Lee. *Bolton and Wodehouse and Kern: The Men Who Made Musical Comedy*. New York: Heineman, 1993.

Everett, William A., and Paul R. Laird, eds. *The Cambridge Companion to the Musical*. New York: Cambridge University Press, 2008.

Ewen, David. *American Musical Theater: A Guide to More than Three Hundred Productions of the American Musical Theater from the "Black Crook" (1866) to the Present, with Plot, Production History, Stars,* Songs, Composers, Librettists, and Lyricists. New York: Henry Holt, 1958.

Flinn, Denny Martin. *Musical! A Grand Tour: The Rise, Glory, and Fall of an American Institution*. New York: Schirmer Books, 1997.

Gänzl, Kurt. *The Encyclopedia of Musical Theatre*. 2d ed. 3 vols. New York: Schirmer Books, 2001.

Gill, Glenda Eloise. *No Surrender! No Retreat! African American Pioneer Performers of Twentieth Century American Theater*. New York: St. Martin's Press, 2000.

Green, Stanley. *Broadway Musicals, Show by Show*. Milwaukee, Wis.: Hal Leonard, 1985.

_____. *The World of Musical Comedy: The Story of the American Musical Stage as Told Through the Careers of Its Foremost Composers and Lyricists*. 4th ed. rev. and enlarged. San Diego, Calif.: A. S. Barnes, 1980.

Hischak, Thomas S. *Boy Loses Girl: Broadway's Librettists*. Lanham, Md.: Scarecrow Press, 2002.

_____. *Word Crazy: Broadway Lyricists from Cohan to Sondheim*. New York: Praeger, 1991.

Kasha, Al, and Joel Hirschhorn. *Notes on Broadway: Conversations with the Great Songwriters*. Chicago: Contemporary Books, 1985.

Kershaw, Baz, ed. *The Cambridge History of the British Theatre*. Vol. 3. Cambridge, England: Cambridge University Press, 2002.

Laufe, Abe. *Broadway's Greatest Musicals*. Rev. ed. New York: Funk & Wagnalls, 1977.

Lewis, David H. *Broadway Musicals: A Hundred Year History*. Jefferson, N.C.: McFarland, 2002.

McLamore, Alyson. *Musical Theater: An Appreciation*. Upper Saddle River, N.J.: Prentice Hall, 2004.

Mordden, Ethan. *Beautiful Mornin': The Broadway Musical in the 1940's*. New York: Oxford University Press, 1999.

_____. *Coming Up Roses: The Broadway Musical in the 1950's*. New York: Oxford University Press, 2000.

_____. *The Happiest Corpse I've Ever Seen: The Last Twenty-five Years of the Broadway Musical*. New York: Palgrave Macmillan, 2004.

_____. *Open a New Window: The Broadway Musical in the 1960's*. New York: Macmillan, 2002.

Sheed, Wilfrid. *The House That George Built: With a Little Help from Irving, Cole, and a Crew of About Fifty*. New York: Random House, 2007.

Suskin, Steven. *More Opening Nights on Broad-*

way: A Critical Quotebook of the Musical Theatre 1965 Through 1981. New York: Schirmer Books, 1997.

_____. *Show Tunes: The Songs, Shows, and Careers of Broadway's Major Composers.* Rev. and expanded 3d ed. New York: Oxford University Press, 2000.

Swain, Joseph. *The Broadway Musical: A Critical and Musical Survey.* 2d ed. Lanham, Md.: Scarecrow Press, 2002.

Traubner, Richard. *Operetta: A Theatrical History.* Rev. ed. New York: Routledge, 2003.

Wilmeth, Don, ed. *Cambridge Guide to American Theatre.* 2d hardcover ed. New York: Cambridge University Press, 2007.

Wilmeth, Don, and Christopher Bigsby, eds. *Post-World War II to the 1990's.* Vol. 3 in *The Cambridge History of American Theatre.* New York: Cambridge University Press, 2000.

Opera

Abbate, Carolyn. *In Search of Opera.* Princeton, N.J.: Princeton University Press, 2001.

Alpert, Hollis. *The Life and Times of "Porgy and Bess": The Story of an American Classic.* New York: Alfred A. Knopf, 1990.

Ashbrook, William, and Harold Powers. *Puccini's "Turandot": The End of the Great Tradition.* Princeton, N.J.: Princeton University Press, 1991.

Barnes, Jennifer. *Television Opera: The Fall of Opera Commissioned for Television.* Rochester, N.Y.: The Boydell Press, 2003.

Bing, Rudolf. *Five Thousand Nights at the Opera.* New York: Doubleday, 1972.

Bourne, Joyce. *Who's Who in Opera: A Guide to Opera Characters.* Oxford, England: Oxford University Press, 1999.

Boyden, Matthew. *The Rough Guide to Opera.* Edited by Joe Staines. London: Rough Guides, 2002.

Bruhn, Siglind. *Saints in the Limelight: Representations of the Religious Quest on the Post-1945 Operatic Stage.* Hillsdale, N.Y.: Pendragon Press, 2003.

Charlton, David, ed. *The Cambridge Companion to Grand Opera.* New York: Cambridge University Press, 2003.

Christiansen, Rupert. *A Pocket Guide to Opera.* London: Faber, 2002.

Cooke, Mervyn, ed. *The Cambridge Companion to Twentieth-Century Opera.* New York: Cambridge University Press, 2005.

Davis, Peter G. *American Opera Singers.* New York: Doubleday, 1997.

Douglas, Nigel. *The Joy of Opera.* London: Andre Deutsch, 2004.

Fredman, Myer. *The Drama of Opera: Exotic and Irrational Entertainment.* Brighton, England: Sussex Academic Press, 2003.

Gallo, Denise. *Opera: The Basics.* New York: Routledge, 2006.

Gilbert, Susie, and Jay Shir. *A Tale of Four Houses: Opera at Covent Garden, La Scala, Vienna, and the Met Since 1945.* London: HarperCollins, 2003.

Grout, Donald Jay, and Hermine Weigel Williams. *A Short History of Opera.* New York: Columbia University Press, 2003.

Grundy Fanelli, Jean. *Opera for Everyone: A Historic, Social, Artistic, Literary, and Musical Study.* Lanham, Md.: Scarecrow Press, 2004.

Griffin, Clive. *Opera.* New York: Collins, 2007.

Hamilton, David, ed. *The Metropolitan Opera Encyclopedia: A Comprehensive Guide to the World of Opera.* New York: Simon and Schuster, 1987.

Hamilton, Mary. *A-Z of Opera.* New York: Facts On File, 1990.

Holden, Amanda, ed. *The Penguin Concise Guide to Opera.* London: Penguin Books, 2005.

McCants, Clyde T. *America Opera Singers and Their Recordings,* Jefferson, N.C.: McFarland, 2004.

Matheopoulos, Helena. *Diva: The New Generation—the Sopranos and Mezzos of the Decade Discuss Their Roles.* Boston: Northeastern University Press, 1998.

Mays, Desirée. *Opera Unveiled: 2007.* Santa Fe, N.Mex.: Art Forms, 2007.

Parsons, Charles H., comp. *Opera Composers and Their Works.* 4 vols. Lewiston, N.Y.: Edwin Mellen Press, 1986.

_____. *Opera Librettists and Their Works.* Lewiston, N.Y.: Edwin Mellen Press, 1987.

Raeburn, Michael. *The Chronicle of Opera.* Rev. ed. London: Thames & Hudson, 2007.

Rasponi, Lanfranco. *The Last Prima Donnas.* New York: Alfred A. Knopf, 1982.

Rutherford, Susan. *The Prima Donna and Opera, 1815-1930.* New York: Cambridge University Press, 2006.

Sadie, Stanley, ed. *The New Grove Dictionary of Opera.* 4 vols. New York: Grove's Dictionaries of Music, 1992.

Sargeant, Winthrop. *Divas*. New York: Coward, McCann & Geoghegan, 1973.

Schoell, William. *The Opera of the Twentieth Century: A Passionate Art in Transition*. Jefferson, N.C.: McFarland, 2006.

Smith, Peter Fox. *A Passion for Opera—Learning to Love It: The Greatest Masters, Their Greatest Music*. North Pomfret, Vt.: Trafalgar Square, 2004.

Weisstein, Ulrich. *Selected Essays on Opera*. Edited by Walter Bernhart. Amsterdam: Rodopi, 2006.

Williams, Bernard. *On Opera*. New Haven, Conn.: Yale University Press, 2006.

Popular Music

Appell, Glenn, and David Hemphill. *American Popular Music: A Multicultural History*. Belmont, Calif.: Thomson Higher Education, 2006.

Barnet, Richard D., Bruce Nemerov, and Mayo R. Taylor. *The Story Behind the Song: 150 Songs That Chronicle the Twentieth Century*. Westport, Conn.: Greenwood Press, 2004.

Bennett, Andy, Barry Shank, and Jason Toynbee, eds. *The Popular Music Studies Reader*. London: Routledge, 2006.

Bloom, Ken. *The American Songbook: The Singers, Songwriters, and the Songs*. New York: Black Dog & Leventhal, 2005.

Bogle, Donald. *Brown Sugar: Over One Hundred Years of America's Black Female Superstars*. New York: Continuum, 2007.

Brackett, David. *The Pop, Rock, and Soul Reader: Histories and Debates*. New York: Oxford University Press, 2005.

Clarke, Donald, ed. *The Penguin Encyclopedia of Popular Music*. 2d ed. New York: Penguin Books, 1998.

DeMain, Bill. *Behind the Muse: Pop and Rock's Greatest Songwriters Talk About Their Work and Inspiration*. Cranberry Township, Pa.: Tiny Ripple Books, 2001.

Durkee, Rob. *American Top 40: The Countdown of the Century*. New York: Schirmer Books, 1999.

Egan, Sean. *The Guys Who Wrote 'Em: Songwriting Geniuses of Rock and Pop*. London: Askill, 2004.

Escott, Colin. *Roadkill on the Three-Chord Highway: Art and Trash in American Popular Music*. London: Routledge, 2002.

Ewen, David. *American Songwriters: An H. W. Wilson Biographical Dictionary*. New York: H. W. Wilson, 1987.

Ferguson, Gary Lynn, comp. *Song Finder: A Title Index to 32,000 Popular Songs in Collections, 1854-1992*. Westport, Conn.: Greenwood Press, 1995.

Friedwald, Will. *Stardust Melodies: The Biography of Twelve of America's Most Popular Songs*. New York: Pantheon Books, 2002.

Friskics-Warren, Bill. *I'll Take You There: Pop Music and the Urge for Transcendence*. New York: Continuum, 2005.

Furia, Philip. *Poets of Tin Pan Alley: A History of America's Great Lyricists*. New York: Oxford University Press, 1990.

Furia, Philip, and Michael Lasser. *America's Songs: The Stories Behind the Songs of Broadway, Hollywood, and Tin Pan Alley*. New York: Routledge, 2006.

Gammond, Peter. *The Oxford Companion to Popular Music*. New York: Oxford University Press, 1991.

Goodfellow, William D. *SongCite: An Index to Popular Songs*. New York: Garland, 1995.

Gottlieb, Jack. *Funny, It Doesn't Sound Jewish: How Yiddish Songs and Synagogue Melodies Influenced Tin Pan Alley, Broadway, and Hollywood*. Albany: State University of New York in association with the Library of Congress, 2004.

Gracyk, Tim, and Frank Hoffmann. *Popular American Recording Pioneers, 1895-1925*. New York: Haworth Press, 2000.

Hill, Dave. *Designer Boys and Material Girls: Manufacturing the '80's Pop Dream*. Poole, Dorset, England: Blandford Press, 1986.

Hischak, Thomas S. *The Tin Pan Alley Song Encyclopedia*. Westport, Conn.: Greenwood Press, 2002.

Holt, Fabian. *Genre in Popular Music*. Chicago: University of Chicago Press, 2007.

Iger, Arthur L. *Music of the Golden Age, 1900-1950 and Beyond: A Guide to Popular Composers and Lyricists*. Westport, Conn.: Greenwood Press, 1998.

Jasen, David A. *Tin Pan Alley: An Encyclopedia of the Golden Age of American Song*. New York: Routledge, 2003.

Jones, Alan, and Jussi Kantonen. *Saturday Night Forever: The Story of Disco*. Edinburgh: Mainstream, 2005.

Jones, Dylan. *Ultra Lounge: The Lexicon of Easy Listening*. New York: Universe, 1997.

Kastin, David. *I Hear America Singing: An Introduction to Popular Music.* Upper Saddle River, N.J.: Prentice Hall, 2002.

Kempton, Arthur. *Boogaloo: The Quintessence of American Popular Music.* New York: Pantheon Books, 2003.

Lanza, Joseph. *Elevator Music: A Surreal History of Muzak, Easy-Listening, and Other Moodsong.* Rev. and expanded ed. Ann Arbor: University of Michigan Press, 2004.

Larkin, Colin, ed. *The Encyclopedia of Popular Music.* 4th ed. 10 vols. New York: Muze, 1998.

_____. *The Virgin Encyclopedia of 70's Music.* London: Virgin Books, 2002.

Lissauer, Bob. *Lissauer's Encyclopedia of Popular Music in America: 1888 to the Present.* 3 vols. New York: Facts On File, 1996.

McAleer, Dave. *Hit Singles: Top 20 Charts from 1954 to the Present Day.* San Francisco: Backbeat Books, 2004.

Melnick, Jeffrey Paul. *A Right to Sing the Blues: African Americans, Jews, and American Popular Song.* Cambridge, Mass.: Harvard University Press, 1999.

Moon, Krystyn R. *Yellowface: Creating the Chinese in American Popular Music and Performance, 1850's-1920's.* New Brunswick, N.J.: Rutgers University Press, 2005.

Nathan, David. *The Soulful Divas.* New York: Billboard Books, 2002.

Pitts, Michael R., and Frank Hoffman. *The Rise of the Crooners: Gene Austin, Russ Columbo, Bing Crosby, Nick Lucas, Johnny Marvin, and Rudy Vallee.* Introduction by Ian Whitcomb. Lanham, Md.: Scarecrow Press, 2002.

Rosen, Jody. *"White Christmas": The Story of an American Song.* New York: Scribner, 2002.

Shapiro, Peter. *Turn the Beat Around: The Secret History of Disco.* New York: Faber and Faber, 2005.

Smith, Kate. *God Bless America: Tin Pan Alley Goes to War.* Lexington: University Press of Kentucky, 2002.

Starr, Larry, and Christopher Waterman. *American Popular Music: From Minstrelsy to MP3.* 2d ed. New York: Oxford University Press, 2007.

Tawa, Nicholas. *Supremely American: Popular Song in the Twentieth Century: Styles and Singers and What They Said About America.* Lanham, Md.: Scarecrow Press, 2005.

Tyler, Don. *Music of the Postwar Era.* Westport, Conn.: Greenwood Press, 2008.

Unterberger, Richie. *Music USA: The Rough Guide.* Edited by Jennifer Dempsey. London: Rough Guides, 1999.

Vaché, Warren W. *The Unsung Songwriters: America's Masters of Melody.* Lanham, Md.: Scarecrow Press, 2000.

Vogel, Frederick G. *World War I Songs: A History and Dictionary of Popular American Patriotic Tunes, with Over Three Hundred Complete Lyrics.* Jefferson, N.C.: McFarland, 1995.

Whitburn, Joel. *The "Billboard" Book of Top 40 Hits.* Rev. and enlarged 8th ed. New York: Billboard Books, 2004.

Wilder, Alec. *American Popular Song: The Great Innovators, 1900-1950.* New York: Oxford University Press, 1972.

Zinsser, William. *Easy to Remember: The Great American Songwriters and their Songs.* Jaffrey, N.H.: David R. Godine, 2000.

Record Companies

Abbott, Kingsley, ed. *Calling out Around the World: A Motown Reader.* London: Helter Skelter, 2001.

Bianco, David. *Heat Wave: The Motown Fact Book.* Ann Arbor, Mich.: Pieran Press, 1988.

Bowman, Rob. *Soulsville, U.S.A.: The History of Stax Records.* New York: Schirmer Books, 2003.

Collis, John. *The Story of Chess Records.* New York: Bloomsbury, 1998.

Dahl, Bill. *Motown: The Golden Years.* Iola, Wis.: Krause, 2001.

Early, Gerald Lyn. *One Nation Under a Groove: Motown and American Culture.* Rev. and expanded ed. Ann Arbor: University of Michigan Press, 2004.

Ertegun, Ahmet, and Greil Marcus. *"What'd I Say?" The Atlantic Story—Fifty Years of Music.* Compiled and edited by C. Perry Richardson. New York: Welcome Rain, 2001.

Escott, Colin, and Martin Hawkins. *Good Rockin' Tonight: Sun Records and the Birth of Rock 'n' Roll.* New York: St. Martin's Griffin, 1992.

George, Nelson. *Where Did Our Love Go? The Rise and Fall of the Motown Sound.* Rev. ed. New York: St. Martin's Press, 2007.

Goldsmith, Peter D. *Making People's Music: Moe Asch and Folkways Records.* Washington, D.C.: Smithsonian Institution Press, 1998.

Gueraseva, Stacy. *Def Jam, Inc.: Rick Rubin, Russell Simmons, and the Extraordinary Story of the World's Most Influential Hip-Hop Label.* New York: One World-Ballantine, 2005.

Hollis, Tim, and Greg Ehrbar. *Mouse Tracks: The Story of Walt Disney Records.* Jackson: University Press of Mississippi, 2006.

Holzman, Jac, and Gavan Daws. *Follow the Music: The Life and High Times of Elektra Records in the Great Years of American Pop Culture.* Santa Monica, Calif.: FirstMedia Books, 1998.

Kahn, Ashley. *The House That Trane Built: The Story of Impulse Records.* New York: W. W. Norton, 2006.

Keane, Bob. *The Oracle of Del-Fi.* Los Angeles: Del-Fi International Books, 2006.

Kennedy, Rick, and Randy McNutt. *Little Labels— Big Sound: Small Record Companies and the Rise of American Music.* Bloomington: Indiana University Press, 1999.

Marmorstein, Gary. *The Label: The Story of Columbia Records.* New York: Thunder's Mouth Press, 2007.

Posner, Gerald. L. *Motown: Music, Money, Sex, and Power.* New York: Random House, 2002.

Ro, Ronin. *Have Gun Will Travel: The Spectacular Rise and Violent Fall of Death Row Records.* New York: Doubleday, 1998.

Scully, Michael F. *The Never-Ending Revival: Rounder Records and the Folk Alliance.* Urbana: University of Illinois Press, 2008.

Smith, Suzanne E. *Dancing in the Street: Motown and the Cultural Politics of Detroit.* Cambridge, Mass.: Harvard University Press, 1999.

Waller, Don. *The Motown Story.* New York: Charles Scribner's Sons, 1985.

Reggae

Barrow, Steve, and Peter Dalton. *The Rough Guide to Reggae.* 3d ed., expanded and completely rev. London: Rough Guides, 2004.

Bradley, Lloyd. *Bass Culture: When Reggae Was King.* New York: Viking, 2000.

Chang, Kevin O'Brien, and Wayne Chen. *Reggae Routes.* Kingston, Jamaica: Ian Randle, 1998.

Cumbo, Fikisha. *Bob Marley and Peter Tosh: Get Up! Stand Up! Diary of a Reggaeophile.* New York: CACE International, 2001.

Davis, Stephen. *Reggae Bloodlines: In Search of the Music and Culture of Jamaica.* New York: Da Capo Press, 1992.

Foster, Chuck. *Roots, Rock, Reggae: An Early History of Reggae from Ska to Dancehall.* New York: Billboard Books, 1999.

Jacobs, Virginia Lee. *Roots of Rastafari.* San Diego, Calif.: Avant Books, 1985.

Katz, David. *Solid Foundation: An Oral History of Reggae.* London: Bloomsbury, 2003.

Mulvaney, Rebekah Michele. *Rastafari and Reggae: A Dictionary and Sourcebook.* New York: Greenwood Press, 1990.

Potash, Chris. *Reggae, Rasta, Revolution.* New York: Schirmer Books, 1997.

Scott, Ricardo. *Scott's Official History of Reggae: The Original Wailers and the Trench-Town Experience.* New York: Cornerstone, 1993.

Stolzoff, Norman C. *Wake the Town and Tell the People.* Durham, N.C.: Duke University Press, 2000.

Thompson, Dave. *Reggae and Caribbean Music.* San Francisco: Backbeat Books, 2002.

Rhythm-and-Blues and Soul Music

Awkward, Michael. *Soul Covers: Rhythm and Blues Remakes and the Struggle for Artistic Identity (Aretha Franklin, Al Green, and Phoebe Snow).* Durham, N.C.: Duke University Press, 2007.

Bogdanov, Vladimir, et al., eds. *All Music Guide to Soul: The Definitive Guide to R&B and Soul.* San Francisco: Backbeat Books, 2003.

Broven, John. *Rhythm and Blues in New Orleans.* Gretna, La.: Pelican Publishing, 1978.

Deffaa, Chip. *Blue Rhythms: Six Lives in Rhythm and Blues.* Urbana: University of Illinois Press, 1996.

Dickerson, James. *Goin' Back to Memphis: A Century of Blues, Rock 'n' Roll, and Glorious Soul.* New York: Schirmer Books, 1996.

George, Nelson. *The Death of Rhythm and Blues.* New York: Penguin, 2003.

Gregory, Hugh. *Soul Music A-Z.* Rev. ed. New York: Da Capo Press, 1995.

Gulla, Bob. *Icons of R and B and Soul.* Westport, Conn.: Greenwood Press, 2008.

Guralnick, Peter. *Sweet Soul Music: Rhythm and Blues and the Southern Dream of Freedom.* New York: Harper & Row, 1986. Reprint. Boston: Little Brown, 1999.

Haralambos, Michael. *Soul Music: The Birth of a*

Sound in Black America. London: Eddison Press, 1974. Reprint. New York: De Capo Press, 1985.

Hirshey, Gerri. *Nowhere to Run: The Story of Soul Music*. New York: New York Times Books, 1984. Reprint. London: Southbank, 2006.

Hoffmann, Frank W. *Rhythm and Blues, Rap, and Hip-Hop*. American Popular Music series. New York: Facts On File, 2006.

Jones, Ferdinand, and Arthur C. Jones, eds. *The Triumph of the Soul: Cultural and Psychological Aspects of African American Music*. Westport, Conn.: Praeger, 2001.

Neal, Mark Anthony. *Songs in the Key of Black Life: A Rhythm and Blues Nation*. New York: Routledge, 2003.

_____. *Soul Babies: Black Popular Culture and the Post-Soul Aesthetic*. New York: Routledge, 2002.

Pruter, Robert, ed. *The Blackwell Guide to Soul Recordings*. Oxford, England: Blackwell, 1993.

Ripani, Richard J. *The New Blue Music: Changes in Rhythm and Blues, 1950-1999*. Jackson: University Press of Mississippi, 2006.

Rosalsky, Mitch. *Encyclopedia of Rhythm and Blues and Doo Wop Vocal Groups*. Lanham, Md.: Scarecrow Press, 2000.

Shapiro, Peter. *Soul—One Hundred Essential CDs: The Rough Guide*. London: Rough Guides, 2000.

Shaw, Arnold. *Honkers and Shouters: The Golden Years of Rhythm and Blues*. New York: Collier Books, 1978.

Tee, Ralph. *Who's Who in Soul Music*. London: Weidenfeld and Nicolson, 1991.

Vincent, Rickey. *Funk: The Music, the People, and the Rhythm of the One*. New York: St. Martin's Griffin, 1996.

Ward, Brian. *Just My Soul Responding: Rhythm and Blues, Black Consciousness, and Race Relations*. Berkeley: University of California Press, 1998.

Werner, Craig. *A Change Is Gonna Come: Music, Race, and the Soul of America*. Ann Arbor: University of Michigan Press, 2006.

_____. *Higher Ground: Stevie Wonder, Aretha Franklin, Curtis Mayfield, and the Rise and Fall of American Soul*. New York: Random House, 2005.

Wexler, Jerry, and David Ritz. *Rhythm and the Blues: A Life in American Music*. New York: Knopf, 1993.

Whitburn, Joel. *The Billboard Book of Top 40 R and B and Hip-Hop Hits*. New York: Billboard Books, 2006.

_____. *Joel Whitburn Presents Top R and B Singles, 1942-1999*. Menomonee Falls, Wis.: Record Research, 2000.

_____. *Joel Whitburn's Top R and B Albums, 1965-1998: Rhythm and Blues*. Menomonee Falls, Wis.: Record Research, 1999.

Rock

Auslander, Philip. *Performing Glam Rock: Gender and Theatricality in Popular Music*. Ann Arbor: University of Michigan Press, 2006.

Bangs, Lester. *Main Lines, Blood Feasts, and Bad Taste: A Lester Bangs Reader*. New York: Anchor, 2003.

Bennett, Andy, and Kevin Dawe, eds. *Guitar Cultures*. Oxford, England: Berg, 2001.

The "Billboard" Illustrated Encyclopedia of Rock. Rev., updated, and expanded paperback ed. New York: Billboard Books, 2002.

Brackett, Nathan, and Christian Hoard, eds. *The New "Rolling Stone" Album Guide*. 4th ed. New York: Simon & Schuster, 2004.

Brown, Pete, and H. P. Newquist. *Legends of Rock Guitar: The Essential Reference of Rock's Greatest Guitarists*. Milwaukee, Wis.: Hal Leonard, 1997.

Budnick, Dean. *Jambands: The Complete Guide to the Players, Music, and Scene*. San Francisco: Backbeat Books, 2003.

Campbell, Michael, and James Brody. 2d ed. *Rock and Roll: An Introduction*. Belmont, Calif.: Thomson Schirmer, 2008.

Carson, David A. *Grit Noise and Revolution: The Birth of Detroit Rock and Roll*. Ann Arbor: University of Michigan Press, 2005.

Cateforis, Theo, ed. *The Rock History Reader*. New York: Routledge, 2007.

Charlton, Katherine. *Rock Music Styles: A History*. New York: McGraw Hill, 2008.

Christgau, Robert. *Christgau's Consumer Guide: Albums of the Nineties*. New York: St. Martin's Griffin, 2000.

_____. *Christgau's Record Guide: Rock Albums of the Seventies*. Boston: Ticknor & Fields, 1981.

_____. *Christgau's Record Guide: The Eighties*. New York: Pantheon, 1990.

_____. *Grown Up All Wrong: Seventy-five Great Rock and Pop Artists from Vaudeville to Techno*. Cambridge, Mass.: Harvard University Press, 1998.

_____. *Stranded: Rock and Roll for a Desert Island*. Cambridge, Mass.: Da Capo Press, 2007.

Clifford, Mike, ed. *The Harmony Illustrated Encyclopedia of Rock.* 7th ed. New York: Harmony Books, 1992.

Covach, John. *What's That Sound? An Introduction to Rock and Its History.* New York: W. W. Norton & Co., 2006.

DeCurtis, Anthony. *In Other Words: Artists Talk About Life and Work.* Milwaukee, Wis.: Hal Leonard, 2005.

_____, ed. *Present Tense: Rock and Roll and Culture.* Durham, N.C.: Duke University Press, 1992.

DeCurtis, Anthony, and James Henke with Holly George-Warren. *The "Rolling Stone" Illustrated History of Rock and Roll.* 3d ed. New York: Random House, 1992.

DeRogatis, Jim, and Carmel Carrillo, eds. *Kill Your Idols: A New Generation of Rock Writers.* Fort Lee, N.J.: Barricade Books, 2004.

Dettmar, Kevin J. H. *Is Rock Dead?* New York: Routledge, 2006.

Editors of *Rolling Stone.* *"Rolling Stone": The Decades of Rock and Roll.* Photographs from the Michael Ochs Archives. San Francisco: Chronicle Books, 2001.

_____. *The "Rolling Stone" Interviews.* New York: Warner, 1971.

_____. *The "Rolling Stone Interviews," 1967-1980.* New York: St. Martin's Press, 1989.

Escott, Colin, ed. *All Roots Lead to Rock: Legends of Early Rock 'n' Roll.* New York: Schirmer Books, 1999.

Firth, Simon, Will Straw, and John Street, eds. *The Cambridge Companion to Pop and Rock.* New York: Cambridge University Press, 2001.

Friedlander, Paul, and Peter Miller. *Rock and Roll: A Social History.* 2d ed. Boulder, Colo.: Westview Press, 2006.

George-Warren, Holly, Patricia Romanowski, and Jon Pareles, eds. *The "Rolling Stone" Encyclopedia of Rock and Roll.* 3d ed., rev. and updated for the twenty-first century. New York: Fireside, 2001.

Gillett, Charlie. *The Sound of the City: The Rise of Rock and Roll.* 2d ed. New York: Da Capo Press, 1996.

Gordon, Robert, and Peter Guralnick. *It Came from Memphis.* New York: Atria Books, 2001.

The Greenwood Encyclopedia of Rock History. Westport, Conn.: Greenwood Press, 2006.

Hedges, Dan. *British Rock Guitar.* New York: Guitar Player Books, 1977.

Helander, Brock. *The Rockin' Fifties: The People Who Made the Music.* New York: Schirmer Books, 1998.

Holm-Hudson, Kevin. *Progressive Rock Reconsidered.* London: Routledge, 2001.

Hoskyns, Barney. *Hotel California: The True-Life Adventures of Crosby, Stills, Nash, Young, Mitchell, Taylor, Browne, Ronstadt, Geffen, the Eagles, and Their Many Friends.* Hoboken, N.J.: Wiley, 2007.

_____. *Waiting for the Sun.* New York: St. Martin's Press, 1996.

Johnstone, Nick. *A Brief History of Rock and Roll.* New York: Carroll & Graf, 2007.

Kiersh, Edward. *Where Are You Now, Bo Diddley? The Stars Who Made Us Rock and Where They Are Now.* Garden City, N.Y.: Doubleday, 1986.

Lazell, Barry. *Punk! An A-Z.* London: Hamlyn, 1995.

Loder, Kurt. *Bat Chain Puller: Rock and Roll in the Age of Celebrity.* New York: Cooper Square Press, 2002.

McKeen, William, ed. *Rock and Roll Is Here to Stay: An Anthology.* Introduction by Peter Guralnick. New York: W. W. Norton, 2000.

McNutt, Randy. *Guitar Towns: A Journey to the Crossroads of Rock 'n' Roll.* Bloomington: Indiana University Press, 2002.

Marcus, Greil. *Mystery Train: Images of America in Rock and Roll.* 4th ed. London: Faber and Faber, 2000.

Markowitz, Rhonda. *The Greenwood Encyclopedia of Rock History.* 6 vols. Westport, Conn.: Greenwood Press, 2006..

Marsh, Dave. *The Heart of Rock and Soul: The 1001 Greatest Singles Ever Made.* New York: Plume, 1989.

Martin, Bill. *Avant Rock: Experimental Music from the Beatles to Björk.* Chicago: Open Court, 2002.

Mayes, Elaine. *It Happened in Monterey: Modern Rock's Defining Moment.* Culver City, Calif.: Britannia Press, 2002.

Miller, James. *Flowers in the Dustbin: The Rise of Rock and Roll, 1947-1977.* New York: Fireside/Simon & Schuster, 2000.

Moore, Allan F. *Rock, the Primary Text: Developing a Musicology of Rock.* Brookfield, Vt.: Ashgate, 2001.

Morrison, Craig. *Rock and Roll.* American Popular Music series. New York: Facts On File, 2006.

Peterson, Charles. *Screaming Life: A Chronicle of the Seattle Music Scene*. New York: HarperCollins, 1995.

Rees, Dafydd, and Luke Crampton. *Encyclopedia of Rock Stars*. New York: DK, 1996.

Reid, Jan. *The Improbable Rise of Redneck Rock*. New ed. Austin: University of Texas Press, 2004.

Robins, Wayne. *A Brief History of Rock, off the Record*. New York: Routledge, 2008.

Schaffner, Nicholas. *The British Invasion: From the First Wave to the New Wave*. New York: McGraw-Hill, 1983.

Schinder, Scott, and Andy Schwartz. *Icons of Rock: An Encyclopedia of the Legends Who Changed Music Forever*. Westport, Conn.: Greenwood Press, 2008.

Spencer, Chris, Zbig Nowara, and Paul McHenry, comps. *Who's Who of Australian Rock*. 5th ed. Noble Park, Vic.: Five Mile Press, 2002.

Spitz, Mark, and Brendan Mullen. *We Got the Neutron Bomb: The Untold Story of L. A. Punk*. New York: Three Rivers Press, 2001.

Starr, Larry, and Christopher Waterman. *American Popular Music: The Rock Years*. New York: Oxford University Press, 2006.

Strausbaugh, John. *Rock 'Til You Drop: The Decline from Rebellion to Nostalgia*. London: Verso, 2001.

Strong, Martin Charles. *The Essential Rock Discography*. New York: Canongate US, 2006.

Studwell, William E., and D. F. Lonergan. *The Classic Rock and Roll Reader: Rock Music from Its Beginnings to the Mid-1970's*. New York: Haworth Press, 1999.

Stuessy, Clarence, and Scott Lipscomb. *Rock and Roll: Its History and Stylistic Development*. Upper Saddle River, N.J.: Prentice-Hall, 2008.

Sumrall, Harry. *Pioneers of Rock and Roll: One Hundred Artists Who Changed the Face of Rock*. New York: Billboard Books, 1994.

Thompson, Dave. *Better to Burn Out: The Cult of Death in Rock 'n' Roll*. New York: Thunder's Mouth Press, 1999.

Tosches, Nick. *Heroes of Rock 'n' Roll*. New York: Harmony Books, 1991.

_____. *Unsung Heroes of Rock 'n' Roll*. New York: Da Capo Press, 1999.

Traum, Artie, and Arti Funaro. *The Legends of Rock Guitar*. New York: Oak, 1986.

Walker, Michael. *Laurel Canyon: The Inside Story of Rock and Roll's Legendary Neighborhood*. New York: Faber & Faber, 2006.

Walser, Robert. *Running with the Devil: Power, Gender, and Madness in Heavy Metal Music*. Hanover, N.H.: Wesleyan University Press, 1993.

Ward, Ed, Geoffrey Stokes, and Ken Tucker. *Rock of Ages: The "Rolling Stone" History of Rock and Roll*. New York: Summit Books, 1986.

Wenner, Jann S., ed. *Twenty Years of "Rolling Stone": What a Long, Strange Trip It's Been*. New York: Straight Arrow Press, 1987.

Woodstra, Chris, John Busch, and Stephen Thomas Erlewine, eds. *Classic Rock*. New York: Backbeat Books, 2007.

Zimmerman, Keith. *Sing My Way Home: Voices of the New American Roots Rock*. San Francisco: Backbeat Books, 2004.

Rockabilly

Cooper, B. Lee, and Wayne S. Haney. *Rockabilly: A Bibliographic Resource Guide*. Metuchen, N.J.: Scarecrow Press, 1990.

Jandrow, Richard E. *What It Was Was Rockabilly: A History and Discography, 1927-1994*. Worcester, Mass.: Boxcar, 1995.

McNutt, Randy. *We Wanna Boogie: An Illustrated History of the American Rockabilly Movement*. Hamilton, Ohio: HHP Books, 1989.

Morrison, Craig. *Go Cat Go! Rockabilly Music and Its Makers*. Urbana: University of Illinois Press, 1998.

Naylor, Jerry, and Steve Halliday. *The Rockabilly Legends: They Called It Rockabilly Long Before It Was Called Rock 'n' Roll*. Milwaukee, Wis.: Hal Leonard, 2007.

Poore, Billy. *Rockabilly: A Forty-Year Journey*. Milwaukee, Wis.: Hal Leonard, 1998.

Women and Music

Ammer, C. *Unsung: A History of Women in American Music*. Westport, Conn.: Greenwood Press, 1980.

Bernstein, Jane A., ed. *Women's Voices Across Musical Worlds*. Boston: Northeastern University Press, 2004.

Briscoe, James, ed. *Contemporary Anthology of Music by Women*. Bloomington: Indiana University Press, 1997.

Childerhose, Buffy. *From Lilith to Lilith Fair*. New York: St. Martin's Griffin, 1998.

Claghorn, Gene. *Women Composers and Songwriters: A Concise Biographical Dictionary.* Lanham, Md.: Scarecrow Press, 1996.

Cook, Susan C., and Judy S. Tsou, eds. *Cecilia Reclaimed: Feminist Perspectives on Gender and Music.* Urbana: University of Illinois Press, 1994.

Cooper, Sarah, ed. *Girls! Girls! Girls! Essays on Women and Music.* Washington Square, N.Y.: New York University Press, 1996.

Dickerson, James L. *Go, Girl, Go! The Women's Revolution in Music.* New York: Schirmer Trade Books, 2005.

Emerson, Isabelle. *Five Centuries of Women Singers.* Westport, Conn.: Praeger, 2005.

Evans, Liz, ed. *Women, Sex and Rock 'n' Roll: In Their Own Words.* London: Pandora, 1994.

Fuller, Sophie. *The Pandora Guide to Women Composers: Britain and the United States, 1629-Present.* London: Pandora, 1994.

Gaar, Gillian G. *She's a Rebel: The History of Women in Rock and Roll.* Seattle, Wash.: Seal Press, 1992.

Glickman, Sylvia, and Martha Furman Schleifer, eds. *From Convent to Concert Hall: A Guide to Women Composers.* Westport, Conn.: Greenwood Press, 2003.

Grattan, Virginia L. *American Women Songwriters: A Biographical Dictionary.* Westport, Conn.: Greenwood Press, 1993.

Gray, Anne K. *The World of Women in Classical Music.* La Jolla, Calif.: WordWorld, 2007.

Green, Lucy. *Music, Gender, Education.* New York: Cambridge University Press, 1997.

Hirshey, Gerri. *We Gotta Get Out of This Place: The True, Tough Story of Women in Rock.* New York: Grove Press, 2001.

Jezic, Diane Peacock. *Women Composers: The Lost Tradition Found.* 2d ed. New York: The Feminist Press, 1994.

Juno, Andrea. *Angry Women of Rock.* New York: Juno Books, 1996.

Koskoff, Ellen, ed. *Women and Music in Cross-Cultural Perspective.* New York: Greenwood Press, 1987.

Lewis, Lisa A. *Gender Politics and MTV: Voicing the Difference.* Philadelphia: Temple University Press, 1990.

Marcic, Dorothy. *Respect: Women and Popular Music.* New York: Texere, 2002.

Marshall, Kimberly, ed. *Rediscovering the Muses: Women's Musical Traditions.* Boston: Northeastern University Press, 1993.

Mellers, Wilfred Howard. *Angels of the Night: Popular Female Singers of Our Time.* New York: Blackwell, 1986.

Moisala, Pirkko, and Beverley Diamond, eds. *Music and Gender.* Urbana: University of Illinois Press, 2000.

O'Brien, Lucy. *She Bop: The Definitive History of Women in Rock, Pop, and Soul.* New York: Penguin Books, 1996.

_____. *She Bop II: The Definitive History of Women in Rock, Pop, and Soul.* London: Continuum, 2002.

O'Dair, Barbara, ed. *Trouble Girls: The "Rolling Stone" Book of Women in Rock.* New York: Random House, 1997.

Pendle, Karin, ed. *Women and Music: A History.* 2d ed. Bloomington: Indiana University Press, 2001.

Raha, Maria. *Cinderella's Big Score: Women of the Punk and Indie Underground.* Emeryville, Calif.: Seal Press, 2005.

Sadie, Julie Anne, and Rhian Samuel, eds. *The Norton/Grove Dictionary of Women Composers.* New York: W. W. Norton, 1994.

Sherman, Dale. *Twentieth Century Rock and Roll Women in Rock.* Burlington, Ont.: Collector's Guide Publishing, 2001.

Whiteley, Sheila. *Women and Popular Music: Sexuality, Identity and Subjectivity.* New York: Routledge, 2000.

Woodworth, Marc, ed. *Solo: Women Singer-Songwriters in Their Own Words.* New York: Delta Books, 1998.

World Music
Alves, William. *Music of the Peoples of the World.* Belmont, Calif.: Thomson Schirmer, 2006.

Bakan, Michael B. *World Music: Traditions and Transformations.* Boston: McGraw-Hill, 2007.

Bebbington, Warren. *The Oxford Companion to Australian Music.* New York: Oxford University Press, 1997.

Bohlman, Philip V. *World Music: A Very Short Introduction.* Oxford, England: Oxford University Press, 2002.

Bordowitz, Hank. *Noise of the World: Non-Western Musicians in Their Own Words.* New York: Soft Skull Press, 2004.

Broughton, Simon. *World: One Hundred Essential CDs, the Rough Guide.* London: Rough Guides, 2000.

Broughton, Simon, Mark Ellingham, and John Lusk, eds. *The Rough Guide to World Music.* 3d ed. London: Rough Guides, 2006-   .

Copland, David. *In Township Tonight! South Africa's Black City Music and Theatre.* Rev. ed. Chicago: Chicago University Press, 2007.

Danielson, Virginia. *The Voice of Egypt: Umm Kulthum, Arabic Song, and Egyptian Society in the Twentieth Century.* Chicago: University of Chicago Press, 1997.

Dawe, Kevin, ed. *Island Musics.* Oxford, England: Berg, 2004.

Erlmann, Veit. *Music, Modernity, and the Global Imagination: South Africa and the West.* New York: Oxford University Press, 1999.

_____. *Nightsong: Performance, Power, and Practice in South Africa.* Chicago: University of Chicago Press, 1996.

Everett, Yayoi Uno, and Frederick Lau, eds. *Locating East Asia in Western Art Music.* Middletown, Conn.: Wesleyan University Press, 2004.

Farrell, Gerry. *Indian Music and the West.* New York: Oxford University Press, 1997.

Fletcher, Peter. *World Musics in Context: A Comprehensive Survey of the World's Major Musical Cultures.* New York: Oxford University Press, 2001.

Green, Garth L., and Philip W. Scher, eds. *Trinidad Carnival: The Cultural Politics of a Transnational Festival.* Bloomington: Indiana University Press, 2007.

Lavezzoli, Peter. *The Dawn of Indian Music in the West.* New York: Continuum, 2006.

McGovern, Adam, ed. *MusicHound World: The Essential Album Guide.* Photographs by Jack and Linda Vartoogian. Includes a compact disc. Detroit: Visible Ink, 2000.

McNeil, Adrian. *Inventing the Sarod: A Cultural History.* Calcutta, India: Seagull, 2004.

Malmström, Dan. *Introduction to Twentieth Century Mexican Music.* Uppsala, Sweden: Institute of Musicology, Uppsala University, 1974.

Melvin, Sheila, and Cai Jingdong. *Rhapsody in Red: How Western Classical Music Became Chinese.* New York: Algora, 2004.

Mitchell, Tony. *Popular Music and Local Identity: Rock, Pop, and Rap in Europe and Oceania.* London: Leicester University Press, 1996.

Muller, Carol Ann. *South African Music: A Century of Traditions in Transformation.* Santa Barbara, Calif.: ABC-Clio, 2004.

Nettl, Bruno, and Ruth M. Stone, eds. *The Garland Encyclopedia of World Music.* 10 vols. New York: Garland, 1998-2002.

Neuman, Daniel M. *The Life of Music in North India: The Organization of an Artistic Tradition.* Detroit, Mich.: Wayne State University Press, 1980.

Nickson, Chris. *The NPR Curious Listener's Guide to World Music.* New York: Berkley, 2004.

Nidel, Richard. *World Music: The Basics.* New York: Routledge, 2005.

Raja, Deepak S. *Hindustani Music: A Tradition in Transition.* New Delhi: D. K. Printworld, 2005.

Ritchie, Fiona. *The NPR Curious Listener's Guide to Celtic Music.* New York: Berkley, 2004.

Roberts, John Storm. *Black Music of Two Worlds: African, Caribbean, Latin, and African-American Traditions.* New York: Schirmer Books, 1998.

Schnabel, Tom. *Rhythm Planet: The Great World Music Makers.* New York: Universe, 1998.

Taylor, Timothy D. *Global Pop: World Music, World Markets.* New York: Routledge, 1997.

Titon, Jeff Todd, ed. *Worlds of Music: An Introduction to the Music of the World's Peoples.* 5th ed. Belmont, Calif.: Schirmer/Thomson Learning, 2009.

Wald, Elijah. *Global Minstrels: Voices of World Music.* New York: Routledge, 2007.

Wallis, Geoff, and Sue Wilson. *The Rough Guide to Irish Music.* London: Rough Guides, 2001.

White, Douglas. *Dictionary of Popular Music Styles of the World.* Lawndale, Calif.: Douglas White Music Research, 1998.

Glossary

a cappella: Sung without instrumental accompaniment.

A side: The side of a single (a 45-rpm record, a cassette, or a CD single) containing the song that is intended to be promoted and played on the radio. *See also* forty-five.

a tempo: Literally, "in time," or in the main tempo of the piece.

***aaba*:** The most common popular song format, consisting of thirty-two bars, where the *a* sections are usually eight bars and the *b* (or bridge) section offers a contrast to the *a* section by using a different melody, different chords, or sometimes a contrasting theme as expressed in the lyrics.

absolute pitch: *See* perfect pitch.

accelerando: A musical notation directing musicians to quicken the tempo gradually.

accent: Stress; emphasis of one tone or beat over others.

accentato: A musical notation meaning "with emphasis."

accompaniment: The music or instrumental part played with the main or more important part; may be harmonic or rhythmic or both.

accordion: A musical instrument in the reed-organ family that combines wind and keyboard to produce sound, strapped to the front of the player. *See also* harmonica.

acousmatic reduction: The mental isolation of sounds from the sources that produce them, in an attempt to concentrate on their inherent characteristics as opposed to their relationships to objects and situations. Coined by Pierre Schaeffer.

acoustic: Generally used to mean "nonamplified" or "nonelectric." Originally used to refer to instruments that produce sound without electronic modification ("acoustic guitar") but expanded to include performances played on nonelectric instruments. In actuality, most "acoustic" performances rely on amplification through microphones and electronic "pickups" on acoustic instruments.

acoustics: The study of sound, its physical properties, and how it interacts with materials in the environment, as in musical instruments and music halls.

ad libitum: From the Latin for "at liberty," a musical notation directing the performer to use his or her own discretion and emotion to dictate speed and manner of execution.

adagio: A musical notation indicating a slow, restful, leisurely tempo.

additive and divisive time systems: Two ways of thinking about and executing musical rhythm that highlight the differences in Western, Euro-American approaches to music (divisive, or subdivided into fractions of a whole, and additive, adding beats in a twelve-beat line).

adult contemporary (AC): A term for a radio format that is similar to the older term "easy listening." Aimed at an older and more conservative audience than the rock-and-roll audience, it includes artists whose work is pleasant and nonthreatening. It overlaps with Top 40 and light rock. The music of the Carpenters, Anne Murray, and Peter Cetera could be termed adult contemporary.

affrettando: A musical notation directing performers to play in a hurrying manner.

agile: A musical notation directing performers to play swiftly.

agitato: A musical notation directing performers to play in an agitated manner.

album: A collection of songs or musical works in one recording, normally performed by one singer, band, orchestra, or other group. The term originally referred to the long-playing (33 rpm) vinyl record format and later compact discs. Albums may be simple compilations of unrelated pieces or tied by a theme or concept (hence the term "concept album"). The Beatles' *Sgt. Pepper's Lonely Hearts Club Band* and the Who's *Tommy* (a "rock opera") were early concept albums. *See also* compact disc; digital versatile disc; long-playing (LP) album.

album cut: A song (or track) recorded to be part of an album, not intended for release as a single.

aleatoricism: The practice of leaving sounds to the

performer (that is, to chance); often referred to as aleatory music.

alla breve: A musical notation directing performers to play in cut time, that is, two beats per measure or the equivalent.

alla marcia: A musical notation directing performers to play in the style of a march.

allargando: A musical notation directing performers to play more slowly or broadly.

allegretto: A musical notation directing performers to play in a somewhat lively manner (more quickly than andante but more slowly than allegro).

allegrissimo: A musical notation directing performers to play very quickly, but not as quickly as presto.

allegro: A musical notation directing performers to play rapidly, in a lively manner.

alteration: The raising (augmenting) or lowering (diminishing) of a tone by a half step.

alternative: A term that began to be used in the early 1990's for an approach to rock music that avoided mainstream rock's commercialism and show-business aspects. The term has been applied to a wide range of styles and artists, from R.E.M. to the Replacements, Jane's Addiction, Nirvana, and Nine Inch Nails. Many so-called alternative artists experienced mass-market success, so the line dividing alternative and mainstream artists has become somewhat blurred.

alto: Literally, "high," used to refer to a voice range higher than tenor but lower than soprano.

AM radio: "AM" stands for "amplitude modulation," a technical term for a type of radio transmission. The first commercial AM radio station, KDKA in Pittsburgh, began broadcasting in 1920. AM radio was the standard type of radio transmission until the late 1960's, when FM began to be widely used for music programming. The Top 40 radio format developed as an AM format. *See also* FM radio; Top 40.

American Society of Composers, Authors, and Publishers (ASCAP): A professional association of U.S. composers, songwriters, lyricists, and music publishers that licenses and distributes royalties earned by its members' copyrighted works and works to advance its members' interests.

amplifier: "Amp" for short, an electrical device that makes an audio signal louder. Guitar amplifiers color the sound of the electric guitar in distinctive ways, whereas the amplifiers used in sound reinforcement ("PA systems," short for "public-address systems") are intended to reproduce sound as accurately as possible.

andante: A musical notation directing performers to play moderately slowly, literally "at walking speed."

anthem: Originally a hymn of praise or loyalty, as in "The Star-Spangled Banner," the U.S. national anthem. The term "rock anthem" has been applied to rock songs that have inspirational and, usually, sing-along qualities. For example, Queen's "We Will Rock You" and "We Are the Champions" are frequently heard at sporting events.

antiphon: A call-and-response format, often found in liturgical compositions and consisting of choral responses.

appassionato: A musical notation directing performers to play passionately.

aria: A well-developed solo vocal piece performed in an operatic work; in this context, arias form a genre with many specialized subgenres. More generally, any elaborate song or melody for solo voice.

arioso: A musical notation directing performers to play in the manner of an aria or melodiously.

arpeggio: Literally, "like a harp"; a musical notation directing performers to play the notes of a chord in quick succession rather than simultaneously.

arrangement: The way a song is structured or orchestrated. "Arranging" a song involves deciding such things as what instruments will be included, whether there will be an instrumental solo, whether there will be harmonies, and how many sections the song will have. *See also* instrumentation; orchestration.

arranger: A musician who specializes in the arrangement of musical instruments, voices, notes, and other elements, whether human or technological, for the performance of a particular musical work.

art rock: *See* progressive rock.

artists and repertoire (A&R): The department of a record company in charge of artists and material. The A&R person may discover new artists, guide artists' careers, influence album content, and approve single releases.

ASCAP: *See* American Society of Composers, Authors, and Publishers.

atonal: Not organized according to a qualitative distinction between consonance and dissonance or around a central pitch; not structured according to a particular key or mode. Characterizes the music of Arnold Schoenberg and his followers as well as other avant-garde composers. *See also* Second Viennese School; serial music; twelve-tone music.

augmented: A tone that is raised by a half step. *See also* alteration.

augmented seventh chord: A dominant seventh chord with a raised fifth added to it.

avant-garde music: Generally, any musical form that is recognized as new, experimental, or otherwise unclassified in a genre. Often identified with so-called serious music rather than popular music, avant-garde may combine musical genres and sometimes other media and may be used to refer to any of a broad variety of movements.

axe: Musical jargon used to refer to one's instrument, including the voice. Most often connected with jazz and other popular musical forms.

B section: *See* bridge.

B side: The side of a single that contains a song not intended for single release; also called the "flip side." Sometimes the B side is a track that is not available elsewhere, intended to encourage purchase by fans who already have the album.

backbeat: Either the second or the fourth beat in 4/4 time, often used in rock and roll, in which those beats are routinely accented.

balalaika: A three-stringed instrument, commonly called a Russian guitar based on its prominence in Eastern European folk music.

ballad: A slow, melodic tune typically accompanied by lyrics telling a story, usually of love or other personal circumstances.

ballet: In the classical sense, a dance and musical performance with dancers often on point, developed in the sixteenth and seventeenth centuries in Western Europe, particularly France and Italy, and spreading from there. Ballet is perhaps the most rigorous and disciplined form of dance, displaying difficult, controlled, and highly ex-

pressionistic movement by solo, paired, or group performers, and as theater it often tells a story supported by program music composed specifically for it. Ballet may also, however, include more abstract, avant-garde works, as initiated in the twentieth century by choreographers such as Isadora Duncan, for whose work Aaron Copland composed music. Hence "ballet" has proved to be a flexible and evolving concept, denoting any extended, spectacular combined dance-and-music program considered "high" or "serious" art.

bandleader: The conductor of a band, often its founder and a coperformer.

bandoneón: A type of large accordion, often used in Latin American bands. *See also* accordion.

banjo: An instrument with a fretted neck and drumlike body and four or five strings that can be strummed or plucked, characteristically used in performances of country and folk music.

bar: *See* measure.

Baroque: A style of music arising during the seventeenth and early eighteenth centuries, grand in style, elaborate in design, heavily ornamented, written to strict formulas, and emotional in effect. The term is borrowed from the art and architectural forms that exhibited similar characteristics.

bass: The lowest register or line in a piece of music, whether performed by an instrument or the voice, often supporting the main melodic line but in some forms (such as the fugue) taking over the dominant line. Also refers to various musical instruments designed to perform in this range, such as bass violin and bass guitar, as well as to the lowest voice range.

beat: The primary unit of musical rhythm. In divisive (Western) time systems, several beats form a measure, depending on the signature: four beats in 4/4 time, two in 2/4 time, three in 3/4 time, and so on. In additive musical systems, such as much traditional African music, beats may be added to form a line, as in a twelve-beat line.

bebop: A style of jazz that emerged in the mid-twentieth century from the performances of Thelonious Monk, Dizzy Gillespie, Kenny Clarke, Charlie Christian, Bud Powell, and others and influenced jazz well into the twenty-first century. The style uses the chord progressions of standard tunes as the springboard for lively improvisations with long, irregular, syncopated phrasing, augmented chords, and an emphasis on instrumental virtuosity over melodic expression.

bel canto: Literally referring to "beautiful singing," a style of operatic singing that emerged in the seventeenth century, saw its heyday in the nineteenth, and was revived in the mid-twentieth by such divas as Maria Callas. Often associated with sopranos, this form is characterized by rich melodies, florid vocal ornamentation, fast cadenzas and scales, and an emphasis on virtuosic technique over volume.

big band era: The period from the late 1920's to the early 1940's when popular music was dominated by large, orchestra-like bands playing swing music. Bandleaders such as Louis Armstrong and Tommy Dorsey epitomized the genre.

Billboard: A weekly music industry publication that contains information about record contracts and new releases and that maintains a series of charts reflecting sales and airplay for single and album releases. For example, the "Hot 100," launched in 1958, lists the week's one hundred most popular mainstream single recordings based on retail sales.

blocked-key technique: A style of playing chords and melody in parallel, alternating between diatonic and diminished chords. Also known as "locked hands" technique.

blue-eyed soul: Bluesy or soulful material performed by artists of European descent. The term has been applied to the music of the Righteous Brothers, the Rascals, Mitch Ryder, Hall and Oates, and others.

blue note: A flatted (lowered or minor) third, fifth, or seventh chord or tone between the traditional major and minor scales of Western music.

bluegrass: A country music subgenre featuring unamplified stringed instruments, close-pitched harmonies, and rapid improvisation. The violin ("fiddle") and mandolin are generally featured instruments. Bill Monroe (of Bill Monroe and the Blue Grass Boys) is considered the father of bluegrass music.

blues: A form of African American folk music that evolved in the late nineteenth century. Blues songs are usually songs of lamentation. The blues refers to both a feeling and a specific song structure. The verse of a blues song generally sings the same phrase twice, then adds a third phrase to complete or answer the thought. Musically, the blues verse is usually a set length (twelve measures, or bars) and has particular chord changes. The blues is central to both rock and roll and jazz. *See also* jazz.

blues rock: A style of music that emerged in the late 1960's as artists reconnected rock and roll with its rhythm-and-blues roots. Influential artists include Eric Clapton, Stevie Ray Vaughan, and the Allman Brothers.

bluesman: A blues musician.

bolero: A type of music, in 3/4 time, based on the Spanish dance of the same name. Maurice Ravel's *Bolero* exhibits some of the characteristics in its accelerating tempo, repetitive measures, and sharp and deliberate movement.

bomba: A musical genre originating in Puerto Rico with African roots, played for the dance of the same name by bands using low-pitched drums for the base beat, higher-pitched drums for synchronization, and maracas. "Bomba" refers to a dancer who, through physically demanding dance moves, challenges the drummer to keep up.

boogaloo: A blend of Caribbean rhythms and African American soul music with both Latin and rhythm-and-blues flavors.

boogie-woogie: A style of piano playing that arose in the 1930's, using steady, repeated eighth notes in the left hand and percussive blues figures and melodic variations in the right hand. *See also* stride.

bootleg: An unauthorized recording of a concert or studio performance that is copied and distributed without the artist's or record company's approval. Recordings may be made by fans smuggling tape recorders or digital devices into concerts, from stolen demo or studio tapes, or by the illegal copying of legitimate releases, with no revenues going to the artist. Bootlegs are often sold and traded among fans, a process expedited with the advent of the Internet.

bop: A rapid-tempo form of jazz that employs percussive, sometimes jerky, shifting stress and convoluted melodic lines. *See also* bebop; hard bop.

bossa nova: A Brazilian musical form, similar to samba but with greater harmonic complexity.

bottleneck guitar playing: A style of playing the guitar by using a bottle, knife, or other object to slide along the strings in order to generate a glissando effect.

boxed set: A collection of two or more vinyl discs, cassettes, or compact discs, intended to provide an overview of an artist's or group's recording career. Boxed sets may include demos, live recordings, alternate versions of songs, and soundtrack material not otherwise readily available.

brass family: An extended family of wind instruments made of brass (or formerly made of brass), such as saxophones, trumpets, cornets, tubas, and other members of the horn family. *See also* horn family.

bravura: A musical notation directing performers to play boldly.

break: A point in a musical piece when a performer plays or improvises solo, usually for only a few bars.

bridge: A passage in a musical piece that connects two major sections of the composition and often is in a different key. In the *aaba* pattern typical of popular songs, the bridge is labeled *b*; hence it is also known as the B section.

brio: *See* con brio.

British Invasion: A nickname for the wave of British bands that became hugely popular in the United States in the mid-1960's. The invasion began with the Beatles' arrival on the U.S. music scene in January, 1964. Many of these British bands were heavily influenced by American rhythm and blues. They adapted it to their own style, evolving partly from British "skiffle" music. The new British style—and the long-haired look and snappy clothes of the bands—had an immense influence on American popular music. British Invasion bands other than the Beatles included the Rolling Stones, the Animals, the Dave Clark Five, the Yardbirds, Chad and Jeremy, Herman's Hermits, the Kinks, Manfred Mann, and the Who.

broken chord: A chord whose notes are played in sequence rather than simultaneously; unlike the notes of an arpeggio, some of the notes in a broken chord may be played together. *See also* arpeggio.

broken time: The playing of a passage of music without an explicit time signature but in an improvised, irregular manner. Often used by drums and basses.

bubblegum: A simple, prepackaged form of music that appeared in the late 1960's, aimed at young teens and subteens—bubblegum chewers. Artists included the Ohio Express ("Yummy Yummy Yummy"), the 1910 Fruitgum Co., and the Archies.

bugalú: *See* boogaloo.

cabaret: A European-style nightclub and related form of musical theater popular in the mid-twentieth century, especially in the period between the two world wars. The type of music featured was generally upbeat, sometimes with an "oompah" rhythm, and focused on mildly taboo or decadent subject matter and emphasizing escapism and entertainment.

cadence: A sequence of chords that can form a turnaround, a section of a tune, or the end of a phrase, section, or the entire composition.

cadenza: A passage of an aria or concerto that highlights the technical virtuosity of an instrumental soloist or solo vocalist.

caesura: A full stop of sound within a musical composition.

call and response: A musical technique, typically used in choral performances, in which a soloist performs a part that invites an answer from the main chorus. This also occurs in jazz combos when performers improvise, playing off one another. *See also* gospel.

calpyso: A type of music indigenous to the Caribbean characterized by a lively double meter and satirical lyrics; popularized in the United States (in a milder form) by Harry Belafonte during the 1950's.

canon: A genre of music in which a melody is played or sung and then imitated by other performers entering at regular intervals, often before the completion of the first melody, and sometimes inverted or at a different tempo. *See also* counterpoint; fugue; round.

cantabile: A musical notation directing performers to play in a flowing (literally, "singing") style.

cantando: *See* cantabile.

cantata: Originally (in the seventeenth century)

used to denote an extended work, of a religious nature, for solo voice. As of the nineteenth century, a term for a short work combining several soloists with chorus and possibly other accompaniment, on either a sacred or a secular subject. *See also* oratorio.

cantor: Literally, a singer; a musical director in a church or the leading singer in a synagogue.

capriccio: A quick, improvisational, spirited piece of music.

capriccioso: A musical notation directing performers to play capriciously, that is, in a lively, unpredictable, whimsical manner.

carol: A song that celebrates Christmas, often with lyrics that tell the story of the birth of Jesus.

cassette: A self-contained plastic cartridge enclosing magnetic recording tape that passes from one reel to another, introduced in 1965. (Previously, anyone wanting to play or record music on tape had to use individual reels of tape.) Prerecorded cassettes were a less expensive, more portable alternative to the vinyl record. Both were replaced by compact discs, which in turn were superseded by digital downloads.

CD: *See* compact disc.

cello: Properly "violincello," a string instrument in the violin family that occupies the tenor position in the strings.

Celtic music: A general term used to refer to both traditional and popularized, commercial music originating in the folk traditions of Scotland, Ireland, Wales, and sometimes Cornwall and Brittany.

cha-cha *or* **cha-cha-cha:** Music, usually in a brisk tempo, with a rhythm designed to accompany the dance of the same name, three quick steps followed by two in a shuffle.

chamber music: Music (generally classical) for between two and ten solo instruments, such as members of the violin family or combinations of strings, winds, and other instruments, each of whose importance is of equal weight.

chanson: French for "song," a genre from mid-twentieth century France notable for its sentimental, nostalgic lyrics that are more important than the melody.

chant: The singing in unison of texts, often liturgical, in a free rhythm similar to that of speech.

charanga music: A style of music originating in Cuba, in which a violin section plays melodic parts with homophonic textures while the piano, bass, and percussion play tightly interlocked ostinato patterns, often with a flute adding another melodic line.

chart: Generally, any musical score, but narrowly a musical score used by jazz musicians in which only the melody, chord symbols, and lyrics appear, leaving the musicians to improvise and elaborate using their instrumental skills and musicianship.

charts: Regularly published rankings of single and album releases, generally based on sales, radio airplay, or a combination. See also *Billboard*.

choir: A chorus, or group of singers who perform together, often broken into different voice-range sections that sing different harmonic parts. "Choir" often appears in church or other religious contexts.

chorale: A hymn designed to be sung by a choir and a church congregation together.

chord: Three or more notes that, when played simultaneously, work together in harmony. *See also* arpeggio; broken chord; chord progression; triad.

chord progression: Several chords played in succession.

chorus: A group of singers who sing together, often broken into different voice-range sections that sing different harmonic parts. Also, a stanza repeated throughout the course of a song as a refrain. Many pop and rock songs have an alternating verse-chorus structure: The words of each verse are different, but the words of the chorus are repeated identically each time. See also *aaba*.

Christian music: Music written specifically for the Christian liturgy or to form part of a church service or other Christian ritual; more recently, any music, whether popular or classical, that invokes Christian themes, relates parts of the Christian story, identifies or celebrates Jesus Christ and biblical icons, or is generally devoted to the advancement of Christianity and its beliefs.

chromatic scale: The twelve tones of the octave, including all letter-named notes in the octave and all half tones between. A scale, in other words, composed completely of half notes. *See also* diatonic.

chromaticism: The quality of using not only whole tones but half tones between. Often used in reference to jazz's blue notes.

clarinet: Any of a family of single-reed wind instruments constructed using a cylindrical metal tube.

classic rock: A nostalgia-based radio format that relies heavily on the same kind of rock and roll music that its listeners, in the thirty-to-fifty age group, listened to when they were teenagers. Among the bands that fit into the classic rock format are Led Zeppelin, the Doors, the Rolling Stones, and the Who.

classical: Refers in a narrow sense to Western music composed in the late eighteenth century that, unlike the Romantic music that followed it, emphasized emotional objectivity, restraint, simple harmonies, and rhythmic and structural symmetry. In the broad sense, used to characterize "serious" music that is considered high art, is performed in established music halls, and falls into a long-standing repertoire of an accepted, mainly Western and European-based canon comprising narrower subgenres from Baroque and classical through Romantic to new music styles. Such bounds are constantly being breached by evolving crossover genres such as jazz, world music, classical repertoires of non-Western cultures, and experimental projects.

clavecin: A French term for harpsichord.

claves: Finger-operated clappers used percussively in Latin American styles of music.

clavichord: An early, rectangular, boxlike keyboard instrument, sometimes with legs and sometimes to be placed atop a table, with strings running parallel to the long side. Tones were produced by pieces of metal called tangets (rather than the hammers of a harpsichord or piano), which would stop a string from beneath, at a point that would result in production of a certain pitch, similar to the way a violinist uses the fingers to hold a string against the neck of the violin.

clavier: The keyboard of a stringed instrument.

clef: The symbol in printed musical notation that appears at the beginning of the staff (the lines on and between which notes are marked) to indicate the pitch range of the notes. The treble (higher-register) clef somewhat resembles an ampersand, while the bass (lower-register) clef resembles a coil followed by a colon.

coda: The end of a section of an entire composition, used only once (that is, not subject to notation instructing repetition of a section). The "ta-dah" sense of some codas has been exaggerrated deliberately by some composers (including Beethoven) to deliberately dramatic or even comic effect.

coloratura: Literally, coloration; used typically to refer to a soprano who employs complex ornamentation in elaborating a vocal line.

combo: A small jazz ensemble composed of different instruments—such as a trio, quartet, or quintet—in which only one instrument plays each part.

common time: A time signature of 4/4 (four beats per measure), notated with a symbol that looks like a capital C. *See also* cut time.

compact disc (CD): Introduced in 1982, the CD is a plastic-coated optical disc on which sound is digitally recorded, to be read and reproduced by a laser. CDs revolutionized the recording industry because they offered better sound reproduction, were more durable, and could hold more music than vinyl LPs or cassettes. The rapid acceptance of CDs in the 1980's and early 1990's surprised even the music industry itself. By the 2000's, other digital formats, including digital downloads from the Internet to portable media players, were beginning to supersede CDs. *See also* album; digital versatile disc; long-playing (LP) album.

comping: Developed during the swing era of the mid-twentieth century, the use of irregularly spaced chords to punctuate a solo jazz improvisation.

con brio: A musical notation directing performers to play with vigor, in a spirited manner.

con dolore: A musical notation directing performers to play with sadness.

con forza: A musical notation directing performers to play with force.

con moto: A musical notation directing performers to play with motion.

con sordina: A musical notation directing performers to play with a mute; also commonly spelled con sordino and con sordini.

concept album: *See* album.

concertmaster: The first violin in an orchestra, who functions as the leader of the first violins and traditionally functions as the conductor's assistant.

concerto: A composition written for a solo instrument, such as the piano or the violin, in which an orchestra provides the accompaniment.

conductor: The director of an orchestra, chorus, or other group of musicians who uses head and arm movements and facial expressions to direct tempo, phrasing, and dynamics during a performance.

conjunto: A genre of traditional Mexican polka music.

consonance: The simultaneous sounding of notes by all instruments in concord or harmony, resulting in a sense that there is no need for further resolution. *See also* dissonance.

contralto: The lowest female singing range, below soprano and alto.

cool jazz: A jazz style of the early 1950's, originated most notably by Miles Davis, that was based on bebop but in which fast tempos were avoided in favor of more subdued forms. The style was adopted by white vocalists and tended to popularize jazz into the dominant white culture of the time. *See also* hard bop.

cornet: A brass wind instrument, with a cup-shaped mouthpiece, keys, and sound emanating from a horn, similar to a trumpet.

counterpoint: A device of musical composition in which two or more melodic lines are executed simultaneously and harmonically intertwine, playing off each other. *See also* polyphony.

counting off: The communication of tempo and meter by counting aloud, often done to initiate a jazz or rock performance.

country: A broad musical genre that evolved from music descended from the folk songs of the southern and western United States. This folk music ultimately came from the musical traditions of America's early English and Scottish settlers. Around the 1930's, country began to evolve from string-band and "hillbilly" music. It was generally called "country and western" from the 1940's to the mid-1960's. Influential figures include Jimmie Rodgers, Roy Acuff, Hank Williams, Chet Atkins, and Marty Robbins. Country went through various evolutions in the 1970's and 1980's, including "outlaw country" and the arrival of the "new traditionalists." By the 1990's, country, rock and roll, and pop had strongly influenced each other, yet major artists such as Garth Brooks and Reba McEntire were still clearly, instantly identifiable as country artists. *See also* Grand Ole Opry.

country and western music: *See* country.

country rock: A style of music that combines elements of country with rock and roll. The term came into use in the late 1960's and early 1970's, when rock artists began to retreat from psychedelic music to a basic, more roots-oriented sound. Influential artists include the Byrds, Gram Parsons, Linda Ronstadt, and the Eagles.

cover: The recording by one artist of a song already recorded by another artist. The term was first used when white performers in the 1950's "covered" songs of black artists, making them more acceptable to white audiences of the time. (Pat Boone's bland cover version of Little Richard's "Tutti Frutti" is often cited.) The term is now widely applied to any artist's re-recording of an old song, either to interpret it differently or simply to capitalize on the song's familiarity.

crescendo: A musical notation directing performers to play gradually louder.

cross-fade: A technique in which one voice or instrument increases in volume while another fades.

crossover: A "crossover" hit is a song that transcends its original genre, reaching new listeners for an artist. It has been most often used to describe songs or artists that are successful on the pop charts in addition to the soul chart or the country chart. For example, many Motown artists had crossover hits on the pop charts during the late 1960's and early 1970's. Country artists such as Kenny Rogers and Dolly Parton have also appeared on the pop charts.

cross-rhythm: The use of more than one time signature (rhythm, such as 4/4 and 3/4) at once in a passage of music, characteristic of jazz.

cut time: The 2/2 time signature, with two half-note beats per measure. In printed music, cut time is denoted on the clef by a broken circle with a line vertically through it, resembling a cents sign and denoting half of "common time," which is notated with a symbol that looks like a capital C. *See also* common time.

da capo: A musical notation directing performers to play from the beginning (literally, "from the head").

debut: The first performance of a musician or a musical composition.

decrescendo: Gradually decreasing in volume. *See also* crescendo.

Delta blues: Named for the Mississippi Delta region where it originated, an early style of blues that came to prominence during the 1930's and 1940's and was instrumentally dominated by guitar and harmonica players. Epitomized by bluesmen such as Charley Patton and Robert Johnson, this style is directly linked to Chicago blues, Detroit blues, and the Memphis soul music and rhythm and blues of the 1960's and later.

demo: Abbreviation of "demonstration." A demo recording, or demo tape, is made by an artist or group to demonstrate its songs and performing style. The goal is usually to catch the attention of a recording company or producer in the hope of signing a recording contract.

diamond: A term applied to record sales by the Recording Industry Association of America (RIAA) to denote more than ten million records sold. *See also* gold; multiplatinum; platinum.

diatonic: The opposite of "chromatic," referring to a melody or harmony that uses an unaltered major or minor scale. *See also* chromatic scale; chromaticism; diminished scale.

digital download: A computer file formatted for music and capable of being transmitted over the Internet.

digital versatile disc (DVD): An optical storage disc with a higher capacity than a compact disc, which can be used to store digital data, including video files as well as audio files. *See also* compact disc.

diminished: Lowered by a half tone.

diminished scale: One of three scales with eighth notes in alternating whole steps and half steps.

diminished seventh: A four-note chord of minor thirds.

disc jockey (DJ): A person who introduces and plays recordings on the radio or in nightclubs. The term came into use in the 1940's. Originally, radio disc jockeys had considerable influence as to what records they played. By the mid-1980's, however, such "playlist" decisions were often being made by professional programming consultants hired by corporations. Club DJs, particularly those in New York City, were instrumental in the development of rap, hip-hop, and various types of electronic music.

disco: Originally a shortened form of the word "discotheque." Disco refers both to a type of dance club and to a style of dance music that became tremendously popular in the second half of the 1970's. A disco is a nightclub where people dance to recorded music, often accompanied by elaborate, computer-controlled lighting effects. The musical genre emerged from these clubs, as did a showy style of dancing, epitomized in the film *Saturday Night Fever* (with music by the Gibb brothers as the Bee Gees).

dissonance: The simultaneous sounding of clashing notes resulting in tension and a sense that there is need for resolution. *See also* consonance.

divisive time system: *See* additive and divisive time systems.

Dixieland: An early style of jazz developed in New Orleans and featuring the combination of trombone, clarinet, and trumpet. A Dixieland band also has a drummer and often a piano player. Dixieland was named for the Original Dixieland Jazz Band, founded in 1912.

DJ: *See* disc jockey.

dolce: A musical notation directing performers to play sweetly.

dolcissimo: A musical notation directing performers to play very sweetly.

dolore: *See* con dolore.

doloroso: A musical notation directing performers to play sorrowfully, plaintively.

doo-wop: A rhythm-and-blues style popular in the 1950's and early 1960's. Doo-wop features male harmonies and nonsense sounds (such as "doo-wop" and "sh-boom, sh-boom") sung in the background vocals. Influential doo-wop artists include Frankie Lymon and the Teenagers, Dion and the Belmonts, and the Marcels.

dotted rhythm: Rhythm that employs dotted beats (which last half again as long as the note indicates) to create syncopation. In musical notation, these beats are indicated by a dot beside the note, to its right.

double time: The effect of doubling the speed of the tempo by dividing each beat in half. In 4/4 time, for example, double time includes eight eighth notes as beats in one measure, rather than four quarter notes.

Down Beat: An influential monthly jazz publication that contains artist interviews and profiles, music reviews, and information for aspiring musicians. *Down Beat* is known for its annual polls naming the top jazz players of the year.

downbeat: The downstroke of a conductor or bandleader to indicate the first stressed beat in a measure; or, the first beat in a measure.

drum machine: A type of synthesizer that produces and repeats drum sounds and patterns. Drum machines were crucial to the development of rap and hip-hop, and they have become widely used in nearly all types of recordings. They are also used in live performances.

dubbing: Recording of new sound to replace or be added to an existing recording. *See also* overdubbing.

duet: A song or other composition written for two vocalists or two instrumentalists.

DVD: *See* digital versatile disc.

dynamics: The loudness, softness, variations in tempo, and other devices a performer uses to interpret music and/or execute the instructions in written music (such as forte, pianissimo, crescendo, decrescendo, allegro, passionato, rubato); also, the same types of interpretations applied to unnotated or unwritten music.

écossaise: A type of counter dance (from the French for "Scottish" but unrelated to Scottish dance), and the two-in-a-measure music written for it.

eight to the bar: Continuous eighth-note rhythm, familiar from the bass (left-hand) piano playing in boogie-woogie.

eighth note: A beat with half the value or duration of a quarter note.

electroacoustic music: Acoustic music that is modified electronically.

electronica: Most often used as a collective term for a variety of electronic-based styles, including house, ambient house, techno, and even industrial. Electronica is derived from dance-music forms, with their heavy use of sampling and computerized rhythm and sound-texture tracks.

elegy: A work, such as a poem or musical composition, written on the occasion of a death for the purpose for memorializing, lamenting, and praising the dead.

encore: As a musical notation, the direction to repeat a section of music; in a concert or musical recital, an extra, often unplanned, piece of music played at the end of the concert in response to the enthusiasm of the audience.

engineer: A music engineer is responsible for the technical aspects of a recording session and works under the supervision of the producer. The engineer places microphones properly, adjusts sound levels and effects, interconnects electronic devices, and troubleshoots problems. Many producers (and some musicians) are also engineers, but some are not. *See also* mixing; record producer.

ethnomusicology: The study of music as a social and cultural phenomenon, as it arises from traditional folk or tribal origins, and the role it plays in daily life, politics, and other social contexts.

étude: Originally, a musical composition written as an exercise solely to improve technique and therefore tending to be short, with emphasis on particular types of passages. Many études, such as the piano études of Frédéric Chopin, have become part of the classical repertoire; eventually, many works intended for performance rather than practice included "étude" in their titles.

experimental music: Any music that does not easily fit into established genres and self-consciously attempts to breach previous generic, technical, or other definitions by a variety of means, such as unconventional uses of instruments (for example, plucking the strings of a piano rather than striking them with keys); using everyday objects, nonmusical media, and other sound sources as traditional instruments; or using unusual time signatures.

exposition: The first section of a multiple-movement composition (notably the sonata), which introduces the work's melodies and themes.

expressionism: In general, a characteristic of any art form in which the emphasis is on the representation of internal, emotional states and responses rather than the external world. Expressionistic music is often atonal, suggesting extreme emotional states.

extended-play single (EP): An EP contains more songs than a standard two-song single but fewer songs than an album—usually between three and six. Sometimes an EP includes an extended remix, or dance mix, of a song on one side. Other EPs are essentially mini-albums; new groups sometimes release an EP independently, since this is much less expensive and time-consuming than recording an album.

falsetto: A male singer's use of his vocal chords to reach the high, female ranges.

fermata: The discretionary holding of a note, or a rest, beyond the value of the beat, often for dramatic effect.

fifth: An interval between two notes consisting of three whole tones and one half tone; for example, the interval from middle C to G above middle C.

film score: All the music that forms the sound track of a film, excluding songs composed for or used within the film. The film score typically includes music that accompanies and signals the emotional response to the action, background music, and music that bridges scenes, and it may be arranged from other compositions as well as the original work of the film-score composer. *See also* sound track; television score.

finale: The section that closes a musical composition; the term often connotes a spectacular or emotional high note.

fingerstyle: A style of guitar playing in which the performer uses the fingers to pick a repeated arpeggio pattern with alternating bass notes to outline the chords.

flat: A note that is diminished by one semitone; also, in musical notation the symbol, resembling a lowercased letter *b*, that follows the note to be flatted.

flat-picking, flat-pick guitar: Introduced by Doc Watson in the 1950's, a strictly alternating plectrum or flat-pick motion allowing transposition of fiddle and banjo tunes to the guitar. This style begat a worldwide fraternity of flat-pick guitarists and enthusiasts.

flattened interval: An interval in which the final scale degree is lowered by one half step; in a flattened fifth, for example, the fifth scale degree is lowered by a half step. Often used in jazz.

flip side: *See* B side.

Fluxus movement: An avant-garde art movement

of the 1960's that advocated blending different artistic media. *See also* performance artists.

FM radio: "FM" stands for "frequency modulation," a technical term for a type of radio transmission. AM ("amplitude modulation") radio was the standard type of radio transmission until the late 1960's. The earliest FM stations were classical stations taking advantage of the greater sound quality of FM. Pop music began to be broadcast on FM radio in the late 1960's, when "underground" rock stations emerged. Because of the clearer sound of FM and the fact that FM signals could easily be broadcast in stereo, by the mid-1970's FM had taken over as the standard pop-music broadcast media. *See also* AM radio.

folk music: Folk music is traditionally sung and played in a simple, direct style and performed on acoustic instruments—primarily guitar, but also violin, banjo, and other instruments. The style descended from European and southern American story songs, or ballads. Woody Guthrie, in the 1930's and 1940's, was one of the first American folk artists to compose his own songs containing social and political commentary. Other influential folk artists include Pete Seeger, Bob Dylan, and Joan Baez. Since the 1960's, the term folk music has sometimes been used in a broader sense that includes the use of electric instruments and the work of singer-songwriters such as Joni Mitchell and Jackson Browne.

folk revival: From the 1930's to the 1950's, the revival of interest in and performance of traditional folk, blues, and country music, often in service of social and political causes, was promulgated by such key figures as Alan Lomax, the Seeger family, and Woody Guthrie, who influenced musicians of the 1960's and 1970's such as Bob Dylan, Judy Collins, and Joan Baez.

folk rock: Music that combines folk-oriented lyrics with rock accompaniment. Bob Dylan's switch from acoustic to electric accompaniment in 1965 horrified folk traditionalists but also defined the folk-rock genre. Other early influential folk-rock artists include the Byrds, Simon and Garfunkel, and the Mamas and the Papas.

form: The overall structure or organization of a musical composition.

forte: In full, fortepiano; a musical notation directing performers to play loudly and forcefully.

fortissimo: A musical notation directing performers to play as loudly as possible.

forty-five (45): A seven-inch vinyl phonograph record. It is called a 45 because it plays at a speed of 45 revolutions per minute (rpm). In the 1950's and 1960's, the terms "single" and "45" were used interchangeably; a single was simply a 45-rpm record containing two songs, the A side and the B (or flip) side. The format was superseded by cassette singles in the 1970's, CD singles in the 1980's, and digital downloads in the early 2000's.

forza: *See* con forza.

forzando: *See* sforzando.

fourth: An interval consisting of two whole tones and one half tone.

free jazz: Emerging during the early 1960's, a style of large-group jazz improvisation, introduced by Ornette Coleman, that was rooted in black cultural nationalism. Coleman's 1960 album *Free Jazz* featured a double quartet (two groups each containing bass, drums, trumpet, and bass clarinet or saxophone) that performed for thirty-seven minutes (both sides of the album), giving space for all eight of the musicians to solo. Still not abandoning a steady beat, "Free Jazz" (the title of the single piece on the album) featured composed unison melodies played by the horns alternating with one of the four horns soloing over the two bassists and two drummers. Occasionally other horns would join the soloist, providing the model for large group improvisation that developed later in the decade. Some free jazz was brilliant, much was mediocre, and in the long run it was not popular, but it did influence later jazz stylings.

front line: In a combo, the horn players; generally, those performers not in the rhythm section.

fugue: A composition written for three to six parts (vocal or instrumental) in counterpoint. After the exposition of the first part, subsequent imitative parts are introduced in a layering that results in increasingly complex counterpoint. *See also* canon; counterpoint; round.

funk: Urban music characterized by a strong, percussive beat and particularly by an emphasis on the bass. Funk combines elements of African music, jazz, rhythm and blues, and rock. Influential funk artists include James Brown, Sly and the Family Stone, and George Clinton.

fusion: Jazz fusion, or simply "fusion," includes characteristics of both jazz and rock. The term came into use in the late 1960's and early 1970's. Fusion employs some of the instruments and techniques (particularly improvisation) associated with jazz while retaining the heavy beat, rhythm, and volume of rock. Influential artists include Miles Davis, Weather Report, John McLaughlin's Mahavishnu Orchestra, Herbie Hancock, and Frank Zappa.

fuzz tone: A sound created by a fuzzbox, a device that distorts the inputted sound signal, making it come out with a fuzzy, "rough around the edges" sound. Used by rock and other popular musicians, especially with guitars, to create special effects.

gamelan: A traditional Indonesian (especially Balinese or Javanese) orchestra that includes gongs, drums, xylophones, and other percussive instruments.

gangsta rap: A form of rap music whose lyrics emphasize gang culture, celebrating resistance against authority, criminal activities, violent lifestyles, sexual promiscuity, and the use of drugs and alcohol.

gaudioso: To be played literally "with joy."

Gebrauchsmusik: German for "useful music," any music that is written to be pedagogically useful to amateur musicians or practically useful to performing ensembles. The notion grew out of a philosophy on the part of musicians in pre-Nazi Germany (such as Paul Hindemith and Kurt Weill) that music should not be composed simply for its own sake but should perform a function useful in daily life or to society as a whole, with emphasis on the masses and subject matter that reflects common needs and concerns.

gentile: A musical notation directing performers to play gently.

gig: The engagement of a musician or musical group to perform, usually for payment. Most often used by jazz, rock, or other popular musicians.

girl group: A pop act composed of female vocalists, usually a lead and two background singers. These groups were often assembled by record companies or producers in the early 1960's to fit a certain sound. Influential girl groups include the Ronettes, the Shangri-Las, the Chiffons, and the Shirelles.

giusto: A musical notation directing performers to play in strict tempo as written.

glam rock: Also known as "glitter rock," glam is a rock-and-roll subgenre that emerged in the 1970's. The artists, both male and female, wore striking makeup and glittering, colorful costumes. David Bowie's look for *The Rise and Fall of Ziggy Stardust* is sometimes considered the epitome of glam rock. A new generation of glam rockers, such as Poison, appeared in the 1980's; they were nicknamed the "hair bands."

glee: Music for three or more solo parts, often to be sung a capella. Groups formed to sing these compositions are known as glee clubs. *See also* a capella.

glissando: A musical notation directing the performer or vocalist to play in a sliding manner from one tone or pitch to another.

glitter rock: *See* glam rock.

gold: A term applied to record sales by the Recording Industry Association of America (RIAA) to denote more than 500,000 records sold. *See also* diamond; multiplatinum; platinum.

golden oldie: The term originated in the 1960's when Top 40 stations would sometimes play an old song—a golden oldie—among current hits. Oldies radio is a radio format that plays songs from the 1950's and 1960's.

gospel: An African American form of religious choral music. Gospel celebrates the joy of spiritual devotion and is believed to have evolved from the call-and-response speaking and singing between the pastor and the congregation in southern black churches. Many great soul singers began their careers as gospel singers, including Wilson Pickett and Aretha Franklin. Mahalia Jackson is often cited as one of the greatest gospel singers of all time.

Grammy Awards: The annual awards presented by the National Academy of Recording Arts and Sciences (NARAS) for particular achievements in the recording industry. Awards are given in a wide array of categories. Major awards include record of the year, album of the year, and song of the year. Winners receive a gold-plated replica of a gramophone.

Grand Ole Opry: Broadcast from Nashville, Tennessee, and founded in 1925, the oldest continuous radio program in the United States, initially featuring exclusively country music but conservatively branching out to include country subgenres. Also, the stage show that grew out of the program, based in Nashville's Grand Ole Opry House and Ryman Auditorium. The Grand Ole Opry's strict generic standards precluded such artists as Elvis Presley, whose rockabilly style proved offensive, and even those who used electronic amplifiers; these conservative standards helped shape the definition of country music in America. Eventually, the relaxing of restrictions on instrumentation solidified the institution's importance and contributed to the revival of country and western music in the United States during the 1990's and beyond. *See also* country.

grand staff: *See* great staff.

grandioso: A musical notation directing performers to play grandly.

grazioso: A musical notation directing performers to play gracefully.

great staff: In musical notation, the full eleven-line staff incorporating the treble, alto, tenor, and bass staffs.

grunge: An "alternative" subgenre that emerged from the Seattle, Washington, music scene, a fusion of punk and metal made popular by bands such as Nirvana and Soundgarden. *See also* alternative.

guaguancó: A type of rhumba music, for the dance of the same name, performed by conga drums, claves, palits (a percussive instrument using wooden sticks to strike a block), a solo vocalist, and a choir to accompany the male and female dancers.

guaracha: A traditional Cuban song, typically in 6/8 or 2/4 time, whose lyrics are slangy and satirical, referencing current events. Popular with big bands and conjunto bands of the mid-twentieth century.

guitar: A family of fretted, stringed instruments played by strumming and picking usually with fingers rather than a plectrum. Related to the lute, it has a flat rather than rounded back and usually six strings. It has many relatives in different ranges, as well as both acoustic and electric forms—the latter dominant in popular and rock music and the former more typical of classical and folk music.

half tone: Also called a half step or semitone, the interval between two tones in the chromatic scale; for example, the interval between C and C-sharp (on a piano, the white key middle C and the black key immediately to its right).

hard bop: In jazz, a subgenre of bebop with emphasis on a driving beat, "street" or urban blues, and rhythm and blues, and admitting more original composition in comparison with the standards favored in bebop. A more urgent delivery than the "cool jazz" favored by white performers and audiences, and in part reacting against it. *See also* cool jazz.

harmonic rhythm: A notion that combines tempo with harmony, referring to the speed with which harmonic chords progress through a piece of music or a performance.

harmonica: A musical instrument in the reed-organ family held in the hands and played by breathing through it, both in and out; also known as a mouth organ.

harmony: Two or more pitches played together (or in quick succession) to accompany a melody or dominant line. Generally these tones are heard as consonant (requiring no further resolution). *See also* consonance; dissonance.

harpsichord: A keyboard instrument, physically resembling the piano, developed in the sixteenth century and eventually superseded by the pianoforte in the eighteenth century. The distinction between the two in effect is that the harpsichord has two keyboards with two strings for each note, and the notes are plucked by plectra rather than struck. However, harpsichords are now being manufactured again and are used not only in the performance of older music but also in new composition.

heavy metal: A form of rock music popular during the 1970's and 1980's, basic in form and characterized by a hard-driving beat, fast and distorted guitar solos, repetitive rhythms, and high volume levels through electronic amplification. Influential artists include Led Zeppelin, Deep Purple, Black Sabbath, and Blue Cheer. Later metal bands include Mötley Crüe, AC/DC, and Metallica.

heldentenor: A tenor who specializes in Wagnerian roles.

heterophony: The personalization of the melody—through the addition of dynamics, variations in tempi, and individual ornamentation—by one or more of the musicians playing a group performance.

hillbilly: The term "hillbilly music" dates back to the 1920's, when it emerged from the mountain regions of Appalachia and the American South. Hillbilly is the primary ancestor of country music. *See also* country.

hip: Also "hep" (an older term), the notion of being "in the know," up to date in one's awareness of, knowledge of, and subscription to current trends, events, and attitudes, especially as these apply to the arts and social culture.

hip-hop: Nearly synonymous with rap music, hip-hop is both a music genre and a cultural phenomenon, born in the late 1980's and coming into its own in the early 2000's. Heavily influenced by funk, rhythm and blues, break dancing, urban street culture, and technical innovations such as turntable manipulation and boomboxes, it has spawned a number of subgenres and typically emphasizes a steady beat on top of which improvised street poetry is spoken, mixed with instrumentals. *See also* rap.

hit: A successful single or album—one that many people buy, which usually means that it is widely played on the radio. In addition, since the mid-1980's, this typically means that videos of the song are shown on television. The definition of "hit" varies from artist to artist; for someone just starting out, reaching the *Billboard* Top 40 is an accomplishment. For an established artist, anything less than a Top 10 song might be considered unsuccessful.

hocket: Based on the Latin for "hiccup," the sharing or division of a melody or a rhythmic line between performers or instruments or sections of a chorus or orchestra, as one hands off the part to another; when the group performs the piece, these parts form an interlocking whole.

homophony: Music sung or performed in unison, created by melody and accompaniment.

honky-tonk: A honky-tonk is a disreputable nightclub or other place of cheap entertainment. As a country-music subgenre, honky-tonk music was very popular in the 1950's and 1960's (Lefty Frizzell, Loretta Lynn, George Jones, Merle Haggard).

hook: A brief but memorable portion of a song, either lyric or instrumental. It is supposed to grab or "hook" the listener into liking and remembering a song.

horn family: A family of wind instruments, made of brass or another metal, featuring a bell at the sounding end and a coiled tube receding to the mouthpiece at the other end, with keyed valves to control pitch (although more primitive one-pitch "natural" horns are included with valve horns in some definitions). The French horn is a prominent example. *See also* brass family.

house band: A band with a steady engagement playing at a particular nightclub. The Doors were the house band at the Whisky-a-Go-Go in Hollywood before beginning their recording career.

house music: A style of dance music that became popular in the late 1980's, named for the Warehouse Club in Chicago, where the style originated. The sound is heavily electronic and repetitive, with heavy, deep bass and drums.

hymn: A song of religious praise and glorification, usually with a simple melody designed to be sung by church congregations and repeated several times with different verses and the same refrain.

imperioso: A musical notation directing performers to play imperiously.

impetuoso: A musical notation directing performers to play impetuously.

impressionism: A general term referring to any type of art that seeks to record the perceiver's fleeting impression of a scene or other sensory perception, rather than provide a detailed representation of reality. In music, this characterization is particularly associated with the work of composer Claude Debussy and those whom he influenced, because his music conveyed a certain dreaminess and his descriptions of some of his own works evoke the work of French Impressionist painters.

impromptu: Any short piano work that is improvised or is composed to give the impression of improvisation, intimacy, and immediacy.

improvisation: The creation of music during a performance as opposed to the playing of written music, often connected with jazz but familiar in other genres as well. The effect is that of unleashing spontaneity, freshness, emotion, and drama in witnessing the onstage "composition" of music and musicality. In group performances, particularly in jazz combos, this type of performance is a regular occurrence, as each player takes a turn at solo performance, springboarding off the main melodic line to depart into variations and related riffs. Bebop jazz groups and rock groups such as the Grateful Dead and Phish are noted for collective improvisation.

indie: An abbreviation for "independent," used to refer to groups, often popular bands, that have not contracted with music producers.

industrial: A variation of house music, dubbed "industrial" because of its machine-like rhythms, use of sounds such as clanking metal pipes, and distorted "metal" guitar.

inner voice: Any submelody that emerges between the main melody and the bass line.

instrumentation: An arranger's choice of instruments, assignment of parts to them, decisions on how many instruments will play, and combinations of them in the performance of a musical work. *See also* arrangement; orchestration.

interlude: Traditionally, a short instrumental work performed between the acts of a play or opera; in an extended sense, a section added to a musical work that is played between solo parts.

intermezzo: A short movement or interlude connecting the main parts of a composition.

interpretation: The expression a performer brings when playing an instrument.

interval: The distance in pitch between two notes.

intonation: The quality of the pitch as it is played or sung, usually with the goal of hitting the pitch accurately but at times with the deliberate intention of approaching it chromatically or with a microtone (a tone slightly off the main pitch). *See also* chromaticism; pitch; tone.

intro: Short for "introduction." A section of music, usually brief, before the main body of the song begins.

inversion: A chord whose root note is not in the base or a voicing with the root note moved up by an octave.

isorhythm: A repeated rhythmic phrase against a changing pitch sequence.

jam, jam session: Slang for an improvised music session, originally referring to jazz rehearsals. "Jam" is also used as a verb, meaning to play hard, often improvising.

jamband: A band that jams, or improvises, during a concert or performance. Early examples include the Grateful Dead; later examples include Phish.

jazz: A type of popular music originating in New Orleans from the African American folk music prevalent in that area. Heavily influenced by blues, the main characteristics of jazz are syncopation, a strong rhythmic beat, and improvisation. Early jazz emphasized melodic improvisation by trumpet, clarinet, and trombone. By the 1950's the saxophone had largely replaced the clarinet, and the roles of the drummer, bassist, and pianist had all expanded. The history of jazz goes back to the early years of the twentieth century, and Dixieland, big-band swing music, bebop, cool jazz, hard bop, and free jazz are among its many subgenres.

jazz fusion: *See* fusion.

jazz standard: A tune that has become part of the standard jazz repertoire, such as "Love for Sale" or "Nights in Tunisia."

jukebox: A machine designed to play any of a variety of records (often in the vinyl 45-rpm format), usually after coins are deposited. Most popular in the 1950's, these machines were often located in soda shops, diners, and other public places where teenagers gathered.

jump or jumping beat: A rapid 4/4 tempo, designed for dancing.

key: The scale and mode in which a work is designed to be played, based on a root note, which in most Western scales both begins and ends the scale. Examples include the key of C major and the key of E minor. *See also* mode.

key signature: In musical notation, the markings at the beginning of the staff, following the clef, that indicate the key in which the piece is to be played, including flats and sharps that define the scale.

keyboardist: A musician who specializes in keyboard instruments, such as the piano; often used to refer specifically to musicians who focus on electronic keyboard instruments played in popular recordings.

Klangfarbenmelodie: German for "tone-color-melody," a somewhat vague term coined by Arnold Schoenberg to denote melodies using timbre the way ordinary melodies use pitch. *See also* timbre.

klezmer music: Traditional Jewish melodies performed on the klezmer clarinet.

komabue: A small transverse bamboo flute, indigenous to Japan.

koto: A thirteen-stringed Japanese type of zither.

label: Usually used to mean "record company," as in signing a recording contract with a label. Most labels are parts of huge corporations, but there are also small independent labels. Large record companies often have different labels for different genres, and some highly successful artists establish their own labels, as the Beatles did with Apple Records and Prince did with Paisley Park.

lacrimoso: A musical notation directing performers to play sadly (literally, "tearfully").

lamentando: A musical notation directing performers to play mournfully; synonymous with lamentoso.

larghetto: A musical notation directing performers to play slowly, but not as slowly as indicated by largo.

larghissimo: A musical notation directing performers to play very slowly, more slowly than largo.

largo: A common musical notation directing performers to play broadly, slowly, in a stately manner.

Latin jazz: Jazz that incorporates rhythms, instrumentation, and other elements of traditional Afro-Cuban, Brazilian, and other Latin American genres and stylings, such as bossa nova, samba, conga, or salsa.

lead guitarist: The guitarist providing the guitar melodies and solos for a recording session or live performance. The term came into use to distinguish the lead player from the rhythm guitarist. The term is now sometimes used even if there is only one guitarist in the band. It is sometimes shortened to "playing lead."

legato: A musical notation directing performers to play contiguous notes in a "joined" fashion, smoothly, without breaks or rests between them.

leggiero: A musical notation directing performers to play lightly and delicately.

leitmotif: From German *Leitmotiv* (leading motive), a musical theme that is attached to, and signals to the audience the presence of, a particular character, set of circumstances, or idea, especially in opera.

liberamente: A musical notation meaning freely; synonymous with libero.

libretto: A book of text containing the words of an opera.

lied (*pl.* lieder): From the German for "song," this term has come to be associated with art songs that emerged from the Romantic movement in music during the late eighteenth and early nineteenth centuries, as well as later works for solo vocalists inspired by them.

ligature: In musical notation, a curved line that arches over or under several notes to indicate that they should be played or sung as a phrase. *See also* phrase; slur.

liner notes: The descriptions of the music or recording processes that sometimes appear on the back or inside cover of an album or in a CD booklet.

live recording: A recording made while an artist is performing in front of an audience at a club or concert hall.

long-playing (LP) album: A vinyl record album that plays at 33 rotations per minute (rpm), the primary format for storing and marketing music from the late 1940's to the mid-1980's. *See also* album; compact disc; digital versatile disc.

lute: A stringed instrument with a vaulted or rounded back, a head angled back from the neck, a fretted fingerboard, and a pear-shaped body. A very old instrument, the lute appears in many varieties in different cultures.

luthier: A maker of violins and other stringed instruments.

Lydian mode: A major scale or chord with a raised fourth, the basic jazz scale according to theorist George Russell.

lyrics: The words written for a song.

ma non troppo: A musical notation directing performers to play in whatever way is indicated, "but not too much," that is, not overdone.

madrigal: A contrapuntal song written for at least three voices, usually without accompaniment.

maestoso: A musical notation directing performers to play majestically, in a stately fashion.

maestro: A general term of respect for a musician regarded as a great composer, conductor, or teacher of music.

mainstream: A verb used to characterize the metamorphosis of any formerly specialized genre, popular with a limited group, for the main or dominant population, often in a modified form. Also, a noun used to refer to the main population or market.

major key: One of two major tonal modes, a key or scale in which the third tone of the scale is four half tones above the root key. *See also* minor key.

marcato: A musical notation directing performers to play in a marked, or accented and deliberate, manner.

march: A form of music written for marching in two-step time. Originally the march was used for military processions and eventually it became associated with patriotic music. The premier composer of marches in the United States is John Philip Sousa.

mariachi music: The music performed by a traditional Mexican mariachi band, performed by a variety of guitars, fiddles, and horns.

marimba: A type of portable xylophone originating in Africa and used in Latin American music. It consists of parallel wooden strips with resonators, mounted on a frame and strapped to the front of the performer. These wooden strips are struck with drum sticks to produce the sound. *See also* vibraphone, xylophone.

measure: Also called more informally a bar, a unit of music consisting of all the beats in one full measure, such as four beats in 4/4 time; in musical notation, these units are divided by vertical "bar lines."

medley: Often used in overtures, a composition that incorporates passages from other movements of the composition in its entirety.

melisma: A shift of one or more tones during the singing of a single syllable in a song.

melody: The meaningful and generally pleasing sequence of pitches that form a theme in a song or other musical composition, consisting of an arrangement of single, dominant notes rather than accompanying chords and harmonies.

meter: The arrangement of strong and weak beats

and groups of beats in a musical work, generally denoted by the time signature, such as 4/4, 3/4, or 6/8.

mezza voce: Sung or played with moderation or a subdued (literally, "half") voice.

mezzo forte: Sung or played moderately loudly, or in a fairly strong but not overpoweringly loud voice.

mezzo piano: Sung moderately softly but not as soft as possible.

mezzo-soprano: The voice range falling between soprano and alto.

middle of the road (MOR): Mellow pop music that appeals to a broad audience. *See also* adult contemporary.

minimalism: A style of serious music developed in the 1970's and 1980's by composers such as Philip Glass and Steve Reich, characterized by a devotion to pulse, repetition, and sustained diatonic harmony, often using electronic sounds.

minor key: One of two major tonal modes, a key or scale in which the third, sixth, and seventh tones are diminished by a half tone from the major scale with the same root key. *See also* major key.

minuet: Slow and stately dance in triple time, introduced in the seventeenth century and eliciting many musical works since.

Mississippi Delta: *See* Delta blues.

misterioso: A musical notation directing performers to play in a manner that evokes a sense of mystery.

mixing: The process of combining all the instruments and singing produced during recording sessions into the final version of the song. In the recording process, twenty-four or more tracks of playing and singing are usually recorded. At its simplest, mixing involves setting all the sounds at the right volume levels, adjusting tone, and adding appropriate effects (such as reverb and delay). Mixing is supervised by the record's producer; engineers do much of the hands-on work. *See also* engineer; record producer.

modal jazz: An approach to jazz, developed by Miles Davis, Herbie Hancock, and others, that employs modes such as Dorian and Lydian.

mode: Generally, a reference to either of the two major modes of musical scales, major or minor. More specifically, there are many modes or scales used throughout the ages and in different cultures. Some of the major modes include the Ionian, Dorian, Phrygian, Lydian, Mixolydian, Aeolian, and Locrian, for example. A mode differs from a key in that it describes the progression of tones but does not stipulate the root note. *See also* key.

moderato: A musical notation directing performers to play moderately in a certain way, such as allegro moderato.

modulation: A harmonic progression from one musical key to another.

molto: Italian for "very," often combined with another direction, such as molto vivace.

monophony: One line of sound performed by a single musician or by a group of musicians who are all playing in unison together.

monotone: The repetition of one pitch.

montuno: A portion of a piece during which extended improvisation takes place over a background of repeated interlocking musical figures, with the number of repetitions left open.

MOR: *See* middle of the road.

motif: A primary musical theme developed throughout a work.

moto: *See* con moto.

Motown: A record label founded in Detroit by Barry Gordy, Jr., in 1959. Motown is credited with revitalizing (even reinventing) rhythm and blues in the 1960's and early 1970's. Once the largest African American-owned business in the United States, Motown Records was home to such artists as the Supremes, the Four Tops, Smokey Robinson, Marvin Gaye, and the Jackson 5.

mouth organ: *See* harmonica.

movement: A separate section of a larger composition.

MTV: A cable television network that began broadcasting in 1981, featuring youth-oriented music videos, news, and other specialty programming. MTV (Music Television) revolutionized the music industry by adding a visual element to what had been almost exclusively an audio art form. The first video broadcast on MTV was "Video Killed the Radio Star," by the Buggles. MTV was early accused of racism for showing few videos of black artists; that situation changed when Michael Jackson's videos from *Thriller* were shown extensively.

multimedia artist: An artist who combines media, such as music, film, video, and visual arts, into one work or artistic event.

multiplatinum: A term applied to record sales by the Recording Industry Association of America (RIAA) to denote more than two million records sold. *See also* diamond; gold; platinum.

musical theater: Theater in which music helps drive the narrative forward, usually associated with Broadway and Off-Broadway productions but also encompassing opera and its offshoots.

musicology: The study of all aspects of music, from its genres and forms to its history, science, methodologies, techniques, and technologies.

musique concrète: Introduced by Pierre Schaeffer, music that highlights the musical potential in sounds recorded from the everyday world.

mute: A device that a brass player inserts into the bell of a horn or brass instrument to soften or otherwise alter the timbre.

natural: A symbol in sheet music that directs the performer to play the note unflatted or unsharped where the key signature would normally call for a flat or sharp.

neo-bop: A bebop style employed by trumpeter Roy Hargrove and other jazz instrumentalists of the 1990's that basically returns to bebop.

neoclassicism: Inspired by eighteenth century classical music, musicians of the interwar period (c. 1920-1940) returned to a sparer, more rational (vs. emotional), symmetrically structured music, in part as a reaction to the emotional fervor of World War I. The key composers were Igor Stravinsky, Paul Hindemith, Sergei Prokofiev, and Béla Bartók.

neo-Romanticism: A reaction against the atonal serial music of the early and mid-twentieth century, neo-Romantic music arose in the late twentieth century, reintroducing melody and emphasizing emotion. Neo-Romantic music includes works by David Del Tredici, Ellen Taaffe Zwilich, Nicholas Maw, James MacMillan, György Ligeti, and Krysztof Penderecki.

New Age: A lyrically emotional and primarily acoustic fusion of folk, jazz, and classical music that is intended to accompany meditation and has a relaxed, spiritual quality. The term was coined during the 1980's and the genre—really more a commercial classification—is associated with names as diverse as Will Ackerman, Mike Oldfield, Enya, and Yanni. *See also* adult contemporary; middle of the road; world music.

new music: A loose term, originating in the late 1970's, for new or recently composed serious concert music in the classical vein.

new wave: A late 1970's term for new rock music that was different from 1970's mainstream rock but was not punk, generally being more melodic and less angry. The term was used so vaguely and widely that it had little real meaning. Artists considered to be affiliated with this genre include Elvis Costello, the Talking Heads, Blondie, and the Pretenders.

No.: *See* opus.

nocturne: A musical composition, usually a short work for piano, intended to evoke the evening and night; often it has a pensive, dreamy quality.

nonet: A work for nine instruments.

notation: The notes, staffs, clefs, dynamics notations, and other printed elements that form written music.

note: A tone, pitch, or printed note in sheet music. All these definitions have been used, but in American usage the term most often refers to the symbols printed on a page of sheet music (such as a whole note, half note, quarter note, eighth note, or sixteenth note). *See also* pitch; tone.

number: *See* opus.

obbligato: An extended instrumental solo that accompanies a vocal part, such as an aria.

oboe: A double-reed wind instrument consisting of a cylindrical tube with keyed valves, having a range of about two and one-half octaves starting at B-flat below middle C.

ocarina: About the size of a harmonica, a wind instrument with an oval or potato-shaped body, finger holds, and a mouthpiece.

octave: Eight full tones above the root note, ending on the root pitch, or the distance between one key (for example, middle C) and the next higher same key (C above middle C).

octet: A work for eight instruments.

oldie: *See* golden oldie.

opera: An extended classical music drama of several acts and scenes that advances a story, either tragic or comic, in which all or most of the dialogue is sung.

operetta: A musical drama, shorter than an opera and with a lighter theme or story.

opus: A term used to refer to one of a classical composer's works, which may in turn contain subworks listed with numbers (No.); for example, Beethoven's Sonata in E-flat, Op. 31, No. 3.

oratorio: A work on a religious subject including arias, recitatives, and choral music, but without plot or scenery.

orchestra: A large group of instrumentalists playing together.

orchestration: The arrangement of a musical work not originally composed for orchestra for orchestral performance. *See also* arrangement; instrumentation.

organ: A wind instrument operated by a console resembling a piano but with two keyboards, which works by forcing compressed air through pipes of different lengths in order to produce different pitches and timbres.

ornaments: Tones and figures that do not always appear in written music, used to embellish the principal melodic tone. Examples include grace notes, turns, portamento, vibrato, and modifications of tempo.

ostinato: Literally, "obstinate"; a rhythmic or melodic fragment or theme that repeats throughout a work.

outside: In the standard *aaba* structure of a song, the *a* sections (not the bridge).

overdubbing: To record sound over an earlier recording in order to give the effect of combined sounds. *See also* dubbing.

overture: The introduction to an opera, musical, or symphonic work, often incorporating themes that receive full exposition later in the work.

parlando: Delivered like speech.

part: A line in a contrapuntal work performed by an individual voice or instrument.

partial: A harmonic given off by a note when it is played.

partitioning: Coined by Milton Babbitt, the splitting of musical material into different voices, so that each voice exhibits a certain character as determined by other musical parameters.

passionato: A musical notation directing performers to play passionately.

pastoral: Idyllic, evocative of the countryside or peaceful nature.

pattern: A melodic figure that is repeated throughout a work, often in different keys or using different pitches.

pausa: A rest, when no notes are played.

pedal: A bass line that remains on one note; also, one of several foot-operated levers in a piano or organ used to sustain a note.

pentatonic scale: A major scale, but consisting of only five notes (the fourth and seventh are omitted from the octave), which characterizes many indigenous musical traditions as well as much of jazz.

percussion instruments: Any instrument used in the making of music that is sounded through striking, scraping, or shaking. Includes drums, cymbals, xylophones, maracas, and many other instruments.

perfect pitch: Also known as absolute pitch, the ability to produce or identify a particular note without reference to other notes; also, the production of that note by means of a tuning fork that vibrates at the note's frequency.

performance artists: Artists who combine many traditional arts, both visual and musical, to present an event that forms the artwork, typically related to current events or social issues and often occurring in unusual or public spaces. *See also* Fluxus movement.

phrase: Similar to a phrase or sentence in speech, a short section of music, normally consisting of a few notes or bars, intended to be played as a unit of musical "language." *See also* ligature.

pianissimo: A musical notation directing musicians to play very softly and gently, more softly than "piano."

piano: A musical notation directing musicians to play softly.

piano-vocal score: A score showing vocal parts along with piano arrangement.

pianoforte: A keyboard-operated instrument, commonly called a piano, originally named for its capacity to produce sounds of varying timbres from loud to soft. Arising in the eighteenth century, it physically resembled the harpsichord but with a different acoustical action, with steel-wire strings struck by felt hammers.

pick-up: In a musical work, a note or phrase that opens the piece prior to the first bar.

pitch: The frequency of a note, which determines how high or low it sounds. *See also* note; tone.

pizzicato: Literally "pinched" or "plucked"; a musical notation directing string players such as violinists to pluck the strings rather than bow them.

platinum: A term applied to record sales by the Recording Industry Association of America (RIAA) to denote more than one million records sold. *See also* diamond; gold; multiplatinum.

player piano: A mechanically operated piano that automatically plays music from scrolls.

playlist: The list of songs to be played by a radio station. Station managers or consultants hired by the station's owners generally determine the playlist, which is tailored to the station's format and audience (country, classic rock, and so on).

pocket: Refers to the center or zone of perfect rhythm; "in the pocket" means in perfect time.

poco: A musical notation meaning "a little" and combined with other notations, as in "poco più allegro," a little faster.

polyphony: Music in which two or more different melodies are played at the same time. *See also* counterpoint.

polyrhythms: Several different rhythms employed at the same time.

polytonality: Several different tones or keys played at the same time, often not in harmony. *See also* dissonance.

pop: Derived from the word "popular," the phrase "pop music" originally referred to any style of music popular with a variety of listeners. It also separated "popular" music from serious classical music. As the term evolved, "pop music" has come to mean music intended for mass consumption, with inoffensive, easy-to-remember melodies and lyrics. A Top 40 radio station generally plays pop music. "Pop" is also used to differentiate this type of music from genres such as country, rap, rock and roll, and soul—although they are certainly popular, they are usually differentiated from mainstream pop. *See also* crossover.

pop-rock music: Popular music with an emphasis on rock devices and stylings.

portamento: A mild glissando between two notes for an expressive effect, or approaching a pitch from just above or below it. On stringed instruments (where it is often used), executed by sliding the fingers on the strings.

prelude: Originally, a short piece preceding a more substantial work, or an orchestral introduction to opera that is shorter than an overture. Also, a discrete work for piano or orchestra based on a short theme.

prestissimo: A musical notation directing musicians to play extremely quickly, as fast as possible, faster than presto.

presto: A musical notation directing musicians to play quickly.

producer: *See* record producer.

program music: Music intended to evoke a series of images, a scene, or a narrative, often associated with Romantic music.

progression: The movement of chords in succession.

progressive rock: A style of rock music that was particularly popular in the early 1970's. Progressive rock bands wrote long, complex songs—sometimes entire album sides—that drew on both psychedelic rock and classical music for inspiration. The most successful progressive bands were British, and they included King Crimson; Yes; Genesis; Emerson, Lake, and Palmer; and Gentle Giant. Some recordings by Jethro Tull, the Moody Blues, and Pink Floyd have also been called progressive. The term "art rock" is also sometimes used, but its meaning is somewhat less focused; art rock includes artists such as Roxy Music and Brian Eno.

promotional record: A recording that a record company distributes free to radio stations and reviewers, hoping to generate advance publicity and favorable reviews. Some "promos" contain interviews and nonalbum material and are widely sought after by collectors.

psychedelic rock: A style of rock music popular in the mid- to late 1960's that was intended to be "mind-expanding" and to emulate the effects of hallucinogenic drugs. It used feedback, distortion, unusual instrumentation such as Middle Eastern instruments, and sound effects. Among influential psychedelic bands were the Jefferson Airplane, the Grateful Dead, the Jimi Hendrix

Experience, and early Pink Floyd. The Beatles' *Sgt. Pepper's Lonely Hearts Club Band* and *Magical Mystery Tour* also include psychedelic effects and arrangements.

punk rock: Marked by extreme expressions of anger and social discontent, punk originated in New York, then evolved in working-class London in the mid- to late 1970's. Punk rock was loud, fast, and generally so untrained as to sound sloppy. Punk is credited with reinvigorating rock and roll in the time of disco and heavily produced but bland rock records. Influential artists include the Sex Pistols, the Clash, and the Ramones. Other punk acts included the Germs, the Slits, and Siouxsie and the Banshees.

quartal: Referring to chords based on fourths, associated with jazz greats McCoy Tyner and John Coltrane.

quarter note: The most common musical note, denoting one-quarter of a measure as the primary beat in music written in the 4/4, 3/4, and 2/4 time signatures.

quartet: Four musicians, either vocalists or instrumentalists, who perform together.

quintet: Five musicians, either vocalists or instrumentalists, who perform together.

quote: Within a musical work, a phrase or piece of another work, often by another composer or from traditional folk tunes. Examples include the Shaker hymn "Simple Gifts" in Aaron Copland's *Appalachian Spring*.

R&B: *See* rhythm and blues.

race music: A name for African American popular music—blues and rhythm and blues—that was in use from the 1920's to the early 1950's. The name implied that only African Americans, not white audiences, would be interested in it. Gradually, beginning in the 1950's, white audiences began to hear and enjoy "black music," and the term rhythm and blues (soon supplemented by rock and roll) replaced "race music."

raga music: A traditional mode in Indian music.

ragtime: A genre of music with syncopated rhythms, upbeat tempos, and often catchy lyrics popular at the beginning of the twentieth century. The tunes (called "rags") were performed by such popular musicians as Eubie Blake and

were transformed by the likes of Louis Armstrong into later forms of jazz.

rallentando: A musical notation directing the performer to broaden the tempo. *See also* ritardando.

rap: A genre in which the vocalists are talkers and rhymers, or "rappers," rather than singers. Rap originated in New York in the 1970's. It was heard in nightclubs long before it found its way onto widely distributed recordings. Club disc jockeys, "spinners," teamed with rappers to develop the genre. The Sugarhill Gang's novelty track "Rapper's Delight" is sometimes cited as the first widely popular rap song. Other influential early performers include Grandmaster Flash, then Run-D. M. C. and LL Cool J. By the 1980's rap had become widely popular, and the 1990's and 2000's saw dozens of major rap stars. *See also* hip-hop.

rave: A large, overnight party involving all-night dancing to techno music and extreme light displays, often located in a warehouse or remote, rural location.

rave-up: An extended improvisation based on a twelve-bar blues progression, developed by Eric Clapton.

recapitulation: A reprise.

recital: A concert performed by a soloist, either a vocalist or an instrumentalist.

recitative: In operas and oratorios, a form of singing in a rhythmically free pattern that mimics speech, characteristically used in dialogue to advance the narrative.

record producer: A person in the music business who is charged with creating the sound of an album or single. The producer's duties vary depending on the artist. Producers review the material and suggest modifications, make budget decisions, select session musicians, and generally determine the best way to realize the artist's vision. Among the many well-known producers who have contributed immensely to the sounds of recordings are Phil Spector (who created the "wall of sound") and George Martin (who produced the Beatles). *See also* engineer; mixing.

Recording Industry Association of America (RIAA): The main trade association of the recording industry. The RIAA sets the standard for gold, platinum, and diamond records and serves as a lobbying body for the interests of the industry.

refrain: A phrase or section of a song that is repeated after each of the song's verses. Also called the chorus.

reggae: A Jamaican music form based on repetitive bass, drum, and percussion patterns. Tempos are slow to midtempo, and reggae has a hypnotic effect because of its simple, interlocking instrumental parts and rocking rhythms. In Jamaica it is culturally intertwined with the Rastafarian religion. By the 1970's reggae was popular worldwide but never achieved major success in the United States. Major artists include Bob Marley, Jimmy Cliff, Peter Tosh, and Burning Spear. *See also* rocksteady; ska.

register: Part of the range of an instrument or voice.

relative major and minor keys: The major and minor keys that share the same notes in that key, such as C major and A minor.

relative pitch: The ability, shared by most musicians and singers, to identify pitch as it relates to the other notes around it. *See also* perfect pitch.

repertoire: The collected works mastered and performed by a group or individual musician. Also, the group of works considered to be part of any standard set, such as the classical repertoire or opera repertoire.

reprise: To repeat a portion of a piece after other sections have been played.

requiem: Narrowly, a musical work composed for the occasion of a mass for the dead. More generally, any piece of music composed for a funeral or memorial service, with the qualities of a dirge or hymn.

resonance: The vibration of all notes or strings, after only one is struck, when they have been tuned to frequencies that are in harmony with one another.

responsorial: *See* call and response.

retrograde: Referring to the backward playing, or inversion, of a melody or series.

reverb: An echo produced electronically, or the device that produces this effect.

rhythm: The beats, tempi, and meter of a piece of music, as denoted by its time signature and other musical notation in written music.

rhythm and blues (R&B): A style of African American popular music of the 1940's and 1950's with roots in jazz, blues, and big-band music. R&B was an important precursor to rock and roll.

Early R&B artists include the Orioles, Hank Ballard and the Midnighters, Louis Jordan, and Fats Domino. The term R&B came into vogue again in the 1980's and 1990's; this music is a smooth blend of pop, urban contemporary, and soul, and it generally emphasizes elaborate, skillful singing. *See also* Motown; soul music.

rhythm changes: The chords to "I Got Rhythm" (Gershwin), somewhat modified and simplified. Many jazz tunes use these changes, and every player must know them. There are several variations.

rhythm guitarist: The guitarist providing the rhythmic accompaniment, rather than solo parts, for a recording or performance.

rhythm section: The part of a jazz ensemble that is keeping time. May be the bass, piano, drums, or guitar (or banjo).

riff: A repeated musical phrase. A riff can serve as the rhythmic basis for a song or can support or play against the melody.

ritardando: Gradually growing slower, decelerating.

rock: The terms "rock music" and "rock and roll" are often used interchangeably. However, "rock" sometimes is used to separate the early "rock and roll" of the 1950's and early 1960's from the evolving "rock" music of the late 1960's and after.

rock and roll: A style of music that evolved from rhythm and blues, mixed with country and, to a lesser degree, gospel, big-band, jazz, and even Afro-Cuban music. As big bands went out of style in the late 1940's, smaller groups filled the void with amplified guitars, shouted vocals, and a rapid beat. The music called "rock and roll" (or "rock 'n' roll") began developing clearly in the early 1950's, but the term itself was a sexual slang term in use among African Americans for many years. Among the characteristics of early rock and roll were driving drumming, saxophone solos, electric guitars, and intense, sometimes shouted or screamed, vocals. Early influential artists include Muddy Waters, Chuck Berry, Little Richard, Bo Diddley, Elvis Presley, and Jerry Lee Lewis. *See also* rhythm and blues; rockabilly.

rockabilly: A link between country (or "hillbilly") music and rock and roll. Rockabilly was the first form of rock performed by white musicians. Influential artists include Elvis Presley, Bill Haley and His Comets, Carl Perkins, and Buddy Holly.

rocksteady: A successor to ska and an immediate predecessor of reggae music in Jamaica in the mid-1960's. Like ska, rocksteady emphasizes the offbeat, but unlike ska, it is characterized by vocal harmony groups and dances in a tempo that is slower and more relaxed as well as more syncopated. *See also* reggae; ska.

rolled chord: *See* arpeggio.

Rolling Stone: An entertainment magazine founded by Jann Wenner in 1967. It was originally a weekly on newsprint paper that focused on rock music. For a few years it was very important to rock recording artists and record companies because it was the only mass-market publication that took late 1960's music and the counterculture seriously. *Rolling Stone* later branched out to include all forms of entertainment, fashion, and social commentary.

Romantic: Referring to music that is emotional, expressive, impressionistic, subjective, harmonically lush, and evocative, as opposed to neoclassical or atonal music.

rondo: In classical works, especially sonatas, a repeated principal theme.

root: The first note of a scale or the first note of a triad chord.

round: A type of canon in which the melody is begun by one voice, started again by another voice several measures after the first voice, and perhaps started after another interval by a third voice. Each voice repeats the melody in its own turn, resulting in harmony throughout. *See also* canon; counterpoint; fugue.

rpm: A reference to the number of times a vinyl record makes a full revolution or rotation within one minute when it is being played.

rubato: Literally, "robbed"; a musical notation directing performers to modify strict tempo to emphasize emotion, often a feature of Romantic composition.

run: A rapid, sequential execution of notes up or down a scale.

salsa: Literally meaning "sauce," a genre of dance that combines styles from Cuba, Puerto Rico, Latin America, and North America, including mambo, danzón, guaguancó, cha-cha, and son. The music written for this dance form is highly syncopated, using conga, trumpets, trombones, guitars, claves, and xylophones. It rose to prominence in the 1970's in New York as part of the Puerto Rican and Cuban immigrant culture there and soon spread across both North and Latin America. The genre is a major component of Latin jazz and is often loosely used to refer to Latin jazz. Names associated with salsa include Willie Colón, Celia Cruz, Ray Barretto, Rubén Blades, and Tito Puente.

samba: A Brazilian musical form, based on the dance of the same name, with African origins.

sample, sampling: An electronic process in which a sound or piece of music is digitally recorded. A sample is a sound or bit of music so recorded. Sampling has produced numerous lawsuits by artists whose work has been sampled and reused without their permission—and without their receiving any royalties on the new record sales. Sampling was first widely heard on rap and hip-hop recordings, and it has spread to nearly all genres of pop music.

sarabande: A steady, dignified musical form based on a dance of the same name, developed in Spain.

sarod: A lutelike instrument originating in India.

saxophone: A family of brass single-reed wind instruments with keyed valves. The main forms are alto, soprano, tenor, and bass saxophones. Associated most often with jazz and popular music, although some classical saxophone works have been composed.

scale: A series of tones arranged in a specified order, including major, minor, chromatic, and other scales. *See also* mode.

scat singing: Jazz singing that uses nonsense syllables, usually with rapid-fire phrasing. In scat singing the voice is treated purely as an instrument. Influential artists include Ella Fitzgerald and Louis Armstrong.

scherzo: Literally "joke" or "jest"; a movement in a sonata that is characterized by its light mood, written in triple time. Some scherzi have been written especially as set pieces for piano.

scoring: A virtual synonym for orchestration, but connoting an emphasis on the arrangement of instruments. *See also* orchestration.

Second Viennese School: The group of composers—Arnold Schoenberg, Anton Webern, and Alban Berg—and their pupils who dominated classical music in and around Vienna during the first two decades of the twentieth century. They promulgated theories of music that emphasized atonal, serial, twelve-tone music. *See also* atonal; serial music; twelve-tone music.

segue: A musical notation directing performers to play on, without pausing.

semitone: *See* half tone.

septet: Seven musicians, either vocalists or instrumentalists, who perform together.

sequence: The transposition and repetition of a phrase at different pitches.

serenade: A multiple-movement, light composition written for a small group of instruments designed to soothe or to accompany social events. Also, a song composed to be sung to court a woman.

serial music: Music organized according to specific orderings of the possible values of one or more types of features (such as pitch, rhythm, dynamic [loudness], or articulation). *See also* atonal; Second Viennese School; twelve-tone music.

seventy-eight (78): A ten-inch phonographic record designed to be played at a speed of 78 revolutions per minute (rpm), the standard speed for gramophones. These records were brittle and broke easily, but they were the only medium widely available until LPs were introduced in the mid-1940's.

sextet: Six musicians, either vocalists or instrumentalists, who perform together.

sforzando: A musical notation directing performers to play forcefully or explosively.

shakuhachi: A traditional Japanese flute.

sharp: A symbol in sheet music, resembling a hatch or number mark, informing the performer that the note is to be raised by one semitone.

shed: *See* woodshedding.

sideman: A musician hired to work with a group of which he or she is not a regular member.

singer-songwriter: An artist who writes and performs his or her own music. Before the mid-1950's, it was virtually unheard of for a songwriter to perform his or her compositions publicly: Songwriters wrote songs, and singers sang them. Some early rock and rollers began to write their own songs, however, as did the bands of the 1960's, led by the Beatles and other British Invasion bands. Bob Dylan, with his intense, lyric-driven folk rock, is probably the archetypal singer-songwriter. The label is now widely applied to artists from James Taylor and Jackson Browne to Melissa Etheridge and Beck.

single: A song intended for radio airplay and for individual sale, as opposed to an album cut. A single was originally a forty-five (45) vinyl record, but the term was subsequently applied to cassette singles and CD singles. Having a "hit single" is still the measure of success for many recording artists, but it was most important in the 1950's and 1960's, before albums and album sales became more profitable. *See also* A side; album; compact disc; digital versatile disc; forty-five.

sitar: A three-stringed lute, indigenous to India.

sixteenth note: A beat with one-quarter the value or duration of a quarter note.

ska: A Jamaican form of dance music in 4/4 time with a drumbeat on the second and fourth beats and with a guitar sounding on the second, third, and fourth beats. Ska bands use bass, drums, guitars, keyboards, saxophones, trombones, and trumpets. A predecessor to rocksteady and reggae music. *See also* reggae; rocksteady.

skiffle: A type of folk music with jazz and blues influences, similar to jug band music, that became popular in the 1960's. Skiffle bands were notable for their use of improvised or folk instruments such as acoustic guitars, banjos, kazoos, and washboards.

slide: A glissando or portamento. Also, the moving part of a trombone. *See also* glissando; portamento.

slur: A curved line drawn over two or more notes of different pitches, indicating that they are to be executed in a smoothly connected manner, without a break. *See also* ligature; slur.

solo: A part in a musical piece during which a single instrumentalist or vocalist performs a section designed for an individual role or featuring the performer's instrument. Also, the act of executing such a performance.

sonata: A highly structured musical form for orchestra that classically consists of three or four movements—including an exposition, a development section, and a recapitulation—each with a different tempo, rhythm, and melody. Often the final movement is in the same key or mode as the first.

sonatina: A short sonata, often a piano piece.

song: Generally, any short, melodic work designed to be sung, most often with words, or lyrics. As a musical form, a song often takes the *aaba* form, with *a* constituting the verse and *b* constituting the melodically contrasting refrain or chorus. Songs may also take an *abab'* form.

song cycle: A series of songs that are unified by a theme or narrative or a series of poems that form the lyrics to the songs.

soprano: The highest of the voice ranges (bass, baritone, tenor, contralto, alto, soprano).

sordina: *See* con sordina.

sostenuto: Literally, "sustained"; a musical notation directing performers to play in an extended or lengthened manner.

sotto voce: A musical notation meaning quietly.

soul music: A gospel-influenced genre that evolved from 1950's rhythm-and-blues artists such as Ray Charles and Sam Cooke. James Brown, "soul brother number one," was an early star, and Otis Redding and Aretha Franklin, the "queen of soul," popularized the style in the 1960's. *See also* funk; gospel; rhythm and blues.

sound track: The recorded sounds and music used in a film, from beginning to end. *See also* film score; television score.

southern rock: A country-tinged version of blues rock, but with more metal. Influential artists include the Allman Brothers and Lynyrd Skynyrd. *See also* blues rock.

spirito: A musical notation directing performers to play in a spirited manner.

Sprechstimme: A method of vocalization that is a cross between singing and speech.

staccato: The execution of notes, either by the voice or by a musical instrument, in a very quick, sharp, shortened, and pronounced manner, detached from the next note. In musical notation, the direction to play a note staccato is indicated by a dot beneath the note.

staff: The parallel lines on and between which notes are marked in written music.

standard: *See* jazz standard.

stanza: One verse of a song or poem.

stop time: A type of meter that replaces a note with a rest, as in 4/4 time where the final beat is a rest (1 2 3 rest, 1 2 3 rest).

stride: A jazz piano style of the 1930's, evolved from ragtime, in which the left hand alternates between a low bass note and much higher chords and the right hand plays virtuosic runs, arpeggios, and chords. Epitomized by the performances of Fats Waller, James P. Johnson, Earl Hines, and Count Basie.

string quartet: A chamber group consisting of four stringed instruments: two violins, a viola, and a cello.

subito: A musical notation meaning "suddenly."

substitution: A chord put in the place of a different chord.

suite: A collection of instrumental compositions.

swamp pop: A popular genre in the American South, particularly East Texas and Louisiana, that blends Cajun and rock-and-roll music in romantic, plaintive songs.

swing music: A big-band, jazz-related style that developed in the 1930's, with a prominent beat on counts one and three, resulting in a swinging feel. Associated with Louis Armstrong, Count Basie, Ella Fitzgerald, Glenn Miller, and many others.

symphony: A broad genre, referring to a work composed for orchestra of three or four movements, often in sonata form. *See also* sonata.

syncopation: The placing of emphasis, or stress, on beats that are not usually stressed for the meter used. For example, in 4/4 time, placing the stress on the second and fourth beats (rather than the expected first and third). Also, the displacement of a beat by half a beat before or after to inject spontaneity, ambiguity, or a swinging rhythm.

synthesizer: Any electronic device designed to produce or control music or sound.

tabla: A pair of hand drums indigenous to India.

tablature: A system of musical notation designed to show finger positions rather than notes to be played, used mainly for guitars, violins, and other stringed instruments.

tape work: Any musical composition designed to be performed using a tape recording or incorporating taped sounds.

techno: A dance-music genre that relies on computerized rhythms and sampled sounds ranging from music to noise, said to have originated in Detroit with Derrick May. Originally relatively anonymous dance-club music, techno was eventually popularized by groups such as the Orb.

Tejano: A type of Mexican American, or Tex-Mex, pop music that incorporates elements of folk, country, and rock music. Tejano bands often include an accordion, horns, and guitars.

television score: The music that forms the sound track for a television episode, excluding songs composed for or used within the program (for example, as part of the drama). *See also* film score; sound track.

television theme: A musical composition, usually an instrumental work, designed to introduce and bridge portions of a television program from week to week.

tempo (*pl.* tempi): The rate of speed at which a musical composition is performed.

tenor: The second lowest of the standard four voice ranges (bass, tenor, alto, soprano), typically sung by a man.

texture: A loose and subjective term that describes the combined effects of a musical work's harmonies, rhythms, tones, timbres, and other elements.

theme: A musical "idea" or pattern of melody or harmony that may be restated, developed, built upon, and modified throughout a musical composition.

theremin: A electronic instrument, invented by Léon Theremin, originally called the Etherphon. Constructed with vacuum tubes and antennae, it creates a sirenlike pitch whose frequencies are controlled by moving a hand around the antennae while the other hand operates the volume control. Used to create the eery sound effects accompanying suspenseful scenes in horror and science-fiction movies of the 1950's and early 1960's.

Third Stream music: A term coined by Gunther Schuller in the early 1950's to characterize a supposed confluence of jazz and classical music, developed by musicians such as Eric Dolphy and John Lewis.

timbre: Sometimes called "tone color," for the shading that a performer can apply to pitch by the characterstic tones and vibrations of differ-

ent instruments or the voice. For example, the difference between the way a middle C sounds on a piano and from a trumpet, or the difference between and the vocalizations of an open-mouth middle C and a closed-mouth, or hummed, middle C constitute differences in timbre.

time signature: The numeric symbol in sheet music that indicates the number of beats to a measure. Basic time signatures include 4/4 (four quarter notes to a measure), 3/4 (waltz or triple time, with three quarter notes to a measure), 6/8 (six eighth notes to a measure), and 2/4 (two quarter notes to a measure).

tonality: The tonal characteristics determined by the relationship of the notes to the tone.

tone: A musical sound or the quality of that sound. Also, a sound of a definite pitch. *See also* note; pitch.

tone cluster: Adjacent notes deliberately sounded together. *See also* dissonance; polytonality.

tone color: *See* timbre.

tonic: Also called the keynote, the first tone of a scale.

Top 10: The top ten records or songs on a sales chart or playlist, as on *Billboard* magazine's Hot 100 chart. A Top 10 record is a hit.

Top 40: The top forty records or songs on a sales chart or playlist, as on *Billboard* magazine's Hot 100 chart. A Top 40 record is successful, but it may or may not be considered a true hit.

transpose: To arrange, write, or perform a musical work in a key different from the one for which it was originally written.

treble: The upper vocal range, or the upper clef in sheet music.

tremolo: The rapid alternation between two notes to create a trembling sound, similar to but more deliberate, somewhat slower, and more pronounced than the undulations in a singing voice known as vibrato. *See also* portamento; trill; vibrato.

triad: A three-note chord formed by the root note, the third, and the fifth, such as middle C, E, and G.

trill: Also called a "shake," the very rapid and deliberate alternation between notes, in singing or in playing an instrument, that are either a half tone or a whole tone apart. *See also* tremolo; vibrato.

trio: Three musicians, either vocalists or instrumentalists, who perform together.

triple time: A time signature of 3/4 (three beats per measure); waltz time.

triplet: The playing of three notes in the same amount of time occupied by one or two beats, with the duration of each note of the triplet equal to that of the others, resulting in a deliberate disturbance of the steadiness of the time signature.

tritone: A chord formed by three whole steps.

trombone: A brass wind instrument formed by a narrow cylinder, with two turns or bends, and ending in a bell. Tones are controlled by means of valves and a movable slide, and the instrument's range is an octave below that of the trumpet.

trumpet: Any of a family of brass wind instruments formed by a narrow cylinder with several turns, ending in a bell, and with pitch controlled by keyed valves. Several different types exist. *See also* cornet.

tune: A rhythmic succession of musical tones forming a melody or song; a term preferred by jazz musicians over "song."

tuning: The manipulation of parts of an instrument (such as tightening or loosening the strings of a piano, guitar, or violin) to make them produce the frequencies that result in the correct pitches.

twelve-tone music: A particular type of atonal music in which all the pitches of a composition are derived from a specific ordering of the twelve pitches created for that composition. This was the first type of serial composition, first used by Arnold Schoenberg. *See also* Second Viennese School; atonal; serial music.

unison: The practice of singing or playing at the same time on the same notes.

up-tempo: A fast tempo.

vamp: A simple section like a riff, designed to be repeated as often as necessary, especially one at the beginning of a tune. Also, a constantly repeated bass line over which a solo is played.

variation: A tune or melody played or expanded upon using different rhythms, ornaments, or keys.

veloce: A musical notation meaning "play with velocity," or quickly.

verse: Often the first section of a song; the section of a song that is not the refrain or chorus; in an *aaba* song, the *a* sections. See also *aaba*.

vibraphone: Similar to a xylophone, a percussion instrument with metal bars that is struck, but with the addition of motorized resonators to sustain tone.

vibrato: The rapid alteration between close tones, used as an ornament especially by singers; often deplored as a singing vice when overused.

viol family: A family of stringed instruments related to the violin family, which superseded it. Differences between the two families are mainly in the construction of the instruments. Viols have rounded (vs. flat) backs and hence deeper bodies, more sloped shoulders, fretted necks, c- rather than f-shaped sound holes, and six rather than four strings; the bow and bowing techniques are also different. Members of this family include the treble or descant viol, alto viol, tenor viol, and the bass viol or "viola da gamba."

viola: A string instrument in the violin family that occupies the alto position in the strings.

violin: A string instrument in the violin family that occupies the soprano (first violin) and second-soprano (second violin) positions in the strings. Other members of this family of instruments include the viola in the alto range, the violincello (cello) in the tenor range, and the double-bass in the bass range. *See also* viol family.

violincello: *See* cello.

virtuoso: A musician known for his or her technical skill with voice or an instrument.

vivace: A musical notation directing performers to play briskly, with spirit.

vocalist: A singer or musician who uses the voice to create sound for music.

voice: The human voice; also, a melodic line.

wah-wah pedal: A type of pedal used with electric guitars that alters the signal, creating the effect of a human voice.

waltz: A dance in triple meter (usually 3/4 time) that enjoyed its heyday in the nineteenth century, along with any of the many musical works written to accompany it.

West Coast school: A subgenre of jazz developed in the early 1950's that appealed mostly to white performers, including musicians such as Dave Brubeck, Gerry Mulligan, and Chet Baker. Musical stylings were those of cool jazz, coupled with complex experimental figures, time signatures, and counterpoint.

western music. *See* country music.

whammy bar: A lever attached to the bridge of a guitar that makes it possible for the performer to change or bend pitch and create effects such as vibrato and portamento.

whole note: Any note whose value is that of a full measure, which varies by time signature. A whole note in 4/4 time occupies four beats, whereas a whole note in 3/4 time occupies three.

whole tone: A tone consisting of two half steps.

whole-tone scale: A musical scale consisting only of six whole-tone notes.

woodshedding: Jazz jargon referring to long, sustained solo practicing to master technique.

world music: Originating mainly as a commercial classification for marketing purposes, generally any non-Western music that is either indigenous to those cultures or uses the instrumentation, orchestration, performance techniques, modes and scales, and vocals of those cultures or ethnicities. Also, commercial music that fuses these elements with Western technology and harmonies for appeal to a mainstream audience. Examples include Japanese koto music, Indonesian gamelan music, African *isicathamiya* music, and Indian raga music. *See also* adult contemporary; New Age.

xylophone: A percussion instrument constructed of wooden bars placed parallel to each other, graduating in length from long to short (corresponding to lower and higher notes), and played with two handheld beaters.

yodeling: A type of fast singing characterized by changing back and forth from a natural voice to a falsetto.

Zeitoper tradition: A style of opera that focused on relevant, everyday subjects that would appeal to a diverse audience. Composers such as Ernst Krenek, Paul Hindemith, and Kurt Weill composed in this genre.

zydeco: Popular dance music, based in Louisiana, that grew out of a combination of Cajun and Caribbean music and is played by bands using guitars, accordions, and washboards.

Chronological List of Musicians

The arrangement of 614 personages in this list is chronological on the basis of birth years. All personages appearing in this list are the subjects of the 608 essays in *Musicians and Composers of the 20th Century*. Subjects of multiperson essays are listed separately and include the Everly brothers (Don and Phil), the Gibb brothers (Barry, Robin, and Maurice), the Broadway team of Adolph Green and Betty Comden, the Holland brothers (Eddie and Brian), and the rap team Salt (Cheryl James) and Pepa (Sandra Denton).

1851-1860
Leoš Janáček (July 3, 1854-August 12, 1928)
John Philip Sousa (November 6, 1854-March 6, 1932)
Sir Edward Elgar (June 2, 1857-February 23, 1934)
Arnold Dolmetsch (February 24, 1858-February 28, 1940)
Giacomo Puccini (December 22, 1858-November 29, 1924)
Victor Herbert (February 1, 1859-May 26, 1924)
Gustav Mahler (July 7, 1860-May 18, 1911)
Ignace Jan Paderewski (November 18, 1860-June 29, 1941)

1861-1870
Dame Nellie Melba (May 19, 1861-February 23, 1931)
Claude Debussy (August 22, 1862-March 25, 1918)
Richard Strauss (June 11, 1864-September 8, 1949)
Carl Nielsen (June 9, 1865-October 3, 1931)
Jean Sibelius (December 8, 1865-September 20, 1957)
Ferruccio Busoni (April 1, 1866-July 27, 1924)
Erik Satie (May 17, 1866-July 1, 1925)
Arturo Toscanini (March 25, 1867-January 16, 1957)
Amy Beach (September 5, 1867-December 27, 1944)
Scott Joplin (November 24, 1868-April 1, 1917)

1871-1880
Aleksandr Scriabin (January 6, 1872-April 27, 1915)
Ralph Vaughan Williams (October 12, 1872-August 26, 1958)
Enrico Caruso (February 25, 1873-August 2, 1921)
Sergei Rachmaninoff (April 1, 1873-March 28, 1943)
W. C. Handy (November 16, 1873-March 28, 1958)
Serge Koussevitzky (July 26, 1874-June 4, 1951)

Arnold Schoenberg (September 13, 1874-July 13, 1951)
Gustav Holst (September 21, 1874-May 25, 1934)
Charles Ives (October 20, 1874-May 19, 1954)
Albert Schweitzer (January 14, 1875-September 4, 1965)
Fritz Kreisler (February 2, 1875-January 29, 1962)
Maurice Ravel (March 7, 1875-December 28, 1937)
Bruno Walter (September 15, 1876-February 17, 1962)
Pablo Casals (December 29, 1876-October 22, 1973)
Carl Sandburg (January 6, 1878-July 22, 1967)
Franz Schreker (March 23, 1878-March 21, 1934)
George M. Cohan (July 3, 1878-November 5, 1942)
Sir Thomas Beecham (April 29, 1879-March 8, 1961)
Wanda Landowska (July 5, 1879-August 16, 1959)
Ottorino Respighi (July 9, 1879-April 18, 1936)
Henri Casadesus (September 30, 1879-May 31, 1947)

1881-1890
Béla Bartók (March 25, 1881-September 26, 1945)
Artur Schnabel (April 17, 1882-August 15, 1951)
Leopold Stokowski (April 18, 1882-September 13, 1977)
Igor Stravinsky (June 17, 1882-April 6, 1971)
Percy Aldridge Grainger (July 8, 1882-February 20, 1961)
Karol Szymanowski (October 6, 1882-March 28, 1937)
Zoltán Kodály (December 16, 1882-March 6, 1967)
Mamie Smith (May 26, 1883-August 16, 1946)
Anton von Webern (December 3, 1883-September 15, 1945)
Edgard Varèse (December 22, 1883-November 6, 1965)
Jerome Kern (January 27, 1885-November 11, 1945)

Musicians and Composers of the 20th Century

Leadbelly (January 29, 1885-December 6, 1949)
Alban Berg (February 9, 1885-December 24, 1935)
Otto Klemperer (May 14, 1885-July 6, 1973)
Ma Rainey (April 26, 1886-December 22, 1939)
Charles Seeger (December 14, 1886-February 7, 1979)
Artur Rubinstein (January 28, 1887-December 20, 1982)
Eubie Blake (February 7, 1887-February 12, 1983)
Heitor Villa-Lobos (March 5, 1887-November 17, 1959)
Sigmund Romberg (July 29, 1887-November 9, 1951)
Nadia Boulanger (September 16, 1887-October 22, 1979)
Lotte Lehmann (February 27, 1888-August 26, 1976)
Max Steiner (May 10, 1888-December 28, 1971)
Irving Berlin (May 11, 1888-September 22, 1989)
Maurice Chevalier (September 12, 1888-January 1, 1972)
Lauritz Melchior (March 20, 1890-March 18, 1973)
Paul Whiteman (March 28, 1890-December 29, 1967)
Frank Martin (September 15, 1890-November 21, 1974)
Jelly Roll Morton (October 20, 1890-July 10, 1941)
Bohuslav Martinů (December 8, 1890-August 28, 1959)

1891-1900
Charley Patton (April, 1891-April 28, 1934)
Sergei Prokofiev (April 23, 1891-March 5, 1953)
Cole Porter (June 9, 1891-October 15, 1964)
Adolf Busch (August 8, 1891-June 9, 1952)
Arthur Honegger (March 10, 1892-November 27, 1955)
Darius Milhaud (September 4, 1892-June 22, 1974)
Joseph Szigeti (September 5, 1892-February 19, 1973)
Andrés Segovia (February 21, 1893-June 2, 1987)
Mississippi John Hurt (March 8, 1893-November 2, 1966)
Bessie Smith (April 15, 1894-September 26, 1937)
Dimitri Tiomkin (May 10, 1894-November 11, 1979)
Arthur Fiedler (December 17, 1894-July 10, 1979)
Alberta Hunter (April 1, 1895-October 17, 1984)
Lorenz Hart (May 2, 1895-November 22, 1943)

William Grant Still (May 11, 1895-December 3, 1978)
Carl Orff (July 10, 1895-March 29, 1982)
Oscar Hammerstein II (July 12, 1895-August 23, 1960)
Kirsten Flagstad (July 12, 1895-December 7, 1962)
Paul Hindemith (November 16, 1895-December 28, 1963)
Léon Theremin (August 15, 1896-November 3, 1993)
Virgil Thomson (November 25, 1896-September 30, 1989)
Ira Gershwin (December 6, 1896-August 17, 1983)
Marian Anderson (February 27, 1897-April 8, 1993)
Henry Cowell (March 11, 1897-December 10, 1965)
Sidney Bechet (May 14, 1897-May 14, 1959)
Erich Wolfgang Korngold (May 29, 1897-November 29, 1957)
Memphis Minnie (June 3, 1897-August 6, 1973)
George Szell (June 7, 1897-July 30, 1970)
Blind Lemon Jefferson (July 11, 1897-December, 1929)
Jimmie Rodgers (September 8, 1897-May 26, 1933)
Fletcher Henderson (December 18, 1897-December 29, 1952)
Paul Robeson (April 9, 1898-January 23, 1976)
George Gershwin (September 26, 1898-July 11, 1937)
Shin'ichi Suzuki (October 17, 1898-January 26, 1998)
Umm Kulthum (December 31, 1898-February 3, 1975)
Francis Poulenc (January 7, 1899-January 30, 1963)
Lonnie Johnson (February 8, 1899-June 16, 1970)
Duke Ellington (April 29, 1899-May 24, 1974)
Carlos Chávez (June 13, 1899-August 2, 1978)
Thomas A. Dorsey (July 1, 1899-January 23, 1993)
Sonny Boy Williamson II (December 5, 1899-May 25, 1965)
Sir Noël Coward (December 16, 1899-March 26, 1973)
Silvestre Revueltas (December 31, 1899-October 5, 1940)
Xavier Cugat (January 1, 1900-October 27, 1990)
Kurt Weill (March 2, 1900-April 3, 1950)
Alfred Newman (March 17, 1900-February 17, 1970)

Aaron Copland (November 14, 1900-December 2, 1990)

1901-1910

Jascha Heifetz (February 2, 1901-December 10, 1987)

Frederick Loewe (June 10, 1901-February 14, 1988)

Harry Partch (June 24, 1901-September 3, 1974)

Ruth Crawford Seeger (July 3, 1901-November 18, 1953)

Louis Armstrong (August 4, 1901-July 6, 1971)

Marlene Dietrich (December 27, 1901-May 6, 1992)

Son House (March 21, 1902-October 19, 1988)

Sir William Walton (March 29, 1902-March 8, 1983)

Meredith Willson (May 18, 1902-June 15, 1984)

Sammy Fain (June 17, 1902-December 6, 1989)

Richard Rodgers (June 28, 1902-December 30, 1979)

Bix Beiderbecke (March 10, 1903-August 6, 1931)

Rudolf Serkin (March 28, 1903-May 8, 1991)

Bing Crosby (May 3, 1903-October 14, 1977)

Aram Khachaturian (June 6, 1903-May 1, 1978)

Roy Acuff (September 15, 1903-November 23, 1992)

Vladimir Horowitz (October 1, 1903-November 5, 1989)

Glenn Miller (March 1, 1904-December 15, 1944)

Fats Waller (May 21, 1904-December 15, 1943)

Count Basie (August 21, 1904-April 26, 1984)

Coleman Hawkins (November 21, 1904-May 19, 1969)

Sir Michael Tippett (January 2, 1905-January 8, 1998)

Tex Ritter (January 12, 1905-January 2, 1974)

Harold Arlen (February 15, 1905-April 23, 1986)

Red Nichols (May 8, 1905-June 28, 1965)

Dorothy Fields (July 15, 1905-May 28, 1974)

August Wenzinger (November 14, 1905-December 25, 1996)

Jule Styne (December 31, 1905-September 20, 1994)

Dmitri Shostakovich (September 12, 1906-August 9, 1975)

Franz Waxman (December 24, 1906-February 24, 1967)

Miklós Rózsa (April 18, 1907-July 27, 1995)

Kate Smith (May 1, 1907-June 17, 1986)

Blind Boy Fuller (July 10, 1907-February 13, 1941)

Benny Carter (August 8, 1907-July 12, 2003)

Ethel Merman (January 16, 1908-February 18, 1984)

Stéphane Grappelli (January 26, 1908-December 1, 1997)

Herbert von Karajan (April 5, 1908-July 16, 1989)

Lionel Hampton (April 20, 1908-August 31, 2002)

Leroy Anderson (June 29, 1908-May 18, 1975)

Louis Jordan (July 8, 1908-February 4, 1975)

David Oistrakh (September 30, 1908-October 24, 1974)

Johnny Burke (October 3, 1908-February 25, 1964)

Olivier Messiaen (December 10, 1908-April 28, 1992)

Elliott Carter (b. December 11, 1908)

Ben Webster (March 27, 1909-September 20, 1973)

Maybelle Carter (May 10, 1909-October 23, 1978)

Benny Goodman (May 30, 1909-June 13, 1986)

Burl Ives (June 14, 1909-April 14, 1995)

Lester Young (August 27, 1909-March 15, 1959)

Art Tatum (October 13, 1909-November 5, 1956)

Johnny Mercer (November 18, 1909-June 25, 1976)

Django Reinhardt (January 23, 1910-May 16, 1953)

Samuel Barber (March 9, 1910-January 23, 1981)

Mary Lou Williams (May 8, 1910-May 28, 1981)

Artie Shaw (May 23, 1910-December 30, 2004)

T-Bone Walker (May 26, 1910-March 16, 1975)

Howlin' Wolf (June 10, 1910-January 10, 1976)

Frank Loesser (June 29, 1910-July 28, 1969)

Pierre Schaeffer (August 14, 1910-August 19, 1995)

1911-1920

Jussi Björling (February 2, 1911-September 9, 1960)

Robert Johnson (May 8, 1911-August 16, 1938)

Big Joe Turner (May 18, 1911-November 24, 1985)

Bernard Herrmann (June 29, 1911-December 24, 1975)

Gian Carlo Menotti (July 7, 1911-February 1, 2007)

Bill Monroe (September 13, 1911-September 9, 1996)

Sonny Terry (October 24, 1911-March 11, 1986)

Mahalia Jackson (October 26, 1911-January 27, 1972)

Nino Rota (December 3, 1911-April 10, 1979)

Lightnin' Hopkins (March 15, 1912-January 30, 1982)

Woody Guthrie (July 14, 1912-October 3, 1967)
John Cage (September 5, 1912-August 12, 1992)
Sir Georg Solti (October 12, 1912-September 5, 1997)
Conlon Nancarrow (October 27, 1912-August 10, 1997)
Witold Lutosławski (January 25, 1913-February 7, 1994)
Jimmy Van Heusen (January 26, 1913-February 7, 1990)
Sammy Cahn (June 18, 1913-January 15, 1993)
Benjamin Britten (November 22, 1913-December 4, 1976)
Ernest Tubb (February 9, 1914-September 6, 1984)
Sonny Boy Williamson I (March 30, 1914-June 1, 1948)
Sun Ra (May 22, 1914-May 30, 1993)
Lester Flatt (June 19, 1914-May 11, 1979)
Adolph Green (December 2, 1914-October 23, 2002)
Pops Staples (December 28, 1914-December 19, 2000)
Alan Lomax (January 31, 1915-July 19, 2002)
Muddy Waters (April 4, 1915-April 30, 1983)
Billie Holiday (April 7, 1915-July 17, 1959)
Les Paul (b. June 9, 1915)
Willie Dixon (July 1, 1915-January 29, 1992)
Billy Strayhorn (November 29, 1915-May 31, 1967)
Frank Sinatra (December 12, 1915-May 14, 1998)
Édith Piaf (December 19, 1915-October 11, 1963)
Sir Yehudi Menuhin (April 22, 1916-March 12, 1999)
Milton Babbitt (b. May 10, 1916)
Charlie Christian (July 29, 1916-March 2, 1942)
Pérez Prado (December 11, 1916-September 14, 1989)
Ella Fitzgerald (April 25, 1917-June 15, 1996)
Betty Comden (May 3, 1917-November 23, 2006)
Lou Harrison (May 14, 1917-February 2, 2003)
Robert Merrill (June 4, 1917-October 23, 2004)
Lena Horne (b. June 30, 1917)
John Lee Hooker (August 22, 1917-June 21, 2001)
Thelonious Monk (October 10, 1917-February 17, 1982)
Dizzy Gillespie (October 21, 1917-January 6, 1993)
Merle Travis (November 29, 1917-October 20, 1983)
Elmore James (January 27, 1918-May 24, 1963)
Marian McPartland (b. March 20, 1918)

Eddy Arnold (May 15, 1918-May 8, 2008)
Hank Jones (b. July 31, 1918)
Leonard Bernstein (August 25, 1918-October 14, 1990)
Alan Jay Lerner (August 31, 1918-June 14, 1986)
Professor Longhair (December 19, 1918-January 30, 1980)
Nat King Cole (March 17, 1919-February 15, 1965)
Pete Seeger (b. May 3, 1919)
Art Blakey (October 11, 1919-October 16, 1990)
Ravi Shankar (b. April 7, 1920)
John Lewis (May 3, 1920-March 29, 2001)
Peggy Lee (May 26, 1920-January 21, 2002)
Isaac Stern (July 21, 1920-September 22, 2001)
Charlie Parker (August 29, 1920-March 12, 1955)
Dave Brubeck (b. December 6, 1920)

1921-1930
Astor Piazzolla (March 11, 1921-July 4, 1992)
Hal David (b. May 25, 1921)
Erroll Garner (June 15, 1921-January 7, 1977)
Johnny Otis (b. December 28, 1921)
Jean-Pierre Rampal (January 7, 1922-May 20, 2000)
Renata Tebaldi (February 1, 1922-December 19, 2004)
Elmer Bernstein (April 4, 1922-August 18, 2004)
Ali Akbar Khan (b. April 14, 1922)
Charles Mingus (April 22, 1922-January 5, 1979)
Iannis Xenakis (May 29, 1922-February 4, 2001)
Judy Garland (June 10, 1922-June 22, 1969)
Jean Ritchie (b. December 8, 1922)
Dexter Gordon (February 27, 1923-April 25, 1990)
Doc Watson (b. March 2, 1923)
Tito Puente (April 20, 1923-May 31, 2000)
Albert King (April 25, 1923-December 21, 1992)
György Ligeti (May 28, 1923-June 12, 2006)
Hank Williams (September 17, 1923-January 1, 1953)
Fats Navarro (September 24, 1923-July 7, 1950)
Maria Callas (December 2, 1923-September 16, 1977)
Earl Scruggs (b. January 6, 1924)
Max Roach (January 10, 1924-August 16, 2007)
Luigi Nono (January 29, 1924-May 8, 1990)
Sarah Vaughan (March 27, 1924-April 3, 1990)
Henry Mancini (April 16, 1924-June 14, 1994)
Charles Aznavour (b. May 22, 1924)
Chet Atkins (June 20, 1924-June 30, 2001)

Clara Ward (August 21, 1924-January 16, 1973)
Dinah Washington (August 29, 1924-December 14, 1963)
Bud Powell (September 27, 1924-July 31, 1966)
Celia Cruz (October 21, 1924-July 16, 2003)
Paul Desmond (November 25, 1924-May 30, 1977)
Wes Montgomery (March 6, 1925-June 15, 1968)
Pierre Boulez (b. March 26, 1925)
Dietrich Fischer-Dieskau (b. May 28, 1925)
Bill Haley (July 6, 1925-February 9, 1981)
Oscar Peterson (August 15, 1925-December 23, 2007)
Jimmy Reed (September 6, 1925-August 29, 1976)
Roy Brown (September 10, 1925-May 25, 1981)
Alan Bergman (b. September 11, 1925)
Mel Tormé (September 13, 1925-June 5, 1999)
B. B. King (b. September 16, 1925)
Luciano Berio (October 24, 1925-May 27, 2003)
Sammy Davis, Jr. (December 8, 1925-May 16, 1990)
Sir George Martin (b. January 3, 1926)
Morton Feldman (January 12, 1926-September 3, 1987)
Miles Davis (May 26, 1926-September 28, 1991)
Tony Bennett (b. August 13, 1926)
John Coltrane (September 23, 1926-July 17, 1967)
Chuck Berry (b. October 18, 1926)
Dame Joan Sutherland (b. November 7, 1926)
Antônio Carlos Jobim (January 25, 1927-December 8, 1994)
Stan Getz (February 2, 1927-June 6, 1991)
Leontyne Price (b. February 10, 1927)
Ralph Stanley (b. February 25, 1927)
Harry Belafonte (b. March 1, 1927)
John Kander (b. March 18, 1927)
Mstislav Rostropovich (March 27, 1927-April 27, 2007)
Elvin Jones (September 9, 1927-May 18, 2004)
Fats Domino (b. February 26, 1928)
Lefty Frizzell (March 31, 1928-July 19, 1975)
Tom Lehrer (b. April 9, 1928)
Burt Bacharach (b. May 12, 1928)
Gustav Leonhardt (b. May 30, 1928)
Eric Dolphy (June 20, 1928-June 29, 1964)
Karlheinz Stockhausen (August 22, 1928-December 5, 2007)
Cannonball Adderley (September 15, 1928-August 8, 1975)
Ennio Morricone (b. November 10, 1928)

Bo Diddley (December 30, 1928-June 2, 2008)
Jerry Goldsmith (February 10, 1929-July 21, 2004)
Cecil Taylor (b. March 25, 1929)
Sir André Previn (b. April 6, 1929)
Jacques Brel (April 8, 1929-October 9, 1978)
Ray Barretto (April 29, 1929-February 17, 2006)
Beverly Sills (May 25, 1929-July 2, 2007)
Cy Coleman (June 14, 1929-November 18, 2004)
Bill Evans (August 16, 1929-September 15, 1980)
George Crumb (b. October 24, 1929)
Nikolaus Harnoncourt (b. December 6, 1929)
Toshiko Akiyoshi (b. December 12, 1929)
Ornette Coleman (b. March 19, 1930)
Stephen Sondheim (b. March 22, 1930)
Sonny Rollins (b. September 7, 1930)
Ray Charles (September 23, 1930-June 10, 2004)
Tōru Takemitsu (October 8, 1930-February 20, 1996)
Clifford Brown (October 30, 1930-June 26, 1956)
Odetta (December 31, 1930-December 2, 2008)

1931-1940

Sam Cooke (January 22, 1931-December 11, 1964)
Alvin Lucier (b. May 14, 1931)
João Gilberto (b. June 10, 1931)
George Jones (b. September 12, 1931)
Anthony Newley (September 24, 1931-April 14, 1999)
Sofia Gubaidulina (b. October 24, 1931)
John Williams (b. February 8, 1932)
Otis Blackwell (February 16, 1932-May 6, 2002)
Michel Legrand (b. February 24, 1932)
Johnny Cash (February 26, 1932-September 12, 2003)
Miriam Makeba (March 4, 1932-November 10, 2008)
Carl Perkins (April 9, 1932-January 19, 1998)
Pauline Oliveros (b. May 30, 1932)
Patsy Cline (September 8, 1932-March 5, 1963)
Glenn Gould (September 25, 1932-October 4, 1982)
James Cleveland (December 5, 1932-February 9, 1991)
Little Richard (b. December 5, 1932)
Nina Simone (February 21, 1933-April 21, 2003)
Mile Stoller (b. March 13, 1933)
Quincy Jones (b. March 14, 1933)
Fred Ebb (April 8, 1933-September 11, 2004)
Jerry Leiber (b. April 25, 1933)

Willie Nelson (b. April 30, 1933)
James Brown (May 3, 1933-December 25, 2006)
Mike Seeger (b. August 15, 1933)
Wayne Shorter (b. August 25, 1933)
Conway Twitty (September 1, 1933-June 5, 1993)
Otis Rush (b. April 29, 1934)
Jackie Wilson (June 9, 1934-January 21, 1984)
Dave Grusin (b. June 26, 1934)
Van Cliburn (b. July 12, 1934)
Leonard Cohen (b. September 21, 1934)
Alfred Schnittke (November 24, 1934-August 3, 1998)
Elvis Presley (January 8, 1935-August 16, 1977)
Gene Vincent (February 11, 1935-October 12, 1971)
Herb Alpert (b. March 31, 1935)
Loretta Lynn (b. April 14, 1935)
Peggy Seeger (b. June 17, 1935)
James Cotton (b. July 1, 1935)
Arvo Pärt (b. September 11, 1935)
Jerry Lee Lewis (b. September 29, 1935)
Johnny Mathis (b. September 30, 1935)
Dame Julie Andrews (b. October 1, 1935)
Luciano Pavarotti (October 12, 1935-September 6, 2007)
Roger Miller (January 2, 1936-October 25, 1992)
James Jamerson (January 29, 1936-August 2, 1983)
Glen Campbell (b. April 22, 1936)
Roy Orbison (April 23, 1936-December 6, 1988)
Kris Kristofferson (b. June 22, 1936)
Dave Van Ronk (June 30, 1936-February 10, 2002)
Buddy Guy (b. July 30, 1936)
Rahsaan Roland Kirk (August 7, 1936-December 5, 1977)
Buddy Holly (September 7, 1936-February 3, 1959)
Steve Reich (b. October 3, 1936)
Eddie Palmieri (b. December 15, 1936)
Philip Glass (b. January 31, 1937)
Don Everly (b. February 1, 1937)
Merle Haggard (b. April 6, 1937)
Freddy Fender (June 4, 1937-October 14, 2006)
Waylon Jennings (June 15, 1937-February 13, 2002)
Vladimir Ashkenazy (b. July 6, 1937)
Tom Paxton (b. October 31, 1937)
Etta James (b. James 25, 1938)
Charley Pride (b. March 18, 1938)
Hoyt Axton (March 25, 1938-October 26, 1999)

Frederic Rzewski (b. April 13, 1938)
Duane Eddy (b. April 26, 1938)
Fela Kuti (October 15, 1938-August 2, 1997)
Gordon Lightfoot (b. November 17, 1938)
McCoy Tyner (b. December 11, 1938)
Phil Everly (b. January 19, 1939)
Gerry Goffin (b. February 11, 1939)
Marvin Gaye (April 2, 1939-April 1, 1984)
Hugh Masekela (b. April 4, 1939)
Judy Collins (b. May 1, 1939)
Eddie Holland (b. October 30, 1939)
Grace Slick (b. October 30, 1939)
Wendy Carlos (b. November 14, 1939)
Tina Turner (b. November 26, 1939)
Sir James Galway (b. December 8, 1939)
Phil Spector (b. December 26, 1939)
Smokey Robinson (b. February 19, 1940)
Solomon Burke (b. March 21, 1940)
Herbie Hancock (b. April 12, 1940)
Ricky Nelson (May 8, 1940-December 31, 1985)
John Lennon (October 9, 1940-December 8, 1980)
Pharoah Sanders (b. October 13, 1940)
Dionne Warwick (b. December 12, 1940)
Frank Zappa (December 21, 1940-December 4, 1993)

1941-1950

Joan Baez (b. January 9, 1941)
Plácido Domingo (b. January 21, 1941)
Neil Diamond (b. January 24, 1941)
Aaron Neville (b. January 24, 1941)
Brian Holland (b. February 15, 1941)
Tom Rush (b. February 8, 1941)
Wilson Pickett (March 18, 1941-January 19, 2006)
Ritchie Valens (May 13, 1941-February 3, 1959)
Bob Dylan (b. May 24, 1941)
Martha Argerich (b. June 5, 1941)
Chick Corea (b. June 12, 1941)
Lamont Dozier (b. June 16, 1941)
David Crosby (b. August 14, 1941)
Joseph Shabalala (b. August 28, 1941)
Otis Redding (September 9, 1941-December 10, 1967)
Christopher Hogwood (b. September 10, 1941)
Cass Elliot (September 19, 1941-July 29, 1974)
Paul Simon (b. October 13, 1941)
Art Garfunkel (b. November 5, 1941)
Carole King (b. February 9, 1942)
Buffy Sainte-Marie (b. February 20, 1942)

Lou Reed (b. March 2, 1942)
Aretha Franklin (b. March 25, 1942)
Barbra Streisand (b. April 24, 1942)
Tammy Wynette (May 5, 1942-April 6, 1998)
Curtis Mayfield (June 3, 1942-December 26, 1999)
Charles Dodge (b. June 5, 1942)
Sir Paul McCartney (b. June 18, 1942)
Brian Wilson (b. June 20, 1942)
Gilberto Gil (b. June 29, 1942)
Andraé Crouch (b. July 1, 1942)
Roger McGuinn (b. July 13, 1942)
Jerry Garcia (August 1, 1942-August 9, 1995)
Isaac Hayes (August 20, 1942-August 10, 2008)
Milton Nascimento (b. October 26, 1942)
Daniel Barenboim (b. November 15, 1942)
Jimi Hendrix (November 27, 1942-September 18, 1970)
Paul Butterfield (December 17, 1942-May 4, 1987)
Janis Joplin (January 19, 1943-October 4, 1970)
Gary Burton (b. January 23, 1943)
George Harrison (February 25, 1943-November 29, 2001)
Sly Stone (b. March 15, 1943)
Vangelis (b. March 29, 1943)
James Levine (b. June 23, 1943)
Robbie Robertson (b. July 5, 1943)
Sir Mick Jagger (b. July 26, 1943)
Roger Waters (b. September 6, 1943)
Julio Iglesias (b. September 23, 1943)
Bert Jansch (b. November 3, 1943)
Joni Mitchell (b. November 7, 1943)
Randy Newman (b. November 28, 1943)
Jim Morrison (December 8, 1943-July 3, 1971)
Keith Richards (b. December 18, 1943)
John Denver (December 31, 1943-October 12, 1997)
Jimmy Page (b. January 9, 1944)
Ronnie Milsap (b. January 16, 1944)
Sir John Tavener (b. January 28, 1944)
Roger Daltrey (b. March 1, 1944)
Townes Van Zandt (March 7, 1944-January 1, 1997)
Diana Ross (b. March 26, 1944)
Patti LaBelle (b. May 24, 1944)
Marvin Hamlisch (b. June 2, 1944)
Ray Davies (b. June 21, 1944)
Jeff Beck (b. June 24, 1944)
Peter Tosh (October 19, 1944-September 11, 1987)
Sir Tim Rice (b. November 10, 1944)

Michael Tilson Thomas (b. December 21, 1944)
Stephen Stills (b. January 3, 1945)
Rod Stewart (b. January 10, 1945)
Jacqueline du Pré (January 26, 1945-October 19, 1987)
Bob Marley (February 6, 1945-May 11, 1981)
Eric Clapton (b. March 30, 1945)
Bob Seger (b. May 6, 1945)
Keith Jarrett (b. May 8, 1945)
Pete Townshend (b. May 19, 1945)
John Fogerty (b. May 28, 1945)
Carly Simon (b. June 25, 1945)
Deborah Harry (b. July 1, 1945)
Van Morrison (b. August 31, 1945)
Itzhak Perlman (b. August 31, 1945)
Jessye Norman (b. September 15, 1945)
John Rutter (b. September 24, 1945)
Neil Young (b. November 12, 1945)
Dolly Parton (b. January 19, 1946)
Al Green (b. April 13, 1946)
André Watts (b. June 20, 1946)
Linda Ronstadt (b. July 15, 1946)
Jimmy Webb (b. August 15, 1946)
Barry Gibb (b. September 1, 1946)
John Prine (b. October 10, 1946)
Gram Parsons (November 5, 1946-September 19, 1973)
Jimmy Buffett (b. December 25, 1946)
Patti Smith (b. December 30, 1946)
David Bowie (b. January 8, 1947)
John Adams (b. February 15, 1947)
Sir Elton John (b. March 25, 1947)
Emmylou Harris (b. April 2, 1947)
Laurie Anderson (b. June 5, 1947)
Arlo Guthrie (b. July 10, 1947)
Carlos Santana (b. July 20, 1947)
Sandy Denny (January 6, 1948-April 21, 1978)
James Taylor (b. March 12, 1948)
Sir Andrew Lloyd Webber (b. March 22, 1948)
Kyung-Wha Chung (b. March 26, 1948)
Jimmy Cliff (b. April 1, 1948)
Brian Eno (b. May 15, 1948)
Stevie Nicks (b. May 26, 1948)
Rubén Blades (b. July 16, 1948)
Cat Stevens (b. July 21, 1948)
Robert Plant (b. August 20, 1948)
Jackson Browne (b. October 9, 1948)
Nusrat Fateh Ali Khan (October 13, 1948-August 16, 1997)

Musicians and Composers of the 20th Century

Donna Summer (b. December 31, 1948)
Gil Scott-Heron (b. April 1, 1949)
Billy Joel (b. May 9, 1949)
Bruce Springsteen (b. September 23, 1949)
Will Ackerman (b. November 1, 1949)
Bonnie Raitt (b. November 8, 1949)
Tom Waits (b. December 7, 1949)
Maurice Gibb (December 22, 1949-January 12, 2003)
Robin Gibb (b. December 22, 1949)
Peter Gabriel (b. February 13, 1950)
Karen Carpenter (March 2, 1950-February 4, 1983)
Bobby McFerrin (b. March 11, 1950)
Willie Colón (b. April 28, 1950)
Stevie Wonder (b. May 13, 1950)
Tom Petty (b. October 20, 1950)

1951-1960
Phil Collins (b. January 30, 1951)
Joey Ramone (May 19, 1951-April 15, 2001)
Chrissie Hynde (b. September 7, 1951)
Sting (b. October 2, 1951)
David Byrne (b. May 14, 1952)
George Strait (b. May 18, 1952)
Joe Strummer (August 21, 1952-December 22, 2002)
Lucinda Williams (b. January 26, 1953)
Kitarō (b. February 4, 1953)
Mike Oldfield (b. May 15, 1953)
Danny Elfman (b. May 29, 1953)
James Horner (b. August 14, 1953)
Pat Metheny (b. August 12, 1954)
Elvis Costello (b. August 25, 1954)
Stevie Ray Vaughan (October 3, 1954-August 27, 1990)
Yanni (b. November 14, 1954)
Steve Earle (b. January 17, 1955)
Eddie Van Halen (b. January 26, 1955)
Kool DJ Herc (b. April 16, 1955)
Yo-Yo Ma (b. October 7, 1955)
Tan Dun (b. August 18, 1957)
Hans Zimmer (b. September 12, 1957)
Michael W. Smith (b. October 7, 1957)
Lyle Lovett (b. November 1, 1957)
Grandmaster Flash (b. January 1, 1958)
Ice-T (b. February 16, 1958)
Babyface (b. April 10, 1958)
Prince (b. June 7, 1958)
Esa-Pekka Salonen (b. June 30, 1958)
Béla Fleck (b. July 10, 1958)

Madonna (b. August 16, 1958)
Michael Jackson (b. August 29, 1958)
Joan Jett (b. September 22, 1958)
Julia Wolfe (b. December 18, 1958)
Morrissey (b. May 22, 1959)
Suzanne Vega (b. July 11, 1959)
Kurtis Blow (b. August 9, 1959)
Bono (b. May 10, 1960)
Chuck D (b. August 1, 1960)
Amy Grant (b. November 25, 1960)
Osvaldo Golijov (b. December 5, 1960)

1961-1970
Enya (b. May 17, 1961)
Melissa Etheridge (b. May 29, 1961)
Wynton Marsalis (b. October 18, 1961)
K. D. Lang (b. November 2, 1961)
Pepa (b. November 9, 1961)
Garth Brooks (b. February 7, 1962)
M. C. Hammer (b. March 30, 1962)
Anne-Sophie Mutter (b. June 29, 1963)
Salt (b. March 28, 1964)
D. M. C. (b. May 31, 1964)
Trey Anastasio (b. September 30, 1964)
Joseph "Run" Simmons (b. November 14, 1964)
Dr. Dre (b. February 18, 1965)
Janet Jackson (b. May 16, 1966)
Dave Matthews (b. January 9, 1967)
Kurt Cobain (February 20, 1967-April 5, 1994)
Jeff Tweedy (b. August 25, 1967)
Harry Connick, Jr. (b. September 11, 1967)
LL Cool J (b. January 14, 1968)
Ice Cube (b. June 15, 1969)
Sean Combs (b. November 4, 1969)
Jay-Z (b. December 4, 1969)
Queen Latifah (b. March 18, 1970)
Mariah Carey (b. March 27, 1970)
Beck (b. July 8, 1970)

1971-1980
Mary J. Blige (b. January 11, 1971)
Erykah Badu (b. February 26, 1971)
Tupac Shakur (June 16, 1971-September 13, 1996)
Missy Elliott (b. July 1, 1971)
Alison Krauss (b. July 23, 1971)
Notorious B.I.G. (May 21, 1972-March 9, 1997)
Eminem (b. October 17, 1972)
Snoop Dogg (b. October 20, 1972)
50 Cent (b. July 6, 1975)

Electronic Resources

The following sites were visited by the editors of Salem Press in 2008. Because URLs frequently change, the accuracy of these addresses cannot be guaranteed; however, long-standing sites, such as those of colleges and universities, national organizations, and museums, generally maintain links when sites are moved or updated.

These electronic resources provide information about twentieth century composers, as well as specific genres of music; music museums and societies; music awards and halls of fame; and lists of Web sites and other resources created by music libraries. Many of the sites contain audio clips and video clips, so users can hear and view radio and television shows, musical performances, film excerpts, and interviews.

The majority of the sites are free Web pages, available online for anyone's use. However, a few Web sites, as well as the Oxford Music Online *electronic database, are available only to paying subscribers. Many public, college, and university libraries subscribe to* Oxford Music Online, *or to its predecessor,* Grove Music Online; *readers can consult library Web sites or ask reference librarians about availability.*

The Aaron Copland Collection

http://memory.loc.gov/ammem/collections/copland/

As part of its American Memory project, the Library of Congress has digitized numerous items in its Aaron Copland collection and placed them on the World Wide Web. The first release of the online collection contains about one thousand items, with about five thousand images, dating from 1899 to 1981. The majority of the items in the digitized collection are from the 1920's through the 1950's and were selected from Copland's music sketches, correspondence, writings, and photographs.

African-American Sheet Music, 1850-1920

http://memory.loc.gov/ammem/collections/sheetmusic/brown/

The Library of Congress has digitized 1,305 pieces from Brown University's collection of African American sheet music, dating from 1850 through 1920. Users can browse the collection and access sheet music by song title, subject, or name of composer.

All About Jazz

http://www.allaboutjazz.com/

All About Jazz describes itself as "a site produced by jazz fans for jazz fans," which in this definition includes jazz "newbies" as well as veteran "hipsters." Its contents include a time line outlining significant events in jazz history, news articles and columns, interviews with musicians, photographs, forums where users can express their opinions about jazz, and reviews of new and reissued compact discs. The Musicians section has a search engine that enables users to locate information about a specific musician, including a biography, news articles, and Web links. Users also can retrieve data via a list of instruments or a list of jazz styles, such as blues, big band, Latin/world, and Brazilian, among others.

All Music

http://www.allmusic.com/

This site's title best describes its contents: *All Music* is a comprehensive, easy-to-use, one-stop source of information about every conceivable genre of music. Users can access pages about specific genres, such as jazz, rock, rhythm and blues, rap, country, blues, world, electronica, and classical; these pages describe the genre and its subgenres and feature links to additional information about top performers and artists, albums, and songs. The search engine enables users to retrieve data about specific artists or groups, albums, songs, and classical works; information about each artist or group includes a biography, discography, and a list of songs or classical compositions.

American Classical Hall of Fame

http://www.americanclassicalmusic.org/intro.html

The hall of fame, located in Cincinnati, Ohio, honors musicians who have made significant contributions to American classical music. Its Web site contains an alphabetical list of inductees, with birth and death dates and audio clips of selected performances for each one.

American Jazz Museum

http://www.americanjazzmuseum.com/

"The premiere jazz museum in the United States," is how this Kansas City, Missouri, museum describes itself on its Web site. In addition to information about the museum itself, the site features video clips of jazz on film and a memorial to Charlie Parker, with a video clip of him and Dizzy Gillespie performing "Hot House."

The American Society of Composers, Authors, and Publishers (ASCAP)

http://www.ascap.com/index.html

ASCAP's Web site contains several informative features for users desiring to learn more about composers. The Audio Portraits series contains interviews in which songwriters discuss the creative process. There also are separate sections that provide news items, biographies, and other information about concerts, film and television music, jazz, musical theater, music from Nashville, pop/rock, and rhythm and soul.

Billboard

http://www.billboard.com

The online version of the music industry trade magazine contains news items, information about artists and the *Billboard* Music Awards, and music videos. The site also provides current and former charts of the top-selling songs and albums in a wide variety of genres.

BMI (Broadcast Music Inc.)

http://bmi.com/

BMI, a performing rights organization that collects and distributes royalties, features a range of music-related content on its Web site. In addition to news items, there is information about recent music awards and data about specific musical genres, including urban, country, jazz, Latin, film and television, musical theater, classical, rock, and singer-songwriters. The site also features audio and video podcasts of interviews with BMI members.

Bossa Nova

http://www.bossanova-web.tv/

A simple and informative overview of Brazilian bossa nova music, with text available in Portuguese and French as well as English. The site contains a time line of bossa nova-related events from 1956 through 1966, audio samples of many well-known bossa nova songs, and video clips of performances by Antônio Carlos (Tom) Jobim, Stan Getz, João Gilberto, and other musicians and composers.

Broadway: The American Musical

http://www.pbs.org/wnet/broadway/hello/elements.html

Included on the Web site for the Public Broadcasting System (PBS), *Broadway: The American Musical* was created to accompany a series of programs with that title. The site allows users to view the series. It also contains text describing the history of the Broadway musical play; a time line outlining major musical theater events during the century from 1904 to 2004; and descriptions of notable musicals. The Stars over Broadway section contains biographies of composers, lyricists, and writers, among other figures; these pages feature video interviews and audio clips of songs.

Classical Archives (subscription Web site)

http://www.classicalarchives.com/

Subscribers to this site can listen to recordings and audio files of music written by almost 2,100 composers, including many from the twentieth century. Its biographies, lists of major works, and selected musical definitions are available free of charge.

Classical.com (subscription Web site)

http://www.classical.com/

The name of this subscription site is somewhat misleading; it features music and information about some jazz and world music artists, as well as data about classical composers and musicians. Subscribers have access to more than 120,000 recordings of works by artists in these genres, and many of the recordings can be downloaded. *Classical.com* also provides biographies, program notes, and more than twelve thousand composer images.

The Classical MIDI Connection: The Twentieth Century

http://www.classicalmidiconnection.com

This site offers music MIDI files. MIDI, or musical instrument digital interface, is a digital technology that allows electronic musical instruments and computers to communicate with one another and makes that music available via the Web. The site has an alphabetized list of composers with links to MIDI files of their music. The twentieth century period page contains links and MIDI files for Richard Rodgers, Leonard Bernstein, Samuel Barber, Benjamin Britten, and other composers.

The Classical Music Pages
http://w3.rz-berlin.mpg.de/cmp/classmus.html

Orchestra conductor Matthew Boynick has compiled this site providing, in his words, "everything you need about classical music—its history, biographical information about composers (with portraits and short sound examples), explanations of the various musical forms and a dictionary of musical terminologies." Some of the site's content comes from the respected *Grove Concise Dictionary of Music*, edited by Stanley Sadie. The Musical Epochs page allows users to retrieve information about several twentieth century composers, including Gustav Mahler, Richard Strauss, Claude Debussy, Arnold Schoenberg, Alban Berg, Anton Webern, Belá Bartók, Igor Stravinsky, John Cage, Luigi Nono, and Witold Lutoslawski. Composer information is also retrievable from the Composers Index, which features a separate list of Women Composers.

CMT (County Music Television)
http://www.cmt.com/

CMT's Web site is a comprehensive resource for information about country music. It features news items and audio files of selected country songs. It also contains information about artists and groups that can be accessed via a search engine or by an alphabetical listing; the data about each artist or group includes a biography, discography, news items, lyrics to some of the performers' songs, information about related artists, and links to related Web sites.

Country Music Hall of Fame
http://www.countrymusichalloffame.com/site/

The Web site for the Nashville, Tennessee-based museum contains a brief history of both country music and the Grand Ole Opry. The museum's Country Music Hall of Fame is a veritable "who's who" of the genre, and users can obtain biographi-

cal information about the many musicians who have been inducted.

Delta Blues Museum
http://www.deltabluesmuseum.org/high/index.asp

As explained in its Web site, the Delta Blues Museum is located in the "land where blues began"—Clarksdale, Mississippi, in the Mississippi Delta. In addition to information about the museum's exhibits and activities, the site enables users to view or listen to *Delta Blues Museum's Uncensored Blues Podcast*, a look at the early history of recorded blues. Each show in the podcast includes a series of rare prewar blues tracks and some discussion of those songs.

DownBeat Magazine
http://www.downbeat.com/

The online version of the venerable jazz magazine contains news items, reprints of some of the magazine's articles, and other information about jazz musicians and composers.

The Film Music Society
http://www.filmmusicsociety.org/

The society's Web page includes a page called Resources and Links, which provides links to the Web sites of many film composers and songwriters. Harold Arlen, Burt Bacharach, Henry Mancini, Ennio Morricone, and Randy Newman are among the composers included in the list of links.

Folk Music Home Page
http://www.jg.org/folk/folkhome.html

A great deal of material is gathered in this site, including links to Web pages by and about artists and groups, organizations devoted to folk music, folk music festivals, and specific instruments. The page entitled By Location provides links to information about folk music in the United States, Mexico, South and Central America, Europe, Canada, Australia, New Zealand, Morocco, India, and Iran.

Grammy.com
http://www.grammy.com/

Grammy.com, the Web site of The Recording Academy, contains information about the academy's Grammy Awards, including an archive of past winners. With the help of a search engine, users can retrieve information about winners for a specific year or genre, or for a specific artist or song title. The site also contains information about the Latin Academy of Recording Arts and Sciences, including the organization's Latin Grammy Awards.

Hip Hop Galaxy: Hip Hop and Rap Music Culture
http://www.hiphopgalaxy.com/
Hip Hop Galaxy contains news items, blogs, reviews of newly released compact discs, and the lyrics of some rap and hip-hop songs. The Artists, Rap and R&B Divas, and Groups sections provide biographical information about many rap and hip-hop musicians, including Tupac Shakur and Notorious B.I.G.

International Alliance for Women in Music
http://www.iawm.org/index.htm
The alliance aims to increase awareness of women's contributions to music. Some of the pages in the alliance's Web site were still being developed as of June, 2008, but the site eventually will contain information about its members' music and samples of music by women composers.

International Bluegrass Music Museum
http://www.bluegrassmuseum.org/index.htm
The International Bluegrass Music Museum, located in Owensboro, Kentucky, includes information about bluegrass music on its Web site. In addition to an historic overview of bluegrass music, there are brief biographies about musicians who have been elected to the museum's Hall of Honor, such as Bill Monroe, Earl Scruggs, and Lester Flatt.

International Rockabilly Hall of Fame
http://rockabillyhall.org/
Users can take a virtual tour of the museum, located in Jackson, Tennessee, and see some of the memorabilia housed there. They also can listen to samples of early rock and roll/rockabilly music.

Jammin' Reggae Archives
http://niceup.com/index.html
Everything anyone has wanted to know about reggae—in one convenient place. Among its contents, the site features a group of pages outlining the history of reggae and other types of Jamaican

music; numerous pages about reggae icon Bob Marley; links to other Web sites about a vast range of reggae artists; and links to sites with MP3 reggae content that can be legally downloaded for free.

The Leonard Bernstein Collection
http://memory.loc.gov/ammem/lbhtml/lbhome.html
The Library of Congress has digitized some of its huge collection of Bernstein-related memorabilia as part of its American Memory project, a series of digitized collections available on the World Wide Web. The online Leonard Bernstein Collection makes available 85 photographs; 177 scripts from his television program, *Young People's Concerts;* 74 scripts from his *Thursday Evening Previews*, the lectures he delivered before conducting concerts of the New York Philharmonic Orchestra; and more than 1,100 pieces of correspondence.

Marion Anderson: A Life in Song
http://www.library.upenn.edu/exhibits/rbm/anderson/index.html
The Annenberg Rare Book and Manuscript Library at the University of Pennsylvania, which maintains Marion Anderon's personal papers, including letters, music scores, programs, photographs, and sound recordings, has digitized some of this collection and mounted it on its Web site. The site provides a biography; audio and video excerpts of performances, interviews, recordings, and home movies; scores from Anderson's music collection; and photographs.

Memphis Rock 'n' Soul Museum
http://www.memphisrocknsoul.org/home.htm
The museum features an exhibition about the birth of rock and soul music, created by the Smithsonian Institution, which tells the story of pioneering rock and soul musicians. Additional information about the music of Memphis, Tennessee, can be found on the Web site for the Stax Museum of American Soul Music (see below).

Motown Historical Museum
http://www.motownmuseum.com/
The history of the Motown Record Corporation is explored in this museum, located in Detroit, Michigan, the original home of the record label. The

museum's Web site provides an overview of the company's history and biographies of some of its artists, among them Stevie Wonder, Diana Ross, and Smokey Robinson.

Movie Music Dot Com

http://www.moviemusic.com/

In addition to selling compact discs of film soundtracks, *Movie Music Dot Com* provides information about film music, film composers, and reviews of soundtracks. With the help of the search engine, users can pull down a list of composers and find links to information about the films they have scored. The site's directory at http://www.moviemusic.com/directory/ contains links to related Web sites, including official and unofficial composer sites.

MTV (Music Television)

http://www.mtv.com/

Along with information about the network's programs, MTV's Web site features music videos. Users can select the name of an artist or group from an alphabetized list to retrieve these music videos, as well as biographies, photographs, and news items about that individual or group.

The National Jazz Museum in Harlem

http://www.jazzmuseuminharlem.org/

The National Jazz Museum in Harlem seeks to preserve the legacy of jazz in this New York City neighborhood. As described in the museum's Web site, "Outside of its native New Orleans, no community has nurtured jazz more than Harlem. Duke Ellington, Benny Carter, Thelonious Monk, Charlie Parker, Charles Mingus, Count Basie, John Coltrane, Billie Holiday—all of their unique sounds reverberated throughout these fabled streets." The site offers an overview of the museum's exhibits and activities.

National Music Museum

http://www.usd.edu/smm/

Located on the campus of the University of South Dakota in Vermillion, the National Music Museum and Center for Study of the History of Musical Instruments maintains numerous collections with more than 13,500 American, European, and non-Western instruments from a range of historical

periods and cultures. These instruments include several twentieth century electric guitars and a group of five hundred instruments made in the late nineteenth and early twentieth centuries by the C. C. Conn Company of Elkhart, Indiana.

New Orleans Jazz National Historic Park

http://www.nps.gov/jazz/

The national park aims to educate people about the history, culture, and people that "helped shape the development and progression of jazz in New Orleans." Its Web site contains information about local musicians, most notably Louis Armstrong; places in the city that played significant roles in jazz history; and an historical overview of New Orleans jazz and the city's early band leaders.

Opera Glass

http://opera.stanford.edu/

Stanford University has created this site about all things opera. The site includes an index of more than 3,500 opera composers and the operas they have written. For some composers, such as Richard Strauss and Leoš Janáč, there are individual pages, with lists of the composer's operas and other dramatic music, links to related Web pages, and bibliographies.

Oxford Music Online (subscription electronic database)

http://www.oxfordmusiconline.com/public/

In March, 2008, the highly regarded *Grove Music Online* electronic database was redesigned, expanded, enhanced, and renamed *Oxford Music Online*. The new database serves as a gateway not only to the former *Grove Music Online* but also to numerous reference subscription products created by Oxford University Press. The redesigned site contains 50,000 subject articles and biographies; links to databases of recorded music and biographies, including the *Oxford Dictionary of National Biography*; and 500 audible musical examples. The full texts of *The Oxford Companion to Music* and *The Oxford Dictionary of Music* have also been added, as has the full text of *Encyclopedia of Popular Music*, which covers popular musicians, genres, record companies, music festivals, and songs for rock music and other genres in the twentieth and twenty-first centuries. The site's searching features have been improved, with all of the articles on a single subject grouped together and retrievable via a single query. The first article for each subject is the primary article from *Grove Music Online*, and will be regularly updated; the remaining articles derive from more specialized directories, including *The New Grove Dictionary of Opera* and *The New Grove Dictionary of Jazz*.

Piero Scaruffi

http://www.scaruffi.com/

Piero Scaruffi, a cognitive scientist and music historian, has compiled several Web sites about rock, jazz, classical, and new music. This page provides shortcuts so users can readily access these sites by the specific musical genre. The information on the site is written in both English and Italian, and some of the Italian pages lack English translations. However, the English-language pages contain a wealth of data about the history of blues, jazz, rock, and new music; biographies of composers; chronologies; and discographies.

Public Domain Music

http://www.pdmusic.org/

This collection of MIDI and text files of lyrics for American music in the public domain contains a separate page featuring American popular songs from 1900 through 1922, with compositions by Harry von Tilzer, George M. Cohan, Irving Berlin, and other composers of popular music. The page about the blues features a number of selections from the early twentieth century, and the page about ragtime piano music includes compositions written between 1897 and 1923 by Scott Joplin and other composers.

The Red Hot Jazz Archive: A History of Jazz Before 1930

http://www.redhotjazz.com/index.htm

The name of this site is something of a misnomer, as this multimedia collection of essays, film clips, and sound files contains not only voluminous information about early American jazz but also features information about blues music. Users can access data about bands led by Louis Armstrong, Duke Ellington, Eubie Blake, Jelly Roll Morton, Paul Whiteman, Tommy Dorsey, and other bandleaders. The site also provides pages of information about individual musicians.

Rock and Roll Hall of Fame Museum

http://www.rockhall.com/

The Cleveland-based facility hosts the annual Rock and Roll Hall of Fame induction and features numerous exhibits dedicated to the history of rock and roll. Its Web site contains a list of five hundred songs that shaped rock and roll; an overview of the music of Ohio; and information about some of the architects of rock music, such as Les Paul. There also is a biography of each musician or group that has been inducted into the Rock and Roll Hall of Fame, as well as a time line, bibliography, and list of essential songs for each inductee.

Rolling Stone

http://www.rollingstone.com

Rolling Stone magazine's Web site features an encyclopedic collection of materials about rock and roll, rap, and other popular genres of music. Users can click on the word "Artists" to retrieve a page that allows them to search for artists by name, or they can obtain information by accessing an alphabetized list of artists. Searching is a bit tricky: Artists are listed alphabetically by their first names, so David Bowie, for example, is listed under "D," while Tupac Shakur is listed under "T." In addition, many rock groups, like the Beatles or the Rolling Stones, are listed with the word "the" in front of their name and alphabetized under "T." Once users figure this out, they will be rewarded with a wide range of information, including a biography of each artist or group, an archive of *Rolling Stone* articles about the artist, album reviews, photographs, discographies, and links to other Web sites. The site also allows users to watch videos and listen to some of the artists' most popular songs.

Society of Composers, Inc.

http://www.societyofcomposers.org/

The society, as explained on its Web site, is "an independent organization concerned with the fellowship, collaboration, career goals, and objectives of new and contemporary music composers and those interested in topics related to composition." The site offers information about the society's annual Student Competition and its other activities.

Songwriters Hall of Fame
http://www.songwritershalloffame.org/

As of 2007, about 350 composers were inducted into the hall of fame. Inductees represent three different musical eras: early American song, 1600-1879; Tin Pan Alley, 1880-1953; and rock and roll, 1953-present. The institution's Web site provides an historical overview of these eras, and it offers biographies, photographs, lists of songs, and recommended recordings for each inductee. In addition, the Songwriters Friends section contains biographies and audio clips of numerous singers.

Soul Tracks
http://www.soultracks.com/

Since its inception in 2003, this Web site has, in its own words, "been designed to provide useful information and updates on the greatest classic soul artists and to introduce readers to the next generation of soul music singers." It features news items, reviews of newly released compact discs, and artist biographies.

Stax Museum of American Soul Music
http://www.soulsvilleusa.com/

The museum is housed in the original site of Stax Records in the heart of "Soulsville U.S.A."—otherwise known as Memphis, Tennessee. In addition to information about the museum and its exhibits, the site features a brief history of Soulsville, describing the importance of Memphis in soul music history, and information about Stax Records, including some of the label's artists, such as Otis Redding, Isaac Hayes, and Booker T. and the M.G.'s. Additional information about Memphis music can be found on the site for the Memphis Rock 'n' Soul Museum (see above).

The Twentieth Century Composers
http://www.wwnorton.com/college/music/enj9/shorter/20century/composers.htm

This no-frills site features some of the text contained in *The Enjoyment of Music*, the title of several editions of books published by W. W. Norton & Company. The five-page site contains photographs of about thirty-five twentieth century composers, and it allows users to retrieve biographies, lists of major works, and links to related Web sites. Some of the pages also feature audio clips of the compos-

ers' works. John Adams, Pierre Boulez, Leonard Bernstein, Aaron Copland, George Gershwin, and Sergei Prokofiev are among the featured composers.

William P. Gottlieb: Photographs from the Golden Age of Jazz
http://memory.loc.gov/ammem/wghtml/wghome.html

Gottlieb was a writer and photographer for *Down-Beat* magazine. This Web site contains some of his photographs from the magazine, documenting the jazz scene from 1938 to 1948, primarily in New York City and Washington, D.C. It features several thousand photographs of jazz musicians, including Louis Armstrong, Duke Ellington, Charlie Parker, Billie Holiday, Dizzy Gillespie, Thelonious Monk, Benny Goodman, Coleman Hawkins, Ella Fitzgerald, and Benny Carter.

Woody Guthrie and the Archive of American Folk Song: Correspondence, 1940-1950
http://memory.loc.gov/ammem/wwghtml/wwghome.html

The Library of Congress has digitized some of the letters between Woody Guthrie and the staff of the Archive of American Folk Song (now the Archive of Folk Culture, American Folklife Center) at the Library of Congress. Most of these fifty-three letters were written in the early 1940's, not long after Guthrie had moved to New York City and met Alan Lomax, the assistant in charge of the archive. The Web site also features a biography of Guthrie and a time line of significant events in his life.

World Music Central
http://worldmusiccentral.org/

Like most music genre sites, *World Music Central* provides news items, reviews of compact discs and concerts, and articles about its subject. However, there are probably few, if any, sites with information about artists who play the zongura (a Transylvanian guitar), or who specialize in yodeling. Biographies of musicians, along with discographies and links to data about artists who perform similar music, are accessible via a search engine or via alphabetical lists of artists, countries, geographical regions, genres, and instruments.

Worldwide Internet Music Resources
http://library.music.indiana.edu/
    music_resources/

The William and Gayle Cook Library at the Indiana University School of Music has compiled this extensive list of Web sites related to music. The site's Web links are organized by the following categories: individual musicians (all genres) and popular groups, with a separate section for classical performers; composers and composition, including Web sites about specific composers; groups and ensembles (except popular music); other sites related to performance, including sites about awards, festivals, competitions, and instruments; genres and types of music; research and study; journals and magazines; the commercial world of music; and general and miscellaneous sites.

Year of the Blues 2003
http://www.yearoftheblues.org/index.asp

On February 1, 2003, Experience Music Project, in association with The Blues Foundation, initiated a yearlong program of events aimed at celebrating one hundred years of blues music. Several features of the program's Web site were still available to users in 2008, including information about Chicago blues music from 1946 through 1966, British blues artists, and the history of blues music originating in Memphis, Tennessee, the Mississippi Delta, and the Piedmont. Users also can listen to *The Blues: The Radio Series*, a thirteen-episode program that was broadcast by Public Radio International in September, 2003.

Rebecca Kuzins

Indexes

Category Index

List of Categories

Kurt Weill, 1609
John Williams, 1620
Meredith Willson, 1633
Julia Wolfe, 1641
Iannis Xenakis, 1649
Frank Zappa, 1661

Classical Musicians
Marian Anderson, 24
Martha Argerich, 32
Daniel Barenboim, 70
Sir Thomas Beecham, 93
Jussi Björling, 126
Adolf Busch, 182
Maria Callas, 198
Enrico Caruso, 219
Kyung-Wha Chung, 242
Van Cliburn, 251
Arnold Dolmetsch, 370
Plácido Domingo, 374
Jacqueline du Pré, 386
Arthur Fiedler, 437
Dietrich Fischer-Dieskau, 443
Kirsten Flagstad, 450
Sir James Galway, 470
Nikolaus Harnoncourt, 583
Jascha Heifetz, 606
Christopher Hogwood, 628
Vladimir Horowitz, 654
Herbert von Karajan, 758
Otto Klemperer, 784
Serge Koussevitzky, 796
Wanda Landowska, 811
Lotte Lehmann, 829
James Levine, 846
Yo-Yo Ma, 891
Dame Nellie Melba, 938
Lauritz Melchior, 940
Robert Merrill, 956
Anne-Sophie Mutter, 1002
Jessye Norman, 1039
David Oistrakh, 1047
Luciano Pavarotti, 1091
Itzhak Perlman, 1097
Leontyne Price, 1138
Jean-Pierre Rampal, 1172
Mstislav Rostropovich, 1236
Arthur Rubinstein, 1248
Pierre Schaeffer, 1278

Andrés Segovia, 1320
Rudolf Serkin, 1323
Beverly Sills, 1348
Sir Georg Solti, 1379
Isaac Stern, 1401
Leopold Stokowski, 1420
Dame Joan Sutherland, 1453
Shin'ichi Suzuki, 1456
George Szell, 1458
Joseph Szigeti, 1461
Renata Tebaldi, 1483
Léon Theremin, 1488
Michael Tilson Thomas, 1490
Arturo Toscanini, 1503
André Watts, 1597
August Wenzinger, 1613

Conductors
John Adams, 5
Vladimir Ashkenazy, 44
Daniel Barenboim, 70
Sir Thomas Beecham, 93
Elmer Bernstein, 118
Leonard Bernstein, 120
Nadia Boulanger, 145
Pierre Boulez, 147
Ferruccio Busoni, 184
Pablo Casals, 223
Arthur Fiedler, 437
Glenn Gould, 524
Percy Aldridge Grainger, 528
Nikolaus Harnoncourt, 583
Bernard Herrmann, 620
Christopher Hogwood, 628
Leoš Janáček, 703
Herbert von Karajan, 758
Otto Klemperer, 784
Serge Koussevitzky, 796
Gustav Leonhardt, 840
James Levine, 846
Sir Yehudi Menuhin, 948
Alfred Newman, 1023
Sir André Previn, 1134
Sergei Rachmaninoff, 1161
Mstislav Rostropovich, 1236
John Rutter, 1255
Esa-Pekka Salonen, 1263
Sir Georg Solti, 1379
Leopold Stokowski, 1420

George Szell, 1458
Léon Theremin, 1488
Michael Tilson Thomas, 1490
Arturo Toscanini, 1503
Bruno Walter, 1575

Cornetists
Bix Beiderbecke, 96
W. C. Handy, 580
Red Nichols, 1029

Country and Country-Western Musicians
Roy Acuff, 2
Eddy Arnold, 42
Chet Atkins, 46
Hoyt Axton, 49
Garth Brooks, 159
Jimmy Buffett, 173
Glen Campbell, 202
Maybelle Carter, 216
Johnny Cash, 226
Patsy Cline, 255
John Denver, 352
Steve Earle, 393
Melissa Etheridge, 421
Don Everly, 426
Phil Everly, 426
Freddy Fender, 434
Lester Flatt, 452
Lefty Frizzell, 462
Merle Haggard, 559
Emmylou Harris, 585
Lightnin' Hopkins, 648
Waylon Jennings, 715
George Jones, 737
Alison Krauss, 798
Kris Kristofferson, 803
K. D. Lang, 814
Lyle Lovett, 879
Loretta Lynn, 887
Roger Miller, 969
Ronnie Milsap, 971
Bill Monroe, 984
Willie Nelson, 1015
Dolly Parton, 1082
Carl Perkins, 1095
Charley Pride, 1140
Bonnie Raitt, 1166

Geographical Index

List of Geographical Regions

Africa
Fela Kuti, 805
Miriam Makeba, 911
Hugh Masekela, 929
Joseph Shabalala, 1326
Umm Kulthum, 1531

Argentina
Martha Argerich, 32
Daniel Barenboim, 70
Osvaldo Golijov, 515
Astor Piazzolla, 1109

Australia
Percy Aldridge Grainger, 528

Dame Nellie Melba, 938
Dame Joan Sutherland, 1453

Austria
Alban Berg, 104
Nikolaus Harnoncourt, 583
Herbert von Karajan, 758
Fritz Kreisler, 800
György Ligeti, 855
Gustav Mahler, 907
Artur Schnabel, 1281
Arnold Schoenberg, 1287
Franz Schreker, 1291
Max Steiner, 1398
Anton von Webern, 1603

Bangladesh
Ali Akbar Khan, 768

Belgium
Jacques Brel, 153
Django Reinhardt, 1188

Brazil
Gilberto Gil, 498
João Gilberto, 501
Antônio Carlos Jobim, 721
Milton Nascimento, 1008
Heitor Villa-Lobos, 1562

Canada
Leonard Cohen, 264

Musicians and Composers of the 20th Century

Hungary
Béla Bartók, 74
Zoltán Kodály, 788
Sigmund Romberg, 1228
Miklós Rózsa, 1244
Sir Georg Solti, 1379
George Szell, 1458
Joseph Szigeti, 1461

Iceland
Vladimir Ashkenazy, 44

India
Ali Akbar Khan, 768
Ravi Shankar, 1331

Ireland
Bono, 142
Enya, 419

Israel
Daniel Barenboim, 70
Itzhak Perlman, 1097
Arthur Rubinstein, 1248

Italy
Luciano Berio, 109
Ferruccio Busoni, 184
Enrico Caruso, 219
Gian Carlo Menotti, 945
Ennio Morricone, 989
Luigi Nono, 1037
Luciano Pavarotti, 1091
Giacomo Puccini, 1153
Ottorino Respighi, 1191
Nino Rota, 1240
Renata Tebaldi, 1483
Arturo Toscanini, 1503

Jamaica
Jimmy Cliff, 253
Kool DJ Herc, 791
Bob Marley, 917
Peter Tosh, 1507

Japan
Kitarō, 782
Shin'ichi Suzuki, 1456
Tōru Takemitsu, 1467

Korea
Kyung-Wha Chung, 242

Lithuania
Jascha Heifetz, 606

Mexico
Carlos Chávez, 233
Conlon Nancarrow, 1006
Silvestre Revueltas, 1193
Carlos Santana, 1272
Charles Seeger, 1303

Middle East
Daniel Barenboim, 70
Itzhak Perlman, 1097
Arthur Rubinstein, 1248
Umm Kulthum, 1531

Netherlands
Gustav Leonhardt, 840
Frank Martin, 923

Nigeria
Fela Kuti, 805

Northern Ireland
Sir James Galway, 470
Van Morrison, 994

Norway
Kirsten Flagstad, 450

Pakistan
Nusrat Fateh Ali Khan, 770

Panama
Rubén Blades, 130

Poland
Wanda Landowska, 811
Witold Lutosławski, 884
Ignace Jan Paderewski, 1063
Arthur Rubinstein, 1248
Karol Szymanowski, 1463

Puerto Rico
Ray Barretto, 72
Tito Puente, 1157

Romania
György Ligeti, 855
Iannis Xenakis, 1649

Russia
Vladimir Ashkenazy, 44
Irving Berlin, 114
Sofia Gubaidulina, 546
Vladimir Horowitz, 654
Aram Khachaturian, 765
Serge Koussevitzky, 796
Sergei Prokofiev, 1149
Sergei Rachmaninoff, 1161
Mstislav Rostropovich, 1236
Alfred Schnittke, 1284
Aleksandr Scriabin, 1298
Dmitri Shostakovich, 1340
Isaac Stern, 1401
Igor Stravinsky, 1435
Léon Theremin, 1488

Scotland
David Byrne, 190
Bert Jansch, 707

South Africa
Miriam Makeba, 911
Hugh Masekela, 929
Joseph Shabalala, 1326

Spain
Pablo Casals, 223
Plácido Domingo, 374
Julio Iglesias, 674
Andrés Segovia, 1320

Sweden
Jussi Björling, 126

Switzerland
Frank Martin, 923
August Wenzinger, 1613

Ukraine
David Oistrakh, 1047
Dimitri Tiomkin, 1496

Personages and Groups Index

Musicians and Composers of the 20th Century

Red Hot Peppers, 999
Red Hot Red. *See* Paul, Les
Red Nichols and His Five Pennies, 1029
Redding, Otis, 1178-1180
Ree, Sister. *See* Franklin, Aretha
Reed, Jimmy, 1180-1182
Reed, Lou, 1182-1185
Reich, Steve, 1185-1188
Reid, Antonio "L. A.," 58
Reiner, Fritz, 451
Reinhardt, Django, 1188-1191
Reiniger, Robert Meredith. *See* Willson, Meredith
Respighi, Ottorino, 1191-1193
Return to Forever, 299
Revolution, the, 1143
Revueltas, Silvestre, 1193-1196
Rey del Mambo. *See* Prado, Pérez
Rhubarb Red. *See* Paul, Les
Rice, Sir Tim, 866, 1196-1197
Richards, Keith, 429, 691, 1197-1200
Riddle, Nelson, 269, 1232
Ridenhour, Carlton Douglas. *See* Chuck D
Ritchie, Jean, 1200-1202
Ritter, Tex, 1202-1205
Roach, Max, 162, 1205-1209
Robertson, Robbie, 1209-1211
Robeson, Paul, 1211-1213
Robinson, Mamie. *See* Smith, Mamie
Robinson, Ray Charles. *See* Charles, Ray
Robinson, Smokey, 1213-1216
Robu. *See* Shankar, Ravi
Roche, Pierre, 51
Rodgers, Jimmie, 1216-1220, 1515
Rodgers, Richard, 570, 1220-1224
Rolling Stones, 691, 1197
Rollins, Sonny, 1225-1228
Romberg, Sigmund, 1228-1230
Romeos, 383
Ronstadt, Linda, 1231-1233
Ross, Diana, 385, 1233-1236
Rostropovich, Mstislav, 1236-1240
Rota, Nino, 1240-1244
Roxy Music, 416
Roy Acuff and His Smokey Mountain Boys, 3

Rózsa, Miklós, 514, 1244-1247
Rubén Blades y Seis del Solar, 130
Rubén Blades y Son del Solar, 130
Rubinstein, Artur, 1248-1251
Run, Reverend. *See* Simmons, Joseph "Run"
Run Love. *See* Simmons, Joseph "Run"
Runaways, the, 718
Run-D. M. C., 332, 1351
Rush, Otis, 1251-1253
Rush, Tom, 1253-1255
Rutter, John, 1255-1258
Rzewski, Frederic, 1258-1260

Saddlemen, the, 562
Saddler, Joseph. *See* Grandmaster Flash
Sager, Carole Bayer, 60, 62
Sainte-Marie, Buffy, 1261-1263
Sallyangie, the, 1049
Salonen, Esa-Pekka, 1263-1265
Salt, 1266-1267
Salt-n-Pepa, 1266
Sandburg, Carl, 1267-1269
Sanders, Pharoah, 1270-1271
Santana, 1272
Santana, Carlos, 1272-1274
Sassy. *See* Vaughan, Sarah
Satchmo. *See* Armstrong, Louis
Satie, Erik, 509, 1275-1278
Saud, Sulaimon. *See* Tyner, McCoy
Savio, Dan. *See* Morricone, Ennio
Schaeffer, Pierre, 1278-1280
Schlesinger, Bruno. *See* Walter, Bruno
Schnabel, Artur, 1281-1284
Schnittke, Alfred, 1284-1287
Schoenberg, Arnold, 104-105, 107, 148, 1287-1291
Schönberg, Arnold Franz Walter. *See* Schoenberg, Arnold
Schreker, Franz, 1291-1294
Schubert, Franz, 444
Schuller, Gunther, 974
Schwartz, Arthur, 440
Schweitzer, Albert, 1294-1296
Scott-Heron, Gil, 1296-1298
Scriabin, Aleksandr, 1298-1301
Scruggs, Earl, 453, 1301-1303

Scruggs, Mary Elfrieda. *See* Williams, Mary Lou
Scryabin, Aleksandr. *See* Scriabin, Aleksandr
Seeger, Charles, 311, 1303-1307
Seeger, Mike, 1306-1308
Seeger, Peggy, 1306, 1309-1311
Seeger, Pete, 1306, 1311-1314
Seeger, Ruth Crawford, 1304, 1315-1318
Seger, Bob, 1318-1320
Segovia, Andrés, 1320-1323
Sensei, Suzuki. *See* Suzuki, Shin'ichi
Serkin, Rudolf, 183, 1323-1325
Shabalala, Joseph, 1326-1328
Shakur, Tupac, 288, 1328-1331
Shankar, Ravi, 508, 1331-1335
Shaw, Artie, 1335-1337
Shenandoah, 550
Shorter, Wayne, 1337-1340
Shostakovich, Dmitri, 158, 1237, 1340-1344
Sibelius, Jean, 185, 1344-1348
Sills, Beverly, 1348-1350
Silver, Horace, 137
Silver Bullet Band, 1318
Silverman, Belle Miriam. *See* Sills, Beverly
Simmons, Russell, 141
Simmons, Joseph "Run," 1351-1352
Simon, Carly, 1353-1355
Simon, Paul, 1327, 1355-1358
Simon and Garfunkel, 475, 1355
Simon Sisters, 1353
Simone, Nina, 1358-1360
Sinatra, Frank, 345, 1361-1363
Singer, Jóska. *See* Szigeti, Joseph
Singing Brakeman. *See* Rodgers, Jimmie
Sissle, Noble, 135
Sista, 410
Slava. *See* Rostropovich, Mstislav
Slick, Grace, 1364-1366
Slim Shady. *See* Eminem
Slowhand. *See* Clapton, Eric
Sly and the Family Stone, 1426
Smith, Bessie, 1366-1369
Smith, Buster, 81
Smith, Harry, 389

Musicians and Composers of the 20th Century

Works Index

Listed below are titles of albums, compositions, songs, symphonies, and many other works discussed in the text of *Musicians and Composers of the 20th Century*. These works are followed by a musician's name in parentheses. The page numbers that follow represent the location of discussion of the work in relation to the musician appearing in parentheses. It is important to note that these parenthetical names are not intended to represent the composers or other "authors" of the works listed—which are often not solo productions but instead the product of songwriting teams, bands and other musical groups, and collaborations between lyricists and songwriters—but rather one of the musicians associated with the work. The individual listed parenthetically after each title therefore represents the musician who is the focus of discussion on the page listed.

"C. C. Rider" (Rainey, Ma), 1166
Cabaret (Ebb, Fred), 395
Cabaret (Kander, John), 757
Cabildo (Beach, Amy), 85
"Call It Stormy Monday (But Tuesday Is Just as Bad)" (Walker, T-Bone), 1572
"Call Me" (Harry, Deborah), 597
"Calle luna calle sol" (Colón, Willie), 282
Calypso (Belafonte, Harry), 100
Camelot (Andrews, Dame Julie), 30
Camelot (Lerner, Alan Jay), 845
Camelot (Loewe, Frederick), 874
Campana sommersa, La (Respighi, Ottorino), 1192
"Can I Get a Witness" (D. M. C.), 333, 1352
Canciones de Mi Padre (Ronstadt, Linda), 1232
Candide (Bernstein, Leonard), 122
"Candy Man Blues" (Hurt, Mississippi John), 666
"Cannonball Rag" (Travis, Merle), 1514
Can't Quit the Blues (Guy, Buddy), 557
Cantata No. 2 (Webern, Anton von), 1606
Canticum Sacrum (Stravinsky, Igor), 1437
Canto sospeso, Il (Nono, Luigi), 1038
Cape Fear (Bernstein, Elmer), 119
Cappello di paglia di Firenze, Il (Rota, Nino), 1242
Caprice viennois, Op. 2 (Kreisler, Fritz), 802
"Car Song" (Guthrie, Woody), 554
Car Wheels on a Gravel Road (Williams, Lucinda), 1625
"Caravan" (Ellington, Duke), 407
Carbon Copy Building (Wolfe, Julia), 1642
Carmina Burana (Orff, Carl), 1058
Carousel (Hammerstein, Oscar, II), 572
Carousel (Rodgers, Richard), 1223
Carpenters, The (Carpenter, Karen), 209
Casablanca (Steiner, Max), 1400

Cat and the Fiddle, The (Kern, Jerome), 764
Cat-Women of the Moon (Bernstein, Elmer), 118
Catch a Fire (Tosh, Peter), 1508
"Cathedral" (Van Halen, Eddie), 1539
Catherine Wheel, The (Byrne, David), 191
"Cathy's Clown" (Everly, Don), 428
Cats (Lloyd Webber, Sir Andrew), 868
"Cayuco, El" (Puente, Tito), 1159
Cello Concerto in E Minor (Elgar, Sir Edward), 404
Celtic Requiem (Tavener, Sir John), 1477
Centerfield (Fogerty, John), 458
"C'est la Vie" (Berry, Chuck), 125
"Chain of Fools" (Franklin, Aretha), 460
Chain works (Lutosławski, Witold), 886
Chamber Concerto (Ligeti, György), 857
Chamber Music No. 1 (Hindemith, Paul), 626
Chamber Symphony (Schreker, Franz), 1293
"Change Is Gonna Come, A" (Cooke, Sam), 293
Change Your World (Smith, Michael W.), 1375
Chantefleurs et chantefables (Lutosławski, Witold), 886
"Characteristic Blues" (Bechet, Sidney), 88
Chariots of Fire (Vangelis), 1537
"Charleston Rag" (Blake, Eubie), 135
Chase, The (Brooks, Garth), 160
Cheap Imitation (Cage, John), 195
"Cheeseburger in Paradise" (Buffett, Jimmy), 174
"Chega de saudade" (Gilberto, João), 501
"Chega de saudade" (Jobim, Antônio Carlos), 721
Chess (Rice, Sir Tim), 1197
Chester and Lester (Paul, Les), 1090

Chicago (Ebb, Fred), 396
Chicago (Kander, John), 757
Child of Our Time, A (Tippett, Sir Michael), 1500
Children's Songs (Leadbelly), 822
Chinatown (Goldsmith, Jerry), 514
"Cho-Cho-San" (Whiteman, Paul), 1617
"Choo Choo Ch' Boogie" (Jordan, Louis), 754
Chôros (Villa-Lobos, Heitor), 1564
Chorus Line, A (Hamlisch, Marvin), 566
Christmas Gift for You from Phil Spector, A (Spector, Phil), 1390
Christmas Music of Johnny Mathis, The (Mathis, Johnny), 933
"Christmas Rappin'" (Blow, Kurtis), 141
Christmas with Babyface (Babyface), 59
Christophe Colomb (Milhaud, Darius), 966
Christophorus (Schreker, Franz), 1293
Chronic, The (Dr. Dre), 367
Chronic 2001, The (Dr. Dre), 367
"Cigarettes and Coffee Blues" (Frizzell, Lefty), 463
Cinderella (Andrews, Dame Julie), 30
Cinéma (Satie, Erik), 1277
Cinema Paradiso (Morricone, Ennio), 990
Circle Game, The (Rush, Tom), 1254
Circles (Berio, Luciano), 112
Citizen Kane (Herrmann, Bernard), 622
City of Angels (Coleman, Cy, Larry Gelbart, and A. E. Hotchner), 271
Clash, The (Strummer, Joe), 1445
Claude Bolling: Suite for Flute and Jazz Piano (Rampal, Jean-Pierre), 1173
Clifford Brown and Max Roach at Basin Street (Roach, Max), 1207
Cloak, The (Puccini, Giacomo), 1155
Close to You (Carpenter, Karen), 208